# Learning C#
# Programming
# with Unity 3D

# Learning C# Programming
## with Unity 3D

Alex Okita

CRC Press
Taylor & Francis Group
Boca Raton   London   New York

CRC Press is an imprint of the
Taylor & Francis Group, an **informa** business

CRC Press
Taylor & Francis Group
6000 Broken Sound Parkway NW, Suite 300
Boca Raton, FL 33487-2742

Version Date: 20140707

International Standard Book Number-13: 978-1-4665-8652-9 (Paperback)

---

**Library of Congress Cataloging-in-Publication Data**

---

Okita, Alex.
    Learning C# programming with Unity 3D / Alex Okita.
        pages cm
    Summary: "Ideal for game programmers with no prior experience with programming languages, this book covers the basics of programming and explains how C# is used to make a game in Unity3D. Interactive examples give C# code meaning. As more complex aspects of C# are explained the interactivity of example games gains depth. Common programming tasks are taught by way of making a game. The final result is a reader who is capable of understanding how to read and apply C# in Unity3D and apply that knowledge to other development environments that use C#"-- Provided by publisher.
    Includes bibliographical references and index.
    ISBN 978-1-4665-8652-9 (paperback)
    1. Computer games--Programming. 2. C# (Computer program language) 3. Unity (Electronic resource) 4. Three-dimensional display systems. I. Title.

QA76.76.C672O43 2014
794.8'1526--dc23
                                                 2014006696

**Visit the Taylor & Francis Web site at**
**http://www.taylorandfrancis.com**

**and the CRC Press Web site at**
**http://www.crcpress.com**

# Contents

# Acknowledgments

Over the past two decades I've had the opportunity to work with many amazingly talented artists and engineers.

Those who have inspired me are Edward, JCAB, Joel, and Eric from Ronin Games. Their skill and expertise kept me on my toes and motivated me to learn new skills. Also from Ronin is Ashish, with whom I was able to get started with writing.

More recently regarding my transition from artist to engineer, I thank Dave Tin Nyo, Anka GranovSkaya, David Bennett, and Jordan Patz. The original Float Hybrid group was one of the most creative collectives I've ever had the opportunity to work with. Never before has there been such a talented group of engineers under one roof—nor will there be one such hereafter.

Along the way, I thank my mother Sandi, who has always been an amazing artist. Finally, I thank April, who was the inspiration for my getting started with this book.

# 1

## Introduction: What This Book Is About

This book was written as an answer for anyone to pick up a programming language and be productive. You will be able to start from scratch without having any previous exposure to any programming language. By the end of this book, you will have the skills to be a capable programmer, or at least know what is involved with how to read and write code.

Afterward you should be armed with the knowledge required to feel confident in learning more. You should have general computer skills before you get started. After this you'll know what it takes to at least look at code without your head spinning.

### 1.1 Why Read a Book: Why This Book May or May Not Be for You

You could go online and find videos and tutorials to learn; however, there is a distinct disadvantage when it comes to learning things in order and in one place. Most YouTube or tutorial websites either gloss over a topic or dwell at a turtle's pace for an hour on a particular subject.

Online content is often brief and doesn't go into much depth on any given topic. It is incomplete or still a work in progress. You'll often find yourself waiting weeks for another video or tutorial to come out.

Most online tutorials for C# are scattered, disordered, and incohesive. It is difficult to find a good starting point and even more difficult to find a continuous list of tutorials to bring you to any clear understanding of the C# programming language.

Just so you know, you should find the act of learning exciting. If not, then you'll have a hard time continuing through to the end of this book. To learn any new skill, a lot of patience is required.

I remember asking an expert programmer how I'd learn to program. He told me to write a compiler. At that time, it seemed rather mean, but now I understand why he said that. It is like telling someone who wants to learn how to drive Formula 1 cars to go compete in a race. In both cases, the "learn" part was left out of the process of learning.

It is very difficult to tell someone who wants to learn to write code where to begin. However, it all really does start with your preparedness to learn. Your motivation must extend beyond the content of this book.

You may also have some preconceived notions about what a programming is. I can't change that, but you should be willing to change your thoughts on the topic if you make discoveries contrary to your knowledge. Keep an open mind.

As a game developer, you should find the act of making a game, or simply learning how to make a game just as fun as playing a game. If your primary goal is only to make that game that you've had in your head for years, then you might have a problem. You may find this book a tedious chore if learning C# is just something in the way of making your game.

Computer artists often believe that programming is a technical subject that is incompatible with art. I find the contrary to be true. Programming is an art, much as literature and design is an art. Programming just has a lot of obscure rules that need to be understood for anything to work.

No, programming is not too hard to learn. Writing a massive multiplayer online role-playing game is quite hard, of course. Learning how to write a simple behavior isn't hard. Like drawing, you start off with the basics, drawing spheres and cubes. After plenty of practice, you'll be able to create a real work of art. This applies to writing code, that is, you start off with basic calculations, and then move on to the logic that drives a complex game.

### 1.1.1  Do I Need to Know Math?

With complex rules in mind, does programming require the knowledge of complex mathematics? Actually, unless you program mathematical software, only a bit of geometry is nice to have. Most of the examples here use only a tiny bit of math to accomplish their purposes. Mathematics and programming do overlap quite a lot in their methodology.

Math taught in schools provides a single solution. Programming results tend to behave a bit like a math proof, but only the proof isn't just another bit of math. Rather, the proof of your code means that your zombies chase after humans. A considerable amount of math required has been done for you by the computer. It is just up to you to know what math to use, and then plug in the right variables.

### 1.1.2  Programming as a Form of Expression

There is a deeper connection between words and meaning in programming. This connection is more mechanical, but flexible at the same time. In relation to a programming language, programmers like to call this "expressiveness."

When you write words in literature, you infer most if not all of the meaning. When programming inference isn't implied, then you're free to define your own meanings for words and invent words freely.

One common merging of art and code appears within a video game. Anytime characters can react to each other and react to user interaction, which conveys a greater experience. An artist, an animator, or an environment designer should have some ability to convey a richer experience to the audience. A character artist can show a monster to his or her audience; but to really experience the creature, the monster should glare, grunt, and attack in reaction to the audience.

### 1.1.3  Games as a Stage with Lights

To do this, we're going to use Unity 3D, a game engine. If you were to write a play, you would not have to build the auditorium for your performance. Building lights and generating electricity to run them would distract you from writing your play. Playwrights don't often build lights and auditoriums from scratch, and there are plenty of venues you could use as your stage, which is where game engines come in. Game engines such as Unity 3D, Unreal Development Kit (UDK), Crytek, and even Game Maker have a lot of the basic functions built for you. They are ready-built stages that allow you to concentrate on making your game, and not on code to run lighting, or even physics.

## 1.2  Personal Information

I maintain a couple of different blogs, as well as a YouTube channel. I started in the 1990s cleaning up sprites for Atari. Back then the job qualifications were basically having Photoshop and a Wacom tablet. Oh, how the times have changed!

I've worked for many different game studios, both 2D and 3D, as an artist. I was exposed to many different software packages including Strata 3D on the Mac and Alias (PowerAnimator) on the SGI (Silicon Graphics International), among many others. I loved learning new 3D modeling, rendering, and animation applications. During my work as an artist, I used Maya, a popular 3D modeling package. Using Maya, I was introduced to the Maya Embedded Language (MEL) script.

After working as a character rigger and technical artist, I learned many programming languages including MAXScript and Python, which helped me to write tools for my fellow artists to use for speeding up production.

I eventually moved into a job as a programmer, which is my primary job function. I wrote prototypes for Microsoft in Unreal using UnrealScript, a programming language much like JavaScript. This game studio was run by John Gaeta and Peter Oberdorfer, who are award-winning movie special effects directors.

I began my career path as an artist, then became a technical artist, and finally a programmer. This seems to be a common trend among a small variety of 3D artists like myself. I know of quite a few folks who have followed the same career path.

During my transition from artist to programmer, I found that there was very little by way of help, documentation, web pages, or similar to complete the transition from an artist to a programmer. Many people assumed that you were either a programmer to begin with or not interested in making that transition. This prompted me to write this book.

## 1.3 A Brief History of Computer Programming: How Programming Came to Be

### 1.3.1 Mechanical Computers

The first programmable computer is arguably the Babbage machine built by Charles Babbage in the 1820s. Being made of tens of thousands of moving parts and weighing several tons, it was a gigantic mechanical calculator that could display a 31-digit number. It was called the Difference Engine, and in 1824 Babbage won a gold medal from the British Astronomical Society for correcting a set of tables used to chart the movement of planets through the sky.

In 1833, a countess named Augusta Ada King of Lovelace, commonly known as Ada Lovelace, met Babbage at a party where she was introduced to the Difference Engine. Several years later, it became evident that she understood the machine better than Charles himself. Despite being housewife to the Earl of Lovelace, she wrote several documents on the operation of the Difference Engine as well as its upgraded version, the Analytical Engine. She is often considered to be the first computer programmer for her work with the Difference Engine and its documentation.

### 1.3.2 Logic

In 1848, George Boole gave us Boolean logic. It would take nearly a century between the Difference Engine and the first general programmable computer to make its appearance. Thanks to George, today our computers count in binary (1s and 0s), and our software thinks in terms of true or false. In 1887, Dorr Eugene Felt built a computing machine with buttons; thanks to him, our computers have keyboards. In the 1890s, a tabulating machine used paper with holes punched in it representing 1s and 0s to record the US census. Back then it saved US$2 million and 6 years of work.

In the 1900s, between Nicola Tesla and Alexander Graham Bell, modern computers were imminent with the invention of the transistor. In 1936, Konrad Zuse made the Z1 computer, another mechanical computer like that of Babbage, but this time it used a tape with holes punched in it like the tabulating machine. He'd later move on to make the Z3 in 1941.

### 1.3.3 Computer Science

In the 1940s, Alan Turing, a British computer scientist, designed and built an encrypted message decoder called the Bombe that used electromechanical switches for helping the Allied forces during World War II. Between the 1930s and the 1950s, Turing informed the computer scientists that computers can, in theory, solve anything calculable, calling this concept *Turing completeness*. All of these components began to lead toward our modern computer.

In the mid-1940s, John Von Neumann demonstrated with the help of his theory that the computer can be built using simple components. This way the software that controls the hardware can add the complex behavior. Thanks to Tesla and Bell, the Z3 was made completely of electronic parts. It included the first use of logic while doing calculations, making it the first complete Turing-complete computer. In 1954, Gordon Teal at Texas Instruments introduced the silicon-based transistor, a key component for building solid-state electronics that are used today in every computer.

### 1.3.4  Software

The Z3 was programmed using Plankalkül, the first high-level programming language, invented by Zuse shortly after he finished building the machine. In 1952, Grace Hopper created the first compiler, software that could translate human-readable words into machine operations. For the first time, the programmer didn't need to know how the transistors operated in the hardware to build software for the computer to run. This opened computer programming to a whole new audience.

Between the 1950s and the 1970s, computers and computer languages were growing in terms of complexity and capability. In 1958, John McCarthy invented LISP at the Massachusetts Institute of Technology (MIT). Object oriented programming appeared in Simula 67 in 1967. Imperative and procedural programming made its appearance in Pascal in 1970.

### 1.3.5  Modern Computer Language

Bell Labs, started by Bell in the 1920s, hired Dennis Ritchie in 1967. In 1974, Ritchie published the C programming language that has become the most popular computer programming language. In 1983, C++ made its appearance as "C with Classes."

In 2001, Microsoft released C#, a combination of several programming language paradigms taking the concepts from C, C++, LISP, Haskell, and others, and incorporating the ideas and concepts into a single language. Today, C# is in its fifth revision, whereas C++ is in its eleventh revision. C# is an evolving language having new features and concepts that make the language richer and capable.

### 1.3.6  The Future of Computer Languages

The International Business Machines Corporation (IBM), a US company founded in the 1920s, is currently engineering new technology using particle physics discovered nearly a century ago. Modern spintronics derived from the work of German physicists in the late 1920s.

Without particle physics and physicists such as Friedrich Hermann Hund, we wouldn't understand quantum tunneling, and the solid-state disk or universal serial bus (USB) thumb drive wouldn't exist. After the discovery and confirmation of the Higgs boson, you might ask "Why bother?" This question might not get a good answer for another hundred years, but it'll be worth it.

C# is not the last computer language; many others have been introduced recently, most notably an entry by Google called Go. Microsoft, not to be outdone, has also introduced F#. There are many relatively new programming languages that have been made popular in recent years. Though the languages are different, the principal concepts are all the same. Once the basic ideas are understood, it is easy to apply the knowledge obtained here to new languages and continue to learn.

Today quantum computers begin to make their appearance. Dealing with today's transistors, we send and receive determinate values. Quantum computers don't work with 1s and 0s; rather they store multiple values between 0 and 1. To deal with this, new programming languages are currently being developed.

## 1.4  C#: A Flexible Programming Language

There are plenty of programming languages, and each language was created to fulfill different roles. Modern programming languages in use today are often described by their paradigms. A paradigm can be explained as a sort of writing style; each style follows a different set of rules.

### 1.4.1  C# Paradigm

In poetry, a haiku follows a 5-7-5 syllable tempo. A sonnet follows an iambic pentameter with 10 syllables per line and rhymes in a specific pattern. Not all prose needs to end in rhyme like haiku, but many do. Rhyming and tempo are paradigms used in poetry.

Modern programming paradigms include object oriented, functional, imperative, and logic programming. Some programming languages use one or more of these paradigms together. For instance, F# is an imperative, object oriented, and functional language. However, Haskell is purely functional.

C# (pronounced "see sharp") is a combination of many different paradigms. As the name infers, C# is a C-style language and primarily expressed using the object oriented paradigm. How C# expresses its different paradigms, and how you choose to write with it, is greatly up to you. Due to this flexibility, C# offers a variety of uses even after you're done with this book.

You may have heard of C++, another multiparadigm language. It is often used by programmers who need detailed control over memory management and many other aspects of their final product. This attention to detail and design is required to produce a refined final product.

C# is an imperative language, that is to say, it does operations in order. It is also object oriented, so each object is allowed to do things on its own. Finally, it is also memory managed, so your computer's memory is organized for you. However, it does provide the flexibility to manage memory if you require that level of control. Just as well, C++ has recently added garbage collection features to match C#.

## 1.4.2 Unity 3D: A Brief History of Game Engines

A game engine is basically software that provides many of the basic functions that are commonly used to build a video game. Most game engines allow for rendering either 2D or 3D shapes by importing files generated in a third-party software such as Blender, or 3D Studio Max or Maya, if you can afford them. Another function often found in a game engine is the ability to write software for the game engine to run. Unity 3D allows you to write software to run your game in C#.

3D game engines have a relatively short history in general computing. Their evolution has been hot and fast. Starting around the 1990s, the 486 processor finally made its way into the general populace as a processor fast enough to allow for everyone to play 3D games. Or at least pseudo-3D, 2D images drawn in the shape of three-dimensional geometry. The technology for true 3D polygons would take a few more years to make it onto the average person's desktop.

Pseudo-3D was used to describe skewing and scaling flat sprites or 2D images to appear as though they were in 3D space. True vertex transformation wouldn't appear in popular video game engines on the PC with games such as Quake 1 till 1995. This was greatly with the help of faster and enhanced graphics processors. The modding community took Quake 1 and created many new additions and full conversions.

When powerful graphics processing units (GPUs) were introduced, it opened the floodgates for many more 3D games to make their appearance. At first, these games functioned only on million-dollar computers, but thanks to 3dfx, nVidia, and Maxtrox in the late 1990s, the GPU quickly took over being a requirement for any 3D game. At that time, id Software, run by John Carmack, quickly came to the forefront of the 3D gaming engine technologies that introduced many concepts such as spline surfaces, complex shadows, and lighting with Quake 2.

Around 1998, Epic Games's Unreal Engine and Valve Software's Source Engine took off with the launch of Unreal Tournament and Half-Life. More modding and conversions exploded onto the scene. Many successful game modifications including Counter-Strike would go on to be one of the most played online multiplayer games Valve Software would publish for years to come.

Before the availability of dedicated GPU and cheap RAM, computers didn't have enough free resources to support a game engine and editing tools. Often the game itself required so much of the computer that; there was little room left for any extras, such as particle editors or just-in-time compiling.

The modding community influenced business, making Unreal 2 and Source more modder friendly. Garry's Mod and Unreal Editor changed how game engines were made by adding tons of user-friendly tools. Many users bought games specifically to "mod," or modify, and create new games.

It is not a surprise that at this time many game engines would show up on the scene to cater to the modding community and the independent game developer. The large game engines found themselves top heavy by focusing on large publishers. Companies such as RenderWare and Gamebryo found themselves poorly positioned to compete against newcomers who focused on the independent developers such as Unity 3D.

With the independent game developer in mind, many game engines focused on affordability and cross-platform development. Tools such as Game Maker, UDK, and of course Unity 3D allowed for many more people to learn and build games without the multimillion-dollar investment formerly required for game production.

### 1.4.3 Why Use Unity 3D to Learn?

*Making a game is more fun than making accounting software.* Having fun learning is more important as getting high test scores. After a test, you pretty much forget the anguish of studying all night and what it was for. So there is no reason to make learning menial work because studying should not be boring.

Once learning becomes entertainment, the lessons become something you want to remember. As a fun experience, you remember the experience longer. I've found that learning how to write game artificial intelligence (AI) and behaviors is the best way to retain programming experience.

Programming lessons are often taught using stiff diagrams and simple math problems with little or no applicable use. How often have you actually needed to know where trains would meet leaving two different cities at two different speeds? Experience shows that readers lose interest in any example involving grade-point averages or a train leaving from New York.

Unity 3D offers examples by blowing things up. Calculus and vector examples are usually explained using grids and lines. These concepts are lost by abstract pictures that lack meaning or application. In this case, we'll use math to solve for where a bad guy needs to throw a grenade in order to hit a moving target.

Finally, we'll end up with both knowledge that will help build a game and skills needed to write software outside of Unity 3D. With any luck, we'll also have fun while learning. Some of these examples may even help with your math classes.

Unity 3D also provides us with a complete set of tools we can use in our code quickly and easily. These tools are a part of the Unity 3D application programming interface (API). The Unity 3D API is filled with useful things such as commonly used routines, data structures, and classes. These parts of the API are often called a library. We'll learn what all that means in the remaining chapters.

### 1.4.4 How Does Unity 3D Use C#?

Unity 3D has very few built-in functions when it comes to making things interactive. Everything is done through various programming languages such as Boo, C#, and JavaScript. Boo is a part of old Unity 3D programming, which is a language that came about when Unity 3D was first introduced. JavaScript is a common programming language used by many web developers. That is why it was first used several versions ago to attract a wider audience of web developers looking to get into 3D game development.

Unity 3D integrated C# to attract an even wider group of developers by using a more universally used programming language. C# is used by a large community of programmers. Unity 3D is also a cross-platform game engine, and a developer working on either OS X or Windows can both share and use files for Unity 3D. C# is exactly the same on both Mac and PC, so there is no concern over what operating system you're going to use.

#### 1.4.4.1 How to Tell Unity 3D What to Do

Unity 3D and MonoDevelop are going to be our integrated development environment (IDE). IDEs come in many different forms. Many professional Windows programmers use Visual Studio and Apple developers use Xcode in OS X. IDEs provide several functions that make programming easier by highlighting the lines of code and automatically filling the commonly repeated tasks.

When it comes to learning about the nuts and bolts of programming, you're basically learning about how your computer thinks, or in more general terms, how your computer does what it is told. Somewhere along the way you'll realize how unintelligent your computer is and how smart good programmers are.

Programming is basically writing detailed instructions on what to do and when. A big part of programming is figuring out where to put information; we'll call this data management. Then you use logic to determine what to do with the data. Programming logic is organized into algorithms found in statements organized into functions.

Unity 3D provides a complete set of tools to create characters and objects that your code can interact with. These assets all live in the project directory as many separate files or entities that you can control through code. Unity 3D provides scene files; 3D models; particle systems for explosions, fire, and other special effects; and tools to create and edit all of these things. It is largely up to you to learn these different systems on your own, but this book covers the code part of things.

## 1.5 What Is Programming?

*It's all about writing code.* Programming is a process in which we organize data and use logic to do something with those data. The data are everything a computer can store; they can range from numbers to zombie characters in a video game. You do this by writing text into files called source code. Source code written into text files replaces punch cards used by the computing machines half a century ago.

When data are combined with logic and then written into a single file, they're called a class. Classes are also data, and as such can be managed with more logic. Classes are used to create objects in the computer's memory and can be duplicated to have a life of their own.

Classes are used to build objects. Each piece of data within the class becomes a part of that object. Different chunks of data inside of a class are called class members. Class members can also be chunks of logic called functions or methods. If that is not clear right now, don't worry we'll go into detail on that in Chapter 2.

In a game with a horde of zombies, each zombie is duplicated or instanced from a zombie class. Each zombie has unique values for each attribute or data element in the class. This means hit points, and locations are unique for each duplicate zombie object. Objects created from a class are called instances.

Similar to families, objects can inherit properties from one another. The child sometimes called a subclass inherits attributes from its parent. For instance, the child created from a zombie may inherit the parent's hunger for brains. To be useful, the child zombie can also add new objects and change the objects it inherited from its parent class. As a result, now the child zombie might have tentacles that the parent didn't have.

Objects talk to each other through events and messages. Shooting at zombies can create an event, or in programmer terms, it "raises" an event. The bullet impact event tells the zombie class to then take necessary steps when hit by a bullet. Events command the class to take actions on its data, which is where functions come in.

Functions, also known as methods, are sections of logic that act on data. They allow your class to create additional events and talk to yet more objects. As the player presses the trigger and moves the joystick around, yet more events can be raised and messages can be sent. Events and messages allow the player to interact with your world; logic events and objects together build your game.

### 1.5.1 What Does C# Look Like?

A game in Unity 3D is made up of many different C# files. Each file can be referred to as a "class" and end with the .cs file extension (which stands for C Sharp). This isn't a class like those that are taught. It is more akin to biology in which classes are categories that define different groups of organisms.

Controller.cs
Visual C# Source file
268 KB

Explosion.cs
Visual C# Source file
33.7 KB

Monster.cs
Visual C# Source file
100 KB

Player.cs
Visual C# Source file
67.2 KB

Projectile.cs
Visual C# Source file
33.8 KB

Weapon.cs
Visual C# Source file
67.1 KB

A basic game might have several different classes, each one named according to its purpose. Each one of these classes contains the text that is your actual C# code. Just so you know, by default Windows will hide the extensions of your files. As a result, if classes appear as simply Weapon or Monster and there is no extension.cs, then you should go into the Tools menu, select Folder Options/View, and enable file extensions.

### 1.5.2  Learning to Copy and Paste

*"A good artist creates, a great artist steals."* There are code examples for you to copy and paste into your project. The content of this book and all downloadable content are no different. This means that you'll have to understand what the code is doing to interpret it to fit your needs.

Every programmer does this habitually. It is important to learn how to do this since it is something that you actually need to do in many cases not only to learn but also to get any unfamiliar task done.

Programming is a constant learning process. It is a language to command computers. Anytime you learn a new language, there will be plenty of words which you'll have to look up. Add to this the fact that every programmer gets to make up new words, and you've got a language that you'll always need a dictionary for.

When some code is shown, you'll be expected to copy that code into your project. With your fingers ready on the keyboard, you'll want to get in the habit of typing. There is a reason why programmers are usually fast typists. This is also cause for programmers to be picky about what keyboard they prefer.

In most cases, the projects in this book will be in some state where you can read text that is already in place. Most of the projects are in a more complete state, where you'll be able to run them and see an intended result.

As a programmer I've gotten used to searching the Internet for example code. Once I've discovered something that looks useful, I copy that code and paste it into a simple test case. After I've wrapped my head around what the code is doing, I rewrite it in a form that is more suited for my specific case.

Even if the code involves some fun trick, I'll learn from that code. As I learn new tricks, I grow as a programmer. The only way to learn new tricks is to find the necessity to solve a new problem for which I haven't already figured out a solution. Finding solutions to problems is a fundamental part of being a programmer.

## 1.6 Compiling: Turning Words into Computer Instruction

Once your source code is finished, it is time to compile. Compiling is the process of taking all of your source files and building bytecode. Unity 3D uses Mono, as it is a compiler to generate the bytecode, but Unity 3D does this automatically. Mono is an open-source compiler that runs on many different processors and operating systems.

The combination of central processing unit (CPU) and operating system is often called a platform. Each platform requires a unique native machine code to execute or run. Building code for each platform is called a target. Unity 3D converts the bytecode into a native machine code and can target Mac, PC, Android, and iOS.

Native machine code is the set of instructions that directly talk to the CPU and operating system. Unity 3D is a simple way to generate the complex set of instructions for your computer to run. Code that talks directly to the hardware is referred to as "low-level" programming.

There are layers of software between you and the computer's hardware. When writing C# for games using Unity 3D, your code is compiled by Mono. Unity 3D then takes the bytecode from Mono and compiles for a target platform into a native machine code.

Both Unity 3D and Mono are the layers underneath your code and the computer's hardware putting you on a higher level. This is often referred to as a computer layer abstraction. That is why C# is usually considered a high-level programming language.

Programming at a lower level requires much more knowledge of memory management and a wide variety of other APIs that might include graphic cards, physics, sound, and everything else that runs a game. Writing for a layer involves an in-depth knowledge of both the layers below and above the one you're writing for.

The computer hardware, such as CPU, graphics card, memory, and storage, live on the lowest level. Above them is the basic input/output system (BIOS) and software that starts the hardware when you press the Power button. Above that is your computer's operating system and drivers that talk to the hardware. Finally, Unity 3D lives above the operating system, and then your code lives above Unity 3D.

That is why we're going to use Unity 3D to write games, and not starting from scratch in raw C++. Otherwise we'll have to spend a few years learning about physics, rendering, and assembly language, or the instruction set that your CPU uses to think.

## 1.7 What We've Learned

As a result, we've figured out what C# is, and what learning how to program will require of you. If you haven't already downloaded Unity 3D from the website https://github.com/badkangaroo/UnityProjects, then do so, as the upcoming chapters will be hands-on tutorials.

Unity 3D is free; there are no fees or royalties that need to be paid to the Unity 3D developers ever. If you want to port your games to iOS or Android that will require a Unity 3D Pro license, then you'll need to pay up. Until then, the free license is all you'll need for learning and sharing your game with your peers on your computer.

## 1.8 Leveling Up

The computer systems in place today have evolved from machines with moving parts. Telling these machines what to do involved setting knobs and switches. Today, we use text organized into statements and logic.

It is difficult to imagine a time when computers were so slow that simple calculations involved waiting for clattering switches to finish moving around to produce an answer. Today, computers complete many billions of calculations in a single second. All too often we take for granted that computers rely on the same concepts and systems that were built nearly a century ago.

Understanding how computers work puts into context how we write software. It is possible to write software without this understanding, but it is harder to appreciate how it works.

# 2

## Before You Begin

This book focuses on learning C# and the fundamentals involved with programming a computer language. However, it does not necessarily focus on using Unity 3D to complete a specific game. You're not required to make any purchases, since this book assumes that you're using the free version of Unity 3D.

## 2.1 What Will Be Covered in This Chapter

Since this is a light chapter, it does not focus more on the C# language. Before we get to know C#, we're going to need to make sure that you're ready with Unity 3D; otherwise you're not going to be able to follow along with the content of the rest of this book.

If you are already familiar with Unity 3D, then this chapter might be a bit of an extra review. If you think you already understand how a scene works and how to attach scripts to objects, then you can skip ahead to the next chapter.

- We'll go over where to get and how to install the Unity 3D game engine.
- We'll go over how to get around in the Unity 3D game engine editor.
- We'll look at how to read C# code.
- Finally, before moving on we'll see how to make use of C# within Unity 3D.

The chapters that discuss Unity 3D will remain focused on how the code works and interacts with software that usually involves C#. There are plenty of books that do focus on Unity 3D's game development tools. It is recommended that you also obtain some reading materials to help you learn the rest of the Unity 3D tool set.

For the tutorials in this book I'll be working in Windows. If you're running C# on a Mac, you can follow along with most of the tutorials as most of the tools will work in the same way in both operating systems. Unfortunately, some features of .NET outside of these tutorials are not supported across both platforms. Truth be told .NET has had a wide acceptance on every operating system, so its support is quite universal.

Most of the elements of the Unity 3D tools such as particle systems, animation systems, and other components such as lighting and sound are not covered in this book. However, this book enables you to add any interactivity with those elements of the engine. By the end of this book, you should be able to intuitively know how to look up what's involved with playing a sound when the player clicks buttons or fires weapons.

We will be encountering a lot of what is called source code. Source code is the term given to the text that is entered into a file by the programmers. Samples of this code, and in many cases a complete source, are provided. A sample of source code will look like the following:

```
using UnityEngine;
using System.Collections;
public class Example : MonoBehaviour {
        //Use this for initialization
        void Start () {
        }
        //Update is called once per frame
        void Update () {
        }
}
```

If the sample makes no sense at all, don't worry, after just a few chapters you'll be more comfortable looking at all of the new punctuation and formatting. Each character space and word has a special meaning. To programmers this formatting of characters is called *syntax*. If you've written something like HTML or even JavaScript, some of this might seem familiar.

It is important that you take care to notice the syntax—the placement of words and punctuation. Each curly brace, colon, and period is important. Forgetting a period or a semicolon will keep all of your code away from working. To help us along in our programming adventure, you'll be introduced to a new software tool called MonoDevelop that looks like the one shown below.

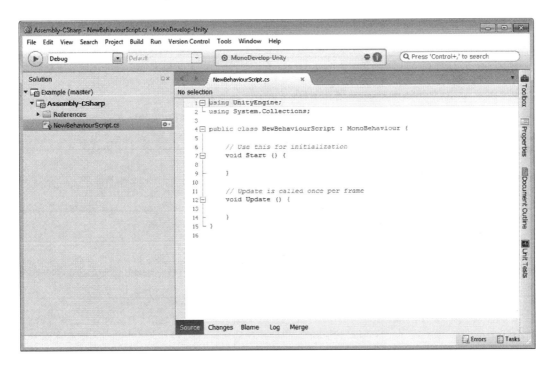

MonoDevelop is an open-source software that is installed along with Unity 3D. Both the free and professional versions of Unity 3D use the same version of MonoDevelop. This is commonly referred to as an integrated development environment (IDE). You could use another text editor such as Notepad, but many of the examples will require MonoDevelop for a complete understanding.

We will be spending a lot of time writing code and observing each line to interpret what each line is for. More importantly, we'll be thinking about why the code works and the alternate methods of accomplishing the same task. One important topic we'll also be looking at is how a line of code can break and how to fix it. There are many common mistakes all programmers make, which we may also get used to them early on.

Just as important we'll take a look at how the code misbehaves and what common mistakes can take place. Error messages are not a huge problem; they act as clues that inform you where you need to fix your code. You can expect a lot of errors when you first get started; in many cases, a single line may have more than one error, so there might be multiple fixes before you're able to move on.

Alternate methods are important so you know that each task you approach isn't solved with a single solution. Approaching a problem is more important than memorizing and regurgitating the same solution when you see a similar problem again. In the real world, no two situations will be exactly alike. Each time you need to solve a problem, you'll need to invent a unique solution.

Programming is a creative process that allows for any number of different methods to accomplish a single task. Each variation of code has pros and cons. Each line of code may vary depending on the programmer; in this case, you may feel differently about what code to use and why you prefer it. Always use the version which you find easier to read and understand.

No doubt if you're really going to get into making games with Unity 3D, you'll want to get an additional book that focuses on building assets, scenes, and effects. If you don't already know your way around Unity 3D, we should have a brief introduction to the Unity 3D interface that we're most concerned about when it comes to writing our scripts.

## 2.2 Downloading and Installing: It Is Free

Download Unity 3D from http://unity3d.com/unity/download, which will bring you to a menu of download options. I picked the free version and ignored any additional options. At the bottom of the page is a large Download button which I used to download the latest version of Unity 3D.

As of this writing, UnitySetup-4.3.0.exe was the latest version which I was prompted to download. The file is just over 1.2 gigabytes, and depending on your download speed, this might take a while to finish downloading. It is worth getting the latest version, as many features and options are always added with every new update.

After the download is finished, start it up and go ahead with the installation process. Hopefully, you'll have the access rights to your computer to do this. I've left everything at the default settings and pressed Next a few times. Eventually you'll get to a progress bar that tells you how far along the installation has gone. As updates come out, feel free to download and install them as well. The C# programming language rarely changes so drastically that any of the code shown in this book will break.

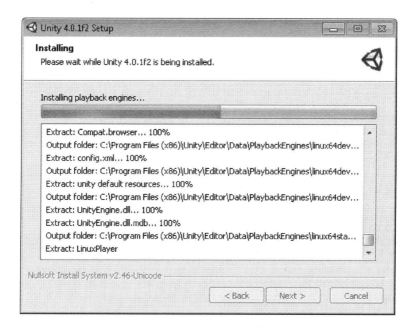

If you're asked to install any additional support files, click Yes, as we may want to refer to these later on. Either way you'll be able to find additional information on the Unity 3D website and download any missing files.

Once the installation is finished, you'll be able to start up Unity 3D. The setup will install Unity 3D and MonoDevelop as well as many related support files. There will also be a large example file that includes many assets and completed script files. We may make some references to this later in the book.

## 2.3  Unity 3D Overview: What We're Looking At

Let's start with a brief overview of the user interface (UI) and where to create the files you need to work on and then how to edit them. We'll be creating a new project for each chapter, and for your convenience they'll also be available on the Internet for downloading. We'll also be creating a lot of C# files, so we'll see that there are a few different ways to do this.

There are no differences between how the free and professional versions interact with C#. All of the examples in this book are based on the free version. The screenshots and visual examples may lack some of the visual flair that the professional version allows for, but it has no effect on the C# we'll be learning.

When starting up for the first time, you'll be prompted with the following dialog:

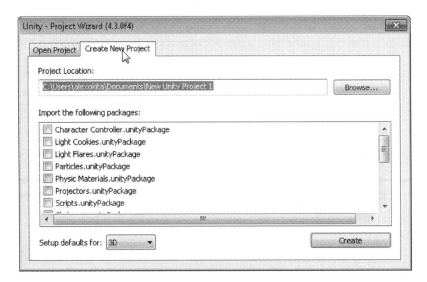

Select Create New Project and put the contents of the new project into your Documents directory. This directory can live anywhere and can be moved later on. We just need to find somewhere to put a project to begin.

### 2.3.1 The Main Panel

Once the project is set, the main editor panel will open. The Unity 3D interface is divided into five major parts: (1) toolbar, (2) Hierarchy panel, (3) Scene and Game view, (4) Inspector panel, and (5) Project and Console panel. Each panel is labeled with a panel at the top left.

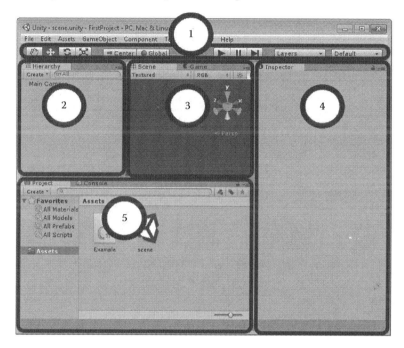

#### 2.3.1.1 Toolbar

Label 1 in the figure shows us the toolbar, consisting of the navigation or manipulation tools and the Play, Pause, and Step Forward buttons. We will be using the Play in Editor button to test our code. When this button is pressed, the Game panel will automatically come to the front. All of the code in the scene will begin to run. This is important because we'll be using Unity 3D to test all of the code we will be writing.

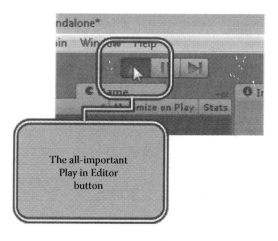

The all-important Play in Editor button

### 2.3.1.2 Hierarchy Panel

Label 2 shows us the Hierarchy panel. In a new scene, you'll only have a Main Camera. The Hierarchy panel shows you all of the different objects that are going to make your game scene. Any zombies, environments, camera lights, and sounds can be found in this panel once they're in the scene. When any object is parented to another, it can be found by expanding the parent object with the triangle. In the following example, you'll find a piggy parented to a house.

### 2.3.1.3 Scene and Game View

Label 3 shows us both the scene and game views. The scene is more like a construction view of the game. The Game panel is the view of the game through the Main Camera. The difference here is that the Scene panel cannot be seen by the player, only you as the creator of the game can access the scene view. With this view, you'll be able to place and arrange any object light and zombie you like.

### 2.3.1.4 Inspector Panel

Label 4 shows us the Inspector panel. By selecting an object in either the hierarchy or the scene view, you'll be able to look at their various properties. Things such as a transform, which show the object's position, rotation, and scale in the scene, can also be altered by you to edit the scene.

Take note of the Add Component button in this panel. This is one of the many ways in which we can assign a C# file to an object in the scene. If this seems a bit confusing, don't worry, we'll get back to what Components and GameObjects are in a moment.

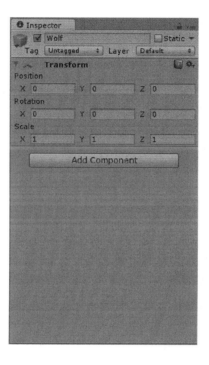

### 2.3.1.5 Project and Console Panel

Finally, label 5 shows us the Project and Console panels. The project view shows us all of the various assets we create to add to a scene. When we save a scene, it then turns into an asset for us to open from the project view. As we create new C# files, they too will be shown to us in the project view.

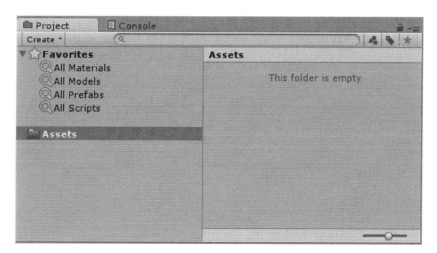

The last but most important part is the Console panel. By clicking on the Console panel, the console view will be brought forward. This view displays all of the information that is being created by the C# code we write. Any problems, warnings, and errors will be presented in this panel.

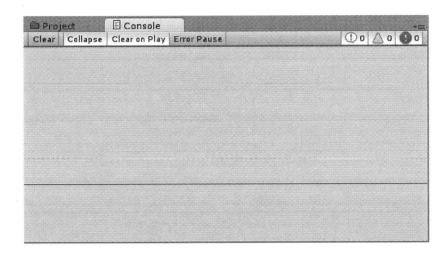

The panels can be easily moved around. To get back to the default layout, select Window→ Layouts→Default.

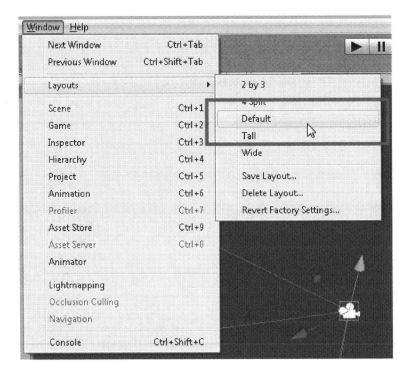

The Unity 3D installer also installed MonoDevelop, the IDE used to edit code. We haven't seen this yet as it doesn't open until you need to edit a C# or other script file used by Unity 3D. We'll get to that soon enough. Before that, we'll want to make sure that we're not too surprised by what we're about to get into.

## 2.3.2 Creating a New Project

Open Unity 3D and you'll be prompted with the Unity 3D Project Wizard. For your own sake, I'd suggest you keep a separate directory aside for all of your Unity 3D projects. In this directory, we'll be creating many different projects. Each project should be kept in a subdirectory named after the chapter it is created for. Example: "UnityProjects/chapter1/" should be where you keep your work for chapter1. Normally, each project will be quite small, usually less than a megabyte. Most music files and images will take up much more space than the Unity 3D projects you'll be creating.

Select New Project in the File menu. This will open the following dialog:

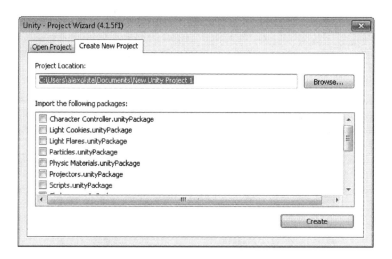

It is up to you to find an appropriate directory for your project. Make sure the path isn't too long as long path names can occasionally cause problems. If you're on Windows, the default project location happens to be your Documents folder\New Unity 3D Project. This will be fine for our examples.

| Name | Date modified | Type | Size |
|------|---------------|------|------|
| Assets | 2/1/2013 12:11 AM | File folder | |
| Library | 2/2/2013 10:21 PM | File folder | |
| ProjectSettings | 2/1/2013 12:11 AM | File folder | |
| Temp | 2/2/2013 10:23 PM | File folder | |
| Assembly-CSharp.csproj | 2/2/2013 10:23 PM | Visual C# Project f... | 4 KB |
| Assembly-CSharp.pidb | 2/1/2013 12:02 AM | PIDB File | 14 KB |
| Assembly-CSharp-vs.csproj | 2/2/2013 10:23 PM | Visual C# Project f... | 4 KB |
| ExampleProject.sln | 2/2/2013 10:23 PM | Microsoft Visual S... | 2 KB |
| ExampleProject.userprefs | 2/1/2013 12:02 AM | USERPREFS File | 1 KB |
| ExampleProject-csharp.sln | 2/2/2013 10:23 PM | Microsoft Visual S... | 2 KB |

Click on the Create button, which restarts Unity 3D and opens a new project. Unity 3D creates many different files for each new project. It creates a main project directory with all of the related assets located in subdirectories. Most software development tools for other games follow a similar pattern. This method allows for several people working on the game at the same time. Each person can edit different parts of the same project and work together.

### 2.3.3  A New Unity 3D Project

You will find that four different directories—Assets, Library, ProjectSettings, and Temp—and several support files may occupy an active Unity 3D project directory. Some of the files will not show up after you've run the game or edited some source files in MonoDevelop. We'll get to what all that means in a moment.

#### 2.3.3.1  Assets Directory

The primary location for all of your C# files and any other game objects such as 3D models, 2D textures, and sounds will be somewhere in this directory. If a file isn't located in this directory, your game will not be able to access it.

Often when a project gets bigger, it is a good idea to create some subdirectories for your game. The organization of these different files is up to you, but most of the time all of the source code will live in its own directory.

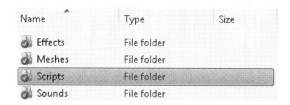

You might be inclined to put all asset resources together in one place. For instance, a hero might have a Hero directory with his sounds, models, textures, and scripts grouped together. This does make things more difficult to share. A weapon or sound effect might have to be shared by more than one character, so it makes more sense assuming that every resource can be shared.

This assumption goes the same for your code. You should write code as though it were something that were sharable among every asset in the game. If you're able to make a bit of software that enables a zombie to wander through a town searching for fresh brains, then you should be able to make a toaster oven do the same and reuse the same code for both.

To make finding specific types of assets easier to locate, there is a search highlighter in the Project panel.

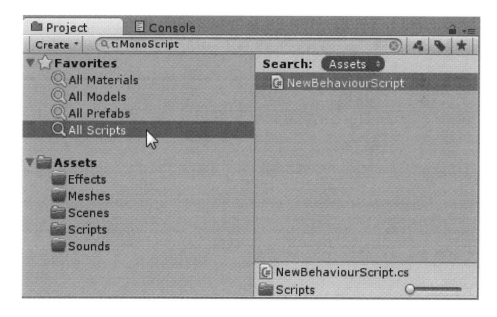

Select All Scripts and the right side of the panel shows all script assets in your project.

### 2.3.3.2 Library Directory

Next to the Assets directory in the computer's file browser is the Library directory. This contains the glue which Unity 3D uses to tie assets and logic together behind the scenes. Your editor preferences, platform settings, and many other bits that game engines need are placed here. It is very rare that any user will ever need to go in here to make any modifications, so it is best to avoid messing with the contents of this directory.

### 2.3.3.3 Project Settings Directory

When any asset is imported into Unity 3D, it goes through a sort of filter and setup. Mostly, with things such as 3D models and textures, a lot of mashing of the bits must take place before they're game ready. Unity 3D does nearly all of this automatically. Even importing a box mesh from a 3D content creation tool requires some processing before you can drop it into a Unity 3D Scene.

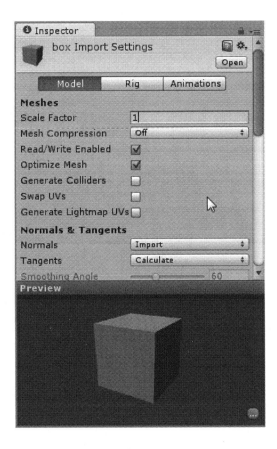

Scale factor, optimization, and many other aspects can be set when importing the model. All of these settings are remembered in the ProjectSettings directory. If you're a 3D artist, then you might know a bit about what all of the above-mentioned settings mean. If not, then rest assured, there will be very little 3D art talk in this book. We're here to write code, not sculpt polygons.

### 2.3.3.4 Temp Directory

Data caches, writing temp files, and other operating system maintenance-related stuff get thrown into the Temp directory. Unity 3D is a complex system made of many different components. For everything to flow together nicely, there's a lot of temporary work involved.

Between the Library, ProjectSettings, and Temp directories, we've got a lot of extras that Unity 3D generates all on its own. This is not unlike many other programming environments. Cache files, debugging files, and intermediate resources often get piled up in even the most simple programming project.

The only directory we're concerned with is the Assets directory, so we'll just stick to messing around in one place.

### 2.3.4 Summary

Unity 3D has a diverse set of tools, all of which are useful once you've decided to go ahead and build a game. The engine has been used to create everything from 2D side-scrolling games to 3D first-person shooters. Fantasy role-playing games and top-down strategy games have all been produced and published using the Unity 3D Game Engine.

It is best for you to look around online for some additional information on the editor itself. There's plenty of cool stuff that you can do once you follow some of the online tutorials that cover the basics of the editor. Topics on surface materials particles and animation will not be covered in this book so it is a good idea to get into the different aspects of the editor to understand the most out of Unity 3D once you've gotten through a portion of this book.

To be an independent game developer, you'll have to cover the breadth of skills that are usually taken on by different team members in a larger game production cycle. As a lone wolf game developer, you have to take on a variety of tasks, not just the code.

If you're an artist looking to add programming as a skill on top of your current skill list, then the rest of the editor's functions will come more easily. That being said, it is still a good idea to know your way around Unity 3D if you're new to this game engine.

## 2.4 Sample Code

Most code will be shown in small samples called code fragments. Fragments, as the word infers, are small parts of a whole code sample. Complete code samples will be shown when it is necessary to show how a completed source file will look like. If only one or two lines change in a complete file, only the changed lines will be shown as a code fragment. Here's an example of a complete source file:

```
using UnityEngine;
using System.Collections;
public class Example: MonoBehaviour {
        //Use this for initialization
        void Start () {
        }
        //Update is called once per frame
        void Update () {
        }
}
```

The above example shows a new C# file generated by Unity 3D. We'll observe how it is created in a moment. What's important is that you could copy the text carefully into a new text file, named `Example.cs`, and use it as is. First let's see how a fragment will look like and then we'll go into how this is done.

### 2.4.1 Code Fragments

The following example shows a fragment of code taken from the completed source file:

```
        //Use this for initialization
        void Start () {
              //A new line of code appears!
        }
```

You should be able to identify where the code was taken from. After identifying where its original is, you should be able to see what's changed or added. This means you should make the same changes in your version of the source code.

A fragment is intended to showcase smaller, more important components of a complete code sample. Rather than reading through the completed source file and looking for the change, a fragment will help you find the important differences when a new concept is shown.

Not all examples in the book will start with a complete source file. Often, the code fragment will require only one line to represent the concept being explained. The context of the code sample and your ability to understand the context should be sufficient by the time you begin to see those examples.

Also worth noting, most of the programming examples will not make a visual impact in the scene inside of Unity 3D. There isn't a single command to make monsters appear or dragons breathe fire. Programming is the manipulation of data with logic, not magic.

If the changes are added correctly, your version will function the same way as described by the tutorial you're reading. A code fragment cannot function on its own. The rest of the code is required by Unity 3D to run without errors.

Once a concept has been introduced, you'll be required to remember how it is used. Later lessons will again reinforce the concept that learning how to program is a skill-building process. To program a complete game, you need to combine the different ideas taught here to write your own code. Building upon your own skill will not only expand your understanding of C#, but once concepts have been learned, you'll be able to apply them to other programming languages.

Occasionally, I'll refer to how C# differs from other programming languages. I'll leave it up to you to investigate what the other languages look like on your own. This provides a context as to why C# looks or acts in a particular way and how other programming languages solve the same problem. In most cases, you may find that many programming languages look and behave quite similar.

## 2.4.2 Are Errors Bad?

Don't be afraid to make mistakes. The code you write can not break Unity 3D or your computer. At least nothing you'll learn from this book will enable you to do so.

As a matter of fact, it is often good to produce errors. The errors tell us what we can and cannot do. Programmers often ask themselves, "Will the compiler let me do this?" which may produce an error. If not, then the programmer will continue his thought with "huh, I guess it will, so that means I can …"

Creating and fixing errors tells us what the compiler expects from us. It is a sort of a conversation between the programmer and the computer, for example, the programmer asking questions in the form of a code statement and the computer replying with an error to the programmer who asks for things the computer can't do.

### 2.4.2.1 Compile-Time and Run-Time Errors

There are two general cases of errors: compile-time and run-time errors. Compile-time errors often include syntactical errors that are usually found right away by Unity 3D before the code is even run. These are shown in the Console panel which we'll show you in a bit. When you get a syntax error, it is usually caused by an unexpected or misplaced character. There are many cases in which compile-time errors can pop up, far too many to list here. However, compile-time errors (sometimes called parser) occur when the code itself is written incorrectly.

Run-time errors happen once the game is run. These errors are usually created by a misunderstanding of what the code is able to do. When Unity 3D comes across a statement that contains unexpected data or tries to do something mathematically impossible, for example, divide by zero, we get a run-time error. Such errors are usually a bit harder to fix as they only show up upon specific conditions in the game. For these we can mark the statement in MonoDevelop and tell Unity 3D to stop when it gets there. Once that happens, we can inspect every bit of data and its value. This will help find and fix any problems that exist.

Errors simply stop Unity 3D from running your code. Some properly written code may follow correct syntax, but might require you to force Unity 3D to close using the task manager, but this is rare and often easy to fix. Read the code samples carefully as you enter them into MonoDevelop.

To fix the error, you have to just find what character was mistyped and replace it with a correction. To test if the error is fixed, go back to Unity 3D from MonoDevelop. If no errors or warnings are produced, then your code is clear of syntactical errors. We'll see this in action soon enough.

### 2.4.3 How to Follow Along

Many examples will require that you use both MonoDevelop and read Unity 3D's output window. We'll be switching back and forth often for each tutorial. When working in Unity 3D, you might need to have the editor take up a lot of screen space for having access to all of the different parts of the Unity 3D interface. Primarily we'll need to see the Console output panel and the Inspector panel. This is often why programmers like having multiple monitors. One monitor with their code and the other monitor with an editor open showing them the resulting behaviors.

I'd suggest taking in a single chapter at a time and then letting the information sink in a bit. I'd also want you to perform experiments on your own to gain a better understanding of what you just learned. If you can make assumptions about something you've learned and step beyond what was taught in the chapter, then I'd say you have a usable grasp of the chapter.

Without following each chapter and skipping around, you might find yourself reading terms that are unfamiliar. I try my best to build up from one chapter to the next. So try not to skip too far ahead of yourself unless you find yourself being bored and unchallenged; in that case, you skim through each chapter till you find something you're not already familiar with.

### 2.4.4 Summary

We're going to have to do a lot of reading and writing. Sorry, that's just the case when it comes to code. If this doesn't detract from the experience of learning, then great! Otherwise you're going to have to just get over the fact that programming involves a lot of typing and thinking at the same time. If you're used to doing that sort of thing, then great!

## 2.5 Working with C#: Game Engines

Unity 3D is a game engine. You will be writing code that runs inside of this game engine. So you're writing software that's run inside of another piece of software. What this means is that your code operates a layer further from your computer's hardware resources.

**NOTE:** What do I mean by further from the computer hardware resources? This is where the term "high-level programming" comes from. At the lowest level is the actual computer hardware. Programmers at this level are actually building silicon chips.

At one level above the silicon are things such as bus and motherboard that everything is either plugged into or soldered on. At another level above those are things that tell the motherboard what to do when power is turned on and how to look for data storage to launch operating systems from and everything else that happen when the computer is turned on.

Once this level finds an operating system, it hands over the tasks to the lowest level of your computer operating system where drivers and other hardware to software interfaces come into play to get your computer running. Once the computer gets booted and your operating system is properly talking to all of the hardware components, it is ready for software applications to start running. At this level your software is usually not talking to any computer hardware directly, but it is talking to the software that runs the operating system.

Unity 3D is a software that talks to the operating system; when you write your game software, your code usually talks directly to Unity 3D but not to the operating system or computer hardware. Your code is being run with many other layers of software between you and the hardware. Similar to so many mattresses between you and the floor, there is more padding between you and any of the complexities that run your computer.

When your code is compiled, it turns into a machine language. The details here are simplified as there's a bit more going on under the hood, so we won't go further into the details. The game code is made up of many different objects called classes. Classes are composed of data (also known as variables), logic (also known as functions or methods), and a name (also known as an identifier).

Functions and data work together inside of Unity 3D to make your game experience come to life. This coordinated effort can then be packaged and turned into a new program that you can publish to any number of computer platforms including browsers, game consoles, and mobile devices.

C# has a few simple parts that we'll be studying later in this chapter. As a part of an exercise, we'll have to learn how to read a bit of code. One unappreciated part of reading code are the line numbers. These numbers are most likely found to the left of your code.

```
1   using UnityEngine;
2   using System.Collections;
3   public class Example : MonoBehavior
4   {
5           public int SomeInt;
6           public int OtherInt = 7;
7           //Use this for initialization
8           void Start ()
9           {
10                  print (MyFunction (1, 2));
11          }
12
13          // Update is called once per frame
14          void Update ()
15          {
16
17          }
18
19          int MyFunction (int a, int b)
20          {
21                  return a + b;
22          }
23  }
```

Each line of code is numbered accordingly. And here we can see that lines 1 and 2 of the code are required to access libraries or software that has already been written by many engineers to empower your code with a vast wealth of software.

At line 3, you'll find what is called a class declaration. This serves as a good overview of what to expect in the remaining chapters, so don't worry if this seems like a lot of unfamiliar information.

Continuing down you'll find some public variables at lines 5 and 6. At line 7, you'll find a comment describing the use of void Start (), which is the first line of code declaring a function. Inside the function at line 8, you'll find a statement that will be executed when the Start () function is called.

At lines 14 through 17, you'll find another function named Update () that doesn't do anything right now, and at line 19, you'll find another function named MyFunction (). At line 22, you'll find the closing curly brace that closes the Example class.

## 2.5.1 Getting Project Files

Cloud file services are becoming more and more common on the Internet. They allow you to store files online and then synchronize them on your computer. They also allow you to share files from computer to computer.

Files have been provided for each chapter by links to various cloud file services. You don't need to sign up for anything to access these links, provided they will allow you to download them without an account.

In my case, I'm keeping all of my projects on GitHub. It's up to you to decide where to keep your projects. We'll see how to download a project and open it in Unity 3D in a moment. Information on additional download locations will be available on the blog associated with this book at http://okita.com/Unity/, which also has updates for this book.

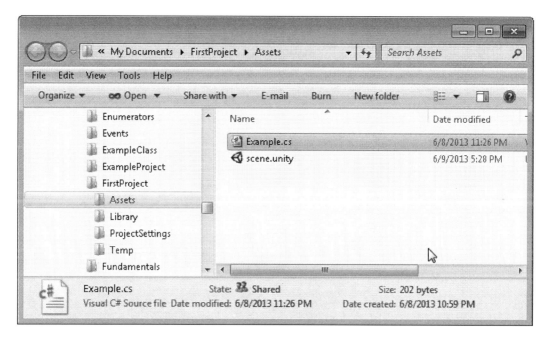

Cloud file systems such as SkyDrive and Dropbox offer a system that allows you to keep your project files both locally on your computer's hard disk and on a remote server. The projects have been made available on several services to make it easy for you to find them.

Without having to install any additional software, you can grab all the projects at once from GitHub.

Open a web browser and follow the link https://github.com/badkangaroo/UnityProjects, which will send you to the latest version of the projects used in this book.

Looking to the lower right of the information, you'll find a Download ZIP button, which will start downloading the project files of this book. Unzip the archive somewhere easy to remember, and you'll be able to open different projects in Unity 3D.

### 2.5.2 Creating and Assigning a New C# File: Now It's Your Turn

Let's start by opening the EmptyProject found in the downloaded project files. This can be done by opening Unity 3D and selecting Open Project in the File menu. In the following panel, click on the Open Other button on the lower left. Navigate to the directory called EmptyProject, then click on the Select Folder button. Projects in Unity 3D are a collection of various files located in a few different folders. We're most concerned about the Assets directory where all of our C# files live.

   C# files are basic text files. It is possible to open Notepad or any other simple text editor and create a new file from scratch, but it is easy to have Unity 3D create a clean, error-free starting file to work from. Right click on the Project panel and select Create→C# Script from the pop-up menu.

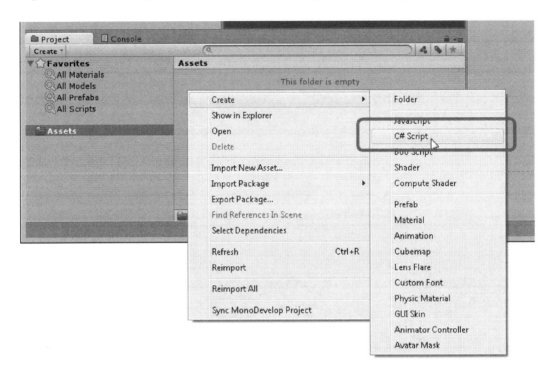

This will create a new C# file in the Assets directory in your project. We'll go into organizing these files with a bit more logic later, but for now we'll just leave it in the Assets directory. Alternatively, you can use the menu and select Assets→Create→C# Script to create a script in the Assets directory.

This will create a file called NewMonoBehaviour, which needs to be renamed as Example to follow along. If you unselect the file, it'll be created as NewMonoBehaviour. This means you'll need to change the file name both in the Assets directory and in the class once it is opened in MonoDevelop. We will cover how this is done in a moment.

   To the right in the Inspector panel, you'll notice some new code. This is a preview of the content of your new file. Selecting different objects both in the Assets panel and in the game scene will prompt different options to appear in the Inspector panel.

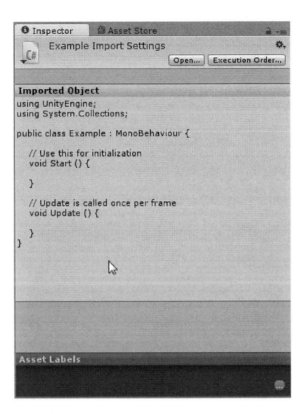

The Inspector panel will be useful for many different things, so we'll be using this quite a lot. Another panel is the Console; at the moment there's not going to be much in it, since we haven't told Unity 3D to put anything in it. We'll also be making extensive use of the Console panel throughout the remainder of this book.

Don't bother trying to edit your code in the Inspector panel. This only serves as a preview to your code, so you might get a clue as to what the code is for. Editing the code is best done in an IDE which we'll jump into next.

Double click on the C# Example file in the Project panel to open MonoDevelop.

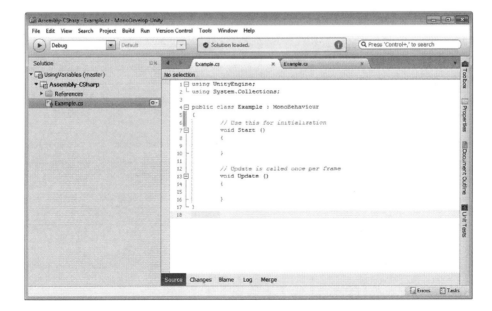

This is where we will be spending most of our time. An IDE is a software made specifically for editing code. MonoDevelop is a popular IDE that has many modern features such as *automatic code completion* and *syntax highlighting*. We'll get to know how to use these features as we read on.

### 2.5.3  Naming Your New File

Just to make sure we're off to a good start, the name of the C# file should match the name of the class. For example, if the file name was called `PeanutButter.cs`, you need to make sure that the class name matches.

Observe the line that reads as "`public class Chocolate : MonoBehaviour {`." When I mean the file name, I do mean the actual file located on the disk in your operating system. To get to these files, right click on the object in Unity 3D's Project panel to get to additional options. In Windows, select Show in Explorer from the right-click window.

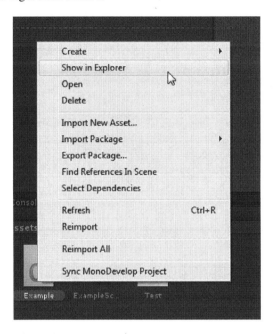

If the name of the file doesn't match the name of the class, you'll get a class definition error when the script is used in the game. Also you can simply click on the name of the file in the Unity 3D's Project panel to rename it.

```
1    using UnityEngine;
2    using System.Collections;
3
4    public class Chocolate : MonoBehaviour
5    {
6            // Use this for initialization
7            void Start ()
8            {
9
10           }
11
12           // Update is called once per frame
13           void Update ()
14           {
15
16           }
17    }
18
```

If the name of the file matches the name of the class, we're in a good position to get started. Keep this file around as we're going to be using it in Chapter 3. Once the class name and the file name match up, you can move on. If the class is named NewMonoBehaviour, change its name to match the file name.

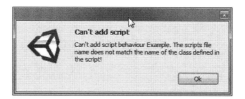

**NOTE:** Some programmers will tell you that C# isn't a real programming language. To some effect it lacks the dirty work of memory management, but that's only a small part of the picture. C# in relation to Unity 3D is being utilized to extend the engine with the content for your game. Due to this, your code will not compile into stand-alone software.

To be fair, you'll be doing a lot of the same work that goes into building a game from scratch. However, a lot of hard work for building a 3D rendering engine that draws 3D objects to the screen, lighting, physics, and particles was already done before you started writing your code. And it is your code that will be run on top of an already sophisticated environment and a vast resource of code that allows you to interface with objects in the game engine.

### 2.5.4 Using Your New File

To assign the C# file to an object in the scene, you can drag it from the Project panel onto an object in the scene. This seems to be pretty simple, but the object might not be in view, or it might be too small to easily select.

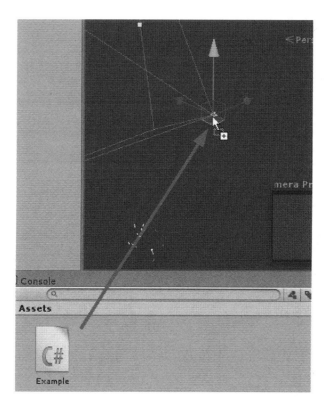

You can also drop it on an object in the Hierarchy panel. Everything in the scene is found here.

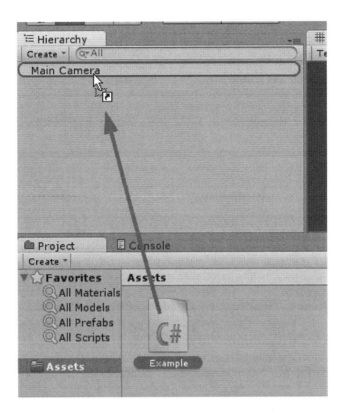

With a selected object in the scene, the Inspector panel will update its properties.

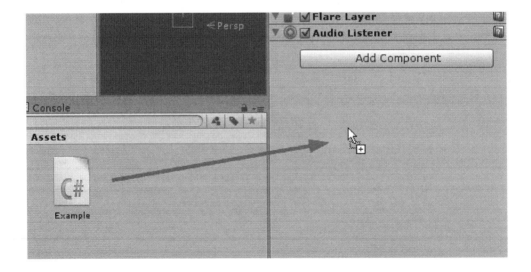

Dropping the `Example.cs` file anywhere under the other properties in the Inspector panel will also add it to the selected object. If that's not enough, then you can press the Add Component button on a selected object in the scene and pick Scripts to select any scripts available in your project.

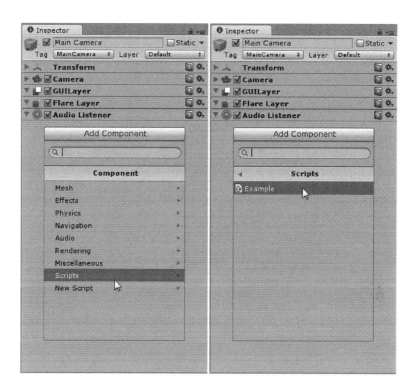

Using the Add Component button, you can even create, name, and add a script all at once! This has become my preferred system of creating and adding scripts to objects in a scene. It does everything all at once. After this it is just a matter of moving the script from the root of the Assets directory into a more organized directory.

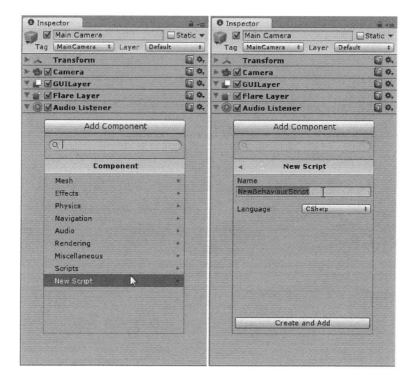

There are plenty of ways to use the editor, but any one of the methods of assigning a script to an object in the scene will work just fine. The end result is that our script will be attached to an object in the scene. As soon as the Start Game button is pressed, your code will go live.

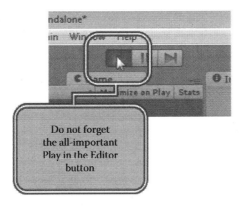

Press the button again to stop the game and your code from running.

After a script has been added to an object in the scene, it becomes a component of that object. All of the components of the object appear as additional rollouts in the Inspector panel. To edit a script component added to the object in the scene, you can double click on the component.

As an alternative you can click on the gear icon and select Edit Script from the pop-up menu.

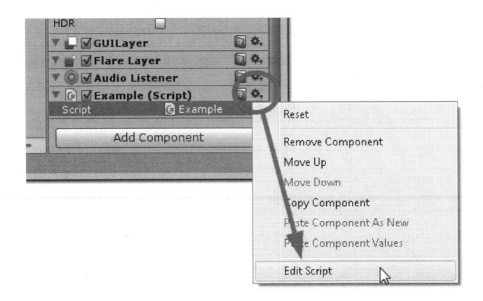

And finally, by clicking on the script attached to the component, the file in the Assets directory will highlight pointing out where the script lives in the project.

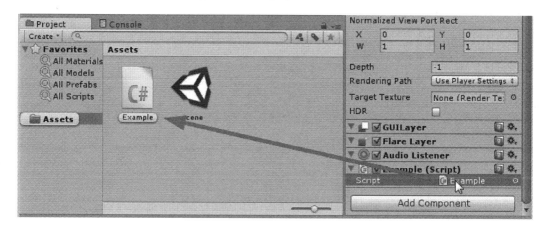

If a script becomes detached from a script component, the script can be replaced or changed by clicking on the little circle to the right of the script name.

Clicking on this little interface widget will open the following dialog showing you all of the available scripts in the project.

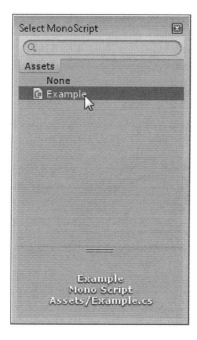

Selecting a script in the panel by double clicking will assign the script to the missing slot in the Inspector panel. To remove an unwanted script or script component, right click on the title of the component and select Remove Component.

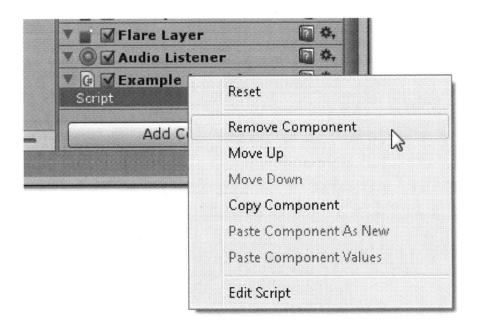

### 2.5.5 Unity 3D Tools

To get an idea of what to expect in the remaining chapters, we can drop in a few simple shapes into the scene. Select GameObject→Create Other→Cube to drop a cube into the scene viewport. To pan around in the scene, press the Q button. Use the left mouse button in the scene viewport to pan around. The mouse wheel zooms the cube, and the right mouse button enables WASD translation navigation and mouse-look mode.

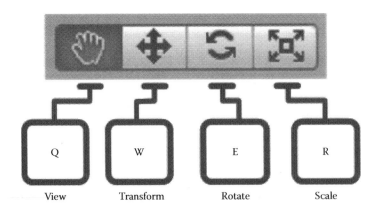

The W key enables the object translation mode. Select any tool aside from the View tool and you'll be able to box select or directly click on an object in the scene. Shift + Box select adds to your selection. Press the Ctrl key while making a selection and you will unselect the next selected item.

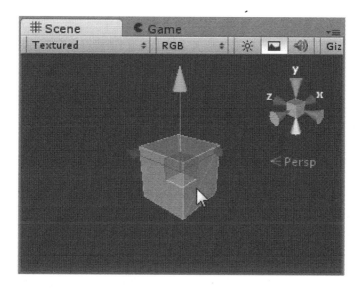

The Transform tool allows you to pick and drag the object around in the scene.

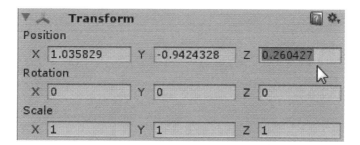

You'll be able to watch the Position values change under the Transform tab in the Inspector panel as you manipulate the cube. The numbers can also be entered directly into the X, Y, and Z fields of the Inspector panel if you want to have a precise control over an object's placement.

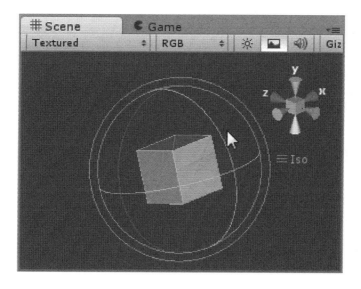

The E key will turn on the Rotation tool. Like the Transform tool, you can watch the object's rotation update in the Inspector panel as you manipulate the object in the scene.

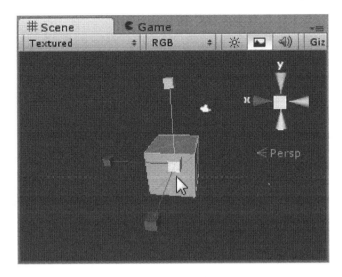

The R key activates the Scale tool and you can change the size of an object or enter the values in the Inspector panel. All three of these tools allow you to pick and drag on various parts of the Manipulation tool in the scene. This changes the manipulation's behavior by constraining the action to one or two axes of freedom.

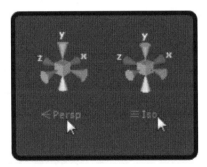

On the top right of the Scene Viewport is a little widget that allows you to switch between various views of your scene. Top front and side views can be accessed quickly by clicking on one of the cones on the widget's cube. To change between a perspective and a parallel camera view, click on the Persp/Iso icon to toggle how the scene is rendered.

### 2.5.6 Running Live Code

While the game is running, you're allowed to reach into the game through the Scene panel. You can select and move objects while the code is being updated. You can also use the Inspector panel to manipulate a selected object's parameters and variables.

Once you stop the game, any changes you made to anything in the scene are immediately reverted to whatever settings they had just before you started the game. This might mean losing some settings which you have tuned while playing the game.

If the settings were saved every time you stopped the scene, then testing a scene would be more troublesome. Going through a level shooting all of the zombies means that the next time you start the level again, everything would already be dead.

### 2.5.7 Saving a Scene

All of the changes we've been doing have been created and applied to objects in a scene. After adding objects to a scene such as lights, cameras, and other objects, it is time to save the scene. The standard Save dialog instructs you to save and name the scene. The default location for a scene is the Assets directory in the project. It is possible to create a subdirectory in the Assets directory called Scenes or something similar; however, for our use, we'll save the scene in the Assets directory of the project.

### 2.5.8 Opening a Scene

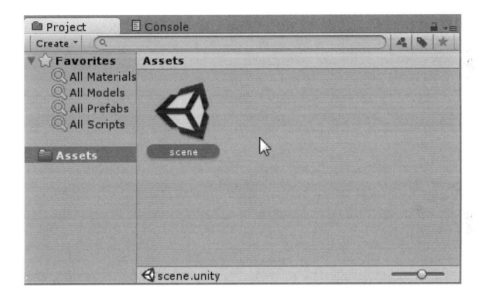

While working with each and every tutorial of this book, there's always going to be a scene file named Scene. Throughout the book, the tutorials will begin with the Scene file found in the downloaded project. To open the scene simply, double click on the scene icon located in the Project panel under the Assets directory. You can also select File→Open Scene to open any scene in the project.

### 2.5.9 Summary

Creating and assigning a new C# file to an object doesn't require so much work. There are plenty of ways to do this within the Unity 3D editor. Once we add some code to the new C# file we're just a button press away from seeing our code in action. With some of the tutorials in this book, you'll be expected to create a new project, create new scripts, and assign the scripts to an object in a scene. With some of the more detailed tutorials, a completed version of the scene will be provided for you.

Amazingly enough, other professional tools for building things for Windows, Linux, or OS X all involve a similar process for creating desktop software. There's almost always a lot more footwork involved with getting started. Templates, frameworks, and other IDE setup processes are required before being able to even get something to print out to a Console panel.

Learning C# with Unity 3D is one of the shortest routes from typing to execution that I can think of that has the most interactive results. The editor itself allows you to interact with variables and values in real time. Selecting an object in the scene editor and changing numbers in the Inspector panel allow you to have a direct connection to your code and see the changes in behavior in real time. This kind of interaction is only possible in the real-time nature of a game engine.

## 2.6  What We've Learned

So far, we've gotten to do a bit of setup and preparation. Getting Unity 3D up and running is necessary, and if you've gotten stuck somewhere, make sure that you check the Internet for any solutions. Naming files and classes correctly is also necessary to get your code to work. A single spelling error can break your code and nothing will work. Also remember that the upper- and lowercase letters matter a great deal. Naming your file the same as the class is also important as a mismatch will also break your code and produce errors.

Programming is a highly rewarding endeavor. Don't let a small hitch bring you down. As you accumulate knowledge, writing code will only get easier. After you've learned one programming language, it is much easier to learn another.

I hope that after you've managed to wrap your head around C#, you'll be able to take the knowledge earned here, look at other programming languages, and feel a need to learn more. If you're an artist, adding the cool tricks that programming can offer to your palette of skills will only make you richer. And I mean richer in more than just the depth of skill.

## 2.7  Leveling Up

Get ready for some new concepts. Telling computers what to do and how to do it takes a lot of work. Computers aren't very bright; they're actually downright dumb. They do exactly what you tell them to do. So if you get unexpected behaviors, it is up to you to make yourself more clear.

Of course, this all involves talking to a computer in its language, something that we should be able to do a part way into this book. Once we've got through the basics, we should be able to tell the computer simple commands and get expected results.

Once you feel that you've gotten to a saturation point while reading this book, it is best to put this book aside for a bit and practice some of the concepts you've just learned. If you feel that you've explored all you can on your own, it is time to come back and pick up where you left off.

# 3

## *First Steps*

This section will cover many basic terms and some of the basic ideas behind writing proper code. C# is among the many different programming languages which use the same words and concepts to convey instructions to the computer. Once we get through the first few chapters we'll be introduced to some more of the basics which are directly related to reading and writing code.

Before we can get to that we'll need to cover some of the terms and concepts that hold true for many different programming languages, not just C#. The methods and systems that allow converting words into executable code require fairly strict rules.

When writing English or chatting online we tend to ignore formatting and punctuation. The brevity allows for faster communication, though only because we as humans have learned many new words and can use context to better interpret the contractions and acronyms in the written form of English used online or in text messages. Computers aren't so smart as to be able to interpret our words so easily.

Unity 3D is a 3D game engine. By 3D we mean three dimensions, which means we have an $x$, $y$, and $z$ coordinate space. 2D or two-dimensional game engines like Game Maker only use $x$ and $y$. This is the difference between a cube and a square. One has depth to each shape and the other does not.

Later on we will be working with three-dimensional vectors. Unity 3D uses Euclidian vectors to describe where objects are located in a scene. When a position is described in terms of $x = 1$, $y = 2$, and $z = 3$, you should understand that this describes a position in 3D space.

## 3.1 What Will Be Covered in This Chapter

We'll go over the specifics of the most basic parts of the C# programming language. The C# language has a great deal in common with other programming languages, so much of the knowledge here is transferable to many other programming languages:

- Tokens, the smallest elements of C#.
- How statements, giving tokens meaning.
- Important words that exist in C# with specific functions.
- How to use white space and proper formatting.
- How statements are grouped together into a code block.
- How classes are organized and what they're used for.
- What a variable is and how it's used.
- Types and how they behave when converted between one another.
- Commenting on code and leaving messages to yourself and others within the code.

## 3.2 Review

In Chapter 2 we looked at some short sample code examples. Before going too much further we'll want to make sure that we are able to open each of the different projects in Unity 3D to follow along.

Near the end of Chapter 2 we had to venture onto GitHub to grab the projects. There are some alternative locations on the Internet to find the projects for this book. These "cloud" services, as they are called, are available to everyone with an Internet connection. They're all public and openly available and they can be updated. If you discover a typo or any errors in the process that weren't intended then you can feel free to find the author's web site and post a note to the forum.

Before continuing you should be able to run Unity 3D, create and open C# files, and attach the C# files to an object in a scene. Once all of this is done, you should be able to press the Play in Editor button without any errors. You should also be able to manipulate objects in the scene using the various navigation tools in the editor.

If any of this seems unfamiliar go back and review Chapter 2; we'll be doing quite a lot here which depends on your being able to move objects and create and edit C# files. It's time to get into what code is, so keep calm and carry on!

## 3.3  Tokens

In written English the smallest elements of the language are letters and numbers. Individually, most letters and numbers lack specific meaning. The next larger element after the letter is the word. Each word has more meaning, but complex thoughts are difficult to convey in a single word.

To communicate a thought, we use sentences. The words in a sentence each have a specific use, as seen in the diagram below. To convey a concept we use a collection of sentences grouped into a paragraph. And to convey emotion we use a collection of many paragraphs organized into chapters. To tell a story we use a book, a collection of chapters.

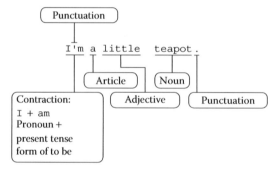

Programming has similar organizational mechanisms. The smallest meaningful element is a token, followed by statements, code blocks, functions, followed by classes and namespaces and eventually a program, or in our case a game. We will begin with the smallest element and work our way up to writing our own classes. However, it's important to know the very smallest element to understand how all the parts fit together before we start writing any complex code.

### 3.3.1  Writing C#

C# is an English-based programming language; like any other C-like programming language it can be broken into tokens, the smallest meaningful fragment of text that the computer can understand. Tokens are made of a single character or a series of characters. For instance, in a simple statement like the following there are five tokens.

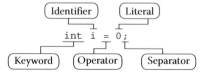

Tokens can be categorized as a *keyword, identifier, literal, operator, separator,* and *white space.* The above statement contains five tokens with spacing provided with white space. The keyword `int` is followed by the identifier i. This is followed by an operator = which assigns the identifier on the left of the operator and the value of the literal 0 on the right. The last token ; is a separator which ends the statement. White spaces and comments, which we have yet to cover, are not considered tokens, although they can act as separators.

It's important that proper formatting or style be used. Let's examine a sample of code:

```
int i = 0; int j = 1;
```

The code shown above is two statements, the separator keeps the computer from misreading the code as a single statement. However, there are humans involved with writing code, and thus code needs to be readable by humans, or any other life-form which might read your code. Proper code means following a specific formatting style. We'll dive into more about proper code style later in this chapter.

Each group of characters, or text, is converted by a *lexical analyzer*, sometimes called a *lexer*, in the computer and turned a *symbol*. This process is called *tokenization*, or as a computer scientist would say, a lexer tokenizes your code into symbols. Once tokenized, the symbols are *parsed*; this process organizes the tokens into instructions for the computer to follow. This unique vocabulary does frame programmers as a strange group of alien beings with a language all to themselves; I promise, however, conversations about lexical analyzers don't come up very often when talking with most programmers.

This may seem like a great deal of work and we are jumping ahead into more complex computer science topics, but all of this happens behind the scenes so you don't need to see any of this taking place. It's important to understand what a compiler does, and how it works so you can write code in a way that the computer can understand. This is why a simple typo will stop the lexer from building code. We'll get to writing code to be analyzed, tokenized, and parsed soon enough.

A computer can't interpret or guess at what it is you're trying to do. Therefore, if you mistype int i = 0: and not int i = 0; the last token cannot be converted by the lexer into a proper symbol, and thus this statement will not be parsed at all. This code results in an error before the code is even compiled.

### 3.3.2 Separator Tokens

The most common separator is the ;, semicolon. This mark of punctuation is used to end a code statement. Other separators come in pairs. Curly braces are used in pairs to separate groups of code statements. The opening curly brace is the { with the pointy end pointed to the outside of the group; this is paired with the } which closes the curly brace pair.

Parentheses start with the ( and end with the ) while square brackets start with [ and end with ]. The different opening and closing braces, brackets, and parentheses have specific purposes and are used to help identify what they are being used for. There are angle brackets < and > as well; these are used to surround data types. And don't forget both single quotes ' ' and double quotes " ", which are used in pairs as well to surround symbols called strings.

**NOTE:** In many word processors a beginning and an ending quote (" and ") are often used. The lexical analyzer doesn't recognize these smart quotes, so the text editor for programming uses straight quote marks (") instead. These subtle changes aren't so subtle once you realize that letters, numbers, and every other character used in programming are all parsed as American Standard Code for Information Interchange (ASCII) or unicode transformation format (UTF)-8, 16, or 32. Both ASCII and UTF are names given to the database of characters that the computer uses to read text. Computers don't use eyes to read. Rather, they use a database of numbers to look up each character being used. Therefore, to a computer " looks more like 0x201C and " like 0x0022, if we were using UTF-16.

Curly braces are used in code to separate statements. Parentheses are usually used to accept data. Square brackets are often used to help identify arrays. We'll get into arrays later, but imagine something like a spreadsheet or a graph paper till we get to their explanation.

```
int[] arrayNumbers = {1, (int) 3.0, 9000};
```

The above statement assigns three numbers to an array. The curly braces contain a pair of statements separated by a comma. The second statement in the curly braces is converting a number with a dot (.) into a number without a dot in it. This will take a bit of explanation, but it's good to get used to seeing this sort of thing. We'll get to what an array is soon enough, as well as a dot operator.

Often, when learning to program you'll see many strange tokens which might not seem to have any meaning. It's up to you to observe every token you come across and try to understand what it does. If none of the statements makes sense that's fine. At this point you're not expected to know what all this means yet, but you soon will.

### 3.3.3 Operator Tokens

Operators are like keywords but use only a few non-word characters. The colon or semi-colon is an operator; unlike keywords, operators change what they do based on where they appear, or how they are used. This behavior shifting is called operator overloading, and it's a complex subject that we'll get into later. It's also important to know that you can make up your own operators when you need to.

Commas in C# have a different meaning. They're used to separate different data values like `Vector3(x, y, z)` or `for(int i = 0, j = 1; ; i++, j++)`.

```
public class Example : MonoBehaviour {
```

Here, the : was used following the name of the class to inform the compiler we're going to be adding to a preexisting class called `MonoBehaviour`. In this case, : will tell our class to extend `MonoBehaviour`. This means to build upon a class which already exists. We're creating a new child object related to `MonoBehaviour`; this is a class that was created by the developers at Unity 3D.

### 3.3.4 Other Operator Tokens

Operators in general are special characters that take care of specific operations between variables. Notation or the order in which operators and variables appear is normally taught with the following notation or mathematic grammar: $a + b = c$. However, in programming the following is preferred: $c = a + b$; the change is made because the = operator in C# works differently from its function commonly taught in math class.

The left side of the = operator is the assignment side, and the right side is the operation side. This puts the emphasis on the value assigned rather than how it's assigned. The result is more important than how the problem is solved since the computer is doing the math. In programming the above example should be read as "c is assigned a plus b."

### 3.3.5 Literals

Literals come in many different forms; similar to operators which appear as things like +, -, or = literals are the tokens that often go between them. Numbers are considered literals, or tokens that are used in a literal manner. Numbers can be called numeric literals.

When something is put into quotes, as in "I'm a literal," you are writing a string literal. Literals are common throughout nearly all programming languages and form the base of C#'s data types. Right now, we're dealing with only a few different types of literals, but there are many more we will be aware of soon.

### 3.3.6 Transitive and Non-Transitive Operations

In math class it's sometimes taught how some operations are transitive and others not. For instance $2 + 3 + 4$ and $4 + 3 + 2$ result in the same values. Where each number appears between the operators doesn't matter, so the + operator is considered transitive. This concept holds true in C#. Results change when we start to mix operators.

```
int a = 1 + 2 - 4 + 7;//a = 6
int b = 7 + 4 - 2 + 1;//b = 10
```

This code fragment shows two different results using the same operators but with different number placement. We'll see how to overcome these problems later on when we start using them in our game. Operator order is something to be aware of, and it's important to test each step as we build up our calculations to make sure our results end up with values we expect.

To ensure that the operations happen as you expect, either you can use parentheses to contain operands or you can do each calculation. We'll dive further into more detail with a second look at operators later on, but this will have to wait till we have a better understanding of more of the basics of C#.

### 3.3.7 Putting It All Together

Coming up with all of the systems that make up a fully functional class for use in a game takes a great deal of work, and that's what the folks over at Unity 3D have taken care of for you. Classes often work together to share and manipulate data. There are exceptions to this rule, but C# allows for many different writing styles and paradigms.

When you create data you've produced components of an object. In general you've created something that can be reused many times. Once you have created a zombie by adding in brain-seeking logic and how many bullets are required to stop him, it's only a matter of duplicating that zombie to create a mob to terrorize your player.

As we proceed we'll become more familiar with what it means to use classes as objects; the tutorials will be aimed at making sure that this is all clear.

```
void MyFunction()
{
    int i = 0;
    while(i < 10)
    {
        print(i);
        i ++;
    }
}
```

Let's break this code sample down. The first word is `void`, which is a keyword. `MyFunction` is an identifier we created. It's called `MyFunction` because we need to identify this function by some name we can remember.

The word used to identify the function could be practically anything; in this case, we're calling it `MyFunction`. Now that we know the parts of this line we should observe that this particular arrangement of tokens `void MyFunction()` is called a function declaration statement.

The parentheses after the identifier are operators used when we need parameters for our function. The parameters are discussed in Section 3.3.2. For now, take in the fact that both opening ( and closing ) parentheses are necessary after identifiers which are used to declare functions. They're really useful; trust me.

To begin the contents of the function we start with curly braces, the opening { and closing } curly braces. Everything that the function will do must be contained between the two braces. Any text appearing outside of them will not be part of the function. The code contained in the curly braces becomes the function block of code or code block.

The first statement in the function's code block is `int i = 0;` this is an assignment statement, where we declare `int i` and then use the = to assign `i` a value of 0. This is then separated from the next statement with the `;` operator.

The assignment statement is followed by `while(i < 10)`, which is called a looping condition. We'll read more on looping conditions later in Section 4.12. This looping statement is followed by an opening { (curly brace). This indicates a code block specifically written for the while loop.

The contained block contains the statement `print(i);`, which is a function call using `i` as a parameter or argument. After the print function call is `i++;`, which applies the post-increment operator `++` to the variable `i`. This code block is ended with the closing `}` (curly brace).

The `while` code block and the `int = 0;` are both within the `MyFunction()` code block. To make the code more readable, tabs are added to indicate a separation between each section of code. Now bask in the knowledge that we've got words to describe everything presented in the above code sample. We may not understand everything that has been written, but we've got some vocabulary where we can get started.

### 3.3.8 What We've Learned

Programmers are meticulous about syntax. They have to be. The following two statements are very different : `int myint0 = -1;` and `Int my 0int = - 1:`. The first one will compile; the second one has at least five errors. You may not be able to spot the problems in the second statement, but by the end of the next section you will.

When trying to ask a programmer questions it's best to limit your subject and consider your words carefully. Asking "how would I write a video game where you shoot zombies with a flame thrower" involves so many different concepts it's impossible for anyone to tell you where to start. Most likely, you might be told to go to school, or at best you might get a link to a book on Amazon. Either way, you're asking for too much in a single forum post.

If you formulate a smaller question like "How do I attach flames to a zombie after it's been hit by a projectile?" you're more likely to get an answer. When talking to a programmer, you'll have to use similar wording. The more specific your question, the more likely you'll get the answer you were looking for.

## 3.4 Statements and Expressions

When reading a book or story you extract meaning from an ordered chain of words. In a similar way, computers extract commands from a chain of ordered instructions. In English we call this a sentence; programmers call this a *statement*. A statement is considered to be any chunk of code which accomplishes some sort of task separated by a semicolon.

At the center of any given task is the *algorithm*, not to be confused with a logarithm. An algorithm is a systematic process that accomplishes something. In many ways you can think of it as a recipe, or rather a recipe is an algorithm for making food.

It can take just one or two statements to accomplish a task, or it could take many hundreds of statements. This all depends on the difficulty of a given task. Each individual statement is a step toward a goal. This is the difference between spending a few minutes frying an egg, or spending an hour baking a souffle. Each step is usually fairly simple; it's the final result that matters.

Like sentences, statements have different forms. Statements can declare and assign values to variables. These are called *declaration* and *assignment* statements. These statements are used to set up various types of data and give them names.

### 3.4.1 Expressions

The subjects of your statements are called *identifiers*. An *assignment statement* is used to give an identifier a value. When you read "Jack is a boy and Jill is a girl," you've mentally assigned two subjects their genders. In C# this might look more like:

```
gender Jack = male;
gender Jill = female;
```

Assignment statements often incorporate some sort of operation. These are called *expressive statements*. Different from expressing an emotion, expressions in code look more like "x + y." Expressions process data. After processing, the result of an *expression* can be assigned to a variable. We'll learn more about variables and assignments in Section 3.10.2.

A collection of statements is called a *code block*, not like a roadblock which might stop your code, but more like a building block, anything that's used to build. When writing a story, we call a collection of sentences a paragraph. The statements in a block of code work with each other to accomplish a task.

### 3.4.2 How Code Is Executed

When a class is created, all of its instructions are not carried out at the same time. As it's been explained, each collection of parts in a class is made up of lines of text called *statements*. Each statement is carried out in order. Where the computer starts is usually dependent on which collection of statements it's told to start with. You're in charge of how the code is started.

Unity 3D provides us with a function called Start (), which we'll go into later. However, this is the preferred place to begin our code using Unity 3D. Once Start () is called, the computer goes to the first line in Start () and begins to carry out the instructions written there. As the computer gets to each statement the computer starts on the left of the statement and works its way to the right. Basically, a computer reads code like you're reading this sentence.

Other development environments often use Main() as their first place to begin running the code. When you start writing software in other environments you'll most likely start with Main(). We don't have to get into that right now, but it's good to know once you're done with this book.

### 3.4.3 Thinking in Algorithms

An algorithm is a step-by-step process. This lends itself to being written in an imperative programming language like C#, which executes operations one at a time and in order. Algorithms are written with statements starting at a beginning statement and finishing that statement before moving on to the next.

Just because we know what an algorithm is doesn't mean it's any easier to create one. Therefore, how do we go about writing the all-important algorithm? The first thing should be how you might accomplish any given task by hand.

As an example, say we're a computer surrounded by a mob of zombies. Thankfully, computers are very fast so we can do a lot before the zombies can get to us. With this in mind we're going to want to focus on the zombie closest to us. Unfortunately, computers are also very dumb, so there's nothing which allows us to just guess at which one is the closest.

First, we're going to need to know how far away every zombie is from our point of view. Therefore, the computer would probably start with measuring the distance from itself to every zombie available to make a measurement to. After that we're going to have to compare zombies and distances, so we'll start with the first zombie we found and compare its distance to the next zombie we found.

If the next zombie is closer we'll have to remember that one as being the closest one we've come across. Otherwise, if the next one is farther away, then we can forget about him and move on to the next zombie and compare numbers again. Once we've gone through all of the zombies, we should have identified the zombie who is the closest one to us.

The process which we just thought through is an algorithm for finding the zombie closest to us. It's not complex, but we had to do a few steps to get to it. First, we needed to get a list of all the zombies we needed to sort through. After that it was an iterative process, by which we needed to remember one zombie as the closest one, then compare others against him to decide whether or not he would retain the status of being the zombie nearest to us. We'll be going over many of these problem-solving thought processes as we learn how to program.

This algorithm would look something like the following code block:

```
void Update () {
    float closestDistance = Mathf.Infinity;
    GameObject closestGameObject = null;
    GameObject[] allObjects =
    (GameObject[]) GameObject.FindSceneObjectsOfType(
    typeof(GameObject));
    foreach(GameObject g in allObjects) {
```

```
        if (g.name != this.name) {
            float distance = (g.transform.position -
            this.transform.position).sqrMagnitude;
                if(distance < closestDistance) {
                    closestDistance = distance;
                    closestGameObject = g;
                }
            }
        }
    Debug.DrawLine(this.transform.position,
    closestGameObject.transform.position);
}
```

We won't cover the entirety of how this code works, as we are yet to discuss the bulk of what's going on here, but in short we are indeed creating a list of objects called `allObjects`. Then we enter a loop where we compare the distance of each object against the one we've decided was the closest. If we find a closer object then we change the `closestGameObject` to the compared object.

Just for a proof of concept we draw a line from the object. Because the script is attached to the object, we draw a line from the object the script is attached to toward the object selected as the closest. The scene will look something like this:

Programming is a lot more about a thought process than it is about processing. In other words, programming is less about how to do multiplication as it is about what to do with the result of a multiplication process. In your everyday life we take for granted the everyday things we do on a regular basis. However, take a moment and really consider the complexity involved with something as simple as breathing.

Your diaphragm is receiving signals from your autonomic nervous system, causing several chemical reactions in the diaphgragm's muscle tissue, which then pull proteins toward one another causing it to contract. This in turn creates a lowered air pressure in your lungs, which pulls in air. There's a whole number of chemical processes which then allow the oxygen in the atmosphere to enter your blood stream. Thankfully, all of this happens without our thinking of it because of chemistry and physics. In programming, nothing is so automatic.

### 3.4.3.1 Wash, Rinse, Repeat

In our every day life we see instructions written everywhere. However, if we follow instructions too closely we'd run into problems with our everyday lives. If you interpreted, for example, the instructions on most shampoo labels like a computer we'd run out of shampoo the first time we used it.

To interpret the "wash, rinse, repeat" instructions like a computer we'd wash our hair, rinse it; then wash our hair then rinse it; then wash our hair then rinse it; … ; you get the picture. You'd continue the process until you've run out of shampoo. Because there are no further instructions, once the shampoo has run out, a computer would send out an error of some kind. There wasn't a number given for how many times the instructions should be followed; there was no way to *terminate* the process, as a programmer would say. A computer would need to have the "shampooing" process killed to stop washing its hair. Simply put, computers lack common sense.

Here's a simple scenario: A spouse tells the programmer to go to the grocery store and says "Get some bacon, if there's milk get three." The programmer comes home with three packs of bacon, and no milk. If this makes sense, then you're thinking like a programmer. There are conditions to tell the programmer to get three bottles of milk if it was available; just the fact that there was milk meant bringing home 3× bacon.

### 3.4.4 What We've Learned

Programmers are often a group of literal thinkers. The thought process a programmer uses is different from what the artist uses. In terms of order of operation, programmers take things one step at a time. This process in programming terms is an imperative procedure, a step-by-step process in which operations are carried out in a linear fashion.

As an artist or newcomer to programming, this imperative process can be a bit out of the ordinary. With some time and practice, however, this paradigm of thinking will become second nature. The approaches a programmer and an artist would take to solve a problem often diverge.

To learn how to write code is to learn how to think like a programmer. This may sound a bit awkward, but perhaps after some work, you'll understand why some programmers seem to think differently than everyone else.

## 3.5 Keywords

*Keywords* are special words, or symbols, that tell the compiler to do specific things. For instance, the keyword `class` at the beginning of a line tells the compiler you are creating a class. A *class declaration* is the line of code that tells the compiler you're about to create a new class.

The order in which words appear is important. English requires sentences and grammar to properly convey our thoughts to the reader. In code, C# or otherwise, programming requires statements and syntax to properly convey instructions to the computer.

```
class className
{
}
```

Every class needs a name; in the above example we named our class `className`, although we could have easily named the class `Charles`. When a new class is named the name becomes a new *identifier*. This also holds true for every variable's name, though *scope* limits how long and where the variable's identifier exists. We'll learn more about variables and scope soon.

You can't use keywords for anything other than what C# expects them to be used for. There are exceptions, but in general, keywords provide you with specific commands. Altogether in C# there are roughly 80 keywords you should be aware of, we don't need to go over all of them now, so instead we'll learn them as we come across them.

### 3.5.1 Class

To create a class named `Charles` we used the keyword `class`. The keyword commands C# to expect a word to identify the new class. The following word becomes a new identifier for the class. In this case `Charles` is used to name the class. Keywords often precede a word, and the computer uses the word following as its identifier.

The contents of `Charles` are defined between curly braces. After the class definition the opening curly brace { is followed by any statements that `Charles` needs to be a proper `Charles`. When you're finished defining the contents of `Charles`, you use the closing curly brace } to indicate you're done with defining the `Charles` class.

```
class Charles {}
```

It's important to note that keywords start with lowercase letters. C# is a case-sensitive programming language, and as such, `Class` and `class` are two different things. In C# there is no keyword `Class`; only `class` starting with a lowercase c can be used. More of the same goes for every keyword in C#.

Writing a new class or any function starts off as a nonlinear process. By this I mean you write out `class Charles {}` with both curly braces. When writing a sentence in English we don't write the period at the end of a sentence first, for example, when we would write something like "It was a dark and stormy night." We don't start with "It." and then go back and add the rest of the sentence later, between "It" and the period.

However, programming works this way: "`class Charles {}`" begins with the start of the class indicated with the open curly brace { and the end of the class indicated by the closing curly brace }, after which we go back and add the body later. Not everything works in this way, and it takes a bit of getting used to before you understand the flow. Certainly, however, this will come naturally after some practice.

Now we have a new class called `Charles`, which has no data and does nothing. This is to be expected since we haven't added any data or functions yet. You can also use the terminology this class is identified as `Charles`.

This class can't be used directly by Unity 3D. It lacks some of the necessary additions needed by the Unity 3D game engine to directly interact with this class. To be specific, this class doesn't have enough information to allow Unity 3D to know what to do with the contents of this class. However, there are methods which make a minimal class, such as `Charles`, quite useful inside of Unity 3D, but we need to cover a great deal of ground before we can do that.

In section 2.4 we looked at a complete source file, `Example.cs` which is ready for use in Unity 3D. However, it's important to know what creates a minimal class before adding all of the rest of the keywords and declarations which make it actually do anything in Unity 3D, our game engine.

Keep in mind no two classes can share the same name. We'll go further into detail about class names and what's called a namespace later on. The contents of the class are contained in the following pair of curly braces. All of the variables and functions that live in between the opening curly brace { and the closing brace } become the contents of the class object.

Other keywords which we'll come across in this chapter include keywords that indicate a variables type. Some variable keywords which will be covered in the next chapter or two are as follows.

```
int
float
string
```

These keywords indicate a type of variable. There are many more, but we're just going to look at these as an example. An `int` variable looks something like the following:

```
int i = 0;
```

A float looks like this:

```
float f = 3.14159f;
```

A string is used to store words like this:

```
string s = "some words in quotes";
```

If `int` and `float` seem similar, it's because they both deal with numbers, but as we will see, numbers behave quite differently when computers use them. Keywords are used quite often, and they are case sensitive. Therefore, `int` and `Int` are different things, and thus using `Int i = 0;` will not work. Only `int` is recognized as a keyword, and there has been no definition written to tell C# what `Int` is. Keywords are also used to indicate special changes in code behavior. The keyword `if` is what is used to control code execution based on a conditional statement.

```
if ( i < 10 )
{
      // Code goes here.
}
```

As you are introduced to more and more keywords, we'll be expanding our ability to create new code as well. Keywords make up the complex vocabulary that is required to use C#.

### 3.5.2  What We've Learned

This was a short section, but it covered a fundamental component of a C# construct. Classes are both construction instructions and rules for objects to obey. Writing a complex class takes a step-by-step approach.

Keywords are an important component of any programming language. Some languages have very few keywords. Lisp has a mere 18 keywords, C# has about 76, and COBOL has over 400 words reserved for special purposes.

Most programming languages use the same keywords for similar purposes. The `var` keyword is often used to indicate that a variable is being declared. Because of the similarities between programming languages, once you've learned one language, it's often easy to pick up and learn new languages.

---

### 3.6  White Space

White space refers to the spaces between words and lines. When typewriters were still in fashion, new lines were entered by pushing on a lever which pushed the roller that held onto the paper to reposition the hammers with letters on them back to the beginning of the next line. Now, these are called line feeds, new lines, or returns.

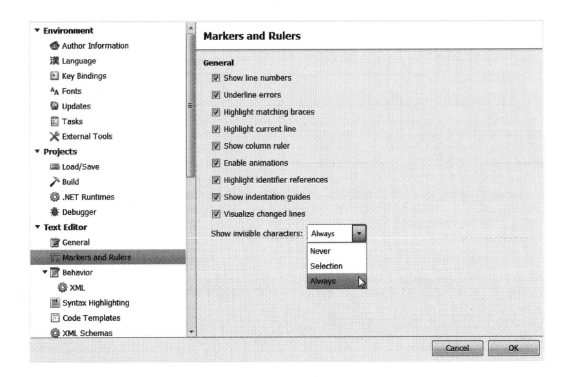

Like letters and numbers, white spaces are also characters entered into your code. To see them along with the rest of your text in MonoDevelop, select Tools → Options, and in the Text Editor section select Markers and Rulers. Select Always from the Show invisible characters Dialog Box. Going back to your script, you should see faint dots, arrows, and \n marks spaced throughout your code.

```
1 ⊟ using·UnityEngine;\n
2 └ using·System.Collections;\n
3     \n
4 ⊟ public·class·WhiteSpace·:·MonoBehaviour\n
5   {\n
6   |————————//·Use·this·for·initialization\n
7 ⊟ |—————void·Start·()·{\n
8   |    \n
9   |—————}\n
10     \n
11  |—————//·Update·is·called·once·per·frame\n
12 ⊟ |—————void·Update·()·{\n
13  |    \n
14  |—————}\n
15 └ }\n
16  <EOF>
```

In many cases the new lines and spaces and tabs are there only to help make the code more readable. And depending on where or what a programmer was taught, the white spaces will be used differently. For instance, adding white space after a function declaration is unnecessary and the location of the curly braces can pretty much be moved anywhere before or after the contents of the function itself. Leaving the white spaces showing isn't necessary, but it's good to know what white space means when talking to a programmer. If none of this makes sense right now, it will later.

```
 1  using UnityEngine;
 2  using System.Collections;
 3
 4  public class WhiteSpace : MonoBehaviour
 5  {
 6      // Use this for initialization
 7      void Start ()
 8      {
 9
10      }
11
12      // Update is called once per frame
13      void Update ()
14      {
15
16      }
17  }
18
```

The placement of curly braces is easy to change; these decisions often lead to debates on standards among programmers. In reality there's little difference either way. However, keeping your own code consistent helps you read your code and find errors faster.

It's important to remember that if you're going to be working with more classically trained programmers they might have a headache when reading poorly formatted code. It's best to copy your programmer friends' style before coming up with your own way to format your classes and functions. No doubt, before the end of this book you will have formed opinions of your own when it comes to the use of white space and formatting your own code.

Normally, code might look a bit like the following:

```
void MyFunction()
{
    int i = 0;
    while(i < 10)
    {
        print(i);
        i ++;
    }
}
```

This looks like a readable collection of statements. However, the compiler could care less about how you use white space. Therefore, here is what would this code sample look like without the unnecessary white space:

```
void MyFunction(){int i = 0;while(i<10){print(i);i++;}}
```

There are still some necessary white space characters used to separate the different tokens in the function. There is the space between `void` and `MyFunction`, and the space between `int` and `i`. In the latest version of MonoDevelop saving a file automatically reformats your code into a more proper format. Rather than fight this it's better to let it format your code, though this isn't always an option with other editors.

To turn this feature off you can select Tools → Options.

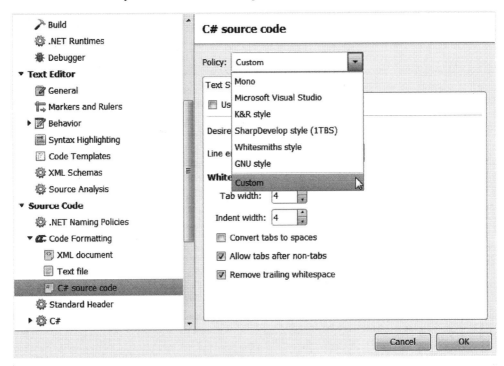

And change some of the behaviors MonoDevelop will follow when saving a file. In an already existing project, for example, you have to change these properties in the project settings.

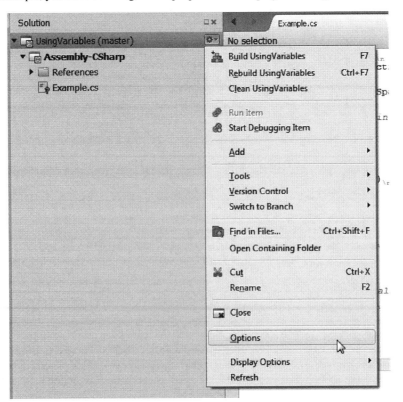

These options all follow different coding styles; you'll want to pick one that suits your taste. Likewise, if you're working in a team you'll want to come to some decision as a group to avoid starting a formatting war.

In any case the white space is required after the use of a keyword. Keywords are unique words reserved for C#. If we used `voidMyFunction()` then there would be an error stating something about not knowing what a `voidMyFunction()` is.

White space is also used to make code more readable. Without the white space the code becomes more difficult to interpret.

```
imagineforamomentwhatenglishwouldlooklikewithoutanyspacesorpunctuation
```

White space should also be used as needed. I once worked with a programmer who would put a few pages of white space between different functions. He said it made it easier to focus on what he was looking at, when there was only one line of code on the screen at a time. Of course, this drove other programmers nuts. It's hardly a common practice.

Although he had a point, being able to focus on one code block at a time is important, but there's a thing called code folding that we'll learn about later on to help make your code more easy to organize.

### 3.6.1 Pick a Flavor

Between programmers there's often a discussion of code style. Many heated debates might flare up based on the use of white space. The differences are entirely based on style and in most cases have no effect on the efficacy of the code. In the following fragments the { is placed in different places.

```
void MyFunction () {
    //some code here...
}
void aDifferentFunction ()
{
    //some more code here...
}
```

The execution of the two functions will perform equally, but the placement of the first curly brace { can make the code more or less readable depending on what you're comfortable with. Unity's developers offer us the first version, but for clarity we'll stick to the second version.

The finer points on where variables appear in a statement or how many statements can appear on a single line are usually dictated by how a programmer has learned to write code. Old school programmers prefer no line of code extending beyond 80 characters. This limit formed in 1928, when IBM punch cards had only 80 columns to poke holes in the paper. Though it's unlikely you'll have to work with an old curmudgeon, but just in case, at least now you know why they might be grumpy.

Today, there's no physical limit other than what would make a statement difficult to read. If a single line of code spans several widths of your screen it's probably unreadable. In these cases it's better to break apart your statement into a few smaller statements. This will help keep the code more readable. Within the confines of this book we're somewhat more limited by space, so we too will be limiting the length of our statements based on the width of the margins of the book.

Likewise, if you've got a lovely 4k monitor you might be comfortable reading mile-long lines, but if you're stuck on a low res laptop then you might hate having to scroll left and right just to read a single statement. Consider the fact that not everyone has a giant monitor.

Interpreting your own code several days or weeks after you've written it is just as important as handing your code off to someone else, with that person being able to read it. There are many times when I've come back to a project written several weeks ago and needed to spend a few minutes trying to figure out what I was thinking when I wrote the code. Sometimes, it takes only a few days for me to forget about the code I've written. Worse yet, if I write the code half asleep then I might forget what I was doing before I've even reached the end of a statement.

In the end it's up to you to pick what you'll stick to. However, it's considered rude to pick through someone else's code and reformat it. Code can sometimes become quite personal, and reformatting code might end up feeling like someone sneaking into your bedroom and reorganizing your sock drawer.

### 3.6.2 What We've Learned

White space and formatting are important to creating a clean easy-to-read class. Every large company will have a set of rules for their programmers to follow. These coding standards, as they are called, are usually maintained by a lead programmer and can vary from company to company.

Smaller teams of engineers can have a less restrictive set of rules, but this often leads to some confusion and large bodies of unreadable code. Everyone has his or her own coding style and preferences. If there is an established set of coding standards, then it's best to follow it.

So far as this book is concerned, it's best that you learn how to make your code work before concerning yourself with strict coding rules. Code formatting and style are important. How you express yourself through code is up to you, so long as it works. Getting your code to work is a big enough challenge; style and proper formatting will come naturally with time as you see the benefits of different code styles, and how they contribute to your code's readability.

## 3.7 Code Blocks

Blocks are collections of statements grouped together when they're evaluated. This evaluation of code is usually controlled by an opening and closing curly brace. C# programmers often use tabs to indent different blocks of code. This makes the different blocks more readable. Some languages like python rely on the tabs to indicate separate blocks of code.

Getting used to how tabs are used is essential for writing readable code. Next, we'll use a logic control statement followed by a block of code. The block for this `if` statement is indented to the right to indicate it's confined within the logic control statement.

```
if (true)
{
    //code goes here
    //im also a part of the code
}
```

If we take a look at a more complex section of code we can see why it's important to differentiate code by using tabs. When looking at code it might not be apparent, but programmers are very fastidious about text layout. Each programmer has a preferred style, but it's safe to say that most, if not all, programmers hate seeing badly formatted code.

```
int i = 7;
int j = 13;
if (i < 13){
int j = 7;}
```

In the above example we can clearly see `int j` being set twice. What isn't obvious is why it's declared twice. All of the lines start at the same position and look crowded. Programming tools offer many text layout options, so white space is used to separate different blocks of code.

```
int i = 7;
int j = 13;
if (i < 13)
{
    int j = 7;
}
```

By adding in some white space we can make the `if` statement more visible. Adding white space around our blocks of code is important to maintain readability. There are also blocks of code that can live within another block of code. In general it's all related to the same block. Blocks inside of a block are called nested code blocks. White space is used to separate the nested code from the block it's found in.

```
if(true)
{
    //all of the code
    //im also a part of the code
    if(true)
    {
        //im another block of code
        //living inside of a bigger
        //block of code
    }
    //yep more code here too
}
```

The block of code following the second `if` statement is considered to be nested inside of the first block of code. This is because of the placement of the first opening curly brace { and the related closing curly brace }. You form hierarchies by placing the different curly braces within one another.

```
if(true)
{
//all of the code
//im also a part of the code
if(true)
{
//im another block of code
//living inside of another
//block of code
}
//yep more code here too
}
```

Poorly indented curly braces make for confusing code; the above code is still valid, but it's less readable compared to the previous version. Most code-editing tools will automatically add in the proper number of indents for you. It's something you'll have to get used to when writing your own code.

We'll go into further detail as to what this all means later. Just gather from this discussion that a bunch of statements appearing between a pair of curly braces is considered a block of code.

### 3.7.1 What We've Learned

Much of programming involves proper use of style and a great deal of white space to accomplish that style. So far we've just been covering vocabulary, but without that vocabulary we can't have a proper conversation about programming. This too includes talking to other programmer friends, who will have a hard time understanding you if you can't speak in their language.

## 3.8 Classes

The most important part of any C# program is the class. Classes here are not the sort that students go to; rather, they are classes in terms of classification. Classes in C# appear in several different forms. Some are called partial classes, and some classes can even appear inside of another class; these classes are called nested classes.

A class is a collection of instructions and data. The instructions can be referred to as functions or methods. The data stored in a class is called a field or property. All of the naming aside, what's important is what classes do and how they're used.

Classes are flexible and easily changed, but this flexibility is not without some complexity. As we've seen before, the class declaration can contain a lot more than the following example. However, much of the complexity comes later in this book, when needed.

When you approach a game or any sort of programming task it's important to first collect data, and then figure out how to use the data. In most programming paradigms it's best to start off with variables at the beginning of your new class. For instance, in this pseudo code we might want to know what day it is before going out:

```
Time day = today;
if (day == Friday)
{
    PartyTonight = true;
}
```

We start off with getting a day, and then deciding what to do tonight based on the day. We should refrain from partying and then checking what the day is unless we want to show up for work late. We'll go into more detail on this topic later on, after we've learned about how to use a variable in a class properly.

### 3.8.1 Objects

Object oriented programming (OOP) was invented to associate data and logic into nicely packaged bundles of code. When you write a class in C# you're creating blueprints and instructions for a new object. Any number of objects can then be constructed based on your blueprints. Programmers use the term *instantiate* when talking about creating an object from the class blueprint.

Each instantiated object is an *instance* of the class from which it was constructed. The class is not itself one of the instances created by it. The newly created object contains all of the functions and data written into the class.

To make this clear, a class in of itself is not an object, just a plan for making objects. We start with a C# class which contains instructions to build an object.

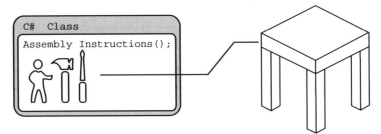

Classes can be simple, or complex. A class might be nothing more than a container for some data. On the other hand a class can also contain behaviors for a complex boss who plans to crash a comet into the earth, or any other instruction for world domination.

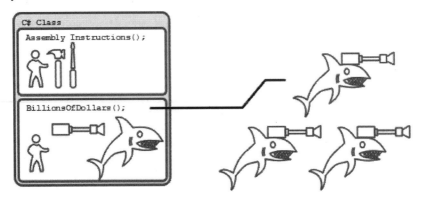

Just as important, a class can create more than one instance of an object. This process is called *instancing*. Each instance is created from the same blueprint and thus behaves the same as all the other instances of the same class. Each instance can have unique values. In Unity 3D, each instance of an object can have unique positions in 3D space.

OOP is particularly useful for video games. Individual classes can address different aspects of your game. A zombie class can be instanced many times to create a mob of mindless zombies. Likewise, a solitary class can be written to manage how to move your player's character around when keys or buttons are pressed. A separate class can manage inventory and how to deal with items.

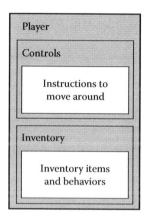

Monsters, and bullets, cameras, and lights all have classes from which they are created. Almost every object you see in any level in Unity 3D can be instanced from a class. An instance of an object communicates to another object through *messages* and *events*.

When people in the real world deal with household items they are rarely concerned with how they function. Knowing how a toaster works has little effect on the toaster's performance. We put bread in a toaster, push down on a button, and wait for a delicious toast.

A toaster, however, is more than a button and a receptacle for bread. It's a collection of wires, heating elements, transformers, and other electrical components which are hidden under a shiny cover. We interact with an *abstraction* of a toaster, never dealing with the insides ourselves.

Abstraction presents only the parts we need to accomplish a given task and hides the rest. To make toast we need a place to put bread and a button to start the machine. The toaster does its work and toast happens, or at least it should.

Messing with the insides of the toaster class isn't recommended; that's why there are labels telling us to keep forks out of the toaster. To protect a human class from fumbling around with the insides of a toaster class the toaster is protected by *encapsulation*.

Encapsulation is the term used to define to how classes hide data and functions from the outside world. To interact with the toaster we must use the toaster's *interface*, but there are other objects in the kitchen which have buttons, and the human class is very good at pushing buttons.

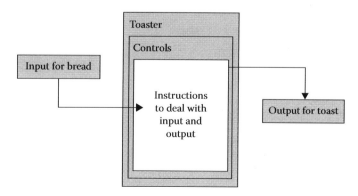

When you put bread into a blender and press a button you will get a very different result from the toaster, but they are both kitchen appliances and use the same power outlet. They're both made of metal and run on the same electronics, but they do different things.

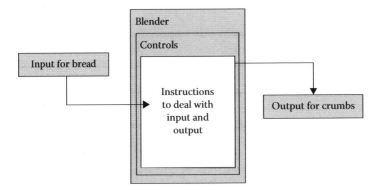

When and where it's possible, a programmer will reuse as much code as possible. A blender and a toaster could share similar components, only the operation carried out on a slice of bread is different when they are used. The capability to change the contents of an operation is described as *polymorphism*.

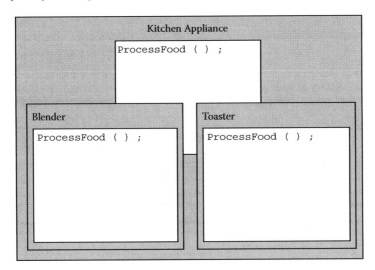

A generic kitchen appliance would be a place to put food and a button to press to process food. Each version of a kitchen appliance does different things to food. A wise programmer would make sure that all of the appliances inherit from the generic kitchen appliance.

*Inheritance* allows many classes to share common attributes and behaviors. If you wanted a toaster with more than one slot and a knob to adjust the darkness of your toast you would want to inherit the original toaster's functions first. This means that the base of both Toaster and Blender is a Kitchen Appliance. A dual slot toaster inherits from Toaster, which inherits from Kitchen Appliance. This in turn means that if any changes are made to Kitchen Appliance that change or addition is inherited by all of the sub-classes inheriting from Kitchen Appliance.

This would mean inheriting the original toaster's electronic systems, casing, and original button. All of these components may also be made from other classes. This would mean only changing one electronic part to adapt a toaster for sale, say, in Europe.

*Aggregating* many different classes into a single class allows another layer of flexibility. By aggregating many separate components or classes into a single useful toaster or blender means you can more easily swap individual parts for new behaviors. A toaster is the aggregate total of many smaller parts.

You may find yourself writing code for a zombie or a toaster and see some similarities between those things and other objects in your game. When your player attacks a zombie or a toaster, they may both break apart. Both the zombie and toaster can share functions related to getting attacked.

As far as your code may be concerned, one object chases after you trying to eat your brains, and the other object turns bread into delicious toast. Keep this in mind when you start writing your own code. Even though some things may seem unrelated, maybe even humans and zombies can both enjoy toast.

### 3.8.2 What We've Learned

I'll let this sink in a little bit. Being new to programming is usually a very intimidating experience. Having to learn any new language is a daunting task. Because much of programming is taught in English we've got a slight advantage. At least the mentioned 80 keywords aren't written in a foreign language.

The main take away from this chapter is the fact that OOP is the process of building objects, instancing them, and then using them. Using objects involves reading data, using logic on the data, and then carrying out tasks based on the logic.

As we move on, feel free to jump back between chapters to refresh your memory if there are concepts which you might have forgotten. It's important to proceed at your own pace; jumping ahead before you're clear on a topic leads to confusion, then frustration, and leading to quitting altogether.

We're here to learn and have fun while learning. Building a game for modern gaming platforms is easy once you've got your head wrapped around this whole C# thing, so stick to it and you'll reap the rewards. Not only will you be able to write your own games from scratch, you'll also be able to write plenty of other apps using other development tools which use C#.

We've also come across a great deal of vocabulary related to classes. If you're not completely clear as to what these words mean we'll be covering chapters dedicated to these more complex concepts. When you're ready it's time to continue learning and getting ready to make some games.

## 3.9 Variables

Programming is a combination of behavior and data. Variables are the little bits of data or information which make up the world. Everything you see in a game scene, and even things that are implicitly assumed, like gravity, can be interpreted as data that can be stored into a variable. Logic behavior can be controlled by comparing values stored in variables.

A variable can be either something that's constantly changing or something you've set once and shouldn't change unless you act on the variable to change it. For instance, an object's location should be updating if it's falling or getting pushed on by other forces in the world. This object's location is a variable, which the programmers at Unity have named `transform.position`. This brings us to how to find a variable.

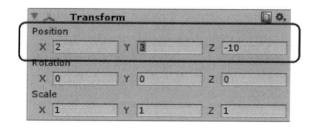

A variable's name is called an *identifier*. For the most part an identifier is a unique word that a programmer, or in this case you, picks to name a variable. An identifier is always something that a programmer invented to describe a variable; it's like naming a new pet or a baby.

### 3.9.1 Identifiers

Identifiers, which are considered symbols or tokens, are words that you invent which you then assign a meaning. Identifiers can be as simple as the letter i or as complex as @OhHAICanIHasIdentifier01. We'll get into properly creating names later on, but *identifier* is the word that's used to name any function, variable, or type of data you create.

When the keyword *class* is used it's followed by another word called an identifier. After properly identifying a function, or other chunk of data, you can now refer to that data by its identifier. In other words, when you name some data Charles you access that data by the name Charles.

```
class MyNewClassImWriting
{
}
```

### 3.9.2 Data

Data, in a general sense, is sort of like a noun. Like nouns, data can be a person, place, or thing. Programmers refer to these nouns as objects, and these objects are stored in memory as variables. The word *variable* infers something that might change, but this isn't always the case. It's better to think of a variable as a space in your computer's memory to put information.

When you play word games like MadLibs you might ask for someone's name, an object, an adverb, and a place. Your result could turn out like "*Garth* ate a *jacket*, and *studiously* played at the *laundry-mat*." In this case the name, object, adverb, and place are variable types. The data is the word you use to assign the variable with.

Programmers use the word type to denote what kind of data is going to be stored. Computers aren't fluent in English and don't usually know the difference between the English types noun and adjective, but they do know the difference between letters and a whole variety of numbers. There are many predefined types that Unity 3D is aware of. If you add that to the ability to create new types of data, the kinds of data we can store is practically unlimited.

The C# built-in types are sometimes called POD, or plain old data. The term *POD* came from the original C++ standard which finds its origin dating back to 1979. POD types have not fundamentally changed from their original implementation.

So far we've used the word type several times. Programmers define the word type to describe the variety of data to be stored. Variables are created using declarations. Declaration is defined as a formal statement or announcement.

Each set of words a programmer writes is called a statement. In English we'd use the word *sentence*, but programmers like to use their own vocabulary. Declaration statements for variables define both the type and the identifier for a variable.

```
public class Example : MonoBehaviour
{
    int i;
}
```

Programmers use a semicolon (;) rather than a period to end the statement. Therefore, if you want to sound like a programmer you can say you can "write a statement to declare a variable of type int with the identifier i." Or if you want to be overly dramatic you can proclaim "I declare a new variable of type int to be known as i!" and so it shall be.

### 3.9.3 Declaring a Variable

Programmers use their own grammar to make complete statements. To ask the computer we'd like some space in memory for a number, we use the following statement. Declaring a variable starts with a type of data followed by the name or identifier we're assigning to the variable.

```
 1 ⊟   using UnityEngine;
 2  └   using System.Collections;
 3
 4 ⊟   public class Example : MonoBehaviour
 5      {
 6              int SomeNumber;
 7              // Use this for initialization
 8 ⊟           void Start ()
 9              {
10
11              }
12
13              // Update is called once per frame
14 ⊟           void Update ()
15              {
16
17              }
18  └   }
19
```

There are three important parts to the statement you see above. First observe the placement of the statement, after the lines. We've added the `int  SomeNumber` after the first line of code `public class Example : MonoBehaviour {`; this is significant because of the first curly brace. Any line of code between the first and last curly brace operator is a part of the `Example` class. Anything outside of the curly braces either supports the `Example` class by external means or is created independently and requires special means to interact with the `Example` class we're writing.

Let's go back to the shampoo example. I've seen some rather vague descriptions for how much shampoo to use at any time. The clause *apply a generous dab* of shampoo means nothing to a computer. Computers like actual numbers; they hate descriptions of a number without a number. Computers would be happier if you said the following by *defining* a generous dab as:

```
float generousDab = 0.33f;
```

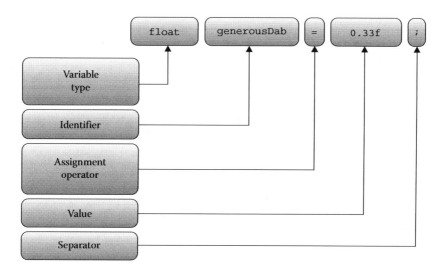

Now we can say we have defined `generousDab` as a type `float`, and then assigned the value `0.33f` to `generousDab`. We will explain what the `f` is doing after the numbers in Section 4.7.1. For now, remember it's just a way to tell C# the value to match the float type it's being assigned to.

The above statement is still rather vague: Does it mean 0.33 fluid ounce or 0.33 gram? This really depends on the hardware a computer would be using to measure an amount of shampoo. It's fair to say that computers would have a hard time washing hair without the help of robotic parts.

Now that we know what parts are required to make a variable declaration, what can we do with them? Once a variable has been declared and assigned it can be reassigned at any time.

```
int i = 0;
i = 1;
```

On the second line the variable i is no longer 0; it's 1 now. If we check what value is being stored at i we'd find a 1. So long as i is not assigned again, i will retain its value.

```
i = 2;
```

And, of course, i is no longer 1; it's 2 now. The variable will retain whatever the last assignment was until it's changed again. Once a variable has been declared with int i;, it cannot be declared again. Consider this bit of code:

```
int i = 0;
int i = 1;//invalid, i has already been declared!
int i = 2;//still won't work, stop trying.
```

This code leads to conflicts in memory, as we're trying to create a declaration for i twice.

### 3.9.3.1 A Basic Example

In a very simple class you need to declare variables inside of the curly braces. In the following example, declaring the variable outside of the curly braces will create invalid code.

```
class SomeClass
{
    int SomeNumber;
}
```

Once the code has an invalid character or line of code the rest of the class will be broken and won't compile.

```
int SomeNumber;
class SomeClass
{
}
```

We are using the keyword int to tell the computer the type of data we want. This is followed by the name of the variable. In this case we're naming the int to SomeNumber. If we were to use programmer speak, we are assigning the identifier SomeNumber to data type int. The last part of our statement is the ; operator. The semicolon is like the period at the end of a sentence. The ; ends the statement, and tells the computer we're done making a statement.

```
class SomeClass
{
    int SomeNumber = 0;
}
```

One classic mistake many, new and old, programmers make is forgetting to add the semicolon to the end of a statement. MonoDevelop will sometimes tell you when there might be an error, but Unity 3D will also stop everything when it finds an error like this.

We've now completed two important tasks. We created a variable identifier giving the variable a way to access the contents of the variable. C# under the hood gave that variable some space in your computer's memory to put an integer. The `int` variable is now defined as `SomeNumber`, an object we can fill with a number with practically any `int` value.

When variables are declared for the first time, or initialized, in C# they are usually immediately given a value. This is not true with all types of variables, but number values are assigned 0 when they are created. For more complex data types their default value is null when they are initialized. This initialization behavior will become useful later when we start inspecting the values of variables.

### 3.9.4 Dynamic Initialization

When we both define and assign a variable we use the term *dynamic initialization*. Some data types automatically give themselves a default value when they are initialized without an assignment. For instance, a Boolean automatically assumes it's false when it's created.

```
class SomeClass
{
    bool SomeBool;
    bool AnotherBool = false;
}
```

In this case, if we were to use `SomeBool` before assigning it then the result would act as though it were initialized false. In the above example both `SomeBool` and `AnotherBool` have the same value. Likewise, most numbers are initialized as 0.

```
class SomeClass
{
    int SomeInt;
    int AnotherInt = 0;
}
```

So in this case both `SomeInt` and `AnotherInt` have the same value. However, this changes when we dynamically assign a value to a variable when initializing.

```
class SomeClass
{
    int SomeInt = 7;
    int AnotherInt = 11;
}
```

When we assign a value to an `int` when it's initialized we skip the default initialization, and the value assumes its assignment when it's created.

### 3.9.5 What We've Learned

Variables are stored in your computer memory. By defining a variable by its type you instruct the computer to set aside a block of memory in the computer's RAM (Random Access Memory) to store data. To access the data you give it a name, or an identifier.

Once the identifier has been defined you can assign or read the data stored in memory through its identifier. In many cases the identifier needs to be unique. Depending on when it was created an identifier might have the same name as one created before it.

When this happens you get an error telling you that a variable has already been defined with that identifier. Changing one or the other's name solves the problem. When creating identifiers we need to consider what they're used for and how to name them.

Some code standards place rules on how an identifier should be named. For instance, a bool might always start with `is` to indicate how it's used. Therefore, a zombie might have `isWalking` or `isRunning`, indicating what it's doing. Other standards might use a prefix `b` for `bools`, so `bWalking` or `bRunning` could be used to indicate the same thing. How you decide to name variables is up to you, but it's good to know what we're about to get into so far as naming variables, which we'll be covering next.

## 3.10  Variable Names

It's important to know that variable identifiers and class identifiers can be pretty much anything. There are some rules to naming anything when programming. Here are some guidelines to help. Long names are more prone to typos, so keep identifiers short. A naming convention for variables should consider the following points.

The variable name should indicate what it's used for, or at least what you're going to do with it. This should be obvious, but a variable name shouldn't be misleading. Or rather, if you're using a variable named `radius`, you shouldn't be using it as a character's `velocity`. It's also helpful if you can pronounce the variable's name; otherwise you're likely to have issues when trying to explain your code to another programmer.

```
int someLong_complex_hardToRememberVariableName;
```

There is an advantage to keeping names as short as possible but still quite clear. Your computer screen, and most computers for that matter, can only fit so many characters on a single line. You could make the font smaller, but then you run into readability issues when letters get too small. Consider the following function, which requires more than one variable to work.

```
SomeCleverFunction(TopLeftCorner - SomeThickness + OffsetFromSomePosition,
BottomRightCorner - SomeThickness + OffsetFromSomePosition);
```

The code above uses many long variable names. Because of the length of each variable, the statement takes up multiple lines making a single statement harder to read. We could shorten the variable names, but it's easy to shorten them too much.

```
CleverFunc(TL-Thk+Ofst,LR-Thk+Ofst);
```

Variable names should be descriptive, so you know what you're going to be using them for: too short and they might lose their meaning.

```
int a;
```

While short and easy to remember, it's hard for anyone else coming in to read your code and know what you're using the variable a for. This becomes especially difficult when working with other programmers. Variable naming isn't completely without rules.

```
int 8;
```

A variable name can't be a number. This is bad; numbers have a special place in programming as much of it has other uses for them. MonoDevelop will try to help you spot problems. A squiggly red line will appear under any problems it spots. And speaking of variable names with numbers, you can use a number as part of a variable name.

```
int varNumber2;
```

The above name is perfectly valid, and can be useful, but conversely consider the following.

```
int 13thInt;
```

Variable names can't start with any numbers. To be perfectly honest, I'm not sure why this case breaks the compiler, but it does seem to be related to why numbers alone can't be used as variable names.

```
int $;
int this-that;
int (^_^);
```

Most special characters also have meanings, and are reserved for other uses. For instance, in C#, a - is used for subtracting; in this case C# may think you're trying to subtract that from this. Keywords, you should remember, are also invalid variable names as they already have a special meaning for C#. In MonoDevelop, you might notice that the word this is highlighted, indicating that it's a keyword. Spaces in the middle of a variable are also invalid.

```
int Spaces are bad;
```

Most likely, adding characters that aren't letters will break the compiler. Only the underscore and letters can be used for identifier names. As fun as it might be to use emoticons for a variable, it would be quite difficult to read when in use with the rest of the code.

```
int ADifferenceInCase;
int adifferenceincase;
```

The two variables here are actually different. Case-sensitive languages like C# do pay attention to the case of a character; this goes for everything else when calling things by name. Considering this: A is different from a.

**NOTE:** Trained programmers are often taught a variation of naming conventions, which yields easier-to-read code. Much of this is dependent on scope, which we will discuss in Section 4.4.4. There are also conventions which always prefix variable names with an indication of what sort of data is stored by that variable.

As a programmer, you need to consider what a variable should be named. It must be clear to you and anyone else with whom you'll be sharing your work with. You'll also be typing your variable name many times, so they should be short and easy to remember and type.

The last character we discuss here is the little strange @ or at. The @ can be used only if it's the first character in a variable's name.

```
int @home;
int noone@home;
```

In the second variable declared here we'll get an error. Some of these less regular characters are easy to spot in your code. When you have a long list of variables it's sometimes best to make them stand out visually. Some classically trained programmers like to use an underscore to indicate a class scope variable. The underscore is omitted in variables which exist only within a function.

You would find the reason for the odd rule regarding @ when you use int, which is reserved as a keyword. You're allowed to use int @int, after which you can assign @int any integer value. However, many programmers tend to use MyInt, mInt, or _int instead of @int based on their programming upbringing.

Good programmers will spend a great deal of time coming up with useful names for their variables and functions. Coming up with short descriptive names takes some getting used to, but here are some useful tips. Variables are often named using nouns or adjectives as they describe an attribute related to what they're used for.

A human character can often have a health attribute. Naming this HealthPoints or NumberOfHealthPoints is sometimes considered too wordy, or even redundant. However, if you and your friends are accustomed to paper role-playing games then perhaps HitPoints would be preferred.

In the end once you start using the name of the variable throughout the rest of your code, it becomes harder to change it as it will need to be changed everywhere it's used. Doing a global change is called *refactoring*, and this happens so often that there is software available to help you "refactor" class, variable, and function names.

**NOTE:** You may also notice the pattern in which uppercase and lowercase letters are used. This is referred to as either BumpyCase or CamelCase. Sometimes, the leading letter is lowercase, in which case it will look like headlessCamelCase rather than NormalCamelCase.

Many long debates arise between programmers as to which is correct, but in the end either one will do. Because C# is case sensitive, you and anyone helping you should agree whether or not to use a leading uppercase letter.

These differences usually come from where a person learned how to write software or who taught that person. The use of intermixed uppercase and lowercase is a part of programming style. Style also includes how white space is used.

When you name variables in Unity 3D the use of CamelCase or BumpyCase will automatically separate the different words indicated by an uppercase letter in the Inspector panel. This doesn't actually affect how the declaration was written. This will only change how your variable's name appears in the Unity 3D editor.

### 3.10.1  UsingVariables in Unity 3D

Open the UsingVariables project in Unity 3D to follow along.

Unity 3D is a great way to demonstrate how these variables work. When you add variables of different types and Unity 3D parses the information, the variables will show up in Unity 3D editor. The Inspector panel we looked at before is useful for a great number of reasons.

```
 1  using UnityEngine;
 2  using System.Collections;
 3
 4  public class Example : MonoBehaviour
 5  {
 6          int SomeInt;
 7          int OtherInt = 7;
 8          // Use this for initialization
 9          void Start ()
10          {
11
12          }
13
14          // Update is called once per frame
15          void Update ()
16          {
17
18          }
19  }
20
```

I've added `int SomeInt;` and then an `int OtherInt = 7;` on the line after. To make these visible to the editor we need to add the keyword "`Public`" before the variable in MonoDevelop.

```
public int SomeInt;
public int OtherInt = 7;
```

The keyword `public` is used to share data outside of the class's encapsulation. With the `public` keyword added before the `int` keyword, the `SomeInt` and `OtherInt` will now appear in the Inspector panel in Unity 3D editor. Don't forget to save the file before jumping back to Unity 3D to observe the changes.

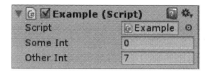

When we added = 7 to the OtherInt we told C# that we're creating a default value to the Object's Script. The first int we declared is initialized to 0 when it's added to the Inspector. Many variable types are initialized with a default value if nothing is provided when they are declared.

Initialization is the process by which variables and other chunks of data are created and stored for the first time in a class object. Initialization can be either automatically declared, like SomeInt, or declared as variables are initialized, such as OtherInt. Later on, we can control how to be more explicit how variables are initialized.

If you make changes to the default values and save the scene, the changes will be saved to the script. To bring them back right click on the script's component title bar and select [Reset] to revert the values to those declared in the script.

In the Inspector panel in Unity 3D we have some new things to look at under the Example script's parameters. Our variables have been added as number fields that we can make changes to. With the new parameters added you can make changes as long as they are valid int values. You might notice that you can't add in a . as this would change the number into something other than an integer.

Integers or int are whole numbers. Numbers which have a decimal in them are not integer values. Such numbers, having values with fractions, have several different names, for example, float, or double. We'll go into some more depth as to what types mean in Chapter 4.

### 3.10.2 Variable Assignment

We stepped through some basic guidelines regarding assignment of variables, but what happens when we change the assignment? The variables' assignment happens one line at a time. The computer starts at the top of the code and works its way down one line at a time. What this means is that the value of a variable shows its changes only after the assignment is made.

For instance, in the following code sample we'll start off with one variable and change its assignment several times and print the results.

```
using UnityEngine;
using System.Collections;
public class Variables : MonoBehaviour {
    //Use this for initialization
    void Start () {
        int MyVariable = 7;
        print (MyVariable);
        MyVariable = 13;
        print (MyVariable);
        MyVariable = 3;
        print (MyVariable);
        MyVariable = 73;
        print (MyVariable);
    }
    //Update is called once per frame
    void Update () {
    }
}
```

With the code included in a new C# script named Variables assigned to the Main Camera in a new scene, we'll get the following output in the Console panel.

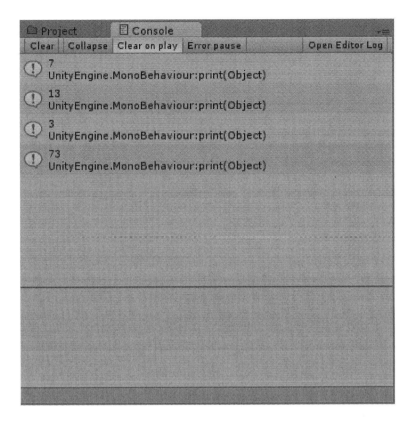

Using the same variable named MyVariable and after assigning it different values, we get different numbers printed to the Console panel. This is because the identifier MyVariable is nothing more than its value; it's just a number. In other words we could use the following code fragment and get the same result from both print outputs.

```
int MyVariable = 7;
print (MyVariable + MyVariable);//prints 14
print (7 + 7);//prints 14
```

If we want to mix variables together we can do that too. Because MyVariable is an integer value, we can treat it like any other integer, or whole number. This can be demonstrated best with another int variable.

```
int MyVariable = 7;
int MyOtherVariable = 3;
print(MyVariable * MyOtherVariable);//prints 21
print(MyVariable * 3);//prints 21
```

Here we'll get an expected 21 printed out to the Console panel from both of the print functions. To be clear, MyVariable * MyOtherVariable and MyVariable * 3 are equivalent; next, let's consider what happens when we assign a variable to another variable:

```
int MyVariable = 7;
int MyOtherVariable = 3;
print(MyVariable * MyOtherVariable);//prints 21
MyVariable = MyOtherVariable;//what's happening here?
print(MyVariable * MyOtherVariable);
```

Now we have MyVariable being assigned the value that is MyOtherVariable. Therefore, let's think through this logic. MyOtherVariable is assigned a value of 3, so if we assign MyVariable a value of 3 the second print function will return `MyVariable * MyOtherVariable`. This means it's actually just 3 * 3, which means 9 will be printed out to the Console panel.

### 3.10.3 Putting It Together

We've named variables and given them assignments. It's about time we start to consider how to apply these new concepts to something useful in Unity 3D. Because variables can be used as the values that they store we'll need to see how that works in Unity 3D.

We'll start off with a basic scene with a little sphere in it; we'll be doing this often. Select the GameObject → Create Other... → Sphere and a sphere will appear in your scene. Create a new C# file named `sphereController` and assign it to the sphere we just created.

Next, open the `sphereController` script in MonoDevelop. To start with, we're going to add in a public variable at the class level. We will be getting to what this all means in Section 4.4.3, but for now what we're doing is making this variable available to the rest of the functions as well as the editor.

```
using UnityEngine;
using System.Collections;
public class sphereController : MonoBehaviour {
    public float Control;
    //Use this for initialization
    void Start () {
    }
    //Update is called once per frame
    void Update () {
    }
}
```

Your code should look like the one above. Now hopping back into Unity 3D you should see Control in the Inspector panel.

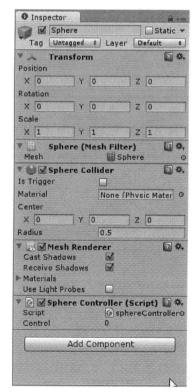

This little thing has a 0 in it and so far that's what we want. We'll be making use of this variable in the
Update () function found in the class. Let's add the following code to the Update () function and
see how it works.

```
    void Update () {
        transform.position = new Vector3(Control, Control + Control,
Control * Control);
    }
```

This will move the sphere such that its x position is simply the number in Control. The y value is
Control + Control and the z value is Control * Control. To play with this simply select the
Sphere in the Hierarchy panel, and then left click + drag on the Control label in the Inspector panel.
Press the Play in Editor button up at the top and watch the update happen as we change the value stored
at Control.

When the Play button is pressed the class we attached to the sphere is immediately instanced into an
object. This process is easily overlooked and taken for granted, but remember, a class is a blueprint for
making objects. Therefore, every class that is attached to a GameObject tells Unity 3D to instance that
class and attach it to the GameObject. So the GameObject behaves as expected.

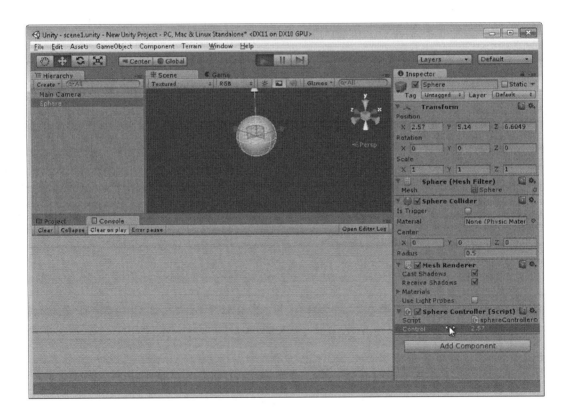

The value that is being modified in the Control script will be directly reflected in the Position under the
Transform information at the top of the Inspector. By adding another variable we can make this even
more interesting.

```
public float OtherControl;
```

Add in another public float OtherControl; on the line following public float Control;
this will add in another value which we can slide around.

```
void Update ()
{
    transform.position = new Vector3(
    Mathf.Sin(Control) * OtherControl,
    Mathf.Cos(Control) * OtherControl,
    Control * OtherControl);
}
```

Play with this for a little bit; just make sure `OtherControl` is a value other than 0. You should see a spiraling ball moving around, thanks to `Mathf.Sin()` and `Mathf.Cos()`. Basically, these two `Mathf` functions return the sine and cosine of control. We've now seen some basic examples of how to use variables in Unity 3D.

An alternative to the above code which is more readable may look like the following:

```
void Update ()
{
    Vector3 vec = new Vector3();
    vec.x = Mathf.Sin(Control) * OtherControl;
    vec.y = Mathf.Cos(Control) * OtherControl;
    vec.z = Control * OtherControl;
    transform.position = vec;
}
```

Another possible option is to use the following:

```
void Update ()
{
    float x = Mathf.Sin(Control) * OtherControl;
    float y = Mathf.Cos(Control) * OtherControl;
    float z = Control * OtherControl;
    transform.position = new Vector3(x, y, z);
}
```

The nuances between the different versions require some understanding of the different data types involved. The variables that you were just introduced to are being put to use in unfamiliar ways. The different uses will become more clear as we are exposed to a more varied set of situations. As we explore the code throughout the rest of the book, we'll become more acclimated to unique uses of different data types.

Of course, there are many things we can try out here, and it's best you try them out on your own. There are many other `Mathf` functions to play with, but we'll leave that for Section 6.5.1.2. For now it's best to explore how variables behave and how we can use them.

### 3.10.4  What We've Learned

We're taking very small steps to start off with. There's a great deal of new concepts for you to absorb and many questions to be asked. If anything up to this point is unclear then take a moment to go back and review.

So far we've become familiar with some basic terms related to writing C#. Learning about programming is somewhat about learning new vocabulary, and we've covered keywords and a few operators and variables. We just added some variables to a C# class object and added it to an object in our Unity 3D scene.

Variables, numbers in particular, demand different amounts of memory based on what type of number is being stored.

C# is an OOP paradigm. Every class is an object. Once we learn how to write our own objects, we'll learn how to read other objects and possibly even begin to understand the complexity laid out in Unity 3D's library.

## 3.11 Types: A First Look

When we assign a variable a value such as int i = 1; we're making an interesting assumption. We assume using 1 automatically infers a value type that matches the variable type. Computers use a wide variety of different types of data for storing numbers.

So far we've been seeing the word int being thrown around as though you know what an int is. In our everyday lives we hardly think there's any difference between numbers 1 and 1.0 or even the word *one*. As humans we can easily conceptualize numbers as units of measure and converting between them. The conversion between the word *one* and the number 1 isn't so easy for a computer.

The keyword int is short for integer. Integers are whole number values. The integer is a C# built-in type. Basically, this means that integers are a fundamental part of C#. Other built-in types include float, double, string, bool, and object. Less commonly used built-in types are char, short, and byte. Altogether, there are 15 different built-in types. All of these, except object and string, are value types.

Every type of data you're able to build must be based on all of these built-in types. The system which creates all of these floats, doubles, and bools is rooted in the origin of computing. Remember the punch tapes and pieces of paper with holes in them? Those were records of 1s and 0s which were fed into computers for storing in the form of mechanical switches, either on or off. The patterns represented numbers or instructions and logic.

Today, we still use the same system of 1s and 0s, or binary, only we don't need to punch holes in paper to tell the computer what to do. The methods of creating and storing the instructions have become many times more complex, but nonetheless the principle of the 1 and 0 are the same. These are called bits; one possible origin for that name is the little bits of paper that were left over from punching all of the holes in the paper cards.

### 3.11.1 Value and Reference Types

The int, float, double, and bool are commonly used value types. The basics of this usage pattern relate to the system that stores and organizes the computer's memory. When you talk about computer storage you use the word *megabyte* or *gigabyte*. Value types are stored with a very specific purpose in mind: to keep track of a numeric value.

**NOTE:** The word *mega* refers to how many millions of bytes a component in your computer can store. *Giga* indicates how every many billions of bytes are being stored. Have you ever thought about what a byte actually is?

A byte is what is called an 8-bit unsigned integer, or a system of using 8 bits to form a number. What this means is that it's a whole number like 0, 7, or 32,767. The word *unsigned* indicates that the number cannot be negative, like −512.

A 1 or 0 in computer terms is called a bit. We won't go into detail on how computers use bits to count, and it's a rather fun thing to learn on your own. However, it's important to know that a byte has a limited range, from 0 to 255. I'll just leave you with the idea that you could count up to 1023 on your 10 fingers if you used binary rather than decimal. Your fingers can be used to represent a 10-bit unsigned integer.

The computer's calculation capabilities used to be far more limited than they are today. An 8-bit game console made in the 1980s had a limited number of colors, 256 to be exact. This limitation was based on the number of bits that the processor could handle. The processor had a limited number of transistors which could be used at any one time. Shortly after, floating point coprocessors were introduced, which had a much larger numeric range allowed, by having closer to 32 bits to work with.

In all of these cases, when you use a value type, that number is actually stored as 1s and 0s in your computer's RAM. This should be considered fairly remarkable. In the past you'd have to go through flaming hoops to store a value. Now you just type in float f = 3.1415926535; and you can measure the circumference of the universe accurately to within the width of a single atom.

What all of these types have in common is that they are stored as a single element. Large values like double gigawatts = 1210000000.0; and double mint = 2.0; use the same amount of memory.

Your computer doesn't assign one double or the other more space in memory. These types are referred to as *primitive types*. The only difference between an `int` and a `float` is the number of bits they use at a time, 8 and 32 respectively; `doubles` use 64 bits.

The `string` and `object` types differ a bit in how they are stored. These types are a composite of any number smaller elements. The bigger a string or object the bigger chunk of memory the computer opens up to place that object or string. These are called *reference types* or sometimes called *nullable types* because C# doesn't look to a single element in memory to get data from it.

We will explain nullable types in Section 4.4.1.2, but in short a nullable type is a space in memory which is reserved for data that has yet to be fulfilled. Primitive or value types are commonly reserved and assigned at the same time. There are systems which allow this to be changed, but we're getting ahead of ourselves for now.

In Unity 3D, a commonly used type is the `Vector3`. Vectors, in the math world, are directions in *x*, *y*, and *z* with a length. Unity 3D uses vectors to keep track of a position in 3D space. The `Vector3` type is a composite of three `float` variables. This means that a `Vector3` is made up of different components. From this, we may infer that a `Vector3` is a *nullable* type. Each float is labeled x, y, and z. However, unlike the primitive types the `Vector3` needs to be instanced. This means that you can't simply use the following syntax.

```
int i = 0;//a valid initialization of an int.
Vector3 v1 = (x = 0,y = 0,z = 0);//not valid initialization.
Vector3 v2 = new Vector3();//this is how it's done.
```

`Nullable` types need to be initialized; that is, they need some form of initial value. We'll go into further detail on this later. It's important to remember there are differences between types when they are being initialized. Later on, as you begin to create and use objects and variables it'll be important to remember how to initialize the different variable types.

### 3.11.2 What We've Learned

There are many different forms which data can take. Each form is called a type. The different forms depend on how they are organized and how they are initialized. Reference or nullable types require some form of initial parameters before they can be used. Value or primitive types usually have an initial value when they are created.

When variables are declared, they are assigned a type. The type changes how the variable behaves and what values it's allowed to store. As we move forward, remembering how types behave is important. C#, and many other C-like programming languages, has specific rules with how to deal with data of differing types.

## 3.12 Strong Typing

This has nothing to do with how hard you type on the keyboard! C# sees a difference between numbers in how they are written. A whole number like 1 is different from 1.0, even though we can think of them as having the same value. Some of these differences can be added by adding a letter. Therefore, `1.0` and `1.0f` are actually different numbers as well.

C# is a *strongly* typed programming language. When a programming language uses strong types you're expected to keep the different types separated. This means that a `1 + 1.0f` can create a problem. Because the two numbers are actually different types of numbers we have to convert one of them to match the other before the operation is allowed to take place.

To convert from one type to another we have to tell C# that we intend to make that conversion from a `1` to a `1.0` by using what's called a *cast operator*. Aside from changing how memory is used, types also limit any problems which might come about when working in a team of programmers.

If one programmer is new to your game and has made assumptions about hit points being in floating point values, he'd quickly find out as soon as he looked that you're using integer values and change how he intends to use those numbers. Value types not only store a value assigned to them but also provide a great deal of information to be inferred by the programmer reading the code.

In Unity 3D a `Vector3 vec = new Vector3(1.0, 1.0, 1.0);` will throw an error. The number `1.0` is called a `double`, which uses 64 bits, whereas `1.0f`, which is a `float`, uses 32 bits. The difference means float `1.0f` is half the size of the double `1.0` in memory. A `Vector3` is made up of three `float` values, not three `doubles`.

Therefore, in terms of declaring a variable and assigning it `float f = 1.0f` and `double d = 1.0;` the same type problems exist as with assigning a `Vector3()`, which is made of three different float values. To properly tell C# you mean a 32-bit version of 1.0 would be to add an `f` after the number: `1.0f` means you want to use the 32-bit version of 1.0 and not the 64-bit version of 1.0. Therefore, to declare `Vector3 vec = new Vector3(1.0f, 1.0f, 1.0f);` is the correct way to assign a proper `Vector3()`.

Confused? I'd imagine so; we'll clear things up in a bit. Just hang in there.

For our purposes of learning how to code, knowing anything about bits may not mean a lot. However, if you ever talk to a programmer it'll be very important that you know the difference. Before getting too far ahead we should know that Unity 3D uses `floats`, `ints`, and `doubles` quite often. There is also a difference between the different data types and that they cannot be simply used interchangeably without consequence.

### 3.12.1  Dynamic Typing

Not all programming languages are so strict with types, but it's a good to get used to working with strict types before learning a more lazily typed programming languages, like Lua (http://www.lua.org/ ). Type conversion is important for learning more complex languages like C, or C++. These languages offer a wider number of platforms and a more detailed level of control.

With dynamically typed languages like Lua or UnrealScript, you can run into strange hard-to-track-down bugs. These are sometimes called "Duck"-typed languages; this refers to the proverb "if it looks like a duck and it sounds like a duck, it's probably a duck." However, when it comes to a type we might see something like this:

```
var i = 1;
if (i)
{
    Console.writeLine("is it true or a 1?");
    i = i * 0.1;
}
```

In the above it's not clear what the variable `i` is supposed to be, is it a `bool` or an `int` or a `double`? When `var` above starts off as an integer but we use it as a bool and then multiply it by a floating point value, what is `i`? What have we turned it into if we want to use it as something else, or how do we turn it back?

As we will see in Section 7.14.4, we are allowed to make some exceptions to the type of a variable. The keywords `var` and `dynamic` do mean you're expecting an unexpected type to be coming, but once it's there, you had better know what to do with it.

### 3.12.2  What We've Learned

We have glossed over the specifics of how numbers work in the computer's memory, but we'll get into that in Section 6.20.2. Superficially, we should know that not all numbers are the same. A byte is 8 bits, a nibble is 4. An int is 32 bits, and an int64 is 64 bits, but that's not all. A float is also 32 bits and a double is 64 bits, but these can't hold the same values as an int or int64.

The float and double use some of their bits called a mantissa to hold the numbers after the decimal. Therefore, 1.01 requires some of the bits to represent the 1, and these are called the significant digits.

The mantissa uses some bits to represent the other 1 in the number. Then there are more bits set aside to tell C# where the dot (.) goes in the number, and these bits are called the exponent. Therefore, with 1.02, the exponent tells the mantissa 2 to move an extra zero after the dot, so 1.02 is the final result.

We take for granted the work going on under the hood to store a simple number. All of this happens thanks to many computer scientists who have worked in the last several decades. Konrad Zuse and John von Neumann introduced a system of floating point representation to computing in the 1940s, with the Z1 and later the Z3. Their system is roughly the same system in use today.

## 3.13 Type Casting, Numbers

This is a simple exercise, but an important one nonetheless. When you start to deal with keeping score, or recording injuries to a monster, it's important that behaviors are predictable. Many problems begin to show up if the math you're using involves mixing numbers with decimal values like floats or doubles, or with integers which have no decimal value.

```
int i = 100;
```

Decimals are not allowed on an `int` value.

```
float f = 100.0f;
double d = 100.0;
```

Decimals are allowed for both `float` and `double`. The only caveat is that a float requires an `f` post fixed to the number when it's assigned.

Converting types between one another is pretty simple when you need to deal with numbers. When we start creating our own classes the task of casting becomes a bit more detailed, but not necessarily more difficult; there's just a bit more work involved. We'll get to that soon enough.

When we go between number types or the built-in value types (POD), we work with things which seem to come with C#. So far we've seen things like `int` and `float`. Integer values like 1, 7, and 19 are useful for counting. We use these for counting numbers of items in an array, or how many zombies are in a scene, for instance. Integers are whole numbers, even though we might be counting zombies whole or not.

Once we start needing numbers with fractions we need to use float values. To get an object's speed or *x*, *y*, and *z* coordinates in space we need to use values like `12.612f`, or `x = 13.33f`, to accurately place an object in space. If not, objects would move around in a scene as though they were chess pieces locked to a grid.

When a float value exists as `0.9f` we lose some values after the decimal when converting the floating point value to an integer.

```
void Start ()
{
    float a = 0.9f;
    int b = (int)a;
    Debug.Log(b);
}
```

If we use the above code in a new script called `Casting.cs` attached to the Main Camera in a new Unity 3D project we'll get the following output to the Console panel.

```
0
UnityEngine.Debug:Log(Object)
Casting:Start () (at Assets/Casting.cs:10)
```

Without the cast operator `int b = a;` we get an error telling us we need to cast the value before assigning it.

```
Assets/Casting.cs(9,21): error CS0266: Cannot implicitly convert type 'float'
to 'int'. An explicit conversion exists (are you missing a cast?)
```

The first part of the error message says "Cannot implicitly convert type," which has a very specific meaning that we'll get to before the end of this chapter, but first let's cover explicit type casting.

### 3.13.1 Explicit versus Implicit Casting

As we have seen, in the Start () function where we declared float a = 0.9f; a was converted to 0. Even though we were only 0.1f away from 1 and 0.9f away from 0 we're left with a 0 instead assigned to int b. To do these conversions we use the explicit casting method, as shown with (int)a;, which explicitly tells C# to convert the value stored at a to a float value. When we are required to use an explicit cast, we're also warned that there may be some data lost in the conversion.

Casting is a process by which C# changes the type of a variable to another type. This may or may not involve a loss of information. In some cases, the conversion doesn't require the explicit cast operator. The following code casts an int to a float.

```
int c = 3;
float d = c;
Debug.Log(d);
```

With the above code we get a 3 printed out to the Console panel. We didn't need to use an explicit casting operator. This is because when we cast from an int, in this case 3, there would be no data loss when it's cast to a float. This is possible through an implicit cast. Implicit casts are allowed only when there is no data lost in the process of converting from one type to another.

There are no integer values which will result in a loss of any value when it's converted to a float. Technically, there are more float numbers between 0 and 1 than there are integer numbers between 0 and 1, or any other sequence of two numbers for that matter.

#### 3.13.1.1 A Basic Example

Create a new project called NumberTypes and assign a C# script to the Main Camera called NumberTypes.cs. In the Start () function include the following code.

```
void Start ()
{
    int a = 1;
    double b = 0.9;
    int c = a * b;
    Debug.Log (c);
}
```

If we look at what is going on here we'll want to think for a moment about what it means. The integer a is set to 1 and double b has 0.9 assigned. We should assume that 0.9 will be assigned to c after the multiplication, but this assignment is stopped by a type conversion error. C# usually gives us pretty clear reasons for its errors. In this case we know there's a cast missing between an int and a double.

```
Assets/NumberTypes.cs(10,21): error CS0266: Cannot implicitly convert type
'double' to 'int'. An explicit conversion exists (are you missing a cast?)
```

The error states we can't implicitly convert a double to an int; why not? 1 certainly looks like 1.0, or so it seems. However, 0.9 can't be turned into an integer. There's no integer between 0 and 1. Even though 0.9 is very close to being 1, it's not.

```
int c = a * (int)b;
```

We use type conversion to tell C# to explicitly change b from a double to an int by preceding the b with (int). What value is going to be assigned to c if it can't be 0.9? The (int) operator is an explicit cast.

```
0
UnityEngine.Debug:Log(Object)
NumberTypes:Start () (at Assets/NumberTypes.cs:11)
```

0 is less than 0.9; we've lost data going from the double value to an integer value. Even though 0.9 is almost a 1, the first int value is 0, followed by values that are cut off by the type conversion. This is why type conversion matters.

We will find other casts which look like this in Sections 6.14 and 6.20, but we're introducing the concept early on as it's a very common problem to come across. The syntax (int) turns a number following this operator into an int. Likewise int i = 0; double d = (double) i ; is a way to cast an int into a double. However, this isn't always necessary.

Some conversions take place automatically as an implicit cast. In the above example we can use the following code without any problems.

```
void Start ()
{
    int a = 1;
    double b = 0.9;
    int c = a * (int)b;
    Debug.Log (c);
    double d = a;
    Debug.Log(d);
}
```

Here we assign double d = a; where a is int 1, which we know isn't a double. This produces no errors. The same goes if we add another line float f = a;. In this case f is a float. These are called implicit casts. An integer value doesn't have a mantissa or an exponent. Both the double and float do have these two possibly large and important values. These two terms were explained at the end of Chapter 2.

When mashing a double into an int we lose the mantissa and exponent. By using an explicit cast, we tell C# that we don't mind losing the data. This doesn't mean that an implicit cast will not lose any data either. An int can hold more significant values than a float. We can observe this with the following lines of code added to the Start () function.

```
Debug.Log(largeInt);
float largeFloat = largeInt;
Debug.Log(largeFloat);
int backAgain = (int)largeFloat;
Debug.Log(backAgain);
```

This code produces the following console output, after a bit of cleaning up:

```
2147483647
2.147484E+09
-2147483648
```

When we start with the value 2147483647 assigned to int we're at one extreme of the integer value. This is the biggest number the int can hold, for reasons discussed in Section 3.11.1, but in short, it's because it's using only 32 bits to store this number.

If we cast this into `largeFloat` we can use an implicit cast, which converts the value from int to float. In this case we see only 2.147484 followed by the exponent E+09, which tells us that the dot (.) is actually nine places over to the right.

When we convert the float back into an int with an explicit cast we get a −2147483648, which is certainly not what we started with. This tells that there's some significant information lost in the conversion from float to int, but there were also numbers lost in the implicit cast from int to float.

This still happens if we remove a digit from the end.

```
int largeInt = 214748361;//cutting off a digit and ending in 1
Debug.Log(largeInt);
float largeFloat = largeInt;
Debug.Log(largeFloat);
int backAgain = (int)largeFloat;
Debug.Log(backAgain);
```

This sends the following numbers to the console:

```
214748361
2.147484E+08
214748368
```

The last digit is changed from 1 to 8. The 8 is coming from some strange conversion when we go from int into float. Even if we look at the numbers being stored in the float value we can tell that there's already a change in value. This tells us that in general, we need to be very careful when converting from one type into another.

Logically, another difficult problem is converting from a string to a number value. When you use `string s = "1";` you're not able to use `(int)s` to convert from a string to an int. The types of data are very different since strings can also contain letters and symbols. The conversion of `(int) "five"` has no meaning to the computer. There's no dictionary which is built into C# to make this conversion. This doesn't mean that there are no options.

```
string s = "1";
int fromString = int.Parse(s);
Debug.Log(fromString);
```

The code added to the `Start ()` function will produce the following number:

```
1
```

There are plenty of options when faced with dealing with significantly different types. The `int. Parse()` function is an option that we can use to convert one value into another. Again, we might be getting a bit ahead of ourselves, but it's important to see that there are many different ways to convert between different types.

### 3.13.2 What We've Learned

In this chapter we used some syntax which has not been formerly introduced. For the sake of seeing what happens to numbers between casting we needed to do this. In Section 6.20, we will cover the details of what happened in this chapter, so don't worry. Everything in this chapter will be explained in detail soon enough.

We've still got a lot to cover about types. It's a bit early to see how they relate to one another and why there is a difference. Once we move into evaluating numbers we'll start to see how the different types interact. Accuracy is one place where we begin to see the effects of type conversion. A float with the value of 0.9 turns into 0 when it's converted to an int.

This chapter is just a cursory look at types. There's a lot more to conversion than just losing some numbers. Later on we'll see what happens when we need to convert between different game play characters like zombies and humans. Many attributes need to have specific conversions but then they're both bipedal creatures.

## 3.14 Comments

Just before the `Start ()` and the `Update ()` functions you'll notice some green text in MonoDevelop. These two lines, which state `//Use this for initialization` and `//Update is called once per frame`, are comments. The `//` operator means that the `//` and anything following it is now invisible to the compiler.

Comments are left as breadcrumbs to help keep notes in your code. Once a new line is started the `//` no longer applies and the next line is now visible.

```
//these are not the lines you are looking for...
```

Programmers use comments for many reasons. Mostly, comments are used to describe what a function is used for. Quite often, comments are left as notes for both the person who wrote the code and for others. Sometimes, when a function is confusing, or isn't always working, a comment can be left as a "to do" list.

Once we start writing our own functions we'll want to leave comments to help ourselves remember what we were thinking when we wrote them. Once in a while, if we need help, we can indicate to our friends our intentions. You can leave comments like `//I'm still working on this, I'll get back to it tomorrow...` if you're still working on some code.

Or you can ask for help: `//help, I can't figure out how to rotate the player, can someone else do this?!` is a simple short comment. Even professional programmers leave comments for their coworkers, letting everyone who may be looking at their work a clue as to what was going on in their code.

In more than one case, the comments in a large code base needed to be cleaned up before releasing to the public. The engineers responsible needed to remove foul language from the comments to avoid any public ridicule. In some instances the comments in the code were also defaming competing game engines.

When a comment requires more than a single line, use the following notation:

```
/* this is a multiline comment
which can carry on to other lines
you can keep on writing anything
until you get to the following */
```

Anything between the `/*` and the `*/` will be ignored by the C# compiler. It's often a good habit for a programmer to introduce a class by leaving a comment at the top of the file. For instance, it's common to see the following in a class written for other people to edit.

```
/* Player class written by Alex Okita
This class manages the player's data and logic
*/
```

The use of comments isn't limited to simple statements. They are often decorated by extra elements to help them stand out.

```
/*****************************************
 * This comment was written by Alex Okita *
 *****************************************/
```

Comments have several other uses which will come in handy; for instance, when testing code you can comment a section of code that you know works and test out new code next to the code commented out. If your test doesn't work you can always clear it out and un-comment the code that does work. We'll play with this idea later in this chapter.

Using comments on the same line of code is also a regular practice.

```
void MyFunction () {
    int someInt = 0;//declaring some regular integer as 0
}
```

We can inform anyone reading our code what a specific statement is doing. Although we want to be smart with how our comments are written, if we add too many comments in our code the actual statements that matter get lost between a bunch of words that don't matter.

Comments are also useful for testing different collections of code. When you're learning about how different behaviors affect the results of your functions it's often useful to keep different versions of your code around. This is often the case when trying to debug a problem and eliminate lines of code without having to completely get rid of them.

```
void MyFunction () {
    int someInt = 0;//I print 0 through 10
    //int someInt = 3;//starts at 3
    //int someInt = 11;//this won't print
    while(someInt < 10) {
        print(someInt);
        someInt++;
    }
}
```

It's possible to test out various test cases using comments to allow you to pick and choose between different statements. In the above code fragment, we've got `someInt` declared three different ways. Depending on which line is left un-commented we can choose between different values.

We can leave another comment on the line after the statement, reminding us what the result was. For covering an entire section of code it's easier to use the /* */ form of commenting.

```
void MyFunction () {
    int someInt = 0;//I print 0 through 10
    //int someInt = 3;//starts at 3
    //int someInt = 11;//this won't work, so leave me out.
    //trying out new code here
    for(i = 0; i < someInt; i++) {
        print(someInt);
    }
    //the code below will do the same thing.
    /*
    while(someInt < 10) {
        print(someInt);
        someInt++;
    }
    */
}
```

In above code, we've commented out the `while` loop following the `for` loop which accomplishes the same task. In this way we can easily switch between the two different loops by switching which loop is commented out. Programmers often leave sections of code in their functions commented out so they verify the validity of the new code they've added in.

The /* */ notation for comments can also be used in smaller places. Anytime the // notation appears everything on the same line is commented out. Using the /* */ notation we can hide a segment of a line of code.

```
    while(someInt </*10*/100) {
        print(someInt);
        someInt++;
    }
```

For instance, we can hide the 10 in the while loop and replace it with another number altogether. The /*10*/ is hidden from the computer so the 100 is the only part of the condition that's seen by the computer. This can easily get a bit more ugly as a single statement can begin to get stretched out and become unreadable.

```
Vector3(/* this is the x variable */1.0f, 2.0f/* <- that was the Y
variable*/,/* the z */3.0f/*variable is here*/);
```

Although the above code is perfectly valid, it's not recommended that something like this appear in your code. When mixing in too many comments a simple declaration can get pretty ugly.

### 3.14.1 Line Numbers

Each line of code in MonoDevelop is indicated in the margin of the editor to the left. When Unity 3D comes across a typo or some unexpected character it's indicated in the Console panel.

```
// Use this for initialization
void Start ()
{
                ?

}
```

In this example I just added in ? in the middle of the Start () function. Unity 3D tells us about this addition with the following output to the Console panel.

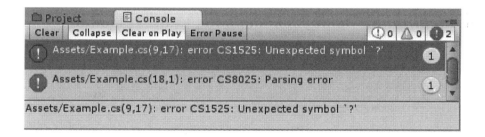

The error tells us: Example.cs(9,17): error CS1525: Unexpected symbol '?'. The (9,17) tells us the position where the error is occurring. The first number is the line number. In the source code mentioned, we added in the ? on the 9th line. The 17 tells us that the character is on column 17, or the 17th character position from the left. If you were to count the number of spaces from the left you'd reach 17 and find the ?, which Unity 3D is erroring on.

This is a more precise example of an error, but we may not always be so fortunate. In general, the line number indicated is more or less a starting place where to start looking for an error. It's difficult to say when and how various errors take place in code, but in general, syntax errors tend to be fairly easy to fix. Difficulties arise when the code itself is using proper syntax but the result is erroneous or deviates from expected behavior.

When this happens we'll have to use other techniques to track down the bugs. We'll save those techniques for when we're ready for them. For now we'll just stick to learning proper syntax and comments.

### 3.14.2  Code Folding

```
1   using UnityEngine;
2   using System.Collections;
3
4   public class Example : MonoBehaviour
5   {
6       /*
7        * Code folding can be handy!
8        * you don't need to have this
9        * open all of the time,
10       * just expand this to see
11       * the rest of the comment!
12       */
13      // Use this for initialization
14      void Start ()
15      {
16
17      }
```

When you add in a long comment using the /* */ notation MonoDevelop recognizes your comment.

```
4   public class Example : MonoBehaviour
5   {
6       /* Code folding can be handy! ... */
13      // Use this for initialization
14      void Start ()
15      {
16          |
17      }
```

Clicking on the little box in the number column will collapse the comment into a single line. This feature comes in most of the modern IDEs, or integrated development environments, meant for writing in C#. This feature is also handy when you're rewriting large segments of code, in that it reduces any distractions.

```
4   public class Example : MonoBehaviour
5   {
6       /* Code folding can be handy! ... */
13      // Use this for initialization
14      void Start ()
15      {
16          //focus on what you're doing!
17      }
18
19      // Update is called once per frame
20      void Update (){...}
24  }
25
```

We can collapse many blocks of code into a single line. If you look at the line numbering following the Update () function you'll see the numbers jump from 20 to 24. This process of collapsing has hidden three lines of code; moreover, this feature will be particularly handy when you need to see two different functions which might have a great deal of code between them.

```
/* Code folding can be handy! ... */
// Use this for initialization
void Start ()
{
        SomeDistantFunction ();
}

// Update is called once per frame
void Update () [...]

void SomeDistantFunction ()
{
        //more code here
                        I
}
```

Here, we can see the SomeDistantFunction() and where it's being used at the same time. If the Update () function wasn't collapsed we might have to scroll up and down to see both the use of the function and the function's contents.

```
void Start ()
{
        for (int i = 0; i < 100; i++) {
                [// code!]
        }        I
}
```

This also works for any instance where the opening curly brace { is followed by the closing curly brace }. This folds the for statement into a more compact form, so we don't have to look at what it's doing. This allows us to focus on the code block we're most interested in focusing on.

### 3.14.3 Summary Comments

```
/// <summary>
/// Clevers the comments.
/// </summary>
void CleverComments ()
{
        /*
         * comments inside
         * of a function
         */
}
```

If you type in three /s over a function, MonoDevelop will automatically add in a summary comment. This will be filled in with an automatically generated comment summary, which is probably going to be wrong, but it's fun to see what it comes up with.

```
///<summary>
///Blends the fruit.
///</summary>
void BlendFruit() {
    int bananas = 2;
    int strawberries = 6;
}
```

Like the other comments the summary comments are also collapsible. MonoDevelop also recognizes many different forms of comment tags.

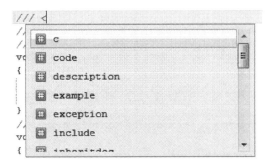

When you add in ///< the above automatic code completion pop-up dialog appears. You can add in description examples and other tags. This feature of MonoDevelop demonstrates how important comments are in a well-written source file. Comments and comment tags have many different options. To avoid writing the rest of this book about comments I'll leave experimenting with the comment tags to you. They are important, but not essential, to learning how C# works.

### 3.14.4 Navigating in Code

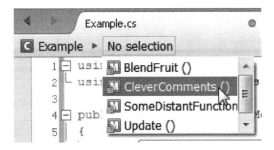

There are also clever ways to get around in a source file. Up at the top of the Editor panel in MonoDevelop is a handy drop-down menu which has a list item for every function in the class. You'll also notice an icon next to each listing.

Add in a `public` keyword before the void `CleverComments()` function and the lock icon goes away. This indicates that the `CleverComments()` function is public. Selecting the item jumps the cursor to the beginning of the function. This comes in particularly handy when dealing with large source files which might have many different functions in them.

### 3.14.5 What We've Learned

Comments are a necessary part of any good source file. When you've written several dozen different C# files you'll find that code written months ago might look alien. I often find myself thinking to myself "What was I thinking when I wrote this?" when I open a file from many months before.

In these cases I hope I wrote in detailed comments, leaving myself at least some clue as to what was going on to lead to the code that has been written; usually, however, I haven't and I need to read through the rest of my code to come up with an understanding of what was going on in my code.

It's time to get back to Unity 3D and start writing something more interesting than comments. We spent a great deal of time in this chapter writing things that are ignored by the computer. It's time to get to writing code that matters.

---

## 3.15 Leveling Up: Moving On to Basics

At this point we've looked at the components that make up C#. We should be able to look at code and identify the different tokens and roughly what they do. The ; is a separator token which ends a code statement. Likewise, we should understand that a : and a ; have different roles in code and cannot be used interchangeably.

Variables have a type, and this type determines how the variable can be used. We should also know that different types cannot interact without explicit conversions between them. Converting between different types can result in loss of data, and thus we should be mindful when doing so.

When we look at a statement, we should be able to identify the different tokens which the statement is composed of. In a statement like `int a = 6;` we should be able to see that we're using five different tokens.

What the different tokens are used for may not be clear, but that information will be presented as we continue. Learning a programming language is just as involved as learning any other language. Just like any language has grammar and vocabulary, C# has syntax, keywords, and structure.

# 4

## Basics: The Building Blocks of Code

After covering the small parts that make up code, it's time to start learning how all of the parts come together to create a behavior. Creating data is easy; keeping the data organized is harder. Adding logic to do something with the data is harder still. That said, it's not impossible; otherwise, no one would write code.

This chapter covers how a statement of code works and where the power that drives the code originates. Programming is much less enigmatic when you understand the mechanisms that drive it. To understand why code behaves the way it does, it's important to know your way around the language.

### 4.1 What Will Be Covered in This Chapter

This chapter is about getting past the details and getting an understanding about the structure of code. This process is somewhat comparable to learning the grammar of the C# programming language. We'll cover the basics about the different types of logic statements and looping statements.

Logic allows you to pick different actions based on the result of a calculation. If you want to tell a human to run away from a zombie or run to a human for help, you'll need logic, to control that human's behavior. Logic takes data, makes a comparison, and chooses which block of code to execute.

Looping statements are able to read and react to more than one or two sets of data. If you're in a room with any number of zombies, you'll want to take them into account all at once. Looping statements are an integral part of any programming language. We'll see why they're so useful in this chapter, in which we discuss the following topics:

- Building up basic concepts
- Creating a new class
- Directives: The keyword `using`
- Functions
- An introduction to scope
- The keyword `this`
- Order of operation
- Logic and operators
- Loops
- Warnings and errors

### 4.2 Review

Before getting ahead of yourself, it's important to remember some of what we just covered. We will be learning many new tokens in this chapter. A token, as we know, is the smallest element that makes up a statement.

Statements are organized tokens that accomplish a task. Tokens can be keywords, or words reserved by C# for special purposes. Some tokens are used to separate statements, and others are used to assign values to variables.

A keyword cannot be used for anything other than what it has been reserved for. Some keywords can be used only in a specific context. Several keywords are used only if you've defined a specific library, where they have been defined; we'll discuss some of these topics later in this chapter.

When you create a variable, you've created a new token. Some variables exist only in the context they were created in; the control of this existence is called scope, something which is coming up in this section as well. As a reminder, when you invent a word to identify a variable that word becomes a new token.

Once created, the token can be used in many different ways; you can apply an operation to a token and use it to assign values to other variables. These operations all happen in a very specific order. Create a variable, execute an operation or an expression, assign the value. This is what makes C# an imperative language.

## 4.3 Building Up a Game Idea: Working with What You Know

Often, when you come up with a game idea it's usually something that sounds familiar yet it's never been done before. When I'm at a convention or a comic book, game, or developer conference, people often like to tell me about their new game ideas. In about 20 years of these often impromptu game pitches, I've heard mostly about World War II (WWII) games usually involving zombies. Hopefully, you've thought of something more original.

At the same time, it's necessary you prune your ideas down to the most simple core game elements play possible. Starting off with an epic massive multiplayer free to play role-playing game (RPG) with app purchases of user-generated content is a mammoth undertaking.

To be honest, I wouldn't know where to start on such a titanic project. With that in mind, when learning any programming language and learning a new game engine, your goals should be in scale to what you know.

Starting off with the programming goal "I'd like to have a game controller move a character around" means you stand a higher chance of success. From there, you can move on to "I'd like the character to shoot a projectile when I press a button." This step-by-step approach gives you the building blocks necessary one day for creating your MMORPG, and it's not recommended that you start with building the next MMORPG/realtime strategy/WWII first-person shooter (FPS) from the get-go.

### 4.3.1 Design from Experience

When programmers think about game design, it's usually in the form of a technical specification. If there are zombies, then we need character controls and some zombie behaviors. If you need a fully automatic chainsaw rocket launcher, you'll need some physics and a pretty cool weapons system. Unity 3D might have the physics and rendering covered, but the rest is up to you.

After accruing a great deal of experience, you can begin to think about more complex game mechanics. It's great to have pie in the sky ideas, but not for your first project. The best games are finished games. The awareness of what is involved with writing a complete game usually comes only after finishing your first project. Only then is it possible to comprehend what's involved with the "Tripple A" or high-budget titles that are produced at large game companies.

You should either finish your project or start on something new. I've started and stopped countless projects. With each project started I get closer to finishing before coming up with another better idea.

This habit is fine, and I encourage the behavior. With each project you tend to approach a similar problem in a slightly different, and often more efficient, way. Because of this approach, you're also learning and growing as a game developer.

#### 4.3.1.1 *Know Yourself*

When you're just getting started it's better to start with your own coding skill. Think to yourself, "I can make a guy that can run, jump, and shoot. I can probably figure out how to make some simple monsters to shoot at. I should make a game where you run, jump, and shoot at monsters." This sounds like a reasonable plan.

Where you begin your code and what you decide to tackle first is determined by what the player does the most often in your game. If you're focused on making a third-person zombie shooter, then you should probably begin with moving a character around on screen with a camera over his shoulder. Once your camera works, move on to the next activity. After shooting, move on to shooting at monsters. Sometime after that, make the monsters react to getting shot.

It's an incremental process; layer one activity onto the next. When the game begins to be playable, you've reached a point where you can begin to add on more interesting behaviors. This process of adding features comes only after the core activity has been achieved.

### 4.3.2 Primary Activity

Deciding what it is that you do most of the time in building a game is usually based on the type of game you're aiming to build. Action games tend to require a great deal of moving around and looking. Puzzle games tend to require a great deal of watching objects move around and looking for patterns.

It's necessary to break your game down into something overly, simplified like moving and looking or watching and pattern matching. The primary activity your player will be doing should be the best functioning part of your code. Quite often, once you start on getting code written, you discover new game play ideas.

As the ideas begin to flow, however, you need to remind yourself that none of them will work unless you get your camera working or your pattern matching down. Maintaining focus is the hardest thing to do as a new programmer. It's also important to remain focused on your ultimate goal: writing a game.

The players' primary activity should be the focus of your game code. You should boil down your ideas into a solid obtainable goal. Only when you've reached the minimal activity to start with, you're ready to move on.

Reading through completed code projects may help you see what you should be working toward. Reading forums online, asking questions, and looking at examples of code helps immensely. Everything you're trying to do in code has most likely been done before, and in many different ways. It's up to you to find the method you're most comfortable with and that matches what you're doing most.

The Unity 3D Asset Store is complementary to your achieving this goal. Many collections of code for various purposes can be found here. If you're looking for a system to control zombies, there might be a good starting point in the store. Reading code downloaded from the store means you'll have Unity-compatible source code, and many examples to learn from for working on your own project.

### 4.3.3 Moment to Moment

Once you've managed to get your primary activity understood, it's time to move on to the moment-to-moment game play. Moment to moment involves thinking about what it is that your player does while doing his or her primary activity.

For a third-person zombie shooter, you'll be mouse clicking to shoot weapons. If you're moving tiles around to match colors, you'll be clicking on tiles. This first action dictates the next set of functions that need to be written to reach your game-making goals.

### 4.3.4 Actions to Functions

The first step to building code is thinking in terms of taking interactions and turning them into code. When you need to read mouse movement, you need to look for something that does that. In most game systems there's usually some input method that exposes the various input systems that the engine can read.

Mouse input, touch input, and in many cases accelerometer, gyro, and even a global positioning system (GPS) can be accessed through functions coded by the engine developers. From there you need to figure out what you want to do with the input. Mouse movements are usually in *x* and *y* coordinates that correspond do a position on the screen. Systems like joysticks often return an *x* and *y* value between −1 and 1.

At first, nothing has to move. You just need to print out the text informing the accomplishment of listening to a mouse click, or recording a mouse position on screen. After you've accomplished reading your input sources, you'll need something to click on, or shoot at. This never has to be fully realized artificial intelligence (AI), or puzzle piece when a simple cube will suffice.

With every step, use a printout to the Console panel to prove you're getting the data you are looking for. Then you should always be using primitive shapes to test out a basic interaction. There's nothing worse than spending a few weeks modeling, rigging, and animating a zombie, only to find out you need to rewrite your code because of something unexpected.

### 4.3.5 Compromise

As mentioned, you might figure out that building a MMORPG with WWII vehicles, zombies, crafting, and user-generated content might be a bit too big for your first project.

At least I hope you figure this out. Once you've decided you need to change plans you need to cut features. Ultimately, this all comes down to how much time you are willing to dedicate to your project.

If you're willing to stick with Unity 3D and C# for the next 20 years then sure, go ahead and make that MMORPGWWII-with-zombies game you've never seen before. Unfortunately, it's likely that you will not see it; no one else will see it either. I have heard of one project where a lone programmer has literally spent over 20 years on one game project. He started in the early 1990s and is still working on his game. He has yet to produce a demo, and will probably spend another 20 years on it. I hate to see people do this, but it's their choice. Once you've written enough code for your first game, you might discover that just wandering around and shooting zombies might be enough to constitute a game. In reality, it is enough to be a game, and you might even be able to finish it before your computer becomes obsolete. If the game isn't fun, however, with this simple activity, then maybe the core of the game isn't actually fun. In any case, you made a game and it's time to start writing another game but maybe this time you will start off with a more interesting game play core.

As an independent developer, or someone working on your own, it's also important to weigh your code time against your art time. Producing art and code takes time, and it's quite difficult to rework and change after a great deal of work has been done. Although code would remain largely the same, to make changes in code to accommodate a minor change in art might take days.

Renaming each joint in a zombie uniquely per requirement of your code would take only a few minutes to correct in your 3D modeling package. Conversely, you the programmer might have to invent a new system for joint location to deal with joints of all the same name, based on some clever concept you haven't even thought of yet. Inventing a new system, or correcting some joint names: hopefully the compromise is easy to make.

### 4.3.6 Starting with Controls

At the beginning of almost every game development project, the player controls are usually the first focus of the game. After all, most games are played by players, so they'll need to be able to control how they play your game.

This should seem obvious, but I've been a witness to some game development that started with realistic physics for breaking objects or amazingly lifelike human motion. In both cases, however, that amazing never-before-seen technology was greatly ignored by the player, or at best taken for granted.

Only a small tech-savvy group of the gaming audience would notice, for example, how glass breaks in a realistic manner, or how a character's feet plants when he turns around. Many developers think that they're breaking ground on realism in gaming. To their player, they're spending thousands of hours not making the game more fun.

Input management is our first goal. You should decide if you're dealing with either keyboard and mouse or touch screen taps and gestures. Testing and iterating on a good input management system takes time and effort. The amount of time usually spans the length of the entire project. Constant tweaks and updates create a constant loop between game play and input.

In Chapter 3, we added a cube to a scene and attached an `Example.cs` script to it. This is actually nearly enough to call a sand box. Depending on your game, you might want to add in a floor and walls. This can be done by adding in some cubes and stretching them out to build a simple room to run around in.

There are many different books already on building games and environments in Unity 3D, and you can defer to those as reference. However, it can't be overlooked that Unity 3D has many different assets already for you to use on the Asset Store. This is a huge bonus for you as a programmer as well.

The Asset Store includes source code written in C#. Downloading free assets from the Asset Store, or even trials, will reveal a wealth of C# techniques both good and bad. After downloading free assets from the Asset Store, it would be difficult to tell what's good and what's bad.

In both cases of good and bad code, code is a very creative art. As in visual crafts like painting and drawing, there are good artists and there are bad ones. The differences also apply to programming. There's plenty of bad code to learn from, or rather learn what not to do. There's also plenty of code that is useful and clever.

Later on, when you've learned more, you'll be able to tell the differences more easily. Large unreadable code assets tend to stand out, as so clean tidy code assets. In general, if you see a great deal of unreadable, uncommented, and messy formatting, you're looking at garbage. If you see clear simple short statements, the chances are you're looking at a winner.

### 4.3.7 What We've Learned

So far we're just getting started. Along our road toward zombie destruction, we're going to need to do a great deal of footwork and studying. Some of what we're about to get into might seem a bit mundane, but it's only the beginning.

We're learning a new language with new words and concepts. With the help of Unity 3D we're going to have a foundation on which pretty much any game can be built. Stick to it and you'll be writing code in no time.

## 4.4 Creating a Class

A class is the set of instructions and tools necessary to build an object. This was mentioned before, but we didn't look at what's involved with writing a new class. To write a new class, open Unity 3D, start a new Project named `MyNewClass`.

To get our heads around what a class is, we're going to write a class inside of a class. This is what is called a nested class. Open the `FirstExample.cs` to follow along.

To write a nested class you start with a *class declaration*. A class declaration is basically the keyword `class` followed by an identifier. As a reminder, an identifier is simply a word you use to name any data you've created. Once a class has been declared, it's a matter of filling it with all of the useful things that classes can do.

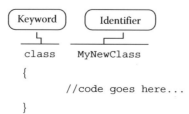

Where does this go? Well, to get started we'll want to have Unity 3D do a bit of footwork for us. Much of this work is done for you by the Unity 3D Editor when you use the Asset → Create → C# Script menu in the Project panel.

This takes a bit of the work out of starting a new file from scratch. There's no difference between the files Unity 3D creates for you this way and the new C# files you create.

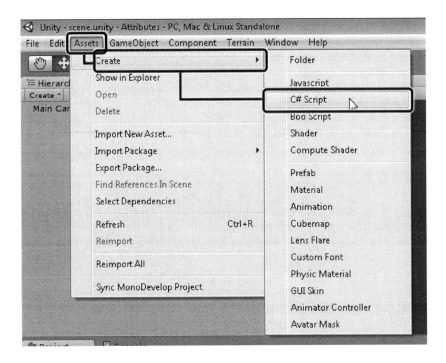

Unity 3D creates a new file, writes some directives, and declares a class, then adds in some base functions to get started. We'll go through the same steps to understand why the file is written like it is. And we'll start with the class declaration.

## 4.4.1 Class Declaration

Classes contain a variety of different objects called members, or *class members*. Variables are accessed by identifiers. When referencing a class the *data members* are sometimes called *fields* or *properties*.

When you fill out a form to log into a web page, you may need to put your name and a password into empty boxes, which are often called text fields because they are fields of data to a programmer. They are open spaces in your computer's memory, into which you put data.

The sections of a class that contain logic and code statements are called *function members*. These are also accessed by their identifiers. Depending on what a function does for the class, it can be categorized as a *method*, a *constructor*, a *destructor*, an *indexer*, a *operator*, a *property*, or an *event*. How these functions differ from one another will be discussed in Sections 5.4.3, 7.13, 4.7.1.1, 7.5, and 7.15.

Classes need to talk to one another for any number of reasons. Zombies need to know where humans are, and bullets need to take chunks out of zombies. Suppose a zombie has a number of chunks left before slain, and the human has a position in the world where the zombie needs to chase him; this information needs to be shared. The availability of the information is called *accessibility*.

Data and function members can be made accessible to each other using the *public* keyword. We'll observe how this works in a moment.

### 4.4.1.1 A Basic Example

C# allows us to create classes within a class. Shown above is a class declaration for `VeryVeryFirstClass`. This is a nested class inside of the `Example` class. For ease of use we'll use a new `Example` class to build a `VeryVeryFirstClass` object. The declaration of the class looks like `class VeryVeryFirstClass {}` that creates a new class that has no members.

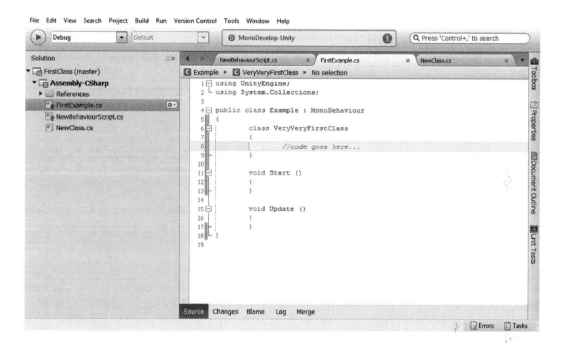

Look just below that and you'll find a line that has the statement `void Start ();` this statement creates a function that is a member of the `Example` class. To create an instance of this class we add `VeryVeryFirstClass FirstClass = new VeryVeryFirstClass ();` to the `Start ()` function.

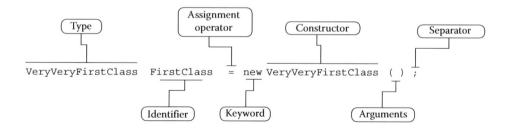

Let's examine the first two words, or tokens. The first token `VeryVeryFirstClass` indicates the type of object we intend to create. The class we created is now a type of data. Once `VeryVeryFirstClass` has been declared as a class, it becomes an instruction to create a new object that can be found by its identifier.

We know a variable is declared by a keyword followed by an identifier like `int i;` a class variable is declared in a similar way: `VeryVeryFirstClass FirstClass`. However, unlike an `int` a class *cannot* be assigned easily.

What differentiates an `int` from a class is how the type is created and then assigned. We'll have to go into detail a bit later when we would have a deeper understanding about data types, but for now, we'll consider an `int` as a fundamental type.

### 4.4.1.2 Value and Reference Types

Although we declared `class VeryVeryFirstClass` we have yet to give it anything to do. For now, there's nothing in `VeryVeryFirstClass`. Once we start adding features to `VeryVeryFirstClass` the task of assigning a value to the class becomes ambiguous. In context:

```
VeryVeryFirstClass FirstClass = 1;//what should this do?
```

What would that mean if `VeryVeryFirstClass` was a zombie? Is the `1` his name, how many hit points does he have, or what is his armor rating? Because C# can't be sure, the computer has no hope of making a guess.

This differentiates a *value type*, like an `int`, over a *reference type*, such as `MyClass`. However, before we go into a chapter about types we need to know more about classes, so we'll get back to the topic at hand.

Therefore, when creating a new instance of a reference type we need to use the form `new SomeClass ();` to assign a variable of type `SomeClass`. Thus, `MyClass myClass = new MyClass ();` is used to create a variable for `MyClass` and assign the variable `myClass` a new instance of the correct class.

To make things clear, `int i` can be assigned in the exact same way we assign `myClass`.

```
int i = new System.Int32();
```

We can use the above statement if we want to make our `int` declarations look the same as our class declarations. This is unorthodox and unnecessary, but it's possible. It's important to know that things like this do exist and that C# is flexible enough to allow us to do this.

### 4.4.2 Adding Data Fields

A data field is any type of information that lives inside of a class. We'll cover what data type really means in Section 6.5.3 but for now we'll assume that data can be pretty much anything, including a number. When a class has data fields added to it, we're giving the class a place that holds onto information and allows the class to remember, or store, some data. For instance, were we to write a zombie for a game we'd need the zombie to know, or store, how many brains it has eaten, or how many whacks it has taken from the player.

```
class VeryVeryFirstClass
{
    int num;
}
```

To add a data field to `VeryVeryFirstClass` we use the same declaration as we would for any other variable. This should be obvious, but since we're writing a class inside of a class this might be a bit confusing. However, when this is declared as `int num;` we're not allowed to use it yet.

### 4.4.3 Access Modifiers and the Dot Operator

To talk to members of a class we use the *dot operator* (.) to tell C# we want to access a member of a class. When a new data field is added to a class it's assigned a type and an identifier. The identifier turns into the word we use after the dot to request access to that data or function.

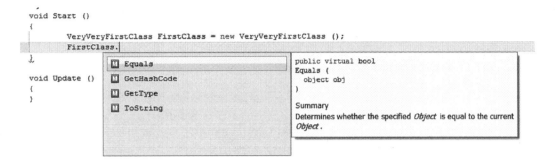

If we try to find the num data field when using MonoDevelop we won't see the num data field in the list of members. To make the int  num accessible we need the public keyword. The public keyword is similar to several other keywords that change the accessibility of a variable within a class; such keywords are called *access modifiers*. There are several access modifiers we'll come to use, but for now we'll just get familiar with the public access modifier.

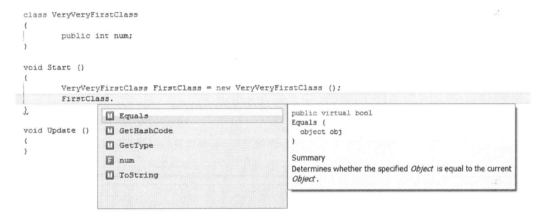

Adding the keyword public before the int  num changes the accessibility to the classes outside of MyClass and allow for other objects to see the data field. The data fields that can be changed this way are called *instance variables* that are unique to each instance of the class.

An instance is a unique version, or object, based on the class from which it was created from. Each instance stands on its own as a new object created from the class it's based on. All of the class members are unique to each instance. There are systems that circumvent this behavior, but we'll get to that in Section 5.5.

To observe this point, we'll create a few instances of the class and set the data fields to different values.

```
class VeryVeryFirstClass {
    public int num;
}
//Use this for initialization
void Start () {
    VeryVeryFirstClass FirstClass = new VeryVeryFirstClass ();
    FirstClass.num = 1;
    VeryVeryFirstClass SecondClass = new VeryVeryFirstClass ();
    SecondClass.num = 2;
    VeryVeryFirstClass ThirdClass = new VeryVeryFirstClass ();
    ThirdClass.num = 3;
}
```

Here, we created three instances of `VeryVeryFirstClass`. Each one has its own num data field and each one can be assigned a unique value. To check this, we could go through a process and print out each one.

```
Debug.Log (FirstClass.num);
Debug.Log (SecondClass.num);
Debug.Log (ThirdClass.num);
```

We could add in these three lines after `ThirdClass.num` was assigned. We could do something a bit more clever by adding a function into the class that does this for us. A class member can be something other than a variable. Functions can also be class members accessible through the dot operator.

```
class VeryVeryFirstClass
{
    public int num;
    public void PrintNum()
    {
        Debug.Log(num);
    }
}
```

Start off by adding a `public void PrintNum()`, and then add in `Debug.Log(num);` to the function, following the example above. We'll get a better look at what function really is in Chapter 5, but this example serves as a quick and dirty introduction come back to a simple function nonetheless.

Next, we can use the function member by using the same dot operator.

```
void Start ()
{
    MyClass FirstClass = new MyClass();
    FirstClass.num = 1;
    MyClass SecondClass = new MyClass();
    SecondClass.num = 2;
    MyClass ThirdClass = new MyClass();
    ThirdClass.num = 3;
    FirstClass.PrintNum();
    SecondClass.PrintNum();
    ThirdClass.PrintNum();
}
```

The `PrintNum()` function is now usable through the dot operator for each instance of `MyClass`. There are many nuances that were skipped over, but we'll go into much greater detail in the rest of this book.

### 4.4.4 Class Scope

Data fields can appear anywhere in your class, though a proper system requires that we keep them together at the beginning of a class. However, it's sometimes simple to organize data with functions that need to use them.

```
class VeryVeryFirstClass
{
    public int num;
    public void PrintNum()
    {
        Debug.Log(num);
    }
    //some other class data field.
    public int OtherNum;
    public void PrintOtherNum()
```

```
    {
        Debug.Log(OtherNum);
    }
}
```

With the above example we can see that OtherNum isn't grouped with num, but rather its declaration is written just before the function that prints it. Where and when class data fields are declared have no effect on whether or not a function can see it. As a matter of fact, the placement of the declaration statements can happen at the bottom of the class, as seen here:

```
class MyClass
{
    public void PrintNum()
    {
        Debug.Log(num);
    }
    public void PrintOtherNum()
    {
        Debug.Log(OtherNum);
    }
    //declared at the end.
    public int OtherNum;
    public int num;
}
```

The functions and data members of a class can appear in any order. This feature might seem contrary to intuition. However, the C# code is fully compliant and functions just fine, ignoring how the different members are arranged. This rule doesn't always hold true, especially once we get into how code itself is executed, but at the class level, or at the class scope, as programmers like to say, the ordering isn't as important.

Not all programming languages will allow this. UnrealScript, for example, enforces all variables live at the beginning of a function. Declaring them anywhere else raises an error. C# understands that formatting is less important than clarity. Declaring variables close to where they are used, however, is important for readability.

### 4.4.5 Class Members

As we add functions and variables to a class, we're adding *members* to the class. In the previous example, num is a member of MyClass. So too are PrintNum() and any other functions or variables included in the class. We can refer to some of the members as public, which means that other classes can access them, while the inaccessible members are private.

In most cases, if public is not used then you can assume the member belongs to private. Private members cannot be accessed from outside of the class, at least not directly. However, functions on the inside or local to the class can modify them freely.

### 4.4.6 What We've Learned

We just covered some of the very basic concepts of what makes up a class. There are plenty of other keywords and some complex concepts that we have yet to even touch on. Later on, we'll get into some of the more clever tricks that classes allow for.

On your own, you should practice creating different data fields and add more functions to your class to get a feel for how they work. As you learn how to use more keywords, you should add them to your own classes to check that you understand how the keywords work.

Example.cs is a class. In this chapter, we created MyClass as a class inside of the Example class. MyClass is an example of a nested class, or a class inside of a class. You're allowed to write multiple nested classes.

```
using UnityEngine;
using System.Collections;
public class Example : MonoBehaviour
{
    class VeryVeryFirstClass
    {
        public int num = 0;
        public void PrintNum()
        {
            Debug.Log(num);
        }
    }
    class AnotherClass
    {
        public int anotherNum = 1;
        public void PrintNum()
        {
            Debug.Log(anotherNum);
        }
    }
    //Use this for initialization
    void Start ()
    {
    }
    //Update is called once per frame
    void Update ()
    {
    }
}
```

We can add as many classes as necessary to any other class. Nested classes can have more classes inside of them.

```
class AnotherClass
{
    public class InsideAgain
    {
        public int insideNum = 0;
        public void PrintInside()
        {
            Debug.Log(insideNum);
        }
    }
    public int anotherNum = 0;
    public void PrintNum()
    {
        Debug.Log(anotherNum);
    }
}
```

We can add class `InsideAgain` to `AnotherClass` if we needed to. So long as the classes are all public we're allowed to use them from outside of the class.

```
void Start ()

{
    AnotherClass.InsideAgain ACIA = new AnotherClass.InsideAgain();
```

```
        ACIA.insideNum = 10;
        ACIA.PrintInside();
    }
```

Using the dot operator from `AnotherClass` we can get to the classes inside of it. This sort of class-in-a-class layout isn't too common, but there's nothing keeping you from doing it. It's important to remember to keep things as simple as possible. With every layer of obscurity, you add a layer of complexity.

The dot operator allows us to access the contents of a class, including classes within classes. The behavior is used throughout C#, and all of the features rely on classes and class members. We'll see how to access the many functions available to us in Chapter 5.

We've been working in a nested class all this time. To show how this works in another class, we can go back to Unity 3D and create a new class next to `Example.cs` called `AnotherExample.cs`. If we open `Example.cs` we have access to the `AnotherExample` class.

```
using UnityEngine;
using System.Collections;
public class AnotherExample : MonoBehaviour {
    //Use this for initialization
    void Start () {
    }
    //Update is called once per frame
    void Update () {
    }
}
```

The above class is the automatically generated class from Unity 3D. This means that in the `Example.cs Start ()` function we're allowed to use the class as though it were any other publically available class. This does mean that there's a completely new C# file alongside the original `Example.cs` file we have been working in.

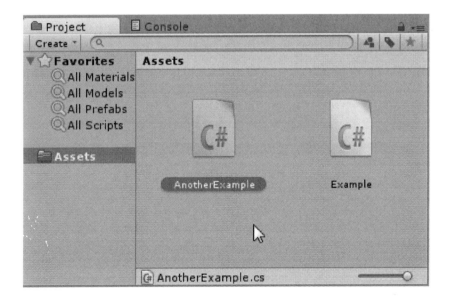

When we write code in the `Example.cs` class the `AnotherExample` class can be accessed from within the `Example` class.

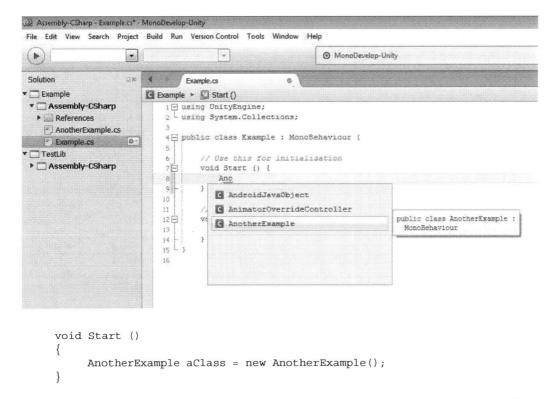

```
void Start ()
{
    AnotherExample aClass = new AnotherExample();
}
```

The above statement in the `Start ()` function of `Example.cs` will create a new instance of the `AnotherExample` class we just created. Classes become accessible throughout the rest of your Unity 3D project. This allows objects and classes to send messages to one another. As soon as they are created, they are able to communicate with one another.

Classes are able to communicate with one another thanks to MonoDevelop's understanding how C# works. Once a class is created its contents can be public or private depending on how they are declared. The scope of a class and its fields are controlled by where they appear.

A class is also able to create and assign its own data. Inside of a function you can create data that's scoped to the function, or to the rest of the class. Once a class is instanced, it becomes an object that allows you to see and manipulate its instanced contents.

With these basic concepts we'll want to explore the different classes which Unity 3D and Microsoft have created to allow us to access the various abilities that are contained in the Unity 3D game engine. Accessing the classes and fields which Unity 3D has provided is quite simple, as we will see in Chapter 5.

## 4.5 Directives

When you start writing code in Unity 3D, or any other programming environment, you must consider what tools you have to begin with. For instance, we might consider that with the .NET (read as "dotnet") framework we get things like `int`, `bool`, `float`, and `double`. These tools are given to us by adding `using System;` to our code.

We also have been taking for granted the use of `using UnityEngine;`; this function gives us another massive set of tools to work with including a ton of work that allows us to use functions and events that are triggered by the Unity 3D game engine itself.

All of these classes, functions, and events are stored in software called a library. Basically, this is code that has been written to enable your code to communicate with Unity 3D. These resources provide a gigantic foundation to build your game on. Much of the difficult math and data management functions in relation to Unity 3D has been written for you.

Knowing what they are and how they are used is important. It's like knowing what tools you have in your toolbox. In Chapter 5, we'll go over their basic use and how to find out more about what they offer.

*Directives* provide the connection between your class and a selected library. Many hundreds of classes, written by the programmers who created Unity 3D, allow you to communicate between the player, the characters, and every other object in the game. In short, a library is software for your software.

```
using UnityEngine;
using System.Collections;
```

In the first two lines of the class we had Unity 3D prepare for us are the directives we needed to get started. The connection between Unity 3D and your code is made, in part, by using directives. A directive makes calls to outside or external resources called libraries.

The libraries that the directives call upon are connected to compiled code. Unity 3D is also connected to the libraries that your code uses. The connection is made by identifying the name of the library after the keyword using is entered.

Libraries live in paths, like a file in a folder on your computer, only they are compiled into a few tightly bundled binary files.

**NOTE:** The initialism *DLL* refers to *dynamically linked library* that is a complete set of software compiled ahead of time for your use. Pretty much every software released these days include many different DLLs that allow the software to be updated and modified by only updating the DLLs they come with. Often some DLLs are located in your computer's operating system's directory but depending on the software involved it too will bring along its own DLLs.

The first line, using UnityEngine;, pulls all of the resources that deal with specific Unity 3D function calls. For instance, moving an object, playing sounds, and activating particle systems are found inside of the UnityEngine library. The functions necessary for making bullets and magic spells work are built into UnityEngine.

As the resources that make up your game are imported into Unity 3D they're made available to your code. The libraries provided by Unity 3D expose all of the imported assets in such a way that they can be found like files on your computer.

The programmers at Unity 3D have taken on the bulk of these complex tasks for you, so you don't have to deal with all of the physics and PhD-level science of rendering 3D graphics. The keyword using is how we tell C# that we're going to ask for a specific library to access.

Many other programming languages do the same thing; for instance, Python uses the statement import module to do the same thing; JavaScript is more wordy, by requiring a path like src = "otherScripts/externalLibrary.js" to access external code.

C++ and C both do the same as C# with the keyword using to access external libraries. In the end, your code has the ability to work with preexisting code stored in nicely packaged libraries. For Unity 3D, this is pretty much necessary.

### 4.5.1 Libraries

Libraries are collections of classes and data that have been bundled into a convenient package with Unity 3D. You can consider them to be similar to a compiled application. A library contains classes that are all accessible through the dot operator, like the classes we wrote in Chapter 3. Inside of MonoDevelop you can take a look at some of the other libraries we can use.

Inside of MonoDevelop, expand the References icon in the Solution explorer. In case the Solution explorer panel isn't open, then use the following menu to show the panel: View → Solution.

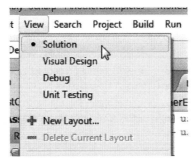

Double click on the `UnityEngine.dll` under the References folder.

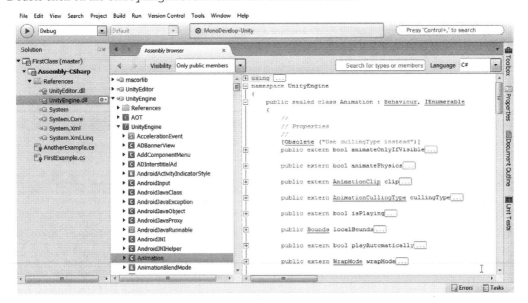

The Assembly Browser will open showing you the various libraries you have access to. In your `FirstExample.cs` class, entering the `using` keyword will prompt a pop-up. The pop-up window prompts you with the many different libraries available to Unity 3D.

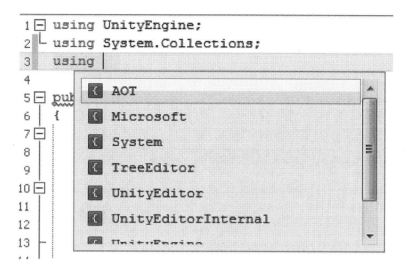

You're then prompted by the various libraries you can add to the project. By adding in `UnityEditor` we can access new functions not previously available without the directive.

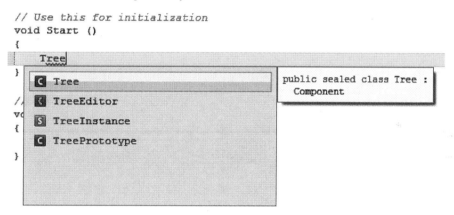

We won't go too far into how to use these other functions. We are just now getting to know the functions we already have. Between both `UnityEngine` and `System.Collections` we've got quite a large set of tools already. Later on, we'll be able to create our own libraries. Within our own libraries, we'll be able to write useful functions that can be used like anything found in `UnityEngine`.

In our `FirstExample.cs` class, we'll use the `Start ()` function and look for a `StreamWriter` function.

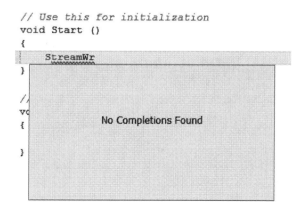

However, the auto-complete pop up shows "No Completions Found" as we start to enter the function we're looking for. Should we use a long-winded version, we would see that it is hidden within System. Within System.IO we find several objects that have Stream in them.

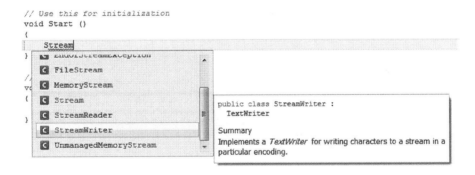

However, if we add in the using System.IO; directive we can shorten our bit of code. The using keyword helps us create a link between the classes within the libraries and our code. The more explicit we are about the objects we're after, the less writing we need to do after the directives have been added.

For this trick, we're going to use the StreamWriter to create a text file.

```
void Start () {
    StreamWriter writer = new StreamWriter("MyFile.txt");
    writer.WriteLine("im a new text file.");
    writer.Flush();
}
```

Using the StreamWriter we create a new object called writer. When the StreamWriter is instanced we pass a parameter with a string used for the file name; in this case, MyFile.txt is given to the new writer object. With the object instanced with the identifier, we use the object and call upon the WriteLine function and give it some text to write into the new file. The line im a new text file. will appear in the MyFile.txt file that Unity 3D will write for us. After that we need to use the Flush(); call to tell the writer to finish its work.

Attach the script onto the Main Camera in the scene and press the Play button to execute the `Start ()` function in the C# class. To find the file, right click on the Assets directory in the Project view.

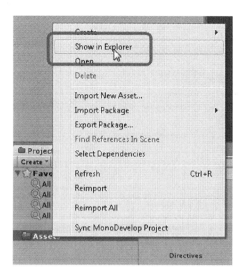

This action should bring up the directory where the new `MyFile.txt` has been written.

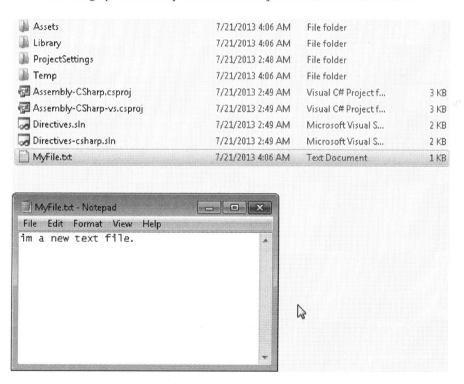

Opening the `MyFile.txt` will open the file in your usual text editor; in my case, it was Notepad. You could imagine writing various bits of information in this, or even begin to read from a text file into your game! This might make writing dialog for an RPG game a bit easier. You wouldn't have to write all of the text into each object or even code in your game. Reading from a text file would make more sense.

Of course, we'll have to do more work to get the most out of reading and writing to text files, but this is just the beginning. We'll move on to more sophisticated tricks later on. This is just a glimpse into what we can do by accessing the different parts of the libraries available to us.

## 4.5.2 Ambiguous NameSpaces

Therefore, we're looking at names of functions from libraries; in theory, each library should have unique names for each function. However, what happens if Unity 3D wrote a function with a specific name that might have existed in another Library?

```
using UnityEngine;
using System.Collections;
public class Directives : MonoBehaviour
{
    //Use this for initialization
    void Start ()
    {
        int UnityRand = Random.Range(0, 10);
    }
}
```

Therefore, if we look at the above code, we have two directives that provide us with a vast wealth of tools to start working with. One of the many tools is a simple random number generator. The `Random.Range();` function was written by the Unity 3D programmers and requires a minimum and a maximum number.

```
using UnityEngine;
using System.Collections;
using System;
```

However, if we add `using System;` to the list of directives, as in the above code sample, we'll get an error in Unity 3D.

```
Assets/Directives.cs(9,33): error CS0104: 'Random' is an ambiguous reference
between 'UnityEngine.Random' and 'System.Random'
```

This means that there's an identically named `Random` function in `System` as well as `UnityEngine`. To resolve this error, we need to be more specific when we use `Random`. Since we might need to use other parts of the `System;` library, we'll want to keep this included; otherwise, we wouldn't have this problem at all.

```
    void Start ()
    {
        int UnityRand = UnityEngine.Random.Range(0, 10);
    }
```

If we change `Random.Range` to `UnityEngine.Random.Range()`, we'll fix the problem of conflicting functions. There will be many times where you might have to change the names of a specific library as well.

## 4.5.3  What We've Learned

Knowing where to look for these functions is something that can be done only by having an investigative hunch. Usually, a quick search on the Internet can drum up a few clues as to what function you need to search for to get a specific task done.

Different libraries provide us with systems which help us add additional functionality to our classes. By default, we're given a rich set of tools to build into our game. Once we need to start reading and writing files to disk for saving lengthy game info or perhaps loading information from a web server, we will require functions that reach beyond the built-in tools that Unity 3D starts us off with.

It should also be mentioned here that the free version of Unity 3D will allow you to use only the `System` and Unity 3D DLLs. The pro version will allow you to use many external libraries for various purposes. With a pro license, you'll be able to use open source libraries for playing with the Microsoft Kinect, or Nintendo Nunchuk.

In addition, it's also possible to write your own DLLs creating libraries for your game. This might allow you to add in platform-specific functions to accelerate various aspects of the game outside of the abilities of the built-in Unity 3D tools or engine.

## 4.6 Functions

Functions, sometimes called methods, contain statements which can process data. The statements can or cannot process data. Methods can be accessed by other statements. This action is referred to as *calling a function* or *making a function call*. In this chapter we touch on the `Start ()`, but we've yet to figure out why the `Start ()` functions work.

So far we've created a class and we gave the class some places to store data. We've even used some of those variables in Unity 3D. We saw how to add a C# class to our game objects in a scene. In Chapter 3, it was a cube in a scene. Then we exposed some more variables to the editor.

This coding, however, hardly makes for a very interesting video game. To add any sort of behavior, we'll need to add in logic. Logic can't be determined without a function to run the logic. The logic needs to process data for anything in the game to happen.

To coordinate this merging of data and logic, we'll need to write some functions.

### 4.6.1 What Are Functions?

In Chapter 3, we talked about the process of shampooing. A second look at the idea of a function is to comprehend the words *wash, rinse, and repeat* in more depth. If you've never heard of the word *wash* before then you're probably dirty, or a computer. Computers need every word defined for them before they understand it.

```
void Wash ()
{
}
void Rinse ()
{
}
void Repeat ()
{
}
```

On a superficial level, we've used the above code to define the three words used to shampoo hair. However, none of the definitions contains any actions. They define the words or identifiers, but when they're used nothing will happen. However, the computer will be able to `Wash (); Rinse (); Repeat ();` without any problems now.

In the `MyClass` we wrote:

```
public void PrintNum ()
{
    Debug.Log (anotherNum);
}
```

which is quite a simple function.

Now that we can write some functions for use in Unity 3D let's get to some real coding. To make use of all of these variables, we need functions. Functions contain the logic in every class. The concept is the same for most object oriented programming languages.

**NOTE:** Functions may look different in different programming languages, but the way they work is mostly the same. The usual pattern is taking in data and using logic to manipulate that data. Functions may also be referred to by other names, for example, methods.

The major differences come from the different ways the languages use syntax. Syntax is basically the use of spaces or tabs, operators, or keywords. In the end, all you're doing is telling the compiler how to convert your instructions into computer-interpreted commands.

Variables and functions make up the bulk of programming. Any bit of data you want to remember is stored in a variable. Variables are manipulated by your functions. In general, when you group variables and functions together in one place, you call that a class.

In Chapter 3, we discussed a bit about writing a class starting with a declaration and the opening and closing curly braces that make up the body. Functions are written in a similar fashion.

We start with the declaration `void MyFunction;` then we add in both parentheses `()` and the curly braces `{}`, indicating to ourselves that we may or may not fill this in later. The first pair of parentheses `()`, doesn't necessarily always require anything to be added. However, the curly braces `{}`, or the body of the function, do need code added for the function to have any purpose.

When writing a new function, it's good practice to fill in the entirety of the function's layout before continuing on to another task. This puts the compiler at ease; leaving a function in the form `void MyFunction` and then moving on to another function leaves the compiler confused as to what you're planning on doing.

The integrated development environment, in this case MonoDevelop, is constantly reading and interpreting what you are writing, somewhat like a spell checker in a word processor. When it comes across a statement that has no conclusive form, like a variable, function, or class definition, its interpretation of the code you're writing will raise a warning or an error. MonoDevelop might seem a bit fussy, but it's doing its best to help.

### 4.6.2 Unity 3D Entry Points

The Unity 3D developers provided us with `MonoBehaviour` which is a class that allows our C# classes to have direct access to the inner workings of the Unity 3D game scene. The `MonoBehaviour` class is a collection of all the functions and data types that are available specific to Unity 3D. We'll learn how to use these parts of Unity 3D in the following tutorials.

**NOTE:** It's also important to know that when learning the specifics of Unity 3D, you should be aware that these Unity 3D-specific lessons can be applied to other development environments. When you use C# with Windows or OS X, you'll be able to write applications for other operating systems for software other than Unity 3D.

Think of `MonoBehaviour` as a set of tools for talking to Unity 3D. Other systems have different sets of tools for making apps for other purposes. Learning how to use the other systems should be much easier after reading this book and learning how to talk to Unity 3D.

When dealing with most other C# applications, you'll need to use `Main()` as the starting point for your C# application. This is similar to many other development environments like C++ and C.

When the class we asked Unity 3D to create was made, Unity3D automatically added in `void Start ()` and `void Update ()` to the class. These two functions are called *entry points*. Basically, the base `MonoBehaviour` class has several functions, that include `Start ()` and `Update ()`, which are called based on events that happen when your game is running.

There are other functions that are also automatically called when MonoBehaviour is used: `Awake ()`, `OnEnable ()`, `Start ()`, `OnApplicationPause ()`, `Update ()`, `FixedUpdate ()`, and `LateUpdate ()`; these functions are commonly called when the object is created and your game is running. When the object is destroyed, `OnDestroy()` is called. There are also various rendering functions that can be called, but we don't need to go over them here.

To better understand what happens during each frame of the game it's best to imagine the game operating a bit like a movie. At the very beginning of the game, when the player presses Start, every actor in the scene with a script based on `MonoBehaviour` has its `Start ()` function called.

Calling a function basically executes the lines of code that live inside of the curly braces that follow the function's declaration. Before the end of the first frame, the `Update ()` functions of each script in the scene are called in no particular order.

At the beginning of the next frame, if there are no new scripts in the scene, the `Start ()` functions are not called. Only `Update ()` functions are called from that point on. Only if new scripts are introduced to the scene are `Start ()` functions called on scripts new to the scene. If there is no code in the `Start ()` function or if there is no `Start ()` function in the script, then nothing happens.

To benefit from anything happening on each frame you'll need to put code into the `Update ()` function. When a class is first introduced into the game world you need to add code into the `Start ()` function. There are several other entry points that we'll be working with. And you'll be able to make use of them all as you see fit. It's important to know that without these entry points your class will be functioning on its own.

Functions all have specific names or identifiers. So far we've seen `Start ()` and `Update ()`, but there are many more functions which we'll make use of throughout this book. The first function we'll make use of the `Log();`, which is a function found inside of the `Debug` class. We'll return in a moment to how this function is used, but first we'll demonstrate how it's used.

If `Debug` is a class, this means that `Log()` is a member of `Debug`. The dot operator allows us to access the `Log()` function found in the `Debug` class.

```
void Start () {
    //This will print out "start" in the Unity Console!
    Debug.Log("start");
}
```

Inside of the `Start ()` function add in `Debug.Log("start");`, as seen in the example above. When the game is started the class will execute the code found inside of the `Start ()` function. This means that the `Debug.Log("start");` statement is executed.

Continuing from the previous FirstExample project, click on the Play button and then click on the Console panel to bring it to the top. You should see the following lines of text in the Console panel.

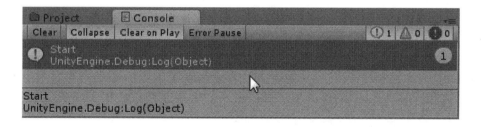

The first line says `Start`, followed by `UnityEngine.Debug:Log(Object)`, which is the expected result. If not, then double check a few different things. First check that the line of code you wrote ends with a semicolon (;) and is not left empty. Next, make sure that you're using quotes around the word: `"Start."`

Then, check that your spelling and case are correct: `Debug` and `Log`. Also make sure you didn't forget the dot operator (".") between `Debug` and `Log`. All of the punctuation matters a great deal. Missing any one of these changes the outcome of the code. This is why syntax matters so much to programmers. Missing one detail breaks everything.

There are a few important things happening here, though many details left out for now. By the end of this chapter everything should be clear.

### 4.6.3 Writing a Function

A function consists of a declaration and a body. Some programmers like to call these *methods*, but semantics aside, a function is basically a container for a collection of statements.

#### *4.6.3.1 A Basic Example*

Let's continue with the FirstClass example project.

```
void MyFunction ()
{
}
```

Here is a basic function called MyFunction. We can add in additional keywords to modify the function's visibility. One common modifier we'll be seeing soon is public. We'll get further into the public keyword in Section 4.13 on accessibility.

```
public void MyFunction ()
{
}
```

The public keyword needs to appear before the return type of the function. In this case, it's void, which means that the function doesn't return anything. Return types are something else that we'll get into in Section 6.3.3, but functions can act as a value in a few different ways. For reference, a function that returns an int would look like this. A return statement of some kind must always be present in a function that has a return type.

```
public int MyFunction ()
{
     return 1;
}
```

The public modifier isn't always necessary, unless you need to make this function available to other classes. If this point doesn't make sense, it will soon. The last part of the function that is always required is the parameter list. It's valid to leave it empty, but to get a feeling for what an arg, or argument in the parameter list, looks like, move on to the next example.

```
public void MyFunction (int i)
{
}
```

For the moment, we'll hold off on using the parameter list, but it's important to know what you're looking at later on so it doesn't come as a surprise. Parameter lists are used to pass information from outside of the function to the inside of the function. This is how classes are able to send information from one to another.

We've been passing an argument for a while now using the Debug class. The Log member function of the Debug class takes a single argument. In Debug.Log("start"); the "start" is an argument we've been sending to the Log function. The Debug class is located in the UnityEngine library and made available because of the using UnityEngine; statement.

We'll see how all of these different parts of a function work as we get to them. Functions are versatile but require to be set up. Luckily, code is easy to build up one line at a time. It's good to know that very few people are capable of writing more than a few lines of code at a time before testing them.

To use a function, you simply enter the identifier followed by its argument list.

```
void SimpleFunction ()
{
    Debug.Log ("simple function is being called");
}
void Start ()
{
    SimpleFunction();
}
```

The placement of SimpleFunction () in the class has no effect on how it's called. For the sake of argument we can use SimpleFunction () anywhere in the class as long as it's been declared at the class scope.

```
void Start ()
{
    SimpleFunction();
}
void SimpleFunction ()
{
    Debug.Log ("simple function is being called");
}
```

Here, we've used SimpleFunction() before it was declared. You may have noticed that Debug. Log(); looks similar to our simple function. The identifier print followed by () with text inside of the parentheses is a commonly used function.

```
int a = 0;
void SetAtoThree ()
{
    a = 3;
}
void Start ()
{
    Debug.Log (a);
    SetAtoThree();
    Debug.Log (a);
}
```

For a function to work, we need to give it some instructions. If we declare an int a and set it to 0, we'll have some data to start with. Create a new function called SetAtoThree(), and then in its code block tell it to set a to 3. If we print a in the Start () function we'll get 0, the value which a was set to in the beginning. Then the function SetAtoThree() was executed, which set a to 3, so when a is printed again its new output is 3.

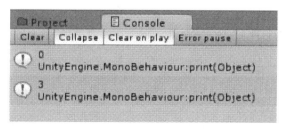

### 4.6.4 More on White Space and Tabs

Tabs are used to delineate the contents of a function. So far, we've been seeing each function written with its contents tabbed to the right with a single tab.

```
void MyFunction()
{
→    //tabbed over once
→    int i = 0;
→    //while statement tabbed over once as well
→    while (i < 10) {
→    →    //contents of the while statement tabbed twice
→    →    print (i);
→    →    i ++;
→    }
}
```

The contents of the function are tabbed over once. The contents of the while statement inside of the function are tabbed over twice, as indicated by the arrows. This presentation helps to clarify that the contents of the while statement are executed differently from the rest of the function.

To help understand how the previous code fragment is read by the computer, we will step through the code one line at a time. This emulates how the function is run when it's called upon. Of course, a computer does this very quickly, but it's necessary for us to understand what the computer is doing many millions, if not billions, of times faster than we can comprehend.

```
void MyFunction()
{
    //tabbed over once
    int i = 0;
    //while statement tabbed over once as well
    while (i < 10) {
        //contents of the while statement tabbed twice
        print (i);
        i ++;
    }
}
```

**NOTE:** For a moment imagine your central processing unit (CPU) was made of gears spinning more than 2 billion times per second. The 2.4 Ghz means 2,400,000,000 cycles per second. A cycle is an update of every transistor in the silicon on the chip: over 2 billion pulses of electrons running through the silicon, every second turning on and off various transistors based on your instructions. Of course, not all of these updates are dedicated to your game; many of the cycles are taken up by the operating system running Unity 3D, so performance isn't always what it should be.

The first line void MyFunction() is identified by the computer and is used to locate the code to execute. Once the function is started the contents of the code begin at the first statement. In this case we reach //tabbed over once, which is a comment and ignored by the computer.

Next we reach int i = 0;, which is a declaration and assignment of a variable that is identified as i, an identifier commonly used for integers. This declaration tells the computer to create a small place in memory for an integer value and it's told that we're going to use i to locate that data.

Following the variable declaration, we get to another comment that is also ignored by the computer. The while (i < 10) { line of code follows the comment and this opens another space in memory for some operations. This also creates a connection to the i variable to check if the while statement will execute. If i is a value less than 10 then the contents will be executed; otherwise, the contents of the while statement are ignored.

Another important character the computer finds is the opening curly brace ({) that tells it to recognize a new context for execution. The computer will read and execute each line in the while statement till it finds a closing curly brace: }. In this new context we'll return to the first curly brace until the while statement's condition is false.

Because i is less than 10, the while statement's condition is true, so we will proceed to the first line of the while statement. In this case, it's a comment that is ignored. This is followed by a print function, which also has a connection to the i variable. Therefore, this line prints to the console the value which is being stored at i. Once the value has been printed to the console the computer moves to the next line down.

The i++; statement tells the computer to look at the contents of i, add 1 to that value, and assign that new value back to i. This means that the new value for i is 1 since we started at 0. Once the computer reaches the closing curly brace we jump back to the top of the while statement.

The contents of the curly braces are repeated until the value for i reaches 10; once the iteration returns 11, the condition of the while statement changes from *true* to *false*. Because 11 is not less than 10, the statements found between the curly braces will not be read. Therefore, the code in the while statement will be skipped. Once the computer reaches the closing curly brace of MyFunction(), the computer stops running the function.

Computers do exactly what they're told and nothing more. The compiler runs using very explicit rules which it adheres to adamantly. Because of this, any strange behavior, which you might attribute to a bug, should point to how you've written your code. In many cases, small syntactical errors lead to errors which the computer will not be able to interpret.

It's greatly up to you to ensure that all of your code adheres to a format the computer can understand. When you write in English, a great deal of the sentiment and thought you put into words can be interpreted by each reader differently. For a computer there's only one way to interpret your code, so either it works or it doesn't.

### 4.6.5 What We've Learned

Function declaration is similar to class declaration. Functions are the meat of where logic is done to handle variables. How variables make their way into and out of a function is covered in Section 6.18. There are many different ways to handle this, but we'll have to handle them one at a time.

On your own experiment with functions like the following:

```
void ATimesA() {
    a = a * a;
}
```

You might want to set int a to a value other than 0 or 1 to get anything interesting out of this. Later on, we'll be able to see how logic and loops can be used to make functions more powerful.

## 4.7 Order of Operation: What Is Calculated and When

Variables and functions work together to make your class operate as a part of your game. As an example, we're going to move an object through space using some simple math. To use numbers correctly, we need to be very specific. Remember, computers do exactly what they're told and nothing more.

Code is executed only when the function the code lives in is called. If the function is never called then nothing in the function will run. Once a function is called, the operation starts with evaluating the code at the top and works its way down to the end of the function one line at a time.

The first order which we've been working with so far is by line number. When code is evaluated each line is processed starting at the top; then it works its way down. In the following example, we start off with an integer variable and perform simple math operations and print the result.

```
void Start ()
{
    int a = 1;
    print (a);//prints 1
    a = a + 3;
    print (a);//prints 4
    a = a * 7;
    print (a);//prints 28
}
```

As you might expect the first line prints 1, followed by 4, and then by 28. This is a rather long-handed method to get to a final result. However, things get a bit strange if we try to shorten this to a single line, as math operators work in a different order than we just used them.

```
void Start ()
{
    int a = 1 + 3 * 7;
    print (a);//prints 22
}
```

After shortening the code to a single line like in this example, we get a different result, 22, which means 3 and 7 were multiplied before the 1 was added. Math operators have a priority when being evaluated, which follows the order of precedence. The multiply and divide operators have a higher precedence than add and subtract.

When evaluating int a, C# looked at the math operators first, and then did the math in the following order. Because the * was seen as more important than the +, 3 * 7 was computed, turning the line into 1 + 21; then, the remaining numbers around + were evaluated, resulting a being assigned to 22, and then ultimately printing that to the Console output.

We'll observe the other behaviors and learn to control how math is evaluated. This section might not be so exciting, but it's worth the while to have this section as a reference. When your calculations begin to have unexpected results, it's usually because of order of operation coming into play and evaluating numbers differently from what you expected.

### 4.7.1 Evaluating Numbers

Calculation of variables is called *evaluation*. As we had mentioned before, each object added to the scene in Unity 3D's editor has several components automatically added when it's first created. To make use of these components, you simply use their name in your code. The first component we'll be using is transform attribute. Transform contains the position rotation and scale of the object. You can see how these are changed when you select the object in the scene and move it around.

You can also enter numbers using the Inspector panel, or even click on the variable name and drag left and right as a slider to modify the data in the field. Moving objects around with code works in a similar manner as entering values in the Inspector panel. The position of the object is stored as three float values called a Vector3.

Operators in C# are the tools that do all of the work in your code. The first set of operators we'll discuss is arithmetic operators.

#### 4.7.1.1 Math

+ –/* and %

The + and − do pretty much what you might expect them to: 1 + 3 = 4 and 1 − 3 = −2; this doesn't come as a surprise. Divide uses the /, putting the first number over the second number. However, the number *type* is important to sort out before we get too much further.

```
28      // Use this for initialization
29      void Start ()
30      {
31          Debug.Log (10 / 3);
32          Debug.Log (10f / 3f);
33          Debug.Log (10.0 / 3.0);
34      }
```

The first line above is a 10/3, which might not return what you would expect. Writing a number without any decimal tells the compiler you're using integers, which will give you an integer result. Therefore, the final result is simply 3, with the remaining one-third cut off since it's rounded down. The second line has an f after the number, indicating we want a float value. The third line without the f indicates a double value. This has twice the number of digits as a float.

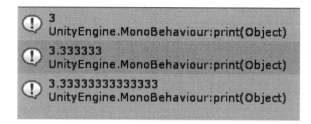

The result here shows the different number of trailing 3s after the decimal. We mentioned in Section 4.4.1.2 that there are different types of numbers. Here is an example of what that really means. An integer is a whole number without any decimal values. A float is a decimal type with only 7 digits in the number; a double is quite a lot bigger, having a total of 15 digits in the number.

```
28        // Use this for initialization
29   void Start ()
30   {
31        Debug.Log (10 / 3);
32        Debug.Log (10f / 3f);
33        Debug.Log (10.0 / 3.0);
34        Debug.Log (10000000.0f / 3.0f);
35        Debug.Log (1000000000000000.0 / 3.0);
36   }
```

Doing this experiment again with larger numbers exposes how our numbers have some limitations.

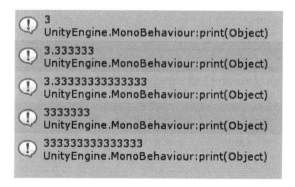

Like the integer, the large doubles and floats only have so many places where the decimal can appear. The number for the double is huge to begin with, but we should have more 3s after the number than are shown with a decimal; where did they go? Keep in mind there *should* be an indefinite number of trailing 3s but computers aren't good with indefinite numbers.

**NOTE:** Computers without special software can't deal with numbers with an unlimited number of digits. To show bigger numbers, computers use scientific notation like E+15 to indicate where significant numbers begin from the decimal point. Games, in particular, rarely ever need to deal with such large numbers. And to keep processes running fast, numbers are limited.

Software applications designed to deal with particularly huge numbers tend to work more slowly as they need to run with the same limitations but instead perform operations on the first part of a number and then another operation on the second half of a number. This process can be repeated as many times as necessary if the number is even bigger. Scientific computing often does this and they have special number types to compensate. There are some additional number types, as well as other data types that aren't numbers. We'll leave the other data types for later (Section 5.3.4). The operators we're dealing with here are mainly for numbers.

Next up is the multiply operator (*). All of the limitations that apply to the divide operator apply to the multiply operator as well. One important thing to consider here is that multiplication is technically faster than division. Therefore, in cases where you want to do 1000/4, the computer is going to be faster if you use `1000 * 0.25` instead.

This difference is a result of how the computer's hardware was designed. To be honest, modern CPUs are so much faster than they used to be, so using a / versus a * will usually make no noticeable difference. Old school programmers will beg to differ, but today we're not going to need to worry about this technicality, though I feel every classically trained programmer wants to scratch out my eyes right now.

Last up is the %, which in programming is called modulo, not percent as you might have guessed. This operator is used in what is sometimes called clock math. An analog clock has 12 hours around it. Therefore, a clock's hours can be considered %12, or modulo twelve, as a programmer might say.

To use this operator, consider what happens when you count 13 hours on a 12 hour clock and want to know where the hour hand will be on the 13th hour. This can be calculated by using the following term: 13%12; this operation produces the value 1 when calculated. Modulo is far easier to observe in operation than it is to describe.

The output from the code below here repeats from 0 to 11 repeatedly. Clocks don't start at 0, but computers do. Therefore, even though `i` is not being reset and continues to increase in value. On each update `i` is not being reset to 0, instead it continues to increment until you stop the game. A programmer would say "int i mod twelve" to describe `i%12` shown here.

```
int i = 1;
void Update ()
{
    int mod12 = i% 12;
    Debug.Log(i + "mod12 = " + mod12);
    i++;
}
```

Programmers are particular about their vocabulary and syntax, so it's best to understand how to think and talk like one. Programmers will usually assume you already know something like this, but it is worthwhile elaborating on the topic. Compilers, however, don't all think in the same way. Therefore, if you're curious and feel like learning other programming languages in the future, you might find that other languages will behave differently.

### 4.7.1.2 Operator Evaluation

As we saw before with `1 + 3 * 7` you may end up with different results, depending on the order in which you evaluated your numbers. To prevent any human misinterpretation of a calculation you can reduce the preceding numbers to `4 * 7` or `1 + 21`. To make our intent clear we can use parentheses.

To gain control, we use the open parenthesis and close parenthesis to change the order of evaluation. For example, we can do this: `1 - 2 - (3 + 4)`. This turns into `1 - 2 - 7`, a whole different result: `-1 - 7` yields `-8`. A simple change in the order of operation can result in a completely different number when evaluated. This sort of thing becomes more important once we start shooting at zombies and dealing out damage. Some monsters might have thicker skin, and you'll want to reduce the damage done by a specific amount based on where he was shot.

### 4.7.1.2.1 A Basic Example

As we saw before, 1 + 3 * 7 will result in 22. We could use the long-winded version and start with a, then add 1 to it, then add 3 to that, and then multiply that by 7 to get 24. There's an easier way.

```
void Start () {
    int a = (1 + 3) * 7;
    Debug.Log (a);
}
```

By surrounding a pair of numbers with parentheses, we can tell the compiler to evaluate the pair within the parentheses before the multiplication. This results in 28, similar to the long-handed version of same math. To elaborate we can add in another step to our math to see more interesting results.

```
void Start () {
    int a = 1 + 3 * 7 + 9;
    Debug.Log (a);
}
```

The code above results in 31 printed to the Console panel. We can change the result to 49 by surrounding the 7 + 9 with parentheses, like in the following.

```
void Start () {
    int a = 1 + 3 * (7 + 9);
    Debug.Log (a);
}
```

The complier computes the 7 + 9 before the rest of the math is computed. Parentheses take precedence over multiplication, regardless of where they appear. It doesn't matter where the parentheses appear, either at the beginning or at the end of the numbers: The parentheses are computed first.

Adding another set of parentheses can change the order of computation as well. Parentheses within parentheses tell the computer to start with the innermost pair before moving on. For instance (11 * ((9 * 3) * 2)) starts with 9 * 3; this turns into (11 * ((27) * 2), which then yields 27 * 2, which turns into (11 * (54)); 11 * 54 turns into 594. This can be switched round by shifting the placements of the parentheses to a different number. Try it out!

```
void Start () {
    int b = (11 * ((9 * 3) * 2)) ;
    Debug.Log (b);
}
```

At this point, you will need to be very careful about the placement of the parentheses. For each opening parenthesis, there needs to be a corresponding closing parenthesis. If you're missing one, then Unity 3D will let you know. It's important to have a sense of what sort of math to use and when to use it.

In this case, where the parentheses encapsulate the entire expression their presence is redundant. Taking out the first and last parentheses will have no effect on the final result. This is true for most operations, but for clarity it's useful to know that they are indeed optional. To be clear about this we can add any number of extra parentheses to the operation and there will be no other effect to the final result, though it may look a bit strange.

```
void Start () {
    int b = (((((11 * ((9 * 3) * 2))))) ) ;
    Debug.Log (b);
}
```

To make things more clear, we can rearrange this expression to be a lot more readable by setting up different variables. For each set of operations we can create a new variable. The operations begin with the first variable; then, after the value is stored, the value is carried to the next time it's used. Just remember, a variable cannot be used until it's been created.

```
void Start () {
    int a = 9 * 3;
    int b = a * 2;
    int c = b * 11;
    Debug.Log (c);
}
```

In this example, we've created a different variable for each part of the math operation. First, we created a 9 * 3 variable assigned to a. After that we multiplied a by 2 and assigned that to b. Finally, we multiplied b by 11 and assigned that result to c. To view the final result, we printed out c to get 594, the same result as the long, fairly obscure operation we started with. This example shows a simple use of variables to make your code more readable.

This seems like we're back to where we started with, at the beginning of this section. To be honest, both methods are perfectly valid. The decision to choose one system over another is completely dependent on which you find easier to understand.

What we should take away from this is the order in which the lines are read. The operations start at the top and work their way line by line to the bottom of the function. As variables are assigned new values, they are kept until they are reassigned.

It's important to note that by creating more than one variable, you're asking the computer to use more space in your computer's memory. At this point we're talking about very small amounts of memory. A classically trained programmer might want to fix this code upon reading it, and then convert it to a single line. To be honest, it does take up plenty more space, not only visually.

When starting a new set of operations, it's sometimes helpful to use a more drawn-out set of instructions, using more variables. When you're more comfortable that your code is doing what you expect it to, you can take the time to reduce the number of lines required and do a bit of optimization. There's nothing wrong with making things work first and cleaning things up later.

### 4.7.2 What We've Learned

Therefore, you've been introduced to variables and you've learned about functions, two big components of programming needed to make a game. Directives will allow your code to talk with Unity 3D, and put meaning behind your variables and functions.

We're using C# and Mono, which is an object oriented programming environment. We just learned objects are all the little bits of info that make up your different C# classes. When we're done with writing some code, Unity 3D will automatically interpret your code for your game.

At this point we've got a pretty strong grasp of the basics of what code looks like and the different parts of how code is written. We've yet to make use of any logic in our functions but we should be able to read code and know what is and isn't in a function.

It would be a good idea, by way of review, to make a few other classes and get used to the process of starting new projects, creating classes, and adding them to objects in a Unity 3D Scene. Once you're comfortable with creating and using new classes in Unity 3D you'll be ready to move on.

---

## 4.8  Scope: A First Look

*Encapsulation* is the term given to where data can be accessed from. The amount of accessibility is called scope. The visibility of a variable to your logic changes depending on where it appears.

Encapsulation can hide, or change the accessibility of data between statements, functions, and classes. Another way to think about it is keeping data on a need-to-know basis. This invisibility is intended for several reasons. One reason is to reduce the chances of reusing variable names.

```
void Start ()
{
        for (int i = 0; i < 10; i ++) {
                print (i);
        }
        // i only exists between the { and }
}
```

For this example, we used the `print()`; function. Thanks to a long history of programming, almost every language has some version of `print`; this function does the same thing as `Debug.log()`; but it just means less typing. There are often many ways to achieve the same result; it's just up to you to pick which one to use.

### 4.8.1 Class Scope

To get a better look at how scope and encapsulation work together, we're going work with the Scope Unity project. Attached to the camera is the Scope Unity project which can be found in the downloaded materials provided. When the scene is run, the code attached to the camera will execute as normal.

```
using UnityEngine;
using System.Collections;
public class Scope : MonoBehaviour {
    int MyInt = 1;
    //Use this for initialization
    void Start () {
        Debug.Log(MyInt);
    }
}
```

The `MyInt` variable exists at the class scope level. `MyInt` can be used in any function that lives in the class scope. The example code you're looking at will produce the following Console output:

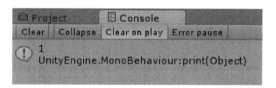

Both `Start ()` and `Update ()` live in the class scope so both can see the `MyInt` variable. Therefore, the following code will send a `1` to the console. Both `Start ()` and the `Update ()` functions will keep sending `1`s to the Console window.

```
using UnityEngine;
using System.Collections;
public class Scope : MonoBehaviour
{
    int MyInt = 1;//this int is in the class scope
    void Start ()
    {
        Debug.Log (MyInt);//Start can see MyInt
    }
```

```
        void Update ()
        {
            Debug.Log (MyInt);//Update can see MyInt
        }
}
```

Placement of a variable at the class scope has little effect on where it's used. The code above can be rearranged easily. The code below will behave in exactly the same way as the code above.

```
public class Scope : MonoBehaviour {
    void Update ()
    {
        Debug.Log (MyInt);
    }
    void Start ()
    {
        Debug.Log (MyInt);
    }
    int MyInt = 1;
}
```

The functions and variables act in the same way, irrespective of where they appear in the class. However, class scope is easy to override with other variables of the same name. This is called variable collision, the effects of which you should be aware of, as discussed in Section 7.4.

```
public class Scope : MonoBehaviour
{
    public int MyInt = 1;//declares MyInt
    void Start ()
    {
        int MyInt = 2;//declares a new MyInt, stomps on the first one
        Debug.Log (MyInt);
    }
}
```

If we declare a variable of the same name in more than one place then it will be overridden by the closest version of our variable. If you were to run this script in your scene, you'd have the Console printout 2 because of the line that preceded the print function call.

There are problems with how variables can collide with one another. And the best way to avoid this problem would be to come up with good names for your variables. Therefore, can we use both versions of MyInt?

```
public class Scope : MonoBehaviour
{
    public int MyInt = 1;//declares MyInt
    void Start ()
    {
        Debug.Log (MyInt);//being used before it's declared.
        int MyInt = 2;//declares a new MyInt, stomps on the first one
        Debug.Log (MyInt);
    }
}
```

The answer is no. The result of such a declaration will be an error: "A local variable MyInt cannot be used before it is declared." You may have expected the first print function to print out the class scope version of MyInt, but this isn't the case.

The variables that live at the class scope happen to still exist even if you stomp on their name with variables of the same name in a function. The keyword `this` preceding the variable unhides the variable that is living at the class scope.

```
void Start ()
{
    Debug.Log(this.MyInt);//class scope version of MyInt
    int MyInt = 3;
    Debug.Log(MyInt);
}
```

By creating an `int MyInt` inside of the `Start ()` function in your class you have effectively hidden the class scoped `MyInt` from the function. Although it can be accessed as `this.MyInt`, the `MyInt` in the function takes precedent.

This example should also highlight that a variable can be used only after it's been initialized. This is a situation best avoided, so it's good to remember what variable names you've used so you don't use them again.

To elaborate, a function starts from the first curly brace ({) and computes one line at a time, working its way from the top, moving toward the bottom till it hits the closing curly brace (}). If a variable is used but if a statement uses a variable before it's declared, an error results.

```
void Start ()
{
    Debug.Log(MyInt);//MyInt doesn't exist yet.
    int MyInt = 3;
}
```

Something that might be obvious but should be mentioned is the fact that you can't reuse a variable name. Even if the second variable is a different type, we'll get the following error in MonoDevelop explaining our error.

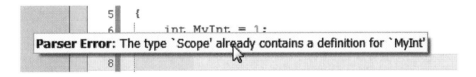

Another effect of creating a variable inside of a function is the fact that another function can't see what's going on. In the following code we declare a `StartInt` in the `Start ()` function. After that we try to use it again in the `Update ()` function, which results in an error.

```
void Start ()
{
    int StartInt = 100;
    print(MyPersonalInt);
}
void Update ()
{
    print(StartInt);
}
```

C# is telling us that we can't use a variable before it's declared. Of course, we did declare it once, but that was in a different function. The `Update ()` function can't see inside of the `Start ()` function to find the `MyPersonalInt` created in the `Start ()` function.

You'll have to keep this in mind once you start writing your own functions. There are two common ways to work with declaring variables. The first is to place all of your variables at the top of the function. This way you ensure that everything you may need to use is already declared before you need them. The second method is to declare the variable just before it's needed.

```csharp
void Start ()
{
    int MyFirstInt = 100;
    int MySecondInt = 200;
    print(MyFirstInt);
    print(MySecondInt);
}
```

In this case, we're being very clear inside of this function about what variables we may use. For short functions this can sometimes be a lot easier to deal with. You can easily sort your variables and change their values in one place. It's also easier to check if you're accidentally reusing a variable's name.

```csharp
void Start ()
{
    int MyFirstInt = 100;
    print(MyFirstInt);
    int MySecondInt = 200;
    print(MySecondInt);
}
```

In this second case, we're using the variable only after it's created. When writing long functions you may find the second method a bit more clear as you can group your variables together near the logic and functions that will be using them.

This is a small example of code style. When reading someone else's code, you'll have to figure out how they think. In some cases, it's best to try to match the style of existing code. However, when you're writing everything on your own, it's best to keep to your own style and decide how you want to arrange your code.

If we declare a variable at the class scope, all functions inside of the class can see, and access, that variable. Once inside of a function, any new variables that are declared are visible only to that function. Some statements can declare variables as well, and those variables are visible only inside of the statement they are declared. Once we get to know about more statements, we'll see how they work, but we'll need to keep scope in mind when we get there.

### 4.8.2 Function Scope

Variables often live an ephemeral life. Some variables exist only over a few lines of code. Variables may come into existence only for the moment a function starts and then disappear when the function is done. Variables in the class scope exist for as long as the class exists. The life of the variable depends on where it's created.

In a previous exercise, we focused on declaring variables and showing them in the Unity 3D's Inspector panel. Then we observed when variables need to be declared to be used without any errors. The placement and `public` keywords were necessary to expose the variables to the Unity 3D editor.

The `public` keyword can be used only at the class scope. This is called class scope as the variable is visible to all of the functions found within the class. Making the variable `public` means that any other class that can see this class can then also have access to the variable as well. We'll go into more detail on what this means and how it's used in a bit.

```
            void Start ()
            {
Parser Error: Unexpected symbol `public' c;
            for (int i = 0; i <
                    print (i);
```

Adding the `public int` within the `Start ()` function will produce an error. You're not allowed to elevate a variable to the class scope from inside of a function. MonoDevelop will inform you of the error: `Unexpected symbol 'public'`; the reason is that variables within a function cannot be made accessible outside of the function.

There are systems in C# to make data within a function accessible, but using the keyword `public` is not it. We'll look into how that's done in Section 6.1. A variable declared inside of a function exists only as the function is used. Variables declared at the top of a function are declared at the function scope. This is to say that the variable is visible to any statement within the function.

```
//Use this for initialization
void Start () {
        int StartInt = 1;
        Debug.Log(StartInt);
}
```

In a function, declaring `int StartInt` is valid, but it's scope is limited to within the function. No other functions can see or directly interact with `StartInt`. There are methods to allow interaction within the function, but we'll get into that in Section 6.3.2.

The functions declared in the class are also a part of the class scope, and at the same level as the variables declared at the class scope level. If a function in a class is preceded by the `public` keyword, it's accessible by name, just like a variable. Without the `public` keyword the function will remain hidden. We'll make use of `public` functions in Section 6.3.2, but it's important to know that a function can be made publicly available, like variables.

Referring to the `Scope.cs` file we created for this chapter, we're going to make use of the functions given to us by the programmers at Unity 3D. The location of a variable in code changes where it can be seen from and how it can be used.

As noted, limiting accessibility of any variable is called encapsulation. The curly braces, {}, and parentheses, (), have a specific context. This context can keep their contents hidden from other sections of code. This means that `Start ()` can have one value for `StartInt`, and if you create a new `StartInt` in `Update ()`, it will not be affected by the `StartInt` in `Start ()`.

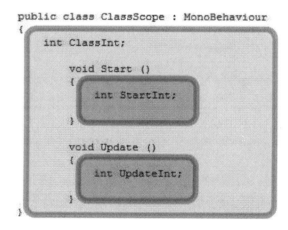

If we look at the above figure we can visualize how scope is divided. The outer box represents who can see `ClassInt`. Within the `Start ()` function we have a `StartInt` that only exists within the `Start ()` function. The same is repeated for the `UpdateInt`, found only in the `Update ()` function. This means that `Start ()` can use both `ClassInt` and `StartInt` but not `UpdateInt`. Likewise, `Update ()` can see `ClassInt` and `UpdateInt` but not `StartInt`.

In the diagram below the boxes represent different levels of scope.

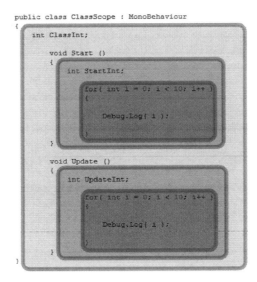

```
public class ClassScope : MonoBehaviour
{
    int ClassInt;

    void Start ()
    {
        int StartInt;

        for( int i = 0; i < 10; i++ )
        {
            Debug.Log( i );
        }
    }

    void Update ()
    {
        int UpdateInt;

        for( int i = 0; i < 10; i++ )
        {
            Debug.Log( i );
        }
    }
}
```

Within each function lies a simple for loop. We'll go into more detail about how a for loop works, but in short, for loops create and use their own variables, which have limited scope and exist only within the confines of the loop. This also means that the for loop inside of the Start () function has access to ClassInt as well as StartInt. Following the same restrictions, the for loop inside of Update () can see ClassInt and UpdateInt, but not StartInt or int i, which exist in the for loop that's been written into the Start () function.

### 4.8.3 What We've Learned

Encapsulation describes a system by which a variable's scope is defined. Depending on where a variable is declared, the scope of the variable changes. Encapsulation prevents variables from overlapping when they're used. Encapsulation, therefore, allows one function to operate independently from another function without our needing to worry about a variable's name being reused.

We'll cover more situations where scope becomes a useful tool to help classes message one another. Encapsulation and scope define a major principle of object oriented programming, and understanding this concept is important to learning how to write C#.

## 4.9 This

What happens when a class needs to refer to itself? In most cases, a class can use its own properties and fields and not get confused what variable is being referred to. For instance, we can take a look at a basic class that might look like the following.

```
public class MyThis {
    float MyFloat;
    public void AssignMyFloat(float f) {
        MyFloat = f;
    }
    public void ShowMyFloat() {
        Debug.Log(MyFloat);
    }
}
```

Here, we have a class which we can add to an Example.cs file. We'll look at public class MyThis and see that it's got a field called MyFloat. We've also got two functions inside of the class that assigns the `MyFloat` field within the `MyThis` class. In the first function, we assign `MyFloat` to a parameter, and in the second function, `ShowMyFloat ()` we simply send the `MyFloat` from within the class to the Console panel. In use, the full code would look like the following.

### 4.9.1 A Basic Example

In the `KeywordThis.cs` file in the Scope project, we'll find the following code.

```
using UnityEngine;
using System.Collections;
public class KeywordThis : MonoBehaviour {
    public class MyThis {
        float MyFloat;
        public void AssignMyFloat(float f) {
            MyFloat = f;
        }
        public void ShowMyFloat() {
            Debug.Log(MyFloat);
        }
    }
    //Use this for initialization
    void Start () {
            MyThis mt = new MyThis();
            mt.AssignMyFloat(3.0f);
            mt.ShowMyFloat();
    }
}
```

In the `Start ()` function we print out 3 to the console. There's no confusion because `MyFloat` is never used in a situation where its name may be confused with another identifier. The situation changes should we change a parameter name in `AssignMyFloat`, for example, from `float f` to `float MyFloat`.

```
public void AssignThisMyFloat(float MyFloat) {
    MyFloat = MyFloat;//ambiguous MyFloat
}
```

If we add the `AssignThisFloat(float MyFloat)` function to the `MyThis` class, we'll get some rather unexpected behavior. If we use this to assign `MyFloat` in the `MyThis` class using the following statements, we will not get the same behavior as before. Unity 3D lets us know something might be misleading by prompting us with the following warning:

```
Assets/KeywordThis.cs(21,49): warning CS1717: Assignment made to same
variable; did you mean to assign something else?
```

To solve this problem, we'll look at some simple solutions.

```
void Start () {
    MyThis mt = new MyThis();
    mt.AssignThisMyFloat(3.0f);
    mt.ShowMyFloat();
}
```

This sends a 0 to the Console panel. This is because in the function `AssignThisMyfloat`, where we assign the `MyThis` variable `MyFloat` to the `AssignThisFloat` argument `MyFloat`, the function assigned the class variable back to itself. The local scope within the function took precedence over the value stored inside of the class. We can correct the behavior by adding the keyword `this` to the function.

### 4.9.2 When This Is Necessary

```
public void AssignThisMyFloat(float MyFloat) {
        this.MyFloat = MyFloat;
}
```

With the addition of the keyword `this` to the function above, we can specify which version of the `MyFloat` variable we're talking about. Running the `Start ()` function again, we'll get the expected 3 being printed to the Console panel. It's easy to avoid the requirement of the `this` keyword. Simply use unique parameter names from the class's variables and you won't need to use the `this` keyword.

There is no unexpected behavior if we superfluously use the `this` keyword anytime we want to. The keyword does as you might expect it will. In both of the versions of the following function, we get the exact same behavior:

```
public void AssignMyFloat(float f) {
        MyFloat = f;
}
public void AssignMyFloat(float f) {
        this.MyFloat = f;
}
```

Of course, we don't want to use both in the same class at the same time, but it's important to know that either version can be used, just not at the same time. The use of `this` can help make the code more readable. In a complex class where we have many different variables and functions, it sometimes helps to clarify if the variable being assigned is something local to the function we're reading or if the variable is a class scoped variable. Using `this` we can be sure that the variable is assigned to a class variable, and not something only in the function.

### 4.9.3 Awkward Names

Naming variables can be difficult. Below we have an awkwardly named variable int `MyBadlyNamedInt` in an awkward class.

```
class MyAwkwardClass
{
        int MyBadlyNamedInt = 0;
}
```

Then we have a function that also happens to have a variable named `MyBadlyNamedInt` inside of it.

```
class MyAwkwardClass
{
        int MyBadlyNamedInt = 0;
        void PoorlyNamedFunction()
        {
                int MyBadlyNamedInt = 7;
        }
}
```

Things get strange if we were to need to call upon the class's badly named int rather than the function's badly named int. The class scoped int `MyBadlyNamedInt` still exists; it hasn't gone away. The same int `MyBadlyNamedInt` inside of the `PoorlyNamedFunction` is interfering with the same int at the class scope.

```
class MyAwkwardClass
{
        int MyBadlyNamedInt = 0;
```

```
        void PoorlyNamedFunction()
        {
                Debug.Log(this.MyBadlyNamedInt);
                int MyBadlyNamedInt = 7;
                Debug.Log(this.MyBadlyNamedInt);
        }
}
```

The `Debug.Log` before or after the declaration of the function's bad `int` will send a `0` to the Console panel. Without the `this` keyword added before the identifier, we assume that we're using the function's named version of the variable.

If the `this` keyword had not been used, then we'd get a conflict with the first use of `MyBadlyNamedInt`. Within the `PoorlyNamedFunction()`, C# has noticed that the `BadlyNamedInt` is declared again and ignores the class scope `int` of the same name.

### 4.9.4 What We've Learned

In general, `this` is a somewhat superfluous keyword. The necessity of using the keyword `this` arises only when a name of a parameter in a function matches the name of a variable in the class where the function's parameter appears.

When naming variables and functions, it's best to keep to a consistent pattern. In general, many people use longer names at the class scope. For instance, the following code uses a pattern of shorter and shorter variable names depending on the variable's scope:

```
        class MyClass {
                int MyInt = 0;
                void MyFunction(int mi) {
                        int mInt = mi;
                        MyInt = mInt;
                }
        }
```

At the scope of the entire class the `int` is `MyInt`. Within the function `MyFunction` in `MyClass` a local variable only visible to `MyFunction` is called `mInt`. The variable from the function's argument list is simply `mi`.

There are obvious limitations to using a convention like shortening variable names. It's very easy to run out of letters and end up with unclear variable names, but it's a simple place to get started.

This isn't a common practice convention by any means; it's one that I've personally become used to using. These sorts of personal conventions are something that everyone needs to invent for his or her individual use. I'd expect you to find your own convention for naming variables.

The flexibility of C# allows everyone to have a personal style of writing code. Identifiers aren't the only place where one can find self-expression through code. Another way to express ones self through code is deciding to use a for–while or do–while loop. Both can be used for the very similar tasks, but the decision is ultimately left to the programmer writing the code.

For any reason should you feel like you prefer one method over another you should follow your own intuition and write how you like to. Programming is a creative process and writing expressive code is a process just like any other form of art.

## 4.10 Turning Ideas into Code—Part 1

When you need to take a task and turn it into code, you need to start off with the first action taken by the player and turn that into something that the computer can use. Or rather collect incoming data and then process it. Often, when this is the input, the input needs to be recorded and dealt with in a meaningful way.

If your primary form of control involves mouse and keyboard, then it's best to start by making sure you can read both the mouse and keyboard inputs. If you're using a touch screen then you need to make sure you can read where and when touch input happens. When using Unity 3D you've got the `Input` class to start with; everything you need will be found in there.

To follow along, start with the IdeasPartOne project from the downloaded projects file provided. In here, we'll look at the `Example.cs` class in the Assets directory.

MonoDevelop makes looking for the code you need easier by guessing what it is you're looking for. Start entering the word `input` and then MonoDevelop guesses what class it is you're going to pull from. If you're unsure where to start looking, a search through a web search engine is a good place to start. Chances are the question you have in your head has been asked on a forum and answered in some way, often with some code to help you toward your goal.

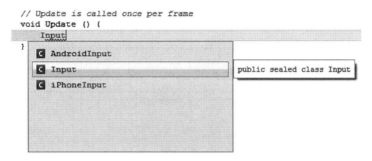

A simple Google search for "Unity 3D How do I read the keyboard" takes you to either the Unity 3D online documentation or to http://answers.unity3d.com; either of these web pages will at least give you a clue or two about what function or class to look at.

Say, for a moment, we want to read the mouse movement; to check we are able to do this, we'd be able to use the print function to see what sort of data we get from the `Input` class.

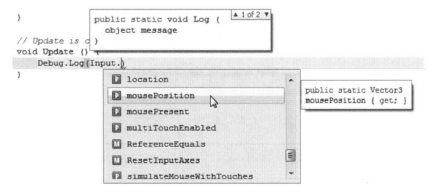

The closest thing we're able to find which might lead to a mouse position seems to be `Input.mousePosition`. The `Input.mousePosition` returns a `Vector3` type variable. A `Vector3` is made of three parts, a float x, y, and z value and we can expect that this is related to the `Input` in some way. To find out what values the `Input.mousePosition` returns we can use the `Debug.Log(Input.mousePosition)`; entered into the `Update ()` function of the `Example.cs` class found in the provided project. To make sure that the `Update ()` function is called we'll attach the `Example.cs` class to the main camera in a new empty scene.

```
void Update ()
{
        Debug.Log (Input.mousePosition);
}
```

While the game is playing, the first and second values printed out to the Console window in Unity 3D change when the mouse is moved. The connection between the mouse and the value returned by `Input.mousePosition` make sense, but how do we use this to control a camera or even a character? We get two fairly big numbers which represent some point on the screen.

```
(445.0, 422.0, 0.0)
UnityEngine.MonoBehaviour:print(Object)
Example:Update () (at Assets/Example.cs:9)
```

Turning the data from `Input.mousePosition` into something, we can use to move a character or camera for a game that requires a bit of manipulation. Before we start using the `Input.mousePosition` values we need to decide what we're going to do with them. In a classic FPS the camera is always under control by the mouse. Therefore, we should start by doing the same.

With the script attached to the camera, we can begin to manipulate various aspects of the object that the code is attached to.

In a new Unity 3D project, we should have the `Example.cs` attached to the Main Camera in the scene. This file will allow us to manipulate the camera with mouse input.

### 4.10.1 Mouse Input

```
using UnityEngine;
using System.Collections;
public class Example : MonoBehaviour {
        //Use this for initialization
        void Start () {
        }
        //Update is called once per frame
        void Update () {
                transform.rotation =
Quaternion.Euler(new Vector3(Input.mousePosition.x, Input.mousePosition.y, 0));
        }
}
```

To get started, we'll use a single line of code in the `Update` () function. The line `transform.rotation = Quaternion.Euler(new Vector3(Input.mousePosition.x, Input.mousePosition.y, 0));` is a long line of code. And it doesn't quite work how you might expect. When you add a few objects into your scene and move the mouse with the game running, you'll see that the camera is indeed spinning around and the mouse is rotating the camera's point of view. However, the behavior isn't exactly the same as that of an FPS.

This is a start, and you might be able to see how quickly we can begin to manipulate objects in a game with familiar systems. However, the refinement to get from here to a full-blown first-person controller takes much more than one line of code. Even so, there are many things to explain in that single line; no doubt there are many questions you might have as to what's really going on here, and that's good.

We will learn what all of that means, but one thing at a time. We still have many different terms to figure out before we get to that.

### 4.10.2 GameObject

If we take a step back from mouse input, we would ask the following question: What is the rotation of the camera? Rotation data is easily accessed by any script attached to the camera object in the scene, but why? When a script is attached to an object in Unity 3D, it becomes a component of that object.

Classes, as we know, can be created as an aggregate of other classes. An object is created from a blueprint, or rather a class. That process of creating an object from a class is called instantiation. And by adding components to a GameObject in the UnityEditor, we're providing Unity 3D with GameObject construction information. This info is used to instruct Unity 3D what objects to instantiate for the GameObject.

Specifically, in code, the C# file you attach is instanced by the GameObject when the game starts. As a matter of fact, practically every object in a Unity 3D Scene is a GameObject. The camera, lights, boxes, and so forth, everything you see in the scene, is a different instance of the `GameObject` class, each one with different attachments.

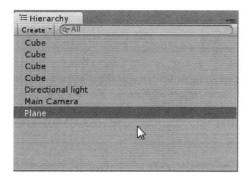

Everything you see in the Hierarchy panel is a GameObject. They are all instances of the `GameObject` class found in the `UnityEngine` library. This point is significant because this means that Unity 3D has done some automatic code generation for you. This is, of course, what a game engine is supposed to do. The Unity 3D engineers put a great deal of work building tools with a pretty User Interface. As a level designer you're able to manipulate your values in your code while the game is running.

GameObject is made up of several other classes. You can see what other classes are being used in the GameObject when it's selected. The Inspector panel shows you some of the classes that are a part of the selected GameObject.

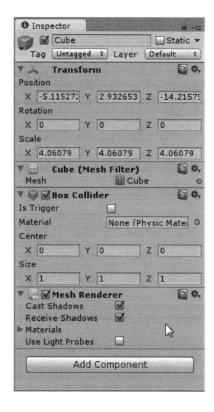

The Transform, Mesh Filter, Box Collider, and Mesh Renderer are all classes that are all members of the GameObject in the scene. To dig another level deeper, Transform has Position, Rotation, and Scale as data members. Each other class listed in the Inspector panel has data members as well. For every script you add to each GameObject, you're adding new data members to the GameObject.

So, to a certain extent, when you add objects to the scene, you're adding code to the scene. When you attach components to a GameObject, you're writing code to instantiate your class in that GameObject. At all levels, every action you take in Unity 3D is calling some class function, or manipulating the data of a member of a class. This goes the same for every other piece of software you use every day; it's all code.

This might seem somewhat existential, but it's to our advantage to understand that a `GameObject` is a class. Every time we add our code as a component, we're telling GameObject to instantiate our class. Once instantiated, our code has become a part of the Unity 3D Scene and can both read and write data to the scene it's in.

Once we get a better grip of the rest of the terms required for writing code, we'll start adding and removing objects in the Unity 3D Scene, but for now, just get used to the idea that everything you do is simply executing some code in Unity 3D.

### 4.10.3 What We've Learned

Figuring out what we have to work with is pretty simple. MonoDevelop assists in various ways, from telling us when we've done something wrong, or what might break. MonoDevelop also provides us with plenty of clues to help us figure out what options we have so far as functions and classes are concerned.

Learning the tricks required to make these clues into functions which do what we want takes a bit of learning and practice. Asking the right questions on forums will only get us so far. By spending time to learn how to use the data we have and how to apply the data through logic, we'll be able to accomplish quite a lot on our own.

To learn how to do all of these things takes time and effort. It's also a good idea to do plenty of research on your own before asking for help. Many problems have already been solved in many different ways. It's up to you to find one that you can work with.

## 4.11 Logic and Operators

Logic allows you to control what part of a function is evaluated based on changes to variables. Using logic, you'll be able to change which statements in your code will run. Simply put, everything you write must cover each situation you plan to cover. Logic is controlled through a few simple systems, primarily the `if` keyword and variations of `if`.

### 4.11.1 Booleans

Using George Boole's logic is a basic tool in nearly every programming paradigm. In C# booleans, or bools for short, are either true or false. It's easiest to think of these as switches either in on or in off position. To declare a `var` as a `bool`, you use something like the following.

To start off, we'll begin with the Bool project in Unity 3D.

```
public class Example : MonoBehaviour
{
        public bool SomeBool;
```

By using `public` you'll expose the boolean variable to Unity 3D's editor. This declaration will also make the variable appear in the Inspector panel like so. The boolean needs to appear here to be seen by the rest of the class an Unity 3D. We'll learn why this is so in Section 4.13 on scope, but we'll digress for now.

`Some Bool` appears in the Inspector as an empty check box. This decision means that you can set the `bool` as either true by checking it on or false by leaving it unchecked. This allows you to set your `public` variables before running the assigned script in the game.

**NOTE:** C# does a pretty good job of automatically initializing many of its built-in types. Number values are always initialized to 0 when they are not given a value. Bools are initialized as false when not given a value. This is handy to know since not all languages do this.

For instance, Lua, another commonly used game programming language, assumes nothing about the value until it's given one. Therefore, when any variable is first declared, it's initialized as nil, which is similar to C#'s behavior when creating a variable of a more complex data type. Though C# calls this uninitialized state null, this means the same as nothing. For good measure, UnrealScript uses the keyword *none* to mean the same as null.

Changes made before the game is run will be saved on that object. For making a game, for example, you can place treasure chests throughout a dungeon and set the amount of gold in each one. This is great since you will not need to make a different script for each treasure chest.

```
public class Example : MonoBehaviour
{
        public int Gold;

}
```

For instance setting a number for gold in the treasure chest will allow you to change the gold in each instance.

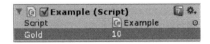

### 4.11.2 Equality Operators

Equality operators create boolean conditions. There are many ways to set a boolean variable. For instance, comparisons between values are a useful means to set variables. The most basic method to determine equality is using the following operator: `==`.

There's a difference between use of a single and a double equals to symbol. `=` is used to assign a value whereas `==` is used to compare values.

### 4.11.2.1 A Basic Example

When you need to compare two values you can use the following concept. You'll need to remember that these operators are called equality operators, if you need to talk to a programmer. The syntax here may look a bit confusing at first, but there are ways around that.

```
void Start ()
{
        SomeBool = (1 == 1);
}
```

There are other operators to be aware of. You will be introduced to the other logical operators later in the chapter. In this case, we are asking if two number values are the same. When the game is started, you'll be able to watch the SomeBool check itself to true. To explain how this works, we'll need to look at the order of operation that just happened. First, the right side of the first single = was calculated. 1 == 1 is a simple comparison, asking if 1 is the same as 1, which results with a true value. Test this out and check for the result in Unity 3D.

To make this a more clear, we can break out the code into more lines. Now, we're looking at a versus b. Clearly, they don't look the same; they are different letters after all. However, they do contain the same integer value, and that's what's really being compared here.

```
void Start ()
{
        int a = 1;
        int b = 1;
        SomeBool = (a == b);
}
```

Evaluations have a left and a right side. The single equal to operator (=) separates the different sides. The left side of the = is calculated and looks to the value to the right to get its assignment. Because 1 == 1, that is to say, 1 is equivalent to 1, the final result of the statement is that SomeBool is true. The check box is turned on and the evaluated statement is done.

```
void Start ()
{
        int a = 1;
        int b = 3;
        SomeBool = (a == b);
}
```

As you might expect, changing the value in one of the variables will change the outcome of this equality test. SomeBool will be clicked off because the statement is no longer true. Or in plain language, Is a equal to b? The answer is no, or as far as SomeBool is concerned, false.

### 4.11.3 If and Branching

In the bool project from the downloaded content, we can control the rotation of the cube in the scene by adding an if logic statement. If statements are sometimes called branching statements. Branching means that the operation of code will change what code is executed.

```
void Start ()
{
     SomeBool = (1 == 1);
     int a = 1;
     int b = 3;
     SomeBool = (a == b);
     if (SomeBool) {
             transform.Rotate (new Vector3 (45f, 0f, 0f));
     }
}
```

The variable SomeBool becomes true once the right side of the statement is evaluated. Before the assignment, it remains in the state it was before the assignment. If you leave the SomeBool variable in the Inspector panel in the editor unchecked, it will check itself on when you run the game. Likewise, we can also show the following.

```
void Start ()
{
     if (true) {
             transform.Rotate(new Vector3(45f, 0f, 0f));
     }
}
```

The if statement is always followed by a pair of parentheses, (), which is followed by an opening and a closing curly brace: {}. The contents of the parentheses tell the compiler whether or not to execute the contents of the following curly braces. If the contents of the parentheses are false, then the contents of the curly braces are ignored.

```
public class Example : MonoBehaviour {
     public bool SomeBool;
     //Use this for initialization
     void Start ()
     {
          if (SomeBool) {
               transform.Rotate(new Vector3(45f, 0f, 0f));
          }
     }
}
```

As you might expect here, by clicking SomeBool to true before the game is run, the object this script is attached to will rotate 45 degrees on the *x*-axis. If not, then the cube will not be rotated when the game is started. Test this out on your own and observe the results.

```
void Update ()
{
     if (SomeBool) {
             transform.Rotate(new Vector3(45f, 0f, 0f));
     }
}
```

Move the code into the Update () function and you'll be able to turn the cube while the game is running; we don't have code yet to turn it back so it's a trick that only works once. We'll find out later how to make this more interesting.

There are many ways to control how booleans are set. The keyword if is used most often to control the flow of your logic. Simply put, if something is true, then do something; otherwise, C# will ignore the statement and move on, and move on, as we have observed. What if we want to do the opposite?

### 4.11.3.1 Not!

If we are looking for a false value to trigger an evaluation of code, we'd need to look for a *not true* to evaluate the `if` statement. This code will look slightly different, as it includes the `!` operator.

```
void Start ()
{
    if (!SomeBool) {
        transform.Rotate(new Vector3(45f, 0f, 0f));
    }
}
```

This change reverses the behavior of the `if` statement. If you leave `SomeBool` as false when the `if` statement is evaluated, then code inside of the curly braces is evaluated. In this case the `!` is called a "not." The not looks for a false value to determine if the `if` statement will be evaluated, or rather it reads the `SomeBool` as what it is not.

We can use this in another way with another equality operator.

```
void Start () {
    int a = 1;
    int b = 1;
    SomeBool = (a != b);
}
```

The `!=` operator is read as "not equal," which looks at the following and returns false. When a = 1 and b = 1, they are equal. `SomeBool` is asking, Is a not equal to b? The answer is false: a is not *not equal* to b. The logic can get a bit awkward, but it's the same as a double negative in English grammar.

### 4.11.4 Flowcharts

Flowcharts, sometimes called activity diagrams, are often used to graph out an algorithm, or flow of logic. This makes a whiteboard in a programmer's office a sort of visual work space for testing out a concept to create a piece of code. There is software available that can reverse engineer code and build a flowchart diagram to help visualize what the code is doing.

In the 1970s, Paul Morrison of IBM wrote a book on flow-based programming. This book takes the idea of following data between nodes connected by lines to write software. Unfortunately, the concept has yet to take hold, and traditional written code remains prominent. The concept is still powerful, and learning how flowcharting works is helpful.

The flowchart involves three parts: a beginning and end, logic, and a sequence. Code we've written so far is like the below:

```
void Update ()
{
    int i = 1;
    if (i < 10) {
        Debug.Log("i is less than 10");
    }
}
```

This code can be translated into nodes with the following diagram:

With some diagramming schemes, however, it's easy to lose some clarity. The more the data added to a diagram, the more confusing it can be. However, in a general form, logic used and the result of that application are easier to understand.

It's because of this simplicity some programmers opt to diagram a complex problem with a flowchart. Once you are able to trace the behavior of your data from start to end, it becomes more clear what your code must do. Using a flowchart as a guide, you can have a better idea what your code must accomplish when you start writing.

Game designers should also be able to explain a specific design decision in terms of a flowchart. When a monster shows up the game designer must be able to explain with simple logic what happens next. User interfaces and even the computer's AI behavior. All of these game events can benefit from having a flowchart as a basis for design decisions.

### 4.11.5 Relational Operators

Bool values can also be set by comparing values. The operators used to compare two different values are called relational operators. We use ==, the is equal symbol, to check if values are the same; we can also use !=, or not equal, to check of two variables are different. This works similarly to the ! in the previous section.

Programmers more often check if one value is greater or lesser than another value. They do this by using >, or greater than, and <, or less than. We can also use > =, greater or equal to, and < =, less than or equal to. Let's see a few examples of how this is used. First, let's add in a `public` variable `int` called `change`. This should appear in the Inspector panel when you select the cube with the attached `Example.cs` script.

Then, add in the `if` statement with the following parameter in parentheses. Then fill in the curly braces with what we've learned so far, setting the `transform.position` to a new vector. This time we're adding the code to the `Update ()` function since it's easier to observe when evaluated frame by frame.

```
public class Example : MonoBehaviour
{
        public int change;
        void Update ()
        {
            bool changed = change > 10;
            if (changed) {
                    transform.position = new Vector3(3f, 0f, 0f);
            }
        }
}
```

Create a `bool` called `changed`, then assign its value to `change` being greater than 10. In the `if` statement, we can decide to evaluate the contents based on `changed` being `true` or `false`. We can shorten this code by skipping the creation and assignment to `change`, by adding the condition directly to the `if` statement's parameter, as in the following.

```
        void Update ()
        {
            if (change > 10) {
                    transform.position = new Vector3(3f, 0f, 0f);
            }
        }
```

This bool can make the code more or less readable, depending on how easily you can read and interpret what the code is doing. Most programmers would prefer that the extra bool changed = change > 10; be omitted, as this means there are fewer lines of code to read. Both versions are perfectly valid; it's up to you to decide on which you need to use based on your own skill.

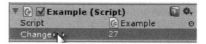

When you run the game, you should be able to click and drag on the change variable to increase or decrease the value of change. Once the value of change is greater than 10, the cube will jump to the location you set in the if statement.

Lowering the change below 10 will not return the cube. This is because we have a statement to move it only when the change value is above 10. To execute another set of code when if returns not true, we need to use the else keyword.

### 4.11.5.1 Else

The else keyword follows the curly braces that if is evaluating. Here, we add in else transform. position is set to new vector3(0,0,0), setting the cube's position to the origin of the world.

```
void Update ()
{
    if (change > 10) {
        transform.position = new Vector3(3f, 0f, 0f);
    } else {
        transform.position = new Vector3(0f, 0f, 0f);
    }
}
```

Running the code again and playing with the value of change will result in the cube jumping to a new position any time change is above 10, and then moving back to the origin when the value is less than 10. However, setting the value to 10 exactly will not fulfill the if statement. To do this, we need to use the following code.

```
void Update ()
{
    if (change >= 10) {
        transform.position = new Vector3(3f, 0f, 0f);
    } else {
        transform.position = new Vector3(0f, 0f, 0f);
    }
}
```

Setting the if statement to change > = 10 means that if the number is 10 or above, then the condition of the statement is true and the first part of the if statement is evaluated. Otherwise, the section encapsulated in the else part of the statement is evaluated. This logic allows for two states to exist. If we need to check for multiple conditions to be set, then we're going to need another case to exist.

```
void Update ()
{
    if (change > = 10) {
        transform.position = new Vector3(3f, 0f, 0f);
    }
```

```
        if (change < 10) {
              transform.position = new Vector3(0f, 0f, 0f);
        }
}
```

We could use two `if` statements to do the same thing, as with the `if-else` statement. This code is going to do the same thing, but this will drive a programmer crazy. The code will also allow for more errors and odd behavior if you get one of the `if` statements wrong.

### 4.11.5.2 Else If

So far, we've observed `if` and `else`. To allow for more than two states, we can use `else if` to further add conditions to our logic.

```
        void Update ()
        {
              if (change > = 10) {
                    transform.position = new Vector3(3f, 0f, 0f);
              } else if (change < = -10) {
                    transform.position = new Vector3(-3f, 0f, 0f);
              }
        }
```

We can leave the code here for you to test. Slide `change` back and forth to numbers greater and less than 10 and –10. This looping will make the cube jump between two positions. If we want to have a default when the change value is between –10 and 10. Next, we'll want a third condition when neither `if` nor `else` is true.

```
        void Update ()
        {
              if (change > = 10) {
                    transform.position = new Vector3(3f, 0f, 0f);
              } else if (change < = -10) {
                    transform.position = new Vector3(-3f, 0f, 0f);
              } else {
                    transform.position = new Vector3(0f, 0f, 0f);
              }
        }
```

With the addition of a final `else`, we catch the case when neither `if` nor `else if` is true. Now, we've got three places for the cube to jump to when playing with the value of the variable `change`. If this logic seems obscure, it's a good exercise to think the steps out loud using plain English. If change is greater than or equal to 10, then transform the cube to 3, 0, 0. Else if the change is less than or equal to negative 10, then set the position to negative 3, 0, 0. Else set the position to 0, 0, 0.

    `if` statements need to begin with `if`. The last statement needs to end with either `else if` or `else`. An `else` that comes before an `else if` will create an error. The final `else` needs to come at the end of a long chain of `else if` statements.

    There are no limits to what can be in each statement, though the logic might lose some of its sensibilities when using different arguments in each statement.

### 4.11.6 Rearranging Logic

Once we start using a multitude of variables combined with logic, we might start to use more variables. It becomes important to revisit a bit about scope, so we can remember how long and where a variable exists.

Download the project from the website https://github.com/badkangaroo/UnityProjects/archive/master .zip and open the LogicScene. Open the `Logic.cs` found in the Project panel that has been attached to a cube found in the game hierarchy. MonoDevelop should launch. A few public variables have been created and should already have A _ Cube, B _ Cube, and C _ Cube assigned in the scene. If not, then it's easy to drag and drop the objects into their slots in the Unity Editor's Attribute Editor panel.

Now, let's focus on the `Update ()` loop, to add some behavior to our little cube friend. A quick search on Google for "Unity change material color" reveals `renderer.material.color = Color.red`. To see if this function works, we'll add it to our first `Update ()`;:

```
void Update () {
    renderer.material.color = Color.red;
}
```

Sure enough, our cube changes to a red color when the game is started. Okay, so we know this function does what we need it to.

```
void Update () {
    Color col = Color.red;
    renderer.material.color = col;
}
```

To have a visible change in the game while it's playing we need to change the color assignment into a variable. However, in this example, we've set it once dynamically when it was declared. Checking again in the game confirms that this works just as well.

```
public GameObject A_Cube;
public GameObject B_Cube;
void Update ()
{
    Color col = Color.red;
    float Ax = A_Cube.transform.position.x;
    float Ay = A_Cube.transform.position.y;
    float Bx = B_Cube.transform.position.x;
    float By = B_Cube.transform.position.y;
    renderer.material.color = col;
}
```

Next, we're going to want to collect some data from the scene from the other cubes placed in the world. We've added an A _ Cube and a B _ Cube to the class. To assign these, create a couple more cubes in the scene and drag them from the hierarchy into the slots in the Inspector panel.

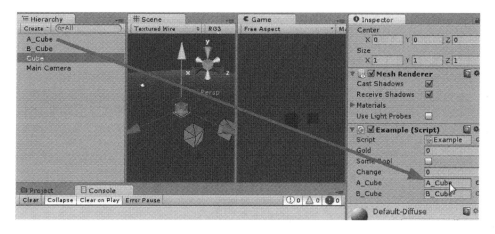

We now have x and y coordinates from both A _ Cube and B _ Cube. Now, to create a simple place-ment puzzle, we can use a bit of logic to manipulate the color of the cube. We're going to check the x coordinate of A against the x coordinate of B. When Ax is greater than Bx, we're going to change the color of the cube from black to blue.

```
public GameObject A_Cube;
public GameObject B_Cube;
void Update ()
{
    Color col = Color.red;
    float Ax = A_Cube.transform.position.x;
    float Ay = A_Cube.transform.position.y;
    float Bx = B_Cube.transform.position.x;
    float By = B_Cube.transform.position.y;
    if (Ax > Bx) {
        col = Color.black;
    } else if (Ax < = Bx) {
        col = Color.blue;
    }
    renderer.material.color = col;
}
```

To see this code in action, go to the Scene panel, select either the A or the B cube, and move it around following the x or red arrow.

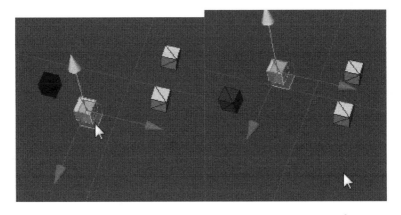

Now moving around either the A _ Cube or the B _ Cube around on the x will switch the color of the cube from blue to black. The placement of the if statement is important. The order in which if statements appear in the code has a direct effect on the final color of the material we're setting. Focus on the first if statement.

```
if (Ax > Bx) {
    float d = Ax + Bx;
    if(d > 5.0f) {
        col = Color.yellow;
    }
    col = Color.black;
} else if (Ax < = Bx) {
    col = Color.blue;
}
```

In the first statement in the code below, we set col = Color.black, before the if (d > 5.0f) statement. If the distance between Ax and Bx is greater than 5, we set the color to yellow. However, in this example, nothing happens.

```
if (Ax > Bx) {
    col = Color.black;
    float d = Ax + Bx;
    if (d > 5.0f) {
        col = Color.yellow;
    }
} else if (Ax < = Bx) {
    col = Color.blue;
}
```

To obtain any effect, we need to change the placement of the code that sets the color. Placing the second if statement inside of the first if statement ensures that the color stays set at yellow before exiting the first if statement. When the second if statement is run, col is set to Color.yellow. Once the statement is finished, the statement exits up one level and then col is set to Color.black and the rest of the if statement is skipped, setting the color to black if the first if statement is true. At first, this might seem obvious to some, but it's important to see firsthand.

### 4.11.6.1 Flawed Logic

```
if (d > 5.0f) {
    col = Color.yellow;
    if (d > 3.0f) {
        col = Color.cyan;
    }
}
```

To better understand this code, we might look at a flowchart:

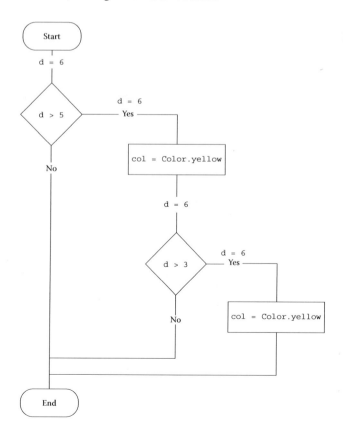

If we look at the second `if` statement, we find that we can add in more logic. Adding in another `if` statement to change the color to `cyan` if d is greater than `3.0f` will always prove true when found inside of the `d > 5.0f` if statement. This means that the cube will never turn `yellow`. To allow for both `yellow` and `cyan`, we'd need to think of a different way to pick when each color appears.

```
if(d > 5.0f) {
    col = Color.yellow;
    if (d > 10.0f) {
        col = Color.cyan;
    }
}
```

With the code changed such that one follows the other, we can set the color to `cyan` when d is greater than `10.0f`. However, there's no reason for doing the code like this.

```
if(d > 5.0f) {
    col = Color.yellow;
}
if (d > 10.0f) {
    col = Color.cyan;
}
```

This code is another version of the same code with one `if` statement not being inside of the other. When using multiple `if` statements, the logic is easier to follow if the `if` statements don't live within one another. There are some additional concepts to avoid when figuring out how to add in another step in logic.

### 4.11.6.2 Unreachable Code

```
if(d > 5.0f) {
    col = Color.yellow;
    if (d < 3.0f) {
        col = Color.green;
    }
}
```

When we add in an `if` statement which checks distance d inside of another distance, check it's easy to create code which will never be reached. Checking if d is less than a value will never be seen if its value is never less than `3.0f` when we're checking for the value being greater than `5.0f`. Such statements are considered unreachable because they are something that the compiler will not be able to catch. It's up to your ability to think out the logic to see when code statements are unreachable.

```
if (Ax > Bx) {
    col = Color.black;
    float d = Ax + Bx;
    if (d < 3.0f) {
        col = Color.green;
    }
    if(d > 5.0f) {
        col = Color.yellow;
    }
    if (d > 10.0f) {
        col = Color.cyan;
    }
} else if (Ax < = Bx) {
    col = Color.blue;
}
```

Rearranging the code to be as flat as possible helps to limit errors like unreachable code. When `if` statements are added inside of another `if` statement we add additional layers of complexity. To reduce the complexity of the code separate the `if` statements to make them easier to read and interpret. Later on, we'll look at some different ways to make this appear a lot cleaner and easier to read.

### 4.11.7 Another Look at Scope

We still have a little bit to review in relation to scope. We've been using the d variable a few times in the first `if` statement. We added the float d = Ax + Bx; inside of the first `if` statement. Every frame this is updated to a new value that is then looked at for each if statement that follows. This raises the question how often can d be used?

```
if (Ax > Bx) {
    col = Color.black;
    float d = Ax + Bx;
    if (d < 3.0f) {
        col = Color.green;
    }
    if(d > 5.0f) {
        col = Color.yellow;
    }
    if (d > 10.0f) {
        col = Color.cyan;
    }
} else if (Ax < = Bx) {
    col = Color.blue;
    if (d < 3.0f) {
        col = Color.magenta;
    }
}
```

Adding in d within the `else if` statement produces an error. After d is declared, its scope is limited to the block of code it was created in. The new `else if` statement creates a new code block, which contains variables that are declared either in the function or within the statement.

We could change d from d = Ax + Bx; to d = Ax − Bx. The declaration is valid, but the use of d is different from before.

```
} else if (Ax < = Bx) {
    col = Color.blue;
    float d = Ay - By;
    if (d < 3.0f) {
        col = Color.magenta;
    }
}
```

If we declare a new d and set it to Ay − By, we don't get any conflicts, but it is confusing to see in your code. At first, d is Ax + Bx, and then it's Ay − By. When you start debugging code, this difference might be missed and can lead to long nights hunting for a single error. If you move the float d declaration outside of the first statement, it becomes visible to both the `if` and the `else if` statements.

Just as awkward, you can use Ax + Bx in both the `if` and the `else if` statements for d. This would be redundant and can also lead to problems if you wanted to change the value for d.

```
float d = Ax + Bx;//moved here for wider scope visibility
if (Ax > Bx) {
    col = Color.black;
    if (d < 3.0f) {
        col = Color.green;
    }
```

```
        if (d > 5.0f) {
             col = Color.yellow;
        }
        if (d > 10.0f) {
             col = Color.cyan;
        }
    } else if (Ax < = Bx) {
        col = Color.blue;
        if (d < 3.0f) {
             col = Color.magenta;
        }
    }
```

With d = Ax + Bx; moved just before the first if statement, it's no longer scoped to within its original code block. This can get deeper by moving float d = Ax + Bx; before both if and else if statements, the value of d can be seen by both logic statements.

```
if (Ax > Bx) {
    col = Color.black;
    float d = Ax + Bx;
    if (d > 10.0f) {
        col = Color.cyan;
        float e = Ay + By;
        if (e > 1.0f) {
             col = Color.green;
        }
    }
} else if (Ax < = Bx) {
    col = Color.blue;
}
```

We can add in another float e, within the if (d > 10.0f) statement.

```
if (Ax > Bx) {
    col = Color.black;
    float d = Ax + Bx;
    if (d > 10.0f) {
        col = Color.cyan;
        float e = Ay + By;
        if (e > 1.0f) {
             col = Color.green;
        }
    }
    if (e > 2.0f) {
        col = Color.gray;
    }
} else if (Ax <= Bx) {
    col = Color.blue;
}
```

Adding a second if statement outside of if (d > 10.0f), which uses the e variable declared before, will produce an error. The variable e exists only within the block of code inside of the if (d > 10.0f). The accessibility of variables follows the same rules as before. Both e and d are no longer visible in the second else if statement since the scope for those variables is contained within the blocks of code they were declared in.

The rules for variable scope are strict. Scope is managed thus to reduce the occurrence of duplication. If a variable wasn't managed like this, then you might end up stomping on a variable declared early on in your code with an unintended value.

### 4.11.8  What We've Learned

Thinking through logic is one of the most difficult parts of programming in general. For now, the logic has been pretty straightforward, but logic can get very tricky quickly. Once things get more difficult, it may be easier to set the booleans ahead of time, like in the first example below, where we use bigChange and use the value after it was set.

One technique to ensure you're forming your logic correctly would be to avoid combining everything into one large if else if statement. Start by making several smaller if statements and then combining them afterward.

```
void Update ()
{
    if(change > = 10)
    {
        transform.position = new Vector3(3,0,0):
    }
    if (change < = -10)
    {
        transform.position = new Vector3(-3,0,0);
    }
}
```

In this code block, we can know that each if statement is being evaluated properly. Finally, we can also set bools ahead of time and watch how they are behaving using the print function.

```
void Update ()
{
    bool bigChange = change > = 10;
    bool lowChange = change < = -10;
    print(bigChange +":"+lowChange);
}
```

With the addition of the +":"+, we can add in the two true and false values together on the same line. To join values together in the print function we use the + operator to merge values. ":" turns the contained : into a string value. Therefore, here, we're merging three values together as strings, or as a programmer might say, "We're appending values" for the print function.

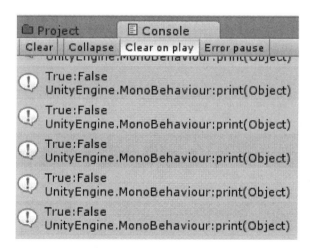

This approach becomes a valuable trick to help you work out your logic when you're writing your code. Try out a few different variations on the code yourself to make sure this all makes sense to you. We'll revisit a few different ways to control logic as we move on to using additional logical operators within the if statement's parameters.

The ability for Unity 3D to allow you to interact with your code through public variables enables you to quickly and easily see how your code behaves. Without this ability, you're left to interacting with code through more code. This gets dull quickly. After a few more programming basics, we're going to dive into the more interesting parts of Unity 3D.

## 4.12 Loops

To follow along, we'll be using the Loops project and looking at the Example.cs file in the Assets directory. The Example.cs has been attached to the Main Camera so that the code will execute when the game is started.

This section is something you may need to return to several times for reference. Learning these different loops is all very different. Most of them accomplish the same thing, but with subtle differences. In general, the for(;;) loop is the easiest to use, and sometimes the fastest.

The Update () function is run once every frame. Within that function, our logic is evaluated, starting at the top moving toward the bottom. Once the function is complete, the next frame begins, and the Update () function is called again to restart the evaluation at the top. This process is then repeated for every frame while the game is running.

To further understand how this process affects our code, we should be able to count the number of frames and thus the number of times the Update () function has been called. To do this, we'll simply create a public int to count the number of times the Update () function has been called.

### 4.12.1 Unary Operators

The term *unary operator* means there's only one operation required. In C#, and many other programming languages, unary operators work only on integers. Integers are best at counting whole values. In this case, we're going to keep track of how many times the Update () function has been called.

Integers are whole numbers, like 1, 2, and 1234. Unlike how numbers are commonly used in written English, in code, no commas are used: "1,234," for example, should be written "1234." Commas are special characters in C#, so the computer will look at 1234 as a 1 followed by a different number 234. We'll go further into the differences between numbers, but we need to know a bit about integers before proceeding. In a new project in Unity 3D start, with the Loops project.

```
public int counter = 0;
void Update ()
{
    counter = counter + 1;
}
```

To start, we should look at how the process looks like in long hand. Adding counter = counter + 1 means we're going to take the previous value of counter and add 1 to it. Some programming languages require this counting method. Lua, for example, needs to increment variables in this manner.

More complex languages like C# can shorten this to a single statement with the use of a unary operator.

```
public int counter = 0;
void Update ()
{
    counter++;
}
```

The unary operator ++ works the same as the long-hand version from the previous statement. When you run the game you can watch the counter value update in the Inspector panel in Unity 3D. After only a few seconds, you can see the counter running up very quickly. Each time the Update () function is called, the counter is incremented by 1.

Another unary operator is the --, which decrements a value rather than increments. Replace ++ with -- and you can watch the counter running down into negative numbers. Each one of these has important uses.

### 4.12.2 While

If we want to run a specific statement more than once in a loop, we need another method. To do this, C# comes with another couple of keywords, while and for. The while statement is somewhat easier to use. It needs only one bool argument to determine if it should continue to execute.

This statement is somewhat like the if statement, only that it returns to the top of the while statement when it's done with its evaluations.

```
using UnityEngine;
using System.Collections;
public class Example : MonoBehaviour
{
        //Use this for initialization
        void Start ()
        {
        }
        //Update is called once per frame
        public int counter = 0;
        void Update ()
        {
                while(counter < 10)
                {
                        counter++;
                        print(counter);
                }
        }
}
```

We start again with public int counter. The while() loop checks if the counter is less than 10. While the counter is less than 10, then, we run the contents of the while statement that increments the counter. Once the counter is larger than 10, the while statement doesn't evaluate its contents. As a programmer might say, the while loop's code block will not be executed.

There is one danger using while statements. If the while statement remains true, it will not stop. In this case, it means that the Update () function will not finish and the game will freeze on the frame. This also means that any input into Unity 3D will respond very slowly as it's still waiting for the Update () function to end. We'll observe how runaway loops behave later on in this chapter.

### 4.12.3 For

To gain a bit more control over the execution of a loop, we have another option. The for loop requires three different statements to operate. The first statement is called an initialization, the second is a condition, and the third is an operation.

```
for (initialization ; condition ; operation)
{
     //code block
}
```

The first argument allows us to set up an integer. After that, we need to have some sort of boolean condition to inform the `for` loop when to stop. The last argument is something that operates on the initialized variable from the first statement in the `for` loop. The following code block is a typical example of the `for` loop statement.

```
void Update ()
{
    for (int i = 0; i < 10; i++)
    {
        print(i);
    }
}
```

Inside of the `Update ()` loop, we can add a for loop that looks like this. After the keyword `for`, we need to add in our three arguments, each one separated by a semicolon (`;`). The first part, `int i = 0`, is the initialization of an `int` for use within the `for` loop. The scope for `int i` exists only within the `for` loop.

```
void Update ()
{
    for (int i = 0; i < 10; i++)
    {
        print(i);
    }
    print(i);//error
}
```

The variable `i` we wrote into the `for` loop is gone once you leave the `for` loop. This point is related to scope. Scope is basically how a variable's existence is managed and when it's allowed to be used. This is just a simple example, and scope has a greater meaning than that shown in the example here.

If you try to use values in the loop outside of the encapsulating curly braces (`{}`), you'll get an error stating you can't use `i` before it's created. At the same time, you're not going to want to declare an `int i` before using one in the `for` loop.

```
void Update ()
{
    int i = 0;//i is going to be used in the for loop
    for (int i = 0; i < 10; i++)
    {
        print(i);
    }
}
```

The second part of the `for` loop is `i < 10`, which is a condition letting the `for` loop know when to stop running. This is similar to the `while` loop we just took a look at. The `for` loop offers alternative uses of its arguments, some uses may seem awkward. This is unorthodox, but you can leave out the initialization section if an `int` value has been declared before the loop.

```
void Update ()
{
    int i = 0;//i is going to be used in the for loop
    for (; i < 10; i++)
    {
        print(i);
    }
}
```

There's not much of a reason for this but it's not going to break anything. The last argument of the `for` loop is an operation which runs after the first two arguments are evaluated. If the second part of the `for` loop is true, then the contents of the curly braces are evaluated. The last part of the expression is `i++` that can also be moved around.

```csharp
void Update ()
{
    int i = 0;
    for(; i < 10 ;)
    {
        print(i);
        i++;
    }
}
```

Unlike the `while` loop that relies on an external variable, the `for` loop contains everything it needs to operate, although, as we've just seen, we can still move the parts of the `for` loop around. If only the condition argument of the `for` loop is used then the `for` loop acts the same as a `while` loop. Although rearranging the parts of a `for` loop like this is not recommended, this does serve as a way to show how flexible C# can be.

Just so you know, a classically trained programmer might have a migraine after looking at this `for` statement, so give him or her a break and just do things normally.

The `while` loop runs only once after the `counter` reaches `10` after the first time it's evaluated. Each time the `Update ()` function is called, the `for` loop starts over again. We can use a slight variation of this using `float` values, though this isn't any different from using integers. Again, it's best to use integer values in a `for` loop, and this is only to show how C# can be changed around freely.

```csharp
void Update ()
{
    for (int i = 0.0f ; i < 10.0f ; i = i + 1.0f)
    {
        print(i);
    }
}
```

### 4.12.4 Do–While

Do–while is another loop to add to our toolbox. We took a look at the `for` and the `while` looping statements in Section 4.12.3. The `for` and `while` loops are the most common and the most simple to use. There are, however, variations on the same theme that might come in handy.

The great majority of the tasks can be handled by the simple `for` loop. However, variations in looping statements are created either to support different programming styles or to conform to changing requirements in different programming styles or to allow for different conditions to terminate the loop.

The `while` and the `for` loops both check various conditions within their parameter list before executing the contents of the loop. If we need to do the check after the loop's execution, then we need to reverse how the loop operates.

```csharp
int i = 0;
do{
    Debug.Log("do " + i.ToString());
    i++;
}while(i < 10);
```

The do–while loop has some subtle differences. For most programmers, the syntax change has little meaning and, for the most part, do–while can be rewritten as a simple `while` loop.

It's worth noting that most programming languages use the same keywords for the same sort of task. Lua, for instance, uses `for` in a similar fashion:

```
for i = 1, 10 do
    print(i)
end
```

However, Lua likes to shorten the conditions of the `for` loop by assuming a few different things in the condition and the operation of i. Other languages like Java, or JavaScript, use `for` and `while` more like C#. Things get really strange only if you look at something like F#:

```
for I = 1 to 10 do
printfn "%d" i
```

Syntax aside, once you know one version of the `for` loop, it's easier to figure out how another language does the same thing. The more basic concepts like booleans and operators also behave the same across languages. Therefore, you won't have to relearn how to use operators now that you know how they're used in C#.

### 4.12.5 Postfix and Prefix Notation

The placement of a unary operator has an effect on when the operation takes place. Placement, therefore, has an important effect on how the operator is best used. This is a difficult concept to explain without seeing in use, so we'll skip right to some sample code.

```
void Start ()
{
    int i = 0;
    Debug.Log(i);//before the while loop = 0
    while(i < 1)
    {
        Debug.Log(i++);//in the while loop = 0
        Debug.Log(i); //called again!= 1
    }
}
```

For various reasons, the i++ is the more standard use of the unary operator. When this code is executed, the first `Debug.Log(i);`, before the `while` loop, will produce a 0, just as when i was first initialized. The first time the `Debug.Log(i);` inside of the `while` loop is called, another 0 is produced in the Unity 3D Console panel. Where things become interesting is at the third `Debug.Log(i);` statement, where we have a different number.

The statement where i++ appears will use the value which i held before it was incremented. After the statement where i++ appears, the value of i will have been incremented. This is the difference between postfix and prefix, where i++ is a postfix notation and ++i is prefix notation. To illustrate this difference, observe the change when we use a prefix notation:

```
void Start ()
{
    int i = 0;
    Debug.Log(i);//before the while loop = 0
    while(i < 1)
    {
        Debug.Log(++i);//in the while loop = 1
        Debug.Log(i); //called again!= 1
    }
}
```

The first version, with postfix notation, produces two 0s and a single 1 before the while loop terminates. The second version produces one 0 and two 1s before the while loop terminates. The choice of which notation to use depends mostly on what value you need i to take when you use it. The syntax difference is subtle, but once it's understood, the effects can be controlled. To make the difference more drastic, we can move the placement of where the unary operation occurs.

```
void Start ()
{
    int i = 0;
    Debug.Log(i);//0
    while(++i < 1)
    {
        Debug.Log(i);//doesn't get reached
    }
}
```

The above statement will produce a single 0 in the Unity 3D's Console panel. The condition to execute the while loop begins as false, where the value for i is not less than 1, thus the Debug.Log() statement is never called. However, if we change things around, we'll get a 0 and a 1 printed to the Console panel.

```
void Start ()
{
    int i = 0;
    Debug.Log(i);//0
    while(i++ < 1)
    {
        Debug.Log(i);//1
    }
}
```

This code block means that the while loop started off true, since the value of i was 0 when evaluated, and only after the evaluation was complete was i incremented. Using the while loop in this way is unconventional, and it might be best avoided even though it's clever.

## 4.12.6 Using Loops

Making use of the loops is pretty simple. In the following use of the while loop, we're counting up a number of cubes. To test out our while loop, we'll create a new cube for each execution of the while loop. To do this, we'll create a new GameObject named box.

To initialize the box, we start with GameObject.CreatePrimitive(PrimitiveType.Cube). This initialization has a couple of new concepts. The first is the GameObject.CreatePrimitive() function. CreatePrimitive()is a function found inside of the GameObject class.

To let CreatePrimitive know what to make, we're using the PrimitiveType.Cube, which is of PrimitiveType; technically, it's an enum, but more on that later. Then, as we've seen before in the while loop, we're incrementing the numCubes variable to make sure that the while loop doesn't run uncontrolled.

```
int numCubes = 0;
//Update is called once per frame
void Update ()
{
    while (numCubes < 10)
    {
        GameObject box = GameObject.CreatePrimitive (PrimitiveType.Cube);
        box.transform.position = new Vector3 (numCubes * 2.0f, 0f, 0f);
```

```
        numCubes++;
    }
}
```

To tell where each cube is created, we move each cube to a new position by setting the box to new Vector3. In Vector3(), we'll take the value of numCubes and multiply it by 2.0f, making sure that each cube is moved to a different x location. Logically, each iteration of numCubes will increment numCubes by 1. Therefore, on the first execution, we'll have 0 * 2.0f that ends with 0. Then, the second time through the while loop, the result will be 1 * 2.0f, then 2 * 2.0f, and so on, until numCubes is larger than 10.

Each time the while loop is evaluated, the box points to a new instance of a cube primitive. The previous iteration of the while loop forgets about the previous instance of the box, which instance box is referencing becomes very important as we don't necessarily want to deal with every instance of the box game object we're thinking about.

An inquisitive person should be asking, Where did CreatePrimitive come from? The answer to that is found inside of the UnityEngine.dll. GameObject is going to be the primary focus of creating any object in the game, as the name might suggest. Expanding the GameObject found inside of the Solution Explorer in MonoDevelop, we find a promising CreatePrimitive function. This is related to how we found Vector3() in an earlier section.

The CreatePrimitive() function expects a PrimitiveType as an argument. Clicking on the PrimitiveType found in the Assembly Browser window, you are presented with the following set of code.

```
using ...
namespace UnityEngine
{
    public enum PrimitiveType
    {
        Sphere,
        Capsule,
        Cylinder,
        Cube,
        Plane,
        Quad
    }
}
```

Here is an enum called `PrimitiveType`. Inside this is `Sphere`, `Capsule`, `Cylinder`, `Cube`, and `Plane`. Each one is a value inside of the `PrimitiveType`. Enums are another generic type that C# makes extensive use of, which we'll introduce in Section 6.6.1. The `CreatePrimitive` function inside of the `GameObject` class is followed by: `GameObject`. This means that it's creating a `GameObject` for you to access. We'll learn about this once we start writing our own classes and functions with return types.

**NOTE:** Looking things up on the Internet is also a huge help. There are many people asking the same questions as you are. If you don't find what you're looking for, then you might just be asking the wrong question, or phrasing it in an obscure way. To find information on CreatePrimitive, search Google using "CreatePrimitive Unity" to get some quick possible answers.

In most cases, the answers are going to be brief and obscure, but they at least serve as an example for what you might need to look for in your own code to complete the task you're trying to complete.

This discussion might be a bit much to swallow right now, so we'll stick with the small bite we started with and get back to the deeper picture later on. For now, let's get back to figuring out more on loops.

### 4.12.7  Loops within Loops

We've created a line of cubes, but how would we go about making a grid of cubes?

Let's move our focus back to the `Start ()` function, so our code is carried out only once. Then we'll write two `for` loops, one within the other. The first `for` loop will use `int i = 0` and the second will use `int j = 0` as their initialization arguments. Then we'll leave the numCubes as a `public int` we can change in the editor. If we set the numCubes in the inspector to `10`, then each `for` loop will iterate 10 times.

```
public int numCubes = 10;
//Use this for initialization
void Start ()
{
    for (int i = 0; i < numCubes; i++)
    {
        for (int j = 0; j < numCubes; j++)
        {
            GameObject box =
            GameObject.CreatePrimitive (PrimitiveType.Cube);
            box.transform.position =
            new Vector3 (i * 2.0f, j * 2.0f, 0f);
        }
    }
}
```

Only in the second `for` loop do we need to create a box; then, in the x and y values of the `Vector3`, we will do some of the same math we did before. This time we'll use the `int i` variable for x and j for y to create a grid. This declaration creates a row and column relation between the two `for` loops. As one iterates through the row, the other inside of the row fills in the column with cubes.

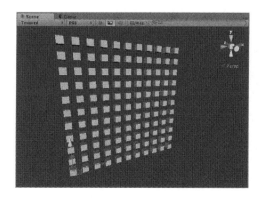

Hop to the Scene panel in the Unity 3D editor to take a look at the grid of cubes that was produced when you pressed the Play button. When the first for loop begins, it gets to the second for loop inside of it. Only after the second for loop is done with its statements of creating 10 boxes will it go back to the first for loop that moves on to the next iteration.

### 4.12.8 Runaway Loops

Loops can often lead to runaway functions. A while loop without any condition to stop it will make Unity 3D freeze. Here are some conditions that will immediately make Unity 3D stop on the line and never finish the frame. Adding any of these will halt Unity 3D, and you'll have to kill the Unity 3D app though the Task Manager.

```
while(true)
{
}
for(;;)
{
}
```

In some cases, these conditions are used by some programmers for specific reasons, but they always have some way to break out of the function. Using either return or break can stop the loop from running on forever. It's worth mentioning that the keyword return is usually used to send data to another function. If there isn't a function waiting for data, it's better to use break.

```
for(;;)
{
        return;
}
while(true)
{
        break;
}
```

There is a specific behavioral difference between return and break. With return you're stopping the entire function and restarting at the top of the function. With break you're stopping only the block of code the break is in.

```
    void Start ()
    {
        Debug.Log("at the start");
        for(;;)
        {
            Debug.Log("before the return");
            return;
            Debug.Log("after the return");
        }
        Debug.Log("at the bottom");
    }
```

Use the above code in the Start () function of a new script in use in a Unity 3D Scene. First of all, we'd get a couple of warnings informing us of some unreachable code. However, that doesn't keep us from testing out the results printed on the Console panel.

```
at the start
UnityEngine.Debug:Log(Object)
Loops:Start () (at Assets/Example.cs:8)
before the return
UnityEngine.Debug:Log(Object)
Loops:Start () (at Assets/Example.cs:10)
```

Therefore, we do get the first line of the Start () function as well as the line before the return executed. However, the two lines following return are not reached. This behavior changes if we replace return with break.

```
void Start ()
{
    Debug.Log("at the start");
    for(;;)
    {
        Debug.Log("before the return");
        break;//not return!
        Debug.Log("after the return");
    }
    Debug.Log("at the bottom");
}
```

We get only one warning of unreachable code, but we do get a third line printed to the Console window.

```
at the start
UnityEngine.Debug:Log(Object)
Loops:Start () (at Assets/Loops.cs:8)
before the return
UnityEngine.Debug:Log(Object)
Loops:Start () (at Assets/Loops.cs:10)
at the bottom
UnityEngine.Debug:Log(Object)
Loops:Start () (at Assets/Loops.cs:14)
```

Therefore, we do get the line after the for loop, but we don't get the rest of the contents from the for loop after the break statement. We'll go into more detail on the specifics of how these functions are used later on, which provides a very short example for break; For instance, we can use the following code to see how a while(true) can be stopped with a specific instruction.

```
void Update ()
{
    int counter = 0;
    while (true)
    {
    counter++;
    if (counter > 10)
    {
        break;
    }
    }
}
```

The counter builds up while we're trapped in the while loop. Once the counter is above 10, we break out of the while loop with the break keyword.

### 4.12.9 Breakpoints: A First Look

To have a better understanding on what we're seeing here, we're going to use a very important feature of MonoDevelop. With the code we just entered in the previous Update () function, we have a while(true) and a counter++ incrementing away inside of it.

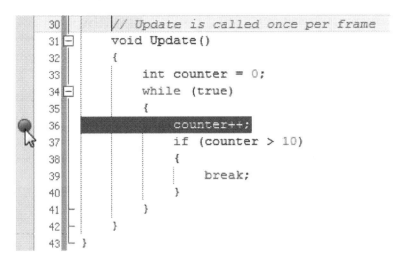

There's a narrow margin to the left of the numbers. The margin is for adding breakpoints. Breakpoints are small bookmarks that help you see exactly what's going on inside of your loop. Click on the line with the `counter++;` and you'll see the line highlight.

Run the code in the scene with the `Example.cs` attached to the Main Camera. While the game is running, select Run → Attach to Process in MonoDevelop. This action will open a dialog box with a list of Unity 3D game engines you might have open. In most cases, you would have only one.

The button is pretty small, but it's there. You can also use the menu (Run → Attach to Process) to open the following dialog.

Press Attach with Unity 3D Editor selected. You may have to bring Unity 3D to the foreground by clicking on it so it updates at least once, but then it will freeze. To speak in programmer jargon, this means "you've hit a breakpoint."

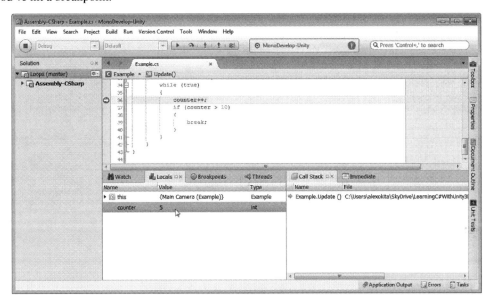

You'll see that the line in MonoDevelop is now highlighted, and a new set of windows has appeared at the bottom of the panel. Select the Locals panel and take a look at the `counter`. There are three columns: Name, Value, and Type, which tell you the `counter` is at `0`, which will tell you the value for `counter` and that it's an `int`.

Press F5 to release the `break` and you'll see the `count` increment by `1`. As soon as the code gets back to the breakpoint, it will stop again. What you're looking at is your code being updated only when you press the F5 key. This is called *stepping through code*. And it's a very important reason why MonoDevelop is to be used with Unity 3D, and not something like Notepad.

You can also hover the cursor over the value you're interested in observing.

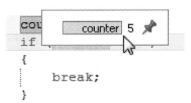

Pressing F5 will show you this value updating with each step. *Debugging* code is a major part of observing how your code is actually working. Breakpoints, and debugging tools like this and debugging tools like the Locals tab are indispensable when it comes to writing complex code.

To stop debugging the code, and let Unity 3D go about its normal work, press the Stop button.

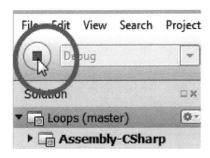

Pressing the little Stop icon will unlink MonoDevelop from Unity 3D and the information that we were watching will stop updating. Unity 3D will also return to regular working order.

### 4.12.10  What We've Learned

The for loop is a tight self-contained method to iterate using a number. The while loop may be shorter, and use fewer parameters, but its simplicity requires more external variables to control. When faced with different programming tasks, it can be difficult to choose between the two loops.

In the end, each loop can be used to do the same thing using various techniques we have yet to be introduced to. Don't worry; we'll get to them soon enough. At this point, though, we have learned enough to start thinking about what we've learned in a different way.

The last major concept we learned was the breakpoint, used to inspect what's going on inside of a loop. Breakpoints can be set anywhere and bits of information can be picked out and inspected while your code is running.

Debugging code is a part of the day-to-day routine of the programmer. Using a debugger that allows you to step through your code's execution allows for a greater understanding of what your code's activity involves. The debugger shows you what your code is actually doing.

## 4.13  Scope, Again

Scope was explored for a bit in Section 4.8, but there is some explaining left to do. We know that some variables exist only for the scope they were declared in. Other variables end up being shown in the Unity 3D Properties editor. This point doesn't explain how one class can talk to another class through a variable, or even whether this was even possible.

### 4.13.1  Visibility or Accessibility

Normally, variables and class definitions are considered to be private. This is usually implied and if you don't tell C# otherwise, it will assume you mean every variable to be private information.

```
private
public
protected
internal
```

There are only four keywords used to change the accessibility of a variable. Each one has a specific use and reason for being. For now, we'll examine the first two keywords in more depth. The keywords private and public are the two most-simple-to-understand ways to change a variable's accessibility.

We've used public before when we wanted a bool to show up in the Inspector panel in Unity 3D.

```
using UnityEngine;
using System.Collections;
public class Example : MonoBehaviour
{
        public bool SomeBool;
        void Start ()
        {
            SomeBool = true;
        }
}
```

We have a `public bool SomeBool;` declared at the beginning of this `Example.cs` code. Because `private` is assumed, we can hide this by simply removing the `public` keyword. At the same time, we can be very explicit about hiding this `bool` by adding the `private` keyword.

```
using UnityEngine;
using System.Collections;
public class Example : MonoBehaviour
{
        private bool SomeBool;//hidden
        bool AnotherBool;     //also hidden
        void Start ()
        {
            SomeBool = true;
        }
}
```

To the editor, there's no real difference between `SomeBool` and `AnotherBool`. The differences will come in later when we look at inheritance. It's important to know about the other keywords that can precede both class and variable statements.

### 4.13.1.1 A Basic Example

For a better observation of a variable's scope, we're going to want to start with a scope project different from before. This time, we'll start with the MoreScope project. In this project, we have a scene file where our Main Camera has the `MoreScope` component added. On a cube in the same scene, we have another script component added called `OtherScope`.

Here's where things get interesting. From the camera, we're able to see the `OtherScope` class. This is indicated by MonoDevelop allowing us to access the `OtherScope` class as we type.

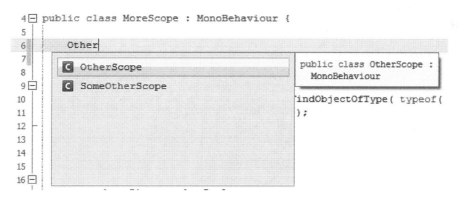

As we begin to type `Other` the class `OtherScope` appears in the Autocomplete pop up. This tells us that there are accessible objects, which we can access from class to class. This is referred to as the global scope.

### 4.13.2 Global Scope

When each class is created in Unity 3D, C# is used to make additions to the global scope of the project. This means that throughout the project, each class will be able to see every other class. This also means we can't have two class files with the same name. If we manage to create two scripts with the same name, we'll get the following error.

```
Assets/OtherScripts/OtherScope.cs(4,14): error CS0101: The namespace
'global::' already contains a definition for 'OtherScope'
```

Here, I've created another directory in Assets called `OtherScipts`. Inside of this directory, I've added another `OtherScope.cs` file, which means that in the project as a whole, there are two `OtherScope` classes. As each new file is created, they're added to the global namespace. This is similar to what would happen should we define two variables with the same name in a class. Changing the name of one of the classes resolves the problem.

Going back to the `MoreScope` class form the beginning of the tutorial we added an `OtherScope` `other`; variable. Next we we want to assign a variable within `other` a value. In the game scene assign the `OtherScope.cs` class to a new `Cube   GameObject` before running the game. In the `MoreScope`'s `Start   ()` function, use the following statement.

```
OtherScope other;
void Start ()
{
        other = (OtherScope)GameObject.FindObjectOfType(typeof(OtherScope));
        Debug.Log(other.gameObject.name);
}
```

Unity's `GameObject` class has a function called `FindObjectOfType()` that will search the scene for any object of the type we're requesting. The statement following the assignment to `other` is `Debug.Log(other.gameObject.name);`, which prints the name of the `gameObject` that the component is attached to in the Console panel. When the game is run, we get the following output.

```
Cube
UnityEngine.Debug:Log(Object)
MoreScope:Start () (at Assets/MoreScope.cs:11)
```

This output indicates that we've correctly found and assigned the variable `other` to the component attached to the `cube` object in the scene. Now let's add some meaningful variables.

```
using UnityEngine;
using System.Collections;
public class OtherScope : MonoBehaviour
{
        public float Size;
        Vector3 mScale;
        //Use this for initialization
        void Start ()
        {
        }
        //Update is called once per frame
        void Update ()
        {
        }
}
```

In the `OtherScope` class, we'll create two variables, one `public float` named `Size` and a `Vector3` called `mScale`. The "m" notation is commonly used by programmers as a short version of "my." Thus "mScale" refers to "MyScale." In the `Update   ()` function of the `OtherScope` class, we'll add the following statements:

```
//Update is called once per frame
void Update ()
{
        mScale = new Vector3(Size, Size, Size);
        gameObject.transform.localScale = mScale;
}
```

This will set the size of the cube object's `transform.localScale` to the `public Size` variable on the *x-*, *y-*, and *z-*axes. In the `MoreScope` class attached to the Camera, we'll add a new `public` variable called `otherScale`.

```
//Update is called once per frame
public float otherScale;
void Update ()
{
        other.Size = otherScale;
}
```

The `Update ()` function in the `MoreScope` class attached to the Main Camera should look like the above code. Because the `Size` variable in the `OtherScope` class was made `public`, it's now accessible through the dot operator. When the scene is run, the size of the `cube` is controlled by the `otherScale` variable assigned to the Main Camera.

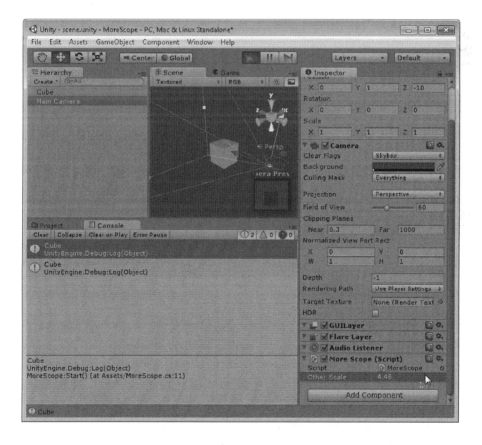

You can click-drag on the `otherScale` variable that has been exposed to the Inspector panel with the Main Camera selected. This action directly affects the size of the `cube` in the scene. Even though there's no visible connection between the two objects, their variables have been connected to one another through a global connection.

Accessing a variable is not the only way a class can manipulate another class. Functions can also be accessed by another class, if they've been made public.

The importance here is that both `MoreScope` and `OtherScope` could see one another. Once they can see each other, the variables inside one another are accessible if they're made public. Could it be possible to declare variables that are accessible globally?

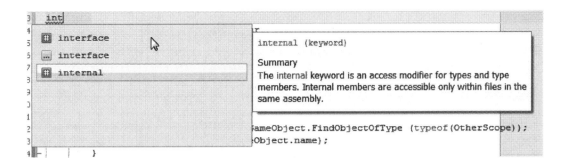

We could try to put a variable outside of a class. This might make it visible to any class that might want to access it. This, unfortunately, won't work. However, this doesn't mean that there are no systems that can make a variable globally accessible. However we'll have to leave off here for now. The systems that allow for globally accessible variables require some steps along the way to fully understand, so we'll get to that stuff soon enough.

### 4.13.3  What We've Learned

Defining public variables allows for interobject communication, which is one of the principles behind object oriented programming. This enables objects to communicate to one another in many unique ways.

Scope and object oriented programming are related. Variable scope is related to object oriented programming. By defining and maintaining scope, you're better able to control how other objects are allowed to communicate.

When working with a team of programmers, it's important to inform all on how your code behaves. You should communicate which variables in your class are allowed to be modified by how they are defined. Making variables public informs everyone that these are the variables allowed to be altered.

By protecting them, you're able to tell others which variables they are not allowed to touch. Much of the time, it's simple to leave things public while testing and making decisions on what needs to be made public. Once you've isolated what can and cannot be altered, it's best to hide variables that shouldn't be changed by outside objects.

## 4.14  Warnings versus Errors

There are two basic events that we will encounter early on in C#. The first are errors, and then we will get to the many warnings. Compile-time errors will stop all your classes from compiling. Because one class can look at and interact with another class, we need to make sure that every class is free from errors before our code can be compiled.

Most of these compile-time errors occurs from typos or trying to do something with the code that can't be interpreted by the lexer. Most of these errors deal with syntax or type-casting errors, which will prevent the rest of the code from working, so it's best to fix these errors before moving on.

At the same time, we'll get many warnings. Some of these warnings can be considered somewhat harmless. If you declare a variable and don't do anything to either assign something to it or use it in any way, then the lexer will decide that you're wasting resources on the variable. This produces a simple unused variable warning.

In some cases, code can still be compiled, but there will be some minor warnings. Warnings usually inform us that we've either written unused code, or perhaps we've done something unexpected. Code with a few warnings will not stop the compilation process, but it will let us know we've done something that might not necessarily work with Unity 3D.

### 4.14.1 Warnings

The most common warning is an alert bringing to your attention a variable declaration without any use. The `MonoDevelop` IDE is quite good at reading your code and interpreting how it's used. A function like the following will produce a warning:

```
void MyFunction()
{
    int j = 0;
}
```

This simply states that `j` is unused, which is true. Nothing is doing anything with it, so is it really necessary? Often, in an effort to write code, you'll be gathering and preparing data for use later on. When we do this, we might forget that we created some data that might have been useful but never did anything with it.

In this case, we might do something with it later on, so it's sometimes useful to comment it out.

```
void MyFunction()
{
    //int j = 0;
}
```

This leaves the variable around in case we need to use it, but it also clears out the warning. Most warnings don't lead to any serious problems.

### 4.14.2 Errors

One most common error occurs when we are dealing with missing variables or incorrect types. These errors show up fairly often when we first start off writing our own functions and aren't used to working with different data types or know how they interact.

```
float f = 1.0;
```

This is a commonly written statement that produces the following error:

```
Assets/Errors.cs(32,23): error CS0664: Literal of type double cannot be
implicitly converted to type 'float'. Add suffix 'f' to create a literal of
this type
```

The fix for the error is included in the error message. The message includes "`Add suffix 'f' to create a literal of this type`," which means we need to do the following.

```
float f = 1.0f;
```

This fixes the error. Many of the error messages give a clue as to what's going on and how to fix the error. Many of these errors show up before the game is run. These are called compile-time errors. Errors that show up while the game is running are called run-time errors.

Run-time errors are harder to track down. Often, this requires a debugging session to figure out where and why an error is happening.

### 4.14.3 Understanding the Debugger

Writing code that works is hard enough. To make sure that the code works, it's often easier to make it readable. To understand how the code works, we often need to add in additional statements to make it easier to debug as well.

To start, we'll want to begin with the DebuggingCode project. We haven't covered declaration of multiple variables in one line; this is because it's bad form, but it's not illegal.

```
//Use this for initialization
void Start () {
    int a, b = 0;
}
```

We can declare both a and b in one statement. In the above, a remains unassigned, and b is now storing 0.

```
//Use this for initialization
void Start () {
    int a, b = 0;
    Debug.Log(a);
}
```

This now produces an error, where a is used before it's assigned; however, the error might not be clear because in the line there certainly is a declaration and an assignment. The assignment is harder to read since it's all happening on one line.

```
//Use this for initialization
void Start () {
    int a = 0, b = 0;
    Debug.Log(a + b);
}
```

This is also valid, but we've done nothing for readability or debugging.

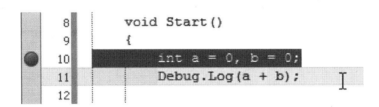

Setting a breakpoint on this line highlights both variables being declared and assigned. This creates a problem if we're trying to find a problem with just one of the variables. This also highlights why we need to change our writing style to help debug our code.

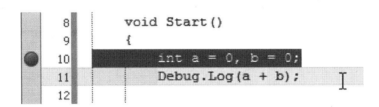

Breaking up the declaration across multiple lines allows for setting a breakpoint on a specific statement rather than a multiple declaration statement. Likewise, debugging a statement like the following is no better.

```
int c = a; int d = b;
```

This line has two statements, but does not have a line break between them. This creates the problem of both readability and debuggability. When you're trying to isolate a problem, it's important to keep each statement on its own line so a breakpoint can be applied to it.

If we continue this exercise, we can take a look at an `ArrayList` that contains different types of data.

```
void Start () {
    ArrayList list = new ArrayList();
    list.Add(1);
    list.Add("this");
    list.Add(1.0);
    list.Add(1.0f);
    //lists can have anything in them!
    foreach(int i in list)
    {
        Debug.Log(i);
    }
}
```

In the list, we have an `int` of `1`, a string `this`, a double `1.0`, and a float `1.0f`. The `foreach` loop requires `int`s and this works fine with the first iteration.

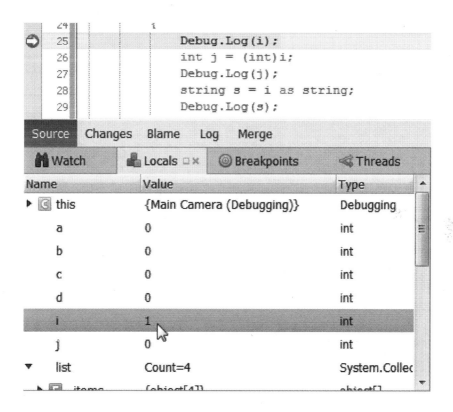

Setting a breakpoint here shows in the Locals panel an `int i` with a value of `1`. So far so good. When we step through the code to get to the next item in the list, we get an error.

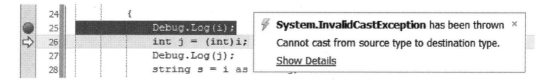

`System.InvalidCastException` shows up in the Locals panel. Since string `this` isn't an `int`, we get an error telling us what error was raised and in what line the error occurred on. This sort of debugging is only a contrived example setup to fail in a known location.

In most instances, problems like this aren't so easy to spot. The warnings and errors are often described with a line number, but it's not always easy to know why the exception was raised. Stepping into the code and checking out values is the only tool we really have to search for problems.

To make things easier on yourself, it's sometimes better to break things out even more.

The object type allows us to cast from the `ArrayList` into different types. By stepping past the assignment of `(int)i` to `j`, we can see what value has been assigned, by hovering over the variable. After this line, string `s` is null.

On the next loop through the `foreach`, we get the expected exception raised, but we have more information.

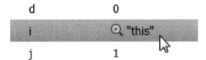

We can see that `i` is storing the value `this` that cannot be cast to an `int`. By making a separation of the value from where it's used, we can get a better idea of what type of data we're looking at. Adding additional lines of code just for the purpose of debugging allows for easier debugging.

Of course, this isn't as efficient as before. We're creating many small variables to be created and stored. This isn't the most optimized way to keep your code, so it's important to learn how to clean your code up to use less memory, but that's for Sections 6.3.2 and 6.15.6.

### 4.14.4 What We've Learned

Working through problems takes a step-by-step approach. Setting your code up for debugging requires some formatting changes to your code to help the debugger do its work. Once the code has been laid out for debugging, it's sometimes easier to read but our code can lose some efficiency.

It's always a good idea to keep your code clean and readable, but it's just as important to help your debugger do its work as well. Seeing the debugger step through your code also helps you understand how your own functions do their work.

When you have a chance to observe your code in operation, it's sometimes easier to see where code can be optimized—for example, when you see the same data being used over and over again. Passing values between variables in a visual sense can help reveal patterns. Once the patterns are seen, it can be easier to produce code that creates and reuses the same value less often.

## 4.15 Leveling Up: Fundamentals

At this point, I can say that you've gained enough of the basic skills to feel confident in your ability to read code and begin to ask the right questions. Just as important, the basics we've covered are shared among most programming languages.

Coming up with clever systems to control data is only a part of the task of programming. A great deal of work is coming up. It's also important to think of clear and concise names for variables. One thing is for sure: There have been plenty of pages written by people trying to wrangle in rampant names for identifiers.

At worst, you might have a situation where humans use health points, zombies hit points, vampires blood units, werewolves silver shots, and each one is simply a record of how many times they take damage before going down. It would be unfortunate for you to have to write functions for each human to shoot at every other type of monster and vice versa.

If someone offers help with your game, looks at your code, and you never hear back from that person again, it's surely due to the confused mess of code he or she got to look at. Some simple guidelines to help with naming have been outlined a number of times by various groups.

### 4.15.1 Style Guides

When faced with the fact that your code will have to eventually be seen by other programmers, it's best to try to avoid some of the embarrassment of explaining every identifier you've written. Furthermore, as a beginner, it's important that you gain some insight into the common practices that classically trained programmers have used throughout their careers. With any luck, books will help you keep up.

A style guide is a reference that often involves preferences involving everything from the placement of white space to naming conventions of identifiers. Official Microsoft style guides for C# provide details on how to name every different type of identifier. This enables us to tell identifiers apart from one another based on their use for variables, functions, or any other construct that C# uses.

As we learn about the different things that identifiers are used for, we'll also want to know how to best name the construct we're creating. A simple Internet search for "C# style guide" will bring up various links, for example, coding standards, guidelines, and coding guidelines.

Once you start working with any number of programmers, it's best to come to some agreement on the practices you'll choose to follow. Everyone learned slightly different methods and ideologies when he or she was introduced to a programming language, even if C# wasn't the first programming language that person learned. This leads to many different styles and conventions.

# 5

## *Fundamentals*

Now that we've covered most of the basic concepts and terms that are commonly taught to new programmers, it's time to learn some of the fundamental concepts that are required to write functioning code. So far, we've learned about the small bits and pieces that are required to understand how to look at code; now it's time to start writing it.

I also find it is important that you compare C# to other programming languages. This comparison helps to contrast C# against languages that might do a similar task in a slightly different way. With such comparison results in mind, we're better able to understand why C# looks the way it does and we'll be better prepared to understand a concept if we look something up on the Internet exemplified in a different language.

Many of the projects that Unity 3D provides as example projects are written with JavaScript. So too are many modules available on the Unity 3D Asset Store. When necessary, you might want to read the code to understand how to use one of the downloaded assets. If you've never seen JavaScript before, you might notice how some of the code will seem familiar, but you might also find much of it to be quite alien.

In the world of computer programming, it's best to have an open mind and be able to at least read through other programming languages. To that end, some examples in this chapter will have code written in other languages shown along with the C# example.

## 5.1  What Will Be Covered in This Chapter

Learning how to add complexity to your code takes time. We'll cover how to make classes communicate with one another on a more global scope. Then we'll learn how to control the flow of our data in more comprehensive ways. Finally, we'll want to understand one of the more useful constructs in C#, the array, and all of it's related forms.

- Review of classes
- Class inheritance
- The keyword *static*
- Jump statements, return, continue, break
- Conditional operators
- Arrays of various types, array lists, jagged arrays, dictionaries
- Strings

## 5.2  Review

The topics covered thus far have a lot in common with programming languages like JavaScript, UnrealScript, Lua, and Java, to name a few. Some of the syntax might look different, but the basic operation of how variables are created and assigned mechanically works the same. For instance, we understand assigning a variable to look like the following statement.

```
int a = 10;
```

In Lua, another commonly used game programming language, you might see something more like

```
local a = 10
```

In JavaScript, we might see something like the following:

```
var a = 10;
```

A language might not use some of the tokens we're used to seeing in C#, but use of a keyword, an identifier, and an assignment operator is the same. This rule also goes for something like a `for` loop. In C#, and many other C-style languages, we're used to using the following:

```
for(int i = 0 ; i < 10 ; i++) {
    //code here
}
```

JavaScript varies slightly, using `var` in place of `int`, but the rest remains the same. However, in Lua, again, we would see something more like the following:

```
for i = 0, 10, 1 do
    print(i)
end
```

Lua tends to omit many of the tokens used to help show how code statements are encapsulated; some prefer the brevity of the language. For a C-style language, the use of curly braces helps visually separate the statements more clearly.

Often, getting to this point is a difficult and unforgiving task. I hope you had some classmates, coworkers, friends, or family members to help you work out some of the exercises. If you're still a bit foggy on some of the concepts, you may want to go back and review. We've covered many cool things so far. For instance, you should be able to identify what the following code is.

```
class SomeNewClass
{
}
```

If you understood this to be a class declaration for `SomeNewClass`, then you'd be right. We should also know that for a class to be useful to Unity 3D, we need to add some directives that will look like the following. To add in directives, we start before the class declaration. We use the keyword `using` followed by a library path and add in both `UnityEngine` and `System.Collections`.

```
using UnityEngine;
using System.Collections;
class SomeNewClass
{
}
```

Directives allow our class to have access to the tools that Unity 3D has to offer. For a Windows app to have access to your computer, you need to use similar directives. For instance, if you want to work with the Microsoft XNA libraries, you'll need to add the following directives.

```
using System.Windows.Threading;
using Microsoft.Xna.Framework;
```

We're still a couple keywords away from a usable class in Unity 3D, though. First, we need to make this class visible to the rest of Unity 3D. To change a class's visibility, we need to add some accessibility keywords.

```
using UnityEngine;
using System.Collections;
public class SomeNewClass
{
}
```

We're almost there, and now we get to a part that might be confusing.

```
using UnityEngine;
using System.Collections;
public class SomeNewClass : MonoBehaviour
{
}
```

What is this : MonoBehaviour stuff that's coming in after our class identifier? You should be asking questions like this. We'll get around to answering this in Chapter 6. MonoBehaviour is another class that the programmers at Unity 3D have written. SomeNewClass is now inheriting from the class MonoBehaviour; we'll dive into what this all means in Chapter 6.

A class is the fundamental system for C#. You're allowed to write classes with nothing in them; for instance, class NothingClass{} is a complete class structure. You can add a single type of data in a class and give it an identifier. In this case, class MyData{int SomeNumber;} is an entire object with one integer value called SomeNumber in it. On the other hand, a file without anything other than int NothingInParticular; is meaningless.

A class can also be a complex monster, with many different behaviors. It's not uncommon for a class to contain several hundred or even a few thousand lines of code. The general practice is for a class to be as small as possible. Once a class grows past a few hundred lines, it's often time to consider breaking the class into several smaller classes of reusable code.

What all of this means in relation to Unity 3D is that we need to write several short classes and add them to the same GameObject. The same goes for any other programming project. The more modular your code is, the easier it is to create complex behavior by creating different combinations of code.

### 5.2.1 Modular Code

In a player character, you might have a MovementController class separated from a WeaponManager class. On top of this, you can choose either a humanAI class or a monsterAI class if you want the computer to take control. A more modular approach provides a wider variety once you've written different classes to manipulate a GameObject in the scene.

The same goes for functions. Rather than having a long algorithm operating in the Update () function, it's better to modularize the algorithm itself. First, you might have some sort of initialization where you obtain the character's mesh and animation system. This should be done in a separate function call rather than being repeated at the beginning of every frame. We'll take a look at a better way to do this later in Section 7.18.

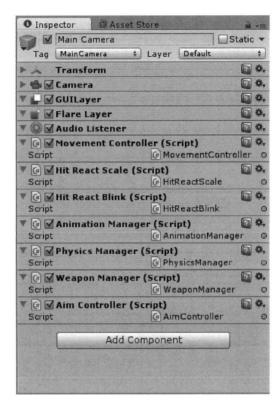

For now, we're reviewing all of the different things we've learned. Next, we are going to want to add in the entry points left in by the Unity 3D programmers called Start () and Update (); to do this, we'll simply add them into the class code block.

```
using UnityEngine;
using System.Collections;
public class SomeNewClass : MonoBehaviour
{
    void Start ()
    {
    }
    void Update ()
    {
    }
}
```

The two functions need to have a return type; in this case, both Start () and Update () return type void. The empty parentheses, (), indicate that they don't accept any arguments. Lastly, both Start () and Update () have nothing between their associated curly braces {} and will not execute any code. To extend this with our own code, we can add a new function.

```
using UnityEngine;
using System.Collections;
public class SomeNewClass : MonoBehaviour
{
    void Start ()
    {
        Debug.Log(MyFunction(7));
    }
```

```
      void Update ()
      {
      }
      int MyFunction (int n)
      {
           return n ;
      }
}
```

If we examine the function we added, we would find we created a new function called MyFunction. This function returns an int, and accepts an arg with type int. In our Start () function, we're using a Debug.Log() function that comes from the Debug class in the UnityEngine library. The Start () function then passes an int 7 to MyFunction(). The MyFunction returns a value n, which is then sent back up to the Debug.Log(), which sends 7 to the Console panel in Unity 3D.

```
using UnityEngine;
using System.Collections;
public class SomeNewClass : MonoBehaviour
{
      void Start ()
      {
           for (int i = 0; i < 10; i++)
           {
                Debug.Log(MyFunction(i));
           }
      }
      void Update ()
      {
      }
      int MyFunction (int n)
      {
           return n ;
      }
}
```

Before moving on, we'll add in one last for loop. If you can guess that this code will print out a 0 through 10 in the Console output panel in Unity 3D, then you're doing great. If you were able to follow along with this example, then you've come quite a long way in understanding the basics behind C#.

Now that we've got most of the basics under our belt, it's time to move onto more interesting things that make C# a powerful language. What differentiates C# from older programming paradigms is the fact that it's an object oriented programming language. Objects make programming powerful, and—if you're not fully informed—confusing.

From here on out, you're going to get into the more interesting capabilities behind C#. The basics we've covered have similar utility in most programming languages. Declaring functions and variables will look the same in many different languages. Order of operation and logic both behave similarly in most modern programming languages.

Try not to limit yourself to learning a single programming language. The science of computers is always changing. New languages are being written, and new business models rely on people who know about the latest developments.

## 5.3 Inheritance: A First Look

Once we've written a new class, we should be thinking toward generalizing what a class can do. When we started our class declarations, we always had : MonoBehaviour added after the class name. This means that our class is inheriting from another class named MonoBehaviour.

Let's take a look at an inheritance project: Open the `Example.cs` file in MonoDevelop and right click on `MonoBehaviour`.

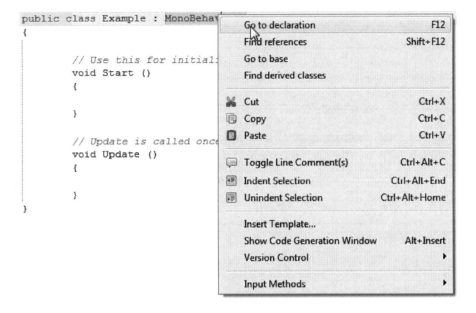

A pop-up with some interesting options appears over the word. Select `Go to declaration`, which brings you to the Assembly Browser. Declaration is used here with the same meaning as when we use a declaration statement to create a new identifier. We've covered declarations before, but in case you forgot, a declaration statement is used to assign a variable a new identifier.

This point should indicate that `MonoBehaviour` is a class that programmers at Unity 3D wrote for us to use. This might be a bit too much information right now, but this is showing you all of the public members that you can access within the class `MonoBehaviour`.

`MonoBehaviour` is a class that is tucked away in a dynamically linked library (DLL), or a dynamically linked library. Unlike the class we will be writing in a moment, a DLL is a prebuilt set of code that cannot be changed. Technically, you can change the contents of a DLL by various hacking methods. You could also get source code from Unity 3D to rebuild the DLL after making changes. However, a DLL is usually something that needs to be updated by its original authors.

The keyword `using` allows us access to the contents of the library where `MonoDevelop` is living inside of. To allow us to inherit from `MonoBehaviour`, we need to add in the `UnityEngine` library with the statement `using UnityEngine;`.

To summarize, `UnityEngine` is a library written by Unity's programmers. This library contains `MonoBehaviour`, a class that is required for our C# code to communicate with Unity's functions. To use the `MonoBehaviour` functions, we tell our class to inherit from it.

### 5.3.1 Class Members

When we write our own classes, they can often be used as an object. There are some cases in which a class wouldn't be used as an object, but for the following examples, we're going to use them as objects. To understand what this means, it's best to see this in practice.

When you declare a class, its identifier is an important name to identify the class by. The keyword `class` tells the computer to hold onto the following word as a new type of data. Each class's identifier basically becomes a new word, much like a keyword, with special meaning.

In addition to the name of the class, all of the contained variables and functions should be considered special components of that new object. Encapsulation determines how easily these contained objects can be used.

Members of a class are not restricted to its functions. Any public variable or function becomes an accessible member of that class. To see how all of this works, we'll need to write some really simple classes in MonoDevelop.

```
using UnityEngine;
using System.Collections;
public class Example : MonoBehaviour
{
    //Use this for initialization
    void Start ()
    {
    }
    //Update is called once per frame
    void Update ()
    {
    }
    public class Cat
    {
    }
    public class PianoCat : Cat
    {
    }
}
```

After void Update (), we're creating a public class Cat. After that, we're creating a new PianoCat class that inherits from Cat. In programming terms, PianoCat inherits from the base class Cat. So far, nothing interesting is happening, at least anything worthy of posting to the Internet.

To see what it means to inherit properties, we need to add some properties to Cat. Let's give our base Cat the ability to meow. Start with Debug.Log("Meow"); in our Cat class. The Debug function is a part of UnityEngine, which is declared way at the top of this file. Our class Cat is still able to reference the libraries that are declared at the beginning of this file.

```
public class Cat
{
    public int Paws = 4;
    public void Meow()
    {
        Debug.Log("meow");
    }
}
public class PianoCat : Cat
{
    public void PlayPiano()
    {
        Meow();//inherited from Cat
    }
}
```

So while PianoCat plays piano in a new function, he can also meow (Meow();), which is a function inherited from Cat.

### 5.3.2 Instancing

To make use of these two classes, we're going to need to do something useful with them.

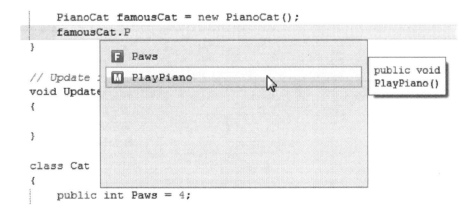

In the first part of our Example.cs class, we've still got our void Start () we can begin to add code to. When we start to enter PianoCat, the auto complete popup provides us with a PianoCat option.

```
//Use this for initialization
void Start () {
     PianoCat famousCat = new PianoCat();
}
```

To make use of a class, we need to create an instantiation of the class. Instancing a class means to construct it from a blueprint. Each instance is a new object created from the class; any changes you do to the instanced version is unique to that instance.

We've created a famousCat with all of the properties of a PianoCat. To make this new cat (famousCat) play piano, we call on the member function found in the PianoCat class.

```
void Start () {
     PianoCat famousCat = new PianoCat();
     famousCat.PlayPiano();
}
```

famousCat.PlayPiano(); is easily added through the handy pop-ups that MonoDevelop gives us. As soon as we add in the dot operator after famousCat, we're given several options, one of which is PlayPiano, but we also get Meow () function.

```
void Start ()
{
    PianoCat famousCat = new PianoCat();
    famousCat.PlayPiano();
    famousCat.Meow();
}
```

Meow is a member function of PianoCat because PianoCat inherited from Cat. Likewise, if we made a NyanCat or HipsterCat based on Cat, they would also inherit the Meow function from Cat. Running the code in Unity 3D returns an expected meow in the Console panel.

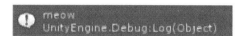

We set the number of paws on Cat to 4; we can use that number through famousCat.

```
public class Cat
{
    public int Paws = 4;
    public void Meow() {
        Debug.Log("meow");
    }
}
```

In our Start () function, in the first class we started with, we can use print () to show how many Paws the famousCat inherited from Cat.

```
void Start ()
{
    PianoCat famousCat = new PianoCat();
    famousCat.PlayPiano();
    famousCat.Meow();
    Debug.Log(famousCat.Paws);
}
```

We've gotten to a point where we'd like to search the entire scene for a specific object. In this case, we should look for every player in the scene. Looking through GameObject, we find the following functions.

- Find (string) : GameObject
- FindGameObjectsWithTag (string) : GameObject[]
- FindGameObjectWithTag (string) : GameObject
- FindWithTag (string) : GameObject
- GetComponent<T> () : T

We can find an object using its name or tag. If we want to find any object that happens to have a player.cs component, we need to know which GameObject it's attached to first. This is quite a puzzle. It's hard to know the name of the object we're looking for if we only know one thing about it. However, there is a more general way to find things.

Of course, we could just use Unity 3D's editor and assign tags, but we wouldn't learn how to do things with code alone. In a more realistic situation, we could just have our game designers assign tags to everything, use the FindWithTag() function, and be done with it.

To give ourselves a better understanding of objects and types, we should go through this process without tags. This way, we will gain a bit more understanding as to what defines objects and types, and how to use null. The null keyword basically means "nothing"; we'll see how that's used in a moment.

```
public sealed class GameObject : Object
```

### 5.3.2.1 A Basic Example

Programmers use the version of the word *inheritance* from genetics, inheriting traits and ability rather than wealth and status. GameObject is the child of Object; we know this because of the operator separating GameObject from Object. In a general sense, all of the code that was written in Object is a part of GameObject.

### 5.3.3 Parent and Child

To show you a basic example of how inheritance works with code, we'll write two new classes. The first is Parent.cs and the second is Child.cs. Create both of these in the Unity 3D project we've been working with. Using the usual right click in the project panel and then the path Create → C# Script is usually the best way. Name the new files according to this tutorial.

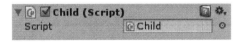

Assign the Child script to a cube in the scene. The class declaration in the Child.cs should look like the following. If there are other scripts on the object in the scene, then you can right click on the script's title and remove the component from the pop-up.

```
public class Child : Parent
{
}
```

Observe that the usual MonoBehaviour following the colon (:) is replaced with Parent. Now to prove that Child inherits the functions found in Parent.cs, we should add a function that the Child. cs can use. This code should appear in the Parent class.

```
    public void ParentAbility()
    {
        Debug.Log("inheritable function");
    }
```

I added this after the Update () function that's created by default when you use the Unity 3D editor to create classes for your project. To see that the function can be used by Child.cs, we'll use it in the Start () function in the Child.cs, as in the following.

```
public class Child : Parent
{
    void Start ()
    {
        ParentAbility();
    }
}
```

`ParentAbility()` is a public class found in the `Parent` class, not in the `Child` class. Running this script when it's attached to an object in the game produces the expected *inheritable function* printout in the Console panel. Remember, there's nothing inside of the `Child` class that has yet to have any new member functions or variables added. If we keep adding new public functions to `Parent`, `Child` will always be able to use them.

Next, add a function to the `Child` class like the following.

```
public void ChildAbility()
{
    Debug.Log("My parent doesn't get me.");
}
```

Then, check if the `Parent` class can use that function.

```
using UnityEngine;
using System.Collections;
public class Parent : MonoBehaviour
{
    //Use this for initialization
    void Start ()
    {
        ChildAbility();
    }
    //Update is called once per frame
    void Update ()
    {
    }
    public void ParentAbility()
    {
        Debug.Log("inheritable function");
    }
}
```

Doing so will produce the following error.

Even though the function is public, the parent doesn't have access to the functions that the `Child` class has. This is an important difference. The other main takeaway from this tutorial is to remember that `Parent` inherited from `MonoBehaviour`, as did all the other scripts we've been working with to this point.

The significance behind this discussion is that `Child.cs` has all of the functions found not only in `Parent.cs` but also in `MonoBehaviour`. One more thing should be noted:

```
public class Parent : MonoBehaviour
{
    public int SomeInt;
    ///other code...
}
```

Adding a public `int` to the `Parent` class will also allow the `Child` class to use the `SomeInt` variable.

```
using System.Collections;
using UnityEngine;
public class Child : Parent
{
    void Start ()
    {
        Debug.Log(SomeInt);
        ParentAbility();
    }
    public void ChildAbility()
    {
        Debug.Log("My parent doesn't get me.");
    }
}
```

`SomeInt` is available as though it were declared as a part of `Child`, because it is. It's important to know that changing anything in the `Child` class will never affect the `Parent` class. Inheritance only works one way: The children of a parent can never change the functions in a parent. Such an occurrence rarely happens in real life as well as in C#.

### 5.3.4 Object

`GameObject`, the class we're looking at, inherits from `Object`. Then `GameObject` adds new functions to on top of anything that already existed in `Object`. As we have just observed from our simple inheritance example, if we find a function in `Object`, we can use it in `GameObject`.

What this means to us is that we may use any interesting functions inside of the `Object` in the Assembly Browser in `Object` as well.

- FindObjectOfType (Type) : Object
- FindObjectsOfType (Type) : Object[]
- FindObjectsOfTypeAll (Type) : Object[]
- FindObjectsOfTypeIncludingAssets (Type) : Object[]
- FindSceneObjectsOfType (Type) : Object[]

Stepping through the thought process, we begin with "I'd like to find an object in the scene, but I might not know what it's called." From that, I would likely look for something called `FindObjects`. The objects I need to find are going to be `GameObjects`, so that does narrow things down a bit. Inside of `Object`, we find a function called `FindObjectsOfType()`, which is probably what we're looking for.

```
GameObject[] gos = GameObject.FindObjectsOfType(typeof(GameObject)) as
GameObject[];
```

In the `Start ()` function, we need to set up an array for every game object in the scene. That's done with `GameObject[]`; the square brackets tell the variable it's an array. We'll cover arrays in more depth in Section 5.9. Then we name it something short, like `gos`, for game objects. Then we can have `Object` run its `FindObjectsOfType` function to fill in our array with every `GameObject` in the scene.

Here's the interesting part, where inheritance comes in.

```
GameObject[] gos = Object.FindObjectsOfType(typeof(GameObject)) as GameObject[];
```

`GameObject.FindObjectsOfType()` works just as well as `Object.FindGameObjectsOfType()`, which should be interesting. There is significance to this finding, as inheritance in C# makes things complex and clever. Keep this behavior in mind in the following example.

Now that we have a list of objects, we need to find the GameObject with the Child.cs attached to it. To do this, we're going to reuse the foreach loop we just covered in Chapter 4.

```
//Use this for initialization
void Start ()
{
    PianoCat famousCat = new PianoCat();
    famousCat.PlayPiano();
    famousCat.Meow();
    Debug.Log(famousCat.Paws);
    GameObject[] gos =
    GameObject.FindObjectsOfType(typeof(GameObject)) as GameObject[];
    foreach (GameObject go in gos)
    {
        Debug.Log(go);
    }
}
```

So now we're up to an array of GameObjects followed by a way of looking at each GameObject. Right now, each monster in the scene knows about everything else in the scene. The Child.cs is a component of the GameObject cube in the scene, as is everything else that the GameObject is made of.

```
Component comp = go.GetComponent(typeof(Child));
```

To find the Child.cs in the ComponentsList of the GameObject called go in the foreach statement, we need to create a variable for it. In this case, we have Component comp waiting to be filled in with a component from the GameObjects in the gos GameObject[] array. That component also inherits from Object.

```
public class Component : Object
```

NOTE: You could enter Component.FindObectsOfType(), and this will work the same as though it were called from Object or GameObject. Inheritance is a complex topic, and right now, we're only observing how functions can be shared from the parent to children, but there's a problem when children try to share. We've used GameObject.CreatePrimitive() to make cubes and spheres. And we know Object has FindObjectsOfType, which both GameObject and Component can use because of inheritance. Therefore, does that mean Object.CreatePrimitive will work?
Actually, no; Object doesn't inherit functions of variables from its children. In programming, parents don't learn from their kids. Suppose GameObject.CreatePrimitive() is a function found in GameObject, and GameObject and Component both inherit from Object; does that mean Component.CreatePrimitive() will work? Again, no; in C#, children don't like to share. C# is a pretty tough family, but rules are rules.

Therefore, now we have a Component in place for the player, and we're setting comp to the go.Get Component(typeof(Player)), which will set comp to the Child.cs component found in the game object, if there is one. We are relying on the fact that not all objects have that component. When the GetComponent(typeof(Player)) fails to find anything, comp is set to null, and it does so reliably.

### 5.3.4.1 A Type Is Not an Object

Type, as we've mentioned, is the name given to a class of an object. Like a vowel, or noun, type refers to the classification of a thing, not the actual thing itself. Semantics is important when dealing with programming, and it's very easy to miss the meanings behind how words are used. For instance, if we need to tell a function the type of a class, we can't simply use the class's name.

```
GetComponent(Player);
```

If the function expected the type player and not the object player, you'd get an error. There's a subtle difference here. The type of an object is not the object. However, it's difficult to say "this is the type Child" and not the "Child" class object. The two things use the same word, so it's easy to confuse.

There is a function that will get the type of an object and satisfy functions that need types and not objects. And that's where typeof(Child) comes in. If we have the object Child typeof(Child), we can put Child into the typeof() function and use that function as the type of Child and not the class Child.

Give the FindObjectsOfType() function a typeof(Child) and it returns an array with every instance of Child in the scene. We can give the Example.cs a GameObject ChildObject; to chase after. Just so we don't get confused what version of the word Player we're looking for we should make it tremendously clear what we're looking for.

### 5.3.5 != null

Add in a GameObject variable for the player at the class scope. The not null check is important. We'll find out why in Section 5.7.4, but for now we'll just observe how it's best used.

```
public class Example : MonoBehaviour
{
    public GameObject ChildObject;
    ///other code…
}
```

Then, in the Start () function, we finish our code with the following:

```
    void Start ()
    {
        PianoCat famousCat = new PianoCat();
        famousCat.PlayPiano();
        famousCat.Meow();
        Debug.Log(famousCat.Paws);
        GameObject[] gos =
        GameObject.FindObjectsOfType(typeof(GameObject)) as GameObject[];
        foreach (GameObject go in gos)
        {
            Debug.Log(go);
            Component comp = go.GetComponent(typeof(Child));
            if (comp != null)
            {
                ChildObject = go;
            }
        }
    }
```

The new section is if (comp != null); our ChildObject is the game object with the go where comp is not null. Sometimes, phrases like "component is not null" are unique to how programmers often think. Their vocabulary may seem unfamiliar at first, but they will grow accustomed to it soon enough. As we start to use little tricks like "!= null," we'll start to understand why programmers often seem to use a language of their own.

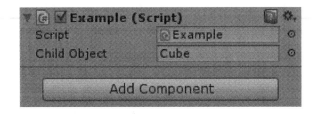

We can run the game, and check the `ChildObject` variable. We'll see that it's `Cube`, and if we check, we'll find that the cube with the `Child.cs` attached to it is the one that we're looking for.

[something] != null is commonly used to know when something has been found. When the something is not empty, you've found what it is you're looking for. This is a useful trick to apply for many different purposes.

### 5.3.6 What We've Learned

Using data to find data is a commonplace task in programming. With Unity 3D, we have plenty of functions available which make finding objects in a scene quite easy. When monsters go chasing after players, we need to have a simple system for allowing them to find one another.

Computers don't use senses like we do. They have another view of the game that can't be compared to how we, as players, perceive the world. By searching through data, and using algorithms, the computer-controlled characters require a different set of parameters to operate.

In one sense, the computer has complete knowledge over the game world. How that world is perceived by the computer requires our instruction. A monster's ability to understand its environment depends on our code.

## 5.4 Instancing

An important feature of C# and many C-like programming paradigms is the use of a class as a variable. When we use a class as a variable, it's created as a new object. Some of these classes are values, which means that the function itself can be used to assign to variables, and many classes are used as values. Using a class as an object which is itself a value is at the heart of object oriented programming.

To make use of a class, or object, variable, we often need to create a new instance of the class. Instancing is basically creating space in memory for a class of a more complex data type. We do this in the same way we create a variable for a more simple data type. However, when assigning a value to the variable of this sort, we need to change things up a bit.

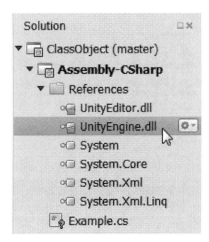

The `Vector3` class is located in the guts of the `UnityEngine` library. We can also see what else the `UnityEngine` library has by double clicking on the `UnityEngine.dll` located on the Solution panel in MonoDevelop. This opens the Assembly Browser. Inside there, you'll find the `UnityEngine.dll`, which you can then expand to find the contents of the DLL.

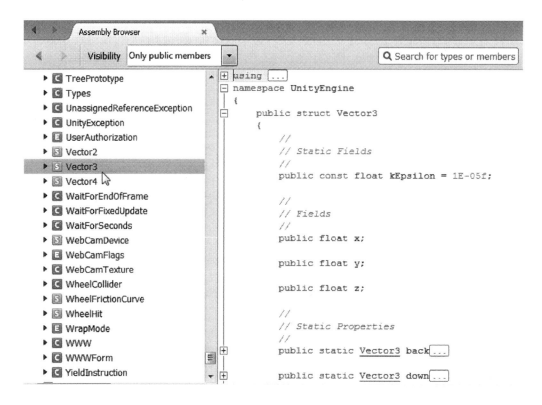

Expand this again and scroll down; you will find that the contents are arranged alphabetically to make things easier to find. Expand the `Vector3` class to reveal its contents; you'll find many additional objects inside of the `Vector3` class.

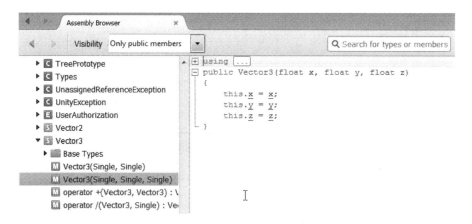

Don't let this cacophony of information bewilder you. We only need to deal with a small portion of these objects to get started. Later on, we'll be able to browse the classes in each one of these DLLs and look for classes we can include in our code.

### 5.4.1 Class Initialization

The reason why we don't need to create an instance for an `int` or a `bool` is that they are built-in types found in the system library. We can also create our own types for our own game. Yes, we get to invent new types of data. For instance, you'll need a player type and a monster type.

For these new types, we'll want to store the status of their health and possibly their ammunition. These bits of information can be any value; however, they are usually `ints` or `floats`. Of course, to store a player's location in the world, we'll want to include a `Vector3`, inferring that a type can contain many other non-primitive types. Eventually, everything in the game will have a class and a type of its own.

In C#, the built-in types do not need a constructor. We'll get into constructors when we start instancing objects later in this chapter. Plain old data types (PODs) include not only the built-in types but structures and arrays as well. The term came from the C++ standards committee, and was used to describe data types that were similar between C and C++. This term can be extended to C# that shares the same POD types.

### 5.4.2 New

The `new` keyword is used to create a new instance of a class. Some data types that fulfill a variable, do not need the `new` keyword. For example, when you declare an `int`, you simply need to set it to a number, as in `int i = 7;`. This declaration creates space in memory for an `int` named i, and then sets the value for i to 7. However, for more complex data types, like a vector, you need to give three different float values. Unity 3D calls a 3D vector a `Vector3`, because there are three values stored in it: x, y, and z.

**NOTE:** Unity 3D also has a Vector2 and a Vector4 type. These are instanced in the same way as a Vector3, but have more specific uses. Vector2 only has an x and y value; Vector4 has an additional vector, w, after x, y, and z.

Normally, in 3D space, you'd need only a Vector3, but when dealing with something called quaternions, you'll need the extra fourth number in a vector; we'll get into this a bit later on.

Remember, declaring a variable starts with the type followed by the name we're assigning to the variable. Normally, you'd start with something like `Vector3 SomeVector;`. Where the difference comes in is assigning a value to the variable. To do this, we start with the `new` keyword, followed by the Vector3's initialization.

### 5.4.3 Constructors

To follow along, we'll use the ClassObject Unity 3D project and examine the `Example.cs` file in MonoDevelop. Constructors add an extra, but necessary, step when using a variable type that's derived from an object class. With many classes, there are different ways in which they can be initialized with a constructor. Most initializations can be done without any parameters, as in the following example.

```
void Start ()
{
    Vector3 vector = new Vector3();
}
```

The use of a pair of parentheses after the type refers to a constructor, or a set of parameters that can be used to build the instance when it's created.

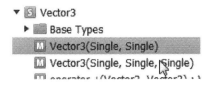

Looking at the Assembly Browser again, we can see that there are two Vector3() functions under the Vector3 class. The constructors are named the same as the class. There's always going to be an assumed () version, with no parameters for construction. After that, there can be any number of alternative constructors. In this case, there are two additional constructors created for Vector3().

We should also note that float is another name for single, as seen in the Assembly Browser. The word *double*, which we've mentioned in Section 4.5, has twice the amount of space in memory to store a value than a single; a single is a 32-bit floating point, and a double is a 64-bit floating point value. More on that when we cover how numbers are stored.

We can add information, or parameters, when initializing a new Vector3 type variable. Parameters, also known as arguments, are values that have been added to the parenthesis of a function. The different parameters are setting variables within the class we're instancing. Inside of a Vector3, there is an x, a y, and a z variable. Like the variables we've been using, like SomeInt, Vector3 is a class that has its own variables. When using parameters, we can get some guides from our integrated development environment (IDE).

If you look at the top right of the pop up, you'll see some indicators, you'll see an up and down triangle before and after a "1 of 3". The indicator numbers the different ways a Vector3 can be created. The up and down arrow keys on your keyboard will change which methods we can use to create a Vector3 class. The third one down has a float x, y, and z in the argument list for the Vector3 type. This is related to the class's constructor.

```
// Use this for initialization
void Start()
{
    Vector3 vector = new Vector3()
}

// Update is called once per fram
void Update()
{

}
```

```
public Vector3(        ▲ 3 of 3 ▼
    float x,
    float y,
    float z
)
```

After the first parenthesis is entered, (, a pop-up will inform you what parameters you can use to initialize the Vector3 we're creating. This information comes from the UnityEngine.dll we looked at earlier. As you fill in each parameter, you need to follow it with a comma to move to the next parameter.

You should use the up and down arrows to switch between constructor options. The second option requires only an x and a y; this leaves the z automatically set to 0. As we start using other classes that need different initialization parameters, it's useful to know what sort of options we have available.

To use the vector we created, we'll assign the object in Unity's Transform, in the Position component, to the vector variable we just assigned. This assignment will move the object to the assigned Vector3 position. We'll go into further detail on how to know what a component expects when assigning a variable when we start to explore the classes that Unity 3D has written for us.

```
void Start ()
{
    Vector3 vector = new Vector3(1, 2, 3);
    transform.position = vector;
}
```

When this class is attached to the Main Camera in the scene and the Play in the Editor button is pressed, we will see the following in Unity 3D. Notice entries for Position in Transform roll out in Inspector.

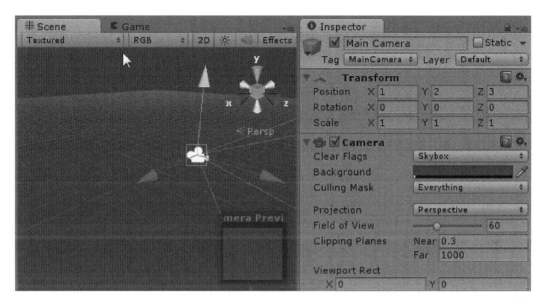

The declaration and initialization of a new vector requires an extra step. For instance, this situation can be translated into English as follows: "I'm making a new Vector3, and I'm naming it to vector. Then I'm assigning the x, y, and z to 1, 2, and 3. Then, I'm setting the position in the Transform component to vector." Likewise, the shorter version could simply be "I'm setting the Position in the Transform component to a Vector3, with x, y, and z set to 1.0f, 2.0f, and 3.0f."

NOTE: Natural language programming, like the English translation above, has been tried before. However, the compiler's job would be to both interpret and translate English into byte code, and this has proven to be quite tricky. Interpretation of English is part intuition and part assumption. Neither of these abilities can be easily programmed into software to work consistently and perfectly predictably.

Various ways to program computers using different formatting options to make code more human readable have been tried many times. In the end, the formatting almost always ends up using more and more keywords, which restrains the programmer, by taking away the options and freedoms that are allowed when fewer rules are applied.

You can also use an initialized vector without assigning it to a variable name first. This is perfectly valid; when Position in the object's Transform component is set, it's automatically assigned a Vector3 that's created just for the position.

```
void Start ()
{
    transform.position = new Vector3(1, 2, 3);
}
```

Once a new class has been initialized, you can modify the individual variables found inside of the Vector3 class. A variable found in a class is referred to as a member variable of the class. We'll go into more detail in Section 6.3.2 about what sort of variables and functions can be found in a class that

Unity 3D has written for your benefit. To change one of these variables inside of a class, you simply need to assign it a value like any other variable.

```
void Start ()
{
    Vector3 vector = new Vector3(1, 2, 3);
    vector.x = 1.0f;
    transform.position = vector;
}
```

There's an interesting difference here. An f has been used: the 1.0f is assigned to the x member of vector. This informs the compiler that we're assigning a float type number to vector.x and not a double. By default, any number with a decimal with no special designation is assumed to be a double number type.

We'll dive into the significance of the difference later on. To tell Unity 3D we're assigning a float to the x member of vector, we need to add the suffix f after the number. This changes the number's type to float. This is related to type casting, which we will cover in Section 6.5.3.

We can also assign POD as an object.

```
        int i = new int();
        Debug.Log(i);
```

Adding this after the previous code block, we'll get 0 sent to the Unity 3D Console panel. We don't need to do things like this for all data types, but it's interesting to see that it's possible. Most data types can be initialized in this way. There are some tricky constructors, like string, which need some additional work for us, to understand the parameter list. The details here will have to wait till Section 6.4 in the book.

### 5.4.4 What We've Learned

The example in this section sets the x of the vector to 1.0; the y and the z are left at 0.0; however, the values for y and z were assigned by C# when the class was first initialized. Setting variables in the class is controlled by how the class was written. The visibility of the variables in the Vector3 class is determined in the same fashion as we declare variables in classes that we have written ourselves. We can make changes to the x, y, and z float variables in the Vector3 class because of their public declaration.

Each nuance and use of the C# language takes some time to get used to. When certain tasks are shortened into easier-to-write code, the code ends up being harder to read. However, most of the harder tasks often have a commonly used format. These shorthand formats are sometimes called idioms.

Idioms in English do not often make the most sense when logically analyzed, but they do have specific meanings. Much like in English, programming idioms might not make sense when you look at them, but they do have a specific meaning when in use. As we make further progress, you'll be introduced to some of the more commonly used idioms in C#.

## 5.5 Static

The static keyword is a keyword that ties all instances of a class together. This allows all instances of a class to share a common variable or function. When you see static next to a function, this means you don't need to make a new instance of the class to use it. Because static functions and variables are class-wide, we access them in a slightly different way than an instance of a variable or function.

There is a static function found inside of Input called GetKey(), which we will use. The last keyword is bool, after public and static. We've seen bool before, but this is used as a return type. When we write our own functions, we'll also include our own return type, but just so you know, return types are not limited to bool. Functions can return any data type, and now we'll take a look at how this all works.

### 5.5.1 A Basic Example

Let's start with the Static project; begin by opening the scene in the Unity 3D Assets Directory. The Main Camera in the scene should have the Player component attached.

```
using UnityEngine;
using System.Collections;
public class Player : MonoBehaviour
{
    //Use this for initialization
    void Start ()
    {
    }
    //Update is called once per frame
    void Update ()
    {
        //add in a check for the A key
        bool AKey = Input.GetKey(KeyCode.A);
        if (AKey)
        {
            Debug.Log("AKey");
        }
    }
}
```

The code here will send the following to the Console panel in Unity 3D.

```
AKey
UnityEngine.Debug:Log(Object)
Player:Update () (at Assets/Player.cs:15)
```

The `KeyCode` class has a public variable for each key on your computer's keyboard. Each variable returns true when the key on the keyboard is pressed. The `Input.GetKey()` function returns the `bool` value based on which the key is checked in the `KeyCode` class. We assign the `bool AKey` to the returned value from the `Input.GetKey(KeyCode.A);` function. The statement `if (AKey)` then executes the `Debug.Log("AKey");` which then prints out `AKey` to the Unity Console window. The `GetKey()` function is a member of the `Input` class and is accessed by using the `.` or dot operator. Now that we're reading libraries we need to know how to get to the members of the classes we're looking at.

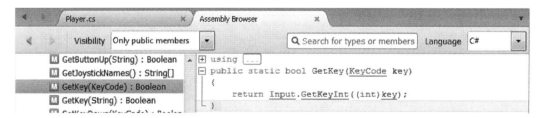

Select the `GetKey()` and go to the definition of this function. You can do this by right clicking on the word and selecting Go To Definition in the pop-up. This will open the Assembly Browser, where we'll be shown the function's definition. We're shown `public static bool GetKey(KeyCode key)` as the function's definition.

This process provides us with the beginnings of a player controller script. Filling in the rest of the WASD keys on the keyboard will allow you to log the rest of the most common movement keys on your keyboard. The Input class is found in `UnityEngine` that was included in this class with the `using UnityEngine` directive at the top of the class.

From previous chapter lessons, you might imagine we'd need to create an instance of `Input` to make use of its member functions or fields. This might look like the following:

```
void Update ()
{
    Input MyInput = new Input();
    bool AKey = MyInput.GetKey(KeyCode.A);
    Debug.Log(AKey);
}
```

While this syntactically makes sense, you're better off not creating new instances of the Input class. The `GetKey()` function is `static`, so there's no need to create an instance of `Input` to use the function. This will make more sense once we write our own static function later in this chapter. However, should we actually try to use `MyInput` as an object, we'd have some problems.

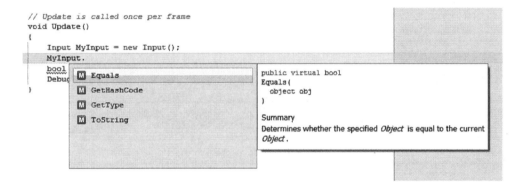

When we check for any functions in the `MyInput` object after it's been instanced, we won't find anything useful. The only things available are universal among all things inheriting from the object class. We'll get to what the object class is in Section 6.13.4, about inheritance, but for now, just assume that these functions will appear and act the same for pretty much anything you are allowed to make an instance of.

The lack of functions or variables is due to the fact that all of the functions and variables have been marked as `static`, so they're inaccessible through an *instance* of Input. Statically marked functions and variables become inaccessible through an instance. This inaccessibility is related to an object's interface and encapsulation. This doesn't mean that they are completely inaccessible, however; but to see them, we'll need to write our own class with our own functions and variables.

### 5.5.2 Static Variables

Let's start off with a simple concept: a `static` variable. Using our previous analogy of toasters, each new toaster built in a factory has a unique identity. Each unit built would have a different serial number. Once in someone's house, the number of times the toasters have been used, when they are turned on and begin to toast, and their location in the world are all unique to each toaster. What they all share is the total number of toasters that exist.

The `static` keyword means that the function or variable is global to the class it's declared in. Let's make this clear; by declaring a variable as `static`, as in `static int i;`, you're indicating that you want to use the `int i` without needing to make an instance of the class that the variable is found in.

Variables that are unique to each instance of a class are called *instance variables*. All instances of the class will share the static variable's value regardless of their instanced values.

If we create a mob of zombies, we might find it important to maintain a certain number of zombies. Too many and the computer will have problems keeping up. Too few and the player will go around with nothing to shoot at. To give ourselves an easier time, we can give each zombie a *telepathic* connection with all other zombies. A programmer would call this a *static variable* or a *static function*.

As we've seen, variables usually live a short and isolated life. For instance, the variable used in the ever-powerful `for` loop exists only within the `for` loop's code block. Once the loop is done, the variable in the `for` loop is no longer used and can't be accessed outside of the loop.

```
for (int i = 0; i < 10; i++)
{
    print(i);//prints 1 to 10
}
//i no longer exists
print(i);//error, i is undefined
```

Now that we're creating objects based on classes, we need to make those classes interact with one another in a more convenient way. To keep track of the number of undead zombies in a scene, we could have the player keep track; as each zombie is created or destroyed, a message could be sent to the player.

The `Player` class keeping track of important `zombie` data is awkward. `Zombie`-related data should remain in the `zombie` class, unrelated classes should not depend on one another in this way. The more spread out your code gets, the more problems you'll have debugging the code. Creating self-contained classes is important, and prevents a web of interdependent code, sometimes referred to as spaghetti code.

Remember that when an object is created it's instanced from a single original blueprint, which can include some variables that are shared between each instance of the class. With static variables instanced cases can talk to the blueprint for a common connection between any new instances made from it.

### 5.5.2.1 A Basic Example

```
using UnityEngine;
using System.Collections;
public class Zombie : MonoBehaviour
{
    static int numZombies;
    //Use this for initialization
    void Start ()
    {
        numZombies++;
    }
}
```

Here, in a pretty simple-looking zombie class, we've got a `static` keyword placed before an `int` identified as `numZombies`. This statement turns `int numZombies`, which would normally be confined to this class alone, to an `int` that's shared among all zombies. As Unity 3D creates more zombies, each zombie has its `Start ()` function called once the class has been instanced: `numZombies` increments by 1.

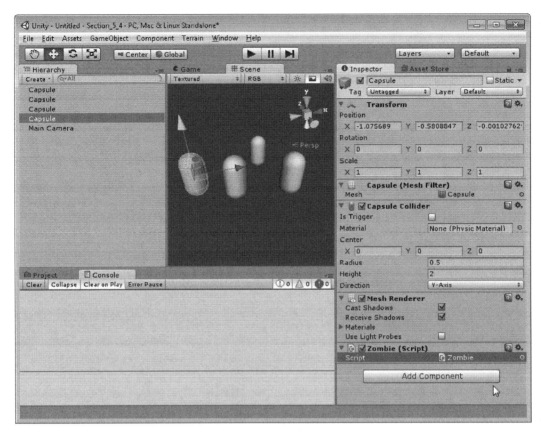

With the above code attached to a collection of four different capsules, we'll be better able to see how many zombies there are in the scene through code. Just be sure that each capsule has the zombie script attached.

```
void Start ()
{
    numZombies++;
    Debug.Log(numZombies);
}
```

The Debug.Log() function in each Zombie's Start () function prints out the numZombies int value. Each new instance of a Zombie increments the same numZombies variable.

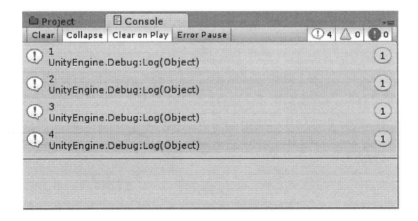

Based on how many zombies are around, you can change a zombie's behavior, making them more aggressive, perhaps. Maybe only after five zombies have been spawned, they'll join one another and perform a dance routine. Having a shared property makes keeping track of a similar variable much easier.

```
using UnityEngine;
using System.Collections;
public class Zombie : MonoBehaviour {
    int numZombies;//no longer static
    //Use this for initialization
    void Start () {
        numZombies++;
        Debug.Log(numZombies);
    }
}
```

When the same code is run without `static` before the numZombies variable, the following output is the result:

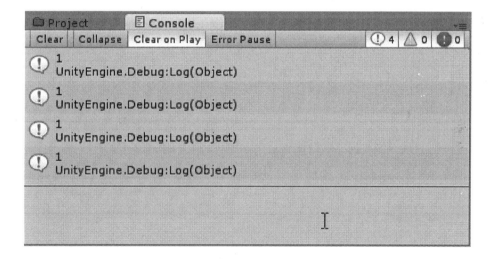

The numZombies value us independent to each instance of the zombie class. When each new Zombie instance is created it's numZombies int is initialized independently to 0. When the Start () function is called in each zombie instance the numZombies value is incremented independently from 0 to 1. Therefore when white, rob and stubbs call their own Start () function their own instance of the numZombies int is incremented, numZombies doesn't get incremented for all zombies because it's not static.

This is an interesting concept here. Up to this point, we've been thinking of classes as encapsulated independent entities. With the static keyword, there's a way to keep the separated objects connected to one another through a variable. This raises the question: Can this be done with functions?

### 5.5.3 Static Functions

Static functions act on behalf of all instances of the class they are a member of. They work only with static variables of the class. If we extend our zombie class with a new static function, we can use the zombie class to call a static function that can read static variables. To make the static function accessible to other classes we need to make the `static` function `public` as well.

```
using UnityEngine;
using System.Collections;
public class Zombie : MonoBehaviour
{
    static int numZombies;
    //int numZombies;//no longer static
    //Use this for initialization
    void Start ()
    {
        numZombies++;
        Debug.Log(numZombies);
    }
    //Logs number of zombies to the console
    public static void CountZombies()
    {
        Debug.Log(numZombies);
    }
}
```

Then we'll add a call to `Zombie.CountZombies();` to find out how many zombies have been created in the `Update ()` function of the Player class, by adding it to the `if(AKey)` code block.

```
using UnityEngine;
using System.Collections;
public class Player : MonoBehaviour
{
    //Use this for initialization
    void Start ()
    {
    }
    //Update is called once per frame
    void Update ()
    {
        //add in a check for the A key
        bool AKey = Input.GetKey(KeyCode.A);
        if (AKey)
        {
            Debug.Log("AKey");
            //calls the static function in Zombie
            Zombie.CountZombies();
        }
    }
}
```

Now when the A key on the keyboard is pressed, we'll get a count printed to the Console panel indicating the number of zombies in the scene along with the `Debug.Log("AKey");` console log.

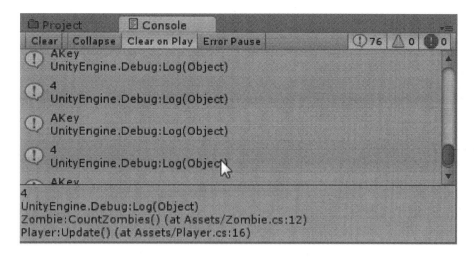

The 4 being printed out comes from the `public static void CountZombies();` function call being made to `Zombie`, not from any of the instances of the zombie class attached to the capsules in the scene.

To call static functions, you use the class name, not the name of an instanced object made from the zombie class. As you can see, there's more than one way the class identifier is used. Up to this point, we've been using the class name mostly as a way to create an instance of that class. With a static function or variable, the class identifier is used to access that static member of the class.

### 5.5.4 Putting It All Together

To complete our `Player` class we should add the rest of the key presses required to move. And add in a few places to store and use the position of the player.

```
public class Player : MonoBehaviour {
    //store the position of the player
    Vector3 pos;
    //Use this for initialization
    void Start () {
        //set the position to where we start off in the scene
        pos = transform.position;
    }
    //Update is called once per frame
    void Update () {
        bool WKey = Input.GetKey(KeyCode.W);
        bool SKey = Input.GetKey(KeyCode.S);
        bool AKey = Input.GetKey(KeyCode.A);
        bool DKey = Input.GetKey(KeyCode.D);
        if(WKey) {
            pos.z += 0.1f;
        }
```

```
        if(SKey) {
            pos.z -= 0.1f;
        }
        if(AKey) {
            pos.x -= 0.1f;
        }
        if(DKey) {
            pos.x += 0.1f;
        }
        gameObject.transform.position = pos;
    }
}
```

At the class level, we need to create a new `Vector3` variable to update each frame. Therefore, `Vector3 pos;` will store a new `Vector3`, using which we'll be able to update individual values. In the `Start ()` function of the player class, we'll want to set the initial value of pos to where the object starts in the scene. The value for that is stored in `transform.position;` this goes the same for almost any `GameObject` that Unity 3D has in a scene.

With the start of any task, we're in need of collecting and holding onto data. Therefore, in the `Zombie.cs` class, we're going to add in a few new variables.

```
    public static int numZombies;
    public bool die;
    public GameObject player;
    public float speed = 0.01f;
```

We're going to use `bool die` to destroy a zombie when he gets too close to the player. Perhaps the zombies are self-destructive zombies; we'll just go with a simple method to decrement the `numZombies` value for now. Then, we're going to need to keep track of the player with a `GameObject player` variable. Making the `bool die` public, we'll be able to test this from the editor.

To fill in the data that we created, we're going to need to use the `Start ()` function of zombie.

```
    void Start ()
    {
        player = GameObject.Find("Main Camera");
        numZombies++;
        Debug.Log(numZombies);
    }
```

So we're adding `player = GameObject.Find("Main Camera");` to use the `GameObject`'s static function called `Find()`. It's not important at the moment to know how or why this function works. We're more interested in how to use the player object, or rather the Main Camera in the scene.

Once we've added those lines, it's time to add some work to the `Update ()` function in the zombie class.

```
    void Update ()
    {
        Vector3 direction =
        (player.transform.position - transform.position).normalized;
        float distance =
        (player.transform.position - transform.position).magnitude;
    }
```

We're going to want to get a couple of bits of more information that need to be updated in each frame. First is `direction;` we get the `Vector3 direction` by subtracting the player's position from the zombie's position. This value is then `.normalized;` to give us a value constrained to a value which doesn't exceed a value of 1 in any direction.

After that, we need to get the distance from the zombie to the player. This is done by calculating the player's position minus the zombie's position; we then use `.magnitude;` to convert that `vector3` to a `float distance`. We'll go further into how these sorts of functions work later on.

After building up some data for the rest of the function we use, we can then set up some statements to take action.

```
Vector3 move =
transform.position + (direction * speed);
transform.position = move;
```

Next, we'll take `direction` and then multiply it by one of the variables we set up ahead of time. `float speed = 0.01f;` is being used to multiply `direction`, such that `move` is slowed down. Therefore, we create a new variable called `move`, then set the `transform.position` of the zombie to `transform.position + (direction * speed);`, which will move the zombie toward the player, slowly.

From there, we can then use the distance to check for when to make the zombie die.

```
if(distance < 1f)
{
        die = true;
}
```

We'll just make an arbitrary distance of `1f`. Therefore, if the distance is less than this number, we set `die` to `true;`, to complete the statement. When `die` was declared at the beginning of the class `public bool die;` it was automatically initialized to `false`. To be more clear, we could have used `public bool die = false;`, but it's unnecessary as new `bool` values are always initialized to `false` when they're created, unless dynamically initialized otherwise.

```
if(die)
{
    numZombies--;
    Destroy(gameObject);
}
```

Last, setting `if (die)` is `true`, we will then decrement `numZombies` by 1 using `numZombies--;`. This takes the previous value of `numZombies`, reduces it by 1, and then sets `numZombies` to the new value of `numZombies - 1`. After that, we use the `Destroy()` function to destroy the `gameObject` that the script is attached to.

The complete `Update ()` function in `Zombie.cs` should look like the following.

```
void Update ()
{
    Vector3 direction =
    (player.transform.position - transform.position).normalized;
    float distance =
    (player.transform.position - transform.position).magnitude;
    Vector3 move = transform.position + (direction * speed);
    transform.position = move;
    if (distance < 1f)
    {
        die = true;
    }
    if (die)
    {
        numZombies- ;
        Destroy(gameObject);
    }
}
```

This code creates a movement that pushes the capsule toward the Main Camera in the scene. To show that numZombies static is accessible to any new script in the scene, we'll create a new ZombieSpawner. cs file and drop it into the scene with a new cube object.

I've created a new cube by selecting GameObject → Create Other → Cube. After the cube is dropped into the scene, I moved it back to the center of the world by setting *x*, *y*, and *z* to 0 under the Transform component in the Inspector panel. After that, I added a new script to it called ZombieSpawner.cs.

In the new .cs file, I've added the following code to the Update () function.

```
void Update ()
{
        if (Zombie.numZombies < 4)
        {
                GameObject go =
                GameObject.CreatePrimitive(PrimitiveType.Capsule);
                go.AddComponent(typeof(Zombie));
                go.transform.position = transform.position;
        }
}
```

In the if(Zombie.numZombies < 4) statement, check the static numZombies value in the zombie class. This is a direct access to that value from ZombieSpawner.cs, which is possible only because the value is set to static, because of which we've got the ability to check its value from any other class.

When the value is less than 4, we follow the statement that tells the script to create a new GameObject go. This creates a new PrimitiveType.Capsule, which then has a Zombie component added to it.

When you click the play icon at the top to begin the game in the editor, we'll get the following behavior.

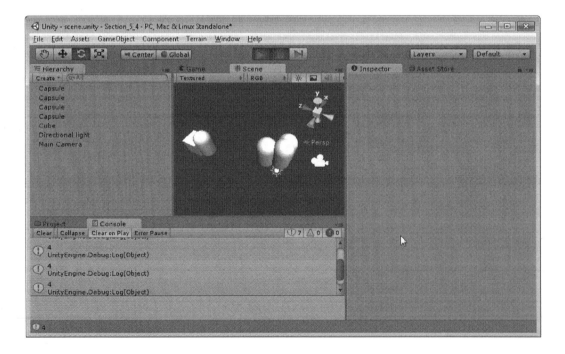

When you check out the Scene panel with the game running, you'll be able to watch the cylinders move toward the Main Camera object. When they get close enough, they pop out of existence. As soon as the capsule is gone, another one is spawned at the cube object.

### 5.5.5 What We've Learned

Using static functions certainly layers on quite a distinctive level of complexity on an already complex understanding of what a class is. Not only do classes have functions talking to one another, they also have the ability to share information. It's important to know that you can have classes without any static variables or functions at all.

You should use a static variable only if all of the classes of the same type need to share a common parameter. This goes the same for a static function. We'll go further into how static functions can help in Section 6.11, when we get back to some of the more complex behaviors, but for now, we'll leave off here.

Moving forward, we'll want to keep in mind that C# has static variables and functions for a specific reason. There are efficiency and optimization considerations to keep in mind as well. For instance, the player's `transform.position` is the same for each zombie. Each zombie doesn't need to have its own instance variable for the `player`. We could have easily converted the `Vector3 pos;` in the player class to a `static` value.

```
public static Vector3 pos;
```

The `static Vector3 pos;` variable could then be used by the zombies in the following manner.

```
Vector3 direction = (Player.pos - transform.position).normalized;
float distance = (Player.pos - transform.position).magnitude;
```

This certainly works, and it might be considered easier to read. This would even make the `GameObject player;` obsolete since `Player.pos` is a static value, and you don't need to use `GameObject.Find()` to begin with. This type of optimization should be thought of as you look at your code and discover new ways to make it more efficient and easier to read.

## 5.6 Turning Ideas into Code—Part 2

We've gotten pretty far. At this point, we're about ready for some everyday C# programming uses. To get to the point, beyond the lessons here, we're already capable of putting all of the lessons we've learned to this point to get the beginnings of a simple game going.

To start with, I've added a plane, a directional light, and some cubes to my scene found in the FPSControl project. Each object was positioned using the editor so that the Main Camera has something to look at. The objects were added using the `GameObject` menu.

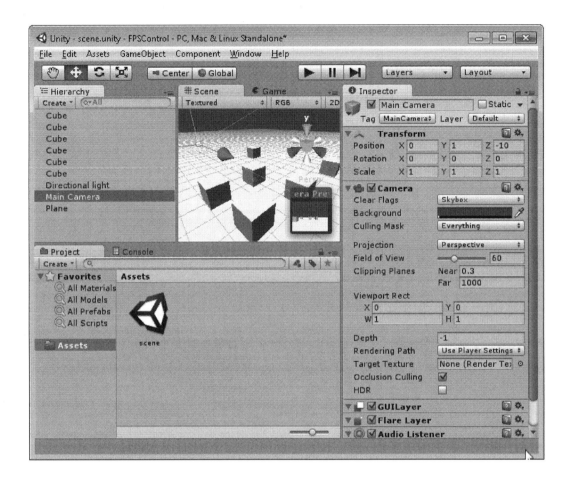

This gives us a basic scene to get started with. To build the very basics of a first-person camera controller for the Main Camera, we'll start off by adding a `FPSAim.cs` to the Main Camera object. I like using the Add Component button in the Inspector panel.

This will get us a new C# script to get started with. To move the camera, we'll want to get a feel for the sorts of data we'll be using to make the camera move around. First, we'll want to check out what data the Input class will give us. Starting off with `Input.mousePosition`, we can see that we'll want a `Vector3`. Input has many static variables and functions we can use; we'll look at the other available variables and functions in a moment.

```
// Update is called once per frame
void Update()
{
    Vector3 mousePosition = Input.mousePosition;
}
                    public static Vector3 mousePosition { get; }
```

Therefore, a `Vector3 mousePosition` will be useful here. However, a mouse is a 2D device, so what does the data coming out of the mouse look like?

```
void Update ()
{
    Vector3 mousePosition = Input.mousePosition;
    Debug.Log(mousePosition);
}
```

Add in a `Debug.Log()` for the `mousePosition` that we have assigned to the `Input.mousePosition`. Remember that the variable `mousePosition` we're assigning to the `Input.mousePosition` and the latter need to have matching types. With this `Debug.Log()` running, we get many numbers streaming out on the x and the y, with no z values coming in other than 0.0. This is pretty much what I'd expect; my mouse doesn't have any way to detect how far from the mouse pad the mouse is, so I wouldn't expect any numbers from the z value. Therefore, it's time to isolate the data into a more simple-to-use variable.

```
void Update ()
{
    Vector3 mousePosition = Input.mousePosition;
    float mouseX = mousePosition.x;
    float mouseY = mousePosition.y;
}
```

Therefore, now, I've boiled down the incoming `mousePosition` to a new `mouseX` and a `mouseY` so that I can more easily deal with each axis on its own. Now, we should look at the local rotation of the camera.

```
Debug.Log(transform.localRotation);
```

This gives us an interesting output. Thanks to our working within a game editor, we can fiddle with the camera in the game. Click the play icon and we'll switch over to the Game view. In the Inspector panel, we can play with the different values in the Transform component of the camera.

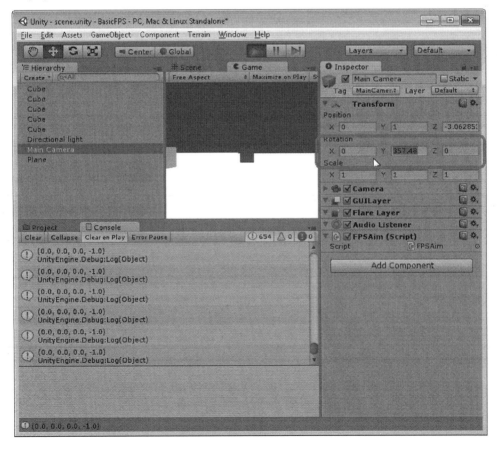

When we drag the `Rotation Y` value, we see the numbers streaming out of the Console panel. The rotations of an object are stored as a quaternion rotation value. Quaternions are special types of vectors that have four values. These values are used to both rotate and orient an object. With an xyz rotation, you're left with an ambiguous upward direction. Without going too deep into quaternion mathematics and topics like the gimbal lock, we'll digress and get back to using Euler rotations, something much easier to deal with.

Thankfully, Unity 3D programmers know that not everyone understands quaternions so well.

```
Debug.Log(transform.eulerAngles);
```

There's a `transform.eulerAngles` value that we can read instead of quaternions. From this data, we get numbers that reflect the values, which we see in the Transform component in the Inspector panel. Putting the mouse together with the `transform.eulerAngles` of the camera, we're able to aim the camera. However, first, how can we effect the camera's rotation using `eulerAngles`?

```
transform.eulerAngles = new Vector3(30,0,0);
```

To test the above function, we'll make a simple statement to set the `transform.eulerAngles` to a new `Vector3(30, 0, 0);` to see if this has the desired effect.

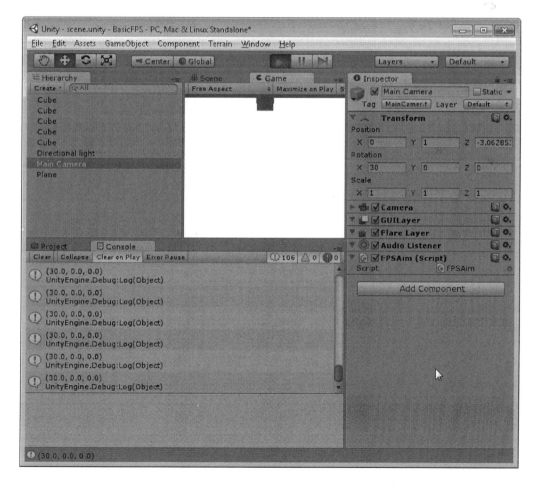

Running again tells us that yes we can aim the camera up and down using this number. We could simply map the `mouseY` to the `eulerAngle X` and see what this does.

```
transform.eulerAngles = new Vector3(mouseY,0,0);
```

However, this makes the camera move up and down a lot more than what we might want. We could reduce the amount of movement the `mouseY` has by multiplying it by a small value.

```
transform.eulerAngles = new Vector3(mouseY * 0.1f,0,0);
```

However, this doesn't have the right effect either. With this, we're limited by the size of our monitor. When the mouse gets to the top of the monitor, we're stuck and can't look up or down any further than our monitor lets us. Perhaps we've got the wrong data!

### 5.6.1 Input Manager

Where is Input coming in from anyway?

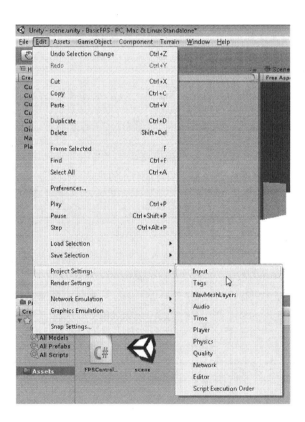

Hunting around in the Unity 3D editor, we find the Input manager at following menu path: Edit → Project Settings → Input; with this selected, we get an update in the Inspector panel. This shows us some interesting bits of information.

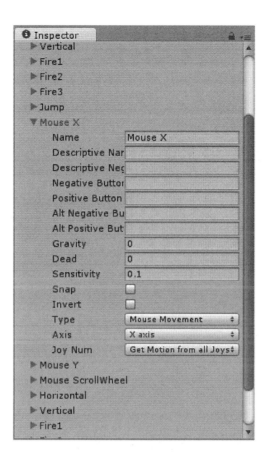

Hey, it's a `Mouse X`, as well as several other types of input. Perhaps we should be looking at this for our Input data. Therefore, before we get too far, it should be clear that most of this is findable with a few short web searches for Unity 3D Input manager queries. We find in the Unity 3D manual an example showing us how to use `Input.GetAxis("Mouse X")`,, so we should start there.

```
void Update ()
{
        float mouseX = Input.GetAxis("Mouse X");
        Debug.Log(mouseX);
        transform.eulerAngles = new Vector3(0, mouseX, 0);
}
```

If we try to use the code as is, we'll get some sort of jittery movement in the camera as we move the mouse left and right. Looking at the Console panel gives us an interesting set of numbers coming out of the `mouseX` variable.

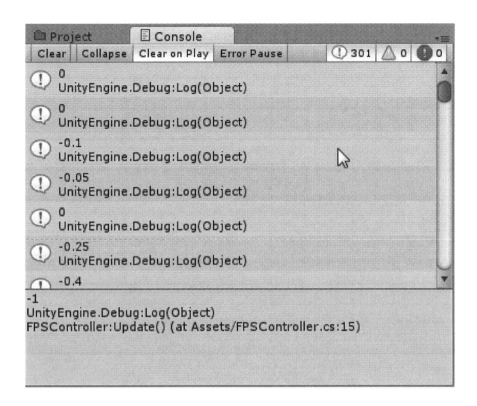

We see a fluctuation between 0 and −0.1 or more when moving in one direction and positive values when moving in the other. Perhaps this means that we should be adding the number to the rotation of the camera rather than trying to use it as a set value. To make this change, we'll keep the mouseX value around beyond the scope of the Update () function.

```
float mouseX;
void Update () {
        mouseX += Input.GetAxis("Mouse X");
        Debug.Log(mouseX);
        transform.eulerAngles = new Vector3(0, mouseX,0);
}
```

This means we'll have a class variable that hangs around and isn't reset every time the Update () function is called. Then we change the mouseX = Input to mouseX + = Input.GetAxis("Mouse X");, which will add the value of the Mouse X input to mouseX.

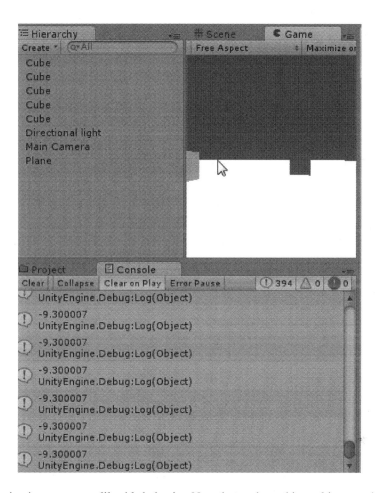

Testing this again gives us a more likeable behavior. Now that we have this working, we should make the same setup for mouseY.

```
float mouseX;
float mouseY;
void Update ()
{
        mouseX + = Input.GetAxis("Mouse X");
        mouseY + = Input.GetAxis("Mouse Y");
        transform.eulerAngles = new Vector3(mouseY, mouseX, 0);
}
```

So far so good. However, now we have up and down inverted. If you're cool with this, then there's no problem, but universally, there's bound to be a preference one way or the other. To avoid this, its best you add in an option for the player to pick using an inverted mouse or not.

```
float mouseX;
float mouseY;
public bool InvertedMouse;
void Update ()
{
     mouseX + = Input.GetAxis("Mouse X");
     if (InvertedMouse)
     {
          mouseY + = Input.GetAxis("Mouse Y");
     } else
     {
          mouseY - = Input.GetAxis("Mouse Y");
     }
     Debug.Log(mouseX);
     transform.eulerAngles = new Vector3(mouseY, mouseX, 0);
}
```

Let's add in an option to allow the user to invert the "Mouse Y" movement. We're still in need of some sort of movement that can be controlled with the keyboard. However, we should get used to the idea of separating our code into different classes, so we'll create a new class just for taking in input from the keyboard.

Using a preferred method, I've added in a new C# class called `FPSMove.cs` to the Main Camera. Within `FPSMove.cs`, we can check for an `Input.GetKey()` to check for any desired keyboard input.

```
void Update ()
{
    if(Input.GetKey(KeyCode.W))
    {
        transform.position + = transform.forward;
    }
}
```

We'll use this to add to our `transform.position` a `transform.forward`, but wow, we are moving fast! We should fix this with some sort of `speed` multiplier.

```
public float speed;
void Update ()
{
    if(Input.GetKey(KeyCode.W))
    {
        transform.position + = transform.forward * speed;
    }
}
```

By making the `speed` variable public, we can play with the value in the editor.

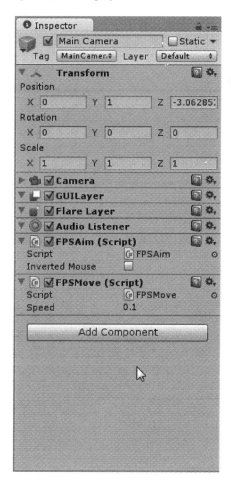

This code will allow us to slowdown the movement to a more controllable rate. With a bit of fiddling, we can get to the final FPSMove.cs code in the Update () function.

```
public float speed = 0.1f;
void Update ()
{
      if (Input.GetKey(KeyCode.W))
      {
            transform.position + = transform.forward * speed;
      }
      if (Input.GetKey(KeyCode.S))
      {
            transform.position - = transform.forward * speed;
      }
      if (Input.GetKey(KeyCode.A))
      {
            transform.position - = transform.right * speed;
      }
      if (Input.GetKey(KeyCode.D))
      {
            transform.position + = transform.right * speed;
      }
}
```

We've taken the transform.forward and used - = to move backward and + = to move forward. Likewise, since there's no transform.left, we need to use transform.right. Then, use transform. position - = to move left and + = to move to the right.

Therefore, where did transform.forward and transform.right come from? If we look at the transform.forward static value in Transform, we can go to the forward declaration.

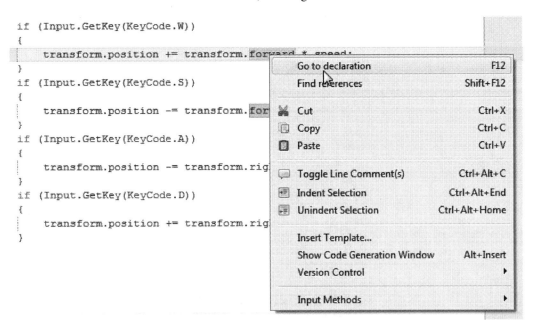

From here, we'll be taken to the Assembly Browser. This works for transform.rotation as well.

We'll notice that there's also a `right` and an `up`. Many other static values are found here. It's important to learn how Unity 3D has organized the data in each class such that we can make use of them. Remember, this is a game engine, and as such we have access to many of the commonly required forms of data that game designers need. This data structure is an example of useful data, common only in well-written game engines.

Therefore, now we have the beginnings of a fairly useful pair of C# files that we can attach to any object in a scene. However, first, we should limit the camera from going through the ground. If we add a `Rigidbody` and a `Capsule Collider` to the Main Camera, the object will collide with the ground and anything else with a physics collider.

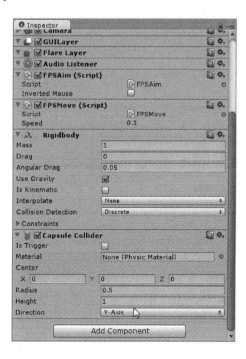

Physics colliders are complex data structures that solidify objects in a game. We can use these structures to make objects feel and act heavy. You might notice that with our new setup, we're sliding around a little bit like we're walking around on ice. This is because our `Rigidbody` has a Drag of 0 by default. Changing this to 1 will keep the camera from sliding around so much.

At this point, we've got a pretty usable beginning to a first-person camera. We can keep adding in new variables to make this more sophisticated, but for now, we'll leave off here. I'll leave the cool stuff up to you. Perhaps a `speed` variable on the `FPSAim` would be called for to make the mouse aim quicker.

### 5.6.2 What We've Learned

The process of writing code often takes a bit of getting used to. This exercise involves a great deal of looking at and testing various sources for data and trying to find results that we can use. By setting up and testing `Debug.Log()`, we can check to see if the data we want is going to be the data we can use.

Before we get too far, it's important to search the Internet for solutions that others have come up with. From their code, we can extract some ideas we can use for our own purposes. Even something as simple as finding the name of a function can help us test and try out a function to see if it's something we can use.

The process might be repetitive, but it's a lot like drawing or painting on a canvas. The first line drawn is usually covered by iterative layers of paint covering one idea with another. One concept to come away with here is the fact that we separated the mouse aim from the keyboard movement. Why was this done, and is it the best way to write C# in general?

There are always going to be arguments for writing a single large set of code versus many smaller more modular pieces of code. One argument for smaller files is the fact that each one can stand on its own. This means you can try out different forms of aim controls and mix them with the keyboard controls without having to rewrite the keyboard control.

However, should you need to have the two interact with one another, you might need to find more clever ways to have separate objects communicate with one another. In this case, a single file is more straightforward. However, there are simple ways for objects to talk to one another.

This also means you can add in a new script for, say, `FPSPrimaryWeapon.cs` that handles the left mouse button. Perhaps an `FPSJump.cs` and maybe even a `FPSSecondaryWeapon.cs` can be added. This means that as you add in new functions, you add in new CS files. As you come up with new versions of each function, you can handle the updates and changes without having to make changes to the other files—make your code modular.

## 5.7 Jump Statements

Suppose you're in the process of looking for a specific color of crayon in a large assortment of art tools. After grabbing handfuls of different pencils and pens, you find the crayon you want and stop looking through the rest of your bin. You've just used a jump statement, and returned to your work with the colored crayon of your desire.

The keywords `break` and `continue` come in particularly handy when sorting through a list of objects. Like `return`, these keywords stop the function from further execution or they jump to a different part of the same function. `return` has the additional feature of coming out of a function with a value. We have looked at these keywords briefly before, but it's important to get a better understanding of `break`, `continue`, and `return` in use.

`continue` in particular restarts a loop from the top and then continues the function again, whereas `break` stops the block of code it's in altogether.

### 5.7.1 Return

We need to love the `return` keyword. This keyword turns a function into data. There are a couple of conditions that need to be met before this will work. So far, we've been using the keyword `void` to declare the return type of a function. This looks like the following code fragment.

```
void MyFunction()
{
        //code here...
}
```

In this case, using `return` will be pretty simple.

```
void MyFunction()
{
        //code here...
        return;
}
```

This function returns `void`. This statement has a deeper meaning. Returning a value makes a lot more sense when a real value, something other than a void, is actually returned. Let's take a look at a function that has more meaning.

The keyword `void` at the beginning of the function declaration means that this function does not have a return type. If we change the declaration, we need to ensure that there is a returned value that matches the declaration. This can be as simple as the following code fragment.

```
int MyFunction()
{
        //code here...
        return 1;//1 is an int
}
```

This function returns `int 1`. Declaring a function with a `return` value requires that the `return` type and the declaration match. When the function is used, it should be treated like a data type that matches the function's return type.

#### 5.7.1.1 A Basic Example

Here is a quick review class that has a function declared as `int MyNumber()`in the `Start ()` function.

```
using UnityEngine;
using System.Collections;
public class Example : MonoBehaviour {
        int MyNumber() {
                return 7;
        }
        //Use this for initialization
        void Start () {
                int a = MyNumber();
                print (a);
        }
        //Update is called once per frame
        void Update () {
        }
}
```

When this code block is attached to the Main Camera in the scene, 7 is printed to the Console panel. The function `MyNumber()` returned 7 when it was called. When we add some parameters to the function, we can make the `return` statement much more useful.

```
int MyAdd(int a, int b) {
      return a + b;
}
//Use this for initialization
void Start () {
      int a = MyAdd(6, 7);
      print (a);
}
```

In this fragment, we have `int MyAdd(int a, int b)`, which we then assign to `int a` in the `Start ()` function. This prints 13 to the console when run. We can skip a step to make the code a bit shorter.

```
void Start () {
      print (MyAdd(6, 7));
}
```

This code produces the same 13 being printed to the Console panel and should make it clear that the function can easily be used as a value.

## 5.7.2  Returning Objects

We can get something more interesting out of a function once it begins to return something more substantial than a simple number—this would be a better way to use `return`. Therefore, in the case of getting a zombie from a function, we'd want to define a zombie first.

As a simple example, select GameObject → Create Other → Capsule to drop a simple capsule in the scene.

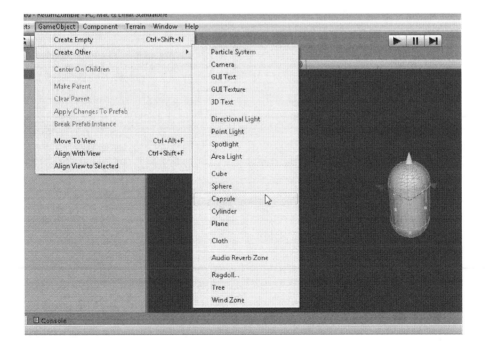

From here, we're going to want to add a script component to the cylinder. In the Inspector, select Add Component → New Script, and then enter `Zombie`, to name the new script and make sure the type is set to `CSharp`. This will represent what will eventually turn into zombie behavior. Of course, the work of writing proper artificial intelligence for zombies is something that will have to wait till after this exercise. This creates a new `Zombie.cs` class, which is now a component of the capsule `GameObject` in the scene.

Open the JumpStatements project and open the scene found in the Assets Directory in the Projects panel. On the Main Camera, attach a new script called `ReturnZombie`, which will serve as the example for testing a function that will give us the zombie in the scene. In the `ReturnZombie` script, we'll add a function that returns a `Zombie`.

```
using UnityEngine;
using System.Collections;
public class ReturnZombie : MonoBehaviour
{
        //Use this for initialization
        void Start ()
        {
        }
        //Update is called once per frame
        void Update ()
        {
        }
        //returns a zombie
        Zombie GetZombie()
        {
                return (Zombie)GameObject.FindObjectOfType(typeof(Zombie));
        }
}
```

### 5.7.3 A Class Is a Type

Our function that returns a `Zombie`, is at the end of our Unity 3D C# default template. We've called our function `GetZombie()`, and we're using a simple function provided in `GameObject` called `FindObjectOfType();`, which requires a *type* to return. The different classes we create become a new type. Much as an int is a type, a `Zombie` is now a type based on the fact that we created a new class called `Zombie`. This goes the same for every class we've created, which are all types.

To inform the `FindObjectOfType()` function of the type, we use the function `typeof(Zombie)`, which tells the function that we're looking for a type `Zombie`, not an actual zombie. There's a subtle difference between telling someone we'd like a thing that is a kind of zombie, not a specific zombie. We'll get into the specifics of types in Section 6.5.3 that focuses on dealing with types, but we're more interested in `return` at the moment, so we'll get back to that.

After making sure that we're getting a `Zombie` from the function, we use `return` in the function to fulfill the `Zombie GetZombie()` return type. We're not using `void` since our `return` actually has something to return. Using this becomes quite interesting if we add a use to the function. In the `ReturnZombie Update ()` function, add in the code to draw a debug line from the camera to the function.

```
        //Update is called once per frame
        void Update ()
        {
                Debug.DrawLine(transform.position,
                GetZombie().transform.position);
        }
```

`Debug.DrawLine()` starts at one position and goes to another position. The second position is a function's `transform.position`. If you look into the Scene panel, you'll see a white line being drawn between the camera and the capsule with the `Zombie` component added to it.

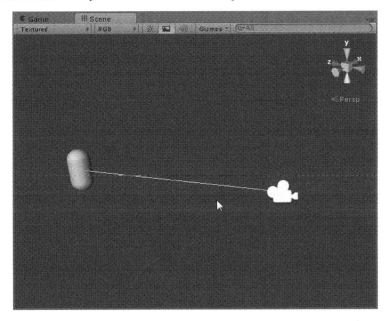

This remarkably means that the `GetZombie().transform.position` is returning the value as though the function is the `Zombie` itself, which has some interesting consequences. Having classes, or rather objects, communicate between one another is a particularly important feature of any programming language. Accessing members of another class through a function is just one way our objects can talk to one another.

This reliance on the function breaks if there are no zombies in the scene. If we were to deactivate the capsule by checking it off in the Inspector panel, we'd effectively remove the capsule from existence.

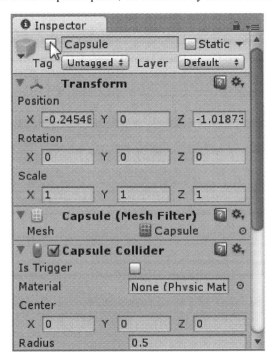

Unchecking here while the game is running will immediately bring up an error.

```
NullReferenceException: Object reference not set to an instance of an object
ReturnZombie.Update () (at Assets/ReturnZombie.cs:12)
```

A `NullReference` is caused when the return type of the function has nothing to return. Errors aren't good for performance and we should handle the problem more effectively. We need to make our use of the function more robust.

```
void Update ()
{
    Zombie target = GetZombie();
    if (target != null)
    {
        Debug.DrawLine(transform.position,
        target.transform.position);
    }
}
```

If we add in a check to see if `Zombie` is null, we'll be able to avoid giving the `Debug.DrawLine()` function nonexistent data. Therefore, we create a local variable to the function. Add in `Zombie target = GetZombie();` and now we have a variable that can be either null or a zombie.

### 5.7.4 Null Is Not Void

There is conceptual difference between void, which is *nothing*, and null, which is more like *not something*. The word *void* means there is no intention of anything to be presented, whereas *null* implies that there can be something. We may add `if(target != null)` and can say that `target` can be empty or it can be `Zombie`. When target isn't a `zombie`, `target` is null; when it is there, it's `Zombie`.

We may add `if(target != null)`—in more readable English, "if the target is not null"—and then conditionally execute the following code block. In the case where we have a target, we can draw a line from the camera's `transform.position` to the target's `transform.position`. This code alleviates the error, and thus we don't have to worry about sending `Draw.DebugLine` an error-inducing null reference.

### 5.7.5 What We've Learned

Functions that return class objects are quite useful. All of the properties that are associated with the class are accessible through the function that returns it. There are various jump statements that have different results.

The `return` statement has a clear purpose when it comes to jumping out of a function. Not all `return` jump statements need to be followed by a value. If the function is declared as `void MyFunction()`, the `return` statement only needs to be `return;` without any value following it.

We'll cover more jump statements in a following chapter.

## 5.8 Operators and Conditions

Conditional operators allow you to ask if more than one case is true in an `if` statement. If you decided to go for a swim on a cold day on the sky being clear, then you might end up freezing. Your *jump in a pool* `if` statement should include temperature in addition to the sky.

## 5.8.1 Conditional Operators && and ||

The `if` statement in pseudocode might look something like the following: If (temperature is hot and sky is clear) {go swimming}. To translate that into something more C# like, you might end up with the following.

```
void Start ()
{
    float temp = 90f;
    bool sunny = true;
    if (temp > 60 && sunny)
    {
        print("time to go swimming!");
    }
}
```

If the temperature is above 60 and it's sunny, then it's time to go swimming. Zombies might not have that sort of thought process, but your player might. Silly code examples aside, the `&&` operator is used to join together multiple conditions in the `if` statement shown. This operator is in a family of symbols called conditional operators, and this particular operator is the *and* operator.

### 5.8.1.1 A Basic Example

To get a better understanding how this operator works, we'll break things down into a simplified example. To follow along, start with the Conditional project and open the scene from the Assets Directory. We could start with two different `if` statements. This means we have to use more curly braces and lines of code to complete a fairly simple task.

```
//Use this for initialization
void Start ()
{
    if (true)
    {
        if (true)
        {
            print("this could be more simple.");
        }
    }
}
```

Using more than one `if` statement should look a bit clumsy. The reason for using conditional operators is to simplify the number of `if` statements you can use in a single line. Rather than spreading out various test conditions across multiple `if` statements, you can reduce the `if` statement into a smaller more clear statement.

```
void Start ()
{
    if (true && true)
    {
        print("both sides of the && are true");
    }
}
```

Inside of the `if` statement are two different boolean cases. Only if both sides of the *and* conditional operator are true will the `if` statement will execute. If either side is false, then the `if` statement will not be evaluated.

```
void Start ()
{
    if (false && true)
    {
        print("I won't print...");
    }
}
```

The above statement has one false statement and will not be evaluated. All of the conditions in the `if` statement's arguments need to be true for the encapsulated instructions to execute. This logic can be further extended with more than one conditional operator.

```
void Start ()
{
    if (true && true && true)
    {
        print("I will print!");
    }
    if (true && true && true && true && true && true && false)
    {
        print("I won't print!");//one false at the end blew it
    }
}
```

Of course, there are no limits to how many arguments will be accepted in a single `if` statement. This absence of limit allows for more complex decision making, but we can make things even more interesting by adding in the other conditional operator *or*.

```
void Start ()
{
    if (true || false)
    {
        print("I will print!");
    }
}
```

The `||`, or double bar, is used to indicate the conditional *or* that is used to evaluate an `if` statement if either boolean is true. The only case where the *or* will not allow the `if` statement to evaluate is when both sides are false.

```
void Start ()
{
    if (false || false)
    {
        print("I won't print!");
    }
    if (false || false || true)
    {
        print("I will print!");
    }
    if (false || false || false || false || false || false || true)
    {
        print("I will print!");//just needs one true to work!
    }
}
```

When both sides of the or operator are false, then the contents of the `if` statement will not be evaluated. If there are more than two statements, any one of the statements being true will execute the contained instructions. The and operator and the or operator can work together, but the logic may get muddy.

```
void Start ()
{
    if (false || true && true)
    {
        print("I will print!");
    }
}
```

It's hard to immediately guess what might happen when you first look at the code. To make things more clear, we can use parentheses in pairs in the `if` statement, like we did with numbers earlier.

```
void Start ()
{
    if ((false || true) && true)
    {
        print("I will print!");
    }
}
```

Evaluating this `if` statement works in a way similar to how math works. The (`false || true`) is evaluated to result in `true`. As long as there is at least one `true`, the `||`, or *or*, returns `true`. This then turns into [`true`] `&& true` being evaluated for the `&&` and the conditional operator. This means that since both sides of the `&&`, or and, operator are true, the `if` statement will evaluate the code between the two curly braces.

Conditional operators are usually used when comparing numbers. Let's take a very contrived scenario, where we have an `enemyHealth` and `myHealth`.

```
void Start ()
{
    int enemyHealth = 10;
    int myHealth = 1;
    bool ImStronger = MyHealth > EnemyHealth;
    if (ImStronger)
    {
        print("I can win!");
    }
}
```

With the code above, the relational operator tells us we are clearly at a disadvantage. However, we can add some additional information to make a better-informed decision.

```
void Start ()
{
    int enemyHealth = 10;
    int myHealth = 1;
    bool imStronger = myHealth > enemyHealth;
    int enemyBullets = 0;
    int myBullets = 11;
    bool imArmed = myBullets > enemyBullets;
    if (imStronger || imArmed)
    {
        print("I can win!");
    }
}
```

If we are better armed than our enemy, then we should have a better chance at winning. Therefore, in this case, if imStronger or imArmed then it's possible "I can win!". There's just a simple mental leap to read "||" as "or" as well as "&&" as "and."

### 5.8.2 What We've Learned

Conditional operators are the controls used for executing your instructions. It's often easier to break out the logic into different parts before using them. For instance, consider the following conditions when looking at some vectors. If we're going to execute a set of instructions only when a target object is above the player, we could create a simple boolean ahead of time for use later on.

```
void Update ()
{
        bool isAbove = target.transform.position.y > transform.position.y;
}
```

The bool isAbove will be true when our target object is higher than the transform.position of the class we're working in. Then we might add the following code to check if the target is in front of our position (bool isInFront).

```
void Update ()
{
        bool isAbove = target.transform.position.y > transform.position.y;
        bool isInFront = target.transform.position.z > transform.position.z;
}
```

We're simplifying this, so that we're assuming anything with a greater z is in front of the object we're working in. Either way, we've got two nicely named booleans that offer us something we can then use to set another boolean called isInFrontAndAbove.

```
void Update ()
{
        bool isAbove = target.transform.position.y > transform.position.y;
        bool isInFront = target.transform.position.z > transform.position.z;
        bool isInfrontAndAbove = isAbove && isInfront;
}
```

With this one boolean, we can then use a third parameter to check if our target is to the left or right of our object. We can set both with one check.

```
void Update ()
{
        bool isAbove = target.transform.position.y > transform.position.y;
        bool isInFront = target.transform.position.z > transform.position.z;
        bool isInfrontAndAbove = isAbove && isInfront;
        bool isLeft = target.transform.position.x < transform.position.x;
        bool isInFrontAndAboveAndLeft = isInfrontAndAbove && isLeft;
        bool isInFrontAndAboveAndRight = isInfrontAndAbove && !isLeft;
}
```

We can use the !, or not, in our conditionals as well. The last bool that checks for isInfrontAndAbove, also checks for *is not left*, which means that the object must be *in front* and *above* but not *left*. This leaves the only other possibility, which is that the target must be to the right.

Getting all of the logic straight is much harder when we try to bunch all of the possibilities into a single `if` statement. For example, for the `isInFrontAndAboveAndRight` boolean, we might end up with a statement a bit like the following:

```
void Update ()
{
        bool isInFrontAndAboveAndRight = (target.transform.position.y >
transform.position.y && target.transform.position.z > transform.position.z &&
! target.transform.position.x < transform.position.x);
}
```

A single statement so long might be considered poor form. Though there are other ways to make this easier, it's best to keep things short and readable.

## 5.9 Arrays: A First Look

Arrays are nicely organized lists of data. Think of a numbered list that starts at zero and extends one line every time you add something to the list. Arrays are useful for any number of situations because they're treated as a single hunk of data.

For instance, if you wanted to store a bunch of high scores, you'd want to do that with an array. Initially, you might want to have a list of 10 items. You could in theory use the following code to store each score.

```
int score1;
int score2;
int score3;
int score4;
int score5;
int score6;
int score7;
int score8;
int score9;
int score10;
```

To make matters worse, if you needed to process each value, you'd need to create a set of code that deals with each variable by name. To check if `score2` is higher than `score1`, you'd need to write a function specifically to check those two variables before switching them. Thank goodness for arrays.

### 5.9.1 Fixed-Sized Arrays

An array can be initialized as a fixed-sized array, or an array can be created to be a resizable; we'll get to these types of arrays in Section 5.12. A fixed-sized array is easier to create, so we'll cover that first. Dynamic arrays require a more interesting step, where an array object is instantiated before it's used.

Arrays are a fundamental part of computer programming, in general. Without arrays, computers wouldn't be able to do what they're best at: repeating a simple task quickly and consistently. We'll be covering a few different types of arrays in the next few Sections 5.11 and 5.12, and we'll be starting with the simplest type of array: the fixed-sized array.

#### 5.9.1.1 A Basic Example

Let's start with the Arrays project and open the scene. The concept is simple in theory, but it's so much easier to see what's going on if you use the following code and check out what's going on in the Unity 3D

Inspector panel. Attach this script to the Main Camera in an empty scene, and then take a look at what shows up.

```
using UnityEngine;
using System.Collections;
public class ArraysAFirstLook : MonoBehaviour
{
        public int[] scores = new int[10];
}
```

The inclusion of the square brackets tells the compiler you're creating an array of ints and naming it `scores`. Because we're working with a built-in type of an int, each value stored in the array is initialized to 0. A new `int[]` array needs to be created before it's assigned to the `scores` array.

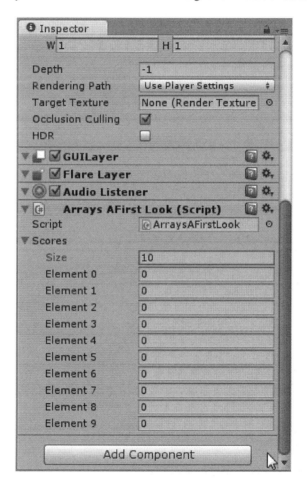

The best part is that the `scores` array is handled as a single object; we'll get into what that means in a moment. Rather than write a function to process one number value at a time we can write a function to deal with the array and process all of the number values at once. We'll take a look at a simple sorting method in Section 7.9.4.

Assigning scores to `int[10]` creates an array with 10 items. As you might imagine, you can make larger or smaller arrays by changing the number in the square brackets. There aren't any limitations to the size you can assign to an array. Some common sense should apply, however; an array with many trillions of values might not be so useful.

Each chunk of data in the array is located by what is called an *index*. The index number is an integer value since it's not useful to ask for a value between the first and second entry in the array. Arrays can be created from something other than ints as well.

```
public string[] strings = new string[10];
public float[] floats = new float[10];
```

Both these statements create valid types of arrays. You are also allowed to create new data types and make arrays of those as well. An n array can be created for any type, not just numbers and strings. This isn't necessarily a requirement. We can use any valid identifier to use for an array.

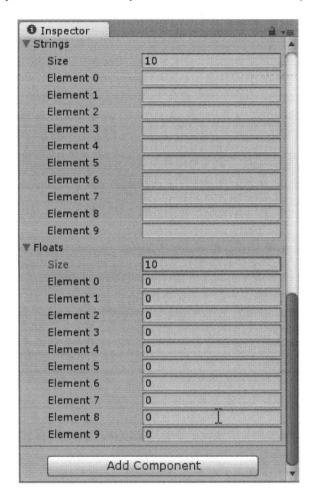

It's important to notice the difference between types. Floats, ints, and numbers in general will have 0 as the default value in the array when they are created. Strings, on the other hand, are initialized with nothing in the array; they are *null*, or, rather, they have no value assigned. You'll need to remember that an array can contain only a single type across all of its entries. Therefore, an array of strings can contain only strings, an array of ints can contain only ints, and so on.

```
public string[] TopScoreList = new string[10];
```

The convention of using a plural does make for a more easily read variable name, but by no means is it necessary for identifying an array. Again, it's up to you to come up with readable variable names, and it's nice to use plurals for identifying an array.

```
public class MyClass
{
}
public MyClass[] MyClasses = new MyClass[10];
```

This creates a new class called `MyClass`, which for this example is a class of nothing. It's important that both sides of the `MyClasses` statement match. In the example above an array was created for the `MyClass` type. Unfortunately, because Unity 3D isn't aware of what to do with MyClass, the array doesn't show up in the Inspector panel. Later on, we'll figure out some ways to make this sort of information show up in Unity 3D.

What makes an array in Unity 3D more interesting is when we do not assign a number to set the size of the array. We can add the following statement to the list of other variables we've already added.

```
public GameObject[] MyGameObjects;
```

If we simply leave an array unassigned, we're free to set the size afterward. Select the Main Camera and click on the lock icon at the top right of the Inspector panel. This will prevent the Inspector from changing when you select something else in the scene. Then, select the other objects in the scene and drag them down to the `MyGameObjects` variable in the Inspector.

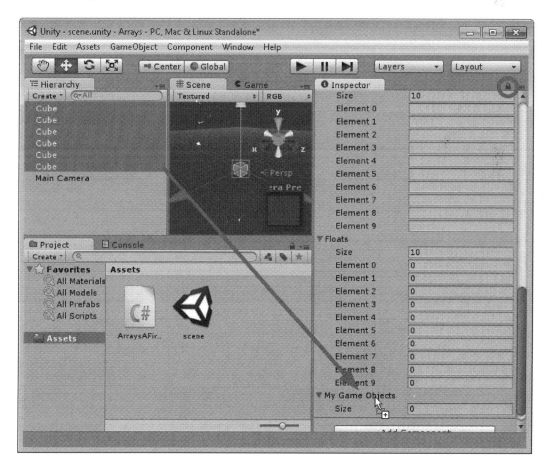

This action sets the size of the array once objects have been dragged into the array. However, this doesn't mean that the code is aware of the size of the array. The size of an array cannot easily be changed once it's been created. Therefore, how do we know how many objects are in an array? This can be accessed by the `.Length` property of the array type.

In the `Start ()` function, we can use the following statement:

```
void Start ()
{
    Debug.Log(MyGameObjects.Length);
}
```

Click the play icon and observe the Console panel. The `Debug.Log` command will print out how many objects had been dragged into the array.

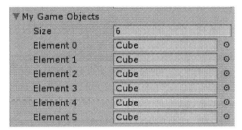

The number should reflect what is being observed in the Inspector panel, where we dragged objects into the array.

```
6
UnityEngine.Debug:Log(Object)
ArraysAFirstLook:Start () (at Assets/ArraysAFirstLook.cs:16)
```

So far so good, but how do we use this? Now that we have an array of game objects from the scene, we're able to manipulate them in a `for` loop.

```
void Start ()
{
    Debug.Log(MyGameObjects.Length);
    for (int i = 0; i < MyGameObjects.Length; i++)
    {
        MyGameObjects [i].name = i.ToString();
    }
}
```

This code changes the names of the game objects in the array to a number. The property of the array `.Length` returns an integer value which we can use for a few different reasons, the most practical use being to set the number of iterations in a `for` loop.

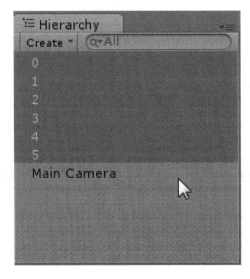

## 5.9.2 Foreach

This loop also happens to reflect how the objects are organized in the array. As we had experimented before with loops, we can use the array in a multitude of ways. We can also iterate over an array using the `foreach` loop. Once we've changed the names of each object, we can tell one from the other by its name.

### 5.9.2.1 A Basic Example

```
void Start ()
{
    Debug.Log(MyGameObjects.Length);
    for (int i = 0; i < MyGameObjects.Length; i++)
    {
        MyGameObjects [i].name = i.ToString();
    }
    foreach (GameObject go in MyGameObjects)
    {
        Debug.Log(go.name);
    }
}
```

The `foreach` statement is dependent on the type of data found on the inside of the array. Therefore, we use `GameObject go` to set up a place to hold each member of the `MyGameObjects` array while in the `foreach` loop. If we wanted to iterate over an array of a different type, we'd have to change the parameters of the `foreach` loop. Therefore, to iterate over an array of ints which was declared `int[] MyInts;`, we'd need to use `foreach(int i in MyInts)` to iterate over each member of that array.

Of course, the variable's name can be anything, but it's easier to keep it short. To use `foreach(int anIntegerMemberFromAnArray in MyInts)`, for example, would be a bit of work to key in if we wanted to do a number of operations on each int found in the array. Then again, there's nothing preventing us from spending time being verbose. We'll cover the `foreach` loop in more detail in Section 6.11.5.

## 5.9.3 Dynamic Initialization

```
void Start ()
{
    float[] DynamicFloats = new float[10];
}
```

We can also initialize a new array in a function. This means that the array exists only while in the scope of the function and can't be accessed from outside of that function. It's important to know that the size of an array is determined ahead of its use. When the array is declared in this way, the size or rather the number of objects the array can contain is set.

Here, we split the initialization into two statements. The first line tells C# we are creating a `float[]` variable identified as `DynamicFloats`. Then, we need to populate this floats array with a new array. The array floats is then assigned a new float array of 10 indices. We cannot switch this assignment to a different type.

```
Float[] DynamicFloats;
DynamicFloats = new int[10];
```

Changing the type creates an error, which we'll have to fix. There are clever ways to avoid this, but we'll get into that in Section 6.14.

We can also use a variable to set the length of the array.

```
public int ArrayLength;
//Use this for initialization
void Start ()
{
    float[] DynamicFloats = new float[ArrayLength];
}
```

This code sets the length of the dynamically defined array. This can be helpful once we need to make our code more flexible to change for various game design settings. On the other hand, we can populate an array with predetermined information.

```
public int[] Primes = new int[]{1, 3, 5, 7, 11, 13, 17};
```

The above statement declares and sets an array that has seven members and assigns each number to a low prime number value. *These even show up in the Inspector panel in Unity 3D.*

### 5.9.4 Using the While Loop with Arrays

Iterating through our array is pretty simple. We've covered some basic loops that handle arrays quite well. If we use a simple `while` loop, we can process each value stored in a fixed array.

```
void Start ()
{
    int[] scores = new int[10];
    int i = 0;
    while(i < 10)
    {
        print(scores[i]);
        i++;
    }
}
```

At this point, all of the values are indeed zero, so we get 10 zeros printed to our Console panel. However, there are a few interesting things to point out here. First of all, `int i` is initialized to 0 ahead of the `while` loop. We'll get into what this means later on, but remember for now that arrays start at zero. The next interesting thing is how the numbers stored in `scores[]` are accessed.

### 5.9.4.1 Setting Array Values

```
scores[0] = 10;
```

We can set the value of each index of scores to a specific value by accessing the scores by their index. When the scores array was initialized as `int[10]`, scores now has 10 different `int` number spaces. To access each value, we use a number 0 through 9 in square brackets to get and set each value. The `while` loop starts at 0 because we started with an `int i = 0;` before entering the `while` loop.

```
void Start ()
{
    int[] scores = new int[10];
    int i = 0;
    while(i < 10)
    {
        scores[i] = Random.Range(0, 100);
        print (scores[i]);
        i++;
    }
}
```

With this code, we're using a function called `Random` and using its member function `Range`, which we're setting to a value between `0` and `100`. The index is picked by using the `i` that was set to `0` before the loop started. The loop starts with `scores[0]` being set to a random number between `0` and `100`.

At the end of the while block, the `i` is incremented by 1 and the `while` loop begins again. The next time, though, we are setting `scores[1]` to a random number between `0` and `100`.

### 5.9.4.2 Getting Array Values

Each time, we're getting the value from `scores[i]` to print. We can make this a bit more clear with the following example.

```
void Start () {
    int[] scores = new int[10];
    int i = 0;
    while(i < 10)
    {
        scores[i] = Random.Range(0, 100);
        int score = scores[i];//getting a value from the array
        print (score);
        i++;
    }
}
```

If we add in the line `int score = scores[i];`, we'll get the score to the value found in `scores[i]`. Each value remains independent of the other values stored in the array. Because we're able to use the entirety of `scores[]` as a single object with index values, we're able to accomplish a great deal of work with fewer lines of code.

Arrays are simple objects with lots of uses. We'll get into a pretty interesting use in Section 5.11.3, but for now, we'll have to settle with playing with some numbers in the array.

### 5.9.5 What We've Learned

Arrays are useful for more than just storing scores. Arrays for every monster in the scene will make it easier to find the closest one to the player. Rather than dealing with many separate variables, it's easier to group them together. Arrays are used so often as to have special loops that make dealing with arrays very simple.

## 5.10  Jump Statements: Break and Continue

Loops are often used to iterate through a series of matching data. In many cases, we're looking for specific patterns in the data, and we'll change what we want to do depending on the data we're sifting through. In most cases, a regular if statement is the easiest to use. When our logic gets more detailed and we need to add more complex behaviors to our code, we need to start adding in special keywords.

When we come across the one thing we're looking for, or maybe the first thing we're looking for, we might want to stop the for loop that might change our result. In this case we use the break; keyword.

### 5.10.1  A Basic Example

To start with, we'll want to begin with the Example.cs file, fresh from the JumpStatementsCont Unity 3D project. To the Start () function of the Example.cs file, we'll add the following code.

```
//Use this for initialization
void Start ()
{
    for (int i = 0; i < 100; i++)
    {
    print(i);
    if (i > 10)
    {
        break;
    }
    }
}
```

When we run this code, we'll get a printout from 1 to 11, and since 11 is greater than 10, the for loop will stop. In the for loop's second argument, we've got i < 100, because of which we would assume that the print(i); would work till we hit 99 before the for loop exits normally. However, since we have the if statement that breaks us out of the for loop before i reaches 100, we only get 1 to 11 printed to the console. Of course, there are reasons for using break other than cutting for loops short.

#### 5.10.1.1  Continue

```
    void Start ()
{
        for (int i = 0; i < 100; i++)
        {
            print(i);
            if (i > 10)
            {
                print("i is greater than 10!");
                continue;
            }
        }
    }
```

### 5.10.2  ZombieData

The keyword break is often used to stop a process. Often, when we go through a group of data, we might be looking for something specific; when we find it, we would need to process it. If we create an array of zombies, we'll need to assign them some specific zombie behaviors. Therefore, we might create a new `ZombieData.cs` class that could include some zombie information.

```
using UnityEngine;
using System.Collections;
public class ZombieData : MonoBehaviour
{
     public int hitpoints;
}
```

Here's a very simple zombie class that has nothing more than some hitpoints. I'll leave the rest up to your game design to fill in. Then, in a new `Example.cs` script, I've added in some logic to create a bunch of game objects. Some of them have `ZombieData`; some don't.

```
using UnityEngine;
using System.Collections;
public class Example : MonoBehaviour
{
     public GameObject[] gos;
     //Use this for initialization
     void Start ()
     {
         gos = new GameObject[10];
         for (int i = 0; i < 10; i++)
         {
             GameObject go =
             GameObject.CreatePrimitive(PrimitiveType.Cube);
             Vector3 v = new Vector3();
             v.x = Random.Range(-10, 10);
             v.z = Random.Range(-10, 10);
             go.transform.position = v;
             go.name = i.ToString();
             if (i% 2 == 0)
             {
                 go.AddComponent(typeof(ZombieData));
             }
             gos [i] = go;
         }
     }
     //Update is called once per frame
     void Update ()
     {
     }
}
```

The for loop in `Start ()` creates 10 new game objects temporarily stored as go. This is done with `GameObject go = GameObject.CreatePrimitive(PrimitiveType.Cube);`; we're creating 10 cube primitives. Then, we create a new `Vector3()`, with `Vector3 v = new Vector3();`. Once v is created, we give x and z a new value between −10 and 10 using `Random.Range(-10,10);` and then assign the v to the new game object go with `go.transform.position = v`. For clarity, we give each go a new name after its iterative number from the for loop by using `go.name = i.ToString();`. Once the new game object go is created, we assign it to an array at the class level called gos.

Then, we get to `if(i%2 == 0) {go.AddComponent(typeof (ZombieData));`, which assigns a new `ZombieData` object to each go if i%2 is 0. The i%2 is a clever way to check if a number is even or odd. Therefore, in this case, if the number is even, then we assign a new `ZombieData`; otherwise, no `ZombieData` is assigned. This means half of the cubes are not zombies.

### 5.10.3 Foreach—Again

In a normal game setting, you might have many different types of objects in a scene. Some objects might be zombies, whereas others might be innocent humans running away from the zombies. We're creating a number of game objects to simulate a more normal game setting.

```
//Update is called once per frame
void Update ()
{
      foreach (GameObject go in gos)
      {
            ZombieData zd =
(ZombieData)go.GetComponent(typeof(ZombieData));
            if (zd == null)
            {
                continue;
            }
            if (zd.hitpoints > 0)
            {
                break;
            }
            print(go.name);
            zd.hitpoints = 10;
      }
}
```

Now, just for the sake of using both `continue` and `break` in some logical fashion, we use the array to check through our list of game objects using `foreach(GameObject go in gos)`. The first line, `ZombieData zd = (ZombieData)go.GetComponent(typeof(ZombieData));`, assigns a `ZombieData` to the variable `zd`. The next line does something interesting.

Here, `null` is useful; in this case, if the object in the array has no `ZombieData`, then `zd` will not be assigned anything. When `zd` is not assigned anything, its data remains `null`. Therefore, in this case, if there's no zombie data assigned to the object in the array, we're looking at *then continue*, or in this case, *go back to the top of the loop, and move on to the next item in the array*. `Continue` means stay in the loop but skip to the next item.

If `zd` exists, then we move to the next line down and we don't hit `continue`. Therefore, we can check if `zd.hitpoints` is greater than 0; if it is, then we'll stop the loop altogether. Otherwise, we'll go and print out the game object's name and then assign 10 hitpoints.

The result of this loop prints out the even-numbered named game objects, and assigns them 10 hitpoints, but it does this printout and assignment only once. If a zombie's hitpoints were to fall below 0, then the zombie's name would be printed out and his hitpoints would be reassigned to 10.

For an AI character, it would be useful to know what objects in the scene are zombies. And your zombies should know what objects in the scenes are players. In your zombie behavior code, you might use something like the following.

```
if (playerController == null) {
      continue;
}
```

This code is used to skip on to the next object in the scene, which might be a player. Likewise, you could do the following with `null`.

```
if (playerController != null) {
      attackPlayer();
}
```

This statement would be just as useful. Likewise, you can do things before using `continue`. If your zombie needed a list of characters in the scene, you would want to add them to an Array List., which is different from an `Array` and you would want to add them to an `array` first.

```
HumanData hd = (HumanData)go.GetComponent(typeof(HumanData));
If (hd != null) {
       allHumans.Add(go);
continue;
}
```

In the above example, we'd check the `go` if it's got a `HumanData` component. If it does, add it to an array list called `allHumans`, and then continue to the next object in the list.

### 5.10.4 What We've Learned

The previous section was a simple use of `break` and `continue`. As more complex situations arise, then using the JumpStatements comes in more handy. The jump statements are often used while searching through an array of many different kinds of objects.

When reading through other people's code, it's often useful to do a search for various keywords when you're interested in seeing how they are used. By searching for `continue;` or `break;`, you might find several different uses that might have not come to your mind immediately.

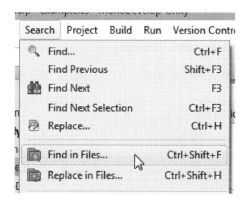

If you've downloaded some code assets from the Asset Store, you can use the following path to sort through their code base to find various places where more unique keywords are used: Search → Find in Files. Much about what is covered in this book is to introduce minimal uses for various features of the C# language.

Discovering the many different ways code can be used comes with experience, and it is something that cannot be taught in a single volume of text. The process of learning different programming features is like looking at a tool box and knowing what a screw driver looks like. It's an entirely different process to understand how it's best used.

## 5.11 Multidimensional Arrays

```
Int[,] TwoDimensionalArray;
```

An array is a single list of objects. Each entry is identified in the array by an index. By adding an additional index, we're allowed to create an additional depth to the array. When working with a single-dimensional array, we can get several simple attributes about the contents of that array.

```
void Start () {
       GameObject[] oneDimension = new GameObject[5];
       for(int i = 0; i < oneDimension.Length; i++) {
              Debug.Log(i);
       }
}
```

With the above statement, we get an output, showing us 0 to 4 printed to the Console panel in Unity 3D. Using `oneDimension.Length`, we get a value representing the number of items in the array. At the moment, though, we have not added anything to the contents of each index. This situation is altered with the following change to the array's declaration.

```
GameObject[,] twoDimension = new GameObject[2,3];
for(int i = 0; i < twoDimension.Length; i++) {
    Debug.Log(i);
}
```

With the above statement, we get 0 to 5 printed to the Console panel in Unity 3D. The `Array.Length` parameter simply returns the total number of items in the array, but we're not able to get any specific information on how the indices are arranged. To get a better feel for the contents of the array, we might consider the `TwoDimensionalArray;` as a grid of two columns by three rows.

### 5.11.1 Columns and Rows

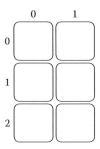

As shown in the above image, we have a 2 by 3 grid as a representation of the `GameObject[2, 3]` array. Each box holds onto a `GameObject`. A multi dimensional array has its place in programming, though it is rare, and the coding is usually better handled using a couple of single-dimensional arrays. However, it's more convenient to pass a single multi dimensional array to a function than it is to pass two different single-dimensional arrays.

To utilize this array, we'll want to populate the array with some `GameObjects`.

### *5.11.1.1 A Basic Example*

Let's begin with the MultiDimensionalArray project in Unity 3D and open the scene.

```
void Start ()
{
    GameObject a = new GameObject("A");
    GameObject b = new GameObject("B");
    GameObject c = new GameObject("C");
    GameObject d = new GameObject("D");
    GameObject e = new GameObject("E");
    GameObject f = new GameObject("F");
    GameObject[,] twoDimension =
    new GameObject[2, 3]{{a, b, c}, {d, e, f}};
}
```

Notice how the array is assigned. There are two sets of curly braces, a pair of curly braces in a set of curly braces. We group three items into two subgroups, and assign them to the 2D array. The notation {{}, {}} is used to assign a 2 by 3 array with 6 GameObjects.

Next, we'll add a function to sift through the 2D array.

```
void InspectArray(GameObject[,] gos)
{
    int columns = gos.GetLength(0);
    Debug.Log("Columns: " + columns);
    int rows = gos.GetLength(1);
    Debug.Log("Rows: " + rows);
    for (int c = 0; c < columns; c++)
    {
        for (int r = 0; r < rows; r++)
        {
            Debug.Log(gos [c, r].name);
        }
    }
}
```

With this code, we'll get an idea of what types of loops will work best with a 2D array. First off, we have a function with one argument. The function InspectArray(GameObject[,] gos) takes in a 2D array of any size. Therefore, a GameObject[37,41] would fit just as well as the GameObject[2,3] that we are using for this tutorial.

We're then using gos.GetLength(0); to assign our columns count. The GetLength() array function takes a look at the dimensions of the array. At index 0 in [2, 3], we have 2, which is assigned to columns. Next, we use GetLength(1); to get the number of rows in the 2D array.

Using two for loops, one inside of the other, we're able to iterate through each one of the objects in the 2D array in a more orderly manner. Without a system like this, we're in a more difficult situation, not knowing where in the array we are.

```
void Start ()
{
    GameObject a = new GameObject("A");
    GameObject b = new GameObject("B");
    GameObject c = new GameObject("C");
    GameObject d = new GameObject("D");
    GameObject e = new GameObject("E");
    GameObject f = new GameObject("F");
    GameObject[,] twoDimension =
    new GameObject[2, 3]{{a, b, c}, {d, e, f}};
    InspectArray(twoDimension);
}
```

At the end of the `Start ()` function, we can make use of the `InspectArray()` function and get a log of the items in each position in the 2D array.

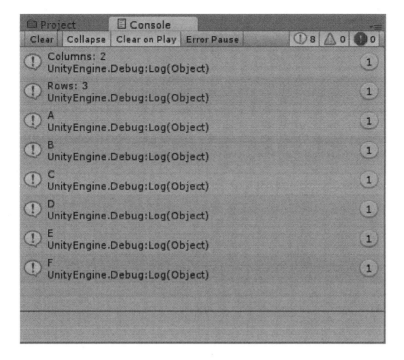

## 5.11.2  A Puzzle Board

Puzzle games often require a great deal of 2D array manipulation. To start a project, we can use the Grid2D project. The code in the `Grid2D.cs` class will begin with the following:

```csharp
using UnityEngine;
using System.Collections;
public class Grid2D : MonoBehaviour
{
    public int Width;
    public int Height;
    public GameObject PuzzlePiece;
    private GameObject[,] Grid;
    //Use this for initialization
    void Start ()
    {
        Grid = new GameObject[Width, Height];
        for (int x = 0; x < Width; x++)
        {
            for (int y = 0; y < Height; y++)
            {
                GameObject go =
                GameObject.Instantiate(PuzzlePiece) as GameObject;
                Vector3 position = new Vector3(x, y, 0);
                go.transform.position = position;
                Grid [x, y] = go;
            }
        }
    }
}
```

The `PuzzlePiece` on the script will need a prefab assigned to it. This means you'll have to drag the Sphere object in the Project panel to the variable in the Inspector panel. Select the Game object in the Hierarchy panel and drag the Sphere object in the Project panel to the puzzle piece variable in the Inspector, as shown below:

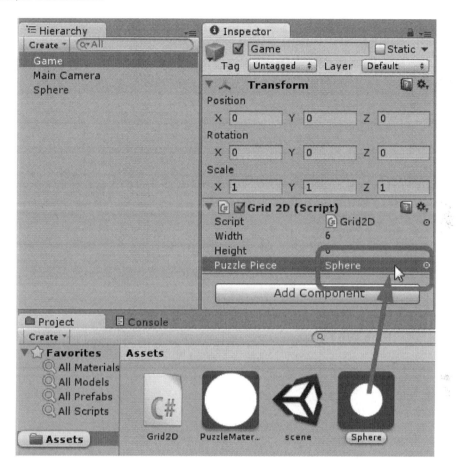

In the `Grid2D.cs` class, the first variables we're going to look at is the `public int Width` and `public int Height`. These two variables are made visible to the Inspector in the Unity 3D editor. I've set both of these to 6 in the Inspector panel. This is followed by a `GameObject`, which we'll fill the grid with. The last variable is a 2D array, which we will fill with the `GameObject PuzzlePiece`.

In the `Start ()` function, we'll add an initialization for the grid with `Grid = new GameObject[Width, Height];` to set up the 2D array so we can use it. Every fixed-sized array, whether 1D, like a `GameObject[]`, or 2D, which looks like the above `GameObject[,]`, needs to be initialized before it's used. Before being initialized, the array is `null`, which means it's lacking any size or any place for us to put anything into the array.

To fill in the array, we use the following code block added to the `Start ()` function.

```
for(int x = 0; x < Width; x++) {
    for(int y = 0; y < Height; y++) {
        GameObject go = GameObject.Instantiate(PuzzlePiece) as GameObject;
        Vector3 position = new Vector3(x, y, 0);
        go.transform.position = position;
        Grid[x, y] = go;
    }
}
```

This code has two functions; the first `for` loop iterates through each position along the x; inside of each x position, we make a column for y with another `for` loop. At each position, we create a new `GameObject`. `Instantiate(PuzzlePiece)` as `GameObject`; to assign to `GameObject go`. When `GameObject.Instantiate()` is used, an object of type object is created. To be used as a `GameObject` type it must be cast. Without the cast, you'll get the following warning in the Unity 3D Console panel:

```
Assets/Grid2D.cs(14,28): error CS0266: Cannot implicitly convert type
'UnityEngine.Object' to 'UnityEngine.GameObject'. An explicit conversion
exists (are you missing a cast?)
```

This error is telling us we need to cast from `Object` to `GameObject`, quite a simple fix even if you forget to do this ahead of time.

After making a new instance, we need to use the x and y to create a new `Vector3` to set the position of each puzzle piece. Use `Vector3 position = new Vector3(x, y, 0);` to create a new `Vector3` for each position. Once the new `Vector3` position has been created and assigned to `position`, we can tell the `GameObject go` where it should be in the world. This is done with the statement that follows: `go.transform.position = position;`.

Once the `GameObject` has been created and positioned, we can assign it to the `GameObject [,]` array with `Grid[x, y] = go;`, where we use x and y to pick which index in the 2D array the `GameObject` is to be assigned to. Once this is done, we can use the `Grid[x,y]` to get a reference to the puzzle piece. To pick a puzzle piece with the mouse, we're going to need to modify the camera's settings.

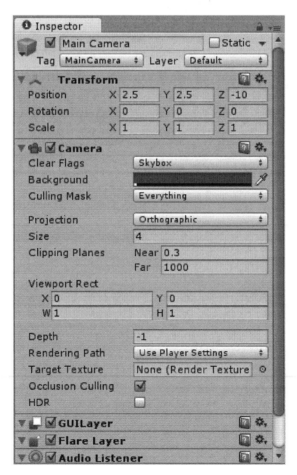

Three changes are required; the first is Projection, which we'll change from Perspective to Orthographic. This will mean that lines will not converge to a point in space. *orthographic* projection means that the line where the mouse appears over the game will be parallel with what the camera is looking at. We'll also want to resize the camera to match the grid. Setting this to 4 and repositioning the camera to 2.5, 2.5, and 10 allows us to see the grid of puzzle pieces.

```
void Update ()
{
    Vector3 mPosition =
    Camera.main.ScreenToWorldPoint(Input.mousePosition);
    Debug.DrawLine(Vector3.zero, mPosition);
}
```

In the Update () function on the Grid2D.cs class, we can use the following statement to convert mousePosition on the screen into a point in space near the puzzle pieces. To help visualize this scenario, we'll draw a line from the origin of the scene to the mouse point with Debug.DrawLine(). Here, the grid started off with the for loop int x = 0; and the inner loop started with int y = 0;, where the x and y values were also used to assign the position of the puzzle pieces.

The first puzzle piece is at position 0, 0, 0, so the Debug.DrawLine starts at the same position. We should have a line being drawn from the origin to the end of the cursor.

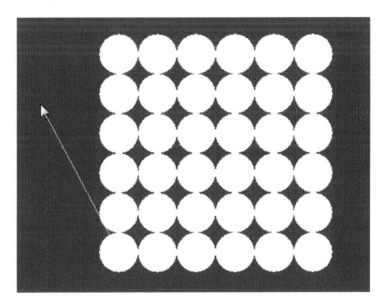

Now, we need to do a bit of thinking. To pick one of the puzzle pieces, we have a Vector3 to indicate the position of the mouse cursor; the position correlates roughly to the x and y position of each puzzle piece. The Grid[x,y] index is an integer value, so we should convert the Vector3.x into an int and do the same for the y value as well.

We can add the following two lines to the Update () function after getting the mouse position.

```
int x = (int)(mPosition.x + 0.5f);
int y = (int)(mPosition.y + 0.5f);
```

This will do two things. First, it takes the mPosition and adds 0.5f to the value coming in. When casting from a float to an int, we lose any values past the decimal point. Therefore, float 1.9 becomes int 1. The desired behavior would be to round the value up to the next whole number if we're close to it. Therefore, adding 0.5f to the float value will ensure that we will get a better approximation to an expected integer value.

These int values can now be used to pick the `PuzzlePiece` with `Grid[x,y];`. This can be done with the following code.

```
GameObject go = Grid[x,y];
go.renderer.material.SetColor("_Color", Color.red);
```

The statement `GameObject go = Grid[x,y];` works, but only when the cursor is over a puzzle piece. When the cursor is over a puzzle piece, we turn its material color to red. When the cursor is no longer over a puzzle piece, we get a bunch of warnings informing us we're selecting an index that is out of range.

### 5.11.3  Checking Range

```
IndexOutOfRangeException: Array index is out of range.
Grid2D.Update () (at Assets/Grid2D.cs:27)
```

This is true when the cursor is at −4, 7; there is no assigned object to the `Grid[-4,7]`; we've only assigned from 0 to 6 on the x and 0 to 6 on the y. These errors should be resolved before as move on. This can be done with an `if` statement or two.

```
if(x > = 0) {
    if(y > = 0) {
        if(x < Width) {
            if(y < Height) {
                GameObject go = Grid[x,y];
                go.renderer.material.SetColor("_Color", Color.red);
            }
        }
    }
}
```

This code checks first that x is at least 0, and then does the same for y. After that, we check that x is less than the width we chose initially, and do the same for y. However, this is a messy bit of code. It works just fine but we can clean this up. There's nothing happening if only x < = 0; none of the `if` statements require any special actions to occur. They all contribute to the same assignment and color change statements at the end. That's how we know they can be reduced to one `if` statement.

The reduced statement looks like the following:

```
if(x > = 0 && y > = 0 && x < Width && y < Height)
{
    GameObject go = Grid[x,y];
    go.renderer.material.SetColor("_Color", Color.red);
}
```

Much better. Therefore, this code works to highlight every game object we touch, but the objects remain colored red. The puzzle piece should return to white when the mouse is no longer hovering over them; how would we do that? The logic isn't so simple. We could pick every other object and set it to white, but that's impractical. Strangely, the solution is to set all of the objects to white, and then color the current object red.

```
for(int _x = 0; _x < Width; _x++)
{
    for(int _y = 0; _y < Height; _y++)
    {
        GameObject go = Grid[_x, _y];
        go.renderer.material.SetColor("_Color", Color.white);
    }
}
```

Iterate through all of the game objects in a similar way to how we instantiated them. Because this code is sharing a function with x and y, where we converted the float to an int, we need to make new versions of x and y for this function; therefore, we'll use _ x and _ y to create a new variable for the for loops. With this, we set them all to white. After resetting all of the puzzle pieces to white, we move to the next function that sets them to red. The completed Update () function looks like the following:

```
void Update () {
    Vector3 mPosition =
    Camera.main.ScreenToWorldPoint(Input.mousePosition);
    int x = (int)(mPosition.x + 0.5f);
    int y = (int)(mPosition.y + 0.5f);
    for(int _x = 0; _x < Width; _x++)
    {
        for(int _y = 0; _y < Height; _y++)
        {
            GameObject go = Grid[_x, _y];
            go.renderer.material.SetColor("_Color", Color.white);
        }
    }
    if(x > = 0 && y > = 0 && x < Width && y < Height)
    {
        GameObject go = Grid[x,y];
        go.renderer.material.SetColor("_Color", Color.red);
    }
}
```

We're not so interested in what our scene looks like in the middle of the Update () function, just how the scene looks like at the end. None of the intermediate steps appears in the scene, until the Update () function has finished. This means we can do all sorts of unintuitive actions during the course of the Update () function, so long as the final result looks like what we need.

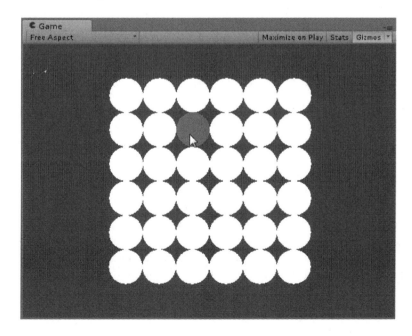

Now, we have a very simple way to detect and pick which puzzle piece is selected in a grid of objects using a 2D array and a Vector3. Of course, the strategy used here may not fit all situations. In addition, applying various offsets for changing the spacing between each object might be useful to make differently proportioned grids. Later on, you will want to add in additional systems to check for color to determine matches, but that will have to wait for Section 5.11.4.

To finish off this exercise, we'll want to move the code we wrote into a function, which would keep the `Update ()` function tidy, keeping a regularly updated function as simple looking as possible. This approach to coding also allows a function to be called from outside of the `Update ()` function.

```
//Update is called once per frame
void Update () {
    Vector3 mPosition =
    Camera.main.ScreenToWorldPoint(Input.mousePosition);
    UpdatePickedPiece(mPosition);
}
void UpdatePickedPiece(Vector3 position)
{
    int x = (int)(position.x + 0.5f);
    int y = (int)(position.y + 0.5f);
    for(int _x = 0; _x < Width; _x++)
    {
        for(int _y = 0; _y < Height; _y++)
        {
            GameObject go = Grid[_x, _y];
            go.renderer.material.SetColor("_Color", Color.white);
        }
    }
    if(x > = 0 && y > = 0 && x < Width && y < Height)
    {
        GameObject go = Grid[x,y];
        go.renderer.material.SetColor("_Color", Color.red);
    }
}
```

With the code moved into its own function, our `Update ()` loop is made a bit more easy to read. We're very specific about what is required to update the picked piece. We just need to remember to rename `mPosition` to a position inside of the new function. We can also extend the new function to return the piece that has been picked. By breaking apart a long string of code into smaller, more simplified functions, we're able to gain more flexibility and allow for changes more easily later on.

### 5.11.4 What We've Learned

Multi dimensional arrays can be a bit of a pain to work with, but after some practice, the logic becomes more clear. Puzzle games that use a grid of colored objects to match up often use a 2D array to check for patterns.

We could expand the concept to more than two dimensions as well. Using the previously defined `GameObjects`, we could make a 3D array that looks like the following:

```
GameObject[,,] threeDimension = new GameObject[4,3,2]
{
        { {a,b}, {c,d}, {e,f} },
        { {a,b}, {c,d}, {e,f} },
        { {a,b}, {c,d}, {e,f} },
        { {a,b}, {c,d}, {e,f} }
};
```

Something like this is easier to produce using code to fill in each value, but it's important to be able to visualize what a [4,3,2] array actually looks like. Though a bit impractical, these sorts of data structures are important to computing, in general. Outside of video game development, multi dimensional arrays become more important to data analysis.

Large database systems often have internal functions that accelerate sorting through arrays of data in more logical ways. Of course, if you're thinking about building a complex RPG, then multi dimensional arrays might play a role in how your character's items and stats are related to one another.

## 5.12 Array List

Fixed-sized arrays are great. When you create an array with 10 indices, adding an 11th score or more will be cause for some rethinking. You'd have to go back and fix your code to include another index. This would be very inefficient, to say the least. This is where an array list comes in handy. An `ArrayList` is initialized a bit differently from a more common fixed-sized array.

```
ArrayList aList = new ArrayList();
```

An `ArrayList` is a C# class that has special functions for building lists that allow for changes in the number of values stored. An `ArrayList` is not set to a specific size. Rather than having to pick an index to put a value into, we merely use the `ArrayList` function `Add();` to increase the number of objects in the `ArrayList`. In addition, an array has a type associated with it.

An array like `int[]` `numbers` can store only a bunch of ints. An `ArrayList` can store any variety of object types. Another feature which we'll find out later is that an array, not an `ArrayList`, can have multiple dimensions, for instance, `int[,]` `grid = new int[8,8];`, which creates an 8 by 8 array. An `ArrayList` cannot be used like this.

The drawback with an `ArrayList` is the fact that we're not able to populate the list ahead of time. With the fixed-sized array, we've been getting to know thus far that we're able to assign each index a value ahead of time; for instance, consider the following:

```
public int[] numbers = new int[]{1, 3, 5, 7, 11, 13, 17};
```

We know that this statement will appear in the Inspector panel with seven numbers in a nice UI roll-out. An array list doesn't allow for this behavior, as it needs to be created and then populated after its creation. The reason why Unity 3D allows us to assign values to objects in a scene is the scene file. The scene itself has had special data or metadata added to the scene. The scene now has specific bindings created to tie the data you've created to the class attached to an object.

To simulate this in a more common Windows app, you'd have to create a secondary file that stores specific settings. When the app is started, the settings need to be read in and then assigned to the classes as they are instanced into the scene. Unity 3D has done much of the specific bindings for you, which allows your game to have scenes with arranged objects and unique settings for each object.

```
int i = 3;
aList.Add(i);
```

The identifier inherits the `ArrayList` member methods. The Add method is used to append a value to the end of the `ArrayList` object. The `aList` from the above code fragment is now an `ArrayList` with one item. With this, we're able to use the `aList` object.

```
print(aList[0]);
```

This statement will send 3 to the Console panel, as you might expect. In practice, the `ArrayList` type is often used to collect an unknown number of objects into something more manageable. Once we've gathered the objects we're looking for, it's easier to deal with the multitude of objects. Therefore, if there are between 0 and 100 zombies in a room, we can have different behaviors based on the number of zombies found. If we want to convert the `ArrayList` into a regular array, we'd need to do some copying from the `ArrayList` to the array.

In addition to allowing for any number of objects, we can also consume any variety of types in the array.

### 5.12.1 A Basic Example

To observe how an `ArrayList` is used, it's best to see it all in action; therefore, we'll start with the ArrayLists project in Unity 3D. In the scene, we can have any number of cube game objects. Should the number of objects be something that can't be predetermined, we'd want to use an `ArrayList` to store a list of them.

```
using UnityEngine;
using System.Collections;
public class ArrayLists : MonoBehaviour {
    //store all the game objects in the scene
    public GameObject[] AllGameObjects;
//Use this for initialization
    void Start () {
        //creates an array of an undetermined size and type
        ArrayList aList = new ArrayList();
        //create an array of all objects in the scene
        Object[] AllObjects =
GameObject.FindObjectsOfType(typeof(Object)) as Object[];
        //iterate through all objects
        foreach(Object o in AllObjects)
        {
            //if we find a game object then add it to the list
            GameObject go = o as GameObject;
            if(go != null)
            {
                aList.Add(go);
            }
        }
        //initialize the AllGameObjects array
        AllGameObjects = new GameObject[aList.Count];
        //copy the list to the array
        aList.CopyTo(AllGameObjects);
    }
}
```

Attached to the camera among all of the scattered cube objects is the above script. This behavior adds everything in the scene to an array. If it's an object, then we add it to the array. Afterward, we iterate through the array using `foreach (Object o in AllObjects)`, which allows us to check if the object in the `AllObjects` array is a `GameObject`. This check is done using `GameObject go = o as GameObject;`, and the following line checks if the cast is valid. If the cast is valid, then we add the object to our array list `aList`. This is done using the same `aList.Add()` function we used before.

After the iteration through the list, we end up with a final pair of steps. The first is to initialize a regular `GameObject` array to the size of the `ArrayList`. Then, we need to copy the `aList` to the freshly initialized `GameObject` array with `aList.CopyTo()`.

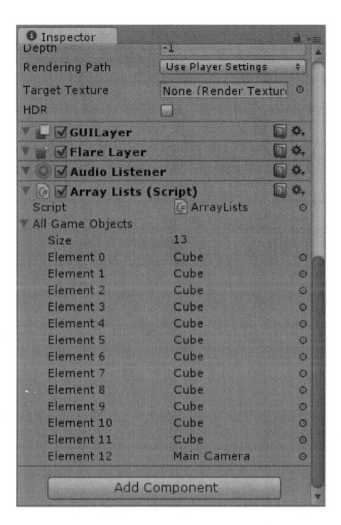

The final result is an `ArrayList` of each game object in the scene. If we skip the cast checking of whether `Object o` is a `GameObject`, then we get an invalid cast error. This happens only when we try to copy the `aList` to the `GameObject` array. We can do the following in the iteration to populate the `aList` without any problems.

```
//iterate through all objects
foreach(Object o in AllObjects)
{
        aList.Add(o);
}
```

This code simply adds everything that `GameObject.FindObjectsOfType()` finds to the `ArrayList` `aList`. This tells us that `aList` ignores the type that it's being filled with. To see what this `foreach` loop is doing, we can use the following modification:

```
//iterate through all objects
foreach(Object o in AllObjects)
{
    Debug.Log(o);
    aList.Add(o);
}
```

Here, we log each `o` to the console. We get many many more objects than you might have guessed. In the scene I've created, there are 76 different lines printed to the Console panel. The list includes the game objects as well as there are many dozens of other objects that are added to the `ArrayList`, too many to spell out in this case. A regular array can accommodate only one type at a time. And a `GameObject[]` array can have only `GameObjects` assigned to each index.

Since we might not necessarily know how many `GameObjects` reside in the final list, we need to dynamically add each one to the `ArrayList`, and wait till we stop finding new `GameObjects` to add. Once the list is done with iteration, we can then use the final count of the `aList`, using `aList.Count`, to initialize the `GameObject` array. The `ArrayList` has a function called `CopyTo`, which is designed to copy its contents to a fixed-sized array; therefore, we use it to do just that, with the last two statements:

```
//initialize the AllGameObjects array
AllGameObjects = new GameObject[aList.Count];
//copy the list to the array
aList.CopyTo(AllGameObjects);
```

### 5.12.2 ArrayList.Contains()

`ArrayList.Contains()` is a static function of `ArrayList`. The `ArrayList` type has several useful functions aside from just copying to an array. Say, we add a `public GameObject SpecificObject;` to the `ArrayLists` class. Then we can drag one of the cubes in the scene to the variable in the Inspector panel.

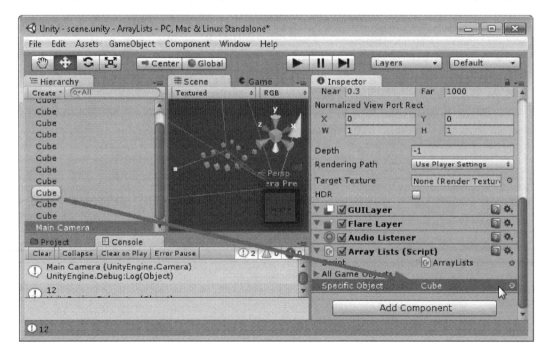

Now, we have an object and a populated array list. This allows us to search the array list for the object.

```
if(aList.Contains(SpecificObject))
{
    Debug.Log(aList.IndexOf(SpecificObject));
}
```

We can use two different array list functions. The first is `Contains()` and the second is `IndexOf()`. The `Contains()` function searches through the array list and returns `true` if it finds the object and `false` if the object isn't in the list. The `IndexOf()` function returns the index where the `SpecificObject` is found. Therefore, if the array list has the `specificObject` at index 12, the `Debug.Log` above returns 12.

### 5.12.3 Remove

The object that the script is a component of is found by `this.gameObject`, or simply, `gameObject`. Therefore, we may remove the object doing the searching from the list with the `Remove()` function. The statement that effects this behavior would look like the following:

```
if(aList.Contains(gameObject))
{
    aList.Remove(gameObject);
}
```

This statement reduces the size of the array list and takes out the Main Camera, which has the array list's component attached. With the camera removed, the copied array now has only cubes in it.

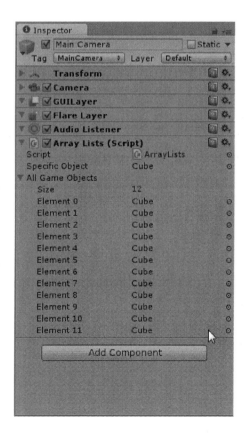

If the goal is to filter the scene for specific objects, then the array list serves as a great net to fill with the types of data you need. If you don't know ahead of time how many objects you are going to find, then an array list is a useful utility class that allows for some interesting tricks. Therefore, we've looked at removing and finding an object in an array list, but we don't need to stop there.

### 5.12.4 Sort and Reverse

Let's add public int [] messyInts = {12,14,6,1,0,123,92,8}; to the class scope. This should appear in the Inspector panel, where we can see that messyInts is indeed a collection of messy ints. To copy the messyInts into a new ArrayList, we use AddRange();.

```
ArrayList sorted = new ArrayList();
//this adds the messyInts to the new ArrayList
sorted.AddRange(messyInts);
//command to sort the contents of the ArrayList
sorted.Sort();
//puts the new sorted list back into the messyInts array
sorted.CopyTo(messyInts);
```

With the above code added to the Start () function, we get the following result once the game is run.

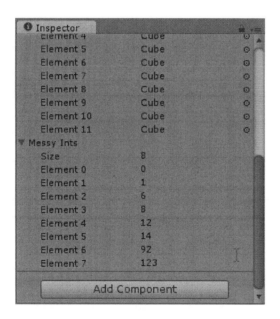

The elements of the array have been sorted, starting at the lowest and ending with the highest. The sort function is a nicely optimized sort function. You might expect this from the experienced computer scientists working on the C# library we've been using. If we want to reverse the order in which the numbers are sorted, then we can use the sorted.Reverse(); function.

```
ArrayList sorted = new ArrayList();
sorted.AddRange(messyInts);
sorted.Sort();
sorted.Reverse();//flips the array list over
sorted.CopyTo(messyInts);
```

Having some numbers rearranged is great, but there's little inherent value to the numbers if there are no associated objects in the scene that relate to the numeric values. The Sort() function is good for simple matters where the data that's sorted has no association with anything in particular outside of the array. However, should we want to compare `GameObjects` in the scene, we might need to do something more useful.

### 5.12.5 What We've Learned

Making a custom sorting system requires some new concepts, which we have yet to get to. A specific type of class called an interface is required to create our own system of sorting. We could use this class in many different ways and take advantage of the power behind C#'s library.

A performance issue comes up with array lists. We may add objects to an `ArrayList` by simply using `MyArrayList.Add(someObject);`, which is easy. When we need to see what's in that array list, we begin to have a few problems.

As this was mentioned at the beginning of this chapter we didn't find out what happens if we use the following.

```
arraylist aList = new ArrayList();
aList.Add(123);
aList.Add("strings");
```

We have an issue with the above code fragment. If we assumed the `ArrayList` would only contain numbers; multiplying 123 by "strings" would result in an error. Of course we can't multiply these two very different types. We'd need to do a few tricks to check if we're allowed to multiply two objects from the `ArrayList`. First, we'd check if both are indeed numbers, if they are then we can proceed with a multiplication statement. If not, then we'd have to find another two objects which are numbers or we'd get an error.

This process takes time, and if the array list is big, then we'd be spending a great deal of time on checking object types. If we use a regular array, we can be sure that each object in the array is the same type, or possibly null. Checking against null for each object in the list is an extra step in the process. Reducing the number of steps your function need to work will speed up your functions and code will run faster.

When dealing with arrays, we might need to stuff an array into an array. Each array inside of an array can be of a different size. Imagine array A to be 10 items long. At A[0], you can create another array B that is, for example, 3 items long. If each index of A is of a different size, you've created what is called a jagged array.

## 5.13 Strings

Strings are collections of letters. C# has no concept of what words are so a string is nothing more than a collection of meaningless letters. When you use a string, it's important to remember that the data stored in it is not like words.

### 5.13.1 Declaring a String

Basically, strings are presented to the computer by using the `"` or `'` operator. Strings act somewhat like an array, so we've held off till after we looked at arrays before getting to strings. Later on, strings will become a bit more useful, once we start naming `GameObjects`.

Strings can be used as user names and will be useful if you wanted to use them for dialog windows when talking to characters in a role-playing game. Being able to process strings is a useful skill to have for many general purpose programming tasks.

#### 5.13.1.1 A Basic Example

Let's start with the Strings project in Unity 3D and open the scene in the Assets folder.

```
string s = "Something in quotes";
```

This statement creates a string with the identifier s and then assigns `Something in quotes` to s. Strings have several additional functions that are important. Be careful to not use smart quotes, which word processors like to use. Quotes that have directions are not the same as the quotes a compiler is expecting. Words in special quotes ("words") actually use different characters when written in a word processor.

The compiler expects a different character. The character set that most word processors use is different from what C# uses to compile. For instance, if you hold down Alt and enter four numbers on the number pad, you'll get a special character.

```
//Use this for initialization
void Start ()
{
    string s = "Something in quotes";
    print(s);
}
```

Printing the s results in a predictable output to the Console panel.

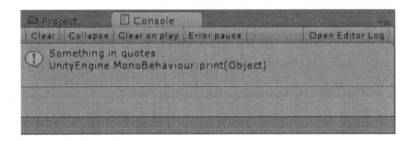

There's not a whole lot unexpected happening here. However, we can do something with strings that might unexpected.

```
s + = "more words";
```

We can add this statement just before the `print(s);` and get a different result. When we run the game, we get the following Console output.

```
Something in quotesmore words
UnityEngine.MonoBehaviour:print(Object)
Example:Start () (at Assets/Example.cs:8)
```

We forgot to add in a space before the *more* in `"more words";`, so it ran into the word quotes. White space is important to how we use strings. There's no logic to what's happening when we add more words to a string. To correct this, we need to add a space before *more* and we'll get a more expected result: `"more words"`.

Strings do have some tricks that make them very useful. The string class has many member functions we can use, like `Contains`.

```
string s = "Something in quotes";
bool b = s.Contains("Something");
print (b);
```

This returns true; the word `"Something"` is contained in the string stored in s. Use any other set of letters which doesn't appear in our string and the console will print false.

We can also do the following.

```
string s = "First word" + "Second word";
```

This statement will print out what you might expect.

```
First word Second word
UnityEngine.MonoBehaviour:print(Object)
Example:Start () (at Assets/Example.cs:7)
```

For argument's sake, we'll try another operator in the string declaration.

```
string s = "First word" - "Second word";
```

Here, we're going to try to subtract `"Second word"` from the first. Of course, this doesn't work and we get the following error.

```
Assets/Example.cs(6,23): error CS0019: Operator '-' cannot be applied to
operands of type 'string' and 'string'
```

So why does the + work and not the − in our declaration? The answer is operator overloading. Operators change their meaning depending on the context in which they appear. When the + is placed between two strings, we get a different result than when we put the + between two numbers. However, strings are rather particular. It's rather difficult to say for sure what it would mean to subtract one word from another. Computers are horrible at guessing.

### 5.13.2 Escape Sequences

Strings in C# need to be handled very differently from a regular word processor. Formatting strings can be somewhat confusing if you treat C# like any other text format.

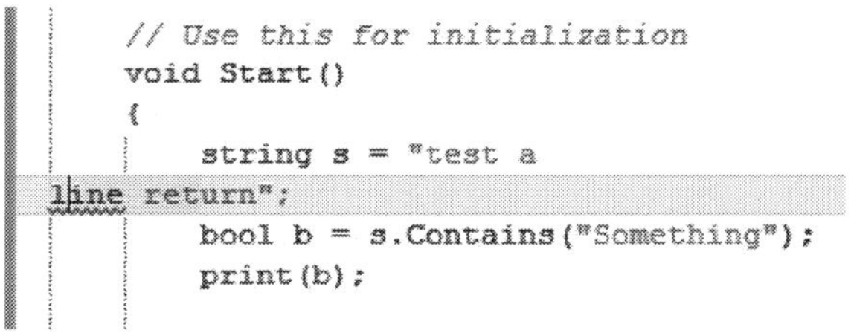

```
// Use this for initialization
void Start()
{
    string s = "test a
line return";
    bool b = s.Contains("Something");
    print(b);
```

If you want to add in a line return, you might end up with a mess as in the above image. Sometimes called line feeds, or carriage returns, these line returns tend to break C# in unexpected ways. To add in line feeds into the string, you'll have to use a special character instead.

I should note that the latest version of MonoDevelop will show an error when you make bad decisions like the above. Not all IDEs will try so hard to fight your bad formatting. Much of the time, software like Notepad++ or Sublime Edit will be more programmer friendly but will not alert you when you're doing something that will break the parser.

```
string s = "First line\nSecond Line";
```

Escape sequences work to convert two regular text characters into more specialized characters without needing to mess up your code's formatting. The \n creates a "new line" where it appears in the string. A \t adds a tab wherever it appears.

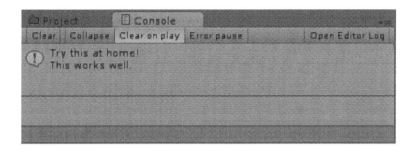

Unity 3D diverges a bit from most C# libraries as it doesn't implement all of the different escape sequences that are generally included. For instance, \r is carriage return, as is \f that are generally included in other common .NET development environments. The \n, which creates new line sequence, is more commonly known.

In old mechanical type writers, a carriage return is a lever that would both push a roll of paper and add in a new line at the same time: hardly something you see around today, unless you're a street poet. Not all of these escape characters work, but there are several others which you'll find useful.

```
print("\"I wanted quotes!\"");
```

To get double quotes to print in your console, you'll use the \" escape sequence. Here's a list of regular escape sequences.

| | |
|---|---|
| \a | (beep) |
| \b | Backspace |
| \f | Formfeed |
| \n | New line |
| \r | Carriage return |
| \t | Tab |
| \v | Vertical tab |
| \' | Single quote |
| \" | Double quote |
| \\ | Backslash |
| \? | Literal question mark |

In addition to these escape sequences, we have additional three types that are used less often but are just as important. C# and Unity 3D will recognize some hexadecimal characters that are accessed with \x followed by two hexadecimal values. We'll find out more about these hex values and other escape sequences in a later chapter. Using hexadecimals is another way to get the more particular characters often found in other languages.

### 5.13.3 Verbatim Strings: @

In some cases, it's useful to use the @ operator before a string. This tells C# that we're really not interested in formatting or not being able to make modifications to our string, like string s = "this \nthat";, which would result in the following:

```
this
that
```

The verbatim operator when used with strings—string s = @"this \nthat";—actually just prints out like the following:

```
this \nthat
```

This also means something as strange looking as

```
void Start () {
    string s = @"this
    that and
    the other";
    Debug.Log(s);
}
```

prints to the console

```
this
    that and
    the other;
```

Notice that the console output includes all of the characters following the @" symbol. This is allowed because of the verbatim operator. When using Debug.Log(), the verbatim operator can be used to format your strings to include new lines wherever you may need them.

### 5.13.4 String Format

Strings that contain information can easily be created; it's often the case when trying to track the behavior of a creature in the scene.

### 5.13.5 What We've Learned

We're not going to be building any word-processing software within Unity 3D. It's not something that sounds all that fun, and there are better environments for doing that. As far as strings are concerned, we're better off using them as seldom as possible.

Very few game engines dwell on their text-editing features, Unity 3D included. If you're planning on having your player do a great deal of writing and formatting to play your game, then you might have a tough time. For most purposes, like entering character names or setting up a clan name, the string class provided will have you covered.

## 5.14 Combining What We've Learned

We just covered some basic uses of loops. The for and the while loop have similar uses, but the for loop has some additional parameters that can make it more versatile. We also covered some relational, unary, and conditional operators.

Together with if, else if, and else, we've got enough parts together to do some fairly interesting logic tests. We can start to give some interesting behavior to our statements. For instance, we can make the placement of the zombies check for various conditions around in the environment before creating another zombie.

### 5.14.1 Timers

In the Timers project in the Unity 3D projects folder, we'll start with the Example.cs file attached to the Main Camera in the scene. Let's say we want to create a specific number of zombies, but we want to create them one at a time. To do this, we should use a timer; therefore, we should start with that first.

```
void Update ()
{
    print (Time.fixedTime);
}
```

If we start with `Time.fixedTime`, we should see how that behaves by itself. We get a printout to the console starting with 0, which then counts up at one unit per second. Therefore, if we want some sort of action 3 seconds later, we can set a timer to 3 seconds from 0.

```
void Update ()
{
    if (Time.fixedTime > 3)
    {
        print("Time Up");
    }
}
```

If `Time.fixedTime` is greater than 3, `"Time Up"` is repeatedly printed to the console. However, we want that to print only once, since we want only one thing to happen when our `if` statement is executed. To do this, we should add in some way to increment the number we're comparing `Time.fixedTime` to.

```
float NextTime = 0;
void Update ()
{
    if (Time.fixedTime > NextTime)
    {
        NextTime = Time.fixedTime + 3;
        print("Time Up");
    }
}
```

With a class scoped variable called `NextTime`, we can store our next `"Time up"` time and update it when it is reached. Running this code prints `"Time up"` once the game starts. If `NextTime` was declared to 3, then we'd have to wait 3 seconds before the first `Time Up` is printed to the console.

Therefore, now, we have a timer. We should next add some sort of counter, so we know how many times the `if` statement was executed.

```
float NextTime = 0;
int Counter = 10;
void Update ()
{
    if (Counter > 0)
    {
        if (Time.fixedTime > NextTime)
        {
            NextTime = Time.fixedTime + 3;
            print("Time Up");
            Counter-- ;
        }
    }
}
```

First, add in `int Counter = 10` to store how many times we want to run our `if` statement. If the `Counter` is greater than 0, then we need to check our `Time.fixedTime` if statement. Once the timer is reset, we need to decrement our `Counter` by 1. Once the counter is no longer greater than 0, we stop. There's a cleaner way to do this.

```
float NextTime = 0;
int Counter = 10;
void Update ()
{
    if (Counter > 0 && Time.fixedTime > NextTime)
```

```
        {
            NextTime = Time.fixedTime + 3;
            print("Time Up");
            Counter-- ;
        }
    }
```

We can reduce the extra if statement checking the counter value. To merge if statements, use the &&
conditional operator. If either side of the && is false, then the if statement is not evaluated. Because
there's no code in the if statement checking the counter, there's no reason why it can't be combined with
the if statement it's containing.

Now, we have a timer and a counter. We can make this more useful by exposing some of the variables
to the editor.

```
public float NextTime = 0;
public float Timer = 3;
public int Counter = 10;
void Update ()
{
    if (Counter > 0 && Time.fixedTime > NextTime)
    {
        NextTime = Time.fixedTime + Timer;
        print("Time Up");
        Counter-- ;
    }
}
```

Add in public before some of the existing variables, and for good measure, let's get rid of the 3 which
we're adding to Time.fixedTime and make that into a variable as well. This is common practice; use
some numbers to test a feature, and then once the feature roughly works, change some of the numbers
into editable parameters that may be handed off to designers.

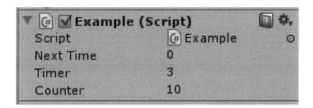

Now we can replace print("Time Up"); with a more useful function. Once we've got the chops, we'll
start replacing boxes with zombies, the code below serves as a good example for now.

```
    public float NextTime = 0f;
    public float Timer = 0.5f;
    public int Counter = 10;
    void Update ()
    {
        if (Counter > 0 && Time.fixedTime > NextTime)
        {
            NextTime = Time.fixedTime + Timer;
            GameObject box =
            GameObject.CreatePrimitive(PrimitiveType.Cube);
            box.transform.position = new Vector3(Counter * 2f, 0, 0);
            Counter-- ;
        }
    }
```

This little block of code will slowly pop a new cube into existence around the scene origin. We're using Counter to multiply against 2 so each box object will appear in a different place along the *x* coordinate.

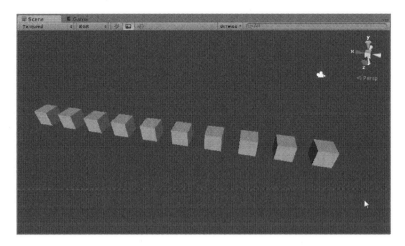

You can speed up the process by lowering the timer value we just added. What if we wanted to have more than one box created at each counter interval? This objective can be accomplished using either a `while` or a `for` statement being run inside of the `if` statement.

```
public float NextTime = 0f;
public float Timer = 0.5f;
public int Counter = 10;
void Update ()
{
    if (Counter > 0 && Time.fixedTime > NextTime)
    {
        NextTime = Time.fixedTime + Timer;
        int randomNumber = Random.Range(1, 10);
        for (int i = 0; i < randomNumber; i++)
        {
            GameObject box =
            GameObject.CreatePrimitive(PrimitiveType.Cube);
            box.transform.position =
            new Vector3(Counter * 2f, i, 0);
        }
        Counter-- ;
    }
}
```

Adding in the `for` loop is the easiest way to do this. `Random.Range();` is a new function that returns a number between the first argument and the second argument. We're just testing this out so we can use any number to start with.

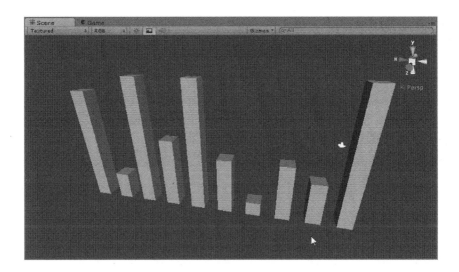

Okay, looks like everything is working as we might have expected. We should take out the numbers we're using in the Random.Range() and make them into more public parameters for use in the editor.

```
public float NextTime = 0f;
public float Timer = 0.5f;
public int Counter = 10;
public int MinHeight = 1;
public int MaxHeight = 10;
public float HorizontalSpacing = 2f;
public float VerticalSpacing = 1f;
void Update ()
{
    if (Counter > 0 && Time.fixedTime > NextTime)
    {
        NextTime = Time.fixedTime + Timer;
        int randomNumber = Random.Range(MinHeight, MaxHeight);
        for (int i = 0; i < randomNumber; i++)
        {
            GameObject box =
            GameObject.CreatePrimitive(PrimitiveType.Cube);
            box.transform.position = new Vector3(Counter *
            HorizontalSpacing, i * VerticalSpacing, 0);
        }
        Counter-- ;
    }
}
```

Adding more variables to control spacing will also make this more interesting.

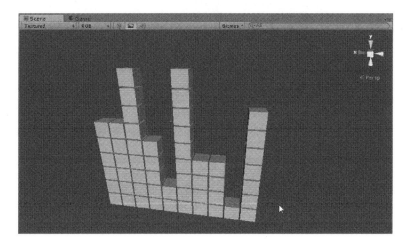

By tweaking some of the parameters, you can build something that looks like this with code alone! The reason why we should be exposing so many of these variables to the editor is to allow for creative freedom. The more parametric we make any system, the more exploration we can do with what the numbers mean.

If you feel adventurous, then you can add in a second dimension to the stack of cubes.

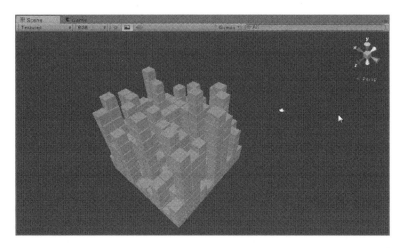

Look at that. What started off as some cube-generating system turned into some 3D pixel art city generator.

```
public float NextTime = 0f;
public float Timer = 0.5f;
public int Counter = 10;
public int MinHeight = 1;
public int MaxHeight = 10;
public float HorizontalSpacing = 2f;
public float VerticalSpacing = 1f;
void Update ()
{
    if (Counter > 0 && Time.fixedTime > NextTime)
    {
        NextTime = Time.fixedTime + Timer;
        for (int j = 10; j > 0; j- )
```

```
        {
            int randomNumber = Random.Range(MinHeight, MaxHeight);
            for (int i = 0; i < randomNumber; i++)
            {
                GameObject box =
    GameObject.CreatePrimitive(PrimitiveType.Cube);
                box.transform.position =
                    new Vector3(Counter * HorizontalSpacing,
                        i * VerticalSpacing,
                        j * HorizontalSpacing);
            }
        }
        Counter-- ;
    }
}
```

If we spend more time on this, then we can even start to add on little cubes on the big cubes by setting scale and position around each of the cubes as they are generated. We won't go into that right now, so I'll leave that on to you to play with.

## 5.14.2 Adding in Classes

The GameObject box is limited by what a box generated by GameObject can do. To learn a more complex behavior, we should change this from GameObject to a more customized object of our own creation.

After the Update () function, add in a new class called CustomBox.

```
    class CustomBox {
public GameObject box = GameObject.CreatePrimitive(PrimitiveType.Cube);
    }
```

In this CustomBox class, we'll add in the same code that created the box for the previous version of this code; however, we'll make this one public. The accessibility needs to be added so that the object inside of it can be modified. Next, replace the code that created the original box in the Update () function with the following:

```
CustomBox cBox = new CustomBox();
cBox.box.transform.position = new Vector3(Counter * HorizontalSpacing, i *
VerticalSpacing, j * HorizontalSpacing);
```

Note the cBox.box.transform.position has cBox, which is the current class object and then .box, which is the GameObject inside of it. The box GameObject is now a member of the CustomBox class. To continue, we'll add in a function to the CustomBox class to pick a random color.

```
    void Update ()
    {
        if (Counter > 0 && Time.fixedTime > NextTime)
        {
            NextTime = Time.fixedTime + Timer;
            for (int j = 10; j > 0; j- )
            {
                int randomNumber = Random.Range(MinHeight, MaxHeight);
                for (int i = 0; i < randomNumber; i++)
```

```
            {
                CustomBox box = new CustomBox();
                box.box.transform.position =
                new Vector3(Counter * HorizontalSpacing,
                    i * VerticalSpacing,
                    j * HorizontalSpacing);
                box.PickRandomColor();
            }
        }
        Counter-- ;
    }
}
```

Check that the color-picking function is public; otherwise, we won't be able to use it. Then check that the color set is done to the box  GameObject inside of the CustomBox class. Add in a cBox.PickRandomColor(); statement to tell the cBox variable to pick a new color for the box GameObject.

```
CustomBox cBox = new CustomBox();
cBox.box.transform.position = new Vector3(Counter * HorizontalSpacing, i *
VerticalSpacing, j * HorizontalSpacing);
cBox.PickRandomColor();
```

The function now tells each box to pick a random color after it's put into position.

We're starting to do some constructive programming and getting some more interesting visual results. Next, we're going to need to make these things start to move around. To do that, we're going to need to learn a bit more about how to use our if statements and some basic math to get things moving.

### 5.14.3 What We've Learned

We're starting to build more complex systems. We're iterating through custom classes and putting them to some use. Adding functions to classes and using them in for loops is a fairly flexible and reusable setup.

We should be a bit more comfortable reading complex algorithms in the functions we read on forums and in downloaded assets. If we come across something new, then we should be able to come up with some search terms to find out what we're looking at.

## 5.15 Source Version Control

We've talked a bit about working with other programmers. However, we have yet to talk about how this is done. You could consider simply talking with one another and work together on a file at the same time. This could mean trading time at the keyboard, but this is simply not practical.

The best concept for working with a team of programmers is source control. Sometimes called revision or version control, the concept is basically being able to keep track of code changes and keeping a history of all of your source files.

Version control means retaining the state of an entire project, not just one file at a time. Tracking the history of a project also means that you can move forward and backward through the history of the tracked files.

Source code, or the code base on which your game is built, is, in essence, a collection of text files. Text remains ordered from top to bottom. Line numbers and code structures are easily recognized by software and where changes appear good, source control software can recognize the differences between revisions.

### 5.15.1 Modern Version Control

Today, there are many different version control systems used by software engineers. You may have heard of the term *Open source*, which is a general term used to describe hardware, or software that has been made publicly available for modification or use.

With open source software, a legally binding agreement is made between the creators of the original code base to the community at large to allow for use and distribution of the concepts and systems that have been made public. Open source software, in particular, is often distributed on what is called a repository.

Public repositories, or repos, like GitHub, SourceForge, and BitBucket, offer free storage space and version control options. GitHub uses a commonly used software called Git, so it has become a popular free service for many open and closed source projects.

Closed source projects are private repositories used by studios to retain the rights to their code and keep their project secret. Large companies and games are usually closed source projects, which protects their intellectual property and keeps their systems and methods out of the public domain.

### 5.15.2 The Repository

A repository is a central location where revisions of code and the most current version of the code can be found. A repo stores a code base. Many publicly available repositories allow for contributions by any number of users. These changes can be submitted and integrated into the code base to fix bugs and allow for the community at large to help solve complex problems.

A repository can also be made private on a local server for internal development. This limits access to those who can communicate with the server. Most game studios tend to keep their code and methods secret from the public.

A private repo can also be useful for a solitary developer. Source control is useful for many different situations. As a solitary developer, it's all too easy to make a change and break everything. It's also easy to forget what the code looked like before everything broke. If you had a backup to refer to, a fix will come easier, by reverting to a previous version of the project. Source control for an individual can be indispensible for this reason.

Your code base includes every C# file you've written along with any supporting text files that your code might reference. Source control is not limited to text. Binary files like audio clips and textures can also retain revision history.

Source control has been around for quite some time. It's difficult to say when the history of source control began, but you can assume it's been around for nearly as long as using text to write software on a computer has been around.

Today, many professionals use the likes of Perforce or possibly Microsoft's Team Foundation Server. Though capable, they're both quite expensive. On the free side, in terms of cost, there are many alternatives for the independent game developer. Among the most common are SVN, GIT, and Mercurial. Each system involves a slightly different philosophy, giving each one different advantages.

The general idea behind source control involves setting up another computer as a server to host your code base. The host can be on the Internet, usually provided free of cost. The host can also be a personal computer you've set up at home. If the host is connected to the Internet, the contents are usually available to the public, such as the files provided for this book.

It's also handy to keep a backup of your work on a separate computer. A simple NAS, or network attached storage, device might be all you need. A NAS is a small box that looks a bit like an external hard disk. You can plug it into your home WiFi router, stream music and video from it, and use it to host your source control software. A quick Internet search for "Git on a NAS" or "SVN on a NAS" will turn up some results on how this can be done.

Binary files are called so because they contain computer-formatted binary data. Binary data complicates source control because revisions of a binary file cannot be merged together. In general, source code works only on text files.

### 5.15.3  GitHub

For this book, we'll be using a popular system called GitHub; otherwise, I'd need to leave my laptop online so you can access my computer to download the files. I've got American broadband, so downloading anything significant from my computer is impossible anyway.

Git stores the history of your project locally. All of the changes, history, and revision information is stored for easy access. This means that every change is retained locally as well.

This doesn't mean much for text files, as each change means a few lines of code. Images and other binary files, on the other hand, can add up. Keep this in mind when working on a large game project that might involve many hundreds of binary assets.

With large projects, the Git repo can be several gigabytes in size. This will increase if there are many image source files, like multilayered Painter or many large, dense Blender files. In general, binary files like that might be better suited for something like Dropbox or Skydrive.

Dropbox retains a history for each file every time it's changed, you can go into the Dropbox history and revert or restore a file from its revision history. This isn't source control; you can't have two files merge together or multiple people working on a file at the same time. You can with Git, but only with text files.

Git is a vast topic that can span a nice thick book all to itself. It's unfortunate that all of the references on Git assume you're already familiar with source control topics in general. Complicate this with the fact that the authors of the Git documentation assume you're a pro with Linux-style terminal commands.

### 5.15.4  What We've Learned

We still have some work left to do. We've gotten through the setup of GitHub and are ready to do some work. To get your own repo set up, we'll need to go through a few more steps, but I promise this part is super easy.

After setting everything up, we need to learn how to commit changes and push them to your own repo.

### 5.15.5  Project Files

A project is the complete collection of all involved source files. A repo can host any number of projects or even a directory containing any number of projects. Each project includes the directory structure and all related assets.

When a new Unity 3D project is created, the Assets Directory should be under source control. This means any changes to a file found in the Assets Directory on your computer can be tracked and any number of revisions recorded.

After a source control system is set up—we will get to this in a moment—and source files have been written, it's time to check-in your work. A check-in is a submission of work to source control, which means that anyone with access can get an update of your work from the host.

It's easy to rename, move, or delete any file or directory from source control, so there's no need to worry about making major changes. Every revision is recorded, numbered, and kept in a database. This allows you to revert a file or the entire Assets Directory to an older version of the source code. In most cases, the database keeps track only of changes between revisions; otherwise, at the end of a project, your source control server might have an overwhelming amount of data to track.

## 5.16  Setting Up a Repository

The Unity 3D Pro license has an option to add on an Asset Server module for more money. As an independent game developer, this might not be an option. We'll go through with the free, more commonly used source control system instruction for now.

To get started, you will want to grab the latest version of the GitHub software. This is located at https://github.com/. Here, you can follow the strange little mascot through the download and installation process of their software.

You may create a free account on github.com, which means that you'll be allowed to create as many projects as you like. You'll also be allowed to have an unlimited number of contributors to your project. You'll need to sign up with a user name and password on the GitHub website. Once this is done, you're just about ready to post your work from Unity 3D.

For a private repository, you'll need to sign up with a paid account. Since we're not exactly going to be building the next Call of Duty or Halo with our first project, there's really no reason to worry about anyone stealing our source code. Once you've started a more serious project, you might consider either a subscription with GitHub or building a private Git server.

I'd recommend skipping the command line setup and use the client software for your operating system. Classically trained programmers may tell you this is a mistake, but I'd rather not go through how to operate source control through the command line. Computers have a graphic user interface for a reason.

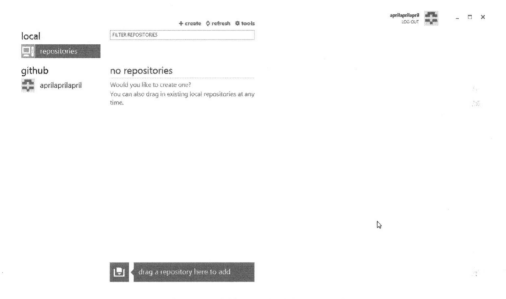

After the GitHub app has started, it's a good idea to double check the settings in the tools → options dialog. To make sure you'll be able to push your files to GitHub, you'll need to check that your user name and email are both filled in.

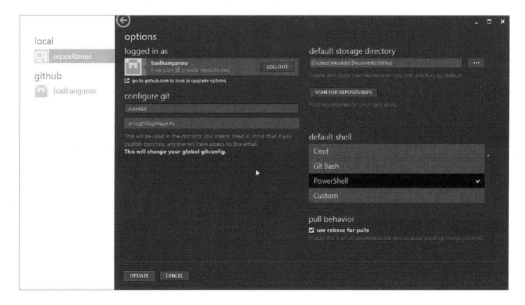

Once set up, it's time to pick a directory for your local repository. This can be changed later on, so any place will do. It's best to start with a new Unity 3D project, or a project that's already under way in Unity 3D. Unity 3D needs to be informed that the files it's generating are to be controlled by some sort of source control. To make this change, select Edit → Project Settings → Editor. The Inspector panel will now display the options for Version Control; select Meta Files to ensure that your Unity 3D project can be managed by Git.

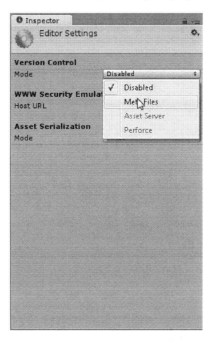

For this example, we'll start with a fresh Unity 3D project. To have something in the repository, I've also created a new C# file. Once the project has been created and Unity 3D has opened, it's simply a matter of dragging the directory on the desktop to the GitHub app.

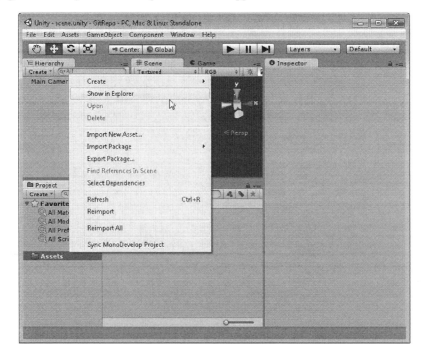

To find the directory, you can right click on the Assets Directory in the Project panel. This opens the directory with the Assets folder in it.

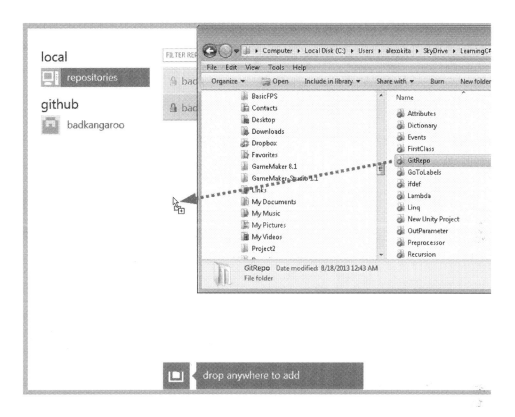

Dropping the file in the panel will begin the repository creation process.

You'll be prompted with a dialog to describe your project; this can be changed later so it's not important to make this meaningful if you're just learning how to use Git. Click on create to push the project to the server.

This action adds the repo to the list of repositories that GitHub is keeping track of. Double click on the new repository entry and you'll be taken to the push dialog. We'll want to make a few modifications to the project before pushing it.

By default, the project will have all of its subdirectories pushed to the server. This can be problematic if we leave all of the default settings. The Temp directory and the Library directories should be excluded from the push. These two directories are managed by Unity 3D and should not be checked in. Each Unity 3D user will have unique versions of these two directories.

Under the tools button, select settings; this opens a dialog box that shows what appears to be some text files.

The left panel shows the ignored files dialog. To make sure GitHub ignores the Library and Temp directories, we add the following two lines:

```
Library/
Temp/
```

This tells GitHub to ignore those directories and your submission will look like the following:

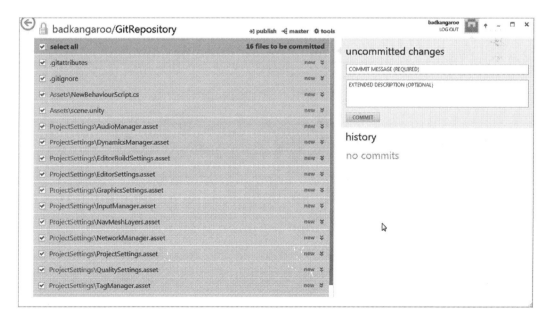

Add some comments; comments are always required.

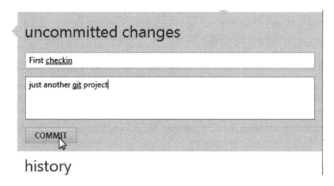

This gives us some clue as to what changes were being made when the check-in was done. After entering a comment, press the COMMIT button. This sounds final, but no code has been submitted to GitHub yet.

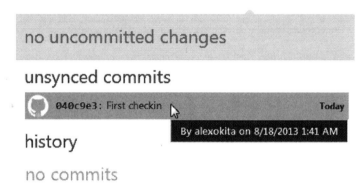

The above image shows unsynced commits; this means that GitHub and our local version are not in sync. To make these changes appear on the trunk, we need to click on the publish button at the top of the panel.

This will upload our changes to the main line source control and make our changes available to the public.

We're almost there!

Only after the in sync button has appeared have we actually submitted our project to GitHub. Once the project is on the GitHub server, it can be shared among any number of other programmers.

For personal use, GitHub is a great way to keep your project's history intact. However, it is a public repository and anything you do will be open to public scrutiny. Again, there are more private ways in which source control can be managed, but this requires a bit more computer software setup on the server, which goes beyond the scope of this book.

### 5.16.1  Push

When we make changes to our local version of the project, we'll want to keep them in sync with the version on the server.

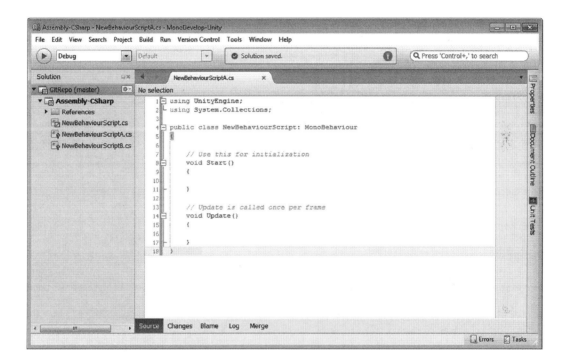

If we add a line to our C# file, we'll also be creating some additional files with the check-in.

### 5.16.2  Gitignore

Often, there are files which we do not want to check-in. These files are usually created locally and will be unique to each user. Local preferences and settings affect only one person at a time and can cause trouble if another person gets the changes. These files should be left out of a check-in and not pushed up to the repo.

Add the `*.csproj` and `*.sln` to the ignored files in the tools dialog box in the GitHub client. This will require a new comment and sync. To check-out our changes, we can expand the changed files in the client.

These show what lines were changed or added. Like before, we have new uncommitted local changes, which we need to push to the server.

Press the sync button at the top to push the updates to the server. From this point on, any programmer who wants to check out your project can download the zip or open the project with the GitHub client and test your game. Everything appears on the GitHub website.

   As you work, you may find other files that will need to be added to the ignore list. These include built files, when you start making APK files for iOS and ADK files for Android. These files shouldn't be checked-in, unless you're working to share a built binary file. These can be quite large in some cases, so it's better to leave them out of the repo.

### 5.16.3 Pull

When you created your GitHub account, your user name becomes a directory under the github.com site. For this book, you'll use https://github.com/badkangaroo/. To find this example repository, you'll add GitRepository/ after the badkangaroo/ user name. On the lower right, there are two options.

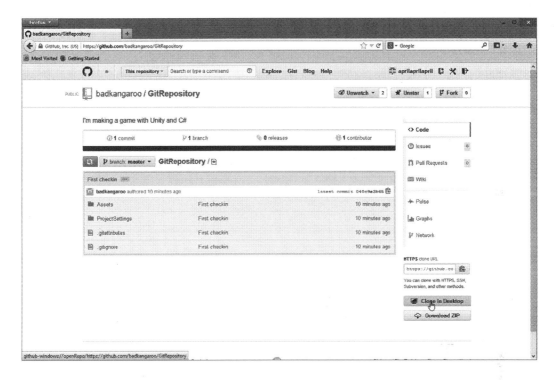

The first is Clone in Desktop; this will open the GitHub software. After a quick sync, the project will be cloned to your computer.

To get this resource another client needs to have the GitHub software installed. Cloning the project makes an exact copy of the latest revision on GitHub to the client's computer. On windows the clone is created in `C:\Users\Username\Documents\GitHub\` followed by the name of the project, so in this case it's `C:\Users\Username\Documents\GitHub\GitRepository` where this can be used as the project directory for Unity 3D. The GitHub website is somewhat similar to this setup https://github.com/Username/GitRepository you'll need to go here to manage the projects settings.

### 5.16.4 Contributors

As the creator of a project, you're the only one who can make modifications to the files in the project. To allow others to make modifications, you'll need to add them as collaborators.

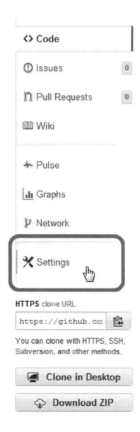

On your GitHub website for the project, select Settings, to the right of your repository. Here, you'll be able to change the name of the directory and pick several other options. To add people to the list contributors, select the Collaborators option.

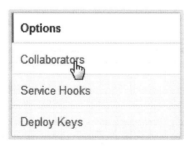

Add in the name they used to sign up for GitHub and now they'll be able to pull your code, make changes, and then push their modifications to the trunk. Users not on this list will not be able to make any contributions to the trunk of the code.

To make a submission, you push your work onto the server. This becomes the root of your source tree. From here on out, the source control server becomes the real home or main line of your project. Any team member should be making his or her contributions to the server, not your computer directly.

Someone needing your latest work would pull it from the server. *Push* and *pull* are commonly used terms when dealing with source control. Other words like *get* and *check-out* refer to pulling source files from the server. *Check-in* or *submit* often refers to pushing data to the server. After their contributions have been checked-in, you'll need to pull them from the server to update your local version to reflect the changes made by other programmers.

If you're working on your own, then you'll be the only one pushing changes. To get the latest projects for this book, I needed to pull only one file from GitHub; this was mentioned in Section 2.5. As files are added and changes are made, GitHub turns into a great location to keep track of your file changes.

Once you've written code, tested it, and are sure that everything is working, it's time to push your changes to the server. Only after the code has been synced can other users pull it from the server and get your changes.

### 5.16.5 What We've Learned

There was a lot to cover in this chapter on how to manage your source code. There's still a lot remaining to learn, when it comes to dealing with complex source control problems. Unless you've started working in a team, it's unlikely you'll have to deal with too many of these issues right away.

You'll be constantly updating the gitignore file; after a few iterations, the number of additions to the gitignore should come less often. Maintaining a clean git repository will help keep things running smoothly.

```
Library/
Temp/
*.csproj
*.sln
*.userprefs
```

The `*.` notation indicates that any file that ends with `.userprefs` or any file that ends with `.sln` should be ignored. The `*` is an old carryover from the DOS command shell; further back, Unix command shells also used the same notation for searching for files in directories.

The GitHub client app is new. It's far from perfect and requires a great deal of updating to make it more user friendly. At every turn, you might have an error prompting you to use a shell. For the uninitiated, this can be frustrating. However, GitHub is popular, and there are humans around who are able to help.

Most likely, you'll be able to search for a problem which many others have encountered and have already asked for help. There are also GitHub alternatives that can interface with the GitHub service.

Even better, there are plug-ins for as little as $5 that integrate with Unity 3D and can directly interface with GitHub from inside of the Unity 3D editor. It's worth some effort to investigate various source control software options as there is no clear winner. Many professional studios prefer using PerForce, a very complete package that includes tools to help merging multiple files. However, at the price its offered at per seat (the term used to describe software licensing), they exclude many independent developers.

## 5.17 Leveling Up: On to the Cool Stuff

We've come further along than most people who set out to learn how to program. By now, you should be able to read through some code and get some idea of how it's working. We've gotten through some of the tough beginnings of learning how to write in C#, but things are just about to get more interesting.

The clever tricks that programmers use to save time are about to start to come into play. If you take the time, you should review Chapters 1 through 4 to strengthen your grasp of the core concepts we've been studying.

There's an interesting topic that hasn't found a place in any chapters yet. If you open the MagicComponent project in Unity 3D, you'll be able to see some interesting behavior. Say we have an object in the scene with a component attached. We'll look at something called `FirstComponent.cs` attached to a cube.

If the Main Camera has a component attached that has a couple of variables that are set for FirstComponent and SecondComponent, how do we add the `GameObject`'s component to that slot in the Inspector panel? We drag it, of course!

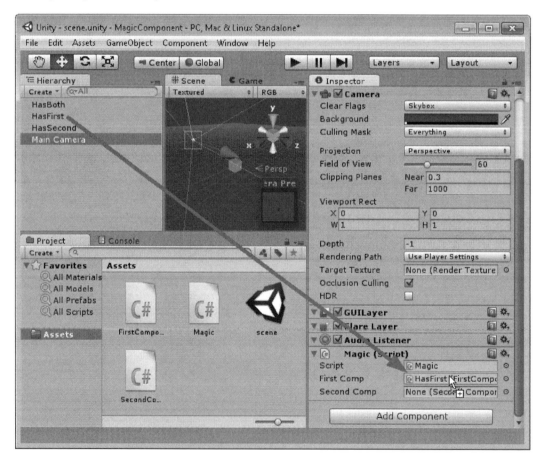

Therefore, even though the variable isn't `GameObject`, you can still drag the object from the scene into the Inspector panel. Unity 3D is clever enough to find a component of the same type as the slot in the Inspector.

This feature also means that any variable changed on the object in the scene will have a direct connection to the `Magic.cs` class that is holding onto the variable. This means a couple of strange things. First, the objects in the scene are actually instances, but they are acting in a rather weird limbo. Second, the connection between variables is stored in some magic data stored in the scene file.

The weird limbo infers that when you drag a class onto an object in the editor, it is immediately instanced. This behavior is unusual in that this only happens in the Unity Editor, your player and the finished game never has any behavior similar to this. The class instances an object and attaches it to the `GameObject` in the scene, as though you used `GameObject.Instance()` or even `new FirstComponent();`, or perhaps `Component.Add();`, and added it to the `GameObject` in the scene.

The fact that the `Start ()` and `Update ()` functions aren't called means that the game isn't running. However, the class is still an instanced object created by the cs file in the Assets Directory. There are editor scripts that do run while the game might not be playing. Editor scripts are often used to help game designers.

Editor scripts can be used to create tools and other fun interfaces specifically for the Unity 3D Editor. These are often not running while the game is playing. We shouldn't venture too far into Unity 3D-specific tricks as this distracts us from learning more about C#, but it's fun to know what to look for if we want to build our own C# tools for Unity 3D.

The strange fact that the variable in `Magic.cs` has a handle on an object in the scene without having to run `GameObject.Find();` or `Transform.Find();` means that there's a lot going on in the scene file. All of this is actually stored in the meta files that seem to be appearing as you work with others on Unity 3D projects.

These meta files are required for these magic data connections between objects in a Unity 3D Scene file. Of course, other file settings and project settings are also stored in these meta files. If you open one, you'll find many things called GUIDs, which stands for globally unique identifiers, and they're used in meta files to find a specific object in the scene and apply settings to them.

It wasn't long ago when game engines referenced everything in the scene by their GUID alone. Today, they're at least hidden from view, but they still affect our lives as game programmers. We can't reference a specific object by name alone. If you've got several objects named `GameObject`, then you're going to have a rough time remembering which one actually has the data you're looking for. Because of this, everything is assigned a GUID and that's just the way it's gotta be.

# 6

## *Intermediate*

Chapters 7 and 8 are big and dense. In many ways, they're exciting as well. Getting into a programming language means discovering many cool tricks. The basics of any programming language have already been covered. To be honest, much of what you need has already been covered.

From here on out, you'll be learning some of the more refined systems that make the C# language elegant and concise. Rather than having long chains of if-else statements, you can use a switch statement. Rather than having a large uncontrolled nest of different variables, you can group them together in a struct.

Don't worry about not making rapid progress; learning is more about the journey than it is about the goal. Of course, if you do have a goal of making a featured mobile game, then by all means speed forth toward your goal. Just try not to skip around too much; there's much stuff that is explained for a reason.

## 6.1 What Will Be Covered in This Chapter

*The long journey begins.* We're going to cover some important concepts here, including the following:

- Pseudocode
- Class constructors
- Arrays
- Enums
- Switch statement
- Structures
- Namespaces
- More on functions
- More on inheritance
- More on type casting
- Some work on vectors
- Goto
- Out parameter
- Ref parameter
- Operator overloading

This chapter discusses a few concepts more than once, or rather, we look at different aspects of type casting, for instance, but we divide the concept over more than one chapter. In between the chapters, we cover a few other concepts that do relate back to the topic. Learning a single concept can mean taking in a few separate concepts before coming back to the original topic.

## 6.2 Review

By now you've been equipped with quite a vocabulary of terms and a useful set of tools to take care of nearly any basic task. Moving forward, you'll only extend your ability and come to grips that you've still got a long way to go. Even after years of engineering software, there's always more to learn. Even once you think you've covered a programming language, another version is released and you need to learn more features.

Aside from learning one language, most companies will eventually toss in a task that involves learning another programming language. In a modern setting, it's likely you'll need to learn some of the programming languages while on the job. This might involve knowing something like Scala or PHP, yet another programming language you'll have to learn.

Learning additional programming languages isn't as daunting as you might think. Once you know one language, it's far easier to learn another. The keyword `var` is used in many other programming languages in the exact same context. It's a keyword used to store a variable. In C#, we see `var v = "things";`, which is similar to JavaScript where `var v = "things";`.

So far the principles that have been covered in this book are general enough such that almost every other programming language has similar concepts. Nearly all languages have conditions and operators. Most languages use tokens and white space in the same way as well.

## 6.3 Pseudocode

In a practical sense, you can do anything you set out to do.

It's just about time now to start trying to think like a programmer. Armed with functions, logic, and loops, we can start to do some more interesting things with Unity 3D. To do this, we're going to learn more about what Unity 3D has in the way of functions which we can use.

There's hardly any feature implemented in a game you've played that you too can't do, given the time. Everything that is being done using Unity 3D is something you too can do. To create a game object, they use the same function we used in Chapter 5.

Programmers start with a task. For this chapter, we're going to move the cube around with the keyboard. Therefore, we're going to do two things: First, we need to figure out how to read the keyboard and then we need to change the cube's position.

### 6.3.1 Thinking It Through

A common exercise is to write pseudocode or at least think about what the code will look like. We need to have a section for reading keyboard inputs, acting on the keyboard inputs, and then moving the cube. This is going to happen on every frame, so we need to put this in the `Update ()` function.

We need at least four inputs: forward, backward, left, and right. Unity 3D is a 3D engine, so we're going to use x for left and right, and z for forward and backward. This might look like the following.

```
bool moveForward
bool moveBackward
bool moveLeft
bool moveRight
```

However, we need to set those somehow with an input command from the keyboard, which might look like the following:

```
moveForward = keyboard input w
moveBackward = keyboard input s
moveLeft = keyboard input a
moveRight = keyboard input d
```

So far everything makes sense. We need to move the cube so that it involves a `Vector3`, since everything that has a position is using `transform.position` to keep track of where it is. Therefore, we should set the `transform.position` to a `Vector3`. We should have an updated position to start with.

```
Vector3 updatedPosition = starting position
```

We should have a `starting position`, so the `Vector3` isn't initialized with 0, 0, 0 when we start. We might want to start in the level somewhere else other than the scene of origin. However, we need to move to the `Vector3` that we're modifying.

```
Transform.position = updatedPosition
```

Now we should think about modifying the `updatedPosition` when a key is pressed. Therefore, something like the following should work:

```
If moveForward updatedPosition.z = updatedPosition.z + 0.1
If moveBackward updatedPosition.z = updatedPosition.z - 0.1
If moveLeft updatedPosition.x = updatedPosition.x - 0.1
If moveRight updatedPosition.x = updatedPosition.x + 0.1
```

We've set positions before with variables, which was pretty easy. Therefore, the only thing we need to figure out is the keyboard input.

### 6.3.2 Class Members

Classes provided by Unity 3D become accessible when you add `using UnityEngine` at the top of your C# code. All of the classes found inside of that library have names which you can use directly in your own code. This includes `Input`, and all of the members of `Input` are imported into your code.

#### 6.3.2.1 A Basic Example

Let's start off with creating a new class that will have some functions in it. We've done this before by creating a new C# class in the Project panel. This can be found in the PseudoCode project from the repository.

```
using UnityEngine;
using System.Collections;
public class Members
{
    public void FirstFunction ()
    {
        print("First function");
    }
}
```

Create a new class called `Members.cs` because we're going to use members of the `Members` class. Then we'll add `public void FirstFunction()` with a basic `print("First Function");` to print to the Console panel when it's used.

There are two classifications for the stuff that classes are made of: data members and function members. As you might imagine, function members are the lines of code that execute and run logic on data. Data members are the variables that are accessible within the class.

In our `Example` class we've been abusing a lot, we'll add in the following line to the `Start ()` function:

```
//Use this for initialization
void Start ()
{
    Members m = new Members();
}
```

This creates what's called an instance. We're assigning m to being a new copy or instance of the `Members` class. The keyword new is used to create new instances. `Members();` is used to tell the new keyword what class we're using. It seems like we're using the class as a function, and to a limited extent we are, but we'll have to leave those details for Section 6.3.3.1.

The m variable that is an instance of the Members class is now a thing we can use in the function. When we use m, we can access its members.

```
// Use this for initialization
void Start()
{
    Members m = new Members();
    m.
}
```

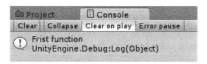

Type "m." and a new pop-up will appear in MonoDevelop showing a list of things that m can do. FirstFunction, as well as a few other items, is in the list. These other items were things that Object was able to do. Accessing the different functions within a class is a simple matter of using the dot operator.

```
void Start ()
{
    Members m = new Members();
    m.FirstFunction();
}
```

Finish off the m. by adding FirstFunction();. Running the script when it's attached to a cube or something in the scene will produce the following Console output. Objects and its members have many uses, though; this might not be clear from this one example.

### 6.3.2.2 Thinking like a Programmer

A peek into a programmer's thinking process reveals a step-by-step process of evaluating a situation and finding a solution for each step. Logic takes the front seat in this case as the programmer needs to not only investigate each function he or she must use but also clean up the thinking process as he or she writes code.

Intuition and deduction is a huge part of programming. The programmer needs to guess what sort of functions he or she should be looking for. With each new development environment, the programmer needs to learn the software's application programming interface, the interface between you (the programmer) and the application you're working with, in this case, Unity 3D.

At this point, we have some basic tools to do something interesting with our game scene. However, to make a game, we're going to read the keyboard mouse and any other input device that the player might want to use. A appropriate place to start would be looking up the word "input" in the Solution Explorer in MonoDevelop.

Dig into the UnityEngine.dll and expand the UnityEngine library. You should find an Input class that looks very promising. From here, we can start hunting for a function inside of input that might be useful for us. At this point, I should mention that programmers all seem to use a unique vocabulary.

The words "Get" and "Set" are often used by programmers for getting and setting values. For getting a keyboard command, we should look for a function that gets things for us. We can find "GetKey" in the numerous functions found in Input.

```
⊞   public static bool GetKey (string name)...
⊞   public static bool GetKey (KeyCode key)...
⊞   public static bool GetKeyDown (string name)...
⊞   public static bool GetKeyDown (KeyCode key)...
⊞   public static bool GetKeyUp (string name)...
⊞   public static bool GetKeyUp (KeyCode key)...
```

There seems to be `string name` and `KeyCode` key for each one of the functions. We did mention that reusing names for things means erasing a previously used name. However, this doesn't always hold true. In the case of functions, when you duplicate a name, you're allowed to share the name, as long as you do something different with the arguments found in parentheses. This is called overriding, and we'll learn more about that in Section 6.13.1. It's just good to know what you're looking at so you don't get too lost.

So now that we've found something that looks useful, how do we use it? The "GetKey" function looks like its `public` function, which is good. Functions with the keyword `public` are functions that we're allowed to use.

The context when using the dot operator in numbers changes an `int` to a `double` or `float` if you add in an `f` at the end of the number. When you add the dot operator after the name of a class found in UnityEngine, you're asking to gain access to a class member. In this case, we found `GetKey` inside of `Input`, so to talk to that function we use the dot operator after `Input` to get to that function.

There were two `GetKey` functions: The first had "KeyCode key" and the second had "string name" written in the arguments for the function. This means we have two options we can use.

When you add the first parenthesis, MonoDevelop pops up some helpers.

```
// Use this for initialization
void Start()
{                   public static bool GetKey(    ▲ 1 of 2 ▼
                        string name
    Members m = m )
    m.FirstFunction();
    Input.GetKey()
}                    ⌷  JointActor2D
                     E  JointProjectionMode
// Update is         S  JointSpring
void Update()        S  JointTranslationLimits2D
{                    S  jvalue
                     F  key:
}                    E  KeyCode              ⸽    public sealed enum KeyCode
```

These help you fill in the blanks. There are many `KeyCode` options to choose from. You can see them all by scrolling through the pop-up. I picked the `KeyCode.A` to test this out. I'm guessing that pressing the A key on the keyboard is going to change something. In the `Example.cs` file, add in the following:

```
void Update ()
{
    bool AKey = Input.GetKey(KeyCode.A);
    Debug.Log(AKey);
}
```

We're setting the bool `AKey` to this function; why a `bool` and why even do this? Remember that the function was designated as a `public static bool`. The last word is the reason why we're using a `bool AKey`. The variable type we're setting matches the return type of the function.

Finally, we're printing out the value of `AKey`. Run the game and press the A key on your keyboard and read the Console output from Unity 3D.

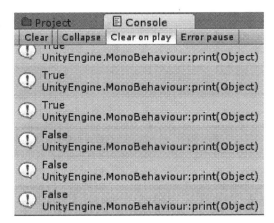

When the A key is down, we get `True`; when it's not down, we get `False`. It looks like our hunch was correct. Our `AKey` `bool` is now being controlled by the `Input` class' member function `GetKey`. We know the return type of `GetKey` because of the `bool` that was written just before the name of the function. We also know how to access the function inside of `Input` through the dot operator.

Let's keep this going. Make a `bool` for `WKey`, `SKey`, and `DKey`. This will allow us to use the classic WASD keyboard input found in many different games. Then we'll make them set to the different `GetKeys` that we're going to use from `Input`.

Now we're going to make our cube move around, so we're going to look at the `Transform` class. To move our cube around, we're going to keep track of our current position. To do this, we're going to make a `Vector3` called `pos` as a class scoped variable.

```
5        public Vector3 pos;
6        // Use this for initialization
7        void Start () {
8            pos = transform.position;
9        }
```

The first thing we want to do is set the `pos` to the object's current position when the game starts. This means we can place the cube anywhere in the scene at the beginning of the game and the `pos` will know where we're starting.

```
12       void Update () {
13           bool AKey = Input.GetKey(KeyCode.A);
14           bool SKey = Input.GetKey(KeyCode.S);
15           bool DKey = Input.GetKey(KeyCode.D);
16           bool WKey = Input.GetKey(KeyCode.W);
17           transform.position = pos;
18       }
```

In the `Update ()` function which is called, we're going to set the `transform.position` of the cube to `pos` in each frame. This means that if we change the x, y, or z of the `pos` `Vector3` variable, the cube will go to that `Vector3`. Now all we need to do is change the `pos.x` and `pos.z` when we press one of the keys.

```
Vector3 pos = Vector3.zero;
void Update ()
{
    bool AKey = Input.GetKey(KeyCode.A);
    bool SKey = Input.GetKey(KeyCode.S);
    bool DKey = Input.GetKey(KeyCode.D);
    bool WKey = Input.GetKey(KeyCode.W);
```

```
        if (AKey)
        {
             pos.x = pos.x - 0.1f;
        }
        if (DKey)
        {
             pos.x = pos.x + 0.1f;
        }
        if (WKey)
        {
             pos.z = pos.z + 0.1f;
        }
        if (SKey)
        {
             pos.z = pos.z - 0.1f;
        }
        transform.position = pos;
    }
```

I've added an `if` statement controlled by each `bool` we created at the beginning of the `Update ()` function. Then we changed the `pos.x` and `pos.z` according to the direction I wanted the cube to move in by adding or subtracting a small value. Try this out and experiment with some different values.

This is not the only solution, nor is it the best. This is a simple solution and rather restricted. The speed is constant, and the rotation of the cube is also fixed. If we want to improve on this solution, we're going to need a better way to deal with many variables.

A big part of programming is starting with something basic and then refining it later on. You start with the things you know and add to it stuff you figure out. Once you learn more, you go back and make changes. It's a process that never ends. As programmers learn more and figure out more clever tricks, their new code gets written with more clever tricks.

### 6.3.3 Return

`return` is a powerful keyword; it's a very clever trick. It's used in a couple of different ways, but certainly the most useful is turning a function into data. If a function doesn't give out data, it's given the return type `void`. For instance, we've been using `void Start ()` and `void Update ()`.

`void` indicates that the function doesn't need to return any data; using the keyword `return` in a function like this returns a `void` or a nothing. Any keywords that precede the `return` type modify how the function operates; for instance, if we wanted to make a function available to other classes, we need to precede the `return` type with the keyword `public`.

#### 6.3.3.1 A Basic Example

Using the `return` keyword gives a function a value. You're allowed to use the function name as though it were the function's return value.

```
    void Start ()
    {
        print(ImANumber());
    }
    int ImANumber()
    {
        return 3;
    }
```

When you run this basic example, you'll see a 3 printed out in the Console panel. To prove that `ImANumber()` is just a 3, you can even perform math with the function. In the following example, you'll get many 6s being printed out to the Console panel.

```
void Start ()
{
    print (ImANumber() + ImANumber());
}
int ImANumber()
{
    return 3;
}
```

Most often when we want to reduce complexity within a single function, we need to separate our code into other smaller functions. Doing so makes our work less cluttered and easier to manage. Once the code has been separated into different smaller functions, they become individual commands that can contain their own complexity.

We're going to reduce the number of lines required in the Update loop. To do this, we'll write our own function with a return type Vector3. Reducing the number of lines of code you have to muddle through is sometimes the goal of clean code.

ImANumber() isn't a variable; it's a function. In other words, you will not be able to assign something to ImANumber() as in the following example:

```
ImANumber() = 7;
```

There are ways to do something similar to this. We'll need to use the contents in parentheses to assign ImANumber() a value for it to return.

### 6.3.4  Arguments aka Args (Not Related to Pirates)

We've seen the use of arguments (also known as args) earlier when we initialized a "Vector3(x,y,z);" with three parameters. To start, we'll write a function that's very simple and takes one arg.

#### *6.3.4.1  The Basic Example*

```
void Start ()
{
    print(INeedANumber(1));
}
int INeedANumber(int number) {
    return number;
}
```

We start with an int INeedANumber (int number) as our function. The contents of this function are filled with int number, indicating two things. First is the type that we expect to be in our function's argument list as well as a name or an identifier for the int argument. The identifier number from the argument list exists throughout the scope of the function.

```
void Start () {
    int val = INeedANumber(3) + INeedANumber(7);
    print (val);
}
int INeedANumber(int number) {
    return number;
}
```

In this second example, we use the INeedANumber() function as a number. It just so happens to be the same number we're using in its argument list. When we print out val from this, we get 10 printed to the Console panel. However, this doesn't have to be the case.

```
int INeedANumber(int number) {
    return number + 1;
}
```

If we were to modify the return value to number + 1 and run the previous example, we'd have 12 printed out to the Console panel. This would be the same as adding 4 and 8, or what is happening inside of the function 3 + 1 and 7 + 1.

### 6.3.4.2 Multiple Args

When you see functions without anything in parentheses, programmers say that the function takes no args. Or rather, the function doesn't need any arguments to do its work. We can expand upon this by adding another argument to our function. To tell C# what your two arguments are, you separate them with a comma and follow the same convention of type followed by identifier.

```
void Start ()
{
    int val = INeedTwoNumbers(3, 7);
    print (val);
}
int INeedTwoNumbers (int a, int b)
{
    return a + b;
}
```

MonoDevelop automatically knows what your argument list looks like and pops up a helper to let you know what you add into the function for it to work. This function then takes the two arguments, adds them together, and then prints out the result to the Unity 3D's Console panel.

Just for the sake of clarity, you're allowed to use any variety of types for your args. The only condition is that the final result needs to match the same type as the return value. In more simple terms, when the function is declared, its return type is set by the keyword used when it's declared.

This also includes data types which you've written. We'll take a look at that in a bit, but for now we'll use some data types we've already seen.

```
int INeedTwoNumbers (int a, float b)
{
    return a * (int)b;
}
```

Mixing different types together can create some interesting effects, some of which might not be expected. We'll study the consequences of mixing types later on as we start to learn about type casting, but for now just observe how this behaves on your own and take some notes. To convert a float value to an int value, you precede the float with the number type you want to convert it to with (ToType) DifferentType, but we'll get into type conversions again later.

So far we've been returning the same data types going into the function; this doesn't have to be the case. A function that returns a boolean value doesn't need to accept booleans in its argument list.

```
bool NumbersAreTheSame (int a, int b)
{
    bool ret;
    if (a == b) {
        ret = true;
    } else {
        ret = false;
    }
    return ret;
}
```

In this case, if both a and b are the same number, then the function returns `true`. If the two numbers are different, then the function returns `false`. This works well, but we can also shorten this code by a couple of lines if we use more than one `return`.

```
bool NumbersAreTheSame (int a, int b)
{
    if (a == b) {
        return true;
    } else {
        return false;
    }
}
```

The `return` keyword can appear in more than one place. However, this can cause some problems. If we return a value based on only a limited case, then the compiler will catch this problem.

```
bool NumbersAreTheSame (int a, int b)
{
    if (a == b)
    {
        return true;
    }
}
```

This example will cause an error stating the following:

```
Assets/Example.cs(16,6): error CS0161: 'Example.NumbersAreTheSame(int, int)':
not all code paths return a value
```

The rest of the possibilities need to have a return value. In terms of what Unity 3D expects, all paths of the code need to return a valid bool. The return value always needs to be fulfilled, otherwise the code will not compile.

### 6.3.4.3 Using Args

Doing all of these little changes repeatedly becomes troublesome, so they leave some things up to other people to change till they like the results. Each function in the `Input` class returns a unique value. We can observe these by looking at the results of `Input.GetKey()`.

```
void Update () {
    print (Input.GetKey(KeyCode.A));
}
```

Once you type in `Input`, a pop-up with the members of the `Input` class is shown. Among them is `GetKey`. Once you enter `GetKey` and add in the first parenthesis, another pop-up with a list of various inputs is shown. Choose the `KeyCode.A`. Many other input options are available, so feel free to experiment with them on your own.

To test this code out, run the game and watch the output in the Console panel. Hold down the "a" key on the keyboard and watch the `false` printout replaced with `true` when the key is down. Using the `print()` function to test things out one at a time is a simple way to check out what various functions do. Test out the various other keys found in the `Input.GetKey()` function.

```
Vector3 Movement(float dist)
{
    Vector3 vec = Vector3.zero;
    if (Input.GetKey(KeyCode.A))
    {
        vec.x -= dist;
    }
    if (Input.GetKey(KeyCode.D))
    {
        vec.x += dist;
    }
    if (Input.GetKey(KeyCode.W))
    {
        vec.z += dist;
    }
    if (Input.GetKey(KeyCode.S))
    {
        vec.z -= dist;
    }
    return vec;
}
```

We should add an argument to the `Movement()` function. With this we'll add in a simple way to change a variable inside of the `Movement()` function and maintain the function's portability. Replace the `0.1f` value with the name of the argument. This means that anything put into the function's argument list will be duplicated across each statement that uses it.

This means we need to pass in a parameter to the argument list in the `Movement()` function. We can test by entering a simple float, which is what the `Movement()` argument list expects.

```
void Update ()
{
    transform.position += Movement(0.2f);
}
```

This means we're just reducing the number of places a number is being typed. We want to make this number easier to edit and something that can be modified in the editor.

```
using UnityEngine;
using System.Collections;
public class Example : MonoBehaviour
{
    public Vector3 pos = Vector3.zero;
    public float speed;
//the rest of your code below...
```

Add in a `public  float` so that the Inspector panel can see it. Then add the variable to the `Movement()`'s parameter list.

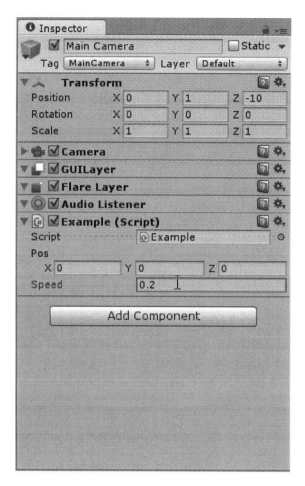

Change the value for Delta in the Inspector panel and run the game. Now the WASD keys will move the cube around at a different speed, thanks to the use of a public variable. There are a few different ways to do the same thing. For instance, we could have ignored using the arguments and used Delta in place of Dist. However, this means that the function would rely on a line of code outside of the function to work. Everywhere you want to use the function, you'd have to write in a public float Delta statement at the class level.

### 6.3.5 Assignment Operators

Operators that fill variables with data are called assignment operators. We've been using = to assign a variable a value in the previous chapters. There are different types of assignment operators that have added functionality.

```
void Update ()
{
    transform.position += new Vector3(0.1f, 0.0f, 0.0f);
}
```

Introduce the += operator to the Vector3. When operators are used in pairs there are no spaces between them. The + operator adds two values together. The = operator assigns a value to a variable. If there was white space between the + and the =, this would raise a syntax error. The += operator allows you to add two vectors together without having to use the original variable name again. This also works with single numbers. An int MyInt += 1; works just as well. Rather than having to use `pos.z = pos.z + 0.1f`, you can use `pos.z += 0.1f`, which is less typing. If you run the code up above, then you'll see your cube scooting off in the positive x direction.

### 6.3.5.1 A Basic Example

As we have seen with the ++ and the – unary operators, the += operator and its negative version, the –=, work in a similar way. One important and easy-to-forget difference is the fact that the ++/–– works only on integer data types. The += and –= work on both integer and floating point data types.

```
float f = 0;
void Update ()
{
    f += 0.25f;
    print(f);
}
```

In this example, the `f` variable will be incremented 0.25 with each update. In the code fragment above, this increase is something that cannot be done with an integer. This is similar to using `f = f + 0.25f`; though the += is a bit cleaner looking. The change is primarily aesthetic, and programmers are a fussy bunch, so the += is the preferred method to increment numbers.

A part of learning how to program is by decoding the meaning behind cryptic operators, and this is just one example. We're sure to come across more mysterious operators, but if you take them in slowly and practice using them, you'll learn them quickly.

```
void Update ()
{
    transform.position += Movement();
}
Vector3 Movement()
{
    return new Vector3(0.1f, 0.2f, 0.3f);
}
```

Rather than using a new `Vector3` to add to the `transform.position`, we want to use a function. To make this work, the function has to have a `Vector3` return type. For a function to return the type, we need to include the keyword `return` in the function.

This function is now a `Vector3` value. Based on any external changes, the value returned can also change. This makes our function very flexible and much more practical. Again, the cube will scoot off to the x if you run this code. This and the previous examples are doing the exact same thing. Don't forget that C# is case sensitive, so make sure the `vec` is named the same throughout the function.

```
void Update ()
{
    transform.position += Movement(0.2f);
}
Vector3 Movement(float dist)
{
    Vector3 vec = Vector3.zero;
    if (Input.GetKey(KeyCode.A))
    {
        vec.x -= dist;
    }
    if (Input.GetKey(KeyCode.D))
    {
        vec.x += dist;
    }
```

```
        if (Input.GetKey(KeyCode.W))
        {
            vec.z += dist;
        }
        if (Input.GetKey(KeyCode.S))
        {
            vec.z -= dist;
        }
        return vec;
    }
```

If += works to add a number to a value, then -= subtracts a value from the number. There are some more variations on this, but they're going to have to wait for Section 8.9.

The Movement() function is portable. If you copy the function into another class, you have made reusable code. As any programmer will tell you, you should always write reusable code. The function operates mostly on its own. It relies on very few lines of code outside of the function. There are no class scoped variables it's depending on, so you need to only copy the lines of code existing in the function.

This function is not completely without any external dependencies. The Input.GetKey function does rely on the UnityEngine library, but there are ways to reduce this even further. To figure out other ways to reduce complexity and dependencies, we need to learn more tricks.

Wherever you need to read input and return a Vector3 to move something, you can use this function. Copy and paste the function in any class, and then add the transform.position += Movement(); into the Update () function of that object, and it will move when you press the WASD keys.

### 6.3.6 What We've Learned

The earlier discussion was an introduction to arguments and return values. We started to learn a bit about how to use members of classes and how to find them. There's still a lot more to learn, but I think we have a pretty good start and enough of a foundation to build on by playing with things in the game engine.

It's time to start having functions talk to other functions, and to do this, we're going to start writing some more classes that can talk to one another. Accessing other classes is going to require some more interesting tricks, and with everything we learn, we expand the tools that we can build with.

## 6.4 Class Constructors

A class is first written as in the following example:

```
class Zombie
{
}
```

We start off with very little information. As we assign member fields and member functions, we create places for the class to store data and provide the class with capability.

```
    class Zombie
    {
        public string Name;
        public int brainsEaten;
        public int hitPoints;
    }
```

The use of these parameters is inferred by their name and use. When we create a new Zombie() in the game, we could spend the next few lines initializing his parameters. Of course, we can add as many parameters as needed, but for this example, we're going to limit ourselves to just a few different objects.

```
    void Start ()
    {
        Zombie rob = new Zombie();
        rob.Name = "Zombie";
        rob.hitPoints = 10;
        rob.brainsEaten = 0;
    }
```

One simple method provided in C# is to add the parameters of the classes in a set of curly braces. Each field in `Zombie` is accessible through this method. Each one is separated by a comma, not a semicolon.

```
    void Start () {
        Zombie rob = new Zombie(){
            Name = "Zombie",
            brainsEaten = 0,
            hitPoints = 10
        };
    }
```

Note the trailing `;` after the closing curly brace. This system doesn't do much to shorten the amount of work involved. With each public data field provided in the `Zombie` class, we need to use the name of the field and assign it. Doing this for every new zombie might seem like a bit of extra work.

While building prototypes and quickly jamming code together, shortcuts like these can inform how we intend to use the class `object`. Rather than coming up with all possibilities and attempting to predict how a class is going to be used, it's usually better to use a class, try things out, and then make changes later.

### 6.4.1 A Basic Example

A class constructor would save a bit of extra work. Open the ZombieConstructor project to follow along. You might have noticed that the statement `Zombie rob = new Zombie();` has a pair of parentheses after the class it's instancing. When a class `Zombie();` is instanced, we could provide additional information to this line. To enable this, we need to add in a constructor to the `Zombie()`'s class. This looks like the following:

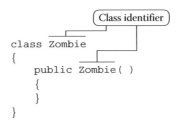

To give this example more meaning, we'll use the following code:

```
class Zombie
{
    public string Name;
    public int brainsEaten;
    public int hitPoints;
    public Zombie()
    {
        Name = "Zombie";
        brainsEaten = 0;
        hitPoints = 10;
    }
}
```

After the data fields, we create a new function named after the class. This function is called a class constructor. The function `public Zombie()` contains assignment statements that do the same thing as the previous class instantiation code we were using.

```
Zombie rob = new Zombie();
```

This statement `Zombie rob = new Zombie();` invokes the `Zombie()` constructor function in the `Zombie` class. When the constructor function is called, `Name`, `brainsEaten`, and `hitPoints` are all assigned at the same time. However, this will assume that every zombie is named "Zombie," has eaten no brains, and has `10` hitpoints. This is not likely the case with all zombies. Therefore, we'd want to provide some parameters to the class constructor function.

```
public Zombie(string n, int hp)
{
    Name = n;
    brainsEaten = 0;
    hitPoints = hp;
}
```

By adding in a few parameters to the interface, we're allowed to take in some data as the class is instanced.

```
void Start ()
{
    Zombie rob = new Zombie("Rob", 10);
}
```

So now when we create a new zombie, we're allowed to name it and assign its hitpoints all at the same time without needing to remember the names of the data fields of the classes. When the constructor is invoked, the first field corresponds to a `string n`, which is then assigned to `Name` with the `Name = n;` statement. Next we will assume that a new zombie has not had a chance to eat any brains just yet, so we can assign it to `0` when it's instanced. Finally, we can use the second argument `int hp` and use that to assign to the `hitPoints` with the `hitPoints = hp;` statement.

### 6.4.2 What We've Learned

Class constructors allow us to instantiate classes with unique data every time a new class is instanced. Putting this into use involves a few extra steps.

```
class Zombie
{
    public string Name;
    public int brainsEaten;
    public int hitPoints;
    GameObject ZombieMesh;
    public Zombie(string n, int hp)
    {
        Name = n;
        brainsEaten = 0;
        hitPoints = hp;
        ZombieMesh = GameObject.CreatePrimitive(PrimitiveType.Capsule);
        Vector3 pos = new Vector3();
        pos.x = Random.Range(-10, 10);
        pos.y = 0f;//optional
        pos.z = Random.Range(-10, 10));
        ZombieMesh.transform.position = pos;
    }
}
```

By adding a mesh to each zombie, we can more directly observe the instantiation of a new zombie in a scene. To make this more clear, we create a vector with a random x and a random z position so that they can appear in different places.

```
void Start ()
{
    string[] names = new string[]{"stubbs", "rob", "white"};
    for(int i = 0; i < names.Length; i++)
    {
        Zombie z = new Zombie(names[i], Random.Range(10, 15));
        Debug.Log(z.Name);
    }
}
```

To make use of the different parameters, we create a new list of zombie names. Then in a `for` loop, we create a new zombie for each name in the list. For good measure, we assign a random number of hitpoints for each one with `Random.Range(10, 15)` which assigns a random number to each zombie between 10 and 15.

```
using UnityEngine;
using System.Collections;
public class Example : MonoBehaviour
{
    //Use this for initialization
    void Start () {
        string[] names = new string[]{"stubbs", "rob", "white"};
        for(int i = 0; i < names.Length; i++) {
            Zombie z = new Zombie(names[i], Random.Range(10, 15));
            Debug.Log(z.Name);
        }
    }
}
```

The full code of `Zombie.cs` should look like the following sample:

```
class Zombie
{
    public string Name;
    public int brainsEaten;
    public int hitPoints;
    GameObject ZombieMesh;
    public Zombie(string n, int hp)
    {
        Name = n;
        brainsEaten = 0;
        hitPoints = hp;
        ZombieMesh = GameObject.CreatePrimitive(PrimitiveType.Capsule);
        Vector3 pos = new Vector3(
        Random.Range(-10, 10), 0,
        Random.Range(-10, 10));
        ZombieMesh.transform.position = pos;
    }
}
```

The only new thing we've added here is the `string[]` object, which we'll get to next. Just so we know what's going on, we show a log of each zombie's name after it's created. We'll go further into arrays in Chapter 7; if the `string[]` is a bit confusing, we'll clear that up next.

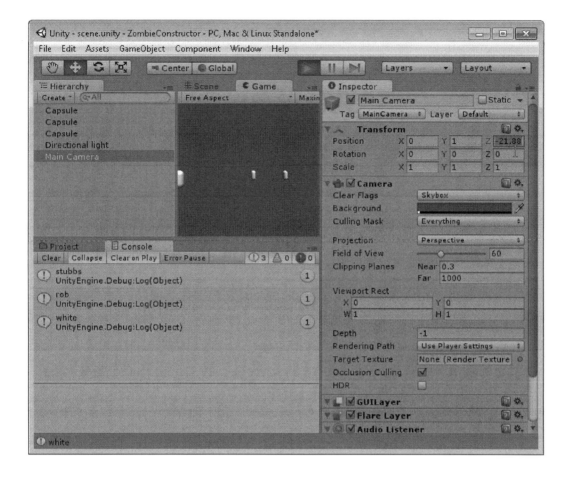

### 6.4.3 What We've Learned

A class constructor is very useful and should almost always be created when you create a new class. We are also allowed to create multiple systems to use a constructor. We'll get around to covering that in Section 6.13.1 on function overrides, but we'll have to leave off here for now.

When building a class, it's important to think in terms of what might change between each object. This turns into options that can be built into the constructor. Giving each object the ability to be created with different options allows for more variations in game play and appearance. Setting initial colors, behaviors, and starting variables is easier with a constructor. The alternative would be to create the new object and then change its values after the object is already in the scene.

## 6.5 Arrays Revisited

By now, we're familiar with the bits of knowledge that we'll need to start writing code. In Chapter 7, we'll become more familiar with the integrated development environment known as MonoDevelop, and we'll go deeper into variables and functions.

Let's start off with a task. Programmers usually need something specific to do, so to stretch our knowledge and to force ourselves to learn more, we're going to do something simple that requires some new tricks to accomplish. If we're going to make a game with a bunch of characters, we're going to make and keep track of many different bits of information such as location, size, and type.

### 6.5.1 Using Arrays in Unity 3D

So far we've dealt with variables that hold a single value. For instance, `int i = 0;` in which the variable `i` holds only a single value. This works out fine when dealing with one thing at a time. However, if we want a whole number of objects to work together, we're going to have them grouped together in memory.

If we needed to, we could have a single variable for each box `GameObject` that would look like the following:

```
public class Example : MonoBehaviour
{
     public GameObject box1;
     public GameObject box2;
     public GameObject box3;
     public GameObject box4;
     public GameObject box5;
     public GameObject box6;
     public GameObject box7;
     public GameObject box8;
     public GameObject box9;
     public GameObject box10;
```

While this does work, this will give a programmer a headache in about 3 seconds, not to mention if you want to do something to one box, you'd have to repeat your code for every other box. This is horrible, and programming is supposed to make things easier, not harder on you. This is where arrays come to the rescue.

```
public class Example : MonoBehaviour
{
     public GameObject[] boxes;
```

Ah yes, much better, 10 lines turn into one. There's one very important difference here. There's a pair of square brackets after the `GameObject` to indicate that we're making an array of game objects. Square brackets are used to tell a variable that we're making the singular form of a variable into a plural form of the variable. This works the same for any other type of data.

```
//a single int
int MyInt;
//an array of ints
int[] MyInts;
//a single object
object MyObject;
//an array of objects
object[] MyObjects;
```

To tell the `boxes` variable how many it's going to be holding, we need to initialize the array with its size before we start stuffing it full of data. This will look a bit like the `Vector3` we initialized in Section 3.10.2. We have a couple of options. We can right out tell the boxes how many it's going to be holding.

```
public class Example : MonoBehaviour
{
     public GameObject[] boxes = new GameObject[10];
```

Or we can initialize the number of boxes using the `Start ()` function and a `public int` variable.

```
public class Example : MonoBehaviour
{
     public int numBoxes = 10;
```

```
public GameObject[] boxes;
//Use this for initialization
void Start ()
{
    boxes = new GameObject[numBoxes];
}
```

In the above code, we're going to add a numBoxes variable and then move the initialization of the boxes variable to the Start () function using the numBoxes to satisfy the array size. In the Unity inspector panel you'll see a field "Num Boxes" appear rather than numBoxes. Unity automatically changes variable names to be more human readable, but it's the same variable.

In the editor, we can pick any number of boxes we need without needing to change any code. Game designers like this sort of stuff. Once you run the game, the boxes array is initialized. To see what is contained in the array, you can expand the boxes variable in the Inspector panel and get the following:

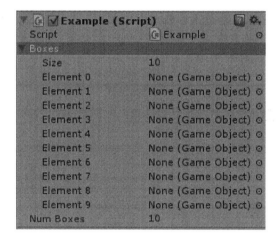

We've got an array filled with a great deal of nothing, sure. However, it's the right number of nothing. Since we haven't put anything into the array of GameObjects we shouldn't be surprised. So far everything is going as planned. Testing as we write is important. With nearly every statement we write, we should confirm that it's doing what we think it should be doing. Next we should put a new cube primitive into each one of the parts of this array.

### 6.5.1.1 Starting with 0

*Zeroth.* Some older programming languages start with 1. This is a carryover from FORTRAN that was created in 1957. Other programming languages mimic this behavior. Lua, for example, is a more modern programming language that starts with 1. C# is not like these older languages. Here we start with 0 and then count to 1; we do not start at 1. Thus, an array of 10 items is numbered 0 through 9.

Now we have an empty array, and we know how many things need to be in it. This is perfect for using a for loop. Numbering in C# may seem a bit strange, but a part of numbering in programming is the fact that 0 is usually the first number when counting.

We get accustomed to counting starting at 1, but in many programming paradigms, counting starts with the first number, 0. You might just consider the fact that 0 was there before you even started counting. Therefore, the first item in the boxes array is the 0th or zeroth item, not the first. It's important to notice that when dealing with arrays, you use square brackets.

```
void Start ()
{
    boxes = new GameObject[numBoxes];
    for (int i = 0; i < numBoxes; i++)
    {
    }
}
```

Right after we initialize the boxes array, we should write the for loop. Then we'll create a new box game object and assign it to the boxes.

```
void Start ()
{
    boxes = new GameObject[numBoxes];
    for (int i = 0; i < numBoxes; i++)
    {
        GameObject box =
            GameObject.CreatePrimitive(PrimitiveType.Cube);
        boxes [i] = box;
    }
}
```

Notice the notation being used for boxes. The boxes[i] indicates the slot in the array we're assigning the box we just made. When the i = 0, we're putting a box into boxes[0]; when i = 1, we're assigning the box to boxes[1] and so on.

Items in the array are accessed by using a number in the square brackets. To check that we're doing everything right, let's run the code and check if the array is populated with a bunch of cube primitives just as we asked. Therefore, if you want to get some information on the fourth cube, you should use boxes[3]; again the 0th, pronounced "zeroth," item makes it easy to forget the index in the array we're referring to.

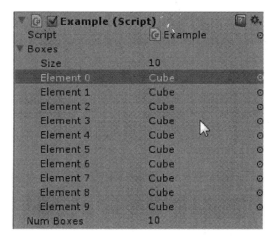

So far this is promising. We created an array called boxes with 10 items. Then we wrote a for loop that creates a box on every iteration and then adds that box into a numbered slot in the boxes array. This is working well. Arrays lend themselves very well for iterating through.

We need to match the variable type with the type that's inside of the array. Because the array boxes[] is filled with type GameObject, we need to use GameObject on the left of the in keyword. To the right of the in keyword is the array we're going to iterate through.

We're accessing all of the array, not just a single item in it, so we don't need to use something like foreach(GameObject g in boxes[0]) which would infer that at index 0 of boxes, there's an array for us to iterate through. Though arrays of arrays are possible, it's not our goal here.

Iterating through arrays with the foreach doesn't give us the benefit of a counter like in the for loop, so we need to do the same thing as if we were using a while loop or a heavily rearranged for loop by setting up a counter ahead of time.

```
//Update is called once per frame
void Update ()
{
    int i = 0;
    foreach (GameObject go in boxes)
    {
        go.transform.position = new Vector3(1.0f, 0, 0);
        i++;
        print(i);
    }
}
```

Let's check our Console panel in the editor to make sure that this is working. It looks like the loop is repeating like one would expect. At the beginning of the Update () function, int i is set to 0; then while the foreach loop is iterating, it's incrementing the value up by 1 until each item in boxes has been iterated through.

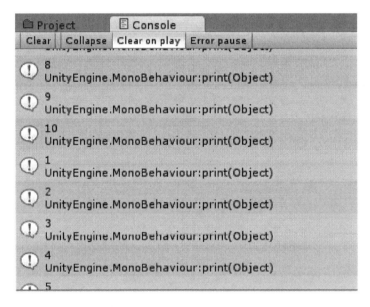

Put the i to some use within the foreach loop statement by multiplying the x of the vector by i * 1.0f to move each cube to a different x location. Note that multiplying any number against 1 is all that interesting, but this is just a simple part of this demonstration. Again, check in the editor to make sure that each cube is getting put in a different x location by running the game.

```
//Update is called once per frame
void Update ()
{
    int i = 0;
    foreach (GameObject go in boxes)
    {
        go.transform.position = new Vector3(i * 1.0f, 0, 0);
```

```
        i++;
        print(i);
    }
}
```

So far everything should be working pretty well. You can change the offset by changing the value that the i is being multiplied by. Or, better yet, we should create a `public` variable to multiply the i variable by.

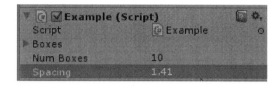

If you create a new `public float spacing` in the class scope, you can use it in your `foreach` loop.

```
go.transform.position = new Vector3(i * spacing, 0, 0);
```

By adding this here, you can now edit spacing and watch the cubes spread apart in real time. This is starting to get more interesting! Next let's play with some math, or more specifically `Mathf`.

### 6.5.1.2 Mathf

`Mathf` is a class filled with specific math function, which we'll need to use fairly often. `Mathf` contains many functions such as `abs` for absolute value, and `Sin` and `Cos` for sine and cosine. To start with, we're going to create a `float` called `wave` and we'll assign that to `Mathf.Sin(i);` which produces a sine wave when we put bob in place of `y` in the `Vector3`.

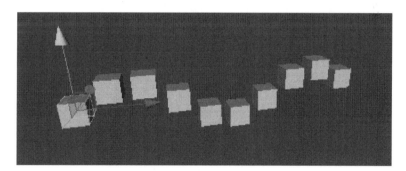

To make this animated, we can use another useful trick from the `Time` class. Let's take a moment to thank all the busy programmers who know how to implement the math functions we're using here. There's more to these functions than just knowing the mathematics behind the simple concept of something like `Sin`. There's also a great deal of optimization that went into making the function work. This sort of optimization comes only from years of computer science experience and lots of know-how and practice. All of the mechanics behind this stuff is far beyond the scope of this book, so we'll just take advantage of their knowledge by using `Mathf`.

```
float wave = Mathf.Sin(Time.fixedTime + i);
go.transform.position = new Vector3(i * spacing, wave, 0);
```

### 6.5.1.3 Time

`Time.fixedTime` is a clock that starts running at the beginning of the game. All it's doing is counting up. Check what it's doing by printing it out using `print(Time.fixedTime);` and you'll just see a timer counting seconds. The seconds will be the same for all of the cubes, but by adding `int i` to each cube's version of `wave`, each one will have a different value for the wave.

We could have had a `public double 1.0` and incremented this with a small value, `0.01`, for instance. This will have a similar effect to `Time.fixedTime`. The difference here is that `fixedTime` is tied to the computer's clock. Any slowdowns or frame rate issues will result in your `Sin` function slowing down as well.

What you should have is a slowly undulating row of cubes. This is also a pretty cool example of some basic math principles in action. We could continue to add more and more behaviors to each cube in the array using this method of extending the `foreach` statement, but this will only get us so far.

Once we want each cube to have its own individual sets of logic to control itself, it's time to start a new class. With the new class, it's important that we can communicate with it properly. Eventually, these other cubes will end up being zombies attacking the player, so we're on the right track.

### 6.5.2 Instancing with AddComponent();

Create a new C# script in the Project panel and name it `Monster`. We're going to create a basic movement behavior using this new script. We're adding this new script to the cube primitive we were making before, but this time the script will be instanced along with the cube.

It's important to understand that `AddComponent()` is a function specific to Unity 3D's `GameObject` class. The `GameObject` is a class written to handle everything related to how Unity 3D manages characters, items, and environments in a scene. Should you leave this comfortable game development tool and move on to some other application development, you will have to most likely use a different function to perform a similar task.

When you have a `GameObject` selected in the game editor, you have an option to add component near the bottom of the Inspector panel. We used this to add the `Example` script to our first cube. This should lead you to thinking that you can also add component with code. Looking into `GameObject`, you can find an `AddComponent()` function with a few different options.

```
//Example.cs
    void Start ()
    {
        boxes = new GameObject[numBoxes];
        for (int i = 0; i < numBoxes; i++)
        {
            GameObject box =
                GameObject.CreatePrimitive(PrimitiveType.Cube);
            box.AddComponent("Monster");//add component here!
            boxes [i] = box;
        }
    }
```

In MonoDevelop, you can enter `box.AddComponent("Monster");` to tell the box to add in the script of the same name. To prove that the script is behaving correctly, add in a `print` function to the `Start ()` function of the `Monster.cs` file.

```
using UnityEngine;
using System.Collections;
public class Monster : MonoBehaviour
{
    //Use this for initialization
    void Start ()
    {
        print("im alive!");
    }
```

When the game starts, the `Example.cs` will create a bunch of new instances of the `Monster.cs` attached to each cube. When the script is instanced, it executes the `Start ()` function. The Console should reflect the fact that the `Start ()` function was called when the script was instanced.

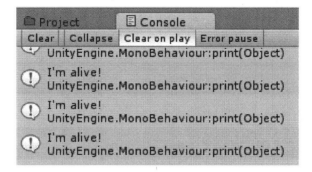

This reduces the amount of work a single script needs to do. Each object should manage its own movement. To do this, each object will need its own script. In the Monster.cs file, we need to replicate some of the variables that we created in the Example.cs file.

```
using UnityEngine;
using System.Collections;
public class Monster : MonoBehaviour
{
    public int ID;
```

Remember that we need to make these public, otherwise another script cannot find them. MonoDevelop is already aware of these variables.

After the box is created, we need to add in the "Monster" class to it. However, that's just half of the task necessary to get our script up and running. We added an ID and a spacing value to Monster.cs, but we have yet to initialize them. We need to get a connection to the component we just added to the box object. To do this, we need to use GetComponent(), but there's a bit more than just that.

### 6.5.3 Type Casting Unity 3D Objects

GetComponent() returns a component type, but it's unaware of the specific type we're looking for. We use some type casting to convert one type to another. Remember from before, we can turn an int 1 to a float 1.0f through type casting.

When type casting between objects or reference types, things get more tricky. A component is about as general as Unity 3D will get. However, we want a type Monster when we get that component back. Therefore, we need to say "I want this component from the box as a type monster." To do this, C# has the keyword as for some basic type casting.

```
    void Start ()
    {
        boxes = new GameObject[numBoxes];
        for (int i = 0; i < numBoxes; i++)
        {
            GameObject box =
                GameObject.CreatePrimitive(PrimitiveType.Cube);
            box.AddComponent("Monster");
            Monster m = box.GetComponent("Monster") as Monster;
            boxes [i] = box;
        }
    }
```

After adding the component, we need to get access to it. Therefore, we create a Monster variable named m. Then we use the GameObject.GetComponent(); function to get an object called "Monster," and we ask that we get it as a type Monster by adding as Monster after we ask for it.

This cast is necessary because `GetComponent()` doesn't necessarily know what it's getting; other than it's some `Component` type, you have to tell it what it's getting. `Monster` and "`Monster`" appear in different places. This is the difference between the word "`Monster`" and the actual class object called `Monster`. The object is what is used after the `as` keyword because we're referring to the type, not what it's called. This might be a little bit confusing, but `GetComponent()` is expecting a string and not a type for an argument.

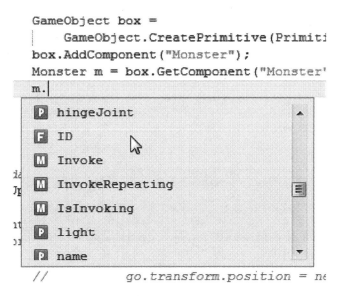

When you enter the `m.`, a dialog box pops up in MonoDevelop. This is a handy helper that shows you all of the things that the object can do. This also shows you any of the `public` variables you may have added to the class. Now that we have a connection to the `Monster` script that's attached to the `box`, we can set a couple of parameters.

```
13        GameObject box = GameObject.CreatePrimitive(PrimitiveType.Cube);
14        box.AddComponent("Monster");
15        Monster m = box.GetComponent("Monster") as Monster;
16        m.ID = i;
17        m.spacing = spacing;
18        boxes[i] = box;
```

We use the dot notation to access the members of the `Monster` class found in `m`. Therefore, `m.ID` is `i` that increments with each new box made. Then the spacing will be the spacing we set in the `Example.cs` file.

```
13        // Update is called once per frame
14        void Update () {
15            float wave = Mathf.Sin( Time.fixedTime + ID);
16            transform.position = new Vector3(ID * spacing, wave, 0.0f);
17        }
```

Add a very similar line of code to the `Update ()` in the `Monster.cs` file and then remove it from the `Update ()` in the `Example.cs` file. The spacing was only set once when the object was created, which you can't update it by sliding on the `Example.cs` file. However, each object is acting on its own, running its own script.

There are a few different ways to use `GetComponent()`, but we'll look at those in Section 6.14 when we need to do more type casting. Not all casting operations work the same. We're going to change a few other things we're doing to make the movement behavior more interesting as well, but we will need to learn a few more tricks before we get to that.

Alternatively, we can assign and get the Monster m variable at the same time with the following notation:

```
Monster m = box.AddComponent("Monster") as Monster;
```

This automatically assigns m as it's assigned to the box component. The component assignment and the variable assignment save a step.

### 6.5.4 What We've Learned

This was a pretty heavy chapter. The new array type was used to store a bunch of game objects, but it could have easily been used to store a bunch of numbers, or anything for that matter. We learned about a foreach loop that is handy for dealing with arrays.

In this chapter, we also made use of some math and found a nice timer function in the Time class. After that, we figured out how to attach script components through code, and then we were able to gain access to that component by GetComponent() and a type cast to make sure it wasn't just a generic component.

There are still a few different data types we need to study. Now that we're dealing with so many types, we're going to learn more about type casting as well.

### 6.6 Enums

If we've got two classes, an Example.cs and a Monster.cs, we've got the Example.cs creating and assigning objects, effectively spawning a Monster. We could take the older version of the Example. cs we wrote and turn it into Player.cs which would give us a total of three objects.

```csharp
using UnityEngine;
using System.Collections;
public class Player : MonoBehaviour
{
    public float Speed = 0.1f;
    //Update is called once per frame
    void Update ()
    {
        gameObject.transform.position += Movement(Speed);
    }
    Vector3 Movement(float dist)
    {
        Vector3 vec = Vector3.zero;
        if (Input.GetKey(KeyCode.A))
        {
            vec.x -= dist;
        }
        if (Input.GetKey(KeyCode.D))
        {
            vec.x += dist;
        }
        if (Input.GetKey(KeyCode.W))
        {
            vec.z += dist;
        }
        if (Input.GetKey(KeyCode.S))
```

```
        {
            vec.z -= dist;
        }
        return vec;
    }
}
```

Therefore, here's the `Player.cs` I'm using for this chapter; we're going to use this to move the little box around in the scene. We'll pretend that the box is a pretty cool-looking monster hunter armed with a sword, shotgun, or double-barreled shotgun.

We may want to rename the `Example.cs` to something like `MonsterSpawner.cs` or `MonsterGenerator.cs`, but I'll leave that up to you. Just remember to rename the class declaration to match the file name. This will spill out monsters to chase the player around. Then the `Monster.cs` attached to each of the objects that the MonsterSpawner creates will then seek out the player and chase him around. At least that's the plan.

**NOTE:** Prototyping game play using primitive shapes is a regular part of game development. This is somewhat related to what has become to be known as "programmer art." Changes to code often mean changes to art. It's difficult to build a game keeping art and code parallel. Often a simple change in code means days of changes to art. It's quite often easier to prototype a game making no requests of an artist. Most of the time, the programmer doesn't even know himself what to ask of an artist.

## 6.6.1 Using Enums

The keyword "enum" is short for enumeration. A programmer might say that an `enum` is a list of named constants. The meaning may seem obtuse. Translated, an enumeration is a list of words that you pick. For our `Monster` to have a better set of functions for its behavior, we're going to create a new `enum` type called `MonsterState`.

We've already interacted with the `PrimitiveType` enum.

```
public enum PrimitiveType
{
    Sphere,
    Capsule,
    Cylinder,
    Cube,
    Plane
}
```

We've also seen that enums can store many different names. For instance, the `InputType` enum had a different enumeration for every key on the keyboard and each input for your mouse or trackpad and controller. Enumerating through a long list of "things" is to help name every possibility with something more useful than a simple numeric index. It's important to remember that enumerations don't need to follow any particular pattern. It's up to you to decide on any organization to keep your enums organized.

In the MoreLogic project, open the `Example.cs` found in the Assets list in the Project panel.

```
    public PrimitiveType primitiveType;
    GameObject obj;
    //Use this for initialization
    void Start () {
        obj = GameObject.CreatePrimitive(primitiveType);
    }
```

At the beginning of the `Example.cs` class, we have a `public PrimitiveType` called `primi-tiveType`. Note the difference in case; the second use of the word is lowercase and is not using a previously defined version of the word `PrimitiveType`.

In the editor, you'll see the availability of a new pop-up of the different `PrimitiveTypes`. In the `Start ()` function, we use the `CreatePrimitive` member function in `GameObject` to create a new object of the selected type.

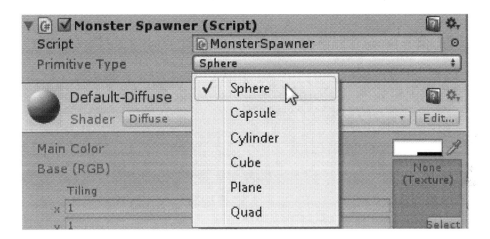

We can extend this more to get a better feel of how enums work for us by creating our own enums. A new `enum` is a new type of data. New data types are easy to create, especially for enums.

```
public enum colorType
{
     red,
     blue,
     green
}
```

In this case, we use the `public` keyword followed by `enum` to tell the compiler we're creating a new `enum` which can be made accessible to other classes. We follow the declaration with a name. In this case, `colorType` is the name of our new `enum`. Following the name of the `enum`, we need to start a new code block with any number of words separated by commas. Just don't add a comma after the last word in the list.

```
public enum colorType{red,blue,green}
```

To be clear, declaring an `enum` doesn't require the line breaks between each word. White space has no effect on how an `enum`, or practically any variable for that matter, is declared. After the new data type is created, we need to create a variable that uses that data type.

```
public enum colorType{red,blue,green}
public colorType myColor;
```

Create a new `public colorType` with the name `myColor` following the declaration of the enum. In the editor, we'll be able to pick the `enum` we want from our new list of words we added to the `enum` `colorType`.

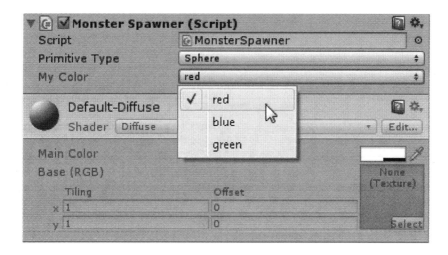

To make use of the enum, we can use several different methods. The system we might already be familiar with is using a bunch of different if statements.

```
obj = GameObject.CreatePrimitive(primitiveType);
if (myColor == colorType.red) {
    obj.renderer.material.color = Color.red;
}
if (myColor == colorType.blue) {
    obj.renderer.material.color = Color.blue;
}
if (myColor == colorType.green) {
    obj.renderer.material.color = Color.green;
}
```

This setup is clumsy; after the obj is created, we check for what word myColor is set to. Compare it against the colorType's options and act when you've got a match. A slightly cleaner solution is to use a switch statement.

Just as a note, if you look at the scene and all you see is a black sphere, you might need to add in a directional light. Without any lights, every object in the scene will appear dark since there's no light to illuminate them. You can add in a light by selecting GameObject → Create Other → Directional Light. This will drop in a light that will lighten up any objects in your scene.

## 6.6.2 Combining What We've Learned

We've been using PrimitiveType.Cube to generate our example monsters. We could just as easily change that to a sphere or anything else in the PrimitiveType enum. As we've seen, the PrimitiveType has some words that reflect what type of Primitive we can choose from. Likewise, we're going to make a list of states for the monster to pick.

```
Public class Monster : MonoBehaviour {
    public enum MonsterState {
        standing,
        wandering,
        chasing,
        attacking
    }
    public MonsterState mState;
```

Enums are declared at the class scope level of visibility. MonsterState is now another new data type. When setting up enum names, it's really important to come up with a convention that's easy to remember.

If you make both the enum MonsterState and mState public, you'll be able to pick the state using a menu in the Unity's Inspector panel. You should consider using enums for setting various things such as weapon pickup types or selecting types of traps.

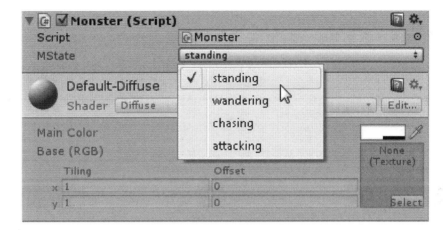

Then, just as we define any other variable, we declare a variable type and give type a name. This is done with the line MonsterState mState; which gives us mState to use throughout the rest of the Monster class. mState is a variable with type MonsterState. In some instances, we may need to ignore what was set in the editor. To set an enum in code rather than a pop-up, we can use the following code. To use the mState, we need to set it when the Monster.cs is started.

```
void Start ()
{
    mState = MonsterState.standing;
}
```

mState is set to MonsterState.standing; this allows us to use mState in the Update () function to determine what actions we should take. Like before, we could use a series of if statements to pick the actions we could take. For instance, we could execute the following code:

```
//Update is called once per frame
void Update ()
{
    if (mState == MonsterState.standing)
    {
        print("standing monster is standing.");
    }
    if (mState == MonsterState.wandering)
    {
        print("wandering monster is wandering.");
    }
    if (mState == MonsterState.chasing)
    {
        print("chasing monster is chasing.");
    }
    if (mState == MonsterState.attacking)
    {
        print("attacking monster is attacking.");
    }
}
```

This will work just fine, but it's rather messy. If we add more enums to the `MonsterState`, we will need more `if` statements. However, there's an easier way to deal with an `enum`, so it's time to learn a new trick.

### 6.6.3 What We've Learned

So far enums have been made to make a list of options. Normally, enumerations are limited to a single option, but this doesn't always have to be the case. Enums are capable of multiple options, which has been discussed throughout this section.

Using an `enum` means to take action based on a selection. An `enum` is actually based on a number. You can cast from an `enum` to an `int` and get a usable value. When this is done, the first name in an `enum` is 0 and anything following is an increment up in value based on its position in the list of enumerations.

Therefore, based on the following code, the logged value is 3 since the first state is 0 and the fourth state is 3.

```
public enum MonsterState
{
     standing,
     wandering,
     chasing,
     attacking
}
public MonsterState mState;
void Start ()
{
     mState = MonsterState.attacking;
     int number = (int)mState;
     Debug.Log(number);
}
```

There are other ways in which the `enum` can be manipulated, but to understand how and why this works, we'll want to cover a few other topics before getting to that.

## 6.7 Switch

The `switch` comes into play fairly often once we have reached more than one condition at a time. For instance, we could come across a situation where we are looking at a lengthy ladder of `if-else` statements.

```
public int i;
void Start ()
{
     if(i == 0)
     {
          Debug.Log ("i is zero");
     }
     else if(i == 1)
     {
          Debug.Log ("i is one");
     }
     else if(i == 2)
     {
          Debug.Log ("i is two");
     }
     else if(i == 3)
```

```
        {
             Debug.Log ("i is three");
        }
        else if(i == 4)
        {
             Debug.Log ("i is four");
        }
        else
        {
             Debug.Log("i is greater than 4");
        }
    }
```

There should be something awkward feeling about this block of code. There is in fact a system in place called a `switch` statement that was made to alleviate the awkwardness of this long chain of if–else statements. The switch starts with the keyword `switch` followed by a parameter `()` that controls a block of code encapsulated by a pair of curly braces `{}`.

```
void Update ()
{
        switch (someVariable)
        {
        }
}
```

The contents of the `switch` statement use the keyword `case`. Each `case` is fulfilled by an expected option that matches the argument in the `switch` parameter.

### 6.7.1  A Basic Example

A `switch` can be used with any number of types. A simple `switch` statement can look like the following code using an `int` like the above if–else chain. This can be found in the SwitchStatement project in the `Example.cs` component attached to the Main Camera.

```
using UnityEngine;
using System.Collections;
public class Example : MonoBehaviour {
    public int i = 1;
    void Start ()
    {
        switch (i)
        {
        case 0:
             Debug.Log("i is zero");
             break;
        case 1:
             Debug.Log("i is one");
             break;
        case 2:
             Debug.Log("i is two");
             break;
        }
    }
}
```

This is a basic `switch` with a `case`. The `case` is followed by 1 or 2 ending with a colon. Before another case, there's a couple of statements, with the last statement being `break;` that ends the `case:` statement.

The first case 1: is executed because i == 1; or in more plain English, i *is* 1 that fulfills the condition to execute the code following the case. The break; following the statements jumps the computer out of the switch statement and stops any further execution from happening inside of the switch statement.

```
int i = 1;
switch (i)
{
    case 1: print("got one"); break;
    case 2: print ("got two"); break;
}
```

When you deal with short case statements, it's sometimes easier to remove the extra white space and use something a bit more compact. Each case is called a *label*; we can use labels outside of a switch statement, but we will have to find out more about that in Section 6.7.5.

The switch statement is a much better way to manage a set of different situations. Upon looking at the switch statement for the first time, it might be a bit confusing. There are a few new things going on here. The general case of the switch is basically taking in a variable, pretty much of any kind. The code then picks the case statement to start. The main condition is that all of the cases must use the type that is used in the switch() argument. For instance, if the switch uses the "mState" enum, you can't use a case where an "int" is expected.

The advantage of switch may not be obvious when looking at the block of code that was written here. The important reason why switch is useful is speed. To step through many different if statements, the contents of each argument needs to be computed.

This means that having a dozen "if" statements means that each one needs to be tested even though the contents of the statement are to be skipped. When using a switch, the statement needs to have only one test before evaluating the contents of the case.

The switch statement can use a few different data types, specifically integral types. Integral types, or data that can be converted into an integer, include booleans or bools, chars, strings, and enums. In a simple boolean example, we can use the following:

```
bool b = true;
switch (b)
{
    case true: print("got true"); break;
    case false: print ("got false"); break;
}
```

With integers where int i = 1; switch(i){} is used to pick the case which will be used. Using integers allows for a long list of cases when using a switch statement.

```
bool b = true;
switch (b)
{
    case true:
        print("got true");
        break;
    case false:
        print("got false");
        break;
}
```

Here i = 1, so case 1: is evaluated and "case 1" is printed. Each appearance of the keyword case is called a case label. Cases are built by using the keyword case followed by the value we are looking for from the variable used in the switch. After the case label is declared, any number of statements can be added. The code following the colon after the case statement is evaluated until the break; statement that stops the switch. The break statement must appear before another case label is added.

## 6.7.2 Default:

What if there's a case that's not included in the `switch` statement? It would be difficult to cover every case for an integer. You'd have to write a case for every and any number. That's where the `default:` case comes in. When dealing with any of the `switch` statements, a default condition can be added when a case appears that isn't handled.

```
int i = 3;
switch (i)
{
    case 0:
        Debug.Log("i is zero");
        break;
    case 1:
        Debug.Log("i is one");
        break;
    case 2:
        Debug.Log("i is two");
        break;
    default:
        Debug.Log("Every other number");
        break;
}
```

With the `default` added, any conditions that aren't taken care of can be handled. If the `default` isn't added, then any unhandled case will be ignored and the `switch` will skip any code from any of the cases. The `default` case is an optional condition when working with the `switch` statement.

Of course, a `switch` statement seems to be most at home when in use with an `enum`. A slightly different variation on the appearance of the `enum` itself is that we need to use the dot operator to compare the incoming value against one of the `enum` values.

```
public enum MyCases
{
    first,
    second,
    third,
    fourth,
    fifth,
    sixth,
    seventh
}
public MyCases cases;
void Update ()
{
    switch(cases)
    {
    case MyCases.first:
        Debug.Log("first case");
        break;
    case MyCases.second:
        Debug.Log("second case");
        break;
    case MyCases.third:
        Debug.Log("third case");
        break;
    case MyCases.fourth:
        Debug.Log("fourth case");
        break;
```

```
            case MyCases.fifth:
                Debug.Log("fifth case");
                break;
            case MyCases.sixth:
                Debug.Log("sixth case");
                break;
            case MyCases.seventh:
                Debug.Log("seventh case");
                break;
            default:
                Debug.Log("other case");
                break;
        }
    }
```

Here we have an elaborate array of cases, each one falling in order based on the enum values for MyCases. Inside of the Unity 3D editor, the C# class provides a useful roll-out in the Inspector panel when assigned to a GameObject.

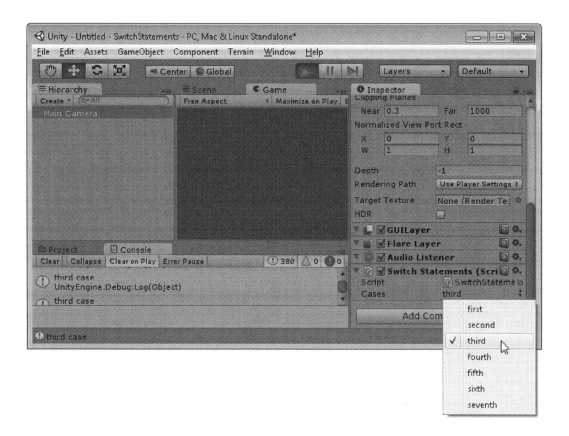

This conveniently gives us the opportunity to pick an enum and watch the Debug.Log() send different strings to the Console panel.

```
public MyCases cases;

void Update ()
{
    switch ( cases )
    {
    case MyCases.first:
        Debug.Log( "first case" );
        break;
    case MyCases.second:
        Debug.Log( "second case" );
        break;
```

It's important that you note what variable is being used in the switch statement's argument. It's often mistaken to use switch(MyCases) with the type in the argument. This of course doesn't work as expected. Here we get the following error:

```
Assets/SwitchStatements.cs(21,25): error CS0119: Expression denotes a 'type',
where a 'variable', 'value' or 'method group' was expected
```

Each case statement must have a break; statement before the next case appears. You can have any number of statements between case and break, but you must break at the end. This prevents each case from flowing into one another. If you forget to add break after the first case statement, then you get the following warning:

```
Assets/SwitchStatements.cs(21,17): error CS0163: Control cannot fall through
from one case label to another
```

It's easy to forget to add these breaks, but at least we are informed that we're missing one. However, we're directed to the beginning of the switch statement. It's up to you to make sure that there's a break statement at the end of each case. It's also required after the default case.

Normally, the default label is the last case at the end of the series of case labels. However, this isn't a requirement. You can write the default label anywhere in the switch statement. Style guides usually require that you put the default at the very end of the switch. Not doing so might invoke some harsh words from a fellow programmer if he or she finds a misplaced default label.

### 6.7.3 What We've Learned

Switch statements are a common combination. Each label is clear and the parameter for the switch is also quite clear. We know what we're expecting and it's obvious what conditions each case needs to be written for.

```
enum cases {
    firstCase,
    secondCase,
    thirdCase
}
cases MyCases;
```

The above enum might be quite contrived, but we know how many labels we need if we use this case in a switch. It should be obvious that our first case label should look like case cases.firstCase: and we should fill in the rest of the case statements in order.

switch statements are limited to a select different types of data.

```
float f = 2.0f;
switch (f)
{
    case f < 1.0f:
        Debug.Log("less than 1.0f");
        break;
    case f > 3.0f:
        Debug.Log("more than 3.0f");
        break;
    default:
        Debug.Log("neither case");
        break;
}
```

The above code might look valid, but we'll get the following error:

```
Assets/Test.cs(15,1): error CS0151: A switch expression of type 'float'
cannot be converted to an integral type, bool, char, string, enum or nullable
type
```

A switch is allowed to use only "integral, bool, char, string, enum, or nullable" types of data. We have yet to cover some of these different data types, but at least we know what a data type is. We do know that we can use ints and enums. In most cases, this should be sufficient.

switch statements should be used when one and only one thing needs to happen based on a single parameter.

```
int a = 0;
int b = 1;
switch (a)
{
    case 0:
    switch (b)
    {
        case 1:
            Debug.Log("might not be worth it");
        break;
    }
    break;
}
```

Having a switch statement nested in one of the cases of another switch statement isn't common. There's nothing really stopping you from being able to do this, but it's probably better to look for a more elegant solution.

```
void Update ()
{
    int a = 0;
    switch (a)
    {
        case 0:
            FirstFunction();
            break;
        case 1:
```

```
                SecondFunction();
                break;
        }
    }
    void FirstFunction()
    {
        Debug.Log("first case");
    }
    void SecondFunction()
    {
        Debug.Log("second case");
    }
```

Using a function in each case is a simple way to keep things tidy, though it's not always clear what's going on. Anyone reading the code will be forced to jump back and forth between the switch and the different functions. However, this does mean that you might be able to make more switch cases within each function in the switch statement.

```
    void Update ()
    {
        int a = 0;
        switch (a)
        {
            case 0:
                FirstFunction(a);
                break;
            case 1:
                SecondFunction();
                break;
        }
    }
    void FirstFunction(int i)
    {
        switch (i)
        {
            case 0:
                Debug.Log("first case");
                break;
        }
    }
    void SecondFunction()
    {
        Debug.Log("second case");
    }
```

The parameter in the switch statement is now in the body of the switch statement. This also means that the parameter can be manipulated before it's used in the case.

```
void Update () {
    int a = 0;
    switch (a)
    {
    case 0:
        a = 1;
        FirstFunction(a);
        break;
    case 1:
        SecondFunction();
```

```
            break;
        }
}
void FirstFunction(int i)
{
    switch (i)
    {
    case 0:
        Debug.Log("first case");
        break;
    case 1:
        Debug.Log("i was incremented!");
        break;
    }
}
void SecondFunction() {
    Debug.Log("second case");
}
```

Because a = 1; appears after we've entered the case and is followed by a break;, case 1: is not triggered, and we don't skip to the second case. The logic might seem cloudy, but it's important that we really understand what's going on here.

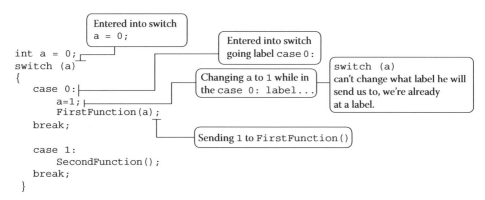

Once inside of the switch statement, the switch cannot change our destination once we've arrived at a label. After we've got to the label, we can change the data that got us there. Once we get to the break; at the end of the case, we leave the switch and move to any statements that follow the switch statement code block.

```
switch (a)
{
case 0:
    a = 1;
    FirstFunction(a);
    continue;//nope!
}
```

A switch is not a loop, so we can't go back to the beginning of the switch by using continue; actually this is just an error telling you that there's no loop to continue to. A switch statement isn't meant to be looped; there are systems that allow this, but in general, these sorts of statements are one-way logic controls. A switch can work only with a single argument.

Something like switch(a, b) could make sense, but this isn't the case. Keeping things simple is not only your goal, but you're also limited by what is allowed. In some cases, the language can force simplicity. In practice, it's best to keep things as simple as possible if only for the sake of anyone else having to understand your work.

### 6.7.4 Fall Through

Using the `break;` statement jumps us out of the `switch`. Therefore, something like the following will execute one or the other statements after the condition and jump out of the `switch`.

```
switch(condition)
{
    case first_condition:
        //do things
        break;
    case second_condition:
        //do something else
        break;
}
```

If we want to, a case can be left empty, and without a `break;` included, anything in the case will "`fall through`" to the next case until the code is executed and a `break;` statement is found.

```
switch(condition)
{
    case first_condition:
    case second_condition:
        //do something else
        break;
}
```

In the above example, if we get to `case first condition:`, we'll simply find the next case afterward and run the code there until we hit the next `break;` statement. It's rare to use this in practice as the conditions included act the same; in this case, both the first and second conditions do the same thing. However, things get a bit more awkward if we need to do something like the following:

```
switch(condition)
{
    case first_condition:
    case second_condition:
        //do something else
        break;
    case third_condition:
    case fourth_condition:
    case fifth_condition:
        //do another thing
        break;
}
```

Here we have two different behaviors based on five different conditions. The first two and the next three cases can result in two different behaviors. Although you might not use this behavior immediately, it's important to know what you're looking at if you see it. There are some catches to how this can be used.

```
switch(condition)
{
    case first_condition:
        //code that is out of place.
    case second_condition:
        //do something else
        break;
    case third_condition:
        //do another thing
        break;
}
```

In the above example, our first condition might have some added code before the second condition. This might visually make sense; go to the first condition, execute some instructions, `fall through` to the next case, do more instructions, and break. However, this behavior isn't allowed in C#.

In order to accomplish what was described, we need to be more explicit.

### 6.7.5 goto Case

```
switch(condition)
{
    case first_condition:
        //code that is out of place.
        goto case second_condition;
    case second_condition:
        //do something else
        break;
    case third_condition:
        //do another thing
        break;
}
```

Using the `goto` keyword allows us to hop from one case in the `switch` statement to another. This allows for an expected `fall through`–like behavior, but also gives us an added functionality of going to any other case once inside of the `switch` statement.

```
switch(condition)
{
    case first_condition:
        //doing something first
        goto case third_condition;
    case second_condition:
        //do something else
        break;
    case third_condition:
        //do another thing
        goto case second_condition;
}
```

The utility of the above statement is questionable. Although the statement is valid, it's hardly something that any programmer would want to read. Bad habits aside, should you see this in someone else's code, it's most likely written as a work-around by someone unfamiliar with the original case.

Aside from being awkward and strange looking, it's important that the `switch` case finally lead to a `break`, otherwise we're caught in the `switch` statement indefinitely. Debugging a situation like this is difficult, so it's best to avoid getting caught in a `switch` statement longer than necessary.

Strange and unusual code practices when working inside of a `switch` statement aren't common, as the regular use of a `switch` statement is quite simple. If you need to do something more clever, it's better to have a `switch` statement that points toward a function with additional logic to handle a more specific set of conditions.

### 6.7.6 Limitations

The `switch` statement is limited to integral types, that is to say, we can only use types that can be clearly defined. These are called integral types and a `float` or `double` is not an integral type.

```
float myFloat = 1f;
switch(myFloat)
{
    case 1.0f:
```

```
        //do things
        break;
    case 20.0f:
        //do something else
        break;
}
```

The above code will produce the following error:

```
Assets/Switch.cs(20,1): error CS0151: A switch expression of type 'float'
cannot be converted to an integral type, bool, char, string, enum or nullable
type
```

Without deferring to a chapter on types, integral types often refer to values that act like whole numbers. Letters and words are included in this set of types. Excluded from the `switch` are floats and doubles, to name some non-integral types. Because a `float` 1 can also be seen as 1.0 or even 1.00000f, it's difficult for a `switch` to decide how to interpret the above example's `myFloat` as being a 1 or a 1.0f.

### 6.7.7 What We've Learned

The `switch` statement is powerful and flexible. Using special case conditions where we use either the `fall-through` behavior or `goto case` statement, we're able to find additional utility within the `switch` statement.

Just because we can doesn't mean we should use `fall-through` or `goto case`. Often, this leads to confusing and difficult-to-read code. The bizarre and incomprehensible `fall-through` or `goto case` should be reserved for only the most bizarre and incomprehensible conditions. To avoid bad habits from forming, it might be better to forget that you even saw the `goto case` statement.

Now that warnings have been issued, experimenting and playing with code is still fun. Finding and solving problems with unique parameters is a part of the skill of programming. Using weird and strange-looking structures helps in many ways. If we're able to comprehend a strange set of code, we're better equipped to deal with more regular syntax.

switch statements can be used with any number of different parameters. Strings, ints, and other types are easily used in a `switch` statement.

```
string s = "some condition";
switch (s)
{
    case "some condition":
        //do things for some condition
        break;
    case "other condition":
        //do something else
        break;
}
```

## 6.8 Structs

We are now able to build and manipulate data. Enums, arrays, and variables make sense. Basic logic flow control systems are no longer confusing. What comes next is the ability to create our own forms of data. The built-in types may not be able to describe what we're trying to do.

Data structures allow you to be specific and concise. By themselves `floats`, `ints`, and `Vector3` are useful. However, copying and moving around each variable individually can look rather ugly. This lack of organization leaves more opportunity for errors.

When having to deal with a complex character or monster type, collections of data should be organized together. The best way to do this is by using a struct, or structure. A `Vector3` is a basic collection of three similar data types: a `float` for x, y, and z. This is by no means the limitation of what a structure can do.

### 6.8.1 Structs

Structures for a player character should include the location, health points, ammunition, weapon in hand, and weapons in inventory and armor, and other related things should be included in the `player.cs`, not excluded. To build a struct, you use the keyword `struct` followed by a type. This is very similar to how an `enum` is declared. What makes a structure different is that we can declare each variable in the `struct` to different data types.

After a structure is built to access any of the `public` components of the structure, you use dot notation. For example, `playerData.hitPoints` allows you to access the `int` value stored in the structure for hitpoints. `PlayerData` now contains all of the vital values that relate to the player.

```
public struct PlayerData {
    public Vector3 Pos;
    public int hitPoints;
    public int Ammunition;
    public float RunSpeed;
    public float WalkSpeed;
}
PlayerData playerData;
```

When you first look at declaring and using a `struct`, there might seem a few redundant items. First, there's a `public struct PlayerData`, then declare a `PlayerData` to be called `playerData`, and notice the lowercase lettering on the identifier versus the type. The first time `PlayerData` appears, you're creating a new type of data and writing its description.

### 6.8.2 Struct versus Class

At the same time, the struct may look a lot like a class, in many ways it is. The principal differences between the struct and the class is where in the computer's memory they live and how they are created. We'll discuss more on this in a moment.

You fill in some variables inside of the new data type and name the data inside of the new type. This new data type needs to have a name assigned to it so we know how to recognize the new form of packaged data. Therefore, `PlayerData` is the name we've given to this new form of data. This is the same as with a class.

The second appearance of the word `PlayerData` is required if we want to use our newly written form of data. In order to use data, we write a statement for a variable like any other variable statement. Start with the data type; in this case, `PlayerData` is our type; then give a name to call a variable of the stated type. In this case, we're using `playerData` with a lowercase p to hold a variable of type `PlayerData`.

A `struct` is a data type with various types of data within it. It's convenient to packaging up all kinds of information into a single object. This means that when using the `struct`, you're able to pass along and get a breadth of information with a single parameter. This matters most when having to pass this information around.

This system of using a `struct` as data means that a `struct` is a value type, whereas a `class` is a reference type. You might ask what the difference between a value type and a reference type is. In short, when you create a `struct` and assign a value to it, a new copy is made of that `struct`. For instance, consider the following:

```
PlayerData pd = playerData;
```

In this case, pd is a new `struct`, where we make another version of `playerData` and copy the contents into pd. Therefore, if we make `PlayerData` pd2 and assign `playerData` to it, or even `playerData`, we'll have yet another copy of that same data in a new variable. Each variable pd, pd2, and `playerData` now all have unique duplicates of the data.

However, should we change `struct` to `class`, we'd have a different arrangement.

```
public class PlayerData {
    public Vector3 Pos;
    public int hitPoints;
    public int Ammunition;
    public float RunSpeed;
    public float WalkSpeed;
}
```

The only change to the above code is changing `struct` to `class`. This is still a perfectly valid C# `class` and appears to be the same as a `struct`, but the similarities cease once a variable is assigned. The differences can be seen in the following simple example. Start by looking at the `ClassVStruct` project and open the `ClassVStruct.cs` component attached to the Main Camera.

```
using UnityEngine;
using System.Collections;
public class StructVClass : MonoBehaviour {
    struct MyStruct{
        public int a;
    }
    class MyClass{
        public int a;
    }
    //Use this for initialization
    void Start () {
        MyClass mClass = new MyClass();
        MyStruct mStruct = new MyStruct();
        mClass.a = 1;
        mStruct.a = 1;
        MyStruct ms = mStruct;
        ms.a = 3;
        Debug.Log(ms.a + " and " + mStruct.a);
        MyClass mc = mClass;
        mc.a = 3;
        Debug.Log(mc.a + " and " + mClass.a);
    }
}
```

In the above code, we have a `struct` called `MyStruct` and a `class` called `MyClass`. Both have a public field called int a; once in the `Start ()` function a new `MyClass()` and a new `MyStruct()` are created. As soon as these classes are created, we assign 1 to the .a fields in both the `struct` and the `class`.

After this, we have an interesting change. Using the `MyStruct ms = mStruct`, we create a copy of the `MyStruct` from mStruct and assign that copy to ms. Doing the same thing to `MyClass mc`, we assign mClass to mc. If we check the value of ms.a and mStruct.a, we get 3 and 1, respectively.

Doing the same thing to mc.a and mClass.a, we get 3 and 3, respectively. How did this happen and why is mc.a changing the value of mClass.a? When a class is assigned to a variable, only a *reference* to the class is assigned. A new copy is not made and assigned to the variable mc.

In the statement `MyClass mc = mClass;`, we assign mc a reference to mClass. This contrasts to `MyStruct ms = mStruct`, where ms gets a copy of the value stored in mStruct. After a struct is assigned, it becomes an independent copy of the struct that was assigned to it. In order to break the reference, we cannot use mc = mClass, otherwise a reference will be created.

```
        MyClass mc2 = new MyClass();
        mc2.a = mClass.a;
        mc2.a = 7;
        Debug.Log(mc.a + " and " + mClass.a + " and " + mc2.a);
```

By making a new instance of `MyClass` called `mc2`, we can assign the value from `mClass.a` to `mc2.a`, which will avoid a reference from being created between `mc2` and `mClass`. The above code prints out the following output:

```
3 and 3 and 7
```

Even though we assigned the `.a` field of `mc2` to `mClass.a`, we lose the reference between `mc2` and `mClass`. When we change `mc2.a` to 7, it has no effect on `mc.a` and `mClass.a`. The differences between the struct and the class is subtle but distinct.

The values of structs are copied when assigned in the `ms = mStruct` fashion. To accomplish the same behavior with a class, we need to assign each field separately with `mc2.a = mClass.a;`. Only in this fashion can we actually make a copy of the value to `mc2.a` from `mClass.a`, not a reference.

### 6.8.3 Without Structs

The alternative to the struct is to use another form of data containment like the array. Each object in the array can hold a different data type, but it must be addressed by its index number in the array. It would be up to you to remember if the walk speed was at index 4 or 3 in the array. Organizational issues make this far too easy to mess up and forget which index holds what data.

Once you start adding new types of data to this method of record keeping, chances are you'll forget something and your code will break. There are languages out there that don't have structs, and this is the only way to manage a collection of data types. Be thankful for structs.

```
public object[] PlayerDataArray;
//Use this for initialization
void Start () {
    PlayerDataArray[0] = new Vector3();//position
    PlayerDataArray[1] = 10;//hit points
    PlayerDataArray[2] = 13;//ammo
    PlayerDataArray[3] = 6.5f;//run speed
    PlayerDataArray[4] = 1.2f;//walk speed
}
```

When another creature comes into contact with the player, it should be given a copy of the entire `PlayerData` stored in `playerData`. This confines all of the data into a single object and reduces the need for making separate operations to carry over different data. To do the same to a class, we'd have to use the same idea of copying each parameter one at a time because of the earlier-mentioned behavior between a class and struct assignment.

### 6.8.4 Handling Structs

We'll start with the Structs project in Unity 3D. In this project, we have a scene with a box and an attached `Struct.cs` component. Structs are best used to contain a collection of data for a particular object. If we wanted to make a simple set of parameters for a box, we might use the following struct:

```
        struct BoxParameters
        {
            public float width;
```

```
        public float height;
        public float depth;
        public Color color;
}
//put the new struct to use and name it myParameters
BoxParameters myParameters;
```

With this added to a new class attached to a box in the scene in Unity 3D, we have a system of storing and moving a collection of data using a single object. Within this object, we've assigned `public` variables for `width`, `height`, `depth`, and `color`.

To make use of this, we can adjust each one of the parameters individually within the structure using the dot operator.

```
//Use this for initialization
void Start ()
{
        myParameters.width = 2;
        myParameters.height = 3;
        myParameters.depth = 4;
        myParameters.color = new Color(1,0,0,1);
}
```

In the `Start ()` function, we can access the `myParameters` variables and assign them values. Once there are usable values assigned to the `BoxParameters myParameters`, we can use them as a variable passed to a function.

```
void UpdateCube(BoxParameters box)
{
        Vector3 size = new Vector3(box.width, box.height, box.depth);
        gameObject.transform.localScale = size;
        gameObject.renderer.material.color = box.color;
}
```

The new function can access the `BoxParameters` passed to it using the same dot accessor and expose values that were assigned to it; the dot is an operator, and not exclusive to just accessors, but properties, functions, and all struct and class members. The first statement creates a `new Vector3 size`. The `size` is then assigned a `new Vector3()`, where we extract the `width`, `height`, and `depth` and assign those values to the `Vector3`'s `x`, `y`, and `z` parameters.

Once the `Vector3` is created, we assign the values to the `gameObject.transform.localScale`. After this, we're also able to change the `gameObject` material's color by assigning the `renderer.material.color` to the `box.color` from the `BoxParameters` values.

To put these two things together, we can make some interesting manipulations in the `gameObject`'s `Update ()` function.

```
void Update ()
{
        float h = (100 * Mathf.Sin(Time.fixedTime))/10;
        myParameters.height = h;
        UpdateCube(myParameters);
}
```

Here we use some simple math `(100 * Mathf.Sin(Time.fixedTime))/10;` and assign that value to `float h`. Then we need to update only one variable in the struct to update the entire `gameObject`.

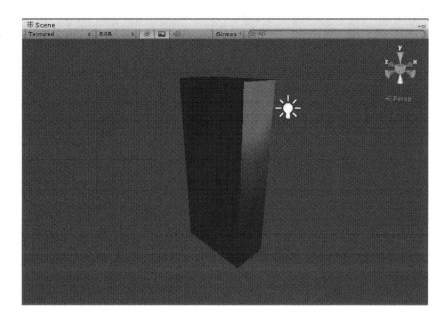

Now we've got a stretching cube. By grouping variables together, we've reduced the number of parameters we need to pass to a function or even the number of functions we would have to use to accomplish the same task.

### 6.8.5  Accessing Structs

If a structure is limited to the class where it was created, then it becomes less useful to other classes that might need to see it. By creating another class to control the camera, we can better understand why other classes need access to the cube's `BoxParameters`.

By moving the `struct` outside of the class, we break out of the encapsulation of the classes.

```
using UnityEngine;
using System.Collections;
//living out in the open
public struct BoxParameters
{
    public float width;
    public float height;
    public float depth;
    public Color color;
}
public class Struct : MonoBehaviour
{
    public BoxParameters myParameters;
    //Use this for initialization
    void Start () {
        myParameters.width = 2;
        myParameters.height = 3;
        myParameters.depth = 4;
        myParameters.color = new Color(1,0,0,1);
    }
    void UpdateCube(BoxParameters box)
    {
        Vector3 size = new Vector3(box.width, box.height, box.depth);
        gameObject.transform.localScale = size;
        gameObject.renderer.material.color = box.color;
```

```
    }
    //Update is called once per frame
    void Update ()
    {
        float h = (100 * Mathf.Sin(Time.fixedTime))/10;
        myParameters.height = h;
        UpdateCube(myParameters);
    }
}
```

From the above completed code of the `Struct` class, we can see that the `struct` has been moved outside of the class declaration. This changes the `BoxParameters` into a globally accessible struct.

```
//living out in the open
public struct BoxParameters
{
    public float width;
    public float height;
    public float depth;
    public Color color;
}
```

When a class is made, its contents are encapsulated within curly braces. The variables or functions created inside of the class contents are members of that class. Should any new `enum` or `struct` be moved outside of that class, it becomes a globally declared object.

Create a new class called `UseStruct.cs` and add it to the Main Camera in the scene.

```
using UnityEngine;
using System.Collections;
public class UseStruct : MonoBehaviour
{
    BoxParameters ThatBox;
    //uses globally accessible BoxParameters struct!
    //Use this for initialization
    void Start ()
    {
    }
    //Update is called once per frame
    void Update ()
    {
        ThatBox =
        GameObject.Find("Cube").GetComponent<Struct>().myParameters;
        gameObject.transform.position =
        new Vector3(0,ThatBox.height*0.5f, -10);
    }
}
```

The new class can see the `BoxParameters` struct because it's not confined within the `Struct.cs` class. The `myParameters` should be made `public` so it can be accessed outside of the `Struct` class. We can then assign `UseStruct`'s `ThatBox` struct the Cube's `Struct.myParameters`. Through some clever use of `ThatBox.height`, we can make the camera follow the resizing of the Cube in the scene with the following statement:

```
gameObject.transform.position = new Vector3(0, ThatBox.height*0.5f, -10);
```

### 6.8.6 Global Access

In practice, it's a good idea to have a more central location for your globally accessible structs and enums. A third class in the project called `Globals.cs` can contain the following code:

```
using UnityEngine;
using System.Collections;
public struct BoxParameters
{
     public float width;
     public float height;
     public float depth;
     public Color color;
}
```

With something as simple as this, we're able to create a central location for all globally accessible information. Starting with simple things such as `public strict BoxParameters`, we can then continu-
ally add more and more useful information to our globally accessible data. Each C# script file need not
declare a class. Although it's common, it's not restrictively enforced that a C# script file contains a class.
Utility files like a `Globals.cs` are handy and can provide a clean system in which each programmer on
a team can find handy structures that can be shared between different objects in the scene.

### 6.8.7  What We've Learned

In Section 6.8.6, we talked about global access. This concept is not that new. When you write a class, in
this case `Structs`, it's accessible by any other class. Therefore, when we assigned `UseStruct` to the
Main Camera in the scene, it's able to use `Structs`.

### 6.9  Class Data

Using a struct is preferred over a class due to how the computer manages memory. Without going into
detail, one type of memory is called the heap and the other is the stack. In general, the stack is a smaller,
more organized, faster part of the memory allocated to your game. The heap is usually larger and can
take longer to access than the stack.

Values can be allocated to the stack, and a struct is a value type; thus, a stack can be accessed faster
than a class. Though often structs and other value types are used in ways that disallow their allocation
to the stack, they go into the heap instead. Classes and other reference data types end up in the heap
regardless.

In a simple function call, the variables that appear in it are all pushed into the stack. As soon as the
function is complete, any of the temporary values created and used inside of the function are immediately destroyed once the function is done executing.

```
void DoThings()
{
     int[] arrayOfInts = new int[100]
     for (int i = 0; i < 100 ; i++)
     {
          arrayOfInts[i] = i;
     }
}
```

The `DoThings()` function does pretty much nothing, but makes an array of ints that are added to the
stack. As soon as this function is done, the array of ints is cleared out. In general, the stack grows and
shrinks very fast. The second object that's added to the stack is the `int i`, which is being used inside of
the `for` loop.

The primary advantage a class has over a `struct` is the addition of a constructor and class inheritance. Aside from that, you're able to add assignments to each variable in a class as it's created.

```
struct MyStruct
{
    public int a = 0;
    public MyStruct()
    {
    }
}
class MyClass
{
    public int a = 0;
    public MyClass()
    {
    }
}
```

The code above produces the following errors:

```
Assets/ClassVStruct.cs(7,28): error CS0573: 'ClassVStruct.MyStruct.a':
Structs cannot have instance field initializers
Assets/ClassVStruct.cs(8,24): error CS0568: Structs cannot contain explicit
parameterless constructors
```

In a struct, you're not allowed to assign values to the fields. Therefore, `public a = 0;` is allowed only in a class. Default values are allowed only in classes. Likewise, the constructor `public MyStruct()` isn't allowed, but it is in a class.

We could easily declare a class that has nothing more than data in it; this will look much like any struct.

```
class PlayerData
{
    public Vector3 position;
    public int hitpoints;
    public int ammo;
    public float runSpeed;
    public float walkSpeed;
}
```

This would do the same things as a struct of the same complexity is concerned. However, a struct has the chance to be a bit faster than a class to access. A struct is also a step up from an enum. The declaration might look somewhat similar, but an enum doesn't allow any values to be assigned to its constituent declarations.

### 6.9.1 Character Base Class

For all of the monsters and players to have an equal understanding of one another, they need to share a common base class. This means that simply they all need to share the same parent class that holds data structures, which all of them are aware of. This concept is called inheritance, and it's something that only a class can do.

```
class Monster
{
}
class Zombie : Monster
{
}
```

The `Zombie` uses the `: Monster` statement to tell C# that the `Zombie` is inheriting from `Monster`. We will go into this again in 6.13 and 6.23, but it's important that we're used to seeing this notation and what it's for.

Once each type of character shares the same parent class, it can use the same data. This is important so that zombies can understand what data makes up a human, and vampires can know to avoid zombie blood. To do this, the zombies need to know how to deal with the player's data structure and the player needs to know how to deal with zombies and vampires.

When we start our game, we're going to have a starting point for the player and for each monster. Classes are a clean way to store data when a game is started. Starting data can include basic chunks of information that don't change, such as minimum and maximum values.

Structs don't allow you to declare values for variables when they are created. Classes, on the other hand, do allow you to assign values. More important, we can make them unchangeable.

### 6.9.2 Const

The const keyword is used to tell anyone reading the class that the value assigned cannot change during the game. The keyword is short for constant, and it means that you shouldn't try to change it either. There are a few different ways which you can assign a value to behave the same as a const, but just by looking at the code, you should know that the following code has a value that shouldn't be changed while playing.

```
class Monster
{
        const int MaxHitPoints = 10;
}
```

If a value is declared to be const, then you should keep in mind how it's used. These are good for comparisons, if a value is greater than MaxHitPoints, then you have a very clear reason for why this value is set.

When you've declared a class and set several const values, this gives the class purposeful location to store all kinds of "set in stone" numbers. One problem with giving a class const values is that they can not be changed after they have been set. So make sure that these values shouldn't need to change once the game is running.

This allows you to create a constant value for the class. To make the value accessible, we need to change the declaration.

```
class Monster
{
    public const int MaxHitPoints = 10;
}
```

The accessor must come before the readability of the variable. Likewise, this can also be made private const int MaxHitPoints. This allows you to set the value when writing the code for the classes. However, if you want to make a variable have a limited availability to set, then we can use a different declaration.

### 6.9.3 Readonly

The readonly declaration allows you to change the variable only when a class is declared or as it's written when it was initialized.

```
public class Monster
{
    public readonly int MaxHitPoints = 10;
    public void SetMaxHP(int hp)
    {
        this.MaxHitPoints = hp;
    }
}
```

The code at the bottom of previous page will produce the following error:

```
A readonly field 'Monster.MaxHitPoints' cannot be assigned to (except in a
constructor or a variable initializer)
```

This means that a `readonly` variable can only be set in a variable, an initializer, or a constructor. This means that the only way to set `MaxHitPoints` can be with the following code:

```
public class Monster
{
    public readonly int MaxHitPoints = 10;
    public Monster(int hp)
    {
        this.MaxHitPoints = hp;
    }
}
```

By using a constructor, we can set the `MaxHitPoints` once, or we can use the value when the variable is declared. Therefore, the first way `MaxHitPoints` can be set is when we use the initialization line `public readonly int MaxHitPoints = 10;` where we set `MaxHitPoints` to 10, or in the constructor where we set the value to the `(int hp)` in the argument list. This differs from the `const` keyword, where we can use the initializer only to set the value of the variable `MaxHitPoints`.

These are only simple uses of the `const` and `readonly` variable declarators. Once you begin reading other programmer's code you've downloaded online or observed from team members, you'll get a better idea of the various reasons for using these keywords. It's impossible to cover every context in a single chapter.

### 6.9.4  What We've Learned

Using these keywords is quite simple, and it makes quite clear what you're allowed to do with them. By understanding what the keywords mean to the accessibility of the variable, you'll gain a bit of insight into how the value is used.

`const` and `readonly` mean that the variable cannot be changed either outside of an initial declaration or as the code is written. This means that the value needs to remain unchanged for a reason. Of course, knowing that reason requires a great deal of context, so it's impossible to lay out every reason here. However, it's safe to assume someone added the declaratory keyword for a reason.

## 6.10  Namespaces

Classes are organized by their namespace. A namespace is a system used to sort classes and their contained functions into named groups. It will be problematic if programmers in the world come up with unique names for their classes and functions. Namespaces are used to control scope. By encapsulating functions and variables within a namespace, you're allowed to use names within the namespace that might already be in use in other namespaces.

### 6.10.1  A Basic Example

A namespace is basically an identifier for a group of classes and everything contained in the classes. Within that namespace, we can declare any number of classes. Starting in the Namespaces project, we'll look at the `MyNameSpace.cs` class and within the new file add in the following code:

```
namespace MyNamespace
{
}
```

A namespace is declared like a class. However, we replace the keyword `class` with `namespace`. This assigns the identifier following the keyword to being a new namespace. A new namespace gives us a way to categorize our new classes under a group identified in this case as `MyNameSpace`.

Inside of the namespace, we can add in a new class with its own functions. Adding a class to the namespace should be pretty obvious.

```
namespace MyNameSpace
{
    public class MyClass
    {
    }
}
```

However, to make the class available to anyone who wants to use the class in the namespace, we need to make it public. Within the class in the namespace, we'll add in a function to make this example complete.

```
namespace MyNameSpace
{
    public class MyClass
    {
        public void MyFunction()
        {
            print("hello from MyNamespace");//oops?
        }
    }
}
```

If we try to use print inside of the new `MyFunction` code block, we'll get the following error:

```
Assets/MyNameSpace.cs(7,25): error CS0103: The name 'print' does not exist in
the current context
```

Of course, this requires some external libraries to pull from, so we'll need to add in a directive to `System`. Our finished example looks like the following:

```
using UnityEngine;
namespace MyNameSpace
{
    public class MyClass
    {
        public void MyFunction() {
            print("hello from MyNamespace");
        }
    }
}
```

## 6.10.2 Directives in Namespaces

Now we need to test out our new namespace and its contained class and function. To do this, we'll need to start a new `Example.cs` and assign it to the camera in a new Unity 3D Scene.

```
using UnityEngine;
using System.Collections;
using MyNameSpace;//adding in a directive to our namespace
public class Example : MonoBehaviour {
```

```
    //Use this for initialization
    void Start () {
    }
    //Update is called once per frame
    void Update () {
    }
}
```

At the end of the directives, add in a new line using `MyNameSpace;` to incorporate the work we just finished. This will give us access to the classes and functions within the new namespace. This should also be a clue as to what a directive is doing.

If you examine the first line using `UnityEngine;`, we can assume there's a namespace called UnityEngine, and within that namespace, there are classes and functions we've been using. Now we should have a way to find the classes within our own `MyNameSpace`.

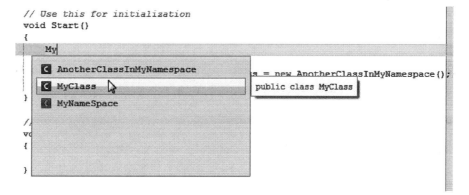

If we go into the `Start ()` function in the `Example.cs` file and add in My…, we'll be prompted with an automatic text completion that includes `MyClass` which is a class inside of `MyNameSpace`. This is reinforced by the highlighted info `class MyNameSpace.MyClass` following the pop-up.

After making a new instance of `MyClass()`, we can use the functions found inside of the class.

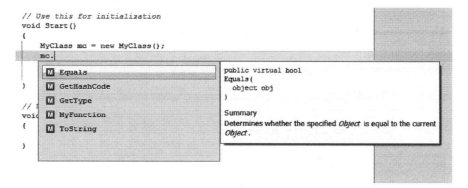

This shows how the functions and classes are found inside of a namespace. Using a new namespace should usually be done to prevent your class and variable names from getting mixed up with identifiers that might already be in use by another library.

```
    void Start ()
    {
        MyClass mc = new MyClass();
        mc.MyFunction();
    }
```

When this code is run, you'll be able to get the following output from the Console in Unity 3D:

```
hello from MyNameSpace
UnityEngine.Debug:Log(Object)
MyNameSpace.MyClass:MyFunction() (at Assets/MyNameSpace.cs:6)
Example:Start () (at Assets/Example.cs:10)
```

This shows where the function was called and what namespace the function originated in. In most cases, you'll create a new namespace for the classes in your new game. This becomes particularly important when you need to use third-party libraries. You might have a function called `findClosest()`, but another library might also have a function with the same name.

If we create C# file named `AnotherNameSpace` and add the following code, we'd be able to observe how to deal with multiple namespaces and colliding function and class names.

```
namespace AnotherNameSpace
{
    using UnityEngine;
    public class MyClass
    {
        public void MyFunction ()
        {
            Debug.Log("hello from AnotherNameSpace");
        }
    }
}
```

Therefore, now if we compare `MyNameSpace` and `AnotherNameSpace`, we're going to have duplicated class and function names. Thus, how do we know which `MyClass` is being used? In the `Example.cs` file, we need to add a new directive to include the `AnotherNameSpace` into the `Example`.

## 6.10.3 Ambiguous References

Coming up with unique names for every variable, class, or function can be difficult. Another class might already use commonly used words like speed, radius, or vector. Namespaces offer a system to help separate your class member names from another class that might already be using the same names.

```
using UnityEngine;
using System.Collections;
using MyNameSpace;
using AnotherNameSpace;
```

This will involve duplicates for `MyClass`, which is cause for some problems. Then Unity 3D will show you the following error:

```
Assets/Example.cs(10,17): error CS0104: 'MyClass' is an ambiguous reference
between 'MyNameSpace.MyClass' and 'AnotherNameSpace.MyClass'
```

Ambiguous references become a common problem if we start to include too many different namespaces. We could possibly fix this by changing the name of the classes in one of the functions, but that wouldn't be possible if the reference came from a dynamic linking library (DLL) or another author's code. We could also change namespaces which we're using, but again, that would be a work around and not a solution.

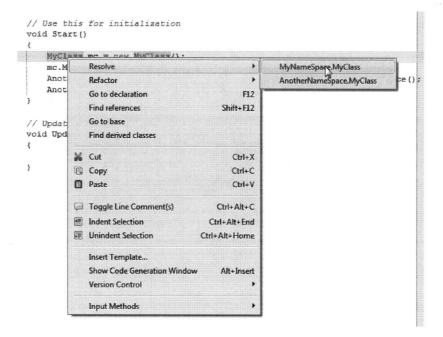

If we hover over the class with the cursor in MonoDevelop, we'll get a pop-up telling us which version is currently being used. Of course, this is just a guess, and a bad one at that. This can be resolved by expanding the declaration. The right-click pop-up has a selection called Resolve.

This will allow us to pick which `MyClass()` we want to use. The resolution is to add on the full dot notation for the namespace we want to use.

```
void Start ()
{
    MyNameSpace.MyClass mc = new MyNameSpace.MyClass();
    mc.MyFunction();
}
```

Of course, it's not the most pretty, but this is the most correct method to fix the namespace we're requesting a `MyClass()` object from. Things can get too long if we need to nest more namespaces within a namespace.

```
using UnityEngine;
namespace MyNameSpace
{
    namespace InsideMyNameSpace
    {
        public class MyClass
        {
            public void MyFunction ()
            {
                Debug.Log("hello from InsideMyNameSpace!");
            }
        }
    }
    public class MyClass
    {
        public void MyFunction()
        {
            Debug.Log("hello from MyNameSpace");
        }
    }
}
```

This example shows a new namespace within `MyNameSpace` called `InsideMyNameSpace`. This namespace within a namespace is called a nested namespace. The following code will work as you might expect:

```
void Start ()
{
    MyNameSpace.InsideMyNameSpace.MyClass imc =
    new MyNameSpace.InsideMyNameSpace.MyClass();
    imc.MyFunction();//hello from InsideMyNameSpace!
}
```

This is long and messy: Is there a way we can fix this? As a matter of fact, there is a way to make this easier to deal with.

### 6.10.4 Alias Directives

Sometimes namespaces can get quite long. Often when you need to refer to a namespace directly you may want to shorten the name into something easier to type. Namespace aliases make this easier.

```
using UnityEngine;
using System.Collections;
using imns = MyNameSpace.InsideMyNameSpace;//shortens a long directive
using AnotherNameSpace;
```

Like a variable `int x = 0;` we can assign a directive using a similar syntax `using x = UnityEngine;` for instance. When we have a namespace nested in another namespace, we can assign that to an identifier as well. To shorten `MyNameSpace.InsideMyNameSpace` to `imns`, we use a statement that looks like `using imns = MyNameSpace.InsideMyNameSpace;` to reduce how much typing we need to use to express which namespace we're using.

```
void Start ()
{
    imns.MyClass imc = new imns.MyClass();
    imc.MyFunction();
}
```

Now we can reduce the declaration of imc to a nice short statement. Of course, unless we have an ambiguous name to worry about, there's no need for being so explicit with the function we're specifically trying to call. With descriptive function and variable names, we can avoid directive aliases.

### 6.10.5 Putting Namespaces to Work

Namespaces allow you to create a new sort of data that can be shared between classes. For instance, in your game you'll most likely have a fairly detailed set of rules and objects that the rest of your game classes will want to share. The best way to keep all of these classes organized is for any sort of shared data to originate from the same namespace.

```
namespace Zombie
{
    using UnityEngine;
    using System.Collections;
    public class MonsterInfo
    {
        public int health;
        public int armor;
        public int attack;
        public MonsterInfo()
        {
            health = 10;
            armor = 1;
            attack = 3;
        }
    }
}
```

Here, we have a new namespace called Zombie that is saved in Zombie.cs in the Assets directory of our Unity 3D project. In this new namespace, we have a class called MonsterInfo that holds three different numbers. An int is used for health, armor, and attack. Once this namespace is created and named, we're able to use any class within it from any other class we create in our game project.

Now if we want to create another monster that uses MonsterInfo to store its game-related information, all we need to do is add using Zombie; in the C# file before the class declaration. Therefore, in a new Monsters.cs file, we add the following code sample. This also goes for any other class that might need to know what a monster's information looks like.

```
using UnityEngine;
using System.Collections;
using Zombie;
public class Monsters : MonoBehaviour
{
    MonsterInfo monster = new MonsterInfo();
    //Use this for initialization
    void Start ()
    {
        MonsterInfo m = monster;
        Debug.Log(m.health);
        Debug.Log(m.armor);
        Debug.Log(m.attack);
    }
    //Update is called once per frame
    void Update ()
    {
    }
}
```

This file now has a class called Monsters, and when it's instantiated, it will create a new MonsterInfo. When the Monsters' Start () function is called, we'll get a list of the health, armor, and attack printed out to the Console panel. This should all be fairly straightforward, but here's where the real use comes into play. To see why namespaces are used, we'll create another C# file called Player.cs, and in the file, we'll also add the using Zombie; statement to import all of the same classes that are used in Monster.cs. With this addition, the player can also have access to the same MonsterInfo data that is being stored in the Monsters.cs.

```csharp
using UnityEngine;
using System.Collections;
using Zombie;
public class Player : MonoBehaviour
{
    public Monsters monster;
    public int attackPower;
    void AttackMonster()
    {
        if (monster != null)
        {
            MonsterInfo mi = monster.monsterInfo;
            Debug.Log(mi.armor);
            if (attackPower > = mi.armor && mi.health > 0)
            {
                monster.TakeDamage(attackPower - mi.armor);
            }
        }
    }
}
```

The access to the monsterInfo is important for the player if he or she needs to know any values from the monster before making an attack. In this case, we create a new function called AttackMonster() where we check for a monster; if we have one, we obtain his monsterInfo by using MonsterInfo mi = monster.monsterInfo; to create a local version of the monsterInfo data.

Then we check on our attackPower, and if we can strike harder than the monster's armor and the monster is still alive, we'll apply some damage to the monster with a function in the monster called TakeDamage();, which means that Monster has a function we need to fill in.

```csharp
//added into Monster.cs
public void TakeDamage(int damage)
{
    monsterInfo.health -= damage;
}
```

We'll add in a simple function called TakeDamage() that takes in an integer value. On the player side, the damage applied is the player's attackPower after we subtract the monster's armor value. This then reduces the monsterInfo.health attribute.

## 6.10.6 Extending Namespaces

Namespaces can be extended quite easily. In another new C# file named ExtendingMyNamespace.cs, we have the following code:

```csharp
namespace MyNamespace
{
    using UnityEngine;
    public class AnotherClassInMyNamespace
```

```
    {
        public void MyFunction()
        {
            Debug.Log("hello from MyNamespace");
        }
    }
}
```

This means that there's a new class called AnotherClassInMyNamespace() in addition to MyClass(). These two namespace files work together, and when the using MyNamespace; directive is used, it allows for both MyClass() and AnotherClassInMyNamespace() to exist side by side. No additional code is needed aside from using MyNamespace;, which is required for Example .cs to see both versions of MyNamespace.

However, there are things to be careful about. If you add class MyClass inside of any other namespace MyNamespace files, you'll get the following error:

```
Assets/MyNamespace.cs(4,22): error CS0101: The namespace 'MyNameSpace'
already contains a definition for 'MyClass'
```

The collection of namespaces acts as one. They aggregate together into a single form when compiled, so even though they are separated into two different files, they act like one.

### 6.10.7 What We've Learned

This is a simple way to allow multiple classes work together by sharing a class through a namespace. Both the player and the monster are aware of monsterInfo, thanks to using the monsterInfo found in the Zombie namespace. We should get used to the idea of adding multiple classes to the Zombie namespace to make it more useful. Things such as ammunition types and weapons should all be added as different classes under the Zombie namespace.

In many cases, it's useful to build a namespace for your game where you'll be creating classes and functions that need to be used throughout your project. Something like CreateZombie() seems like a function that will be called often. If that's the case, then it's often useful to have a namespace called ZombieGame;. By adding using ZombieGame; to all of your classes, they'll all have access to the CreateZombie() function.

The namespace should also contain common structs that every class will need to make use of. Specifics such as a ZombieInfo{} struct could contain position, aggression level, defenses, and weapons. Character spell abilities and effects can be held in the namespace. Basically, anything you need to do often and anywhere should be kept in the namespace.

## 6.11 Functions Again

So far we've been working in either the Start () function or the Update () function because they are entry points. Because of this, they are automatically called by the engine. In a non-Unity 3D Engine program, the default entry point would be something like public static void Main().

### 6.11.1 Parameter Lists

When a function is called, its identifier followed by its parameter list is added to code. Parameters are like little mail slots on the front door of a house. There might be a slot for integers, floats, and arrays. Each slot on the door, or argument in the parameter list, is a type followed by an identifier.

### 6.11.1.1 A Basic Example

If we look at a basic example, we'll see how all this works.

```
using UnityEngine;
using System.Collections;
public class Example : MonoBehaviour {
    int a = 0;
    void Start ()
    {
    }
    void SetA (int i)
    {
        a = i;
    }
}
```

`void SetA (int i)` takes in one parameter of type `int`. This is a simple example of a value parameter; there are other types of parameters which we'll go into next. The value parameter declares the type and an identifier whose scope is limited to the contents of the function it's declared with.

```
    void Start ()
    {
        print(a);
        SetA(3);
        print(a);
    }
```

To use our function, add in the preceding lines of code to the `Start ()` function in Unity 3D. When you start the game, you'll see a 0 followed by a 3. We can do this any number of times, and each time we're allowed to change what value we set A to. Of course, it's easier to use `a = 3` in the `Start ()` function, but then we wouldn't be learning anything.

### 6.11.2 Side Effects

When a function directly sets a variable in the class the function lives in, programmers like to call this a side effect. Side effects are usually things that programmers try to avoid, but it's not always practical. Writing functions with side effects tend to prevent the function from being useful in other classes. We'll find other systems that allow us to avoid using side effects, but in some cases, it's necessary.

```
Class MySideEffect
{
    int a = 0;
    void SetA ()
    {
        a = 5;
    }
}
```

The above `SetA()` function sets `int a` to 5. The `SetA()` function does have a clear purpose, setting A, but there's nothing in the function that indicates where the variable it's setting lives. If the variable lived in another class which `MySideEffect` inherited from, then you wouldn't even see the variable in this class.

Once the complexity in a class grows, where and when a variable gets changed or read becomes more obscure. If a function remains self-contained, testing and fixing that function becomes far easier.

Reading what a function does should not involve jumping around to find what variable it's making changes to. This brings us back to the topic of scope. Limiting the scope or reach of a function helps limit the number of places where things can go wrong.

```
class MySideEffect {
    int a = 0;
    void SetA ()
    {
        a = 5;
    }
    void SetAgain ()
    {
        a = new int();
    }
}
```

The more functions that have a side effect, the more strange behaviors might occur. If an Update () function is expecting one value but gets something else entirely, you can start to get unexpected behaviors. Worse yet, if SetAgain() is called from another class and you were expecting a to be 5, you're going to run into more strange behaviors.

### 6.11.3 Multiple Arguments

There aren't any limits to the number of parameters that a function can accept. Some languages limit you to no more than 16 arguments, which seems acceptable. If your logic requires more than 16 parameters, it's probably going to be easier to separate your function into different parts. However, if we're going to be doing something simple, we might want to use more than one parameter anyway.

```
int a = 0;
void Start ()
{
}
void SetA (int i, int j)
{
    a = i * j;
}
```

We can add a second parameter to SetA. A comma token tells the function to accept another variable in the parameter list. For this example, we're using two ints to multiply against one another and assign a value to a. There isn't anything limiting the types we're allowed to use in the parameter list.

```
int a = 0;
float b = 0;
void Start ()
{
}
void SetA (int i, float j)
{
    a = i;
    b = j;
}
```

The function with multiple parameters can do more. Value parameters are helpful ways to get data into a function to accomplish some sort of simple task. We'll elaborate more on this by creating something useful in Unity 3D.

## 6.11.4  Useful Parameters

Often, we need to test things out before using them. Let's say we want to create a new primitive cube in the scene, give it a useful name, and then set its position. This is a simple task, and our code might look like the following:

```
void Start ()
{
    GameObject g = GameObject.CreatePrimitive(PrimitiveType.Cube);
    g.name = "MrCube";
    g.transform.position = new Vector3(0,1,0);
}
```

Our cube is given a name, and it's assigned a place in the world. Next, let's say we want to make a bunch of different cubes in the same way. We could do something like the following:

```
void Start ()
{
    GameObject g = GameObject.CreatePrimitive(PrimitiveType.Cube);
    g.name = "MrCube";
    g.transform.position = new Vector3(0,1,0);
    GameObject h = GameObject.CreatePrimitive(PrimitiveType.Cube);
    h.name = "MrsCube";
    h.transform.position = new Vector3(0,2,0);
    GameObject i = GameObject.CreatePrimitive(PrimitiveType.Cube);
    i.name = "MissCube";
    i.transform.position = new Vector3(0,3,0);
    GameObject j = GameObject.CreatePrimitive(PrimitiveType.Cube);
    j.name = "CubeJr";
    j.transform.position = new Vector3(0,4,0);
}
```

If this code looks horrible, then you're learning. It's accomplishing a task properly, but in terms of programming, it's horrible. When you intend to do a simple task more than a few times, it's a good idea to turn it into a function. This is sometimes referred to as the "Rule of Three," a term coined in an early programming book on refactoring code.

### 6.11.4.1  The Rule of Three

The Rule of Three is a simple idea that any time you need to do any given task more than three times it would be better served by creating a new single procedure to accomplish the task that has been done manually. This reduces the chance of error in writing the same code more than three times. This also means that changing the procedure can be done in one place.

```
void CreateANamedObject (PrimitiveType pt, string n, Vector3 p)
{
    GameObject g = GameObject.CreatePrimitive(pt);
    g.name = n;
    g.transform.position = p;
}
```

We take the code that's repeated and move it into a function. We then take the values that change between each iteration and change it into a parameter. In general, it's best to put the parameters in the same order in which they're used. This isn't required, but it looks more acceptable to a programmer's eyes.

```
void Start ()
{
    CreateANamedObject(PrimitiveType.Cube, "MrCube", new Vector3(0,1,0));
}
```

We then test the function at least once before writing any more code than we need to. If this works out, then we're free to duplicate the line of code to accomplish what we started off doing.

```
void Start ()
{
    CreateANamedObject(PrimitiveType.Cube, "MrCube", new Vector3(0,1,0));
    CreateANamedObject(PrimitiveType.Cube, "MrsCube", new Vector3(0,2,0));
    CreateANamedObject(PrimitiveType.Cube, "MissCube", new Vector3(0,3,0));
    CreateANamedObject(PrimitiveType.Cube, "CubeJr", new Vector3(0,4,0));
}
```

Again, though, we're seeing a great deal of duplicated work. We've used arrays earlier, and this is as good a time as any to use them. By observation, the main thing that is changing here is the name. Therefore, we'll need to add each name to an array.

```
string[] names = new string[] {"MrCube", "MrsCube", "MissCube", "CubeJr"};
```

The variable declaration needs to change a little bit for an array. First of all, rather than using `type identifier;`, a pair of square brackets are used after the type. The statement starts with `string[]` rather than `string`. This is followed by the usual identifier we're going to use to store the array of strings.

Unlike an integer type, there's no default value that can be added in for this array of strings. To complete the statement, we need to add in the data before the end of the statement. The `new` keyword is used to indicate that a new array is going to be used. The array is a special class that is built into C#. Therefore, it has some special abilities that we'll get into later.

Now that we've declared an array of names, we'll need to use them.

### 6.11.5 Foreach versus For

The `foreach` loop is often our `goto` loop for iterating through any number of objects.

```
string[] names = new string[] {"MrCube", "MrsCube", "MissCube", "CubeJr"};
void Start ()
{
    foreach(string s in names)
    {
        Debug.Log(s);
    }
}
```

The parameters for the `foreach` also introduce the keyword `in` that tells the `foreach` iterator what array to look into. The first parameter before the `in` keyword indicates what we're expecting to find inside of the array. Therefore, for this use of the `foreach` iterator, we get the output in the following page.

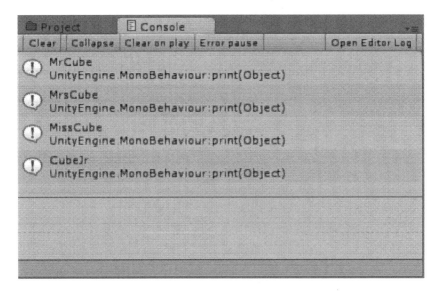

As expected, we get a list of the names found in the array we added. As we add in new functions and variables, it's important to test them out one at a time. This helps make sure that you're headed in the right direction one step at a time. Now we can switch out the `print` function for the clever function we wrote now.

```
foreach(string s in names)
{
     CreateANamedObject(PrimitiveType.Cube, s, new Vector3(0, 1, 0));
}
```

The `foreach` loop in some respects operates in the same way as a `while` loop.

```
     float y = 1.0f;
     foreach(string s in names)
     {
          CreateANamedObject(PrimitiveType.Cube, s, new Vector3(0, y, 0));
          y += 1.0f;
     }
```

It's simple to add in a variable outside of the loop that can be incremented within the loop.

```
string[] names = new string[] {"MrCube", "MrsCube", "MissCube", "CubeJr"};
void Start ()
{
     float y = 1.0f;
     foreach(string s in names)
     {
          CreateANamedObject(PrimitiveType.Cube, s, new Vector3(0, y, 0));
          y += 1.0f;
     }
}
void CreateANamedObject (PrimitiveType pt, string n, Vector3 p)
{
     GameObject g = GameObject.CreatePrimitive(pt);
     g.name = n;
     g.transform.position = p;
}
```

It's not time to admire our clever function. The `foreach` means we can add in any number of names to the array and the tower of cubes will get taller with named boxes.

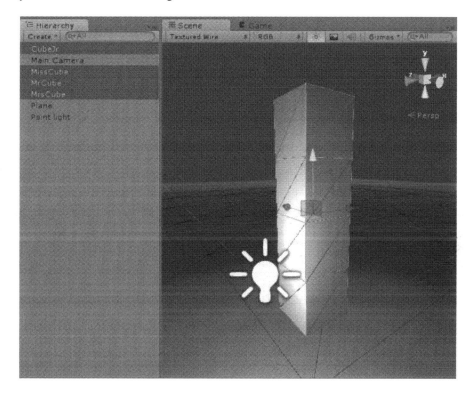

## 6.11.6 What We've Learned

The `foreach` loop is useful in many ways, but it's also somewhat limited. If we had more than one array to iterate through at the same time, we'd have some difficulties. In some cases, it's easier to use a regular `for` loop. Arrays are lists of objects, but they're also numbered.

Arrays are used everywhere. On your own, experiment by adding more parameters to the function and more names to the list. We'll take a look at how to use other loops with multidimensional arrays and even jagged arrays in Chapter 7.

## 6.12 Unity 3D Execution Order

C# is an imperative language, which means that operations are executed in order, first one thing and then another. When Unity 3D makes an instance of a new `gameObject` with `MonoBehaviour` components, each component will have at least five functions called on it before the end of the frame where it was created. Additional rendering calls can be called as well.

Specifically, the `Start ()` and `Update ()` functions in Unity 3D are called in each `MonoBehaviour` in a specific order. Several other functions are also used by Unity 3D, and they each have specific moments when they are called.

A total of eight functions which Unity 3D calls are as follows:

```
Awake()
OnEnable()
Start ()
FixedUpdate ()
```

```
Update ()
LateUpdate ()
OnDisable()
OnDestroy()
```

The order of this should make sense, considering that C# will execute statements in order. However, what happens when another class is instanced in the Awake() function and it too will have its own Awake(), OnEnable(), and Start () functions?

## 6.12.1 A Basic Example

Begin by examining the ExecutionOrder project; the First.cs class will look a bit like the following:

```csharp
using UnityEngine;
using System.Collections;
public class First : MonoBehaviour
{
    void Awake()
    {
        Debug.Log("First Awake");
    }
    void OnEnable()
    {
        Debug.Log("First OnEnable");
    }
    void Start ()
    {
        Debug.Log("First Start");
    }
    void FixedUpdate ()
    {
        Debug.Log("First FixedUpdate");
    }
    void Update ()
    {
        Debug.Log("First Update");
    }
    void LateUpdate ()
    {
        Debug.Log("First LateUpdate");
        //Destroy(this);
    }
    void OnDisable()
    {
        Debug.Log("First OnDisable");
    }
    void OnDestroy()
    {
        Debug.Log("First OnDestroy");
    }
}
```

This prints out the following:

The Console shows that the code is executed in the same order in which we laid them out in the class. When the LateUpdate () function is called, we use Destroy(this); to begin deleting the class from the scene. When the class begins to delete itself, it's first disabled and then deleted.

When a new instance of a MonoBehaviour is created, it will also call its Awake(), OnEnabled(), and Start () functions. Intuitively, it would make sense if you create an object in the Awake() function; the new object might wait till the end of Awake() before it begins its Awake() function. However, this isn't always the case.

```
void Awake ()
{
        Debug.Log("Awake Start");
        this.gameObject.AddComponent(typeof(Second));
        Debug.Log("Awake Done");
}
```

Say we create a new class called Second.cs and have it log its Awake() and Start () functions as well. Then, in the Second.cs class we have the following code:

```
public class Second : MonoBehaviour
{
        void Awake ()
        {
                Debug.Log("Second Awake Start");
        }
        void OnEnable ()
        {
                Debug.Log("Second OnEnable Start");
        }
}
```

This produces the following output:

```
First Awake Start
Second Awake Start
Second OnEnable Start
First Awake Done
First OnEnable
```

Before the `First` class was created, the `Second` was able to get its `Awake()` done and move on to `OnEnable()` without interruption. `First` waited for `Second` to finish its `Awake()` and `OnEnable()` functions before `First` finished its own `Awake()` function. Afterward, `OnEnable()` of the `First` was finally called, even if `Second` took its own time to finish its `Awake()` function.

```
void Awake ()
{
      Debug.Log("Second Awake Start");
      for (int i = 0; i < 1000; i++)
      {
            Debug.Log("wait!");
      }
      Debug.Log("Other Awake Done");
}
```

The `First.cs` class finishes its `Awake()` function, then the `Second.cs` class finishes its `Awake()` function and starts its `OnEnable()`. Then the `First.cs` class finishes its `Awake()` and starts its `OnEnable()` function. The First and Second being their `Start ()` function. Notice that "First Awake Done" doesn't appear until after "Second OnEnable." The "Second OnEnable" is only printed once the "Second Awake Done" is printed, indicating that the `for` loop was able to finish.

When more objects are being created, the order in which these functions are called becomes more difficult to sort out. If you created several different objects, some of them might take even longer or shorter to finish their `Awake()`, `OnEnable()`, and `Start ()` functions. Figuring all of this out takes a bit of thinking things through.

### 6.12.2 Component Execution Order

The execution of classes becomes a bit more confusing when they're attached to a `gameObject` as a prefab. In the scene, adding `Second` and `Third` classes to the Main Camera will show us some unexpected results.

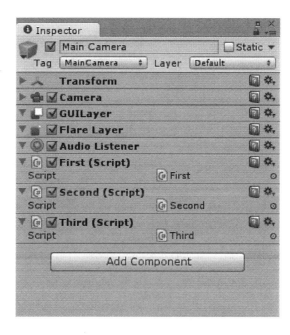

Once all three `MonoBehaviours` have been attached to the Main Camera, we can observe the execution order of the functions found in each class.

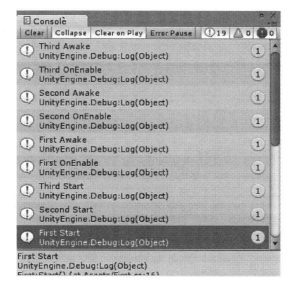

The `Third Awake()` and `OnEnable()` are called before the `Second` and the `First` even though the components look like they've been reordered in the opposite order on the Main Camera. However, this isn't always the case.

In the above screenshot, we swapped the `First` component with the `Second`. Even after changing the order in which they appear in the components list, we get no change in the Console's log output. This tells us that there's no specific order in which the objects are created and how they are ordered in the `gameObject`'s components list. However, there is a simple system in which we can change the execution order manually.

In Unity 3D under the Edit → Preferences → Script Execution Order, we can open a panel that tells Unity 3D how to prioritize when a class is called. By clicking on the + icon on the lower right of the panel, we can add our classes to an ordered list.

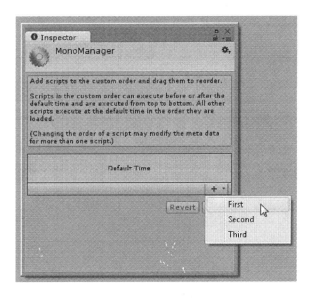

After your classes have been added to the list, you can make any changes by altering the number in the box to the right. Clicking on the – icon removes them from the list. Press Apply once you've added all of your classes to the list.

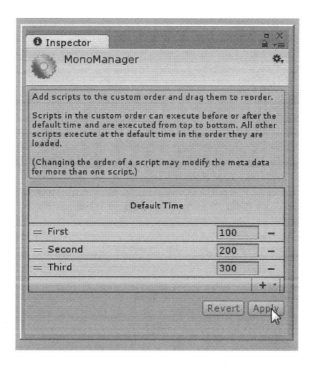

Once the scripts have been added to this list, they are guaranteed to be called in this order, ignoring how they are ordered in the components list on the `gameObject` they've been added to. Playing the scene with the components attached to the Main Camera in any order will always result in the following output:

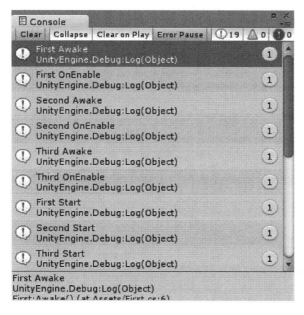

After the scripts order is set, the Console panel shows us a more expected result. Of course, there are other ways to ensure that a class behaves as you might expect, but we will have to hold off on those systems for Section 6.23. For now it's important that we observe how the functions operate and how to best use these behaviors to our advantage.

From observation, we know that we can maintain when each function is called.

### 6.12.3  What We've Learned

In this chapter, we looked at how to manage execution order between multiple classes. For simple projects, this execution ordering system should suffice. However, when you're not inheriting from `MonoBehaviour`, this management system will no longer work.

Once we get into more complex systems that do not inherit from `MonoBehaviour`, we'll build our own system for managing the execution order. There are systems that allow you to better control what functions are called and when, but we'll have to learn a few other things before getting to that.

Unity 3D expects many different things of your classes when you inherit from `MonoBehaviour`. If you include an `Update ()` function, it will automatically be called on every frame. However, when there are too many `Update ()` functions on too many classes running in a scene, Unity's frame rate can suffer.

Once a game gets moving along and creatures and characters are spawning and dying, it's impossible to know when and in what order each function is executed. Each object in the scene should be able to operate on its own. If an object depends on a variable, the value of which needs to be updated before it's used, then you may run into problems reading stale data.

## 6.13  Inheritance Again

Inheriting members of a parent class is only one facet of what inheritance does for your code. The behaviors of the functions also carry on in the child classes. If the parent has functions that it uses to find objects in the world, then so do the children. If the parent has the ability to change its behavior based on its proximity to other objects, then so do the children.

The key difference is that the children can decide what happens based on those behaviors. The data that is collected can be used in any way. A child class inherits the functions of its parent class. When the child's function is executed, it operates the same way as its parent. It can be more interesting to have the child's function behave differently from the inherited version of the function.

### 6.13.1  Function Overrides

The `override` keyword following the `public` keyword in a function declaration tells the child version of the function to clear out the old behavior and implement a new version. We've seen how member functions work when they're used by another class. Now we're going to see how to effect the operation of inherited functions.

#### 6.13.1.1  A Basic Example

Revisiting the `Parent.cs` and `Child.cs` classes again in the ParentChild project, we should add the following code to the `Parent` class. Start by writing three new functions to the `Parent` class. Start with `ParentFunction ()` and then add in a print to say hello.

```
using UnityEngine;
using System.Collections;
public class Parent : MonoBehaviour
{
    void Start ()
    {
        ParentFunction();
    }
```

```
    public void ParentFunction()
    {
        print("parent says hello");
        FunctionA();
        FunctionB();
    }
    public void FunctionA()
    {
        print("function A says hello");
    }
    public void FunctionB()
    {
        print("function B says hello");
    }
}
```

When the `ParentFunction()` is added to the `Start ()` function, this will produce the expected "parent says hello" followed by "function A says hello" and then "function B says hello" in the Console panel in the Unity 3D editor. So far nothing surprising has happened.

The child class is based on the parent class, and we have an opportunity to make modifications by adding layers of code. To make see this modification, we need to reuse the code from the `Parent` class in the `Child` class. Take the `ParentFunction()` and add it to the `Start ()` function of the `Child` class.

```
public class Child : Parent
{
    void Start ()
    {
        ParentFunction();
    }
}
```

Running this will produce the same output to the Console panel as the `Parent` class. Right now, there is no function overriding going on. If we intend to override a function, we should make the `Parent` class allow for functions to be overridden by adding the `virtual` keyword to the function we plan to override.

```
public virtual void FunctionA () {
    print("function A says hello");
}
```

Adding the `virtual` keyword after the `public` declaration and before the return data type, we can tell the function it's allowed to be overridden by any class inheriting its functions. Back in the `Child` class, we have the option to override the virtual function.

```
using UnityEngine;
using System.Collections;
public class Child : Parent
{
    void Start ()
    {
        ParentFunction();
    }
    public override void FunctionA()
    {
        print("Im a new version of function A");
    }
}
```

This has a new instruction for FunctionA(). As you might expect, the output to the Console panel is changed to something new. The Child class will send new data to the Console that should read

```
parent says hello
Im a new version of function A
function B says hello
```

Without the keywords override and virtual, we get the following warning:

```
Assets/Child.cs(11,21): warning CS0108: 'Child.FunctionA()' hides inherited
member 'Parent.FunctionA()'. Use the new keyword if hiding was intended
```

We can try this and watch the resulting output. In the Child class, we'll add in the new keyword. However, the output will remain the same as though the Parent class' version of FunctionA() was being used. This is because the FunctionA() living in the Child class is a new one, and not the one being used by the ParentFunction(). As you can imagine, this can get confusing.

```
public virtual void FunctionA()
{
    print("function A says hello");
}
```

### 6.13.1.1.1 Base

The Child class' version of the function hides the inherited member from its Parent class. Hiding means that the inherited version of the function is no longer valid. When called, only the new version will run. However, we have written code in the Parent class' version of the FunctionA(), which we may or may not want to override. To use the original version, we can add the keyword base to the beginning of the FunctionA().

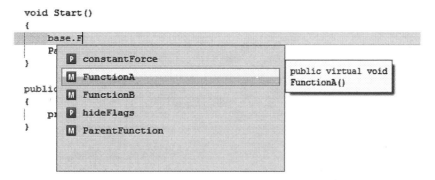

This produces the expected 3 to be printed out in the Console panel. For the Child class to take over the FunctionA() and create its own version of the function, use the override keyword.

```
public override void FunctionA()
{
    print("Im a new version of function A");
}
```

Therefore, when the Start () function calls on the FirstFunction(), the resident version is called resulting in "new version of FirstFunction()" printed in the Console panel in Unity 3D when the game is run. Normally, overriding functions come into play when we have more than one child class that needs to use the same function.

## 6.13.2 Class Inheritance

We've seen a bit about how a function can inherit some attributes from a previous version of a class. To see how this works, create a couple of nested classes in a new C# file named `Monsters`.

```
using UnityEngine;
using System.Collections;
public class Monsters : MonoBehaviour
{
    //Use this for initialization
    void Start ()
    {
    }
    //Update is called once per frame
    void Update ()
    {
    }
    class Monster
    {
        public int HitPoints;
    }
    class Zombie : Monster
    {
        public int BrainsEaten = 0;
    }
    class Vampire : Monster
    {
        public int BloodSucked = 0;
    }
}
```

In the `public class Monsters`, we've added at the bottom a `class Monster` and a `class Zombie` as well as a `class Vampire`. Both `Zombie` and `Vampire` are followed with : `Monster` to indicate that they are both inheriting functions and fields from `Monster`. Note all this is happening within one C# file called `Monsters` (plural).

### 6.13.2.1 Sharing Common Attributes

The whole point of inheritance is the ability to create a general class of object from which child objects can inherit the same properties. If all of the characters in a game are going to share a system for taking damage, then they should all use the same system. Games use "mechanics" as a generalized term for game rules. Often used like "this game's mechanics are fun." Recovering health, taking damage, and interacting with objects should all be added to what is called a *base class*.

Consider building base classes for things such as destructible objects and monsters. Base classes allow for the multitude of objects in your game to have hitpoints and share the ability of the player to interact with them. Breaking down a door and basting away a zombie shouldn't require a different set of code to accomplish the same thing.

By adding `public int HitPoints` to `Monster`, we've given both `Zombie` and `Vampire` a `HitPoints` variable. This is a main strength of why we need to use inheritance. Objects that share common attributes should be able to share that data. We need to make this `public` so that when the class is used, you can access the `HitPoints` variable from outside of the class. To demonstrate, we'll need to make some instances of both the zombie and the vampire.

```
//Use this for initialization
void Start () {
    Zombie Z = new Zombie();
    Vampire V = new Vampire();
    Z.HitPoints = 10;
    V.HitPoints = 10;
}
```

Now Vampires and Zombies have HitPoints. In the Start () function, we'll create a new Zombie named Z and a new Vampire named V. Then we'll give them some starting hitpoints by using the identifier and adding a.HitPoints = 10; to make the assignment. However, if we add in a constructor, we can put the HitPoints = 10; into the constructor for the monster instead! While we're at it, extend the Monster by adding a capsule to its presence. We'll also make him announce himself when he's created.

```
class Monster
{
    public int HitPoints;
    public GameObject gameObject;
    //class constructor
    public Monster()
    {
        HitPoints = 10;
        gameObject =
                GameObject.CreatePrimitive(PrimitiveType.Capsule);
        Debug.Log("A new monster rises!");
    }
}
```

To make use of the HitPoints variable, we will create a function that will deal with damage done to the monster. Adding in a new public function that returns an int called TakeDamage will be a good start.

```
class Monster
{
    public int HitPoints;
    public GameObject gameObject;
    public Monster()
    {
        HitPoints = 10;
        gameObject =
                GameObject.CreatePrimitive(PrimitiveType.Capsule);
        Debug.Log("A new monster rises!");
    }
    public virtual int TakeDamage(int damage)
    {
        return HitPoints - damage;
    }
}
```

In the TakeDamage() argument list, we'll add in (int damage) that will return the HitPoints − damage to let us know how many HitPoints the monster has after taking damage. Now both the Zombie and the Vampire can take damage. To allow the Zombie and Vampire to reuse the function and override its behavior, we add in virtual after the public keyword.

```
class Vampire : Monster
{
    public int BloodSucked = 0;
    public override int TakeDamage(int damage)
    {
        return HitPoints - (damage/2);
    }
}
```

Because vampires are usually more durable than zombies, we'll make the vampire take half the damage that is dealt to him. Use `public override` to tell the function to take over the original use of the `Monster.TakeDamage()` function. This allows us to reuse the same function call on both zombies and vampires. For the `Zombie`, we'll return the default result of the `Monster.TakeDamage()` function by using `return base.TakeDamage(damage);`. The keyword `base` allows us to refer the original implementation of the code.

```
void Start ()
{
    Zombie Z = new Zombie();
    Vampire V = new Vampire();
    Debug.Log (Z.TakeDamage(5));
    Debug.Log (V.TakeDamage(5));
}
```

In the preceding `Start ()` function of `Monsters.cs`, we'll make the following uses of `Z` and `V`. The results of our code in `Start ()` should look like the following:

```
5
UnityEngine.Debug:Log(Object)
Monsters:Start () (at Assets/Monsters.cs:10)
8
UnityEngine.Debug:Log(Object)
Monsters:Start () (at Assets/Monsters.cs:11)
```

This looks useful, though remember that we're dealing with `int` values and not `float`. When we divide `int` 5 by `int` 2, we get 3, not 2.5. When building new objects, the goal is to reuse as much code as possible. Likewise, we can leave the `TakeDamage()` out of the zombie altogether if we don't need to make any changes.

```
class Zombie : Monster
{
    public int BrainsEaten = 0;
}
class Vampire : Monster
{
    public int BloodSucked = 0;
    public override int TakeDamage(int damage)
    {
        return HitPoints - (damage/2);
    }
}
```

However, it's sometimes unclear what's going on and might end up being less obvious when damage is dealt to the two monsters. In the end though, it's up to you to choose how to set up any functions that are inherited from your base monster class.

This should serve as a fair example as to what objects and classes are created in the way they are. When functions and variables are separated in classes, they allow you to compartmentalize for very specific purposes. When you design your classes, it's important to keep object-oriented concepts in mind.

### 6.13.3 Object

Changing behaviors of previously implemented functions is a powerful tool in object oriented programming (OOP) languages. The base class from which all classes in Unity 3D inherit is object. The object class is the base class to which unity can reference. For Unity 3D to be able to interact with a class, it must be based on object first. The .Net Framework provides object as a foundation for any other class being created. This allows every new object a common ground to communicate between one another.

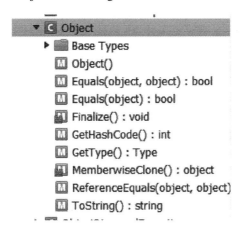

Referring to MonoDevelop and expanding References → UnityEngine.dll, you can find the object class. Inside that you'll find several functions and some variables. If we were to override ToString(), we could add some useful parameters to our monsters to provide a more customized return value.

```
class Zombie : Monster
{
    public int BrainsEaten = 0;
    public Zombie()
    {
        Debug.Log("zombie constructor");
        gameObject.transform.position = new Vector3(1, 0, 0);
    }
    public override string ToString()
    {
        return string.Format("[Zombie]");
    }
}
```

As soon as we enter public override, MonoDevelop will pop up a list of functions that are available to override. Selecting ToString() automatically fills in the rest of the function. If we add in Debug.Log(Z.ToString()); to the Start () function, we'll get the following printed to the Unity's Console panel:

```
[Zombie]
UnityEngine.Debug:Log(Object)
Monsters:Start () (at Assets/Monsters.cs:12)
```

The printout [Zombie] might not be as useful as something more detailed. This does inform us what we're working with but not much more. Then again, if we print out what the vampire to string is, we're not going to get anything more useful since we have yet to provide any specific ToString() functionality.

```
Monsters+Vampire
UnityEngine.Debug:Log(Object)
Monsters:Start () (at Assets/Monsters.cs:13)
```

Therefore, it's often useful to find functions that are already in use and update them to fit our current class. The object class was created with `ToString()`, which provides every object in C# to have some sort of `ToString()` behavior. This also means that we can override `ToString()` with pretty much any class we create.

### 6.13.4 What We've Learned

At this point, we've got a great deal of the basics down. We can write classes and we know how the basics of inheritance work. This is important, as we proceed to use inheriting properties and methods more and more. We've studied a bit of flow control systems using `if` and `switch`, which are indispensable statements.

We've created several classes already, but we've yet to really use classes as objects. In Chapters 7 and 8, we're going to learn the core of what OOP is all about.

Often when you start writing classes for a game, you can get started faster by creating a class for every object. This is sometimes required if you're working with a group of people. Everyone begins by creating classes for his or her own set of objects. Only after a few different classes have been written will it become clear that a base class might exist.

```
//written by programmer A
class Zombie
{
    int afterLife = 10;
    int brainsEaten = 0;
    float stumbleSpeed = 2.1f;
    public void TakeDamage(int damage, bool isFire)
    {
        if(!isFire)
        {
            afterLife -= damage;
        } else {
            afterLife -= damage * 2;
        }
    }
}
//written by programmer B
class TreasureChest
{
    bool Broken = false;
    int damageToOpen = 5;
    int goldCoins = 100;
    public bool BreakChest(int smash)
    {
        if(smash > damageToOpen)
        {
            Broken = true;
        } else {
            Broken = false;
        }
    Return Broken;
    }
}
```

If we look at the above two classes, each written by a different programmer, we might notice that one has a `return bool` if the damage has reached a threshold. The `BreakChest()` function looks for a number greater than its `damageToOpen` value. If it is, then it returns `true`, otherwise the chest remains not `Broken`. The `Zombie` class, on the other hand, has an `afterLife` value that is decremented every time the `TakeDamage()` function is called.

Both work in similar ways, but the `Zombie` decrements the `afterLife` pool, while the `TreasureChest` only requires enough damage to be done in one hit to break. When the two programmers come together to collaborate, they might want to agree on some similar behaviors, and then agree on more generic names for the variables to build a base class.

## 6.14 Type Casting Again

When programmers use the word *integral type*, they mean things that can be numbered. For instance, a boolean can be converted from true and false to 1 and 0; note that this can be done by simply using `int i = 0;` and `bool t = i;` but it's close. Try the following code in the Integrals project:

```
using UnityEngine;
using System.Collections;
public class CastingAgain : MonoBehaviour
{
    enum simpleEnum
    {
        a,
        b,
        c
    }
    //Use this for initialization
    void Start ()
    {
        simpleEnum MySimpleEnum = simpleEnum.b;
        int MyInt = MySimpleEnum as int;
        Debug.Log(MyInt);
    }
}
```

Create an enum type with `enum simpleEnum{a,b,c};` and then create a variable for the `simpleEnum` called `MySimpleEnum` to store the `simpleEnum.b` value. In this case, `simpleEnum.b;` is the second value of the enumerator.

As we try to cast `MySimpleEnum` as `int;` to `MyInt`, we get an error!

```
"Assets/CastingAgain.cs(13,42): error CS0077: The 'as' operator cannot be
used with a non-nullable value type 'int'"
```

The `as` operator can't be used for this because an `int` is not actually an enum. Therefore, we get a conflict here. We're trying to use the enum as though it were already an `int`, which it's not. There is a way to convert different types from one to another.

```
    void Start ()
    {
        simpleEnum MySimpleEnum = simpleEnum.b;
        int MyInt = (int)MySimpleEnum;
        Debug.Log(MyInt);
    }
```

The line `int MyInt = (int)MySimpleEnum;` is using the explicit cast `(int)` to convert the `MySimpleEnum` into the `int` value. This isn't always possible, but in some cases, this will work when an explicit cast has been defined.

Here we get "1" in the Console when we run the game. Remember that numbering lists in C# starts at 0, so the second item in a list will be indexed at 1. Of course, not all explicit conversions work. For instance, you can't turn a Monster GameObject into a `float` value. Zombies aren't just numbers!

### 6.14.1 (<Type>) versus "as"

Here we've started to see a bit of a difference in type casting methods. This is the difference between (<Type>)and as problems that can actually come up during an interview process if you're trying to get a job as a programmer.

We should also note that some casting is also going on when we use float f = 1; where 1 is an int value, but it's accepted into a float f without any question. This is an implicit cast, or rather this is a cast that is accepted without any explicit cast operation. This also works for a double d = 1.0f; where 1.0f is a float value and d is a double.

The two different methods we can use are called *prefix-casting* and *as-casting*. Prefix casting is what the (int) is called; this is also referred to as an explicit cast operator. The as operator works a bit differently than the explicit cast operator.

```
using UnityEngine;
using System.Collections;
public class TypeCasting : MonoBehaviour
{
    class Humanoid
    {
    }
    class Zombie : Humanoid
    {
    }
    class Person : Humanoid
    {
    }
    //Use this for initialization
    void Start ()
    {
    }
    //Update is called once per frame
    void Update ()
    {
    }
}
```

Add in three classes: Humanoid, Zombie, and Person. Make the Zombie and Person inherit from the Humanoid class, and we'll be able to get started with our tutorial. Discovering the differences with as and (<Type>) is significant only once we start getting into the nitty-gritty of doing something with the results of the type casting.

```
    //Use this for initialization
    void Start ()
    {
        Humanoid h = new Humanoid();
        Zombie z = h as Zombie;
        Debug.Log(z);
    }
```

In our Start () function, we'll create a new Humanoid h, which will instantiate a new Humanoid type object identified by h. Then we'll create another object called z and assign h as Zombie to z. This assumes that the Humanoid is a Zombie type object. When we use Debug. Log(z), we get Null.

```
Null
UnityEngine.Debug:Log(Object)
TypeCasting:Start () (at Assets/TypeCasting.cs:16)
```

Compare this result to the following explicit cast operator. If we use the prefix system as in the following example code,

```
void Start () {
    Humanoid h = new Humanoid();
    Zombie x = (Zombie) h;
    Debug.Log(x);
}
```

we get a different result, this time an error:

```
InvalidCastException: Cannot cast from source type to destination type.
TypeCasting.Start () (at Assets/TypeCasting.cs:15)
```

This tells us that a type Humanoid cannot be converted to a type Zombie. This doesn't change when converting between a Person and a Zombie. To create an explicit cast, we need to implement a function to allow the cast to work.

```
void Start () {
    Person p = new Person();
    Zombie z = p as Zombie;
    Debug.Log(z);
}
```

As before, we get a similar error.

```
Assets/TypeCasting.cs(23,30): error CS0039: Cannot convert type 'TypeCasting.
Person' to 'TypeCasting.Zombie' via a built-in conversion
```

We need to add some lines of code to allow us to do this conversion between Zombies and People, referring to Zombies as the zombie monster and People as in a human person.

You can imagine that this would happen quite a lot when playing a zombie game. C# is trying to make changes to the data to conform it so that it matches the type we're asking for it to be converted to. In some cases, the as operator is more appropriate than the prefix operator. A Null is much easier to deal with than an error. This conversion makes sense only when the types are incompatible if there is no conversion possible.

We could do this between ints and floats, no problem aside from losing numbers after a decimal. There are conversions available through C#, but none has been made to convert a Humanoid to a Zombie. There should be some method made available to do so. The conversion work has been written for the built-in data types. The work has not yet been done to convert between a Person and a Zombie, so we shall do this.

## 6.14.2 User-Defined Type Conversion

First, let's modify the Humanoid, which has some hitpoints.

```
class Humanoid
{
    public int hitpoints;
}
```

This way we can have some significant meaning for converting between a Person and a Zombie. We'll assume zombies use negative hitpoints and a person has a positive number for hitpoints. Thanks to inheritance, we can safely assume that both the Person and the Zombie will have a hitpoints property when they derive from the Humanoid class.

Now we'll create a new function in the Person, so we can convert him into a Zombie.

```
class Person : Humanoid
{
    static public implicit operator Zombie(Person p)
```

```
        {
            Zombie z = new Zombie();
            z.hitpoints = p.hitpoints * -1;
            return z;
        }
    }
```

With this we can see that we'll need to add a few new keywords. The keywords `implicit` and `operator` work together to allow us to use the `Zombie` cast when working with a `Person` type object. Now we can check what the `hitpoints` of a `Person` is if it was to be treated as a `Zombie` type object.

```
    void Start ()
    {
        Person p = new Person();
        p.hitpoints = 10;
        Zombie z = p as Zombie;
        Debug.Log(z.hitpoints);
    }
```

Through the `implicit` keyword, we can quite nicely assign the `Zombie z` to the `Person` type. We're also allowed to do something very simple like the following code sample:

```
    void Start ()
    {
        Zombie z = new Person();
        Debug.Log(z);
    }
```

This automatically assigns `z` a new `Person()` that is then implicitly converted to a `Zombie` on the assignment. Likewise, we can use a prefix conversion and get the same result by using an `as` operator.

```
    void Start ()
    {
        Person p = new Person();
        Zombie z = (Zombie)p;
        Debug.Log(z);
    }
```

This seems like the most useful conversion; however, there's a simple problem. What if we expect only a very specific return type from the conversion?

### 6.14.3 Implicit versus Explicit Type Conversion

Explicit casts are used if there is a conversion that might end with some loss of data. Implicit casts assume that no data is lost while converting from one type to another. This can be seen when casting an `int` to a `float`. The `int` value 1 is the same as a `float` value 1.0, so an implicit cast infers that nothing is lost. In some edge cases, there can be data lost, so implicit casts are not perfect, though they are generally reliable.

### 6.14.4 Break

If `break` is not present, then the evaluation continues through the rest of the cases. This might be a bit confusing, but basically the `switch` jumps to the line where the corresponding case appears, and `break` stops the code evaluation and ends the `switch` statement. There are other uses for `break`, but we don't need to go into them right now.

Copy the `Monster.cs` from the enums project into the Assets directory for the current Integrals project. For using an `enum` in the `switch`, we need to use the full `enum` value for the case value.

This means `MonsterState.standing` should be used to indicate the `enum` we are looking for. The `mState` stores the `MonsterState`'s enum values that are being used.

To determine the state our monster should be in, we should collect some data in the scene. We'll need to do a bit of setup with a game scene to collect data from.

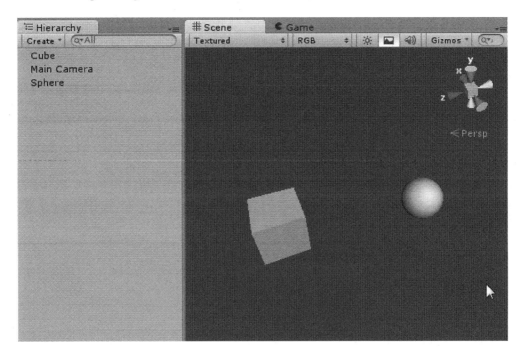

I've added a cube and a sphere to the scene. Then I added the `Player.cs` component to the cube and the `MonsterGenerator.cs` to the sphere. To save some time, you will be able to grab the Unity 3D scene from the website for the book. It's still a good practice for you to do this work on your own.

My `MonsterGenerator.cs` code looks a bit like the following:

```
using UnityEngine;
using System.Collections;
public class MonsterGenerator : MonoBehaviour
{
    public int numMonsters;
    //Use this for initialization
    void Start ()
    {
        for (int i = 0; i < numMonsters; i++)
        {
            GameObject sphere =
                    GameObject.CreatePrimitive(PrimitiveType.Sphere);
            sphere.AddComponent("Monster");
        }
    }
    //Update is called once per frame
    void Update ()
    {
    }
}
```

This code is similar to before where we created 10 objects and attached the `Monster.cs` component to a primitive. Running the game will produce 10 spheres, with `Monster.cs` attached to them.

### 6.14.5 What We've Learned

Using the `explicit` and `implicit` type casts requires a bit of thought. When dealing with a large number of different types, we need to keep in mind what we're trying to accomplish by casting between types. In many cases, we should avoid unnecessary cast operations.

If data needs to be shared between different classes, it's better to create a parent class from which both classes inherit. Rather than requiring specific casts between people and zombies, a new version should be instanced between the two without using a cast.

The zombie–person cast is not the best use case, though it does illustrate how a cast is performed. Most casts should only be between specific data types. It should also be noted that casting is allowed between structs.

```
struct a
{
    static public explicit operator b(a A)
    {
        return new b();
    }
}
struct b
{
    static public explicit operator a(b B)
    {
        return new a();
    }
}
```

Here we can make an `explicit` cast from a to b and back again. Though there's nothing really going on here, a struct is somewhat different from a class, but offers many of the same functionality. Defining `explicit` cast operators is one of the shared abilities between a class and a struct.

---

## 6.15 Working with Vectors

Vector math is something that was taught in some high school math classes. Don't worry; you're not expected to remember any of that. Vector math is easily calculated in C# using the Unity 3D libraries, as vector math is often used in video games. Adding, subtracting, and multiplying vectors are pretty simple in Unity 3D. We'll take a look at how simple vector math is in Unity 3D later on in this section.

There are also many tools added into the `MonoBehaviour` class we've been inheriting for most of the classes we've been writing. Only `Start ()` and `Update ()` have been added to our prebuilt class we've been starting with, but there are many others which we haven't seen yet.

### 6.15.1 Vectors Are Objects

Let's add behaviors to the `MonsterGenerator.cs` we were working with from Chapter 5.

```
public int numMonsters;
//Use this for initialization
void Start ()
{
    for (int i = 0; i < numMonsters; i++)
    {
        GameObject sphere =
            GameObject.CreatePrimitive(PrimitiveType.Sphere);
        sphere.AddComponent("Monster");
        Vector3 pos = new Vector3();
        pos.x = Random.Range(-10, 10);
```

```
                    pos.z = Random.Range(-10, 10);//not y
                    sphere.transform.position = pos;
            }
    }
```

`Random.Range();` is a new function. `Random` is an object that's located in the `MonoBehaviour` parent class. We use this to give us a number between -10 and 10. The two arguments are separated by a comma. The first argument is the minimum number we want and the second number is the maximum value we would want. Then `Random` sets the `x` and `z` to a number between these two values.

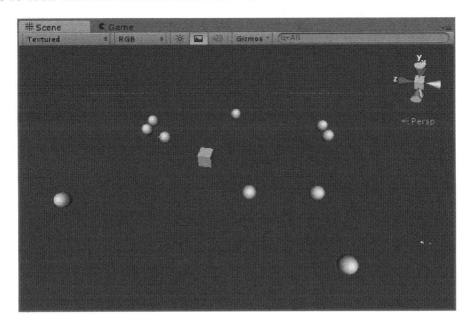

Running the `MonsterGenerator` creates a field of sphere monsters placed randomly in the `x` and `z` directions. As an alternative, we could have put the positioning information inside of the monster himself using the "`Start ()`" function.

### 6.15.2 Stepping through MonsterGenerator

We introduced breakpoints in Section 4.12.9, but this is a good point to come back to how breakpoints are used to see how your code is working. Why does each monster appear at a different place? Let's add in a breakpoint near the first line within the "`for`" statement.

```
 8      void Start()
 9      {
10          for (int i = 0; i < numMonsters; i++)
11          {
12              GameObject sphere =
13                  GameObject.CreatePrimitive(PrimitiveType.Sphere);
14              sphere.AddComponent("Monster");
15              Vector3 pos = new Vector3();
16              pos.x = Random.Range(-10, 10);
17              pos.z = Random.Range(-10, 10);
18              sphere.transform.position = pos;
19          }
20      }
```

Here, I have the breakpoint added on line where the `Monster` component is added. Press the `Run` button and attach MonoDevelop to the Unity 3D thread.

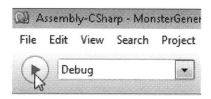

In MonoDevelop, select Run → Start Debugging and then select Unity 3D in the following pop-up panel. Go back to the Unity 3D editor and press the Play button. You may notice not much happening in Unity 3D, which means that MonoDevelop grabbed Unity 3D's thread and is holding it at the breakpoint.

Start stepping through the code. Pressing the F10 key on the keyboard will push the arrow line at a time through the "`for`" statement. After pressing it once, you'll notice that the highlighted line will begin to move over your code. Also notice the data populating the Callstack and the Locals windows that open below the code.

Click on the word "`sphere`." Each instance of the word will highlight and a new dialog box will open up with specifics on the new sphere object. Hover the cursor over "`sphere`" to invoke a pop-up with information on the `sphere` object.

```
for (int i = 0; i < numMonsters; i++)
{
    GameObject sphere =
        GameObject.CreatePrimitive(PrimitiveType.Sphere);
    sp    sphere  {Sphere (UnityEngine.GameObject)}
    Ve
    pos.x = Random.Range(-10, 10);
    pos.z = Random.Range(-10, 10);
    sphere.transform.position = pos;
}
```

Step again and we'll get details on the new `Vector3` called `pos`, which I'm using as an abbreviation of "position." Press F10 to *step over* once to move to the next line.

```
12              GameObject sphere =
13                  GameObject.CreatePrimitive(PrimitiveType.Sphere);
14              sphere.AddComponent("Monster");
15              Vector3 pos = new Vector3();
16              P   pos {(0.0, 0.0, 0.0)}    0, 10);
17                                           0, 10);
18              sphere.transform.position = pos;
19          }
```

It's important to understand that data isn't fulfilled on the line it's created on. Only after stepping one more line with F10 does the data become fulfilled.

```
12              GameObject sphere =
13                  GameObject.CreatePrimitive(PrimitiveType.Sphere);
14              sphere.AddComponent("Monster");
15              Vector3 pos = new Vector3();
16              pos.x = Random.Range(-10, 10);
17              P   pos {(7.0, 0.0, 0.0)}    0, 10);
18              s.                         on = pos;
19          }
```

In the following line, you'll read `pos.x = Random.Range(-10f, 10f);` which means that the `x` value in the `Vector3` named `pos` will be set to a random number between −10 and 10. If we hover `pos` in the line where the `x` is being set, the first value is still `0.0`; this is to change once we press F11 again to move on.

Now that we're another line down, you'll see that the first value of `pos` is now an interesting number, in this case −4.4. The `x` value is now readable after it has been set to the `Random.Range` created the line before. Pressing F10 again, we'll be able to see the `sphere.transform.position` being set to `pos`, which we should check.

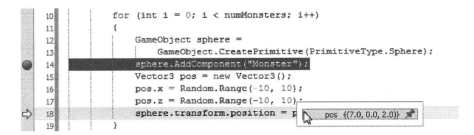

And I get a value for `x` and `z` as 7.0 and 2.0, respectively; you'll get a different value for each since we're using a random number. Keep on pressing F10 and you'll be able to follow the flow of the code as each line highlights again. Each time the line is executed, the values coming from the `Random.Range()` function will be different. This is why the code will scatter the monsters around the `MonsterGenerator`.

As an alternative, we can move the code into the `Monster` itself. If the code was taken out of the `MonsterGenerator` and added into the `Start ()` function of `Monster`, we can remove the "sphere." from the "transform.position" and set the position of the monster directly when it's created.

```
sphere.AddComponent("Monster");
Vector3 pos = new Vector3();
pos.x = Random.Range(-10, 10);
pos.z = Random.Range(-10, 10);
sphere.transform.position = pos;
```

When the object was created in the `MonsterGenerator`, the `transform.position` was a part of a different object. Therefore, we had to tell the object the `transform.position` we wanted to set, and not the position of the `MonsterGenerator`.

The option of where to set the initial position of an object is up to the programmer. It's up to you to decide who and where the position of a new object is set. This flexibility allows you to decide how and when code is executed.

### 6.15.3 Gizmos

While stepping through code helps a great deal with understanding how our code is being executed, visualizing things as they move can be more helpful. That's where Unity 3D has provided us with a great deal of tools for doing just that.

Unity 3D calls its helper objects "Gizmos." Visualizing data is carried out by using Gizmos to draw lines and shapes in the scene. In other game engines, this may be called `DrawDebugLine` or `DrawDebugBox`. In Unity 3D, the engineers added the `Gizmos` class. The members of this class include `DrawLine` and `DrawBox`.

Colored lines, boxes, spheres, and other things can be constructed from the code. If we want to draw a line from the monster to a target, we might use a line between the two so we know that the monster can "see" its next meal. It's difficult to mentally visualize what the vectors are doing. Having Unity 3D display them in the scene makes the vector math easier to understand.

### 6.15.3.1 A Basic Example

The first example in the `Gizmos.cs` in the Integrals project is the `DrawLine();` function that requires two arguments or parameters. The first argument is a start vector followed by an end vector. Start in a fresh `MyGizmos.cs` class and add in a function called `OnDrawGizmos()` after the `Start ()` and `Update ()` functions. The `OnDrawGizmos` can be placed before or after the `Start ()` or `Update ()` function, but to keep organized we'll add it after the preconstructed functions.

```
using UnityEngine;
using System.Collections;
public class MyGizmos : MonoBehaviour
{
    //Use this for initialization
    void Start ()
    {
    }
    //Update is called once per frame
    void Update ()
    {
    }
    void OnDrawGizmos()
    {
    }
}
```

This is what your `MyGizmos.cs` should look like. To see what's going on, create a new `Sphere` GameObject Object using the GameObject → Create Other → Sphere menu, and then add the `Gizmos.cs` component in the Inspector panel.

To draw a Gizmo, we'll need to pick the Gizmo we want to use.

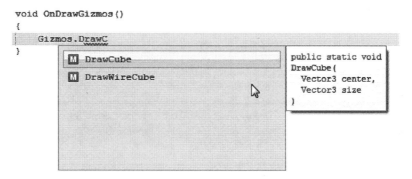

When we start with "`Gizmos.`" we are presented with quite a list of things we can try out. Thanks to MonoDevelop, it's quite easy to figure out how these are used. Each function has some pretty clear clues as to what data types are used and what they are for.

#### 6.15.3.1.1 DrawCube

```
void OnDrawGizmos()
{
    Gizmos.DrawCube ()
}
```

```
public static void DrawCube{
    Vector3 center,
    Vector3 size
)
```

Starting with "DrawCube(" we'll be prompted with a `Vector3` for the cube's center and another `Vector3` for the cube's size. To fulfill the `DrawCube` member function in `Gizmos`, enter the following arguments:

```
void OnDrawGizmos()
{
    Gizmos.DrawCube(new Vector3(0, 0, 0), new Vector3(1, 2, 3));
}
```

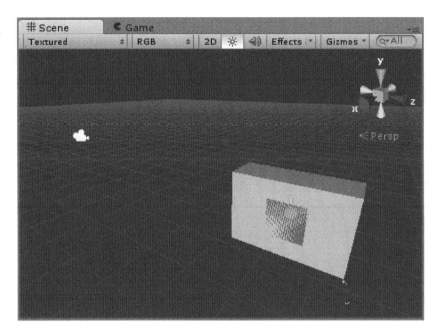

The Gizmo will be drawn with the center point at `Vector3(0,0,0)`, which is the scene's origin, and the size will be `Vector3(1, 2, 3)`, making the object 1 unit wide, 2 units tall, and 3 units deep. Gizmos are pretty interesting as they represent some very useful debugging tools.

### 6.15.3.1.2 DrawRay

Some of the other Gizmo functions require data types we haven't encountered yet, such as rectangles and rays. With a little bit of detection, we can figure out how these work. Let's start off with a `DrawRay` we're presented with (`Ray  r`) as its argument. We can start with a `new  Ray` (and we'll be given a (`Vector3 origin, Vector3 direction`)).

We can fulfill this with `Gizmos.DrawRay(new    Ray(new    Vector3(0,0,0),    new Vector3(0,1,0)));`. This might seem like a bit of a convoluted line to read, so we can make this more easy to read by breaking out one of the arguments.

```
        void OnDrawGizmos() {
            Gizmos.DrawRay(new Ray(
```

> Ray (Vector3 origin, Vector3 direction)

```
void OnDrawGizmos()
{
    Ray r = new Ray();
    r.origin = new Vector3(0, 0, 0);
    r.direction = new Vector3(0, 1, 0);
    Gizmos.DrawRay(r);
}
```

This code will produce a simple white line that starts at the origin and points up in the *y*-axis 1 unit. Rays are useful tools that show an object's direction or angle of movement. We'll take a closer look once we get more used to how Gizmos are used. Assuming the object with the script applied is a cube at the origin of the scene, you'll have a similar effect to the following figure:

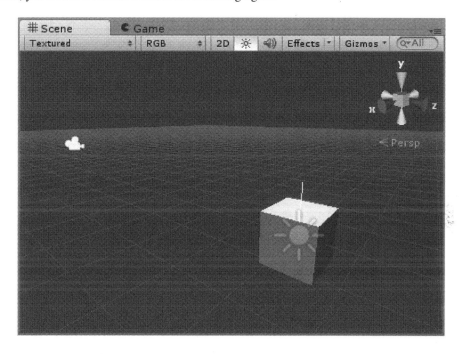

### 6.15.4 Using Gizmos

How to use `Gizmos` may not be obvious. Let's start with the following code located in the `Update ()` function of the `Monster.cs` to draw a line from where the monster is to the origin of the world, or `Vector3(0,0,0);`.

```
//Update is called once per frame
void Update ()
{
    Gizmos.DrawLine(transform.position, new Vector3(0, 0, 0));
}
```

Unfortunately, this produces the following error!

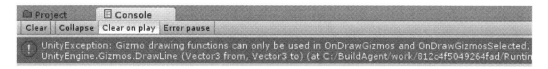

This error does tell us what is wrong. It's expecting the `Gizmos` drawing function to be used in an `OnDrawGizmos` or `OnDrawGizmosSelected` function. Therefore, let's move that line of code into that function. The `OnDrawGizmos` function can be placed anywhere in the class scope.

```
void OnDrawGizmos()
{
    Gizmos.DrawLine(transform.position, new Vector3(0, 0, 0));
}
```

Remember how a child can inherit a function from its parent. There's more to inheritance than simply inheriting functions. We can add to and overwrite the functions given to a class from its parent. This draws a line from `transform.position` to `Vector3(0,0,0)`, which is the origin of the scene.

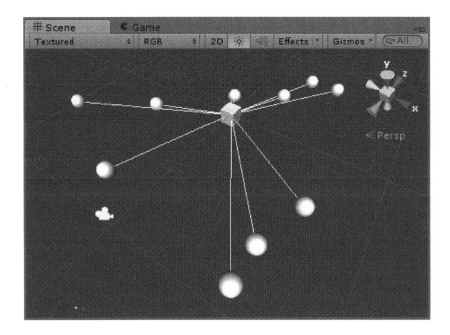

Now we're drawing a bunch of white lines from the center of the monster, or the monster's `transform.position`, to the center of the world or `Vector3(0,0,0)`. If you still have this code around for finding the player, we can make use of the player `GameObject`.

```
public GameObject PlayerObject;
void Start ()
{
    int number = (int)mState;
    Debug.Log(number);
    Vector3 pos = new Vector3();
    pos.x = Random.Range(-10f, 10f);
    pos.z = Random.Range(-10f, 10f);
    transform.position = pos;
    GameObject[] AllGameObjects = GameObject.FindObjectsOfType(typeof
    (GameObject)) as GameObject[];
    foreach (GameObject aGameObject in AllGameObjects)
    {
        Component aComponent = aGameObject.GetComponent(typeof(Player));
        if (aComponent != null)
        {
            PlayerObject = aGameObject;
        }
    }
}
```

`PlayerObject` contains a `transform.position` we can use. As long as an object has a `Player.cs` assigned to it, the `Monster` script will be able to find it. To view the Gizmos in the Game panel, you can turn them on by clicking on the Gizmos button located to the top right of the Game panel.

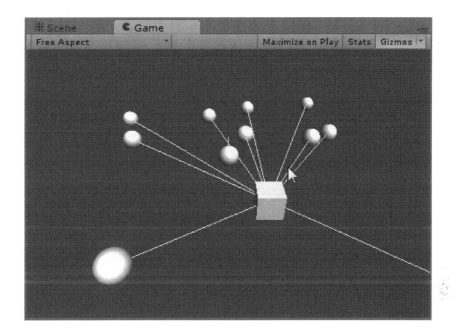

Like before, using the WASD keys will move the cube around in the world and the monsters will be able to draw a line to you. Now the monsters know where you are, but now they have to move toward you. To do this, we need to add in a Vector3 Direction to tell the monster which way to go to get to the player.

A Vector3 Direction needs to be declared at the class level of scope. Remember that it's a variable that's visible to all other functions in the class. This means we can use it again in the OnDrawGizmos () function. The easiest method to calculate Direction is to use Vector3.Normalize. This method found in Vector3 will take a vector and reduce the values to something much easier to deal with.

```
Vector3 Direction;//class scoped variable
void Update ()
{
    Direction = Vector3.Normalize(PlayerObject.transform.position -
transform.position);
}
```

Direction needs to live at the class scope. Variables that are scoped to the entire class can be used by any function in the class. Therefore, when Direction is updated in the Update () function, it will be available to the OnDrawGizmos () function. Now that we know what direction the vector is going in, we need to use it in the OnDrawGizmos () function. To make this clear, we'll consider this in terms of pseudocode.

Using OnDrawGizmos() draw a line in the direction to move toward the center of the object. The center of the object is transform.position, and the direction to move toward is the normalized Vector3 we called Direction. In C#, this translates into the following code:

```
void OnDrawGizmos()
{
    Gizmos.DrawLine(transform.position, transform.position + Direction);
}
```

The first argument is the current transform.position of the monster. This is the starting point of the line. Then we need to set the end point for the line, which starts at the same place, but then it is drawn with the addition of the direction.

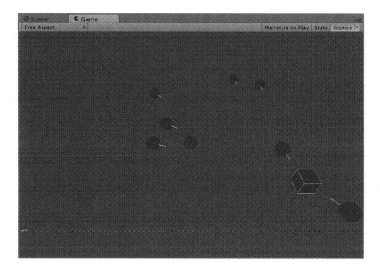

The end result is a bunch of small lines drawn from the center of each monster toward the player. By adding the `Direction` to the `Update ()` function, the line will be recalculated. Now we have a good starting point for adding a `Vector3` in the direction of the player.

The `Direction` we're using ranges from 0 to 1, and traveling a full unit per update is quite a lot. This means we may move over a hundred units per frame. Consider that we may get over a hundred updates per second. Therefore, we need to shrink the `Direction` `Vector3` to a smaller value. A `Vector3` can be multiplied by a single float value that multiplies the x, y, and z equally.

```
Vector3 Direction;//class scoped variable
void Update ()
{
    Direction =
    Vector3.Normalize(
        PlayerObject.transform.position - transform.position
    );
    transform.position += Direction * 0.1f;
}
```

In this example, we're multiplying the `Direction` by `0.01f` that should slow the monster down so we have a chance of running away.

Run away!!! The little sphere monsters will be chasing after the GameObject that has a Player.cs component attached. Before we go further, we should put some limits by using a bit of logic. If we get too close to the player, we should stop moving toward him. If we don't stop, then we'll eventually sit inside of the player. To do this, we'll need to know how far away from the player we are.

```
Void Update () {
    Vector3 MyVector = PlayerObject.transform.position - transform.position;
    float DistanceToPlayer = MyVector.magnitude;
```

Start with a new Vector3 made from subtracting our current position from the position we're headed toward. Then to get the magnitude of that vector, we create a float called DistanceToPlayer and set that to the MyVector.magnitude. If you remember anything from math class, some of this should sound familiar.

Now we have data to make use of with some logic. We'll surround the code that moves the monster with an if statement controlled by some arbitrary number. If we are more than 3 units away from the player, then move toward him.

```
Vector3 MyVector =
PlayerObject.transform.position - transform.position;
float DistanceToPlayer = MyVector.magnitude;
if (DistanceToPlayer > 3.0f)
{
    Direction =
    Vector3.Normalize(PlayerObject.transform.position - transform.
    position);
    transform.position += Direction * 0.1f;
}
```

### 6.15.4.1 Building Up Parameters

Now they should all stop once they get close enough to the player. Based on game design you may want to change this arbitrary distance away from the player, your monster will stop. It's time to start breaking out our hard numbers and making them editable.

```
Vector3 Direction;//class scoped variable
public float AttackRange = 3.0f;
void Update ()
{
    Vector3 MyVector =
    PlayerObject.transform.position - transform.position;
    float DistanceToPlayer = MyVector.magnitude;
    if (DistanceToPlayer > AttackRange)
    {
        Direction =
        Vector3.Normalize(PlayerObject.transform.position -
        transform.position);
        transform.position += Direction * 0.1f;
    }
}
```

Replace the 3f with a public float so it can easily be modified from an outside class. We may change the speed with a public float as well. It's always a good practice to change hard numbers into something that can be changed later on by a design change. Naming the variables also gives more meaning to how the variable is used. You may notice that there aren't any numbers inside of the Update () loop left to parameterize. Now we're thinking like a programmer.

```csharp
Vector3 Direction;//class scoped variable
public float AttackRange = 3.0f;
public float SpeedMultiplyer = 0.01f;
void Update ()
{
    if (mState == MonsterState.standing)
    {
        print("standing monster is standing.");
    }
    if (mState == MonsterState.wandering)
    {
        print("wandering monster is wandering.");
    }
    if (mState == MonsterState.chasing)
    {
        print("chasing monster is chasing.");
    }
    if (mState == MonsterState.attacking)
    {
        print("attacking monster is attacking.");
    }
    //Gizmos.DrawLine(transform.position, new Vector3(0, 0, 0));
    Vector3 MyVector =
        PlayerObject.transform.position - transform.position;
    float DistanceToPlayer = MyVector.magnitude;
    if (DistanceToPlayer > AttackRange)
    {
        Direction =
            Vector3.Normalize(PlayerObject.transform.position -
            transform.position);
        transform.position += Direction * SpeedMultiplyer;
    }
}
```

### 6.15.5 Optimizing

Now we have some optimization we could do. The math we do to MyVector is somewhat redundant. This can be encapsulated and can more directly set the DistanceToPlayer. We can delete the entire line for MyVector by moving the code directly into the line that sets the distance value.

```csharp
float DistanceToPlayer = (PlayerObject.transform.position - transform.
position).magnitude;
```

Likewise, we don't even need the DistanceToPlayer to be calculated before it's used. This means we can do the calculation inside of the if statement's parameters.

```csharp
if (PlayerObject.transform.position - transform.position).magnitude >
AttackRange)
```

Again we can reduce this even more. Calculating the Direction and then using its value may also be done in the line of code where it's eventually used.

```csharp
if ((PlayerObject.transform.position - transform.position).magnitude >
AttackRange)
```

```
{
    transform.position +=
    Vector3.Normalize(PlayerObject.transform.position -
    transform.position) * SpeedMultiplyer;
}
```

Unfortunately, this means that `Direction` is never calculated and it can't be used for drawing the Gizmo. When we reduce our code this much, we start to run into problems. Usually, it's a good practice to create data before it's used. This shortens the length of each line of code and makes your code easier to read.

The line where you stop cutting down lines of code is up to you. It's difficult to say how much you should smash things down. In many cases, when you reduce code to just a few lines, your code's readability is also reduced.

### 6.15.6 What We've Learned

Unity 3D has many tools built in for doing vector math functions. It's a good idea to figure out how they're used. We'll explore as many different uses of these tools as we can, but we're going to be hard pressed to see all of them.

A Gizmo is a handy tool to help see what your code is trying to do. Gizmos draw lines, boxes, and other shapes. You can even have text printed into your 3D scene for debugging purposes. Again, we'll try to use as many of the different Gizmos as we can.

The sort of optimization we did here is in the reduction of lines of code only. There was no actual change to the speed at which the code here was executed. There are some cases in which a line or two should be added to speed things up.

For now we're going to focus on keeping our code clear and readable. Later on, we'll learn some basic programming idioms. Programming idioms are little tricks that programmers often use to reduce complex tasks to just a line or two. They're sometimes rather cryptic, but once you understand them, they're quite useful.

---

## 6.16 goto Labels

We've gone through several of the usually employed logical controls in Section 4.11.3. This time we have the `goto` keyword. It is a commonly misused control statement, and it's about time we learned about how it's used.

The `goto` keyword allows you to skip around in a statement. This includes sending the computer back up in the code to run statements that it has already gone past. When using many `goto` statements, you end up making your code difficult to read as you need to jump around to follow the flow.

A `goto` statement is the keyword `goto` followed by an identifier, which is referred to as a *label*. This looks like `goto MyLabel;` which tells C# which label to go to, in this case as `MyLabel;` which is the identifier followed by a colon.

A `goto` statement should be encapsulated by some sort of logical statement. It's very easy to get caught in a loop with a `goto` statement. This has a similar behavior to `for(;;)` and `while(true)` which will freeze Unity 3D in an endless loop forcing you to kill the process from the Task Manager.

```
void Start ()
{
    StartOver:
        goto StartOver;
}
```

Using a label and a `goto` in this way will create an infinite loop that will require you to kill Unity 3D from the Task Manager. You can assume `StartOver:`, which tells where the computer will jump to in the `Start ()` function when the `goto` tells the function where to jump to. Anything between the identified label and the `goto` command is executed as normal. There's nothing wrong with this statement syntactically, and it's just not very useful. This can be controlled by any code between the label and the `goto` statement.

```
void Start ()
{
     int num = 0;
StartOver:
     num++;
     if(num > 10) {
          goto Stop;
     }
     print ("stuck in a loop");
     goto StartOver;
Stop:
     print ("im free!");
     }
```

This is the same as for(int i = 0; i < 10; i++); only some might find it a bit harder to read. Of course, it's up to you to choose when to use a `goto` statement, but there are some useful cases. Finding a good reason to use the `goto` statement comes with experience in spotting when it might be useful. Because they're tricky to use and to read, most programmers shy away from using them at all. We're learning as much as we can in this book, so we may also learn how it's used.

### 6.16.1  A Basic Example

In the GoToLabels project, we'll start with the `Example.cs` attached to the Main Camera.

```
using UnityEngine;
using System.Collections;
public class Example : MonoBehaviour
{
     public int num = 1;
     void Start ()
     {
          if (num > 0)
          {
               goto MyLabel;//goes to MyLabel
          }
          print("number was less than 0");//gets skipped if num isn't > 0
          MyLabel://goes here when num is greater than 0
          print("I jumped to MyLabel");
     }
     //Update is called once per frame
     void Update ()
     {
     }
}
```

By adding in a `public int num` to the class, we're able to pick the `goto` label we're using. If we set `num` to 0, then both print statements will be executed. If the number is greater than 0, then only the second "I jumped to MyLabel" print function will be executed.

   When we started off with the `switch` statement, we looked at the keyword `case`. The `case` keyword set up conditions which the statement would skip through till a case fits the statement. It then executed the code that followed the case.

switch and goto statements share the : colon notation for labels. However, goto lets you set up labels anywhere in a code block, whereas the switch statement allows labels only within the switch statement. When goto is used, it sends the software to the line following the label it was told to jump to.

## 6.16.2 Zombie State Machine

Let's start by building a simple zombie character in Unity 3D. I created a zombie character using the GameObject → Create Other → Capsule menu. To this I needed to add in a Rigidbody component by selecting Component → Physics → Rigidbody and then change the parameters to the following settings:

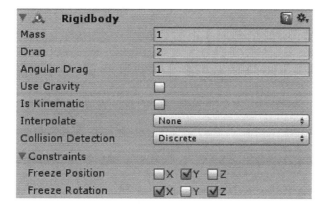

By adding some Drag, we keep the Rigidbody from sliding around on a surface like it were on ice. Then since we're not in need of any Gravity, we turn that off as well. To keep the zombie from tipping over, we need to freeze the X and Z rotations. He still needs to look around, so we'll leave Y unfrozen. Then to keep him on the ground, we'll freeze the Y position.

For fun I've added small spheres for eyes, but made sure to remove the collision component from the sphere objects parented to the Zombie Capsule. You can also create a Material using the Project menu Create → Material.

This can allow you to make the little guy green.

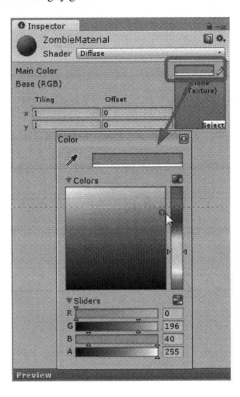

All you need to do once you create the Material and set its color is to drag it onto the Capsule's Mesh in the Scene editor.

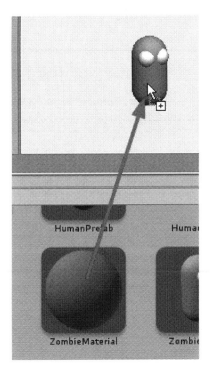

Once a `ZombieState.cs` to the object, the object is dragged from the Hierarchy to the Project panel.

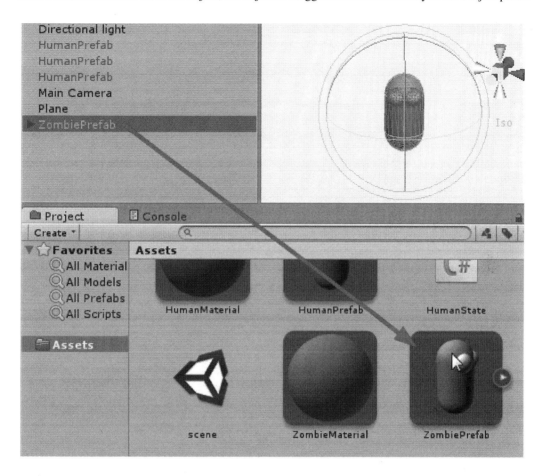

This created a Unity 3D prefab object. A prefab is a nicely packaged object that is an aggregation of different objects. This saves us some time if we need to make changes to multiple instances of the guy in the scene. We just make a modification to one; then we can press the Apply Changes to Prefab button in the Inspector panel, and the changes propagate to the rest of the objects that are from the same prefab.

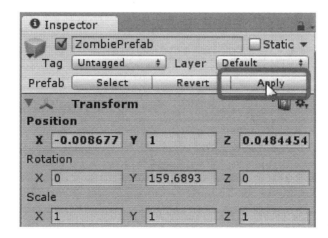

This will update all copies of the prefab in the scene.

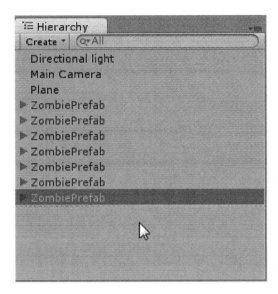

Make multiple duplicates of the ZombiePrefab. Add in a Plane using the GameObject → Create Other → Plane menu so that the zombies have somewhere to walk on. Then set its size to the following settings:

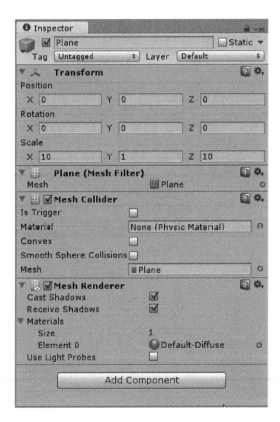

Then for good measure, I've created a Directional light using the GameObject → Create Other → Directional Light menu so that nothing shows up as black. This will give us something to see from the Main Camera.

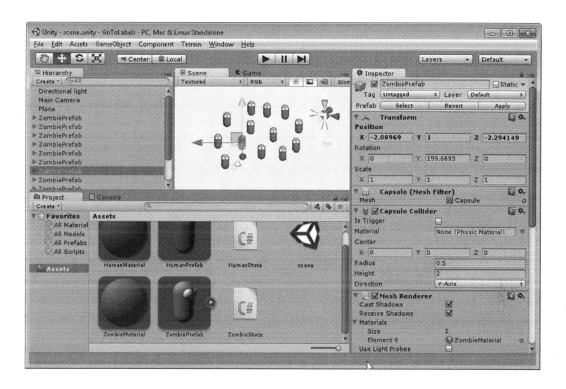

My scene has some extra stuff that we'll get to in a moment. If the zombies don't look up to the latest standards in video game graphics, you're right. This is what is often referred to as "programmer art." If you are an artist, then you might want to spend some time here to spruce things up. However, I'll let you do that on your own.

Labels are traditionally seen as messy. However, in some cases, they can be used quite well, in case of a simple artificial intelligence (AI) behavior. The zombie AI can exist in a limited number of states; in many cases, the states are often stored in an `enum`; we'll start with just two values in the `enum` to begin with. Creating a `ZombieState.cs` is where we will begin. In the new C# file, we'll add in a simple `enum` with the following information and then make a variable to hold the `enum` as follows:

```
enum ZState{
    idleing,
    wandering,
}
ZState MyState;
```

Then to store some additional information, we'll want to have a timer to check how long we'll be in each state. For some basic interesting behaviors, we'll want to have a variable for the closest object and the furthest object away from the zombie. This is considered a fairly standard practice as any specific monster should exist only in one state at a time. The code then turns into a large `switch` statement, with code specific to each state embedded in each segment of the `switch` statement. However, we can use the `switch` statement to simply control which `goto` label we jump to instead.

```
float stateTimer;
float closestDistance;
float furthestDistance;
GameObject closestGameObject;
GameObject furthestGameObject;
```

With these values, we'll be able to build up some interesting zombie's `wandering` and `idleing` behaviors. In the `Start` () function, we need to initialize these values so they can be used later.

```
void Start ()
{
    stateTimer = 0.1f;
    MyState = ZState.idleing;
    closestDistance = Mathf.Infinity;
}
```

The zombie now has a short timer to start off with, and then we'll have an initial state to start in. Then since the `closestDistance` variable is going to start off as 0, we need this to be a large number instead, otherwise nothing will be closer than the default value; this needs to be fixed with a `Mathf.Infinity`, quite a large number indeed. We then add in a `switch` statement at the beginning of the `Update` () function to different labels of `goto` inside of the `Update` () function.

```
void Update ()
{
    switch(MyState)
    {
    case ZState.idleing:
        goto Ideling;
    case ZState.wandering:
        goto Wandering;
    default:
        break;
    }
Ideling:
        return;
Wandering:
        return;
}
```

This creates our basic starting place for building up some more interesting behaviors. If we look at the `Ideling:`, we should add in a system to hold in the loop there for a moment before moving on.

```
Ideling:
    stateTimer -= Time.deltaTime;
    if(stateTimer < 0.0f)
    {
        MyState = ZState.wandering;
        stateTimer = 3.0f;
    }
    return;
```

If we start with a `stateTimer -= Time.deltaTime;`, we'll count down the `stateTimer` by the time passed between each frame. Once this is less than `0.0f`, we'll set the `MyState` value to another state and add time to the `stateTimer`.

```
Wandering:
    stateTimer -= Time.deltaTime;
    if(stateTimer < 0.0f)
    {
        MyState = ZState.idleing;
        stateTimer = 3.0f;
    }
    return;
```

Now we have a system to toggle between each state after `3.0f` seconds or so. The `return;` after the label tells the `Update ()` function to stop evaluating code at the return and start over from the top. To add to the Ideling behavior, we'll create a new function called `LookAround();`.

```
void LookAround()
{
    GameObject[] Zombies = (GameObject[])
    GameObject.FindObjectsOfType(typeof(GameObject));
    foreach (GameObject go in Zombies)
    {
        ZombieState z = go.GetComponent<ZombieState>();
        if(z == null || z == this)
        {
            continue;
        }
        Vector3 v = go.transform.position - transform.position;
        float distanceToGo = v.magnitude;
        if (distanceToGo < closestDistance)
        {
            closestDistance = distanceToGo;
            closestGameObject = go;
        }
        if (distanceToGo > furthestDistance)
        {
            furthestDistance = distanceToGo;
            furthestGameObject = go;
        }
    }
}
```

This function has a few things going on here. First, we have the line at the top:

```
GameObject[] Zombies = (GameObject[])
GameObject.FindObjectsOfType(typeof(GameObject));
```

This looks through all of the `GameObjects` in the scene and prepares an array populated with every game object in the scene called `Zombies`. Now that we have an array, we can iterate through each one looking for another zombie. To do this, we start with a `foreach` loop.

```
foreach (GameObject go in Zombies)
{
    ZombieState z = go.GetComponent<ZombieState>();
```

Then we use `ZombieState z = go.GetComponent<ZombieState>();` to check if the `GameObject` go has a `ZombieState` component attached to it. This ensures that we don't iterate through things such as the ground plane, light, or main camera. To make this check, we use the following lines:

```
if(z == null || z == this)
{
    continue;
}
```

### 6.16.3 This as a Reference to Yourself

Here we're also seeing `z == this`, which is important to point out. The array that is being returned includes all objects in the scene, with a `ZombieState` component attached. This includes the `ZombieState` that is doing the checking.

In the case where you want to check if you are not going to complete any computations based on where you are and you are included in your own data, then it's a good idea to note that you can exclude yourself from being calculated by using this as a reference to the script doing the evaluation. If you were making a distance check to the closest zombie and you are a zombie, then you'd be pretty close to yourself. Of course, that's not what we want to include in our calculations when we're looking for another nearby zombie.

This if statement checks if the z is null, or rather the GameObject go has no ZombieState attached. We also don't want to include the instance of the object itself as a potential zombie to interact with. The continue keyword tells the foreach loop to move on to the next index in the array. Then we need to do some distance checking.

```
Vector3 v = go.transform.position - transform.position;
float distanceToGo = v.magnitude;
```

With Vector3 v = go.transform.position - transform.position;, we get a Vector3, which is the difference between the transform.position of the zombie who is checking the distances to the GameObject go in the array of Zombies. We then convert this Vector3 v into a float that represents the distance to the zombie we're looking at. Once we have a distance, we compare that value to the closest distance and set the closestGameObject to the GameObject if it's closer than the last closestDistance, and likewise for the furthestDistance.

```
if (distanceToGo < closestDistance)
{
    closestDistance = distanceToGo;
    closestGameObject = go;
}
if (distanceToGo > furthestDistance)
{
    furthestDistance = distanceToGo;
    furthestGameObject = go;
}
```

Now we have populated the closestGameObject and the furthestGameObject values.

```
Ideling:
    stateTimer -= Time.deltaTime;
    if(stateTimer < 0.0f)
    {
        MyState = ZState.wandering;
        stateTimer = 3.0f;
        closestDistance = Mathf.Infinity;
        furthestDistance = 0f;
        LookAround();
    }
    return;
```

Now we can add the LookAround(); function to our Ideling: label in the Update () function. We also want to reset the closestDistance and furthestDistance values just before running the function, otherwise we won't be able to pick new objects each time the function is run. After this, we want to use the closestGameObject and furthestGameObject to move our little zombie around.

```
void MoveAround()
{
    Vector3 MoveAway =
    (transform.position -
    closestGameObject.transform.position).normalized;
    Vector3 MoveTo =
    (transform.position -
    furthestGameObject.transform.position).normalized;
    Vector3 directionToMove = MoveAway - MoveTo;
    transform.forward = directionToMove;
    gameObject.rigidbody.velocity =
    directionToMove * Random.Range(10, 30) * 0.1f;
    Debug.DrawRay(transform.position, directionToMove, Color.blue);
    Debug.DrawLine(transform.position,
    closestGameObject.transform.position, Color.red);
    Debug.DrawLine(transform.position,
    furthestGameObject.transform.position, Color.green);
}
```

We want two vectors to create a third vector. One will move us away from the `closestGameObject` and the other will point at the `furthestGameObject`. This is done with the lines at the beginning. We then use the `normalized` value of the `Vector3` to limit the values that these will give us to a magnitude of 1.

```
Vector3 MoveAway = (transform.position -
closestGameObject.transform.position).normalized;
Vector3 MoveTo = (transform.position -
furthestGameObject.transform.position).normalized;
```

A third `Vector3` is generated to give us a direction to go in, which is `Vector3 directionToMove = MoveAway - MoveTo;` this gives us a push away from the closest object and moves the zombie toward the furthest object. We then turn the zombie in that direction by using `transform.forward = directionToMove;` and then we give the zombie a push in that direction as well:

```
gameObject.rigidbody.velocity = directionToMove * 0.3f;
```

The `directionToMove * 0.3f` lowers the speed from 1.0 to a slower value. Zombies don't move so fast, so we want to reduce the speed a bit. To see what's going on, I've added in the three lines:

```
Debug.DrawRay(transform.position, directionToMove, Color.blue);
Debug.DrawLine(transform.position,
closestGameObject.transform.position, Color.red);
Debug.DrawLine(transform.position,
furthestGameObject.transform.position, Color.green);
```

These lines are drawn closest, furthest, and toward the direction of movement and the zombie. This can now be added to the `Update ()` function's `Wandering` label.

```
Wandering:
    stateTimer -= Time.deltaTime;
    MoveAround();
    if(stateTimer < 0.0f)
    {
        MyState = ZState.idleing;
        stateTimer = 3.0f;
    }
    return;
```

With this in place above the `stateTimer` that switches functions, we have a continuous execution of the function while the `Update ()` function is being called. This updates the `MoveAround()` code as though it were inside of the `Update ()` function; by doing this we're able to keep the code clean and independent in its own function.

One note before going on: Make sure that all of the little guys have the same `transform.position.y`, otherwise you'll have individuals looking up or down, which will throw off the rotation values when aiming the zombies at one another.

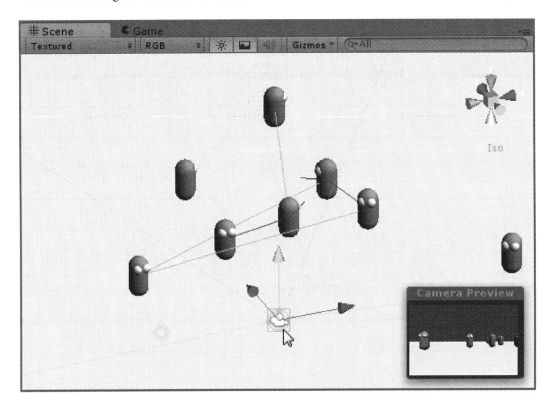

Running this will begin the process of multiple zombies wandering around one another, scooting toward the zombie who is furthest away from him, and pushing away from the one who is closest. This behavior tends to keep them in one general area so long as they don't go too fast in any one direction for too long.

### 6.16.4 HumanState Based on ZombieState

We can easily create a new behavior based on the zombie with the following code in a new `HumanState.cs`:

```
using UnityEngine;
using System.Collections;
public class HumanState : ZombieState
{
}
```

By removing the `Start ()` and `Update ()`, we can create a HumanPrefab, with the `HumanState.cs` file attached rather than the `ZombieState.cs` component.

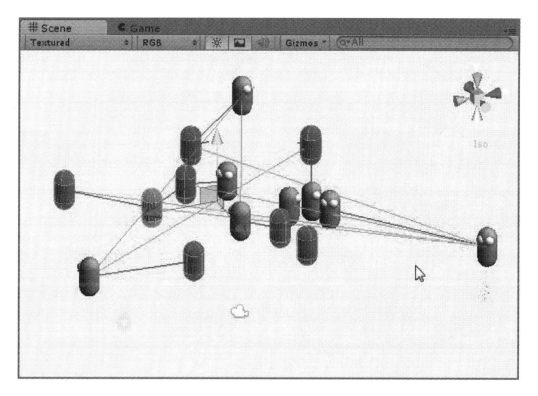

Adding a bunch of humans right now, noted here with the differently colored capsule, we'll get the same behavior as the ZombieState. However, we can make a simple change to the LookAround() function and not touch anything else. First, in the ZombieState.cs, we need to change the LookAround() function so we can enable overriding the function.

```
virtual public void LookAround()
```

Add in virtual and public before the void. This will allow the HumanState.cs to override the function call and allow us to change the behavior. In addition, we'll be accessing some variables in ZombieState, so they too need to be made public.

```
public float closestDistance;
public float furthestDistance;
public GameObject closestGameObject;
public GameObject furthestGameObject;
```

### 6.16.5 The Is Keyword

With these variables made public, we'll be able to use these from the new LookAround(); function in HumanState. In Chapter 5, we covered the as keyword when we were doing implicit casting. The handy use for implicit casting comes into play when we want to check an object's type as a condition statement.

For instance, Zombie z, as we know before, has a ZombieState component. To do a check, we can use the following statement: if (z is ZombieState). We can check if the z is of type ZombieState. If the z is indeed a ZombieState, then we get true, otherwise the if statement is not executed.

```
override public void LookAround()
{
    GameObject[] Zombies = (GameObject[])
    GameObject.FindObjectsOfType(typeof(GameObject));
    foreach (GameObject go in Zombies)
    {
        ZombieState z = go.GetComponent<ZombieState>();
        if(z == null || z == this)
        {
            continue;
        }
        Vector3 v = go.transform.position - transform.position;
        float distanceToGo = v.magnitude;
        if (distanceToGo < closestDistance)
        {
            if(z is ZombieState)
            {
                closestDistance = distanceToGo;
                closestGameObject = go;
            }
        }
        if (distanceToGo > furthestDistance)
        {
            if(z is HumanState)
            {
                furthestDistance = distanceToGo;
                furthestGameObject = go;
            }
        }
    }
}
```

We're adding only two new `if` statements. Inside of the `closestDistance`, we check again to see if the `z` is a `ZombieState`; if it is, then we set the `cloesestGameObject` and distance to that object. If the furthest object is a `HumanState`, then we set the `furthestGameObject` to the furthest object.

What starts off as an evenly distributed mass of humans and zombies like this:

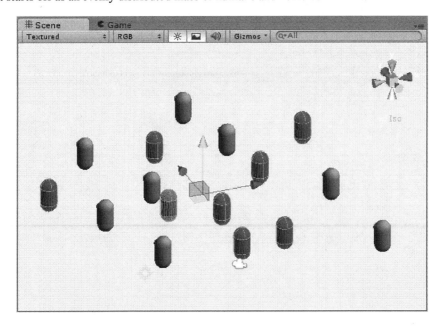

sorts out into a clump of humans wandering away from the zombies.

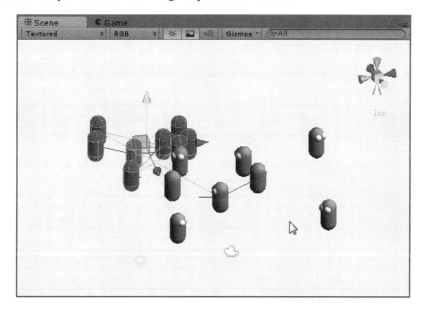

Once enough humans and zombies have been added, we get a more interesting behavior by limiting how far a human is willing to go to join another human.

```
if (distanceToGo > furthestDistance && distanceToGo < 10)
{
    if(z is HumanState) {
        furthestDistance = distanceToGo;
        furthestGameObject = go;
    }
}
```

This turns into the following grouping habit:

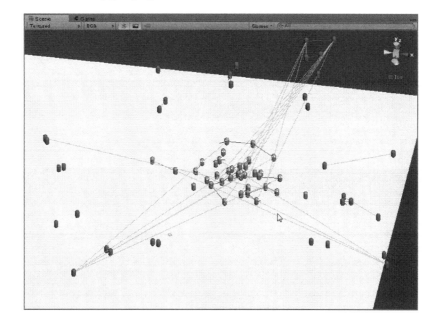

Notice that the humans tend to cluster into smaller groups and pairs. In any case, I encourage you to play with the code to find other emergent behaviors.

### 6.16.6 What We've Learned

Goto labels don't have to be cumbersome to be useful. As a simple divider to a long Update () function, they can work fairly easily and still remain clear so long as the mechanism that switches between labels is clear and contained in one place such as a switch statement.

You can easily make an argument to leave all of the logic within the switch statement and avoid the labels altogether, but this can easily make the switch statement larger and bulkier than necessary as well. In the end, the only difference is readability. If by using labels you make your code easier to follow, then using labels is fine. If your switch statement begins to overflow with different cases, then you might want to try another system outside of the switch, and labels might be a nice option.

On your own it's a good idea to see what this code would look like by adding different states. Perhaps when a zombie gets close enough to a human, that human could turn into a zombie. When a pair of humans gets close to a zombie, then the zombie might turn into a human. Simple mechanics like this can quickly add a very unpredictable level of behavior and emerge into a game mechanic simply through experimentation with the code itself.

## 6.17 More on Arrays

Arrays have a few different descriptions. Your standard array is called a single-dimensional array, which we have dealt with earlier. Other array types include multidimensional and jagged. Arrays can store any type of data; this includes other arrays.

### 6.17.1 Length and Count

Declaring an array is simple and uses a different operator than a class or function to contain its data. The square brackets [and] are used to tell the compiler that your identifier is going to be used for an array. The following statement declares an array of integers:

```
int[] ints;
```

We can dynamically declare an array of ints using the following notation. Use curly braces {} to contain the contents of the array assigned to primes.

```
int[] primes = {1, 3, 5, 7, 11, 13, 17, 23, 27, 31};
```

Arrays have several functions associated with them, which we can use with different loops. To get the number of items in an array, we use the Length property of the array.

#### 6.17.1.1 A Basic Example

We'll go with the MoreArrays project and start with the Example.cs component attached to the Main Camera in the scene provided.

```
int[] primes = {1, 3, 5, 7, 11, 13, 17, 23, 27, 31};
int items = primes.Length;
```

In this example, we assign an int items to the Length of the array. This is a common practice when using an array. We'll see why this is more useful than creating an array of a set length ahead of time in a moment. To use this in a `for` loop, we use the following syntax shown in the following code fragment added to the `Start ()` function:

```
//Use this for initialization
void Start ()
{
    int[] primes = {1, 3, 5, 7, 11, 13, 17, 23, 27, 31};
    int items = primes.Length;
    for (int i = 0; i < items; i++)
    {
        print(primes [i]);
    }
}
```

This code prints out a new line for each number stored in the array. Try this out by assigning the script to an object in a new game scene; I usually pick the Main Camera. Each time the `for` loop iterates, the `int` i moves to the next item in the array starting with the zeroth index. Once the end of the list is reached, the `for` loop exits. We could also use a `while` loop to do the same thing.

```
int j = 0;
while (j < items)
{
    print(primes [j]);
    j++;
}
```

This produces the same output with a few less characters, but the counter `j` required for the `while` loop needs to live outside of the `while` statement's code block. Yet another option, and one that's slightly tailored for an array, is `foreach`.

## 6.17.2 Foreach: A Reminder

With an array of `int`s in our `primes` variable, we can use the following syntax to print out each item in the array:

```
foreach (int i in primes)
{
    print(i);
}
```

This syntax is quite short, simple, and easy to use. The keyword `in` assigns the `int` i variable to each element in the `primes` array it's given.

Which form you use is up to you, but it's important to know that you have more than one option. Of course, you can use any identifier for counting indexes; `int` j could just as easily be `int` index or anything else that makes sense. Though the common convention is to use the `for (int i = 0; i < items; i++)` form for iterating through an array, the `int` i variable initialized in the parameter list of the `for` loop can be used for various things related to the element we're stepping through in the array. We'll be able to use this more often than not when we need to know where we are in the array. If this information isn't necessary, then it's easier to stick to the `foreach` iterator when using an array.

We can declare arrays of different lengths by using different bits of data. Each one is of a different length. Using the `Length` property of each array, it's easier for us to print out each array without knowing how many items are stored in each one.

```
int[] primes = {1, 3, 5, 7, 11, 13, 17, 23, 27, 31};
int[] fibonacci = {0, 1, 1, 2, 3, 5, 8, 13, 21, 34, 55, 89, 144};
int[] powersOfTwo = {1, 2, 4, 8, 16, 32, 64, 128, 255, 512, 1024};
```

Of course, these aren't complete sets of numbers, but that's not the point. They are different lengths, and we don't need to keep track of how many items are stored in each array to print out their contents.

```csharp
void Start ()
{
    int [] primes = {1, 3, 5, 7, 11, 13, 17, 23, 27, 31};
    int [] fibonacci = {0, 1, 1, 2, 3, 5, 8, 13, 21, 34, 55, 89, 144};
    int [] powersOfTwo = {1, 2, 4, 8, 16, 32, 64, 128, 255, 512, 1024};
    ArrayList Numbers = new ArrayList{primes, fibonacci, powersOfTwo};
    int numArrays = Numbers.Count;
    for (int i = 0; i < numArrays; i++)
    {
        int[] Nums = Numbers [i] as int[];
        int items = Nums.Length;
        for (int j = 0; j < items; j++)
        {
            int Num = Nums [j];
            print (Num);
        }
    }
}
```

In the above code fragment, we've added in three different arrays of integers using the `Start ()` function. After that we declare a `new ArrayList` called `Numbers` fulfilled with a `new ArrayList {primes, fobonacci, powersOfTwo};`. This fills the `new ArrayList` with the three different `int[]` arrays, where each `int[]` has a different `Length` property.

`ArrayLists` differ from a regular array in that its `Length` property is called `Count`. Therefore, to get the number of items stored in the `ArrayList`, we use `Numbers.Count` rather than `Length`. This is assigned to an `int numArrays` for use in a `for` loop.

To learn this, we would have to ask on a forum, "How do I get the size of an ArrayList?" Alternatively, we could right click on the ArrayList type and select Go to declaration from the following pop-up:

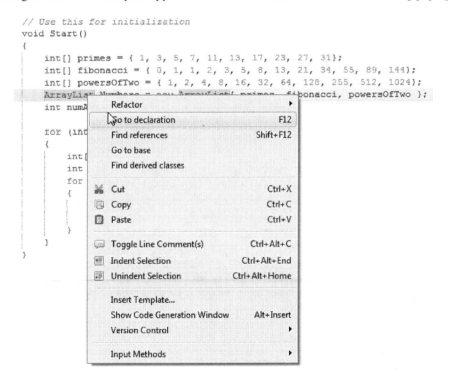

This brings us to the declaration of classes and all of the things that the ArrayList allows us to do. Scroll through the options till we find something we can use.

▼ 🄲 System.Collections
   ▼ 🄲 ArrayList
      ▶ 📦 Base Types
      🄼 ArrayList(ICollection)
      🄼 ArrayList(int)
      🄼 ArrayList()
      🄼 Adapter(IList) : ArrayList
      🄼 Add(object) : int
      🄼 AddRange(ICollection) : void
      🄼 BinarySearch(object, ICompare
      🄼 BinarySearch(object) : int
      🄼 BinarySearch(int, int, object, IC
      🄼 Clear() : void
      🄼 Clone() : object
      🄼 Contains(object) : bool
      🄼 CopyTo(int, Array, int, int) : voi
      🄼 CopyTo(Array, int) : void
      🄼 CopyTo(Array) : void
      🄼 FixedSize(ArrayList) : ArrayList
      🄼 FixedSize(IList) : IList
      🄼 GetEnumerator(int, int) : IEnum

In the Assembly Browser, we'll find a Count property that sounds reasonably usable. It's possible to do many different things with the other options found in the ArrayList class, so we'll experiment with them next. You'll need to remember the Go to definition function in MonoDevelop in order to be a self-sufficient programmer. If it's late at night and you have a final due in the morning, you may not have enough time to wait for an answer on a forum.

Unfortunately, there aren't so many options with the int[] as this brings you to only what an int32 is defined as. Luckily, most of the questions have been asked about how to deal with an array in C#. There is, however, a class definition for Array. This can be found by using the Search field in the Assembly Browser.

From here, you can find all of the functions and properties available to use with the Array type. The ArrayList's count can be used as a condition to stop the for loop. Once we have the ArrayList's count, it's used in the following for loop as the condition to stop the loop.

```
int numArrays = Numbers.Count;
for (int i = 0; i < numArrays; i++)
{
}
```

This code will allow us to iterate through each array stored in the Numbers array list. Next, we need to get the int[] array stored at the current index of the array list. This is done by using the for loop's initializer's int i variable and a cast. ArrayList stores each item as a generic Object type. This means that the item at Numbers[i] is an Object type. In this case, the Object stored at the index is an int[] type.

```
int[] Nums = Numbers[i] as int[];
```

Casting the Object to an int[] is as simple as Numbers[i] as int[];. Without this cast, we get the following error:

```
Assets/Arrays.cs(15,31): error CS0266: Cannot implicitly convert type
'object' to 'int[]'. An explicit conversion exists (are you missing a cast?)
```

This assumes that an Object is trying to be used as an int[], as indicated by the declaration int[] Nums, and to do so, we need to use the as int[] cast. Once Nums is an int[] array, we can use it as a regular array. This means we can get the Nums.Length to start another for loop.

```
int[] Nums = Numbers[i] as int[];
int items = Nums.Length;
for(int j = 0; j < items; j++)
{
```

This loop will begin the next loop printing out each item stored in the Nums integer array. As we did earlier, we use the following fragment:

```
for(int j = 0; j < items; j++)
{
    int Num = Nums[j];
    print (Num);
}
```

This fragment is inside of the first for loop. Using this, we'll get each item of each array stored at each index of the Numbers array list. This seems like a great deal of work, but in truth it's all necessary and this will become second nature once you're used to the steps involved in dealing with arrays.

ArrayLists allow you to store any variety of object. To store an array of arrays, you need to use an ArrayList. What might seem correct to start off with might be something like the following:

```
Array Numbers = {primes, fibonacci, powersOfTwo};
int numArrays = Numbers.Length;
```

In fact, this is syntactically correct, and intuition might tell you that there's no problem with this. However, the Array type isn't defined as it is without any type assigned to it. However, we can use the following:

```
object[] Numbers = {primes, fibonacci, powersOfTwo};
```

This turns each int[] into an object, and Numbers is now an array of objects. To an effect we've created the same thing as before with the ArrayList; only we've defined the length of the Numbers array by entering three elements between the curly braces.

For clarification, we can use the foreach iterator with both the ArrayList and the int[] array.

```
ArrayList Numbers = new ArrayList{primes, fibonacci, powersOfTwo};
foreach (int[] Nums in Numbers)
{
    foreach(int n in Nums)
    {
        print (n);
    }
}
```

This produces the same output to the Console panel in Unity 3D as the previous version; only it's a lot shorter. It's important to recognize the first `foreach` statement contains `int[] Nums in Numbers` as each element in the `Numbers` array is an `int[]` array type.

### 6.17.3 Discovery

Learning what a class has to offer involves a great deal testing. For instance, we saw many other functions in `ArrayList` which we didn't use. We saw `Count` that returned an integer value. This was indicated when the listing showed us `Count: int` in the Assembly Browser.

However, it's good to learn about the other functions found in `ArrayList`. Let's pick the `ToArray() : object[]` function; this sounds useful, but what does it do? More important, how do we find out? The steps here begin with testing various features one at a time.

The return type indicates that it's giving us an object, so let's start there.

```
ArrayList Numbers = new ArrayList{primes, fibonacci, powersOfTwo};
object thing = Numbers.ToArray();
print (thing);
```

This sends the following output to the Console panel:

```
System.Object[]
UnityEngine.MonoBehaviour:print(Object)
Arrays:Start () (at Assets/Arrays.cs:14)
```

The `thing` is apparently a `System.object[]` that was sent to the Console output panel. From this, we learned that `thing` is, indeed, an `object[]`, or rather it's an array of objects. What can we do with this? Let's change this to match what we've observed.

```
object[] thing = Numbers.ToArray() as object[];
print (thing.Length);
```

Now that we know it's an array, let's cast it to being a proper array by adding in a cast. Now the `thing` returns a length. We get 3 sent to the Console panel of Unity 3D when we press the Play game button. But what's going on here? Remember that earlier we had to use `numbers.Count` to get the size of the `ArrayList`. Now we're dealing with a regular `Array`, not an `ArrayList`. Therefore, should we need to use an `Array` and not an `ArrayList`, this function could come in handy! Good to know.

This little exercise is important; a part of learning any new language is testing the code that you discover when browsing through a class' functions. Anything listed in the Assembly Browser is there for a reason. At some point, somebody thought the function was necessary, so he or she added it.

### 6.17.4 Putting It Together

When we're building a game, one important use of an array is storing many different objects and sending them commands in a coordinated manner. We did this earlier by making a line of undulating cubes. However, what if we want to keep track of a number of monsters approaching the player?

The first thing we'd need to do is figure out how to find the monsters. We can do this by keeping track of them as they're spawned, but this would mean there's a sort of master controller both spawning them and keeping track of each one.

Unity's `GameObject` class will come to the rescue. Expand the References folder found in the Solution panel in MonoDevelop.

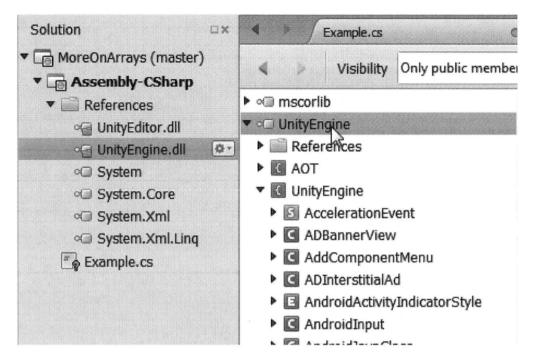

This will open the Assembly Browser, where we'll look for the `GameObject` class we've worked with in the past. If you scroll through the various functions found within the `GameObject` class, we'll come across a few different functions with the word "find" in them.

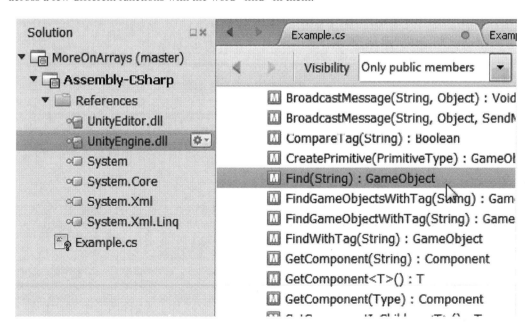

Perhaps we can discover how these are used.

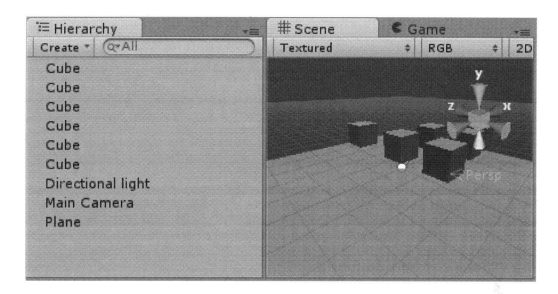

To start our test, I've built a simple scene that includes some cubes. I then created a new C# class called `Monster` and assigned it to each of the cubes. I added in a light to make things a bit easier to see. Finally, I added in a ground cube so that there's something to look at other than the vastness of nothing that exists in an empty level.

To the Main Camera, I've added a new `Example.cs` script so we can begin testing out some new scripting ideas.

To get started with `GameObject.Find()` : `GameObject`, the Assembly Browser tells us that it returns a `GameObject`. Therefore, in the `Start` () function, we'll add in the following code:

```
GameObject go = GameObject.Find("Cube");
print (go);
```

Once we add in the first parenthesis ( after `Find`, we're reminded that it's looking for a `string` that is the name of the `GameObject` we're expecting to return. Let's test out `"Cube,"` since there seem to be many in the scene we're working with. Remember to use an uppercase `C` since that's how it's named in the scene.

The above code fragment added to the `Start` () function produces the following output in the Console panel.

```
Cube (UnityEngine.GameObject)
UnityEngine.MonoBehaviour:print(Object)
Example:Start () (at Assets/Example.cs:9)
```

This output looks promising. Therefore, what can we do with the `Cube` we just found? Our camera knows about something else in the scene, which is pretty important. If a monster is going to find a player, he'll have to find it in code. However, which `Cube` did the camera find?

```
//Update is called once per frame
void Update () {
    GameObject go = GameObject.Find("Cube");
    Vector3 CubePosition = go.transform.position;
    Vector3 Up = new Vector3(0, 10, 0);
    Debug.DrawRay(CubePosition, Up);
}
```

We're going to use the Update () function for this. I've moved my code from the Start () function to the Update () function so we can use the Debug.DrawRay() function we used earlier.

When we run the game, we can take a look at the Scene panel that will draw Gizmos used by the Debug functions. It looks like it's just picking the first Cube at the top of the list of cubes in the Hierarchy panel. This is most likely the case, but that doesn't necessarily mean it's the closest Cube in the scene.

How would we go about finding the nearest Cube to the camera? We'd want a list of all of the cubes, compare their distances, and pick the cube with the smallest distance value. This means we want an array of all of the GameObjects of the Cube in the scene.

The closest function we can find is GameObject.FindGameObjectsWithTag() that returns a GameObject[] array. Therefore, I guess this means each Monster will need a Monster tag assigned. In Unity 3D, to create a new Tag, you select any object in the scene. In the Inspector panel, go under the object's name and open the Tag pull-down menu. Select Add Tag….

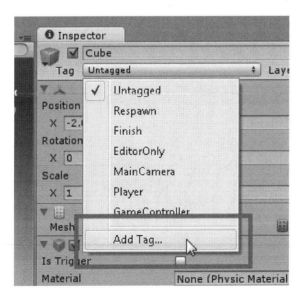

The following Tag Manager panel will open. The Tag Manager is also accessible from the Edit menu: Select Edit → Project Settings → Tags.

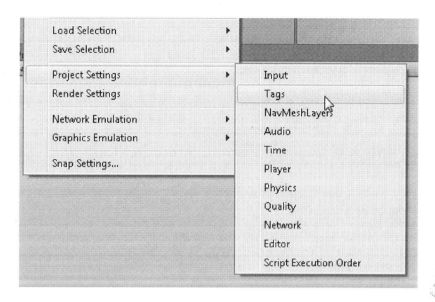

This will take you to the same place. Once there, expand the Tags submenu and add in `Monster` to the zeroth element of the `Tag` array. You may notice that an additional slot will automatically be added when you start typing.

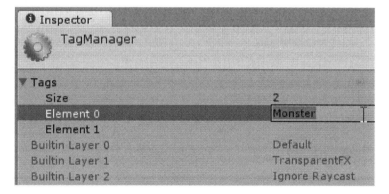

Once this is done, open the `Monster.cs` we created and assigned to each of the cubes in the scene.

```
//Use this for initialization
void Start ()
{
    tag = "Monster";
}
```

In the `Start ()` function in the `Monster` class, I've added in `tag = "Monster";` which sets the tag of any object that the script is assigned to `"Monster."` This is a bit easier than going to each cube in the scene and changing the tag manually. Remember that programmers are lazy.

Moving back to the `Example.cs`, we'll want to test out the `FindGameObjectsWithTag()` function.

```
//Update is called once per frame
void Update ()
{
    GameObject[] gos = GameObject.FindGameObjectsWithTag("Monster");
    print (gos.Length);
}
```

We'll want to have an array of GameObjects[] to fill in with whatever data is provided by the GameObject's function. To double check that there's data in the identifier gos, we'll see if the array has a Length greater than 0 by printing the Length property of the array. Now we get the following output from the Example.cs script.

```
6
UnityEngine.MonoBehaviour:print(Object)
Example:Update () (at Assets/Example.cs:14)
```

Awesome, now we're getting somewhere. Now we're going to get each GameObject's transform.position.

```
//Update is called once per frame
void Update ()
{
      GameObject[] gos = GameObject.FindGameObjectsWithTag("Monster");
      Debug.Log(gos.Length);
      foreach (GameObject g in gos)
      {
           print(g.transform.position);
      }
}
```

This code will print out a bunch of different Vector3 values. Each position isn't that useful, so we're going to do something about that. A distance in math terms is called a magnitude. To get a magnitude, we need to provide a Vector3() and use the .magnitude property of the Vector3() class. This is better explained with some sample code.

```
foreach(GameObject g in gos)
{
     Vector3 vec = g.transform.position - transform.position;
     float distance = vec.magnitude;
     print(distance);
}
```

To get a single vector that informs us of the magnitude of any vector, we subtract one Vector3 from another. We use Vector3 vec = g.transform.position - transform.position; to get the difference between two different vectors. To find vec's magnitude, we use float distance = vec.magnitude; to store that value. Running the above code fragment in the Update () function prints out a bunch of numbers; each one should be a game object's distance from the camera, or whatever you assigned the Example.cs script to in the scene.

Now we collect the different distances and sort through them to find the smallest one. Here's an interesting point. What if there are more or less cubes in the scene? This array may be of any size. Therefore, we'll make sure that we have an array that can adapt to any size; that's where the ArrayList really comes in.

```
void Update ()
{
      GameObject[] gos = GameObject.FindGameObjectsWithTag("Monster");
      ArrayList distances = new ArrayList();
      foreach(GameObject g in gos)
      {
          Vector3 vec = g.transform.position - transform.position;
          float distance = vec.magnitude;
          distances.Add(distance);
      }
      print (distances.Count);
}
```

We're at an appropriate point to iterate the order of operation when it comes to loops. When the Update () function begins, we start with a new array gos that is fulfilled with any number of GameObjects with the tag "Monster." The number of monsters in the scene can change, but since the Update () function starts fresh every time, the array will be updated to account for any changes from the last time the Update () function was called.

Right after that, we declare a new ArrayList of distances. This ArrayList is created anew each time the Update () function is called. Then we hit the foreach() loop. This runs its course, and using the Add function in the ArrayList class, we add in a distance. Once the loop exits, the distances.Count matches the gos.Length. It's important to note that the numbers match up. This means that the first element in distances matches the first element in distances.

This is where it's important to know when to use a for loop versus a foreach loop. We need the index number from the for loop's initialization. We're working with the int i as a number to relate one array to another. To start, we'll use any of the objects from one array and compare that value against the rest of the values.

```
float closestValue = (float)distances[0];
GameObject closestObject = gos[0];
```

If there's at least one value in the array, the rest of the function will work as expected. If there are 0 objects with the tag "Monster," then the rest of the function will produce a great deal of errors. We'll find out how to deal with exceptions in Section 7.12, but for now, keep at least one monster in the scene. To continue, we'll add in a simple for loop using the number of game objects we started with.

```
GameObject[] gos = GameObject.FindGameObjectsWithTag("Monster");
Debug.Log(gos.Length);
float closestValue = (float)distances [0];
GameObject closestObject = gos [0];
for (int i = 0; i < gos.Length; i++)
{
    float d = (float)distances [i];
    if (d < closestValue)
    {
        closestObject = gos [i];
        closestValue = (float)distances [i];
    }
}
```

Here we iterate through each index of the distances[] and gos[] array. We use these to compare a stored value, in this case closestValue, against a value stored in the distances[] array. We prepare the closestValue float variable before the for loop. To store this as a float, we need to convert it from an object type stored in the distances[] array to a float using the (float) cast syntax.

We need to do this once for the first closestValue and once for each element in the distances[] array before we compare the two float values. The second conversion needs to happen within the for loop. You can see the second conversion on the fourth line down in the above fragment.

Once we have two float values, we can compare them. If we come across a value that's smaller than the one we already had, then we assign our closestObject and our closestValue to the values found at the index we're comparing against. If we find no other value smaller than the ones we're currently comparing all of the other objects to, then we've discovered the closest object.

To visualize this, we can add in a handy little Debug.Ray() starting from the closest game object.

```
Vector3 up = new Vector3(0,1,0);
Vector3 start = closestObject.transform.position;
Debug.DrawRay(start, up);
```

We'll start the ray from the `transform.position` of the `closestObject` and shoot a small ray up from it. The completed code should look something like the following:

```csharp
using UnityEngine;
using System.Collections;
public class Example : MonoBehaviour {
    //Use this for initialization
    void Start () {
    }
    //Update is called once per frame
    void Update () {
        GameObject[] gos = GameObject.FindGameObjectsWithTag("Monster");
        ArrayList distances = new ArrayList();
        foreach(GameObject g in gos) {
            Vector3 vec = g.transform.position - transform.position;
            float distance = vec.magnitude;
            distances.Add(distance);
        }
        float closestValue = (float)distances[0];
        GameObject closestObject = gos[0];
        for(int i = 0; i < gos.Length; i++) {
            float d = (float)distances[i];
            if (d < = closestValue) {
                closestObject = gos[i];
                closestValue = d;
            }
        }
        Vector3 up = new Vector3(0,1,0);
        Vector3 start = closestObject.transform.position;
        Debug.DrawRay(start, up);
    }
}
```

This is a handy bit of a fun code to know. As you move the camera around in the Scene editor, you'll notice that the little white ray will jump to the closest cube in the scene.

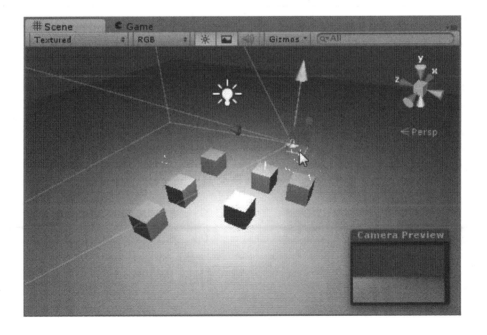

### 6.17.5 What We've Learned

You might be done with arrays, but there's still a few tricks left. We'll leave off here for now and move on to a different topic next. Arrays are a fundamental part of programming in general. A database is not much more than a complex array of different types of data. The principal difference is that a database has some relational connections between one element and another. Arrays without this relational data mean you'll have to keep track of the different relations.

Sorting through numbers is such an important part of general computing that many algorithms do nothing more than sort and organize numbers. Computer scientists spend years trying to speed up these sorting processes. We can't necessarily spend too much time on comparing these different methods of sorting in this book, as the field of study has filled countless volumes of text. If it were not for this importance, companies wouldn't base their entire business on storing, sorting, and organizing data.

You could imagine dealing with a few dozen monster types; each one with different sets of data, stats, and members can quickly become cumbersome to deal with. There are ways to maintain some control; that's where data structures come into play.

---

## 6.18 Out Parameter

We have been thinking that functions return a single value. Another method to get more than one value from a function is to use the `out` keyword in the parameters. The `out` keyword is usable in most situations even if you need only one return value though its use is different from how `return` is used.

```
int getSeven()
{
    return 7;
}
```

The above is a function that basically returns a 7. In use, you might see something similar to the following code fragment:

```
int seven = getSeven();
```

What limits us is the ability to return multiple values. What we'd like to be able to do but can't is something like Lua that looks like the following:

```
function returns7and11()
    return 7, 11
end
local seven, eleven = returns7and11()
```

While Lua has some clever tricks like returning multiple values, we'd have to do some extra work in C# to do the same thing. This is not elegant to say the least, and this does not mention the performance issues that will creep up if something like this is used too often.

```
ArrayList sevenEleven()
{
    ArrayList al = new ArrayList();
    al.Add(7);
    al.Add(11);
    return al;
}
void Start ()
{
    ArrayList se = sevenEleven();
    int seven = (int)se[0];
    int eleven = (int)se[1];
}
```

From the above example, we created a function called seven() that returned a 7. return which is used to provide a system to turn the function into some sort of value, which can be an array, but then we start to lose what sort of data is inside of the array. Because of this, we will run into type safety issues. For instance, we could modify the statement in sevenEleven() to look like the following:

```
ArrayList sevenEleven()
{
    ArrayList se = new ArrayList();
    se.Add(7);
    se.Add("eleven");//oops, not an int!
    return se;
}
```

The parser will not catch the error, until the game starts running and the sevenEleven() function is called and the int eleven tries to get data from the array. You will get this printed out to the Console panel.

```
InvalidCastException: Cannot cast from source type to destination type.
```

This type of error is not something we'd like to track down when you're using an array for use with numbers. Vague errors are rarely fun to figure out. It's best to avoid using anything like the code mentioned above.

### 6.18.1 A Basic Example

In the OutParameter project, we'll start with the Example component attached to the Main Camera as usual. The identifier defined in the argument list in the first function is named s who is assigned the return value from the seven Out () function. So far this is a very simple use of how the return key-word works, which we've seen earlier. However, you might be inclined to get more than one value from a function.

```
void sevenOut(out int s)
{
    s = 7;
}
void Start ()
{
    int i;//new int
    sevenOut (out i);//i is now 7
    print(i);//prints 7 to the console
}
```

You need to do a couple of things before the out keyword is used. First, you need to prepare a variable to assign to the function. Then to use the function, you need to put that variable into the parameters list preceded by the same out keyword. When the function is executed, it looks at the variable's value inside of it and sends it back up to the parameters list with its new value. Of course, we can add more than one out value.

```
void goingOut(out int first, out int second, out int third)
{
    first = 1;
    second = 2;
    third = 3;
}
void Start ()
{
    int i;
    int j;
```

```
        int k;
        goingOut(out i, out j, out k);
        print(i + " " + j + " " + k);
}
```

The above code produces 1, 2, 3 in the Console. Using the function in this way allows you to produce many useful operations on incoming values as well. The additional benefit is the fact that the function can act as a pure function. This means that as long as none of the variables inside of the function rely on anything at the class level, the code can be copied and pasted or moved to any other class quite easily.

```
void inAndOut(int inComing, out int outGoing)
{
        outGoing = inComing * 2;
}
void Start ()
{
        int outValue = 0;
        print(outValue);//writes 0 to the console
        inAndOut(6, out outValue);
        print(outValue);//writes 12 to the console
}
```

This example shows an `inComing` value that is multiplied by 2 before it's assigned to the `outGoing` value. The variable `outValue` is initialized before the function is used and then it's assigned a new value when the function is executed. The `out` keyword is handy and allows for more tidy functions.

### 6.18.2 Simple Sort (Bubble Sort)

Arrays are an integral part of any game. Lists of monsters and values make for an important part of any list of data when making decisions on what to do in an environment. We'll start with a simple scene.

To the Capsule in the scene, attach a new script component named OutParameter; we'll add our new behavior using the `out` parameter here. We're going to create a simple `ArrayList` that will have all of the objects in the scene added to it. Then we're going to create a new `GameObject[]` array that will be sorted based on the distance to the capsule.

Sorting algorithms have a long history in computer programming. Many thesis papers have been written on the topic. However, we're going to make use of a simple sort algorithm to order an array of game objects from the shortest distance to the longest distance.

We'll start with a simple system to get an `ArrayList` of objects in the scene.

```
public GameObject[] GameObjectArray;
//Use this for initialization
void Start ()
{
    ArrayList aList = new ArrayList();
    GameObject[] gameObjects =
    (GameObject[])GameObject.FindObjectsOfType(typeof(GameObject));
    foreach(GameObject go in gameObjects)
    {
        if(go.name == "Sphere")
        {
            aList.Add(go);
        }
    }
    GameObjectArray =
    aList.ToArray(typeof(GameObject)) as GameObject[];
}
```

This creates a new `ArrayList` called `aList` using `ArrayList aList = new ArrayList();` at the beginning of the `Start ()` function. To populate this list, we need to get all of the `GameObjects` in the scene with `GameObject[] gameObjects = (GameObject[])GameObject.FindObjects OfType(typeof(GameObject));`, which does a few different tasks in one statement.

First, it creates a new `GameObject[]` array called `gameObjects`. Then we use `GameObject.FindObjectsOfType()` and assign the function in `GameObject` the `typeof(GameObject);` this returns a new array of every `GameObject` in the scene.

After we get all of our data, we use a `foreach` loop `foreach(GameObject go in gameObjects)` to check through all of the different objects. In the parameters of the `foreach`, we create a `GameObject` `go` that stores the current iteration as we go through the `gameObjects` array. Then we filter the objects and take only the ones named Sphere using the `if` statement `if(go.name == "Sphere")` which adds the `go` to the `aList` array if the names match.

Finally, the `aList` is assigned to `GameObjectArray` which was created at the class scope. The statement is fulfilled by `aList.ToArray()` that takes the argument `typeof(GameObject)`. We then convert the returned data to `GameObject[]` by a cast as `GameObject[];` at the end of the statement.

Now we're ready to sort through the `GameObjectArray` based on distance.

```
void sortObjects(GameObject[] objects, out GameObject[] sortedObjects)
{
    for(int i = 0; i < objects.Length-1; i++)
    {
        Vector3 PositionA = objects[i].transform.position;
        Vector3 PositionB = objects[i+1].transform.position;
        Vector3 VectorToA = PositionA - transform.position;
        Vector3 VectorToB = PositionB - transform.position;
        float DistanceToA = VectorToA.magnitude;
        float DistanceToB = VectorToB.magnitude;
        if(DistanceToA > DistanceToB)
        {
            GameObject temp = objects[i];
            objects[i] = objects[i+1];
            objects[i+1] = temp;
        }
    }
    sortedObjects = objects;
}
```

Here we have a new function added to our class. What we do here is simple and works only if it's iterated a few times. The idea is that we need to discover the distances between two objects in the array. Compare the distances, and if one distance is greater than another, then swap the two objects in the array. As we repeat this, we rearrange the objects in the array with each pass. As this can repeat any number of times, we're doing things in a very inefficient manner, but it's getting the job done. We'll look at optimizing this loop again in this section, in which we go further into sorting algorithms.

The function starts with `GameObject[] objects`, which accepts an array of `GameObjects` called `objects`. Then we start up a `for` loop to check through each object. This begins with `for(int i = 0; i < objects.Length-1; i++);` what is important here is that we don't want to iterate through to the last object in the array. We want to stop one short of the end. We'll see why as soon as we start going through the rest of the loop.

Next we want to get the location of the current object and the next object. This is done with `Vector3 PositionA = objects[i].transform.position;`. Then we use `Vector3 PositionB = objects[i+1].transform.position;` to get the next object in the list. You'll notice `objects[i+1]` adds 1 to i that will reach the end of the array. If we used `i < objects.Length`, and not `i < objects.Length-1`, we'd be looking at a place in the array that doesn't exist. If there were 10 objects in the scene, the array is `Length 10`, which means that there's no `objects[11]`. Looking for `objects[11]` results in an index out of range error.

Then we get some vectors representing the object's position minus the script's position. This is done with `Vector3 VectorToA = PositionA - transform.position;` and `Vector3 VectorToB = PositionB - transform.position;`. Then these are converted to magnitudes, which is a math function that can be done to a `Vector3`. This gives us two `float` values to compare `float DistanceToA = VectorToA.magnitude;` and `float DistanceToB = VectorToB.magnitude;`.

Finally, we need to compare distance and do a swap if A is greater than B.

```
if(DistanceToA > DistanceToB)
{
    GameObject temp = objects[i];
    objects[i] = objects[i+1];
    objects[i+1] = temp;
}
```

We use a `GameObject temp` to store the `object[i]` that is going to be written over with the swap. The swap begins with `objects[i] = objects[i+1];` where we will for a single statement have two copies of the same object in the array. This is because both `objects[i]` and `objects[i+1]` are holding on to the same `GameObject` in the scene. Then to finish the swap, we replace the `objects[i+1]` with `temp` that holds onto `objects[i]`.

To send the sorted array back, we use `sortedObjects = objects;` and the `out` parameter pushes the array back up out of the function into where it was called on. To check on the sorting, we'll use the following code in the `Update ()` function:

```
void Update ()
{
    sortObjects(GameObjectArray, out GameObjectArray);
    for(int i = 0; i < GameObjectArray.Length; i++)
    {
        Vector3 PositionA =
        GameObjectArray[i].transform.position;
        Debug.DrawRay(PositionA, new Vector3(0, i * 2f, 0),
        Color.red);
    }
}
```

Call on the new function, sortObjects(GameObjectArray, out GameObjectArray). Woah! You can do that? Yes you can! You can have both in and out parameters reference the same array variable. What this will do is that it will take in the array, sort it, and send it back out sorted! Once the array has been sorted, it can be sorted again and again.

### 6.18.3  Simple Sort Proof

To test our sort, we'll use a for loop. Each higher value in the array will hold onto a different model. The furthest model will be the last in the array and thus have the highest index in the array. The closest object will be at GameObjectArray[0], and the furthest one will be at the end of the array. Therefore, if there are 10 objects in the scene, the furthest object will be at GameObjectArray[9]. Remember that arrays start at 0, not 1.

So we'll get the position of the current object with Vector3 PositionA = GameObjectArray[i]. transform.position;. We then use this value in a Debug.DrawRay function. This looks like Debug.DrawRay(PositionA, new Vector3(0, i * 2f, 0), Color.red); where we take the starting position PositionA and draw a ray up from it with new Vector3(0, i * 2f, 0) that tells it to draw a straight line up. The length of the line is i * 2f, or twice the int i.

In the Scene panel with the game running, you'll see the following:

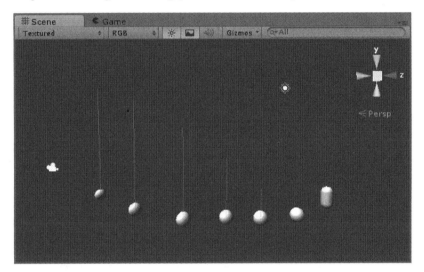

As you move the Capsule with the script applied around in the scene, you'll notice the length of the lines changing based on the distance away from the capsule. This means that you can use this sort algorithm to place a priority on which object is closest and which is the furthest away based on its index in the array.

### 6.18.4  What We've Learned

We should leave off here for now; sorting is a very deep topic that leads into the very messy guts of computer science. The algorithm isn't complete and lacks any efficiency. It's effective, but only superficially. The only reason why this works at all is the fact that Update () is called many times per second.

The first time through the sortObjects() function, the sort is not complete. Only neighboring differences will be swapped. If the first and last objects need to be swapped, all of the objects between them must be swapped several times before the full array can be arranged properly. Proper sorting algorithms usually require several iterations. The speed at which they can do their job depends greatly on how it was implemented. Different implementations have different names.

Most of the commonly used sorting algorithms have names such as bubble sort, heap sort, or quick sort. What we did here is a simple implementation of a bubble sort. This means we looked at the first two elements in the array, and if one had some greater value than the other, we swap them.

For games such as tower defense, or anything where a character needs to shoot at the closest target and then move on to the next closest, we can use sorting to help provide the character with some more interesting behaviors. Perhaps he can target more than one object with different weapons at the same time. Maybe the character can simply shoot at the closest three objects. The great thing about writing your own game is that you can explore behaviors like this freely, but only once you understand how to use the code you're writing.

There are many different ways to accomplish the same task, and you're not limited to the `out` parameter. We could have done the following instead:

```
GameObject[] sortObjects(GameObject[] objects)
{
    for(int i = 0; i < objects.Length-1; i++)
    {
        Vector3 PositionA = objects[i].transform.position;
        Vector3 PositionB = objects[i+1].transform.position;
        Vector3 VectorToA = PositionA - transform.position;
        Vector3 VectorToB = PositionB - transform.position;
        float DistanceToA = VectorToA.magnitude;
        float DistanceToB = VectorToB.magnitude;
        if(DistanceToA > DistanceToB) {
            GameObject temp = objects[i];
            objects[i] = objects[i+1];
            objects[i+1] = temp;
        }
    }
    return objects;
}
```

Here we simply `return` the objects and make sure that we use `GameObject[] sortObjects(GameObject[] objects);` however, this isn't fun. We wouldn't have been able to see the `out` keyword in action using an interesting behavior. We're not limited by how our functions operate with C#. We're able to use its flexibility to test out various ideas, not only with game play but with the language itself.

Of course in the end, we're required to keep our code as simple as possible. The `out` keyword is best used when we can't return a single value. In the case with a single return value, the later version of `sortObjects` where we simply return the sorted array is more readable.

One last thing before moving on is to remember that sorting is usually quite expensive. In this example, we don't notice how long this is taking since there aren't many objects to sort through. Try the example again with several hundred objects in the scene.

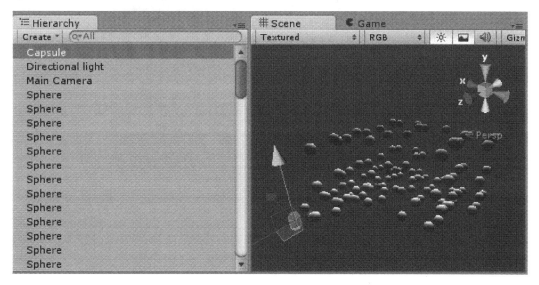

You'll be able to actually watch the red lines rearrange themselves in the array as you move the capsule around!

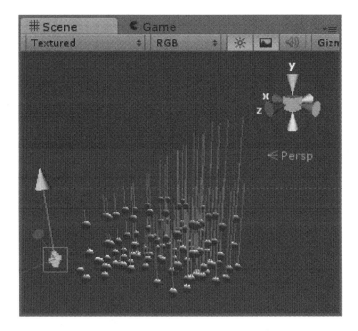

Here we start on one side of the group of spheres.

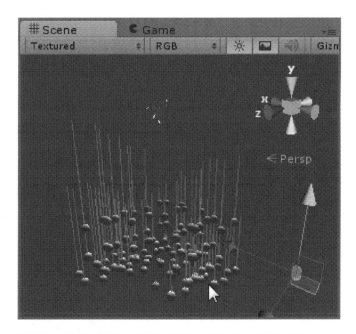

Quickly move the capsule with the script attached to the other side of the spheres. You'll be able to watch the red lines change as the array is sorted.

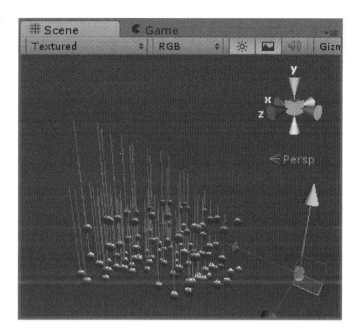

After a few moments, the array is sorted and the lines stop changing in length, indicating that the sorting is done. Since we don't have a condition to stop the sorting, the function is still being called, so this process takes up much of central processing unit (CPU) time, but if you're a nerd, it's fun to watch!

Just in case use the following adjustment to the DrawRay call:

```
Debug.DrawRay(PositionA, new Vector3(0, i * 0.1f, 0), Color.red);
```

This makes the lines shorter and easier to see.

## 6.19 Ref Parameter

The ref keyword, which is short for *reference*, works with variables in a slightly less intuitive way than we have experienced to this point. This is related to how we've been thinking about variables. In the usual case, we use the statement x = 1;, and now when we use x, we can assume we're dealing with the value it's storing.

The difference with ref enters when we start to manipulate the data stored under an identifier. If we use a statement like x = 1; y = x;, we aren't actually taking x and putting it into y. What's really going on is that y is looking at the value that x is holding onto and changes its own value to match what x is storing.

In memory, y is storing a 1 and x is storing a different 1. The statement x = 1; ref y = x; would actually mean that y is now looking at the identifier, not the value being stored at the location of x. If ref y is looking at the identifier and not the value, were we to modify y, the action is going to take place in the contents of x.

This may seem a bit hard to understand, and to be honest, it is. This concept is one that takes a while to get used to and that is why some programming languages are more difficult to learn than others. However, the concept becomes more apparent when we see the code in action.

## 6.19.1 A Basic Example

The `ref` keyword acts somewhat like the `out` keyword. In practice we'll see how they differ with the following example code fragment.

```
public int x;
void RefIncrementValue(ref int in)
{
    in += 1;
}
void Start ()
{
    print(x);//before executing the ref function
    RefIncrementValue(ref x);
    print (x);//after executing the ref function
}
```

The code above takes in the `ref` of x which is assigned `in` by the parameters of the function. The `in` argument now has a direct connection to the contents of x. When `in += 1` is executed, the value that x was holding is incremented. After the function is completed, the value of the original x has been modified.

Here's a bad way to do the same thing using side effects.

```
public int x;
void IncrementX()
{
    x += 1;
}
void Start ()
{
    print(x);//before calling the increment function
    IncrementX();
    print(x);//after calling the increment function
}
```

The biggest problem with this is the fact that the increment function works only on the x variable. What this means is that you can now reduce the number of functions that affect any particular variable. Otherwise, we'd need a function for every variable we want to modify.

```
public int x;
public int y;
void RefIncrementValue(ref int inValue)
{
    inValue += 1;
}
void Start ()
{
    print(x);
    print(y);
    RefIncrementValue(ref x);
    print(x);
    RefIncrementValue(ref y);
    print(y);
}
```

With the above code, we can easily manipulate any value sent to the `RefIncrementValue()` function. Hopefully, you're thinking to yourself, "wow, I wonder how I can use this?" and you'd be on the right track. The `ref` keyword is in particular an interesting keyword. In many cases, a function is best when there are no side effects.

### 6.19.2 Code Portability Side Effects

When you've started writing code, it's better to reuse as much as you can to help speed along your own development. Often you'll find simple tricks that help with various tasks. When programmers talk about reusing code, we need to think about how a function works.

If a function relies on the class it was written in, then it becomes less portable. When a function can operate on its own, it becomes more utilitarian and more portable.

```
using UnityEngine;
using System.Collections;
public class Example : MonoBehaviour {
    int a = 1;
    int b = 3;
    int ReliesOnSideEffects()
    {
        return a + b;
    }
    void Start ()
    {
        print (ReliesOnSideEffects());
    }
}
```

In this Example class, we're adding a + b and returning the result. For this function to operate properly if used by another class, we'd also have to copy the two variables in the class used to complete its task. Portable code shouldn't have to do this to work. We have plenty of options that work.

```
using UnityEngine;
using System.Collections;
public class Example : MonoBehaviour {
    int a = 1;
    int b = 3;
    int AddsNumbers(int x, int y) {
        return x + y;
    }
    void Start () {
        print (AddsNumbers(a, b));
    }
}
```

This version accomplishes the same task, adding a to b, but the function we're using requires no outside variables. With something like this, we're more able to copy and paste the function in a class where it's needed. We're allowed to try out many different iterations of this simple task. Once the task gets more complex, we're going to explore more options.

### 6.19.3 What We've Learned

In Section 6.18, we covered the out keyword, and here we learned the ref keyword. A decision must be made between which keyword to use for each situation. In most cases, the out keyword is going to be more useful. In the case where we create a variable with a limited scope, it's better to use out.

```
void someFunction(out i)
{
    i = 7;
}
```

```
void Start ()
{
    int localInt = 0;
    someFunction(out localInt);
    print(localInt);
}
```

If we were to create a variable that existed only within the Start () function, for example, we'd need to use only the out keyword. This limits where the variable is being changed. However, if we need to use a variable with a wider scope which more functions are going to see, then we'd want to use the ref keyword.

```
int classInt = 0;//can be seen by both functions
void someFunction(ref i)
{
    i = 7;
}
void Start ()
{
    someFunction(ref classInt);
}
void Update ()
{
    print(classInt);
}
```

Should a variable be accessed across more than one function, then we'd need to modify the original variable, so ref is more useful in this situation. Of course, there are other ways to do the same task. The someFunction() function can return a value, or it can modify a variable using the ref keyword as shown in the following code fragment:

```
int classInt = 0;
int someFunction()
{
    return 7;
}
void Start ()
{
    classInt = someFunction();
}
void Update ()
{
    print (classInt);
}
```

This works perfectly well, but then we're limited to a single return value. If we had something more complex in mind, we'd need to use either out or ref should we need more than a single return value. For instance, if we needed two or three values, we might have to use something like this:

```
void someFunction(out x, out y)
{
    x = 7;
    y = 13;
}
void Start ()
{
    int firstInt = 0;
    int secondInt = 0;
```

```
        someFunction(out firstInt, out secondint);
        print(firstInt + " " + secondint);
}
```

As we've seen, there are plenty of options when we begin to get familiar with how C# works. It's important to not let all of the options confuse us. At the same time, it's good to know how to do a single task in different ways, should we find one more convenient than another.

In addition, `ref` also allows you to use the variable within the function. This means that `ref` has both incoming and outgoing availability.

In the end, though, it's up to you to decide how to write and use functions and how they change values. How you decide to do this allows you to express your own ideas and methods through code. Different programming languages have different levels of expressiveness or expressivity. Basically, some languages are more strict, while others allow for more than one way to carry out any given task.

The expressivity of C# is fairly high, allowing you to try out many different methods to do the same thing. There are more common practices, but by no means should you feel limited to a commonly used syntax. If you feel that a less commonly used syntax is more helpful, by all means use it.

---

## 6.20 Type Casting Numbers

We need to know more about a variety of different data types and how they're used before we can begin to understand how and why type casting is important. At this point, we need more casting from one type of data into another. Now that we've had a chance to use a wide variety of different data types, it's time we started learning why converting from one type to another is necessary.

We casted from object to float, but why is this required? C# is a *type-safe* programming language. What this means is that your code is checked for mixed types before it's compiled into machine-readable code. This is done to prevent any errors that show up while the code is running. When converting between types that are similar, we don't usually see too many errors. In the following code sample, we demonstrate why we don't want to use an integer for setting an object's position.

```
using UnityEngine;
using System.Collections;
public class TypeConversion : MonoBehaviour
{
    public int Zmove;
    //Use this for initialization
    void Start ()
    {
    }
    //Update is called once per frame
    void Update ()
    {
        transform.position = new Vector3(0,0,Zint);
    }
}
```

The result of this is a cube that snaps from one location to another. Assign a script named `TypeConversion.cs` to a cube in a new scene. Start the game and then use the Scene editor to observe the cube's movement when the `Zmove` is modified. The cube hops from point to point. Integers can't hold fractions. However, there are other types that do. The `float` type is a number type that stores the position of a decimal point.

Simply put, an integer is a whole number such as 1, 2, and 3. A fraction can have a value between 1 and 2, for example, 1.5625. Therefore, if we change from an `int` to a `float`, we'll get a more smooth movement when we modify the Zmove value. However, what happens when we cast a float to an int?

```
void Update ()
{
    int Zint = (int)Zmove;
    transform.position = new Vector3(0, 0, Zint);
}
```

In this code fragment, we start with a modifiable Zmove, and then in the Update (), we create a cast from Zmove to Zint. This results in the same choppy movement we observed before. However, you may see that there's some information lost in translation.

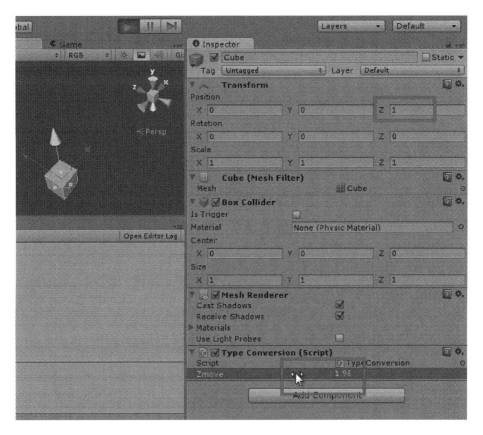

The input from Zmove is at 1.96; however, the actual Z position of the cube in the scene is sitting at 1. This is what is meant by data loss. Everything after the decimal is cut off when moving from a float to an int. In Section 4.7, we looked at some math operators and what happens when 1 is divided by 5. The results ended up giving you different number of places after the decimal. When converting from int to float, we don't need to use a cast.

```
public float Zmove;
//Update is called once per frame
void Update ()
{
    float Zfloat = Zmove;
    transform.position = new Vector3(0, 0, Zfloat);
}
```

In particular, notice that `float Zfloat = Zmove;` didn't need an `int`-to-`float` cast like `(float)` `Zmove` even though `Zmove` was an `int`. This is because there's no data lost. A smaller data type like an `int` will fit into a `float` without any chance of data being lost. When data can convert itself from a smaller type into a larger type, this is called an *implicit cast*.

### 6.20.1 Number Types

This leads us to numbers having a size. In fact, so far we've used `int` and `float`, and there was even mention of a `double`. However, why do these have a size related to them and how is an `int` smaller than a `float`? This is a computer science question, and to explain this, we need to remember how computers count.

In the old days, when computers had moving parts, instructions were fed to them using a flat piece of physical media with holes punched into it. Each hole in the media represented either a 0 or a 1, which was then converted back into decimal numbers which we use in our everyday life. The primary limitation in these old computers was size, and to hold big numbers, computers needed to be physically bigger.

Each number was stored in a series of switches. In 1946, the Electronic Numerical Integrator and Computer (ENIAC) used flip-flop switches to store a number; imagine a light switch, with *on* being a 1 and *off* being a 0. Each group of switches was called an accumulator and it could store a single 10-digit number for use in a calculation. Altogether with 18,000 vacuum tubes and weighing over 25 tons, the ENIAC could store a maximum of 20 numbers at a time.

Because programming languages have such a deep-rooted history with limited data space, numbers today still have similar limitations. On your PC, you might have the memory to store many hundreds of billions of numbers, but this doesn't hold true for every device. Every year new smaller, more portable devices show up on the market, so it's good to be aware that forming bad habits of wasting data space will limit the platforms you can write software for.

### 6.20.2 Integers

It's important to know how computers convert 1s and 0s into decimal numbers. To explain, let's start with a 4-bit number. This would be a series of four 1s or 0s. A zero would be as simple as 0000. Each place in the number is a different value. The first place is either a 1 or a 0, the second 2 or 0, the third 4 or 0, and the fourth 8 or 0. Each whole number between 0 and 15 can be represented with these 4 bits.

To demonstrate 0101 means 2 + 8 or 10. An interesting change is to shift both 1s to the left to get 1010 that translates to 1 + 4 or 5. This is called a bit shift, or in this case a shift left. The number 15 looks like 1111. It just so happens that a 4-bit number is called a *nibble*. A nibble also happens to easily represent a single hex number.

Hex numbers are used often when dealing with assigning colors on a web page. Hex numbers range from 0 to 9 and include an additional A through F to fill in the last six digits. A color is denoted by three 8-bit numbers for red, blue, and green. An 8-bit number is called a *byte*. Each color gets a range from 0 to 255. This turns into a two-digit hex number. Therefore, 0 is 00 and 255 is FF in hex.

#### 6.20.2.1 Signed Numbers

Today C# uses numbers starting with the *sbyte* up to the decimal. The sbyte is a number from −127 to 127, and the byte is a number from 0 to 255. The *s* in the sbyte is an abbreviation of the word *signed*. Therefore, you can actually call an sbyte a *signed byte*.

This is an important difference: Signing a number means it can be either positive or negative. However, you lose half the maximum range of the number since one of the 1s and 0s is used to tell the computer if the number is positive or negative. If we use the first bit to represent the signedness of a number in terms of our nibble, this turns 0100 into positive 1, while 1100 turns into negative 1. Negative 3 is 1110 and negative 7 is 1111, or "negative + 1 + 2 + 4."

| sbyte | 8 bits | −128 to 127 |
|---|---|---|
| Byte | 8 bits | 0 to 255 |
| Short | 16 bits | −32,768 to 32,767 |
| Unsigned short | 16 bits | 0 to 65,535 |
| Int | 32 bits | −2,147,483,648 to 2,147,483,647 |
| Unsigned int | 32 bits | 0 to 4,294,967,295 |
| Long | 64 bits | −9,223,372,036,854,775,808 to 9,223,372,036,854,775,807 |
| Unsigned long | 64 bits | 0 to 18,446,744,073,709,551,615 |

The above table represents most of the useful varieties of integer numbers. None of these have a decimal point in them to represent a fraction. Numbers that do have a decimal are called floating point numbers. So far we've used `float` and `double` as well; only that it hasn't been so obvious.

### 6.20.3 Floating Point

Floating point numbers have been a focus of computers for many years. Gaining floating point accuracy was the goal of many early computer scientists. Because there are an infinite possibilities of how many numbers can follow a decimal point, it's impossible to truly represent any fraction completely using binary computing.

A common example is π, which we call pi. It's assumed that there are an endless number of digits following 3.14. Even today computers are set loose to calculate the hundreds of billions of digits beyond the decimal point. Computers set aside some of the bits of a floating point number aside to represent where the decimal appears in the number, but even this is limited.

The first bit is usually the sign bit, setting the negative or positive range of the number. The following 8 bits is the exponent for the number called a mantissa. The remaining bits are the rest of the number appearing around the decimal point. A float value can move the decimal 38 digits in either direction, but it's limited to the values it's able to store.

We will go further into how numbers are actually stored in terms of 1s and 0s in Section 8.9. For now just understand that numbers can represent only a limited number of digits. Without special considerations, computers are not able to handle arbitrarily large numbers.

To cast a `float` into an `int`, you need to be more explicit. That's why C# requires you to use the cast and you need to add the `(int)` in `int Zint = (int)Zmove;`. The `(int)` is a cast operator; or rather `(type)` acts as a converter from the type on the right to the type needed on the left.

### 6.20.4 What We've Learned

There's still a bit left to go over with numbers, but we'll leave off here for now. A CPU is a collection of transistors. The computer interprets the signal coming from each transistor as a switch which is either on or off.

Computers collect these transistors into groups to accomplish common tasks. A floating point unit (FPU) is a collection of transistors grouped together to assist in floating point number processing. A graphics processing unit (GPU) is a variety of different groups of transistors specifically used to compute computer graphics.

These groups of transistors are built with highly complex designs. Their organization was designed by software to accomplish their task quickly. Software was used to build the hardware designed to run more software. It all sounds a bit of catch-22, but at least we have some historic reference where all of this comes from.

## 6.21 Types and Operators

Most of the operators we've been using compare equality. This works just fine when dealing with numbers. However, we can use operators on types that are not numbers, but which comparative operators can we use?

For number types, we can use relational operators. This affords us the ability to set booleans by using greater than >, less than <, greater than or equal to ≥, and less than or equal to ≤. All of these operators produce a boolean result.

```
float a = 1.0f;
float b = 3.0f;
bool c = a > b;//false
bool d = a < b;//true
```

As you might imagine, all of the math operators such as add +, subtract −, multiply ×, divide /, and modulo % work on any number type data. However, we can also use the + on the string type.

```
//Use this for initialization
void Start ()
{
        string a = "hello";
        string b = ", world";
        print (a + b);//prints hello, world
}
```

In the print() function, we use (a + b) to join the two strings together. However, we cannot use multiply, subtract, divide, or modulo on strings. But, we can use some of the comparative operators.

```
//Use this for initialization
void Start ()
{
        string a = "hello";
        string b = ", world";
        print (a == b);//prints False
}
```

In the print(a == b); function, we get False printed to the Console in Unity 3D. Likewise, we can use numbers and compare their values as well. We can also use the not equal (!=) operator on strings.

```
//Use this for initialization
void Start ()
{
        string a = "hello";
        string b = ", world";
        print (a != b);//prints True
}
```

The comparative operator (!=), or not equal operator, works on strings as well as numbers. Knowing which operators takes a bit of intuition, but it's important to experiment and learn how types interact with one another.

### 6.21.1 GetType()

We can also compare data types. This becomes more important later on when we start creating our own data types. To know how this works, we can use the data types that are already available in C#.

```
//Use this for initialization
void Start ()
{
        int a = 7;
        string b = "hello";
        print (a.GetType() != b.GetType());//prints True
}
```

The built-in types in C# have a function called `GetType();`, which allows us to check against what type of data each variable is. In this case, an `int` is not equal to a `string`, so the Console prints out `True` when the game is started.

```
//Use this for initialization
void Start ()
{
        int a = 7;
        string b = "7";
        print (a.ToString() == b);//prints True
}
```

Even though we have two different types here, we can convert an `int` to a `string` by using the `ToString()` function in the `int` data class. Here we've got an `int` 7 and we're comparing it to the `string` "7"; when the `int` is converted to a `string`, the comparison results in `True` printed to the Unity's Console panel when run. We can do some more simple type conversions to confirm some basic concepts.

```
//Use this for initialization
void Start ()
{
        int a = 7;
        float b = 7.0f;
        print (a == b);//prints True
}
```

### 6.21.2  More Type Casting

We can compare `ints` and `floats` without conversion. This works because C# will convert the `int` to a `float` implicitly before the comparison is made. However, C# does know that they are different types.

```
//Use this for initialization
void Start ()
{
        int a = 7;
        float b = 7.9f;
        print (a == b);//prints False
        print (a == (int)b);//prints True
}
```

We can force the cast using the `(int)` on b that was assigned 7.9, which we know is clearly greater than 7. However, when we cast `float` 7.9 to an `int`, we lose the numbers following the decimal. This makes the cast version of the comparison true.

Can we cast a string to a number data type?

```
//Use this for initialization
void Start ()
{
        int a = 7;
        string b = "7";
        print (a == (int)b);//doesn't work
}
```

No, there's no built-in method to allow us to change a `string` data type into an `int` or any other number type. Therefore, type conversion has limitations. However, don't let this get in your way. Comparing values should used with like types to begin with. What else can we compare?

```
GameObject a = GameObject.CreatePrimitive(PrimitiveType.Capsule);
GameObject b = GameObject.CreatePrimitive(PrimitiveType.Capsule);
print (a == b);//False?
```

What is being compared here? Well, these are actually two different objects in the scene. Even though they share a good number of attributes, they are not the same object. A more clear way to compare two instances of a game object is to use the following fragment:

```
GameObject a = GameObject.CreatePrimitive(PrimitiveType.Capsule);
GameObject b = GameObject.CreatePrimitive(PrimitiveType.Capsule);
print (a.GetInstanceID());
print (b.GetInstanceID());
print (a.GetInstanceID() == b.GetInstanceID());//False
```

Here we're being more specific as to what we're comparing. If every object in the scene has a unique instance ID, then we're going to more clearly debug and test what's being compared when we need to check objects in the scene for matches. When we compare objects in the scene, which don't have a clear comparison, there's usually a method to allow us to make a more readable difference between objects.

```
GameObject a = GameObject.CreatePrimitive(PrimitiveType.Capsule);
GameObject b = a;
print (a == b);//True
```

In this case, yes, they are the same object, so the behavior is correct. However, again we should do the following to ensure that we're comparing something more easily debugged.

```
void Start () {
        int a = GameObject.CreatePrimitive(PrimitiveType.Capsule).
GetInstanceID();
        int b = a;
        print (a);
        print (b);
        print (a == b);//True
}
```

The above code produces the following output in the Console panel:

```
-3474
UnityEngine.MonoBehaviour:print(Object)
TypeCasting:Start () (at Assets/TypeCasting.cs:10)
-3474
UnityEngine.MonoBehaviour:print(Object)
TypeCasting:Start () (at Assets/TypeCasting.cs:11)
True
UnityEngine.MonoBehaviour:print(Object)
TypeCasting:Start () (at Assets/TypeCasting.cs:12)
```

Now we're looking at something that makes more sense. It's always important to understand what our code is doing. In some cases, it's unavoidable, but there's nearly always a method that's available to give us data that we can read.

In the case where we are looking to see if they are GameObjects, we'd need to check for type. This means that we can make sure that we're looking for GameObjects. To do this, we need to check if one object's type matches another object's type.

```
void Start ()
{
        GameObject a = GameObject.CreatePrimitive(PrimitiveType.Capsule);
        GameObject b = GameObject.CreatePrimitive(PrimitiveType.Capsule);
        print (a);
        print (b);
        print (a.GetType() == b.GetType());//True
}
```

There is a very important difference here. We're starting with two objects of type GameObject. This allows us many more options than an int type. GameObjects contain many more functions that allow for many more complicated comparisons. GameObject a and GameObject b can be checked for their type. Therefore, a.GetType() and b.GetType() will return the same GameObject type. The significant difference here is the fact that the type of data in memory has a type, that is to say, there's a form or shape that each data has in the computer's memory.

Therefore, GameObjects have an associated type; this also means that we can make our own types. So far with every class we write, we are creating new types of data. To see this concept in operation, it's best to write a couple of simple classes to test. Let's look at what other types are for a moment.

```
        int c = 1;
        Debug.Log(c.GetType());
```

The above code sends the following output to the Console panel:

```
System.Int32
UnityEngine.Debug:Log(Object)
TypeCasting:Start () (at Assets/TypeCasting.cs:14)
```

We've discovered that c is a System.Int32, so what are a and b?

```
UnityEngine.GameObject
UnityEngine.Debug:Log(Object)
TypeCasting:Start () (at Assets/TypeCasting.cs:14)
```

The GameObject a is a UnityEngine.GameObject, which is the same as b. Because they are of the same type of data, the check from a == b is true. We should investigate a few other types. Let's see the following code fragment:

```
        float c = 1.0f;
        Debug.Log(c.GetType());
```

With the above code, we get the following debug information sent to the Console panel :

```
System.Single
UnityEngine.Debug:Log(Object)
TypeCasting:Start () (at Assets/TypeCasting.cs:14)
```

Even though the type we're using is called float, C# interprets it as a System.Single.

```
        System.Single c = 1.0f;
        Debug.Log(c.GetType());
```

### 6.21.3 Type Aliasing

We could use the above code in place of float, but float is the naming convention that started with C#. Therefore, we'll give in to convention and use float rather than System.Single, even though both are acceptable by C#. The word float came from someone early on in C# who decided to add a type alias. We can add our own type aliases with a using statement.

```
using UnityEngine;
using System.Collections;
using MyOwnIntType = System.Int16;
```

Along with the directives we're used to seeing at the top of our classes, we can add in another using directive. Adding using MyOwnIntType, we can assign it to System.Int16; which turns our identifier MyOwnIntType into a System.Int16.

```
MyOwnInt c = 1;
Debug.Log(c.GetType());
```

Using the above fragment produces the following Console output:

```
System.Int16
UnityEngine.Debug:Log(Object)
TypeCasting:Start () (at Assets/TypeCasting.cs:15)
```

Therefore, the float was assigned to System.Single somewhere in the depths of Unity 3D. It's unlikely that we're going to find out where the convention of using float is a Single, but it's important to know how the keyword was assigned. The fact is that the float keyword, even though it has become superfluous in programming, is still just the alias given to a System.Single.

Likewise, int or double and some other keywords we commonly use are just aliases to simplify our code. Other systems have aliased the system types with words such as bigint, smallint, and tinyint as mappings to different numbers of bytes held for the integer value.

Therefore, now that we know a bit where types come from and how to convert one type into another, it's time to put this to some use.

### 6.21.4 Boxing and Unboxing

*Boxing* is the term that programmers use when a generic container is used to assign a multitude of types. Once it's discovered what has been "put in a box," we can decide what to do next. When the data is pulled from the variable, you "unbox" the data once you know what it is and what to do with it.

For instance, we can get all of the objects in a scene and put them into an array GameObject[] allObjects. This includes the Main Camera and any lights in the scene as well as any monsters, players, and environment objects. If you look through the list for anything that has a Zombie() class attached, you can then take the closest GameObject with a Zombie component and carry out any operations involving that particular object. This unboxes that one Zombie from the array and allows you to interact with it.

## 6.22 Operator Overloading

What happens if you'd like to do something specific when you add one zombie to another? Operators, like anything else it seems in C#, can have additional functionality added to them. When it comes to dealing with new classes, we need to manage data using methods which we feel fit. In most cases, operator overloading should be considered a bit like voodoo.

```
class Zombie
{
}
void Start ()
{
    Zombie a = new Zombie();
    Zombie b = new Zombie();
    Zombie c = a + b;
}
```

Therefore, this might not be a common scenario, but it's likely that we might want to tell our game what to do in case we would like to add two zombies together to make a third. Say for instance, our zombie had a damage number.

```
class Zombie
{
    public int damage = 10;
}
```

With this value, we might want to add zombie's damages together if we add one zombie to another. In that case, if we had zombie a and b in a scene and a designer decided that it would be cool for them to merge into a bigger zombie, we could go through a process of adding one zombie to another through a function. Intuitively, we might want to use an operator instead.

```
class Zombie
{
    public int damage = 10;
    public static Zombie operator + (Zombie a, Zombie b)
    {
    }
}
```

We start by adding a new function using the pattern we've got used to with accessor property identifier. This time we follow with a type, in this case Zombie followed by operator + to tell C# that we're intending to overload the + operator. In our argument list that we use, enter the left and right sides of the operator we're overloading.

The problem with operator overloading between classes of a nonnumerical value is the fact that there is a loss in readability. For purposes of learning how to do this, we'll ignore this fact; however, do consider operator overloading something best avoided. Most of the time, the operators used on numbers are sufficient and should be left alone. When working on classes you've created, the common math operators should be left to operating on numbers.

### 6.22.1 A Basic Example

With the OperatorOverloading project, open the Example component on the Main Camera and open that in MonoDevelop.

```
public static Zombie operator + (Zombie a, Zombie b)
{
    Zombie z = new Zombie();
    int powerUp = a.damage + b.damage;
    z.damage = powerUp;
    return z;
}
```

Therefore, our designer decides that we need to add Zombie a's damage to Zombie b's damage to produce Zombie c's damage. We add the required statements to fulfill the request into the + operator overloading function. Start by creating an object to return, which fulfills the requirement of the data type inferred after the public static keywords.

Therefore, once we're done adding a's damage to b's damage, we can set our new zombie's z.damage to the added result. Once we're done with all of our adding behaviors, we can return z to the statement where it was called from.

In this case, Zombie c = a + b; where variable c now gets the result of our overloaded + operator.

```
void Start ()
{
    Zombie a = new Zombie();
    Zombie b = new Zombie();
    Debug.Log(a.damage);
    Debug.Log(b.damage);
    Zombie c = a + b;
    Debug.Log(c.damage);
}
```

With the above code, we get the following debug information sent to the Console panel:

```
10
UnityEngine.Debug:Log(Object)
OperatorOverloading:Start () (at Assets/OperatorOverloading.cs:18)
10
UnityEngine.Debug:Log(Object)
OperatorOverloading:Start () (at Assets/OperatorOverloading.cs:19)
20
UnityEngine.Debug:Log(Object)
OperatorOverloading:Start () (at Assets/OperatorOverloading.cs:21)
```

To add some more meaningful context to apply operator overloading, we'll look at a more interesting example.

```
class Supplies
{
    public int bandages;
    public int ammunition;
    public float weight;
    public Supplies(int size)
    {
        bandages = size;
        ammunition = size * 2;
        weight = bandages * 0.2f + ammunition * 0.7f;
    }
}
```

If we have a supply box that is a standard item in our game, we might want to have a simple method to add one supply box to another. In our code, this becomes something pretty interesting when we add a constructor that has a bit of math involved to automatically calculate the weight based on the items in the supply box. Here we're adding some arbitrary weight from the bandages and ammunition to the weight of the supply box.

After the `Supplies` constructor is set up, we're going to add in a behavior for the + operator.

```
public static Supplies operator + (Supplies a, Supplies b)
{
     Supplies s = new Supplies(0);
     int sBandanges = a.bandages + b.bandages;
     int sAmmunition = a.ammunition + b.ammunition;
     float sWeight = a.weight + b.weight;
     s.bandages = sBandanges;
     s.ammunition = sAmmunition;
     s.weight = sWeight;
     return s;
}
```

This simply takes the combination of a's and b's contents and adds them together and sets a new `Supplies` object to the combined values. At the end, we return the new object.

```
void Start ()
{
     Supplies supplyA = new Supplies(3);
     Supplies supplyB = new Supplies(9);
     Supplies combinedAB = supplyA + supplyB;
     Debug.Log(combinedAB.weight);
}
```

If we create two copies of the `Supplies` object and add them together, we get a final result that reacts how you might expect. This works as you might expect with any other math operator. The following code also produces an expected result:

```
Supplies supplyA = new Supplies(3);
Supplies supplyB = new Supplies(9);
Supplies combinedAB = supplyA + supplyB;
Debug.Log(combinedAB.weight);
Supplies abc = supplyA + supplyB + combinedAB;
Debug.Log(abc.weight);
```

The final weight of `supplyA` + `supplyB` with another `supplyA` and another `supplyB` is 38.4 units of weight. The overload is required to be static because this is a function that acts on the `Supplies` object at a class-wide scope. Should we need to go lower into the structure to give us the ability to add bandage `C = bandageA+bandageB;`, we'd need to make a class for that with an operator overload of its own.

## 6.22.2 Overloading *

We're not restricted to overloading a class by a class. As in the above example, we're adding supplies to more supplies. We can overload our `Supplies operator *` with a number.

```
public static Supplies operator * (Supplies a, int b) {
     Supplies s = new Supplies(0);
     int sBandages = a.bandages * b;
     int sAmmunition = a.ammunition * b;
     float sWeight = a.weight * b;
```

```
                    s.bandages = sBandages;
                    s.ammunition = sAmmunition;
                    s.weight = sWeight;
                    return s;
            }
```

In the above example, we take supplies and multiply it by int b. To make use of the new operator, our code would have to look something like the following:

```
            Supplies sm = new Supplies(5);
            Debug.Log(sm.weight);
            sm = sm * 3;
            Debug.Log(sm.weight);
```

In this case, our sm = sm * 3; takes the original and then multiplies it by 3 and accepts the new value for itself. The log for this sends 8 followed by 24 to the Console panel. This also means that we can use the following modification to get 32 printed to the Console panel: sm = sm + sm * 3;.

In addition to the previous examples using + and *, we can also overload the true and false keywords. For operators such as > and <, we can test if one zombie is more dangerous than another.

### 6.22.3 Overloading <

Operators that return a bool value can also be overridden. The operators < and > can be overridden to return a true or false value. The code fragment that accomplishes this is as follows:

```
        public static bool operator < (Zombie a, Zombie b)
        {
                if (a.damage < b.damage)
                {
                        return true;
                } else {
                        return false;
                }
        }
```

Before we can use this, Unity 3D will likely remind us that we're forgetting something with the following error message:

```
Assets/OperatorOverloading.cs(46,36): error CS0216: The operator
'OperatorOverloading.Zombie.operator <(OperatorOverloading.Zombie,
OperatorOverloading.Zombie)' requires a matching operator '>' to also be defined
```

To comply we'll add in the opposite version of the less than < operator overload. Using this we would compare the two zombies in our Start () function with the following statement:

```
        public static bool operator >(Zombie a, Zombie b)
        {
                if (a.damage > b.damage)
                {
                        return true;
                } else {
                        return false;
                }
        }
```

A quick copy/paste and a replacement of less than < to greater than > is all it takes to allow us to use the less than < and greater than > overload. In our `Start ()` function, we can use the following few statements to check if our overload is working.

```
Zombie a = new Zombie();
Zombie b = new Zombie();
a.damage = 9;
if(a < b)
{
    Debug.Log("a has less damage!");
}
```

If the default initialization of the zombie's health is set to 10, then Zombie  a does indeed have less damage left than Zombie b. In this `if` statement, we do get the "a has less damage!" printed to our Console panel. Does this mean that he's more dead than Zombie b? I guess this question is left to the designer on what to do with this information.

However you decide to use overloaded operators is left to how you've decided to work with your classes. In many cases, if you find yourself comparing a few variables between two objects of the same class to execute some block of code, then you should consider using an operator overload. Likewise, if you find yourself adding multiple things together using the + for multiple attributes, then that's another candidate for an overload.

### 6.22.4  What We've Learned

With all of what we just learned, you should be able to see how overriding less than < and greater than > can be useful in terms of sorting. You'd be able to make a sort based on specific properties between classes. Comparing distances and threat levels can be a very interesting behavior.

Some of what we're doing here is a bit awkward and mostly contrived. In general, greater than > and less than < should be used to compare more numeric values. In the above code, comparing two zombies directly is misleading. Are we comparing size, armor, and number of brains eaten? It's impossible to know with the operator alone. In this case, `a.armor > b.armor` would make far more sense.

It's important to always leave the code in a readable state. Simply comparing two classes against one another makes it impossible to know exactly what it is we're comparing. This also goes for any other math operator. In general, math operations are best suited for numbers, not zombies.

## 6.23  Controlling Inheritance

Dealing with various uses for inheritance is key to using any OOP. The key features for OOP include keeping control over each inherited object. Some features should not be directly overridden. It's up to you to decide on how this is maintained, but once you're working in a group, this control is going to be lost.

If someone needs to add behaviors to a class, but you require something like movement to remain consistent between all classes, then you'll have to implement various systems to keep people from breaking your code. Sealed class, often referred to as a final class, cannot be inherited from. This sort of data ends the line as far as inheritance is concerned. This class is used when you want to finalize a class and prevent any further inheritance.

Class inheritance works by layering changes on top of a base class. Each layer can either add new functions or modify functions that are inherited from its base. In general, all of the functions found in the base class are going to exist in any class inheriting from it.

The common metaphor used to describe inheritance is a family tree; however, what more closely describes class inheritance is biological classification or scientific taxonomy. This is a system to organize and categorize organisms into groups such as species, family, and class. Each category is a taxonomic rank.

To biologists the species *Agaricus bisporus*, the average button mushroom, belongs to the genus *Agaricus* of the family Agaricaceae of the order Agaricales in the phylum Basidiomycota in the kingdom Fungi. That's quite a mouthful, even if you don't like them on pizza.

In a very similar way, when you create a `Zombie : MonoBehaviour`, you are creating a class `Zombie` based on `MonoBehaviour`, `Behaviour`, `Component`, `Object`, and `object`. Notice that `Object` with an uppercase O is based on `object` with a lowercase o.

In this ranking and categorizing of mushrooms and zombies, the hierarchy that is formed means there are common traits shared among objects. A death cap mushroom is a fungus like a button mushroom. Both share common traits, reproduce by spreading spores, and have similar structures made of chitin. One of these makes pizza deadly, and the other just makes pizza yummy.

In a similar way, all of the classes we've written based on `MonoBehaviour` share common features, for example, `Start ()` and `Update ()`. From `Behavior`, they inherit `enabled`. From `Component`, they inherit various messaging and component properties. `Object` gives them the ability to instantiate or destroy themselves and find one another. Finally, `object` gives them all `ToString()`.

Nature might take aeons to create a new class of life. For a programmer, a new class in Unity 3D just takes a few mouse clicks. Programmers also have the ability to override how inherited functions behave. However, unexpected behaviors usually result in bugs. To control this, it's best to put preventative measures around inherited functions through encapsulation and special controls.

### 6.23.1 Sealed

The `sealed` prefix to a function is one of the systems that allows you to control how a function is inherited. Once you've written a well-constructed class, it's a good idea to go back and prevent anyone from breaking it. The sealed keyword prevents a class member from being misused by a child inheriting the member.

One commonly written class is a `timer`. The `timer` should have some features such as setting the length of time for the timer, asking for how much time is left, pausing and restarting the timer, and events for when the timer ends and starts.

If you want all of the timers to behave exactly the same, then you'll have to prevent anyone from making any unnecessary modifications to the `timer` class. This is why they need to be sealed. A `sealed` class is meant to prevent any further modifications from the point where it has been sealed.

### 6.23.1.1 A Basic Example

Adding in the `sealed` keyword before the `class` keyword does the trick. Once this is added, no class is allowed to inherit from the class. In the Sealed project, let's look at the `FinalizedObject` class attached to the Main Camera.

```
using UnityEngine;
using System.Collections;
public sealed class FinalizedObject : MonoBehaviour
{
    //Use this for initialization
    void Start ()
    {
    }
    //Update is called once per frame
    void Update ()
    {
    }
}
```

Once in place, you can create another class in an attempt to inherit from it. The following class tries to inherit from the `sealed` class:

```
using UnityEngine;
using System.Collections;
public class InheritFromSealed : FinalizedObject
{
    //Use this for initialization
    void Start ()
    {
    }
    //Update is called once per frame
    void Update ()
    {
    }
}
```

This, of course, produces the following error in the Unity's Console panel:

```
Assets/InheritFromSealed.cs(4,14): error CS0509: 'InheritFromSealed': cannot
derive from sealed type 'FinalizedObject'
```

It would be easy to remove the `sealed` keyword from the class and open it up for basing more classes on it. However, this does inform you that you are indeed making a change that isn't intended. This behavior is meant to limit the amount of tampering of a class written to do something specific. Usually, classes written with `sealed` are for very basic and very widely available functions that shouldn't require any other class to inherit from it.

The key notion is that a class that is widely available should be stable and unchanging. Reliability is key for preventing too many bugs from creeping into your code. All of the different accessibility modifications such as `sealed` are intended to help prevent unexpected behavior. Of course, this doesn't by any stretch of the imagination mean that it prevents bugs completely.

## 6.23.2 Abstract

Related to how classes inherit behavior from their parent class, the `abstract` keyword is another clever keyword. The `abstract` keyword is used to tell inheriting classes that there's a function they need to implement. If you forget to implement a function that was marked as `abstract`, Unity 3D will remind you and throw an error.

### 6.23.2.1 A Basic Example

To inform another programmer, or yourself that you need to implement a specific function, the `abstract` keyword is used. Setting up a class to inherit from helps you plan your classes and how the classes are intended to be used.

```
using UnityEngine;
using System.Collections;
public class Abstraction : MonoBehaviour
{
    abstract class BaseClass
    {
        public int Counter;
        public abstract void ImportantFunction();
    }
    class ChildClass : BaseClass
    {
        public override void ImportantFunction()
```

```
        {
            Counter++;
            Debug.Log(Counter);
        }
    }
    void Start () {
        ChildClass c = new ChildClass();
        c.ImportantFunction();
        c.ImportantFunction();
        c.ImportantFunction();
        c.ImportantFunction();
    }
}
```

The example above creates two nested classes in the `Abstraction.cs` class based on `MonoBehaviour`. The first class is called `BaseClass`. This provides two things: an `int` to count with and an `abstract` function. The `int` is called `counter` and the function has been named `ImportantFunction()`. A class with an `abstract` function in it is required to be declared as abstract as well.

```
abstract class    BaseClass
{
        public int counter;
        public abstract void ImportantFunction();

}
```

The `abstract` keyword implies that the function declared is a stub. This tells the programmer who is inheriting from the `BaseClass` that there's an important function which he or she has to implement. The implementation, however, is left up to the author of the child class.

For instance, if we're making monsters, we'd have a monster base class and some sort of `attackHuman();` function that all monsters will need to do. Vampires, zombies, and werewolves all need to do some `attackHuman()` function. How and what that function entails differs between each monster. How this is implemented depends on the monster and who is writing the function.

When a function is preceded by the `abstract` keyword, the function cannot have a body. This might look like the following:

```
    abstract class BaseClass
    {
        public int Counter;
        public abstract void ImportantFunction()
        {
                //no code allowed
        }
    }
```

Should there be any code at all in the `abstract` `ImportantFunction()`, you'll get the following error:

```
Assets/Abstraction.cs(9,38): error CS0500:
'Abstraction.BaseClass.ImportantFunction()' cannot declare a body because it
is marked abstract
```

This only means to inform you that you cannot implement an abstract function. You must rely on a child class making the implementation. The intent here is to provide a clear and specific structure for all classes inheriting from the BaseClass.

```
class ChildClass : BaseClass
{
    public override void ImportantFunction()
    {
        Counter++;
        Debug.Log(Counter);
    }
}
```

The function in ChildClass that is inheriting from BaseClass needs to use override to inform C# that it is indeed writing the implementation for the important function. The result of this ChildClass is to increment the Counter up by 1, with each call to ImportantFunction() after a Debug.Log() call. When Start () is called in the Abstraction.cs class, we make an instance of the ChildClass and call the important function a few times to get 0, 1, 2, and 3 printed to the Console panel.

To continue we should make a sibling class similar to ChildClass with a different implementation of the ImportantFunction() call.

```
class SiblingClass : BaseClass
{
    public override void ImportantFunction()
    {
        Counter-- ;
        Debug.Log(Counter);
    }
}
```

This time we decrement Counter by 1 each time the function is called. Therefore, if the following lines are added to the Start () function, we can get some set of numbers going up and another set going down.

```
void Start () {
    ChildClass c = new ChildClass();
    c.ImportantFunction();
    c.ImportantFunction();
    c.ImportantFunction();
    c.ImportantFunction();
    SiblingClass s = new SiblingClass();
    s.ImportantFunction();
    s.ImportantFunction();
    s.ImportantFunction();
    s.ImportantFunction();
}
```

This results in the following Console output:

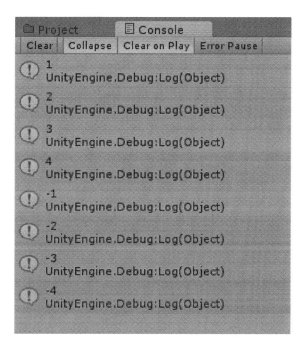

If the classes are considered final, they can be sealed.

```
sealed class ChildClass : BaseClass
{
        public override void ImportantFunction()
        {
                Counter++;
                Debug.Log(Counter);
        }
}
```

This means that the ChildClass can no longer be derived from. However, this doesn't apply to the SiblingClass that hasn't been sealed. The Sibling is considered a branch from BaseClass. One interesting test case we can observe is using sealed on an abstract class. Of course, but adding sealed to the BaseClass looks like the following:

```
abstract sealed class BaseClass
{
        public int Counter;
        public abstract void ImportantFunction();
}
```

This results in both `ChildClass` and `SiblingClass` breaking with the following error:

```
Assets/Abstraction.cs(12,22): error CS0709: 'Abstraction.ChildClass': Cannot
derive from static class 'Abstraction.BaseClass'
Assets/Abstraction.cs(21,15): error CS0709: 'Abstraction.SiblingClass':
Cannot derive from static class 'Abstraction.BaseClass'
```

The `sealed` keyword really means it. Once you've sealed a class, any classes deriving from it will immediately break. Keep this in mind when you start structuring how classes derive from one another. As another interesting experiment, what happens if we want to create the instance of the base class?

```
void Start ()
{
    BaseClass b = new BaseClass();
}
```

We can create instances of each child class based on `BaseClass()`, but we cannot use the `BaseClass` itself. We get an error that looks like the following:

```
Assets/Abstraction.cs(34,46): error CS0144: Cannot create an instance of the
abstract class or interface 'Abstraction.BaseClass'
```

C# is informing us that it cannot create an instance of the `abstract` class or interface `BaseClass`. An interface works in a similar way to an `abstract` class, but with a few more restrictions. All of these mechanisms are there to prevent problematic issues that have come up with different languages. We'll get into the hows and whys of the interface in Section 7.6.4.

### 6.23.3 Abstract: Abstract

The topic should be expanded to look at additional abstract classes inheriting from abstract classes. These can be used to add more diversity to a simple base class. By creating a branch that is also abstract, you can add more data fields and functions to provide a variation on the first idea.

```
abstract class BaseClass
{
    public int Counter;
    public abstract void ImportantFunction();
}
abstract class SecondaryClass : BaseClass
{
    public int Limit;
    public abstract bool AtLimit();
    public abstract void SetLimit(int l);
}
```

Here we have the `abstract class SecondaryClass` that is based on the `abstract class BaseClass`. We are allowed to add some additional fields and functions to this secondary class. The advantage here is that we don't need to make any modifications to the `BaseClass`, as there might be other classes relying on its stability. Keeping code intact is important, and diving into base classes and making changes could cause problems to ripple through the rest of the project.

Changing inheriting classes is simple; change the `: BaseClass` to `: SecondaryClass` and C# will tell you what you need to fix.

```
sealed class ChildClass : SecondaryClass
{
    public override void ImportantFunction()
```

```
            {
                Counter++;
                Debug.Log(Counter);
            }
    }
```

With the inheritance changed here, we get a simple warning:

```
Assets/Abstraction.cs(18,22): error CS0534: 'Abstraction.ChildClass' does not
implement inherited abstract member 'Abstraction.SecondaryClass.AtLimit()'
Assets/Abstraction.cs(19,22): error CS0534: 'Abstraction.ChildClass' does not
implement inherited abstract member 'Abstraction.SecondaryClass.SetLimit(int)'
```

We need to implement the abstract member AtLimit(); and SetLimit(int); which is great; this means that we get to keep our current implementation of ImportantFunction() and we need to add only the missing functions.

```
    sealed class ChildClass : SecondaryClass
    {
        public override void ImportantFunction()
        {
            Counter++;
            Debug.Log(Counter);
        }
        public override bool AtLimit()
        {
            return Counter > = Limit;
        }
        public override void SetLimit(int l)
        {
            Limit = l;
        }
    }
```

Here we've written some simple implementations of AtLimit(); and SetLimit(int); for the ChildClass. To check if we are indeed at the limit, we use return Counter> = Limit;. This works only because Limit is a member of the SecondaryClass and Counter is found in BaseClass. The inheritance allows the ChildClass to use both of these data fields together.

Next we have SetLimit(int); that accepts a number to set the limit. In the Start () function in the Abstraction.cs class, we can add the following code to test our modifications to ChildClass:

```
        ChildClass c = new ChildClass();
        c.SetLimit(2);
        c.ImportantFunction();//prints 1
        Debug.Log(c.AtLimit());//prints False
        c.ImportantFunction();//prints 2
        Debug.Log(c.AtLimit());//prints True
```

This sends the following output to the Console panel in Unity 3D:

```
1
UnityEngine.Debug:Log(Object)
ChildClass:ImportantFunction() (at Assets/Abstraction.cs:23)
Abstraction:Start () (at Assets/Abstraction.cs:52)
False
UnityEngine.Debug:Log(Object)
Abstraction:Start () (at Assets/Abstraction.cs:53)
```

```
2
UnityEngine.Debug:Log(Object)
ChildClass:ImportantFunction() (at Assets/Abstraction.cs:23)
Abstraction:Start () (at Assets/Abstraction.cs:54)
True
UnityEngine.Debug:Log(Object)
Abstraction:Start () (at Assets/Abstraction.cs:55)
```

### 6.23.4 Putting This to Use

We'll start with a construct that's used fairly often for many different game systems.

```
using UnityEngine;
using System.Collections;
public abstract class BaseTimer
{
        public float time;
        public float endTime;
        public float remainingTime;
        public float normalizedTime;
        public abstract void SetTime(float t);
        public abstract bool Ended();
        public abstract void BeginTimer();
}
```

An `abstract BaseTimer` gives us a few interesting things to work with. First off, the big difference here is the fact that we're not using `MonoBehaviour` as our base class for the `BaseTimer`. We're going to make this a base class for use in any number of other classes that will have their own update functions, so we won't need to use an `Update ()` function in this class.

Next we'll make an implementation of this abstract class called `CountdownTimer();`, in which we can set a number of seconds and check for the `Ended()` boolean to become `true`.

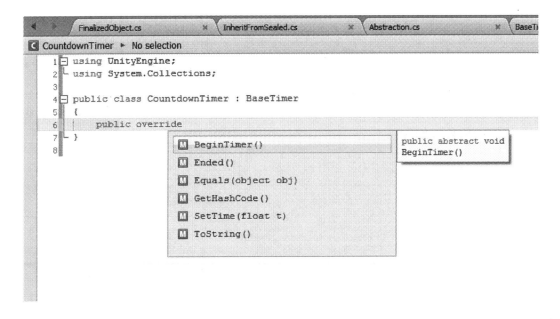

As we begin to populate our new `CountdownTimer` with `public override`, we can make use of MonoDevelop's handy pop-up.

Selecting `SetTime` automatically fills in the rest of the function with some placeholder code. As the functions are stubbed in, the number of functions appearing in the pop-up is reduced to only the remaining functions waiting to be implemented. The seemingly extra functions `ToString()`, `Equals()`, and `GetHashCode()` are described in `Object()`, which is what every class created in Unity 3D is based on by default. These are provided by default and can be ignored.

```
using UnityEngine;
using System.Collections;
public class CountdownTimer : BaseTimer
{
        public override void BeginTimer()
        {
                throw new System.NotImplementedException();
        }
        public override bool Ended()
        {
                throw new System.NotImplementedException();
        }
        public override bool Equals(object obj)
        {
                return base.Equals(obj);
        }
        public override int GetHashCode()
        {
                return base.GetHashCode();
        }
        public override void SetTime(float t)
        {
                throw new System.NotImplementedException();
        }
        public override string ToString()
        {
                return string.Format("[CountdownTimer]");
        }
}
```

With all of the functions we're concerned with stubbed in, we can begin to flesh them out. The first function sets how long the timer will last. For this we'll simply add the following code to replace the system error:

```
public override void SetTime (float t)
{
     time = t;
}
```

This sets the `float` time to t in `SetTime(float);`. From here we can move on to the next function.

```
public override void BeginTimer ()
{
     endTime = Time.fixedTime + time;
}
```

This turns into a pretty simple process of setting up each function with a simple implementation of each function. The only thing to watch out for here is the automatic word replacement happening in MonoDevelop trying to change `time` to `Time`. Next up is the `bool` for the `Ended()` function.

```
public override bool Ended ()
{
     return Time.fixedTime > = endTime;
}
```

When `Time.fixedTime` is larger than or equal to the `endTime`, then the function returns `true`, otherwise the function returns `false`. Now we're about ready to give this a try.

```
CountdownTimer countdown;
void Start ()
{
     countdown = new CountdownTimer();
     countdown.SetTime(3.0f);
     countdown.BeginTimer();
}
void Update ()
{
     if (countdown.Ended())
     {
          Debug.Log("end");
     }
}
```

In the `FinalizedObject.cs` class that was attached to the Main Camera at the beginning of this chapter, we can make use of our new `CountdownTimer` class. We need to make a variable for the `CountdownTimer` so it can be shared between our `Start ()` and our `Update ()` functions. Therefore, a `public CountdownTimer countdown;` is added at the class scope.

Once in the `Start ()` function, we can add in the statement to instantiate a new `CountdownTimer()` with `countdown = new CountdownTimer();`. Follow this with a statement to set the length of the timer and a statement to start it.

Once in the `Update ()` loop, we use the `countdown.Ended()` to check on each update whether or not the countdown has ended. Once it has, we begin to send end to the Console panel. To restart the countdown, we just need to call the `BeginTimer()` function again and wait for `Ended()` to be true again.

### 6.23.5 What We've Learned

We can continue to make variations on the `BaseTimer` class fairly easily. We can make an implementation called `CountupTimer` that will be true until the timer has ended. All we'd have to do is switch one operator in the `Ended()` function and one operator in the `BeginTimer()` function to the following:

```
public override void BeginTimer ()
{
    endTime = Time.fixedTime - time;
}
public override bool Ended ()
{
    return Time.fixedTime < endTime;
}
```

This code changes the behavior and adds a variety of systems which we can use in our game. We added a normalized variable which we can use to show us a value between 0 and 1 when it's queried.

```
public override bool Ended ()
{
    normalizedTime = (endTime-Time.fixedTime)/time;
    return Time.fixedTime > = endTime;
}
```

We can set this by using the above addition to the `Ended()` check. In the `Abstraction.cs` class, we can look at the `normalizedTime` value with the following debug statement.

```
void Update () {
    Debug.Log(countdown.normalizedTime);
    if(countdown.Ended()) {
        countdown.BeginTimer();
    }
}
```

With this change, we can watch the values start near 1.0 and decrease toward 0.0, and reset based on what was used in the `SetTime()` function. This is a very basic timer, but its use can be shared between many different classes. Each class can have any number of timers set up to trigger various changes in behavior.

Zombies can wait for the timer to end before climbing out of the ground after they've spawned. They can set a different timer to tell them how often to search for a new target. Timers can be used for any number of different tasks.

Once a timer has been used in more than a couple of classes, it's time to seal it off to prevent its modification. Any modifications that might change its behavior could result in many different unexpected behaviors from any classes using it.

If any new types of timers are required, it's better to create a new branch and make a new implementation of the `BaseTimer` rather than tweak the timer already in use. It's easy to say that having too many different implementations of a timer class can create a headache for anyone coming in late to the project. If not wisely implemented, each programmer might end up with his or her version of a timer, which isn't optimal.

The coordination of all of this is dependent on how you've structured your team of programmers. Any individual change can have wide-reaching problems if unchecked. C# in general is built to allow for these sorts of behaviors, both better and worse. In the end, it's up to your ability to communicate and share your plans with the rest of your team to keep your code under control.

## 6.24 Leveling Up

*Building up some skills.* We're getting pretty deep into C#. This section contains a great deal of the things that make C# powerful and flexible. A great deal of the code we've learned up to this point allow us to get functional and get some basic work done. Even some of the more complex tasks can be completed with what we already know.

We had a short introduction to the more interesting constructs that make up C#. It's about time we had a short review of constructors, namespaces, and inheritance. We'll also look at more uses of arrays, enums, and `goto` labels. All of these systems make up a part of the skills that every C# programmer uses.

# 7

## Advanced

Chapter 6 was complex and covered many interesting topics. No doubt if you've gotten this far you're willing to find out more about what C# can do. It's difficult to say just how much you can do with what you know. Even with the content of Chapters 1 through 5, you would be capable of quite a lot of things.

Most game logic and control systems need only the fundamentals that have been provided up in Chapters 3 through 6. Once the behaviors need more coordinated events and simultaneous actions, you'll need to learn a few more tricks.

To make your work more predictable and to prevent bugs, you'll need practice; there are also some features that make C# more precise. This is to say that you would be able to enforce your own structure to how you allow others to work with your code in the ways you intended.

Since programming is just reading and writing text, there are many things that can go wrong. A simple misspelling or misplaced dot operator can break everything. There are many systems which you can use to help your fellow programmers follow your instructions through how they interact with what you've written.

### 7.1 What Will Be Covered in This Chapter

Many layers of simple code with layers of basic logic create a complex behavior. C# allows for many different ways to keep your code contained in simple classes and functions. Simple classes and functions are easier to write and debug. Complex behaviors required for game interactions come about when you combine many simple behaviors with interesting logic.

We'll look at the following features in this chapter:

- MonoDevelop's user interface (UI) and navigation of some of their interface widgets
- Further exploration into comments
- More function overloading
- More on base classes
- Optional parameters in functions' argument lists
- Delegate functions
- Class interfaces
- Class constructors again
- Basic preprocessor directives
- Exceptions
- Generics
- Events
- Unity 3D-friendly classes
- Destructors
- Concurrency and coroutines
- Dictionary, `stack`, and queue types
- Callbacks
- Lambda expressions
- Accessors or properties

## 7.2 Review

In the previous chapter, we looked at some interesting material. We were able to overload the regular + and − with some new functionality. We looked at a few new ways to use the argument list in a function and write a loop.

There are some additional concepts worth mentioning. There are several online articles on the allocation of objects to either the `stack` or the heap. The heap is built up in order, but isn't rearranged too often.

When objects are added to the heap, the size of the heap grows. When objects are destroyed, they leave holes in the heap. This leaves gaps between the objects that were not deleted. Suppose we have 100 spaces in memory and object A takes up addresses from 1 to 20, B takes up from 21 to 40, and C takes up from 40 to 60. When object B is removed, spaces 21 to 40 are empty, between A and C. If a new object D is only a bit bigger than 20 spaces, say 22, it needs to find the next biggest place at the end, so D uses 61 to 82. If another object D is created, we're out of luck and the game stops running due to lack of memory.

The `stack`, however, is more organized based on how your code is executed. When a `for` loop is started, the `int i = 0;` parameter is always tossed into the top of the `stack`; as soon as it's no longer needed, it's chopped off, leaving room for the next object to be added to the `stack`.

In the end, memory management is a result of how you've arranged your data. So long as you use structs to move around large amounts of complex data, you'll most likely be allocating them to the `stack`. By instancing too many classes, you're leaving yourself to the heap that can eventually lead to memory problems. There is a problem if a `stack` is passed around in a class, in which case you're still working in the heap.

### 7.2.1 Moving Forward

We don't want to limit our experiences to the lessons we've just managed to get through. There's still plenty left to learn when it comes to the interesting parts of C#. In this chapter, we'll learn how to make C# bend to our will. Or at the very least, we'll come to understand what some of the more complex concepts look like.

We'll find out more about how functions can have different numbers of arguments. We'll even learn how a variable can be a function. Interfaces are special chunks of classes that serve as a template for other classes to follow. Then we'll look into some more interesting uses of those interfaces.

Later on, we'll explore some more possibilities of how arrays can be handled and some simple tricks to make those arrays more manageable. Interfaces come into play again when dealing with arrays. After all, much of what computers are good at is iterating through long lists of data.

Speaking of data, because not all data is the same, we'll need to learn how to make functions more accepting of different types of data and still do what we expect them to. We can generalize functions to operate on practically any type of data.

After this, we'll finish some of the functionality of how C# works and then move on to how to use C# to its fullest. Many of the lessons in the following chapters are transferable to other languages. Modern features such as delegates and lambda functions are common among many other languages. Learning the principles of how modern programming features work in C# is useful in learning any other modern programming language.

Programming languages are as much about communicating to the computer as they are about conveying your thought process to another programmer reading your code.

## 7.3 MonoDevelop

MonoDevelop wasn't written by the programmers at Unity 3D. Its open source software was developed specifically as a multiplatform software engineering tool for the .NET platform developed by Microsoft. Unity 3D has integrated a Mono virtual machine, called a VM, to execute the byte code generated by Mono.

Programmers have their specific tastes in integrated development environments (IDEs). The environment includes libraries and autocomplete and search features. What they all boil down to are basically clever text editors. Old-school programmers prefer to use minimal editors like Vim simply because it's what they're used to.

You can go to http://monodevelop.com/ for more information on what we've been working in all this time. What differentiates an IDE from a text editor is all of the autocomplete functions. The IDE is also constantly reading and interpreting your code, pointing out errors and warnings. These are things that cannot be done so easily in just any text editor.

Visual Studio Professional from Microsoft is one of the most popular and the most expensive IDEs. However, because so many games are written for PC or Xbox, many game engines are written in Visual Studio. C# is a Microsoft invention, so Visual Studio has some great C#-related tools, including a free version of Visual Studio that allows you to do pretty much everything you need for writing a new C# application for Windows.

Unity 3D and MonoDevelop are quite nicely integrated. The libraries and Unity's functions are all readily available to you without any setup. MonoDevelop has several features, which you may have noticed, and to be a proficient programmer, you're going to need to learn how to use them.

The first interesting feature which you'll notice is syntax highlighting. This feature colors words based on how they are used. Keywords and different important symbols will be highlighted to help you read the code. Many programmers change color schemes to suit their different taste; changing schemes is great for aesthetics.

Autocompletion is the next important feature that is useful when trying to remember the names of functions you may be looking for.

### 7.3.1 Find in Files

The search command is another great feature. When working with a large project, it's important to be able to figure out where some name was used. To easily do this task, you can use the Find in Files feature. If we look at the ExecutionOrder project from Section 6.12.1, we can recall that there were many different functions.

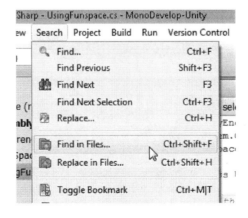

Select Find in Files from the Search menu.

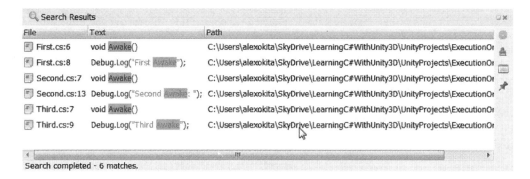

Enter Awake in the Find field.

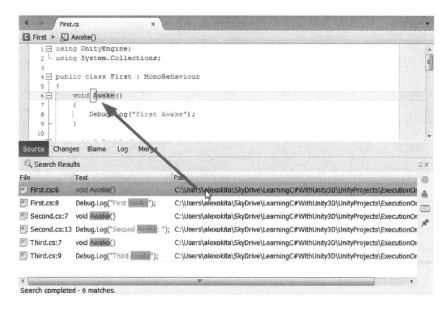

The Search Results panel shows several places where Awake appears throughout your project. This feature can be used to find a specific place in your project where you might have code you want to take a look at.

Double clicking on the Search Results line will open and hop the cursor to the location where the word was found. Leaving the Search Results panel open allows you to hop to every instance of the word Awake. This action allows you to read every line of code where the word appears.

We're also able to change one word to another word.

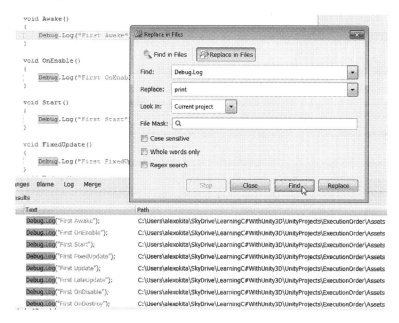

The Replace in Files function allows you to find all of the instances of a word and then replace the word with another word. If we have `Debug.Log()` used throughout a project and want to replace that function with `print()`, you can use this feature.

## 7.3.2 Word Processors

You may be inclined to use something you're already familiar with, like Microsoft Word, or perhaps, if you're into open source software, Open Office. Neither of these applications will do much good for you when it comes to writing software; sorry.

Word and many other word processors don't use the sort of text that a compiler will understand. If you were to open a Word document in MonoDevelop, you might not be able to recognize your work. That's because all of the formatting that goes into setting fonts, colors, and paragraphs nicely are now being read by the compiler. And compilers are ignorant to bold or italic formatting and are easily confused.

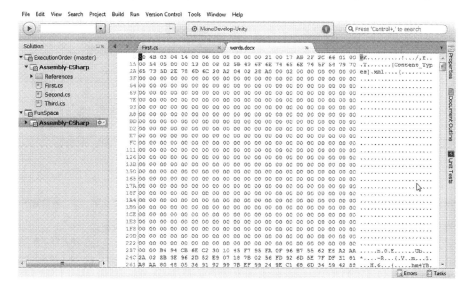

Programmers follow a completely different aesthetic when it comes to reading and writing code, something that you'll be able to somewhat appreciate, by the end of this book.

### 7.3.3 Mono History

Mono is an open source, free-to-use software. Mono is an implementation of the .NET Framework. Microsoft based their .NET Framework for C# language on the European Association for Standardizing Information and Communication Systems (ECMA). As with most European acronyms, the letters have nothing to do with what they stand for.

The Mono compiler was first developed by Miguel de Icaza, Ravi Pratap, Martin Baulig, and Raja Harinath. The compiler had many other contributors that helped improve and standardize how the internals work. Many improvements are continuously added every year.

In an effort to maintain cross-platform compatibility, Unity 3D utilizes Mono 4.0.1, though this is a recent addition. It's this broad platform compatibility that enables Unity 3D to support practically every form of distribution, including browsers, phones, and the most common PC operating systems.

Another commonly used framework is Oracle Systems' Java. Java has taken on many different forms and supports many different devices, including Blue-ray players and other more specific embedded systems. Because of Apple's strict platform requirements, Java has been greatly barred from iOS. Because of this restriction, C# is a better choice for developing mobile games. If you intend to write programs for iOS, you would need to learn Objective-C, but then you'd be trapped to one platform.

After you write code, a compiler interprets the code and converts it into machine-readable language. The compiler first parses or converts your human-readable code into a computer-readable format called an intermediate language.

When your code is parsed, it's scanned for errors and syntax. Once this passes, various optimizations are applied. Extraneous comments, unreachable code, and unused variables are omitted during this conversion. Finally, the intermediate language is generated, which is then converted into machine code specific to the central processing unit (CPU) and operating system.

In the case with Unity 3D, the C# compiler eventually builds a file that is compiled just before the game begins. This library works similar to the libraries that you include in your own C# code. Because the code written for Unity 3D is based on `MonoBehaviour`, Unity 3D is able to make its connections into your code.

The code you write is able to compile to different platforms because it's compiled just before the game begins. Thanks to the .NET technology and Mono, the conversion from your code into machine code can happen when needed without any modification.

You may have become used to the fact that one operating system cannot normally run an application built for another operating system. For instance, you can't natively run an application built for Android on your PC. Even more difficult is emulating another CPU architecture altogether. This is because the binary executable that is produced by a compiler needs to know what to convert your language into ahead of time.

---

## 7.4 Function Overloading

Overloading, in the programming sense, means use of the same function name with different parameter values. Functions, so far, have had a single purpose once they're written. This most directly relates to the parameters which we give them. For example, consider the following.

### 7.4.1 A Closer Look at Functions

If we consider the following code for a moment, it looks like we're trying to write a function that returns half the value of a number fed into the parameter.

```
int a = 8;
float b = 7;
void int HalfInt (int a)
```

```
{
    return a/2;
}
    void float HalfFloat (float a)
{
    return a/2.0f;
}
```

The function `HalfInt()` accepts an `int` and returns that `int` value divided by 2. `HalfFloat()` accepts a `float` value and returns a `float` that's half the value fed into its parameter.

What if we wanted to use the same function name for both? This would certainly make remembering the function's name a lot easier. The function name `HalfValue()` would be a lot easier than remembering `HalfInt()`, `HalfFloat()`, `HalfDouble()`, and anything else we might want to divide into two. We're actually allowed to do this quite easily using function overloading.

### 7.4.1.1 A Basic Example

We'll begin with the FunctionOverloading project.

```
int a = 8;
float b = 7f;
//first version of a function
int HalfValue(int a)
{
    return a/2;
}
//second version of a function
float HalfValue(float a)
{
    return a/2.0f;
}
```

This code might seem a bit awkward, given our learning that once an identifier has been used, it can't be used again for a different purpose. In C# we're allowed to do this with functions. This is one of the few places this is allowed. Stranger still, we can return the same value if needed.

```
int a = 8;
float b = 7;
int HalfValue(int a)
{
    return a/2;
}
int HalfValue(float a)
{
    return (int)a/2;
}
```

In this case, both versions match in both return type and name. The key difference here is the parameter types, so let's have a look.

```
int a = 8;
float b = 7;
int HalfValue(int a)
{
    return a/2;
}
int HalfValue(int a)//oops?
{
    return a * 0.5;
}
```

## 7.4.2 Function Signature

Here, we have the same function written twice, but we get an error this time that the function is already defined! And, as a matter of fact, yes, it has already been defined, once before. A function is defined by not only its identifier but also its parameters. The function name and its parameter list together are called a *signature*.

The return type is not a part of a function's signature. What this means is best illustrated by the following code fragment.

```
int RetVal()
{
    return 1;
}
    float RetVal()
{
    return 1.0f;
}
    void Start ()
{
    int a = RetVal();
    float b = RetVal();
}
```

Unfortunately, C# isn't smart enough to understand that we're asking for one of two different functions here. Because the return type is not included when looking at a function signature, the two functions look the same to C#. The code fragment above results in an error.

## 7.4.3 Different Signatures

So far, we've used a single parameter for all of the above examples. This doesn't need to be the case. We're allowed to use as many different parameters as we require.

```
public static int Reloaded()
{
    return 1;
}
public static int Reloaded(int a)
{
    return 1 + a;
}
public static float Reloaded(int a, float b)
{
    return a/b;
}
void Start ()
{
    int a = Reloaded();
    int b = Reloaded(3);
    float c = Reloaded(3, 2.0f);
    print(a);//prints 1
    print(b);//prints 4
    print(c);//prints 1.5
}
```

The above code uses no parameters in the first version of the function `Reloaded()`; this is followed by a single `int`, and then we're using an `int` and a `float`. However, all three of these have return values. Can we do the same with the `ref` and `out` as well? Let's add the following code to the versions of the above-mentioned functions and see what happens next.

```
public static void Reloaded(int a, ref float b)
{
    b = (float)a/3;
}
void Start ()
{
    float d = 0;
    Reloaded(1, ref d);
    System.Console.WriteLine(d);
}
```

The above code will divide 1 by 3. Then, according to how `ref` works, b is now pointing at the data found at `float  d`. This then manipulates the data at d and assigns it to `(float)a/3`; that changes the 0 to 0.3333333. Another important change is that the function has a `void` return type. This leads us to another possibility.

```
public static double classInt = 13;//class scoped number
public static void Reloaded(double b)
{
    classInt = b;
}
void Start ()
{
    print(classInt);//prints 13
    Reloaded(9.0);//sets the classInt to 9.0
    print(classInt);//prints 9
}
```

It's usually a bad habit to use a class-wide variable in this way, but this code is still perfectly valid. Functions are meant to be as independent of the class as possible. This independence allows them to be more portable. Once we see how class inheritance works, this importance will become clear.

We know what a proper signature for a function looks like. A function's signature is a name and a list of parameters. For a function overload to work, we are allowed to use the same function name, but overloads require that each function have the same name but a different parameter list.

Why is this so important; wouldn't using the same name with different results end up being confusing? As long as the intent remains the same, this is perfectly easy to reconcile; we'll see how this works before the end of the chapter.

### 7.4.4 Putting It Together

By creating functions with overloads, we're allowed to give ourselves some options when using the same function name. Making our code more flexible without adding complexity is possible with very few changes to the function.

```
GameObject CreateObject()
{
    GameObject g = GameObject.CreatePrimitive(PrimitiveType.Cube);
    return g;
}
GameObject CreateObject(PrimitiveType pt)
{
    GameObject g = GameObject.CreatePrimitive(pt);
    return g;
}
GameObject CreateObject(PrimitiveType pt, Vector3 loc)
```

```
    {
        GameObject g = GameObject.CreatePrimitive(pt);
        g.transform.position = loc;
        return g;
    }
    //Use this for initialization
    void Start ()
    {
        GameObject a = CreateObject();
        GameObject b = CreateObject(PrimitiveType.Cylinder);
        GameObject c = CreateObject(PrimitiveType.Sphere, new
        Vector3(2.0f, 3.5f, 1.3f));
    }
```

This code sample was created for an `Example.cs` assigned to an object in the scene. I assigned it to the Main Camera in an empty new scene in the Unity 3D editor. There are three versions of `CreateObject()`, each one having a different signature. In the `Start ()` function, each version is used to demonstrate going from no parameters to two parameters. Of course, you are allowed to add as many parameters as you think are manageable.

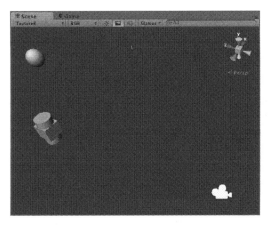

The objects in the image above would be made in the scene based on the three functions we just wrote. We have access to the three objects assigned as a, b, and c in the `Start ()` function, so we can make additional changes to them in the `Start ()` function.

### 7.4.5 Not Quite Recursion

Where function overloading becomes interesting is when a function refers to an overloaded version of itself. The logic here is that a function can be accessed in one of two different forms without needing to write another function. The scenario arises when you have a simple function, say, drawing a word to the screen with some debug lines.

The task starts off with drawing a letter, so first we'll want to build a system for storing letters. We'll also want to create some system to give the collection of array points of a letter to whoever is asking for it. We'll start off with two letters; I'll let you figure out the rest on your own.

### 7.4.6 DrawWord

This DrawWord project example is available with the full alphabet available in the Unity 3D projects downloaded from GitHub along with the rest of the content for this book; but here we'll look at a shorter version of the code.

```
public class Letters {
    public static Vector3[] A = new[]{
        new Vector3(-1,-1, 0),
```

```
            new Vector3(-1, 0, 0),
            new Vector3(0, 1, 0),
            new Vector3(1, 0, 0),
            new Vector3(-1, 0, 0),
            new Vector3(1, 0, 0),
            new Vector3(1,-1, 0)
        };
    public static Vector3[] B = new[]{
            new Vector3(-1,-1, 0),
            new Vector3(-1, 1, 0),
            new Vector3(0, 1, 0),
            new Vector3(1, 0, 0),
            new Vector3(-1, 0, 0),
            new Vector3(1, 0, 0),
            new Vector3(1,-1, 0),
            new Vector3(-1,-1, 0)
        };
    public static Vector3[] ToVectorArray(char c)
    {
        Vector3[] letter;
        switch (c)
    {
        case 'A' :
            letter = A;
            break;
        case 'B' :
            letter = B;
            break;
    }
    }
}
```

Here, we are looking at two letters A and B stored in the form of 3D points in space. The Vector3[] is an array of Vector3s and the A or B identifies the array. They are rather boxy since they're made of only a few points each. The ToVectorArray returns which set of points based on an incoming type char. We'll look at what a char is in a moment.

```
public static void drawWord(char c, float scale, Vector3 position, Color
color)
{
    Vector3[] lines = ToVectorArray(c);
    for(int i = 1; i < lines.Length; i++) {
        Vector3 start = (lines[i-1] * scale);
        Vector3 end = (lines[i] * scale);
        Debug.DrawLine(start + position, end + position, color);
    }
}
```

In the above code, the function drawWord() accepts a char c, as well as a scale, position, and color. This then asks for the lines to draw using the ToVectorArray function. Once the vectors are assigned to the array called lines, the for() loop iterates through each line segment.

The char type is short for character. A char is a single character in a string. Rather, a string is an array of chars. Chars can be only letters, numbers, or symbols; when we use "hello," we are assembling chars to make a word.

For readability, we create a start and an end Vector3 in the for loop. This takes the previous Vector3 and assigns that to start. An important, yet somewhat not-so-obvious, step here is to start the for loop with int i = 1; rather than 0. The start of the line begins with lines[i-1] that means that if the loop begins with `i = 0;`, the first line point will be `lines[-1]` that would give us an `index out of range` error. Remember that an array always starts at 0.

This function isn't only meant to draw a single letter. Instead, we'll write another version of the exact same function with the following code:

```
public static void drawWord(string word, float scale, Vector3 position, Color
color)
{
    //convert to uppercase first
    string uLetters = word.ToUpper();
    char[] letters = uLetters.ToCharArray();
    if(letters.Length > 0)
    {
        for(int i = 0; i < letters.Length ; i++)
        {
            float offset = (i * scale);
            Vector3 offsetPosition = new Vector3(offset + position.x,
position.y, position.z);
            drawWord(letters[i], scale, offsetPosition, color);
        }
    }
}
```

This version of the same function does a couple of things. First we change the function's signature, which means that rather than `char c` as the first parameter, we use `string word` instead. This changes the signature in such a way that this `drawWord` function is now an overloaded version of the first `draw-Word` function. We should convert `string word` into upper case. This conversion to upper case is necessary to convert any lower case letters to allow the `ToVectorArray` function to convert each letter to an array of vectors. Once we have the string converted from something like "abba" to "ABBA" by using `string uLetters = word.ToUpper();`, we're ready for the next step.

To convert this string to an array of chars, we use the statement `char[] letters = uLetters.ToCharArray();`, where the `ToCharArray()` function in string returns an array of uppercase chars. So long as the array comes back with at least one result, we continue to the next `for` loop.

In this `for` loop, we start at the beginning of the char array. To keep the letters from piling up on top of one another, we create an offset, so each letter can start at a new location. This is done with `float offset = (i * scale);`, which we then use to create a new `offsetPosition` Vector3. The x of the `offsetPosition` is the only place where we need this `offset + position.x`; the y and z will just use the parameter at the beginning of the function.

When we use the overloaded version of the function in the function, we use the `char` parameter `drawWord(letters[i], scale, offsetPosition, color);`, where `letters[i]` is passing a `char` to the function rather than a `string`. The overloaded version is automatically detected and the other version of this same function is called.

To see our code in action, add the `DrawWords.cs` class as a component to the Main Camera in a new scene in the Unity Editor.

```
    void Update () {
        Vector3 position = Vector3.zero;
        drawWord ("words are being drawn", 2f, position, Color.black);
    }
```

In the `Update ()` function, I've added a `position` to draw the word at the origin, and I've assigned `2f` to scale up the letters and set `color` to `Color.black;`, so they're easier to see.

The `Letters` class is added after the `DrawWords` class in the same file. Make sure that the Gizmos button on the top right of the game view port is turned on; otherwise, the `Debug.DrawLines()` function will not work.

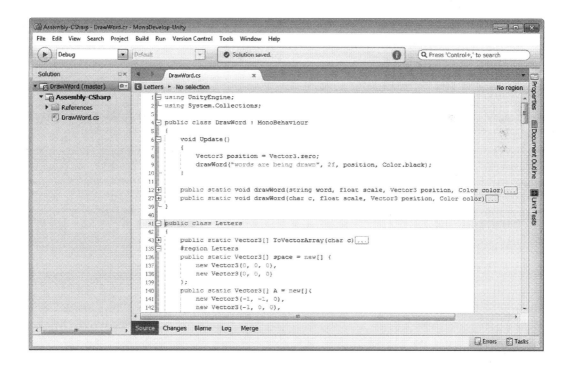

The `drawWord` functions are written inside of the `DrawWord` class. Notice the change in case to prevent the `DrawWord` class from colliding with the `drawWord` function. The `Letters` class is separated into a different public class outside of the `DrawWord` class. This means that it can be accessed by another class; if you wanted to use this for your own project, please feel free to do so.

### 7.4.7  What We've Learned

The above discussion also works as an interesting example of code portability. The `Letters` class is self-contained and doesn't depend on anything other than `UnityEngine` for the `Vector3` data type. Overloading a function should come naturally when you want to use the same function in different ways. This also means that you can simply use `drawWord(someChar, 1.0f, new Vector3.zero, Color.red);` to draw a single character if `someChar` was just a single char object.

---

## 7.5  Accessors (or Properties)

Encapsulation is an important property of any class. Keeping a class protected from mismanagement is critical if you want to keep your sanity when the time to debug anything comes. Consider the following class:

```
class fluffHead
{
    public int MyNumber;
}
```

The `public int MyNumber` is open to anyone who wants to make changes. For the most part, this is just fine. Other objects are allowed to go in and make changes to `fluffHead`'s number anytime. Were the `MyNumber` to be critical for any of `fluffHead`'s functions, then we might start to run into problems. To protect this number, you could add the following:

```
class fluffHead
{
    public readonly int MyNumber;
}
```

This statement changes the read/write ability of `MyNumber` to read only. However, there are a number of drawbacks to this; the most important is the fact that the `doodad` class isn't allowed to change this variable either. Should we want to protect an `int` internally, we should make it `private`, and then make a publically available version which has some checks to block values we don't want.

```
class fluffHead
{
    //internally stored int
    private int mNumber;
    //publically accessible interface for int
    public int MyNumber
    {
        get
        {
            return mNumber;
        }
        set
        {
            if (value > = 0)
                mNumber = value;
            else
                mNumber = 0;
        }
    }
    //constructor
    public doodad()
```

```
        {
            fluffHead = 0;
        }
    }
    void Start ()
    {
        fluffHead fh = new fluffHead ();
        fh.MyNumber = -1;//trying to set to a negative value
        Debug.Log(fh.MyNumber);//it didn't work!
    }
```

Here we have a `private mNumber` and a `public MyNumber`. We'll plan on using one of them inside of the class, whereas we'll make the other publically available. We'll suppose that this number should never be negative. To prevent mNumber from ever getting incorrectly set to a negative number, we'll add in logic to MyNumber to keep the number valid.

### 7.5.1 Value

The placement of mNumber = value; in our code is important. The value keyword is the number where MyNumber is being assigned a value of some type. Where we use the get{} set{} notation, value is a catcher's mitt to snag incoming data. This accounts for any value entering the variable. This could be a struct, a string, or anything at all, so long as the type matches up.

#### 7.5.1.1 A Basic Example

In its most simple form, the get;set; notation can be as simple as follows:

```
    class GetSet
    {
        public int myInt {get; set;}
    }
    void Start ()
    {
        GetSet gs = new GetSet ();
        gs.myInt = 10;
        Debug.Log(gs.myInt);
    }
```

At this point, there's no difference between `public in myInt;` and `public int myInt{get;set;};` the two operate essentially the same way. What we're starting to produce here is a simple system wherein we're allowed to add in some logic to how a value is assigned.

To make full use of the accessor, we need to have two versions of a variable: the public accessor and a value that remains private within the confines of the class. This ensures a certain level of encapsulation that defines what object oriented programming is all about.

```
    class GetSet
    {
        private int myInt;
        public int MyInt {get{return myInt;} set{myInt = value;}}
    }
```

The above code has a `private int myInt` and a `public in MyInt` with an accessor. This is a standard notation that should be used to define a variable for a cleanly encapsulated class. This too operates the same as the previous {get;set;}, only with the idea that it's redirecting an incoming data value from a `public` variable to a `private` variable hidden inside of the class.

458 Learning C# Programming with Unity 3D

### 7.5.2 Set Event

One of the advantages of an accessor is the ability to add logic to how a number is set. In addition to logic is the ability to raise an event. As in Section 7.5.2 from before, we'll want to add the delegate and the event to the GetSet class. Inside of the set element of the accessor, we'll make a check to see if there are functions delegated to the handler and then raise an event.

```
class GetSet
{
      public delegate void MyIntHandler(int i);
      public event MyIntHandler MyIntEvent;
      private int myInt;
      public int MyInt
      {
            get{return myInt;}
            set
            {
                  myInt = value;
                  //raise an event if there are
//any assigned functions
                  if(MyIntEvent != null)
                  {
                        MyIntEvent(myInt);
                  }
            }
      }
}
void Start ()
{
      GetSet gs = new GetSet();
      //assign a function to be raised when the value is changed
      gs.MyIntEvent + = IntChanged;
      //set a value, this wil raise an event!
      gs.MyInt = 10;
}
void IntChanged(int i)
{
      Debug.Log("change! " + i);
}
```

The above code instances the new class and then adds the IntChanged() function to the gs.MyIntEvent inside of the GetSet class. Once the value is set on the following line, we get the following output from the Console.

```
change! 10
```

This is a very useful result of setting a value. Looking closer at how the event is raised brings us some ideas about what this event can be used for.

```
if(MyIntEvent != null)
{
    MyIntEvent(myInt);
}
```

When the event is raised, we're passing in the value of myInt. This means that anytime myInt is set, we're passing the new value to the event. Therefore, if myInt is set to 10, the event is raised knowing the new value 10. Once a proper accessor to a protected variable has been created, we're able to do a few more tricks with our new setup.

### 7.5.3 Read-Only Accessor

When writing a class it's often a good idea to prevent some values from getting set inappropriately. It's not possible to set a variable if its value has been calculated by a function. In these cases, we need to make that variable a read only accessor.

```
class GetSet
{
     public delegate void MyIntHandler(int i);
     public event MyIntHandler MyIntEvent;
     private int myInt;
     public int MyInt
     {
          get{return myInt;}
          set
          {
               myInt = value;
               if(MyIntEvent != null)
               {
                    MyIntEvent(myInt);
               }
          }
     }
     //read only!
     public int doubleInt
     {
          get {return myInt * 2;}
     }
}
```

We could add the above code to the `GetSet` class and have a simple system to get a value that's two times the `myInt` value. Notice too that there's no `set;` included in the accessor. If we try to set `doubleInt` with something like `doubleInt = 1;`, we get the following error:

```
Assets/Accessors.cs(65,20): error CS0200: Property or indexer 'Accessors.
GetSet.doubleInt' cannot be assigned to (it is read only)
```

By omitting `set;`, we've turned `doubleInt` into a read-only variable.

```
void Start ()
{
     GetSet gs = new GetSet();
     gs.MyIntEvent + = IntChanged;
     gs.MyInt = 10;
     Debug.Log(gs.doubleInt);
}
```

This set of code produces the following output:

```
change! 10
20
```

These examples with `get;set;` should expand to quite a variety of useful tricks. We can guard the internal value from bad values. We can raise events when a value is changed. And we can make the value read only by omitting `set;` from the accessor.

## 7.5.4 Simplification

We have several options for getting information from a class. With accessors, we are spared the use of parentheses when we ask for a value from a class or struct.

```
struct AccessorStruct
{
    private int myInt;
    public int MyInt
    {
        get{return this.myInt;}
        set{this.myInt = value;}
    }
    public int GetInt()
    {
        return MyInt;
    }
    public void SetInt(int i)
    {
        MyInt = i;
    }
}
```

We have a couple of options here with the above struct. We can set the value of the `private myInt` variable in the struct by the accessor or a pair of functions. We can set the value of `myInt` to 3 with `SetInt(3);` or `MyInt = 3.`

How does this look in practice?

```
void Start ()
{
    AccessorStruct MyAccessorStruct = new AccessorStruct();
    MyAccessorStruct.MyInt = 3;
    MyAccessorStruct.SetInt(3);
    Debug.Log(MyAccessorStruct.MyInt);
}
```

The simplicity of `MyInt = 3;` certainly means quite a lot. It's a notation that we're used to seeing; however, by the nature of the accessor, we have a great deal of control over what can be done in the accessor's logic.

## 7.5.5 What We've Learned

Accessors are useful for so many reasons. They provide functionality that has already been covered quite a lot, though in a more simple system. There are many powers which the accessor provides us. We'll be exploring some of the other tricks that make coding easier.

Many tricks in C# are made to make your work easier. Convenience offers more than just simplicity. If a trick makes things easier, then you're allowed to make more important decisions. Rather than dwelling on function names and parameters, you're allowed to focus on game play. After all, if you're making a game, the last thing you want to do is spend all your time rewriting code.

## 7.6 Base Classes: Another Look

When we begin to use inheritance and add keywords such as virtual and override onto functions, we begin to add many new layers of complexity onto the use of a class. How we write these class members greatly depends on how we want them to be used.

Depending on who you work with, you might find yourself seeing your code being used in unexpected ways. Often this is the case when you've written functions that have similar-sounding identifiers. Perhaps even misleading function names can be the cause for a great deal of confusion.

It's up to you to keep your code organized to begin with; however, given tight deadlines and poor sleeping habits, this can't always be the case. You can try to add descriptive comments, but these are all too often ignored. Your best option is to just disallow other code from seeing the variables and functions at all.

This topic brings into question why any of these techniques is necessary. Inheritance is a system in which you are able to write a base class and have many different variations of that class exist. The intent is to make a system that allows for a common set of base-level functionality. Based on what's been written, you make additions to, or variations of, that functionality.

To begin we'll look at building up some classes not derived or based on `MonoBehaviour`. This makes them regular C# classes outside of the influence of the normal `Update ()` and `Start ()` behaviors which we commonly see in most C# classes in Unity 3D.

`MonoBehaviour` is not an abstract class, which means that we cannot make an abstract class based on it. An abstract class determines the necessary collections of data that every derived class will need to implement and use. To take a look at how a base class can be used to do some work for us, we'll take a look at a few classes in the `BaseClasses` project available from GitHub.

### 7.6.1 Generalization—Base Classes

Generalization allows us to make some wide-use cases for a class and then allow for more specific cases later on. In general though, if we had little objects running around on a flat plane, we can make some good assumptions about the types of data we would want. If our behavior was nothing more than moving forward and turning left or right, we can add some variables that allow for this and name them appropriately.

A good base class will include some primitive variables but at the same time provide a system for building up the types of behaviors we'll want. This is almost like writing code before it's written, but at least you can jump between classes and make changes when necessary. For our next behavior, we want some generic shapes driven by two numbers: a forward speed and a turn speed. Aside from that the objects should have a very minimal set of instructions to prevent any unnecessary meddling in their activity.

The `BaseClass.cs` class is a fairly detailed class. This data was necessary since we didn't have the usual objects inherited from `MonoBehaviour`. Since we had to generate a great deal of this information from scratch, we needed to add in some accessors and other protections around the different data members to ensure that nothing unexpected might happen. We'll take a look at what happens when these barriers are taken down. The base class we're starting with looks like the following:

```
using UnityEngine;
using System.Collections;
public abstract class BaseClass {
    #region BaseProperties
    private float speed;
    protected float Speed
    {
        get {return speed;}
        set {speed = value;}
    }
    private float turn;
    protected float Turn
    {
        get {return turn;}
        set {turn = value;}
    }
    private Vector3 transform;
    protected Vector3 ChildTransform
    {
        get {return transform;}
```

```
            set {transform = value;}
    }
    private Vector3 rotation;
    protected Vector3 ChildRotation
    {
            get {return rotation;}
            set {rotation = value;}
    }
    private MeshFilter mMeshFilter;
    protected MeshFilter MyMeshFilter
    {
            get{return mMeshFilter;}
            set{mMeshFilter = value;}
    }
    private MeshRenderer mRenderer;
    protected MeshRenderer MyMeshRenderer
    {
            get{return mRenderer;}
            set{mRenderer = value;}
    }
    private Material mMaterial;
    protected Material MyMaterial
    {
            get{return mMaterial;}
            set{mMaterial = value;}
    }
    private Mesh mMesh;
    protected Mesh MyMesh
    {
            get{return mMesh;}
            set{mMesh = value;}
    }
    #endregion
    #region BaseMethods
    public abstract void Initialize(Mesh mesh, Material material);
    public abstract void MoveForward(float spd, float trn);
    public abstract void ChildUpdate ();
    public virtual void Speak()
    {
            Debug.Log("base hello");
    }
    #endregion
}
```

As an abstract class, nothing has been implemented. We have one function called Speak(), which says "base hello." Everything else has been stubbed in to ensure that any class inheriting from BaseClass will have a great deal of work to do. The first region has been set up for many protected and private variables.

In the above class, we use the abstract keyword as well as virtual. In many cases, we might add many variables in anticipation of what we might need. These can be declared as we need them or we might just leave in a bunch of place holders, thinking that we might need them later. Often it's far better to create them as they are needed and decide if it's specific to a child class and move them into a parent class afterward. However, in this example, it's good to see that any number of variables can be added to this class for later use even if they're not necessary for all child classes to use them.

By making accessors for these variables, we've created a barrier between how the variables are set and who can set them. The protected variables are accessible only to members of the class. Other classes that might be trying to change these classes' movement patterns have to go through functions to change these variables. They won't be able to access them directly through a dot operator.

Following the base class, we have a `ChildA` class that inherits from the base class.

```
using UnityEngine;
using System.Collections;
public class ChildA : BaseClass {
    #region ChildA_properties
    protected GameObject me;
    #endregion
    public override void Initialize(Mesh mesh, Material material)
    {
        this.MyMesh = mesh;
        this.MyMaterial = material;
        me = new GameObject(this.ToString());
        MyMeshFilter = me.AddComponent<MeshFilter>();
        MyMeshFilter.mesh = this.MyMesh;
        MyMeshRenderer = me.AddComponent<MeshRenderer>();
        MyMeshRenderer.material = this.MyMaterial;
    }
    public override void MoveForward(float speed, float turn)
    {
        Speed = speed;
        Turn + = turn;
        ChildRotation = new Vector3(0, Turn, 0);
    }
    public override void ChildUpdate ()
    {
        ChildTransform = me.transform.forward * Speed;
        me.transform.localPosition + = ChildTransform;
        me.transform.localEulerAngles = ChildRotation;
    }
    public override void Speak()
    {
        Debug.Log(me.name + " word");
    }
}
```

This class has two important functions: `MoveForward()` and `ChildUpdate ()`. Since we have no access to the `MonoBehaviour` class, we don't get to have either of these. Just as important, we have the `Initialize()` function that replaces the `Start ()` functionality.

## 7.6.2 Specialization

The `Initialize()` function has two arguments: `Mesh` and `Material`. These are then applied to a new `GameObject me`. Here is where the `ChildA` starts to add layers of specialization on top of the `BaseClass`. The term *specialization* comes in whenever we add new properties or behaviors that were not present in the base class. The base class should be as generalized as possible. In our case, our base class is called `BaseClass`, just so we don't forget.

When we add additional behavior to a second `ChildB`, we have another opportunity to add another layer of specialization. In the following case, we add a `color` to our `mMaterial`'s property.

```
using UnityEngine;
using System.Collections;
public class ChildB : ChildA {
    #region ChildB_properties
    private Color mColor;
    public Color MyColor
```

```
    {
        get {return mColor;}
        set {mColor = value;}
    }
    #endregion
    public override void Initialize (Mesh mesh, Material material)
    {
        base.Initialize(mesh, material);
        this.MyColor = new Color(1,0,0,1);
        MyMeshRenderer.material.color = this.MyColor;
    }
}
```

### 7.6.3 Base

As new classes derive from each other, they require only smaller and smaller adjustments to gain added functionality. The specialization adds only thin layers of additional code on top of the base class and any class below. There are some important changes that need to be noted when deriving from a class that has some important functions already in place.

```
    public override void Initialize (Mesh mesh, Material material)
    {
        base.Initialize(mesh, material);
        this.MyColor = new Color(1,0,0,1);
        MyMeshRenderer.material.color = this.MyColor;
    }
```

The first line in the override void Initialize() function is base.Initialize(mesh, material);. Here we have some important new tricks to take a look at. When the keyword base is invoked within a function, it's an indication that we're informing C# that we want to do what's already been done in the previous layer of that code. We can explore what the code looks like with what base. Initialize is actually doing.

```
    public override void Initialize (Mesh mesh, Material material)
    {
        //from ChildA
        this.MyMesh = mesh;
        this.MyMaterial = material;
        me = new GameObject(this.ToString());
        MyMeshFilter = me.AddComponent<MeshFilter>();
        MyMeshFilter.mesh = this.MyMesh;
        MyMeshRenderer = me.AddComponent<MeshRenderer>();
        MyMeshRenderer.material = this.MyMaterial;
        //added to ChildA
        this.MyColor = new Color(1,0,0,1);
        MyMeshRenderer.material.color = this.MyColor;
    }
```

The base keyword tells C# to execute the parent classes' version of the function after the dot operator. The above code is what the function would look like to Unity 3D. Thanks to the base.Initialize, we've done the equivalent of this work without having to worry about any typos. Without invoking base.Initialize(), we'd lose the mesh material and gameObject creation and setup process.

ChildB is based on ChildA and ChildA is based on BaseClass. This means that both ChildB and ChildA are related to one another because they both are also derived from BaseClass. This means that we can address them both as BaseClass objects. If we look at the ManageChildren.cs class, we'll have the following code:

```
using UnityEngine;
using System.Collections;
public class ManageChildren : MonoBehaviour
```

```
{
    public Mesh ChildMesh;
    public Material ChildMaterial;
    BaseClass[] children;
    void Start ()
    {
        children = new BaseClass[2];
        children[0] = new ChildA();
        children[0].Initialize(ChildMesh, ChildMaterial);
        children[1] = new ChildB();
        children[1].Initialize(ChildMesh, ChildMaterial);
    }
    //Update is called once per frame
    void Update ()
    {
        for(int i = 0; i < children.Length; i++)
        {
            children[i].MoveForward(i*0.1f+0.1f, i*3.0f+1.5f);
            children[i].ChildUpdate ();
            children[i].Speak();
        }
    }
}
```

This class is derived from `MonoBehavior` and we have the benefit of the `Start ()` and `Update ()` functions to use. It's worth noting that this is the only class based on `MonoBehavior` active in the scene in which we've added any code to. In `ManageChildren` class, we have a `BaseClass[]` array and an identifier `children`. This means that the array can accept any number of `BaseClass` type objects.

In the `Start ()` function, we instantiate `ChildA()` and `ChildB()` and assign both of them to the `BaseClass[]` array. This is valid since they both derive `BaseClass`. Because `BaseClass` had the abstract functions `MoveForward()` and `ChildUpdate ()`, they can be called in the `Update ()` function in the Manager. This `for` loop provides some motivation to make the two little guys move around.

```
for(int i = 0; i < children.Length; i++)
{
    children[i].MoveForward(i*0.1f+0.1f, i*3.0f+1.5f);
    children[i].ChildUpdate ();
    children[i].Speak();
}
```

This also provides a system for them to speak. What's important here is how both the `ChildA()` and `ChildB()` classes are locked down.

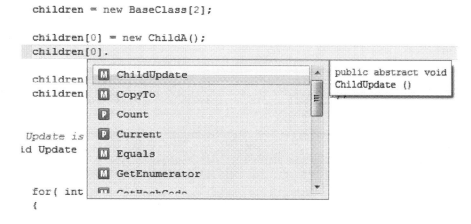

Inside of the Manager, they have just a few exposed functions or variables. Aside from Child-Update (), Initialize(), MoveForward(), and Speak(), the rest of the functions derive from the object. This is great for a few different reasons. The first is the fact that once the code starts working, it's hard to break.

Code usually comes tumbling down when an internal variable is set from many different places. Because options are now limited, your code has to make changes to the internals of a class and therefore its less likely your code will fall apart. Should we not have a BaseClass for the two child objects, we'd have to write our code more like the following:

```
//Update is called once per frame
void Update ()
{
    if(firstChild != null)
    {
        firstChild.MoveForward(0.1f, 3.0f);
        firstChild.ChildUpdate ();
        firstChild.Speak();
    }
    if(secondChild != null)
    {
        secondChild.MoveForward(0.05f, -3.0f);
        secondChild.ChildUpdate ();
        secondChild.Speak();
    }
}
```

Each one would have to be initialized and updated separately. This defeats the purpose of the base class entirely. There are still clever and dangerous tricks that we can use to add functionality to ChildA without needing to expand how much bigger that class might want to be.

## 7.6.4 Partial

If we're in ChildB and decide that ChildA is really missing a scale function of some kind, we can add it without going back to the ChildA class and adding the code there. Although this practice is unorthodox and possibly deviates from strict programming practice, it's still possible.

```
using UnityEngine;
using System.Collections;
//sneaking in some code to ChildA
public partial class ChildA : BaseClass {
    private float mScale;
    protected float MyScale
    {
        get {return mScale;}
        set {mScale = value;}
    }
}
public class ChildB : ChildA {
    #region ChildB_properties
    #region ChildB_functions
}
```

In the ChildA class, we could go in and change public class ChildA : BaseClass and add in the keyword partial so that we have public partial class ChildA : BaseClass. This gives us the ability to tack on last-minute functionality to the ChildA class.

```
using UnityEngine;
using System.Collections;
public partial class ChildA : BaseClass {
    private float mScale;
    protected float MyScale
    {
        get {return mScale;}
        set {mScale = value;}
    }
    protected void SetScale(float scale)
    {
        MyScale = scale;
        me.transform.localScale = Vector3.one * MyScale;
    }
}
public class ChildB : ChildA {
    #region ChildB_properties
    #region ChildB_functions
    public override void Initialize (Mesh mesh, Material material)
    {
        base.Initialize(mesh, material);
        this.MyColor = new Color(1,0,0,1);
        MyMeshRenderer.material.color = this.MyColor;
        //using the SetScale function just added to ChildA
        SetScale(2.0f);
    }
    #endregion
}
```

Therefore, say we needed a system for ChildB to set its scale to some arbitrary new size, we can do that by adding the code locally to ChildB, or we can make sure that anything else deriving from ChildA will also have this ability. This also means that ChildA has that new ability as well.

The result of using partial classes like this tends to scatter code all over the place. This quickly leads to angry nights debugging code. Although, there are some cases in which this can be quite helpful, it's best to start with the best use case for partial in mind.

```
using UnityEngine;
using System.Collections;
public abstract partial class BaseClass {
    public enum Shapes{
        Box,
        Sphere
    }
    private Shapes mShape;
    protected Shapes MyShape
    {
        get{return mShape;}
        set{mShape = value;}
    }
    public abstract void SetShape(Shapes shape);
}
public partial class ChildA : BaseClass {
    public override void SetShape(Shapes shape)
    {
        switch (shape)
        {
        case Shapes.Box:
```

```
                this.me = GameObject.CreatePrimitive(PrimitiveType.Cube);
                break;
        case Shapes.Sphere:
                this.me = GameObject.CreatePrimitive(PrimitiveType.Sphere);
                break;
        }
    }
}
```

Setting up both the base class and the immediate child at the same time reduces the number of places you might have to go in order to find any problem areas in the code. This still isn't the best use case; however, when implementing various interfaces, you can have a different class as a helper for each interface being implemented. This certainly helps separate the different tasks. Suppose, for instance, that the `BaseClass` looked something like the following:

```
using UnityEngine;
using System.Collections;
public abstract partial class BaseClass : IEnumerator, ICollection {
    #region BaseProperties
    #region BaseMethods
}
```

Both the `IEnumerator` and the `ICollection` interfaces are rather complicated. Having `BaseClassIEnumerator.cs` and `BaseClassICollection.cs` would help. Each one would start the same as `BaseClass`, but the contents of each would be related to the interface they are implementing. Thanks to MonoDevelop, we have a quick way to generate the code we need.

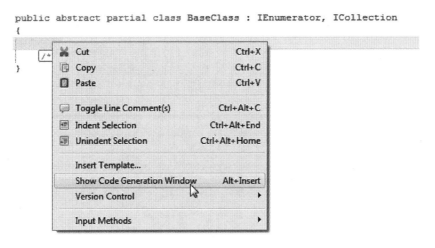

We can invoke the Show Code Generation window with the right click menu. This will open the following pop-up.

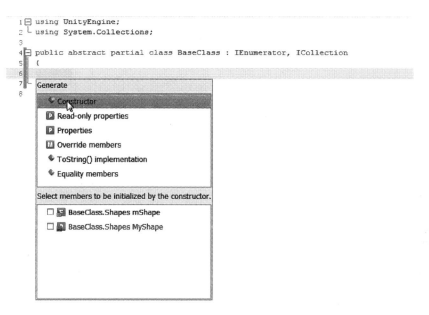

Down around the bottom are the required functions for building the `IEnumerator` interface. After the selections have been made, hit Enter on the keyboard and let MonoDevelop do some work for you. If you need a reminder of which functions are required for the `IEnumerator` interface, you can always just look at the error log in the Console panel.

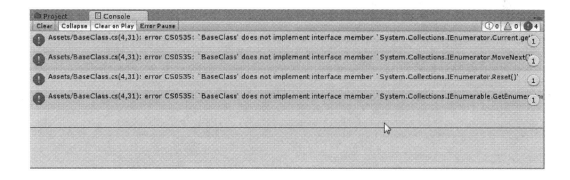

This shows you what interface members are missing.

```
using UnityEngine;
using System.Collections;
public abstract partial class BaseClass : IEnumerator, ICollection
{
    public IEnumerator GetEnumerator()
    {
        throw new System.NotImplementedException();
    }
    public bool MoveNext()
    {
        throw new System.NotImplementedException();
    }
    public void Reset()
    {
        throw new System.NotImplementedException();
    }
    public object Current
    {
        get
        {
            throw new System.NotImplementedException();
        }
    }
}
```

The resulting output into your code is enough to fulfill the IEnumerator, and the process can be repeated with the ICollection interface. Of course, the functions are all just throwing NotImplementedExceptions(); errors, but that's just until you get around to implementing the functions with your own code. MonoDevelop isn't going to do all of the work for you.

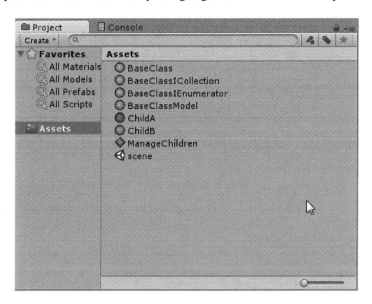

By adding the different partial classes to each one of these different files, the BaseClass is already getting to be quite big. However, the original file has not increased in complexity. Each partial addition has only added complexity to its own portion of the class. All of the new behaviors we've been adding are all being inherited by ChildA and ChildB. This is a remarkable amount of work that can be done with less effort, thanks to our simplifying how classes can be merged as needed.

Normally, Unity 3D would complain that the class name doesn't match the file name. This exception is made for classes not deriving from MonoBehaviour. By avoiding MonoBehaviour, we're more able to take some liberties with the C# language. The partial(), abstract(), and virtual() functions and classes offer a great deal of flexibility not allowed when deriving from MonoBehaviour.

### 7.6.5 Protected, Private, and Public

The accessibility keywords include protected to help shield your code from influence from other classes. This prevents bugs by other programmers from creeping into your code. You may have noticed in ChildB that the variables that were declared in both BaseClass and ChildA are all shown with a different icon in the pop-up.

```
this.MyMesh = mesh;
this.My|
```

- MyMaterial
- MyMesh
- MyMeshFilter
- MyMeshRenderer
- MyScale
- MyShape

```
protected Mesh
MyMesh { get; set; }
```

In ChildB, we declared MyColor as public. This is indicated by the lock icon to the left of the auto-complete list.

```
public class ChildB : ChildA
{
    #region ChildB_properties
    private Color mColor;
    public Color MyColor
    {
        get {return mColor;}
        set {mColor = value;}
    }
    #endregion
    #region ChildB_functions
    public override void Initialize(Mesh mesh, Material material)
    {
        base.Initialize(mesh, material);
        this.MyColor = new Color(1, 0, 0, 1);
        MyMeshRenderer.material.color = this.MyColor;
        //using the SetScale function just added to ChildA
        SetScale(2.0f);
    }
    #endregion
}
```

The rest of the properties are visible, but they have a lock icon, which indicates that these values cannot be seen outside of this class. However, the protected variables aren't even in the list. Remember that there was an mColor mMaterial and a corresponding mProperty for each property in that pop-up list. A protected value means that the value should not be directly modified.

However, we get a different set of variables from another class. Going into the `ManageChildren.cs` class, we see only a few things. If we make a `ChildB()` and look at what properties we have available, we're very limited indeed.

```
children [1] = new ChildB();
ChildB cb = new ChildB();
cb.My
```

```
P  MyColor                                      dMaterial);

                                            public Color
                                            MyColor { get; set; }
```

The only property available is `MyColor`, that's because it was left `public`. The rest are well hidden by the encapsulation provided by C#'s accessibility keywords.

### 7.6.6 What We've Learned

It's difficult to know where to make a split from one class to two. It's often only useful once you've gotten to a point where your update loops begin to have conditions `if(enemyA)//do enemyA things,` `else//do enemyB things`. Once this begins to show up more than once or twice, it's time to break out into a new class.

However, where does the break happen? Does `enemyB` branch from `enemyA` or do you make a subclass for both of them, make both `enemyA` and `enemyB` based on a similar `baseEnemy` and then branch A and B from the base? The logic is difficult to write to begin with, and often you'll end up going back over an old system and writing a new one from scratch.

This is often painful, but it's worth it. The second time, though, is almost always faster than the first time. Organizing everything into a clean simple group and branching with more reliable behaviors always comes once you've got a better understanding of what you wanted to do to begin with.

## 7.7 Optional Parameters

We've been putting a great deal of thought into how functions work and how we can make them more flexible through inheritance and overrides. The different features are not to add complications; they are meant to add flexibility. Once you get used to how the features work, you're allowed to do more things with less work. It's just a matter of understanding how the features work.

Hopefully, you're able to keep up with the break-neck speed at which we've been adding these features. If not, then it's time to practice what you know before going on. This is a pretty simple chapter that adds a pretty simple feature to our C# toolbox. Adding optional features is a pretty simple trick to our functions that often comes up. Normally, when we declare a function, we use syntax like the following:

```
void MyFunction()
{
    //some code here...
}
```

Therefore, we've used a few different variations on how to manipulate the argument list of a function to get a few different uses out of a single function. We're allowed to use a few other tricks that can help make things a bit easier to deal with when making many changes. When the process of writing code gets to a fevered pitch, you're going to be needing to write a great deal of code fast and finding yourself going back to fix things quite a lot.

Say for a moment that you've written a function that appears in many different places but you want to change it. This would mean spending the time to fix it everywhere it's used, and this can be a boring time-consuming chore.

Therefore, you wrote a function that might look something like the following:

```
public GameObject CreateACube(string cubeName, Vector3 position)
{
    GameObject cube = GameObject.CreatePrimitive(PrimitiveType.Cube);
    cube.name = cubeName;
    cube.transform.position = position;
    return cube;
}
//Use this for initialization
void Start ()
{
    GameObject c = CreateACube("bob", new Vector3(10,0,0));
    Debug.Log(c);
}
```

For a moment, let's pretend that the `Start ()` function making use of `CreateACube()` is far too much work to change and we are incredibly lazy. What happens when we need to make some changes to the argument list but we don't want or feel like making many changes everywhere the function appears? For a moment, we want all of the current uses of the function to use the same code, which means that an override will not work.

Suppose there is a request to make a fundamental change to the `CreateACube()` function, which tells us that we need to make a third parameter set the scale of the cube; we have a few options that we've been introduced to. The first option is to make a second version of the `CreateACube()` function with a different signature that might look like the following:

```
public GameObject CreateACube(string cubeName, Vector3 position){
    GameObject cube = GameObject.CreatePrimitive(PrimitiveType.Cube);
    cube.name = cubeName;
    cube.transform.position = position;
    return cube;
}
public GameObject CreateACube(string cubeName, Vector3 position, float
scale){
    GameObject cube = GameObject.CreatePrimitive(PrimitiveType.Cube);
    cube.name = cubeName;
    cube.transform.position = position;
    cube.transform.localScale = new Vector3(scale, scale, scale);
    return cube;
}
//Use this for initialization
void Start () {
    GameObject c = CreateACube("bob", new Vector3(10,0,0));
    //uses the first version of the function
    GameObject d = CreateACube("big_bob", new Vector3(0,10,0), 5.0f);
//uses the second version of the same function
    Debug.Log(c);
    Debug.Log(d);
}
```

This would mean that we have two different versions of the same function, only the second one has some additional statements, to take care of the third parameter. This should bring up the question, Isn't there a cleaner way to take care of any additional parameters without making more than one version of the same function? The answer is an optional parameter.

### 7.7.1 Using Optionals

When a function is used the parameter list allows for default values. There are some simple rules to follow if you want to make some of the arguments in the parameter list optional.

```
public GameObject CreateACube(string cubeName, Vector3 position, float
scale = 1.0f){
        GameObject cube = GameObject.CreatePrimitive(PrimitiveType.Cube);
        cube.name = cubeName;
        cube.transform.position = position;
        cube.transform.localScale = new Vector3(scale, scale, scale);
        return cube;
}
```

The third parameter is float scale = 1.0f. The addition of the = 1.0f predefines the incoming value unless it's overridden by a third parameter's value. In short, if there's no third parameter given, then the float scale parameter is defaulted at 1.0f, and fulfilling all three parameters is not necessary.

Without any modifications to the Start () function's use of CreateACube, we've added a simple override that handles both cases with little additional work. There are, however, some restrictions to how optional parameters are used.

Setting variables in case they're not used in the argument list is an easy way to skip writing several versions of the same function; in case there are different ways, you intend the function to be used. One loss with a predefined parameter is the fact that they will retain their order and value types.

```
public void ParamUsage(int anInt)
{
    Debug.Log("using an int " + anInt);
}
public void ParamUsage(string words)
{
    Debug.Log("using a string " + words);
}
```

For instance, we should remember that using two different signatures altogether can be used without any additional fuss.

```
void Start ()
{
    ParamUsage(1);
    ParamUsage("not a number");
}
```

This would result with two different types being used with predictable results. This works for situations in which this was expected and different types were used from the beginning since there was a predefined reason for the behavior of function's differences. However, does this mean we can add an optional parameter to either of these functions?

### 7.7.1.1 A Basic Example

Let's start with the OptionalParameters project and look at the Example component of the Main Camera in the scene.

```
using UnityEngine;
using System.Collections;
public class Example : MonoBehaviour
```

```
{
    public void ParamUsage(int anInt, float anOptionalFloat = 1)
    {
        Debug.Log("using an int " + anInt + " a float? " + anOptionalFloat);
    }
}
```

The option exists only because the parameter has an assignment in the parameter list. This does not mean that we cannot use regular overrides along with the regular use of the function. Of course, you're not actually required to write an override of any kind to begin with, though we're adding one just to show that it is possible to do so without any adverse or unexpected results.

```
public void ParamUsage(string words)
{
    Debug.Log("using a string " + words);
}
```

This, of course, means that the first version of the `ParamUsage()` example function must use both parameters it's given, which means that when in use we get the same version of the function used twice even though it's being accessed by two different sets of parameters.

```
ParamUsage(1);
ParamUsage(1, 7.0f);
ParamUsage("not a number");
```

This sends the following output to the Console panel in Unity 3D, shown is the next section.

```
using an int 1 a float? 1
using an int 1 a float? 7
using a string not a number
```

### 7.7.2 Optional Arguments

We should check to see if the optional parameter can be made unoptional in a different version of the same function; this would look something like the following:

```
public void ParamUsage(int anInt, float anOptionalFloat = 1)
{
    Debug.Log("using an int " + anInt + " a float? " + anOptionalFloat);
}
public void ParamUsage(int anInt, float aRequiredFloat)
{
    Debug.Log("using an int " + anInt + " a float? " + aRequiredFloat);
}
```

Unity 3D gives us the following error:

```
Assets/OptionalParameters.cs(17,21): error CS0111: A member
'OptionalParameters.ParamUsage(int, float)' is already defined. Rename this
member or use different parameter types
```

The signature combination for the function (int, float) is the same with both versions of the function. Therefore, no, we are not allowed to redefine the function with one using an optional parameter and another using a required parameter of the same type. This should make sense: When you're using the function, the appearance of the use would look the same. Why stop with just one optional parameter?

```
public void ParamUsage(int anInt = 1, float anOptionalFloat = 1)
{
    Debug.Log("using an int " + anInt + " a float? " + anOptionalFloat);
}
public void ParamUsage(string words)
{
    Debug.Log("using a string " + words);
}
```

We can set all of the parameters in a version of the function with defined values, which means that we're allowed to do the following in the Start () function:

```
void Start () {
    ParamUsage();
    ParamUsage(3);
    ParamUsage(9, 7.0f);
    ParamUsage("not a number");
}
```

The first use has no arguments, the second has an int for the first int, the third has an int and a float, and the fourth uses a string, which is a great deal of flexibility. We have four different uses of only two versions of the function. I think at this point we can begin to see how this can be a bit confusing. Are we allowed to make the first parameter optional and the second parameter nonoptional?

```
public void ParamUsage(int anInt = 1, float anOptionalFloat)
{
    Debug.Log("using an int " + anInt + " a float? " + anOptionalFloat);
}
```

This code throws the following error pretty quickly:

```
Assets/OptionalParameters.cs(13,55): error CS1737: Optional parameter cannot
precede required parameters
```

This error message is quite specific. Optional parameters cannot come before required parameters. This seems fair enough. For clarity if we made the first value or set of values optional, it would be impossible to tell the difference between these two functions when they're in use.

```
void pickOne(int a = 1, int b)
void pickOne(int a, int b = 1)
pickOne(1);
```

Therefore, optional parameters must only come after all of the required parameters have been defined, with the exception that we're allowed to make all parameters optional. The above code should be somewhat of a trick question: Which parameter will pickOne actually use? Will pickOne turn a or b into the used parameter? Of course neither, since there would be an error that stops the code from being compiled.

### 7.7.3  Named Parameters

Naming the arguments can be an easy way to make the parameters easier to read. In the case of CreateACube(string name, vector3 position), it's pretty clear what the two parameters are for. And thanks to helpful pop-ups in MonoDevelop, we can get useful reminders telling us what each parameter is for.

```
CreateACube (
    GameObject c    GameObject CreateACube (string     ct
    GameObject d    cubeName, Vector3 position, float scale)  w
    Debug.Log( c
```

A less commonly used feature gives us additional flexibility. If we consider a function that might have several different parameters, some of which might be optional, it's easy to forget the order in which they are expected. Furthermore, if you want to use only one of the optional parameters but don't necessarily want to override any of the others, then we'd have a problem trying to express this.

Consider the following function's signature:

```
public void LotsOfParams(int a = 0, int b = 1, int c = 2, int d = 3)
{
    Debug.Log("a:" + a + "b:" + b + "c:" + c + "d:" + d);
}
void Start ()
{
    LotsOfParams();
}
```

All of the parameters are optional, and not using any of them prints the following line of output to the Console.

```
a:0b:1c:2d:3
```

This should be expected, but if we simply want b to be 99 and leave the rest, we would be required to do the following:

```
void Start ()
{
    LotsOfParams(0,99);
}
```

From this result, we infer that a isn't actually an optional argument. Unfortunately, LotsOfParams(0,99); isn't even an option. We are missing out by not using named parameters. If the parameters from LotsOfParams had names, in this case a, b, c, and d, we can use them in the following manner.

### 7.7.3.1 A Basic Example

Named parameters follow a bit of a different look. Once there are a great deal of parameters, it's easy to forget which is which. By using a named parameter, it's more clear what the value is for and what the assignment is.

```
LotsOfParams(b:99);
```

Just use the name of the argument you want to assign a value to followed by a: and the value you want to assign to it. The order is also ignored so long as the identifiers are used.

```
LotsOfParams(b:99, a:88, d:777, c:1234);
```

This code produces the following output:

```
a:88b:99c:1234d:777
```

The b followed by a and then d before c should look rather confusing, and in practice, it's not the best form to mix arguments so badly. However, there's nothing preventing you from confusing anyone else when reading your code. From the previous CreateACube example, we're allowed to do the following:

```
CreateACube(scale : 6.0f, cubeName : "henry", position : new Vector3(2.0f,
0,0));
```

Starting off with named parameters, we're going to have to use all of the rest of the names. They can be in any order, but once we start off with naming parameters before assigning them, we're stuck with naming all of them before they're assigned. Once the order is messed up, we're unable to tell the function our intent for the data going into the different slots in the argument list. For instance, consider the following two statements:

```
CreateACube("bob", new Vector3(10,0,0));
CreateACube("henry", position: new Vector3(2.0f, 0,0));
CreateACube(position: new Vector3(1.0f, 0,0), "jack" );
```

We created a cube named bob in the first statement, as we have before; we didn't use the name in the second parameter. When we created henry, we didn't use a name in the first parameter where the string is expected. This works fine since the order has been retained. However, if we use position: as the first parameter but then use "jack" to assign the string to an out-of-order position, we get the following error:

```
Assets/OptionalParameters.cs(38,45): error CS1738: Named arguments must
appear after the positional arguments
```

Basically, the position or order of the unnamed arguments must line up with the function's signature. After that names can be used for any remaining arguments in the list.

### 7.7.4  Combining What We've Learned

We've looked at the out and ref parameters, and now we've covered both optional and named parameters in relation to the arguments and functions. We should know a bit about how they should be used together.

If we write a strange combination of out, ref, and some optional parameters, we might come up with something like the following:

```
public void Variations(ref float a, out float b, float c = 10.0f, float
d = 11.0f) {
     b = c/a;
     a = c/d;
}
```

There are a couple of important notes about this: First is the fact that ref cannot have a default value. It might look something like the following:

```
public void bad(ref int a = 1)
{
     Debug.Log ("test: " + a);
}
```

The logic that results in this error is pretty simple. Ref is a keyword reserved to tell the parameter that it's going to assume the place of another variable that already exists. This means that the value that's in the argument list can't be defined as the ref tells the value that it must be modifying something that exists outside of the function.

```
Assets/OptionalParameters.cs(31,40): error CS1741: Cannot specify a default
value for the 'ref' parameter
```

### 7.7.5  What We've Learned

We've got many options. At this point, there are very few things which you might come across in a function's parameter list that will come as a surprise. Keeping your code under control is largely dependent on your discretion and your team's decision making. Coming up with standards may or may not include using named or optional arguments, which are not too common.

Optional arguments are certainly clever, and when used properly, they're readable and easy to understand. Life can continue with or without these types of parameters appearing in your code. There's certainly nothing you can't do without them.

Optional parameters alleviate the necessity of writing additional overloaded functions, which saves some time. This is possibly best suited for a longer function that spans a heavy number of lines of code. In these cases, a repeated block of code is more likely to have errors.

Any time you need to write code again is another chance for a bug to creep in. Overloaded functions, in which one version works and another version doesn't, can lead to long nights searching for which version is being called and why it's broken.

Even in bug fixing, we learn how to write better code. Often having others check your work is a good practice to keep you in line with the rest of the team. Code reviews are a common practice among large companies, especially on high-profile projects in which a small bug can cause big problems.

## 7.8 Delegate Functions

A delegate acts like a data type; just like how both `int` and `double` are number types, a delegate is a type of function. The idea of a delegate is a bit weird. So far we've been thinking of functions as a construct that processes data.

A delegate allows us to use a function in a variable. If you're able to assign a variable to a function, you can use it like data. This means passing it between functions, structs, or classes through a parameter or assignment.

### 7.8.1 Delegates

A clever trick that C# has the ability to do is to store a function into a variable just like it were data. There are a few rules for doing this. The first important step is to ensure that the signature of the variable you're storing a function in and the function you're about to delegate match.

#### 7.8.1.1 A Basic Example

Starting with the Delegates project, we'll look at the `DelegateFunctions.cs` class. First we need to write a new delegate function, which is a sort of a template signature for any function that is to be delegated. This is easier to see in code than to explain. At the class level, add in the following code statement:

```
Example : MonoBehaviour {
//we declared a new delegate called MyDelegate
delegate void MyDelegate();
    void Start (){
    }
    void Update (){
    }
}
```

We've defined a delegate, which is pretty simple; but if you look at the signature, there's not a whole lot going on. We defined the `MyDelegate()` with return type `void` and assigned no arguments in the parentheses. However, we'll go with this as a basic example and take a look at more complex delegates in a moment.

Now that we have a defined delegate, we need to make some functions that match the signature.

```
delegate void MyDelegate();
void FirstDelegate()
{
    Debug.Log("First delegate called");
}
void SecondDelegate()
{
    Debug.Log("Second delegate called");
}
```

It's important that any functions that are going to be used with MyDelegate() have matching signatures. If not, then you'll get an error before the code compiles. To make use of a delegate, you need to make an instance of the function like you would if it were a class object.

```
void Start ()
{
    MyDelegate del = new MyDelegate(FirstDelegate);
}
```

Looking at the statement added to Start (), you should notice a couple of things. MyDelegate is the name of the delegate we defined at the class scope. This defines not only the signature we're going to be matching but also the identifier of the delegate we're going to be using. To make an instance of that delegate, we use its name.

This is followed by an identifier that is defined like any other variable. In this we're using a short identifier del to identify the MyDelegate function. This is then followed by an assignment. We use the new keyword to create an instance of the delegate function MyDelegate(), but then we add in a parameter to a set of parentheses.

We wrote two functions with matching signatures: FirstDelegate() and SecondDelegate(). Choose the FirstDelegate() and add its name to the delegate parameter. This is a bit weird, but it's an overloaded use of parentheses for delegates. After the assignment, del is now a FirstDelegate(). To use it, simply add the following statement:

```
void Start ()
{
    MyDelegate del = new MyDelegate(FirstDelegate);
    del();
}
```

When the computer runs del();, we'll get "First delegate called" printed to our console. Now here comes the interesting part.

```
void Start ()
{
    MyDelegate del = new MyDelegate(FirstDelegate);
    del();
    del = SecondDelegate;//del is reassigned!
    del();
}
```

We can give del a new assignment. To do this, we add del = SecondDelegate; to change what function has been assigned to the delegate del. When del(); is used again, we'll get "Second delegate called" printed to the Console of Unity 3D.

## 7.8.2 Delegate Signatures

Now for a more interesting example. Let's add a delegate with a more interesting signature.

```
delegate int MyDelegate(int a, int b);
public int FirstDelegate(int a, int b)
{
    return a + b;
}
public int SecondDelegate(int a, int b)
{
    return a - b;
}
```

```
//Use this for initialization
void Start ()
{
    MyDelegate del = new MyDelegate(FirstDelegate);
    int add = del(7, 3);
    Debug.Log(add);
    del = SecondDelegate;
    int sub = del(103, 3);
    Debug.Log(sub);
}
```

Here we have assigned a return value and two arguments to the delegate `MyDelegate()`;. To make use of this signature, we wrote two different functions using the same signature: The first function returns a + b and the second function returns a - b, as you might expect.

When `del` is assigned the duty of being the delegate to a function, it should be treated like a function. The clever trick is that now we're allowed to change which function `del` is delegating. There's a more important underlying use for delegates, but it's important to understand the basic setup and use of a delegate first.

The use of delegates involves first matching up all of the signatures to ensure type safety. Once this is done, you're allowed some leeway to make changes but only under some strict rules. We'll come back to that in a later chapter. We've got plenty to work with before we get there.

So far we've used `del = SecondDelegate` to assign a delegate that was created within the `Start ()` function. There's a much more interesting way to assign and use a delegate function.

### 7.8.3 Stacking Delegates

When the delegate is first declared, it's useful to add a variable to store it in at the class scope. This allows other objects in the scene to have access to the delegate.

```
delegate void MyDelegate(int a);
public MyDelegate del;
void FirstDelegate(int a)
{
    Debug.Log("first delegate: " + a);
}
void Start ()
{
    if (del == null)
    {
        del + = FirstDelegate;
        del(3);//prints "first delegate: 3"
    }
}
```

Once in the `Start ()` function, we can check if the variable left for the delegate function is null. If it is, then we can use the + = notation to assign a function to `del`. When `del` is called by another class, the `FirstDelegate` function will be executed. As we write more functions that fit the delegates' signature, we can chain more functions for `del` to execute when called.

```
delegate void MyDelegate(int a);
public MyDelegate del;
void FirstDelegate(int a)
{
    Debug.Log("first delegate: " + a);
}
void SecondDelegate(int a)
```

```
    {
        Debug.Log("second delegate: " + a);
    }
    void Start ()
    {
        if (del == null)
        {
            del + = FirstDelegate;
            del + = SecondDelegate;
            del(3);        //prints "first delegate: 3"
            //and "second delegate: 3"
        }
    }
}
```

This code stacks more functions onto our delegate. When this code is run, we get both `first del-egate: 3` and `second delegate: 3` printed to the Console panel in Unity 3D. The feature sounds cool, but when is it used? More importantly, how does this feature make C# more useful?

Once we get into events and event management, we'll get a clearer picture of what delegate functions are really used for, but it's important to understand how to create and assign delegates before we get to events. Events are basically functions that call other functions when something specific is triggered. Usually collision events and input events need to trigger user-defined events.

This is where delegates become important. The event that was initially written by the Unity 3D programmers doesn't have a specific task because they don't know what you have in mind when a key is pressed or a collision occurs on a game object. They leave the definition of what to do on the event up to you to define in your own function. To use the event, we need to match the signature of the event with our own function. Then we assign the function we wrote to the event written by the Unity 3D programmers.

### 7.8.4 Using Delegates

A `delegate` is basically a type, like any other `int` or `float`. This also means we're allowed to pass them to functions as though they were variables as well. This might be somewhat of a surprise; C# allows for many very surprising behaviors. In a function, you're allowed something as simple as `int AddNumbers(int a, int b);`, but we're also allowed to do something more complex, like the following:

```
using UnityEngine;
using System.Collections;
public class Delegates : MonoBehaviour
{
    delegate int MyDelegate();
    //Use this for initialization
    void Start ()
    {
        UseDelegate(GetThree);
    }
    int GetThree()
    {
        return 3;
    }
    void UseDelegate(MyDelegate mDelegate)
    {
        int gotNumber = mDelegate();
        Debug.Log(gotNumber);
    }
}
```

The above code declares a delegate called `MyDelegate()` that then becomes a type. The type it has turned into is indicated when it's declared; it's signature determines how it's used. `MyDelegate()` must return a type and it has no arguments. This is matched by the function `GetThree()`, which returns an int—in this case 3—and also takes no arguments. When we use the function called `UseDelegate()` in the `Start ()` function, we can use the identifier `GetThree` in the argument list of `UseDelegate()`.

The above example is contrived; the actual use of a delegate is hardly ever so simple. The basic idea of the delegate allows you to pick and choose between functions to assign to another function as an argument. This also means that you can assign a function to a variable almost like any other data type.

A delegate doesn't need to have its function declared ahead of its use.

```
delegate void Del();
//Use this for initialization
void Start ()
{
    Del d = delegate()
    {
        Debug.Log("delegate calling");
    };
    d();
}
```

Just having a function named `Del()` and declaring it as a delegate with `delegate void Del();` is enough to have a signature to work with. In the above `Start ()` function, we create a new instance of that `delegate` with `Del d`. Then we assign it a task to do when `d();` is called.

The formatting of the above code looks a bit peculiar, but we are declaring a function inside of a function. This also means that we can reassign the function after it's used.

```
delegate void Del();
//Use this for initialization
void Start ()
{
    int a = 10;
    Del d = delegate()
    {
        Debug.Log("delegate calling");
    };
    d();
    d = delegate()
    {
        Debug.Log("a/2 = " + a/2);
    };
    d();
}
```

Delegate d is declared and written inside of the `Start ()` function's scope. This means that `int a` declared at the beginning of the `Start ()` function is visible to the `delegate()`'s contents. If `int a = 10;`, we can use the variable a in a delegate's code block. Therefore, `a/2` is calculable inside of the delegate. From the above code, we get both "`delegate calling`" and "`a/2 = 5`" printed in the Console.

```
delegate void Del();
//Use this for initialization
void Start ()
{
    int a = 10;
    Del d = delegate()
    {
        Debug.Log("delegate calling");
    };
    d();
```

```
        d = delegate()
        {
            Debug.Log("a/2 = " + a/2);
        };
        HandlesDel(d);
    }
    void HandlesDel(Del del)
    {
        del();
    }
```

Stranger still now that Del is a type, it can also be passed between functions as an argument. Instead of dealing with d(); at the end of the Start () function, we can also pass d to a function that has the Del type as an argument variable.

The function void HandlesDel(Del del) can accept d as an argument. This means that a function is a type. As a type it can be passed between functions as data. The behavior also has an effect on the data inside of the function. Therefore, data is also something that does work, contains logic, and can perform tasks.

### 7.8.5 What We've Learned

In Unity 3D, delegates are often used to update the state of an object that has been created in the scene. This is best done via events. We'll find out more about that in a few chapters. I'll leave you to play with some delegates for now; using events is going to take up a chapter, so we'll leave that for later.

Transferring data between functions and classes is one thing. Sending functions between functions is another.

```
        delegate int iDel();
```

This statement declares a delegate with a return value of int. This means that when the delegate code is assigned, you need to have a return value.

```
        iDel id = delegate()
        {
            return 12;
        };
```

This doesn't act in the same way, as the body is only stored as a value in id. To use id(), you can do the same as before, and simply use id(); to execute the delegate. Likewise a function can accept iDel as a type.

```
        void AdsiDel(iDel id)
        {
            Debug.Log("adding iDels together: " + id()*2);
        }
```

The above code simply prints adding iDels together: 24 to the Console. It's quite interesting once you accept that functions are actually data types like any other number or letter. This consideration has far-reaching implications. The flexibility has a number of uses as well.

## 7.9 Interface

An interface is a promise that your new class will implement a function from its base class. The implementation of an interface can be made for any method, event, or delegate. Anything that has a signature with an identifier and argument list can be turned into an interface for a base class.

The structure of your code depends on having a consistent plan. With every new function and every new data structure, you're adding to the overall complexity of your game or software. The more people you collaborate with, the more will be the complexity, necessitating some way to stay organized and maintain some sort of consistency. Your game's chance of success is based on your code remaining consistent and stable.

An interface provides a framework that all of the child classes based on it will derive from. An interface is an organizational tool that helps us when sweeping changes are made. Say you decide that all of your zombies now need to have a new feature, for example, their arms needing to be cut off; it will help out in the end if you made an interface for building the body of the zombie when you started.

### 7.9.1 Early Planning

Using an interface should be considered early on. Adding them after many classes have already been written can turn into a nightmare if your different monsters took on a wide variety of implementations, but therein lies the strength of the interface.

An interface is a construct that helps other programmers understand what you've written. These tools are intended to provide a basis for understanding without needing to hover around the rest of your team to explain what your code does. Interfaces provide a system for constructing a class that implements your code.

When we consider why object oriented programming helps us rather than hinders us, we need to remember a few things. First, we need to think of each new class as a progressive evolutionary process to a previous class. Every fundamental change we make to our game has to be reflected on as wide a scale as possible. Second, we need to remember that every object should share as much data as possible. Finally, we need to make sure that all of our objects should be able to interact with one another as closely as possible.

To communicate this interaction and to solidify this unity between characters and properties in our game world, you need to set up some base rules. These rules are best communicated by using an interface. For an interface to make sense, we have to create a class that the rest of the objects in our game will find as their base, a common foundation for all objects in our game to share. Once we begin with some basic design patterns, we'll really understand why interfaces are important, but for now, we'll just take a look at a basic implementation.

### 7.9.1.1 A Basic Example

We'll start with the Interface project, in which we have an `IThink.cs` created in the Assets directory. Unlike many other classes, an interface isn't directly used in Unity 3D. The naming convention always starts with an `I` to indicate that the class is an interface and not necessarily an object for use in the game.

```
public interface IThing
{
    string ThingName {get; set;}
}
```

We've deleted some of the usual starting functions to create an interface. As a common practice, we prefix the interface with an uppercase `I`, though it's not necessary. Inside of our interface, we added an arbitrary string called `ThingName`. Everything needs a name, doesn't it? Of course, you can use any type inside of the interface as an example, but a string is something easy to test, so we'll start with `string ThingName` in our example.

The new syntax we're seeing is called an *interface property*, and the format we're seeing is how a property is created in an interface. Interface properties are consistent identifiers, which all classes that implement the interface will have. Often you might see this done with the following style:

```
string ThingName {get; set;}
```

This looks cleaner, so we should get used to seeing the `get; set;` syntax, as in the above statement. The interface property is used as a system to allow each implementation of the interface to change how the property is used. We can change how the `get` and `set` work, depending on the goal for each implementation. Interface implementations need to be made `public`.

Until we fully implement the `IThing` interface, Unity 3D will be telling us that there are some errors because `Toaster` doesn't implement all of `IThing`. This is corrected by adding in members of the interface.

This can automatically be stubbed out by selecting the Show Code Generation panel with the right click menu in MonoDevelop inside of the `Toaster` class. Select the member in `IThing` and the following template will be generated:

```
using UnityEngine;
using System.Collections;
public class Toaster : IThing
{
    public string ThingName
    {
        get
        {
            throw new System.NotImplementedException();
        }
        set
        {
            throw new System.NotImplementedException();
        }
    }
}
```

This shouldn't be the final code, but it's telling us what we need to provide to complete the implementation.

```
using UnityEngine;
using System.Collections;
public class Toaster : IThing
{
    private string ToasterName;
    public string ThingName
    {
        get
        {
            return ToasterName;
        }
        set
        {
            ToasterName = value;
        }
        //keyword value is specific to the accessor
    }
}
```

We need a private local variable specific to the class to store in the class that holds onto `string name`, which was supplied in the interface. In this case, we use `ToasterName` in the Toaster class. This isolates the local data but uses the interface property for the variable `ThingName` that was created in the `IThing` interface.

### 7.9.1.2 *Using Accessors*

The keyword `value` is used in the `get;` `set;` `{}` function to access the interface's variable. The `get;` `set;` statement is called an accessor statement and is used for interface implementation. The appearance of `get;` `set;` in a class implementing the interface now requires code to be complete. Finally, we can instance the object in Unity 3D by creating an `Example.cs` file attached to the Main Camera in the scene.

```
using UnityEngine;
using System.Collections;
public class Example : MonoBehaviour
{
    //Use this for initialization
    void Start ()
    {
        Toaster T = new Toaster();//create a new Toaster
        T.ThingName = "Talkie";//set the toasters name
        print(T.ThingName);//check the toasters name
    }
    //Update is called once per frame
    void Update ()
    {
    }
}
```

As an example, we create a new `Toaster T`, assign its name to `"Talkie,"` and then print out the name to double check that the accessor is correctly implemented. Notice that we're not using `ToasterName` that was made `private` in the `Toaster` class. The use of `ThingName` and not `ToasterName` is the key reason for why interfaces are important. For every class that implements the `IThing` interface, we must have a system to set a `ThingName`.

If you have programmers adding new monsters, they should be instructed to implement the `IThing` interface. With this rule, their code will not work unless their monster has a `ThingName`. If you make a rule to never check-in code that's broken, you always should confirm your code works before checking it in. Needing to implement an interface to every new object ensures that every object has a `ThingName`. Therefore, if we were to create a new zombie with the same interface, we'd need to do something like in the following example:

```
using UnityEngine;
using System.Collections;
public class Zombie : MonoBehaviour, IThing
{
    private string ZombieName;
    public string ThingName
    {
        get
        {
            return ZombieName;
        }
        set
        {
            ZombieName = value;
        }
    }
    //Use this for initialization
    void Start ()
    {
    }
    //Update is called once per frame
    void Update ()
    {
    }
}
```

This is a new zombie class that is based on `MonoBehaviour`. This means that we're creating a new `ZombieGame` object since we're inheriting from `MonoBehaviour`. We've also implemented the name accessor to follow the IThing interface. Without `public   string   ThingName{get;set;}` defined, we get the following error:

```
Assets/Zombie.cs(4,14): error CS0535: 'Zombie' does not implement interface
member 'IThing.ThingName.get'
Assets/Zombie.cs(4,14): error CS0535: 'Zombie' does not implement interface
member 'IThing.ThingName.set'
```

A programmer needs to know quickly when an error has occurred. I've heard people say "fail fast and fail often" to describe rapid development in small game studios. There are many reasons for this, and finding bugs in your code is one of them. Interfaces ensure that new game objects follow the proper setup you might want to use in your game. We should be careful when instancing a class that is based on MonoBehaviour. Using the following code fragment will give us an error:

```
void Start ()
{
    Toaster T = new Toaster();
    T.ThingName = "Talkie";
    print(T.ThingName);
    //Zombie Z = new Zombie();
    //Zombie is a game Object, new won't work
}
```

The error looks like the following:

```
You are trying to create a MonoBehaviour using the 'new' keyword. This is not
allowed. MonoBehaviours can only be added using AddComponent(). Alternatively,
your script can inherit from ScriptableObject or no base class at all
UnityEngine.MonoBehaviour:.ctor()
Zombie:.ctor()
Example:Start () (at Assets/Example.cs:11)
```

To remedy the error that this produces, we'll have to use `gameObject.AddComponent();`. Therefore, the code should look a bit more like the following:

```
void Start ()
{
    Toaster T = new Toaster();
    T.ThingName = "Talkie";
    Zombie Z = gameObject.AddComponent("Zombie");
}
```

However, we still get an error.

```
Assets/Example.cs(11,24): error CS0266: Cannot implicitly convert type
'UnityEngine.Component' to 'Zombie'. An explicit conversion exists (are you
missing a cast?)
```

Ah, yes, of course! We're adding a gameObject component, so right now we're saying that we'd like a Zombie Z, but we're creating by instancing a gameObject component. Therefore, we need to convert the gameObject component into a Zombie before it's assigned to Zombie Z. This means that our final code fragment in the Example.cs file should look like the following:

```
void Start ()
{
    Toaster T = new Toaster();
    T.ThingName = "Talkie";
    print(T.ThingName);
```

```
        Zombie Z = (Zombie)gameObject.AddComponent("Zombie");
        Z.ThingName = "Stubbs";
        print(Z.ThingName);
    }
```

Now we've created a `gameObject` that uses the `IThing` interface. Both `Toaster` and `Zombie` implement the same interface. Therefore, we can assign both a name and get that name to print. We can ensure that everything using interface `IThing` has a `ThingName` we can get and set.

If you check-in Unity's attribute editor after running the code, you'll notice that a new component has indeed been added to the camera. Because we based `Zombie` on `MonoBehaviour` and implemented the `IThing` interface, we also get the benefit of `Start()` and `Update()` along with compatibility with all `IThing` functionality.

## 7.9.2 Interface Methods

We looked at a basic field property access to interfaces with `ThingName{get; set;}`, but what about functions? To get to that, we're going to add a basic function to the `IThing` interface. Our thing should be able to say hello, or at least print something to the Console.

```
public interface IThing
{
    string ThingName
    {
        get;
        set;
    }
    void SayHello();
}
```

As soon as we add the `void SayHello();` function to the interface, we get a warning in Unity 3D, reminding us that some classes don't implement the `SayHello();` interface member.

```
Assets/Toaster.cs(4,14): error CS0535: 'Toaster' does not implement interface
member 'IThing.SayHello()'
```

To remedy this, we should add the function to the `Toaster`.

```
using UnityEngine;
using System.Collections;
public class Toaster : IThing
{
    private string ToasterName;
    public string ThingName
    {
        get
```

```
        {
                return ToasterName;
        }
        set
        {
                ToasterName = value;
        }
    }
    public void SayHello()
    {
            Debug.Log("howdy doodly do.");
    }
}
```

Because Toaster doesn't have MonoBehaviour to inherit from, you lose print(). Thankfully, Debug.Log() is found in the UnityEngine directives that are handy when it comes to finding useful functions. In your game, you might want to have the sayHello() function play a sound and play some animation to make this function more meaningful. The interesting thing here is that we do need to make any interface members public.

The accessor for ThingName is a public string. The SayHello() function is also public.

```
using UnityEngine;
using System.Collections;
public class Zombie : MonoBehaviour, IThing
{
    string ZombieName;
    public string ThingName
    {
        get
        {
                return ZombieName;
        }
        set
        {
                ZombieName = value;
        }
    }
    public void SayHello()
    {
            print("brains");
    }
    void Start ()
    {
    }
    void Update ()
    {
    }
}
```

In our Zombie, which also implements the IThing interface, add the public SayHello() function as well. Of course, the Zombie doesn't share the same ideas as the Toaster, so his greeting should be different. Having different classes have the same function identifiers but with differing operations within the function is what allows us to maintain consistency.

### 7.9.2.1 Breaking a Fixing

While you're coding up a storm, you'll be writing a great deal of code that need to be constantly updated. It's very common to add a feature to an interface or a base class, and then need to do many code updates. In some cases, your errors may span across multiple files.

Fear not; this is just a part of programming. For instance, when you add a small bit of code to an interface, you'll need to find everything that uses the interface and add the new changes to them. This can be time consuming, but if the feature is important, it's worth the effort.

When you start making changes, it's sometimes easier to let the compiler find the locations where changes need to be made. For instance, when we added the `SayHello()` method to `IThing`, we got some errors telling us what line the error occurred on. If we implemented several classes that used `IThing` as an interface, we'd get multiple errors. Each error informs us where we need to go to add in our changes.

Thankfully, you can double click on the error information in Unity 3D and MonoDevelop will open the file and jump the cursor to the error's location. The errors and warnings are there to help you, not to remind you that you're doing things wrong.

### 7.9.3 Multiple Interfaces

In C# we do not have the ability to inherit from multiple classes. This means to create a zombie bear we can't inherit the members of both a zombie and a bear. However, we can implement both interfaces. For this we need to add in a new class called `IDamage`.

```
using UnityEngine;
using System.Collections;
interface IDamage
{
    int HitPoints {get; set;}
    void TakeDamage(int damage);
    void HealDamage(int damage);
}
```

We've added three members to the interface class `IDamage`. We need to be pretty clear in our coding as to what we're going to use the interface members for.

```
using UnityEngine;
using System.Collections;
public class Zombie : MonoBehaviour, IThing, IDamage
{
    private string ZombieName;
    private int ZombieHitPoints;
    public int HitPoints
    {
        get
        {
            return ZombieHitPoints;
        }
        set
        {
            ZombieHitPoints = value;
        }
    }
```

```
public void TakeDamage(int damage)
{
        ZombieHitPoints - = damage;
        //zombies take damage from baseball bats
}
public void HealDamage(int damage)
{
        return;
        //zombies can't be healed
}
public string ThingName
{
        get
        {
            return ZombieName;
        }
        set
        {
            ZombieName = value;
        }
}
public void SayHello()
{
        print("brains");
}
void Start ()
{
}
void Update ()
{
}
}
```

When we add `IDamage` after `IThing`, we're reminded by warnings popping up in the Unity 3D Console to implement the interface. Therefore, we add in the accessor for the `HitPoints`, and then implement the zombie's version of `TakeDamage()` and `HealDamage()`. It's up to you to decide what happens when you try to heal a zombie.

### 7.9.4 IComparer

Building a collection of interfaces makes sense so long as the interfaces provide necessary functionality. The interfaces provided by C# offer more interesting possibilities in that they can be customized for any suited purpose.

The `ArrayList` isn't complete without having our own method to sort. The sort requires a customized version of the `IComparer` interface. In this interface, we have the `public int Compare()` function that takes two objects. We've added a third term called `Target`. This can be assigned after the `DistanceComparer` has been instanced. Therefore, after `DistanceComparer dc;` has been created with the new keyword, we assign the `Target` to another `GameObject` in the scene.

```
using UnityEngine;
using System.Collections;
public class DistanceComparer : IComparer
{
    public GameObject Target;
    public int Compare(object x, object y)
    {
        GameObject xObj = (GameObject)x;
```

```
            GameObject yObj = (GameObject)y;
            Vector3 tPos = Target.transform.position;
            Vector3 xPos = xObj.transform.position;
            Vector3 yPos = yObj.transform.position;
            float xDistance = (tPos - xPos).magnitude;
            float yDistance = (tPos - yPos).magnitude;
            if (xDistance > yDistance)
            {
                return 1;
            } else if (xDistance < yDistance)
            {
                return -1;
            } else
            {
                return 0;
            }
        }
    }
}
```

The above code has the added `Target GameObject` and some math to check the distance from object x to the `Target` and the distance to object y. Once these two values are found, we compare them. If the distance to the first object is greater, then we return 1; if the value is less, we return -1. If neither of these two cases is fulfilled, then we return 0, inferring that x and y are equal.

The `ArrayList.Sort()` function uses the different 1, -1, and 0 values to move the objects it's comparing. 1 means to move the x object up one in the array, -1 down one in the array, and finally 0 means don't move any objects. Under the hood, the `Sort()` uses what is often referred to as a quicksort algorithm.

### 7.9.5 Using IComparer

In the `Example` component, we'll add the following code to the `Update ()` loop:

```
public GameObject[] SortedByDistance;
void Update ()
{
    ArrayList ObjectList = new ArrayList();
    GameObject[] Objects = GameObject.FindObjectsOfType(typeof
    (GameObject)) as GameObject[];
    foreach (GameObject go in Objects)
    {
        ObjectList.Add(go);
    }
    DistanceComparer dComparer = new DistanceComparer();
    dComparer.Target = this.gameObject;
    ObjectList.Sort(dComparer);
    SortedByDistance = new GameObject[ObjectList.Count];
    ObjectList.CopyTo(SortedByDistance);
}
```

In the above code, we create a new instance of the `DistanceComparer` object. The `gameObject` which has the `Example.cs` component attached is then assigned the `Target` object. This provides the interface with a reference to compare objects in the `ArrayList` to.

Once the `Target` is assigned, we can use the `ObjectList.Sort()` with the `dComparer` in the argument list. This tells the sort to do its work with your new `IComparer` algorithm. This then returns another array that is sorted by distance.

The `SortedByDistance` array is now rearranged not by the order in the scene but by distance! Very quick and easy.

### 7.9.6 What We've Learned

There has already been a great deal of material in this chapter. I doubt you have any urgent need for either toast or brains, but at least we know we can give our characters the option. Interfaces are sort of like promises to reuse both the same identifier and the same signature that were created in the interface.

This ensures that you always get the same implementation for each class that uses the same interface. It would be a good idea to have as few interfaces as necessary. To explain, you shouldn't implement a `IMedPack` interface and an `IShieldPowerup` interface. What should be implemented is an `IPickup` interface. An `IPickup` would cover anything that your player could pick up.

Likewise, an `IWeapon` would be fine to cover anything that shoots, needs to hold ammo, and does anything that a weapon is used for. The `IPickup` could hold information for incrementing ammo, health, armor, or anything else. Classes implementing the `IPickup` interface could decide which they are incrementing, allowing for one or all of the stats to be adjusted when the item is picked up.

We'll get into a few common-looking setups later on when we look at game design patterns. For now try to think on your own what sort of interfaces you'll be implementing.

---

## 7.10  Class Constructors Revisited

Interfaces provide a system to ensure that a class is talked to in a specific way. When we start building more complex classes, we need to use an apparatus to ensure a consistent creation of the class. When we get started with a game where zombies are spawned and chase after the player, we might begin with a single zombie type. Later on we'd want to change this up for more variety. Modifing the amount of damage to destroy a zombie or change its size, shape, and model would all need to be modified according to specific parameters.

If you're working with a team, you're going to be needing to make sure that the class you're writing is created consistently. If you allowed one programmer to directly set the hit points and another one to modify its armor instead, then you might get some unexpected behavior between the two monsters.

This could be mitigated by using a constructor when the monster is first created. You set up a specific set of parameters that have to be used to properly create a zombie.

A class *constructor* is used to set up an initial set of parameters required to instance a new zombie.

### 7.10.1 A Basic Example

In the following code sample in the ClassConstructorsAgain project, find the class Example and create a subclass called MyClass. Within MyClass is a private string name; that isn't directly accessible from outside of the class. Inside of the MyClass declaration is a public MyClass(string n) function that takes in a string parameter. When a class declaration has a function with a matching identifier inside of the class, that function becomes the class's constructor.

```
using UnityEngine;
using System.Collections;
public class Example : MonoBehaviour
{
    //sub class declaration
    public class MyClass
    {
        //sub-class string called name
        private string name;
        //function with same identifier as class name
        public MyClass(string n)
        {
            //assigns the internal name to string n
            name = n;
        }
    }
    void Start ()
    {
        //uses the class constructor, names the class bob
        MyClass mc = new MyClass("bob");
    }
}
```

Without much work, we can standardize the class to require a name when the class is instanced with the new keyword. If you try to create the class without a name with MyClass mc = new MyClass();, you'll get the following error:

```
Assets/Example.cs(20,43): error CS1729: The type 'Example.MyClass' does not
contain a constructor that takes '0' arguments
```

This tells you that you're instancing the class differently than how the class is expected to be instanced. To properly instance this class, you are required to provide a string to assign to the class's name variable. Using function overloading, we're allowed to make more than one signature for the class constructor.

```
    public class MyClass
    {
        private string name;
        public MyClass(string n)
        {
            name = n;
        }
        public MyClass(int n)
        {
            name = n.ToString();
        }
    }
```

This code fragment has two versions of the `public MyClass()` constructor. The second one takes in an `int` parameter and then converts it to a `string` before assigning it to the `private string name`. This allows us to use the following code to create a new class instance.

```
void Start ()
{
    MyClass mc = new MyClass(3);
}
```

If we create a class with this code and use a number for its name, it'll get assigned a 3 to its name as a character, not an `int`. Putting this into practice, we can create some more interesting constructors.

### 7.10.2 When to Create a New Class

Now that we've been working with classes for a few chapters, you might begin to wonder how often you'll need to write a new class. To be honest, it's something that you might end up doing more often than not. Nesting classes within a class is often helpful to organize and control data within a larger class that needs to manage several things at once.

For instance, we might look at creating an endless treadmill for a scrolling shooter. We could begin this task with a treadmill manager, something that would create, move, and destroy elements that need to scroll by. Each object that it creates should manage its own positioning within the treadmill's parameters.

```
using UnityEngine;
using System.Collections;
public class TreadmillManager : MonoBehaviour {
    //Use this for initialization
    void Start () {
    }
    //Update is called once per frame
    void Update () {
    }
}
```

Since there's going to be many objects scrolling by, we'll want an array. Some of the objects might move and fly around; others might be static objects that the player might collide with. Should we have two different nested classes? Or perhaps should we create two new classes?

Actually, we're getting ahead of ourselves. We should focus on one thing at a time. After our class is created, we only need to move it to a new file, once it has grown beyond a reasonable number of functions and fields. Let's start with at the beginning and think our way through. Let's build the start of an `Obstacle` class for our `TreadmillManager` to work with.

```
using UnityEngine;
using System.Collections;
public class TreadmillManager : MonoBehaviour
{
    class Obstacle
    {
        GameObject obstacle;
    }
    private Obstacle[] obstacles;
    public int ObstacleCount = 10;
    //Use this for initialization
    void Start ()
    {
        obstacles = new Obstacle[ObstacleCount];
        //creates a new array of the size requested
        for (int i = 0; i < ObstacleCount; i++)
```

```
        {
            obstacles [i] = new Obstacle();
            //fills in the array with new obstacles
        }
    }
    //Update is called once per frame
    void Update ()
    {
    }
}
```

Now we should allow the obstacle to generate an object for itself.

```
class Obstacle
{
    GameObject obstacle;
    //constructor
    public Obstacle()
    {
        obstacle = GameObject.CreatePrimitive(PrimitiveType.Cube);
    }
}
```

In the nested class `Obstacle`, we add `public  Obstacle()`, which is the constructor for the `Obstacle` class. Every new class has a default constructor. This might not be obvious, but it's true. If a specific constructor isn't provided, then when the constructor is called, nothing interesting happens. However, when we specify what to do when the class is instanced, we get to do clever things such as creating primitives when the class is instanced. The alternative would be something like the following:

```
class Obstacle {
    GameObject obstacle;
    //constructor
    public void InitObstacle() {
        obstacle = GameObject.CreatePrimitive(PrimitiveType.Cube);
    }
}
private Obstacle[] obstacles;
public int ObstacleCount = 10;
//Use this for initialization
void Start () {
    obstacles = new Obstacle[ObstacleCount];
    //creates a new array of the size requested
    for (int i = 0; i < ObstacleCount; i++) {
        obstacles[i] = new Obstacle();
        obstacles[i].InitObstacle();//extra function call
    }
}
```

In the `Start ()` when we fill in the `Obstacle[]` array, we would need to make an additional function call, which would then have to act like a constructor. If we need the obstacle to have a mesh any time it's instanced, we may also add that functionality to the constructor. We have additional options as well. We can set up the correctly written constructor with a parameter.

```
public Obstacle(PrimitiveType primitive)
{
    obstacle = GameObject.CreatePrimitive(primitive);
}
```

When the `obstacles[]` array is filled in, we can add a parameter to the class instancing the call.

```
//Use this for initialization
void Start ()
{
    obstacles = new Obstacle[ObstacleCount];
    //creates a new array of the size requested
    for (int i = 0; i < ObstacleCount; i++)
    {
        obstacles [i] = new Obstacle(PrimitiveType.Sphere);
        //pick a different primitive
    }
}
```

This is clever and far more interesting. Therefore, now our `TreadmillManager` is creating an array of little spheres. We have a couple of decisions to make now that the cubes are being instanced properly and the `TreadmillManager` has something to manage. These guys need to move, so should the `TreadmillManager` move them? Or perhaps they could each move on their own accord.

If the `TreadmillManager` were to keep each one's position, we'd need another array of positions to deal with, then tell each obstacle where it needs to be positioned, and then update each position. If some of the obstacles need to move in a pattern, it would mean additional behaviors and another array. This seems like a bad strategy.

```
class Obstacle
{
    GameObject obstacle;
    public enum MovementType
    {
        Static,
        Wave,
        Left,
        Right
    }
    MovementType movementType;
    //constructor
    public Obstacle(PrimitiveType primitive, MovementType movement)
    {
        obstacle = GameObject.CreatePrimitive(primitive);
        movementType = movement;
    }
}
```

Let's add in a variety of different `MovementType`s. I'm using an enum, which limits us to only a few different possibilities. With enums, we can easily communicate to our designers what to expect when a `MovementType` is selected.

```
void Start ()
{
    obstacles = new Obstacle[ObstacleCount];
    //creates a new array of the size requested
    for (int i = 0; i < ObstacleCount; i++)
    {
        obstacles [i] = new Obstacle(PrimitiveType.Sphere,
        Obstacle.MovementType.Static);
    }
}
```

We'll pick a default `MovementType` for creating the new `Obstacle()` object. For now we'll just pick static, and then we'll add in a function to pick a different movement later on. Let's just add in a simple way to move the obstacle.

```
class Obstacle
{
    GameObject obstacle;
    public enum MovementType
    {
        Static,
        Wave,
        Left,
        Right
    }
    MovementType movementType;
    //constructor
    public Obstacle(PrimitiveType primitive, MovementType movement)
    {
        obstacle = GameObject.CreatePrimitive(primitive);
        movementType = movement;
    }
    //Let's move the obstacle
    public void UpdatePosition(float z)
    {
        if (movementType == MovementType.Static)
        {
            Vector3 pos = new Vector3(0, 0, z);
            obstacle.transform.position + = pos;
        }
    }
}
```

We're adding in a function at the end of the nested class called UpdatePosition() and then giving it a simple parameter for movement speed. In the declaration, we have public void UpdatePosition(float z);. We need to use the function in the parent class, so we have to make the declaration public. Next, we're not too concerned whether or not the function is doing its thing, so it'll return void.

```
//Update is called once per frame
void Update ()
{
    foreach(Obstacle o in obstacles)
    {
        o.UpdatePosition(-0.01f);
    }
}
```

In the parent class, we're adding a new foreach statement to the Update () function that is called each frame. This action moves all of the different spheres at the same rate down the z axis in the scene. This is an instruction sent to each object individually. Superficially this will work out, but there's a more simple method which we can use to give each obstacle the same function.

### 7.10.2.1 Add in a Private zposition Offset

In the Obstacle class, we need to give each obstacle its own zposition.

```
static float zposition;
private float myZposition;
//constructor
public Obstacle(PrimitiveType primitive, MovementType movement)
```

```
    {
        obstacle = GameObject.CreatePrimitive(primitive);
        movementType = movement;
        myZposition = Random.Range(-10f, 10f);
        obstacle.transform.position =
            new Vector3(Random.Range(-10f, 10f),
                Random.Range(-10f, 10f),
                Random.Range(-10f, 10f));
    }
```

When the object's constructor is called, we'll set the `myZposition` to a random number between $-10f$ and `10f`. Once that's done, we'll need to add the `myZposition` to the function where we set the object's position in the game.

```
    public void DrawObstacle()
    {
        Vector3 pos = obstacle.transform.position;
        pos.z = (zposition + myZposition)% 10f;
        obstacle.transform.position = pos;
    }
```

The `pos.z` uses the `static zposition` and the `private myZposition`. This means that each object can potentially have a unique `zposition` from all other objects.

### 7.10.3 Static Functions

In Chapter 5, we saw how `static` can give each instance of a class access to the same variable. Change the `UpdatePosition()` function to merely update a `static` variable called `zposition`.

```
    class Obstacle
    {
        GameObject obstacle;
        public enum MovementType
        {
            Static,
            Wave,
            Left,
            Right
        }
        MovementType movementType;
        static float zposition;
        private float myZposition;
        //constructor
        public Obstacle(PrimitiveType primitive, MovementType movement)
        {
            obstacle = GameObject.CreatePrimitive(primitive);
            movementType = movement;
            myZposition = Random.Range(-10f, 10f);
            obstacle.transform.position =
                new Vector3(Random.Range(-10f, 10f),
                    Random.Range(-10f, 10f),
                    Random.Range(-10f, 10f));
        }
        //move the obstacle
        public static void UpdatePosition(float z)
```

```
        {
            zposition + = z;
        }
        public void DrawObstacle()
        {
            Vector3 pos = obstacle.transform.position;
            pos.z = (zposition + myZposition)% 10f;
            obstacle.transform.position = pos;
        }
    }
```

This code reduces the places where a variable is updated. Each time the static function is called, every instance of the obstacle class gets the change. Using a foreach loop does make things easier, but a static method and a variable are even easier than that. With the current number of variables we have, we'll be seeing every object in the same place. The obstacle GameObject is going to need to get a new position with each frame. Right now, we're going to be setting them all to the same position. Therefore, we'll want to change that with a simple additional step to the creation of the objects.

### 7.10.3.1 Using a Delegate Function

The objects still need to be updated individually. They all share a single variable, but they need to have their own position updated by another function. For our Start () function, add a new delegate function. Rather than using a loop to iterate through each object's function, we'll instead use a delegate function to do that for us.

```
private Obstacle[] obstacles;
public int ObstacleCount = 10;
delegate void UpdateObstacles();//delegate function
UpdateObstacles treadMillUpdates;//the delegate to assign functions
//Use this for initialization
void Start ()
{
    obstacles = new Obstacle[ObstacleCount];
    //creates a new array of the size requested
    for (int i = 0; i < ObstacleCount; i++)
    {
        obstacles [i] =
            new Obstacle(PrimitiveType.Sphere,
                Obstacle.MovementType.Static);
        //assign each objects update to the delegate here
        treadMillUpdates + =
            new UpdateObstacles(obstacles [i].DrawObstacle);
    }
}
```

This will allow us to use a single delegate function to call many other functions rather than using a for loop to iterate through an array. The attempt to keep code tidy and brief is a simple goal but requires many different tricks to achieve.

The statement delegate void UpdateObstacles() creates a signature to instantiate a delegate function. The delegate function is instantiated with the UpdateObstacles treadMill-Updates; line where UpdateObstacles is the type and treadMillUpdates is the identifier.

Once in the for loop in the Start () function, we assign a new UpdateObstacles(obstacles[i]. DrawObstacle); to the treadMillUpdates; identifier. Using the + = operator, we stack the obstacles[i].DrawObstacle function into the treadMillUpdates delegate function. At the end of the for loop, the treadMillUpdates() becomes a single function that calls a stack of other functions. To use the delegate, it's added to the Update () loop as a single statement.

```
//Update is called once per frame
void Update ()
{
    Obstacle.UpdatePosition(-0.1f);
    treadMillUpdates();
}
```

Once all of the object functions have been assigned to the delegate, you need to only use one line to update all of the objects. Obstacle.UpdatePosition() changes the zposition for all of the objects, and now treadMillUpdates() sets the position to the updated data.

```
using UnityEngine;
using System.Collections;
public class TreadmillManager : MonoBehaviour
{
    class Obstacle
    {
        GameObject obstacle;
        public enum MovementType
        {
            Static,
            Wave,
            Left,
            Right
        }
        MovementType movementType;
        static float zposition;
        private float myZposition;
        //constructor
        public Obstacle(PrimitiveType primitive, MovementType movement)
        {
            obstacle = GameObject.CreatePrimitive(primitive);
            movementType = movement;
            myZposition = Random.Range(-10f, 10f);
            obstacle.transform.position =
                new Vector3(Random.Range(-10f, 10f),
                    Random.Range(-10f, 10f),
                    Random.Range(-10f, 10f));
        }
        //move the obstacle
        public static void UpdatePosition(float z)
        {
            zposition + = z;
        }
        public void DrawObstacle()
        {
            Vector3 pos = obstacle.transform.position;
            pos.z = (zposition + myZposition)% 10f;
            obstacle.transform.position = pos;
        }
    }
    private Obstacle[] obstacles;
    public int ObstacleCount = 10;
    delegate void UpdateObstacles();
    UpdateObstacles treadMillUpdates;
    //Use this for initialization
    void Start ()
    {
        obstacles = new Obstacle[ObstacleCount];
```

```
            //creates a new array of the size requested
            for (int i = 0; i < ObstacleCount; i++)
            {
                obstacles [i] =
                    new Obstacle(PrimitiveType.Sphere,
                        Obstacle.MovementType.Static);
                treadMillUpdates + =
                    new UpdateObstacles(obstacles [i].DrawObstacle);
            }
        }
        //Update is called once per frame
        void Update ()
        {
            Obstacle.UpdatePosition(-0.1f);
            treadMillUpdates();
        }
    }
}
```

The completed code for the treadmill effect looks pretty simple now. We're making use of some fairly complex concepts. Delegate functions help reduce the amount of work we need to do to ensure that we're maintaining a consistent flow of data. We could use additional `for` or `while` loops, but this adds complexity and challenges when we need to start adding features. The performance is still pretty good here, even when we pump up the number of obstacles to 1000.

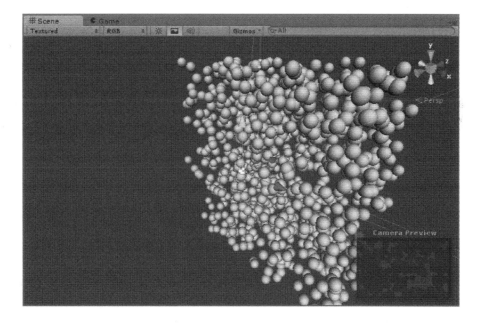

### 7.10.4 What We've Learned

As we add new tricks to our bag, we need to consider how to use them. Even though the tricks are no more than organizational or even for practice, it's important that we use them. Practice is the only way we will get better at the craft of code. With each new tool we learn we should use it.

This might not always work out for the better. In many cases, inappropriate uses of some of these tricks can cause problems for other programmers when they come across your use of some interesting new programming trick. Only after some experience will you be more able to deploy these tricks in an appropriate manner. Until then, use them often until you find a case where you're in need of using a different trick.

## 7.11 Preprocessor Directives

We live in a computer-diverse age where PCs and mobile devices must share code. More important to our everyday lives as a game developer, we must consider the differences between the Unity 3D editor and the Unity 3D game that the editor produces.

The system in place to enable or disable blocks of code is called a preprocessor directive, which acts somewhat like a comment that can use logic to bypass or enable blocks of code.

To use them we'll start in a new unity project called Preprocessor. For our uses, the Unity 3D editor has been our main development testing environment. However, the primary goal of Unity 3D is to produce games, not just learn C#.

### 7.11.1 A Basic Example

To follow along use the Directives project. C and create a new C# file attached to the Main Camera. We'll add the following code to our new C# file:

```
#define TESTING
using UnityEngine;
using System.Collections;
public class Preprocessor : MonoBehaviour
{
    //Use this for initialization
    void Start ()
    {
        #if TESTING
        Debug.Log("just testing");
        #endif
        Debug.Log("normal behavior");
    }
    //Update is called once per frame
    void Update ()
    {
    }
}
```

At the very top of the C# class, we must use a `#define` to create a new directive. In this case, we use `#define TESTING` to indicate that we might be testing specific things in our code. Once a preprocessor directive has been defined, it's then allowed to be used throughout the rest of the class.

Looking further down, we use the `#if TESTING` in the `Start ()` function followed by `Debug.Log("just testing");`, which is followed by `#endif` to end the statements executed by the directive. The result of this code allows us to easily pick chunks of code to switch on and off.

```
just testing
UnityEngine.Debug:Log(Object)
Preprocessor:Start () (at Assets/Preprocessor.cs:10)
normal behavior
UnityEngine.Debug:Log(Object)
Preprocessor:Start () (at Assets/Preprocessor.cs:12)
```

The above code is the output with the `#define TESTING` located at the top of the class. This is where things get more interesting. If we comment out `#define TESTING` and leave the rest of the code alone, we get a result that behaves as though the `Debug.Log("just testing");` isn't there.

You might also notice that as soon as `#define TESTING` has been commented out at the top, the line inbetween `#if TESTING` and `#endif` also looks to be commented out! When the code is run, the `just testing` log will not be sent to the console as TESTING is not defined. Of course, you can check for this case as well. If we leave //#define TESTING commented out, we'll get the testing code working if we use the following preprocessor:

```
#if !TESTING
        Debug.Log("just testing");
#endif
```

The above #if !TESTING, or rather "if not testing," will now send just testing to the Console panel again. Preprocessors like this can be used to completely omit code from compiling, depending on whether or not the code it's around is needed.

```
1    //#define TESTING
2    using UnityEngine;
3    using System.Collections;
4
5    public class Preprocessor : MonoBehaviour
6    {
7        // Use this for initialization
8
9        void Start()
10       {
11           #if TESTING
12           Debug.Log("just testing");
13           #endif
14           Debug.Log("normal behavior");
15       }
```

This is why it's called a preprocessor directive. Based on how the directives are set up, you can have entire sections of code omitted from various versions of the code. It's worth noting that you have to put all of your #define directive statements before any other token appears in the class, so all of the #define statements must appear at the top of the class file.

Using the #if preprocessor is a clever way to manage what code gets executed based on the programmer adding in or taking out various #define directives. In Unity 3D, however, we get a very useful predefined set of directives.

### 7.11.2 UNITY_EDITOR

In the Directives.cs file, take a look at the line where #if UNITY_EDITOR appears.

```
#if UNITY_EDITOR
        Debug.Log("im an editor only message");
#endif
```

The UNITY_EDITOR directive is defined only when the code is being run in the editor. A complete listing of the different symbols that have been defined can be found on the Unity 3D website. The other defined symbols include Unity 3D version number and the platform that the game is running on.

When the game is run in stand-alone mode or on a mobile device, the UNITY_EDITOR directive doesn't exist, so any code inside of any #if UNITY_EDITOR preprocessor directives will skip being compiled into the game. It's often useful to have specific behaviors when running in the editor. This can speed up testing if you find yourself changing numbers while testing in the editor.

```
public int health = 10;
void Start () {
#if UNITY_EDITOR
        health = 1000;
#endif
    }
```

With something like this, we can easily just skip over changing the numbers every time we start the game in the editor. This also prevents us from accidentally checking in code that might affect the final release of the game. We can add on some layers of complexity onto the use of directives.

```
//#define LOWHEALTH
using UnityEngine;
using System.Collections;
public class Directives : MonoBehaviour
{
    //Use this for initialization
    public int health = 10;
    void Start ()
    {
        #if UNITY_EDITOR && LOWHEALTH
        health = 1;
        #elif UNITY_EDITOR
        health = 1000;
        #endif
    }
}
```

Here we can comment in and out the directive definition at the top and switch between LowHealth and Unity _ Editor testing. The first preprocessor statement #if UNITY _ EDITOR && LOWHEALTH only sets when we're running in the editor and we've uncommented out the //#define LOWHEALTH directive at the beginning of the class. The && operator works the same as though we were using it in an if statement.

To make things more clear, we can use parentheses around the preprocessor's condition #if (UNITY _ EDITOR && LOWHEALTH), which will produce the same result. This isn't required; however, programming style might dictate that you use parentheses anyway. To switch between the two statements, we use #elif, which is a preprocessor version of } else if { normally found in the rest of your code.

The difference comes from an old habit that originated from an older less integrated system. An external text editing software actually went through each file and deleted text before it was compiled. Each # command had to be one word for the macro to work properly. The macro has been incorporated into the parser now, but the formatting hasn't changed. We're also looking at #endif rather than a closing parenthesis or curly brace.

It's a whole different language, and to that there are some benefits. It's much more obvious that there's a secondary set of actions taking place on the code. Rather than using something that looks like the following:

```
void Start ()
{
    if (UNITY_EDITOR && LOWHEALTH)
    {
        health = 1;
    }
    else if (UNITY_EDITOR)
    {
        health = 1000;
    }
}
```

Here it's not so clear if these are directives. The real problem here is the fact that this code will be compiled into the shipping game and it's more likely someone might accidentally leave a check box turned on before checking in. Of course, the real issue is the fact that there is extra code being checked into the shipping version of the game that doesn't need to be there.

```
public bool isEditor = false;
```

Of course, we could actually leave these check boxes on or off based on how they are being used. However, the automation provided by simply adding #if UNITY _ EDITOR is much more simple and automatic, and also less prone to mistakes.

### 7.11.3 Warning

When using #define for debug purposes, it's often important to remind yourself to use #undef to turn off any directives that were activated. As a self-serving reminder, #warning can be added after an #if as a reminder in Unity 3D that there are modifications going on with your directives.

```
#define TESTING
using UnityEngine;
using System.Collections;
using System;
public class Directives : MonoBehaviour {
    //Use this for initialization
    void Start () {
        int playerHealth = 100;
#if TESTING
#warning DEBUG is on
        playerHealth = 100000;
#endif
        if(playerHealth < 0) {
            Debug.Log ("player has died");
        }
    }
}
```

After adding this to the code, you'll get a warning once the script has been interpreted by Unity 3D that "DEBUG is on." This text can be anything you like, so long as the warning message you're giving to yourself makes sense. The warning message has no special formatting, so adding a line break in the middle of the message will just break your code.

```
#warning don't add a line
break in the middle of a warning
```

That won't work. Your messages need to stay on the line where the #warning appears. The same goes for the rest of the #define preprocessor directives. As a general rule of thumb, these should be short and in all caps. The all caps notation isn't enforced, although it is common practice. This helps point out where any of these special case definitions are happening in the code.

```
#if TESTING
#warning DEBUG is on
        playerHealth = 100000;
#elif UNITY_EDITOR
        playerHealth = 100000;
#endif
```

The else if equivalent in a preprocessor directive has been shortened to #elif and works in the same way as you might expect with a normal if-else if statement.

### 7.11.4 Organizing

Organization is a constant struggle. In MonoDevelop, you have little boxes for folding code. #region NAME is a useful directive that is used to help keep your development environment sane.

```
 6  public class Directives : MonoBehaviour
 7  {
 8      #region IMPORTANTFUNC
 9      void ImportantFunc()
10      {
11          int j = 10;
12
13          #region SPECIFICPART
14          //lots of stuff here
15          int i = 0;
16          while (i < 10)
17          {
18              //more things...
19          }
20          #endregion
21
22          while (j-- > 0)
23          {
24              //more things...
25          }
26      }
27      #endregion
28
```

Adding regions to your code can help collapse sections of code. Adding too many different #ifdef and #region tags might work against you. Having more hash tags in your code than actual functions defeats the purpose of why these are used to begin with.

```
 6  public class Directives : MonoBehaviour
 7  {
 8      IMPORTANTFUNC
28
```

Though used wisely in a long class, a few regions can help. A #region can be nested inside of another region. Once inside of a region you're able to collapse sections of a long function to help you observe relations between variables that might be far apart.

```
 8      #region IMPORTANTFUNC
 9      void ImportantFunc()
10      {
11          int j = 10;
12
13          SPECIFICPART
21
22          while (j-- > 0)
23          {
24              //more things...
25          }
26      }
27      #endregion
```

In the above code, the #region SPECIFICPART could be quite long. MonoDevelop is also aware of your regions. Notice the small pop-up on the top right of the IDE.

This will help you jump to specific #regions or #if directives, though the danger here is that int j might have been changed before it use in the while loop. There are very specific uses for different pre-processor directives. Some of these directives have limited use, but the directives outlined in this chapter offer the most utility in everyday programming situations. The #pragma is used to tell the compiler what special functions to obey. Since we're using Unity 3D to do this work, it's better to avoid using #pragma altogether since its side effects can lead to plenty of unexpected behaviors.

### 7.11.5 What We've Learned

We will be coming back to some of the preprocessor directives again once we've covered some error handling concepts. In general, preprocessors work on the code in a manner closer to how comments work. Because of this, we can use preprocessor directives to manage different chunks of code based on a single #define at the beginning of a class.

Directives are used for many different things: One of the most common is to manage work with multiple platforms. Using preprocessor directives you can set different settings for screen resolutions based on make or model.

## 7.12 Exceptions

Working with a few warnings such as unused variables is simple enough; having too many of these can create situations where an important warning might be missed. In general, it's best to keep your warnings to an absolute minimum, or at least, no unexpected warnings at all.

There are situations where we might want to get specific warnings. In situations where we try to read a uniform resource locator (URL) from a web page and the server is down, we'd not have our game simply crash or freeze.

There are also situations where you might expect some values to be incorrect. When dealing with a user, you might expect a numeric value and get a letter instead. Rather than freeze and crash the game, you can ignore the input until a correction is made.

### 7.12.1 A Basic Example

Starting in the Warnings Unity 3D project, we have the following Warnings.cs setup in the scene with a simple Update () function. At the class scope, we're using a public string, that will allow you to enter any string value.

```
using UnityEngine;
using System.Collections;
public class Warnings : MonoBehaviour
{
    public string input;
    void Update ()
    {
        int i;
        //give parsing a shot.
        try
        {
            i = int.Parse(input);
        }
        //nope, didn't work...
        catch
        {
            i = 0;
        }
        Debug.Log("i = " + i);
    }
}
```

This code allows us to use any string in the input field, which results in an error. Without the `try{}`-`catch{}` keywords, we'd have an `Update ()` that looks more like the following.

```
void Update ()
{
    int i;
    i = int.Parse(input);
    Debug.Log("i = "+ i);
}
```

As soon as any other character is used in the string field, we'd get a bunch of errors in the Console panel.

```
FormatException: Input string was not in the correct format
System.Int32.Parse (System.String s) (at/Applications/buildAgent/work/
b59ae78cff80e584/mcs/class/corlib/System/Int32.cs:629)
Warnings.Update () (at Assets/Warnings.cs:15)
```

The `try{}` statement makes an attempt to do some process to the input with `i = int.Parse(input);`. Should this fail, the `catch{}` statement picks up that failure and makes a correction. If the `try{}` succeeds, then the `catch{}` isn't called. We can make additional changes to the `try{}` statement even if the initial parse works out.

We can give ourselves more information about what is going wrong with some parameters going into the `catch{}`. To start we'll want to add a new directive at the beginning of the class.

```
using UnityEngine;
using System.Collections;
using System;
```

The addition of `using System` to the directives will open up the `Exception` type to our `catch{}` call.

```
catch (Exception e)
{
    Debug.LogWarning(e);
    i = 0;
}
```

When any invalid inputs are made, we get the following warning:

```
System.FormatException: Input string was not in the correct format
```

This means that we know not only that `try{}` failed, but why it failed. We can create a specific response to the failure. When the failure occurs for different reasons, we can create different catches for each situation.

### 7.12.2 Exception Messages

One of the overrides of the `Exception` class is a message. We can use the message to tell us what situation created the `Exception` and what we can do about it.

```
int CheckInput(string s)
{
    int parsed = 0;
    if(string.IsNullOrEmpty(s))
    {
        throw new Exception("null");
    }
    parsed = int.Parse(s);
    return parsed;
}
```

Let's start with a new function that can check for different types of input problems. With the above code, we're starting with a parsed int that will be assigned the incoming string. An if statement checks if the string coming in is null; if that's the case, then we use the throw keyword and create a new Exception(); with "null" as its parameter. In the Update () function, we'll add in the code to the try{} statement.

```
void Update ()
{
    int i;
    //give parsing a string a shot
    try
    {
        i = CheckInput(input);
    }
    catch (Exception e)
    {
        Debug.LogWarning(e);
        i = 1;
    }
    Debug.Log("i = "+ i);
}
```

The catch{} statements that follow the CheckInput() function will catch the Exception() created before it. This might seem a bit arbitrary, but it's an interesting feature of C#. Here we're seeing a new Exception() object being created, and a catch() statement is getting it without directly telling it to do so. Indeed there's a great deal of underlying architecture that allows for this.

When the above code is run and the Inspector panel has nothing entered in the Input panel, we get the following warning issued to the Console panel in Unity 3D.

```
System.Exception : null
```

Here, null is the string we entered into the Exception when we created it. Because we were able to catch this problem and make decision on how to handle it, we saved the game from an execution error. There are, however, already predefined exceptions that were written for situations where null is a problem.

```
int CheckInput(string s)
{
    int parsed = 0;
    if(string.IsNullOrEmpty(s))
    {
        throw new ArgumentNullException("please enter something");
        //different exception thrown!
    }
    parsed = int.Parse(s);
    return parsed;
}
```

We can catch this specific exception with a catch that is looking for this to be thrown. This becomes more important once we start looking at situations where we require some number to be entered before we can continue.

```
void Update ()
{
    int i = 0;
    //give parsing a string a shot
    try
    {
        i = CheckInput(input);
    }
```

```
        catch (ArgumentNullException e)
        {
            //just catches a null arg
            Debug.LogWarning("null arg! " + e);
            i = 2;
        }
        catch (Exception e)
        {
            //catches any other Exception
            Debug.LogWarning("catch all " + e);
            i = 1;
        }
        Debug.Log("i = "+ i);
}
```

In the `Update ()`, we can add another catch to look for null argument exceptions to be thrown. The above code will set `int i` to 2, should there be no argument in the input field. It's only set up for that one type of exception. The second catch will throw an `Exception` for any other unexpected condition.

```
int CheckInput(string s)
{
    int parsed = 0;
    if(string.IsNullOrEmpty(s))
    {
        throw new ArgumentNullException("please enter something");
    }
    parsed = int.Parse(s);
    if(parsed > 100)
    {
        throw new NotImplementedException();
    }
    return parsed;
}
```

Here we can throw another exception if the parsed value is greater than 100. Throwing a `NotImplementedException()` is more useful for development. However, if we don't make a `catch` specific for this, the `catch(Exception e)` will grab it since `Exception` is the base class for all other exceptions. Using any number greater than 100 will throw the following message:

```
catch all System.NotImplementedException: The requested feature is not
implemented.
```

The situations where this is required mostly come into play when dealing with player input. For instance, an age field can check for anything other than numbers, throw an exception and have a catch, change a value to something reasonable, and display a message.

The `try-catch` system operates more gracefully than a long `if` statement ladder. We could use a `switch` for every situation or even several `goto` statements to deal with different problems. However, the `try-catch` method was specifically designed for dealing with a variety of problems. It's best to use the tools for what they were intended for.

When situations arise that have not been anticipated by a system exception, we're going to need to write our own exception.

### 7.12.3 Custom Exceptions

Working with many different conditions complicates debugging. Finding and dealing with a specific error condition is best dealt with by using custom exception code.

```
public class MyException : Exception
{
    public MyException()
    {
    }
    public MyException(string message) : base(message)
    {
    }
    public MyException(string message, Exception innerException)
        : base(message,innerException)
    {
    }
}
```

We start a new exception with the above class. It's important that we implement all the methods that were implemented in the base Exception class. However, with this we've added no additional information to the base Exception class we're extending. Since we've been dealing with an int, we'll want to add relevant information to our MyException() class.

```
public class MyException : Exception
{
    public int Number;//relevant information
    public MyException()
    {
    }
```

The above fragment includes a new Number variable to which we can implement some use. Of course, this means that to throw our exception, we need to change how it's thrown.

```
int CheckInput(string s)
{
    int parsed = 0;
    if(string.IsNullOrEmpty(s))
    {
        MyException e = new MyException("null");
        e.Number = 0;
        throw e;
    }
    parsed = int.Parse(s);
    if(parsed > 100)
    {
        MyException e = new MyException("too high");
        e.Number = parsed;
        throw e;
    }
    return parsed;
}
```

We can rewrite the CheckInput() function to throw our new MyException at a catch{} statement following the try{} statement. With something more specific for our use, we can begin to make better use of the catch{} statement.

```
void Update ()
{
    int i = 0;
    //give parsing a string a shot
```

```
try
{
    i = CheckInput(input);
}
catch (MyException e)
{
    i = e.Number;
    if(i.
}
Debug.Log("i = "+ i);
}
```

With the above code, we're able to reduce the number of catch{} statements and still get the same functionality. Adding more logic to the catch statement will allow us to better deal with different situations.

```
catch (MyException e)
{
    i = e.Number;
    if(e.Message == "too high")
    {
        Debug.Log("use a lower number");
    } else if (e.Message == "null") {
        Debug.Log("input a number");
    }
}
```

Now once the exception is caught, we can check what situation threw the message, and then react appropriately. In cases where we can't possibly come up with every imaginable situation, we have one last keyword to help us.

### 7.12.4 Finally

To complete our try{}-catch{} statement, we can add a finally{} statement. Since we're not doing anything complex here, all we need is the following:

```
finally
{
    Debug.Log("done!");
}
```

In this situation, the finally{} statement is unnecessary. Where finally comes in handy is with functions that require some clean up afterward.

### 7.12.5 Try–Catch and Finally in Use

To continue with our tutorial, we'll want to add in another directive. This time we're adding System.IO.

```
using UnityEngine;
using System.Collections;
using System;
using System.IO;
```

This code will give us the ability to read or write files to disk. We've neglected the Start () function so far in this example, so we'll want to use it for writing a single file.

```
void Start () {
    FileStream file = null;
```

```
FileInfo fileInfo = null;
try
{
    fileInfo = new FileInfo("C:\\file.txt");
    file = fileInfo.OpenWrite();
    for(int i = 0; i < 255; i++)
    {
        file.WriteByte((byte)i);
    }
}
catch(UnauthorizedAccessException e)
{
    Debug.LogWarning(e.Message);
}
finally
{
    if (file != null)
    {
        file.Close();
    }
}
}
```

With this added to the start function, we use the `try{}` to create a new file called `file.txt`. Once it's created, we open it for writing, and then add in a bunch of characters with `file.WriteByte()`. If we're not allowed to write to this directory, we catch that problem with `UnauthorizedAccessException e` and have Unity 3D let us know if there was a problem. If the file has been written, it's closed with the `finally{}` block.

### 7.12.6  What We've Learned

The notation used here creates a clean and tidy way to create a file, check for problems, and finish the file writing process. The blocks are clear and the proper procedures are followed. We also get an interesting look at all of the different characters in a font.

In the `file.txt`, we get many weird characters before we start to see letters and numbers. Aside from unusual characters, it's important to know how the `try-catch-finally` process works for using network connections.

When setting up a connection through hypertext transfer protocol (HTTP) to get an image from the Internet or models from a web server, we'll want to make sure that the connection didn't disconnect halfway through. Possibly a user name or password was incorrect. All of these situations will need to be caught before we reach a finally{} block and pretend that everything went as expected.

After the file.txt was written, you can get properties on the file and change it to read only. This will throw the exception and you'll get the following error:

```
Access to the path "C:\file.txt" is denied.
UnityEngine.Debug:LogWarning(Object)
Warnings:Start () (at Assets/Warnings.cs:26)
```

This means that the try{} block failed and the catch{} block was activated. When the finally{} block is reached, the file is null and doesn't need to be closed.

There are many different types of exceptions that Unity 3D will be throwing quite often. It's likely that you might need to move an object and want to catch if a number gets out of hand or you suspect a divide by zero exception might be thrown. These situations are easier to work with if you use try{} and catch{}.

## 7.13 IEnumerator

Enumerations are systems in which you might get data from something but it's presented to you only through specific methods. In that case, what the heck is an IEnumerator? The prefixed letter is an I, so there's an interface of some kind, but what does that even mean? An IEnumerator is something that we use on an array of any sort of object.

The problem is something that starts with a long list of items. The usual for(int i = 0; I < array.Length; i++) works fine for most situations, and in fact you can get by with just that. There are cases in which some data is not presented as an array but as an IEnumerator. Extended markup language, which looks a lot like a web page for data, doesn't always present its data to you in the form of an array. We'll find out more about that in a later chapter about reading and writing data.

With cases like this, we are forced to use either a foreach or a while loop. However, the way these loops are used aren't as simple as you might expect. Once you understand how it works, you will find that a large array is really easy to iterate through.

### 7.13.1 Enumeration

Before we make our own enumerator, it's easier to see how it's used. The IEnumerator is an interface with one property and two methods. The only property is called Current, and the two methods we can use are called Reset and MoveNext.

#### 7.13.1.1 A Basic Example

Let's find the Enums class in the Assets directory of the Enums project.

```
using UnityEngine;
using System.Collections;
public class Enums : MonoBehaviour
{
    int[] ints = {3, 7, 11, 13, 17, 23} ;
    //Use this for initialization
    void Start ()
    {
        IEnumerator o = ints.GetEnumerator();
        while (o.MoveNext())
        {
            Debug.Log(o.Current);
        }
    }
}
```

This is a pretty short example of what an IEnumerator does. First we get an array of integers, though the array can be of anything. We're calling the array ints, just to keep things simple. Arrays have a method called GetEnumerator() that returns a type IEnumerator. To use this we can assign a variable, in this case o as a type IEnumerator to ints.GetEnumerator();.

The o variable, which is an IEnumerator, has a few simple functions.

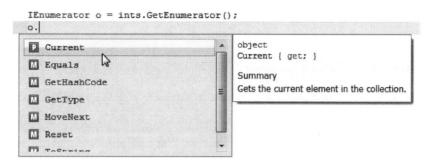

It's important to note that the IEnumerator o is an object. To use it for something else, we'll need to cast it to whatever it is we're expecting. We will need to remember this later on. We can use the IEnumerator o outside of a while loop.

```
int[] ints = {3, 7, 11, 13, 17, 23} ;
//Use this for initialization
void Start ()
{
    IEnumerator o = ints.GetEnumerator();
    o.MoveNext();
    Debug.Log(o.Current);
    o.MoveNext();
    Debug.Log(o.Current);
    o.MoveNext();
    Debug.Log(o.Current);
    o.MoveNext();
    Debug.Log(o.Current);
    o.MoveNext();
    Debug.Log(o.Current);
    o.MoveNext();
    Debug.Log(o.Current);
}
```

This might not be the most efficient way to use an IEnumerator, but this is a good approximation of what's actually happening inside of the while loop. The o.MoveNext(); function call tells o to change the value of o.Current. To make this more clear, we'll add in why the while loop works.

```
int[] ints = {3, 7, 11} ;
//Use this for initialization
void Start ()
{
    IEnumerator o = ints.GetEnumerator();
    if (o.MoveNext())
    {
        Debug.Log(o.Current);
    }
    if (o.MoveNext())
    {
        Debug.Log(o.Current);
    }
```

```
        if (o.MoveNext())
        {
            Debug.Log(o.Current);
        }
        if (o.MoveNext())
        {
            Debug.Log(o.Current);
        }
    }
```

After shortening the array of `int`s to only three items, we'll see what happens if we use `if (o.MoveNext)` to limit if `o.Current` has a value. The array is three items long, so the fourth `if` statement returns false, and a fourth `o.Current` isn't printed. The `IEnumerator` function of an array returns a useful little trick for us to use for tasks involving arrays.

### 7.13.1.2 *What Doesn't Work*

For many of the basic tasks involving arrays, you might use the `foreach` statement. The following code fragment could work on its own if you didn't use a `foreach` statement.

```
    void Start ()
    {
        string[] strings = {"A","B","C"};
        IEnumerator IEstring = strings.GetEnumerator();
        foreach (string s in IEstring)
        {
            Debug.Log(s);
        }
    }
```

With a `foreach` statement, we might expect the `IEstring` to contain something useful as though it were a simple array. However, this is not the case. The `IEumerator` type doesn't actually give access to its contents without providing it directly. Just as interestingly enough, if you were to ask for `IEString.Current`, the first value found has nothing in it.

```
    void Start ()
    {
        string[] strings = {"A","B","C"};
        IEnumerator IEstring = strings.GetEnumerator();
        Debug.Log(IEstring.Current);
    }
```

Try doing the above code sample and you'll get a run-time error message.

```
InvalidOperationException: Enumeration has not started.
System.Array+SimpleEnumerator.get_Current ()
(at/Applications/buildAgent/work/b49ae77dff90f584/mcs/class/corlib/System/
Array.cs:1874)
Enums.Start () (at Assets/Enums.cs:10)
```

The enumeration process has not started, it seems. This requires at least one use of `MoveNext()` before the `IEnumerator` variable's `.Current` object has a value of some kind. As we've seen, there are various ways to use `MoveNext()` to get a value from the `.Current` property in the `IEnumerable` data type.

Take a moment to think about what's going on. The `IEnumerator` is an interface class written by C# programmers. It was created to provide you, the programmer, a method to make a consistent interface that can be incorporated into your code smoothly. Once implemented, other programmers can use your class as they would use any other `IEnumerator`. You can think of it as adding a handy feature to your class. However, to fully implement the feature and make sure that it does what you want it to, you'll need to understand how it's expected to work.

### 7.13.2 Implementing IEnumerator

```
using UnityEngine;
using System.Collections;
public class Enums : MonoBehaviour {
    int[] ints = {3, 7, 11} ;
    class MyEnumerator : IEnumerator {
        //Starting here.
    }
    //Use this for initialization
    void Start () {
        IEnumerator o = ints.GetEnumerator();
        if (o.MoveNext()) {
            Debug.Log(o.Current);
        }
        if (o.MoveNext()) {
            Debug.Log(o.Current);
        }
        if (o.MoveNext()) {
            Debug.Log(o.Current);
        }
        if (o.MoveNext()) {
            Debug.Log(o.Current);
        }
    }
}
```

Starting in the `MyEnumerator` class, we want to add the `:  IEnumerator` interface. This is an interface that is implemented in the `System.Collections` C# library and not specific to Unity 3D. Enumerations, as we've seen, are useful for long lists of objects. It's often useful to store these objects as arrays, but in some cases we might want to add a more direct method to get through a specific list in a class.

The implementation of a new `IEnumerator` requires two classes: The first will be a class that implements the `IEnumerable` interface, which will contain the second class, the `IEnumerator`. For our example, we'll want to start with the first `IEnumerable` class. We'll add some information to this guy as he's going to be a zombie master.

```
using UnityEngine;
using System.Collections;
public class Enums : MonoBehaviour
{
    //zombie master
    class ZombieMaster : IEnumerable
    {
        public static string ZombieMasterName;
        public ZombieMaster(string name)
        {
            ZombieMasterName = name;
        }
    }
    //Use this for initialization
    void Start ()
    {
    }
}
```

We start with a pretty regular class with the addition of the `:  IEnumerable` interface added to the declaration of the class. `IEnumerable` should not be confused with `IEnumerator`. An object that is

IEnumerable means that it's got an IEnumerator in it. This tells us what functions we'll need to add to make the class implement an IEnumerable behavior.

To start we'll want our zombie master to have a name, so in his constructor we'll accept a name when he's created. So far this is just like any other class. And as a reminder, this is just any other class. When we add an interface, we're not changing the type of class we're writing. This class still has the functions of any other zombie or monster for that matter. We're just adding in a new IEnumerable interface to give him an additional C# ability.

```
Assets/Enums.cs(49,46): error CS1061: Type 'Enums.ZombieMaster' does not
contain a definition for 'GetEnumerator' and no extension method
'GetEnumerator' of type 'Enums.ZombieMaster' could be found (are you missing
a using directive or an assembly reference?)
```

Unity 3D is telling us to add in a GetEnumerator method, so we shall.

```
//zombie master
class ZombieMaster : IEnumerable
{
    public static string ZombieMasterName;
    private IZombieEnumerator Enumerator;
    public ZombieMaster(string name)
    {
        ZombieMasterName = name;
        Enumerator = new IZombieEnumerator();
    }
    public IEnumerator GetEnumerator()
    {
        return Enumerator;
    }
}
```

We've got three additions to make a partial implementation. Remember that we need two classes to make our own enumerations. Therefore, we're creating a private IZombieEnumerator Enumerator; variable for the ZombieMaster to hold on to. Then we add that Enumerator's assignment to the ZombieMaster's constructor with Enumerator = new IZombieEnumerator();. This can be done in various other ways, but adding it to the constructor is much easier. Finally, we implement the public IEnumerator GetEnumerator() function, in which we simply return the Enumerator. This is the same object that was created in the constructor.

We'll still be getting a warning from Unity 3D about not knowing what an IZombieEnumerator is, but we'll fix that next.

```
class IZombieEnumerator : IEnumerator
{
    private string[] minions;
    private int NextMinion;
    public object Current
    {
        get {return minions [NextMinion];}
    }
    public IZombieEnumerator()
    {
        minions = new string[]{"stubbs", "bernie", "michael"};
    }
    public bool MoveNext()
    {
        NextMinion++;
        if (NextMinion > = minions.Length)
```

```
            {
                return false;
            } else
            {
                return true;
            }
        }
        public void Reset()
        {
            NextMinion = -1;
        }
    }
```

If you look around on the Internet for implementing an IEnumerator, you'll find a variety of different implementations. Each one has a different advantage, but they all end up behaving the same. This might make writing a good IEnumerable or IEnumerator class easier or harder; since there's no strict rules, you're free to make up your own version.

In the IZombieEnumerator class, we ask for the IEnumerator interface. For a proper interface, we need to have an array to iterate through, which we're calling minions. Then we need to have a counter to pick one of the items in the array, which we're calling NextMinion. Then we need to have a ReadOnly variable called Current to match the interface properties.

The Current property should be read only; therefore, in its interface, we're only implementing get{} and leaving out set{}, which prevents any accidental changes to the array's contents. Inside of Current, we combine the array and the counter with return minions[NextMinion]; for the get value.

As an example, we're creating the array in the IZombieEnumerator's constructor. This implementation can be replaced later on with something more flexible by adding in an array parameter in the argument list of the constructor.

```
public IZombieEnumerator()
{
        minions = new string[]{"stubbs", "bernie", "michael"};
}
```

When you need to use this constructor with an argument, it might look a bit more like the following:

```
public IZombieEnumerator(string[] strings)
{
        minions = strings;
}
```

You just need to remember that you're passing an array, not a single value. Next we need to implement the MoveNext() and Reset() functions inside of the IZombieEnumerator class. The MoveNext() function needs to return a bool and the Reset() needs to return a void. You will get error messages if you're not returning the right value from the function.

```
public bool MoveNext()
{
    NextMinion++;
    if(NextMinion > = minions.Length)
    {
        return false;
    }
    else
    {
        return true;
    }
}
```

The `MoveNext()` increments up the `NextMinion++;` value by 1 each time it's called. If the `NextMinion` value is greater than or equal to the number of items in the array, then you `return false`; otherwise you `return true`. This stops the `foreach` and `while` loops when we reach the end of the array.

```
public void Reset()
{
        NextMinion = -1;
}
```

Next the `Reset()` function sets the `NextMinion` to -1; this might be a bit confusing, but this means that the first iteration of `NextMinion` in the `foreach` and `while` loops is set to 0 when `MoveNext()` is first called.

```
void Start ()
{
    ZombieMaster zombieMaster = new ZombieMaster("bob");
    Debug.Log(ZombieMaster.ZombieMasterName);
    foreach (object obj in zombieMaster)
    {
        Debug.Log(obj.ToString());
    }
}
```

Now your `zombieMaster` is `IEnumerable` and it's got additional properties as well. You can log the `ZombieMaster`'s name and then iterate through his list of minions. You're not limited to a single interface. You're allowed to implement as many interfaces as you feel the need for. Of course, this might make your class large and bulky, so you might want to build a base class with different interfaces implemented, but that's greatly up to you.

It's easy to start off with one or two interfaces, and afterward move each collection of functions and parameters to a different class and inherit from them. We'll go into how to best manage copying and pasting large groups of code from one class into another in a later chapter.

### 7.13.3 What We've Learned

This has been a pretty heavy chapter about implementing the `IEnumerator` and `IEnumerable` interface. It's great practice and it's important to know how to go about implementing an interface from the C# library.

There are many cool tricks that can be added to your classes to make them more feature complete. This does require more thought and time, but in the end your classes will be more useful to the rest of the team of programmers you might be working with.

When to decide to implement one of these programming features is up to you and your team. Sometimes adding a feature might make a simple class too complex. If you're fine with using simple code to avoid the complexity, then you're free to do so. Thankfully, C# allows you to do pretty much anything that's allowed within the language. There aren't any hard and fast rules in the language that limit how it's used.

Interfaces not only tell you what is expected out of your class but also how to get it done. You're allowed to provide the data in any way you feel fit, but it's important to not provide something to start testing with.

On your own you should figure out how to add and remove items in a dynamic array in the `IZombieEnumerator`. You've implemented the required functions and properties to make the `IEnumerator` interface happy, but there's nothing limiting you from adding more features to the class beyond the `IEnumerator` interface.

## 7.14  Generics

When you create a new data structure, you're creating a strict organization and naming of your new data. This begins to run into problems when you need to make small modifications to that structure to suit multiple tasks. As your project gets more complex, your data will become more complex as well.

Thankfully as of C# version 2.0, generics were included to make data flow a bit more easily. In Unity 3D, we get used to doing casts with the following syntax where (float) takes the int 1 and converts it into the expected type to assign to f.

```
void Start ()
{
        float f = (float)1.0;
        Debug.Log(f);
}
```

Of course, this can be avoided if we start off with the correct type to assign by using 1.0f to indicate that we're using a 1.0 as a float and not a double. Although many conversions are automatic between int and float, for example, not all conversions can be done for you.

When faced with making different data structures for different needs, you'll end up with more and more new data types. This leads to more and more mismatching of data. New data types diminish your object's ability to inherit from other objects; therefore, we lose the power of an object oriented programming language.

All of the forms of data we create are based on the Object class, and as such we're able to use Object as a common ground to cast them from. However, we run into problems when casting incorrectly or not knowing what to cast a value to. This is the problem with type-safe programming languages; using an object is an unfortunate work-around to which we should have a better method, to ensure that we don't run into mismatching data.

There is a way to make your data more flexible, and to do this we need generic types.

### 7.14.1  Generic Functions

Generics finally make sense now that we've looked at and used delegates and lambda expressions. Generics allow a function to adhere to the type-safe nature of C# but also allow you to pretend that it matters a little less. In the case of building a game involving a variety of monsters, we could quite readily use a system to organize various items we're using in our game. If we were to think in a world without generics, we'd have to make a few different systems for storing and categorizing items and monsters.

Generics are indicated by a function followed by an identifier to be used to indicate the type expected in the function.

#### 7.14.1.1  A Basic Example

```
using UnityEngine;
using System.Collections;
public class Generics : MonoBehaviour
{
    public void log<T>(T thing)
    {
        string s = thing.ToString();
        Debug.Log(s);
    }
    //Use this for initialization
    void Start ()
```

```
    {
        log(9);
        GameObject g = new GameObject("My name is mud");
        log(g);
    }
    //Update is called once per frame
    void Update ()
    {
    }
}
```

The above code produces a nice log of what was put into it.

```
9
My name is mud (UnityEngine.GameObject)
```

We were able to use both an `int` and a `GameObject` in the `log<T>` function. The function `log<T>(T thing)`, where `T` indicates a placeholder for a type, accepts both `int`s and `GameObject`s. Without the `<T>`, how would this work for various other data types? Let's take a look at a simple alteration that would instantly create a great deal of additional work.

```
    public void logInt(int thing) {
        string s = thing.ToString();
        Debug.Log(s);
    }
```

Suppose we wrote a `logInt` for the `int` type; it might look something like the above code. In the `Start ()` function, we could try to use the following statements:

```
    void Start () {
        logInt(8);
        logInt(5.0);
    }
```

The first `logInt(8);` would pass, however, `5.0` is a `double` and Unity 3D would quickly tell us we're doing it wrong.

```
Assets/Generics.cs(19,17): error CS1502: The best overloaded method match for
'Generics.logInt(int)' has some invalid arguments
Assets/Generics.cs(19,17): error CS1503: Argument '#1' cannot convert
'double' expression to type 'int'
```

Okay, so `logInt` doesn't like `double`s mixed in with its `int`s; that's fair enough; we should know not to mix types by now. Without generics we'd have to write a different function for every type that can be converted to a string and logged to the Console panel. To attempt this would be a huge waste of time, impractical at best. Thanks to `<T>` we don't need to.

### 7.14.1.2 Why T?

We use the identifier `T` to denote a use of the type expected to be reused elsewhere in the function. This is just a convention and not a strict rule. We could break the convention and traditionally trained programmers' brains by writing the same function again with another type identifier.

```
    public void log<LOL>(LOL cat)
    {
        Debug.Log(cat.ToString());
    }
```

This works just fine, but it's hardly appropriate. The T is purely a convention that has stuck around since it was first implemented. This is somewhat like how the for loop is always taught with for (int i; i < 10; i++); in this case, int i just seemed appropriate.

Therefore, in this case, generic type T seemed to match well. Unlike so much of mathematics, the letters we use in programming have much less intrinsic meaning. If this were not the case, then we'd need a whole lot more letters. Therefore, in the end, sticking to the convention T will make any other programmer more easily understand what you're trying to do.

The applied cases often require specific reasons in which no other solution could be found. Creating and assigning delegates like this are often avoided due to the uncommon nature of needing to write specific code for the same function call. However, that is the entire reason for the anonymous expressions for being in use.

On occasion, when you have several classes inheriting behaviors from one another, you'll want one class to react differently than other classes when a function is called. Shoving a wooden stake through the heart of a vampire has a very different effect on a zombie. Calling the same OnStakedThroughHeart() function on both should result in different code being executed.

Normally, you'd just want to have both zombie and vampire use an interface which includes an OnStakedThroughHeart event; however, your player's character might not necessarily care into what monster he's pushing the pointy end of the stake, through. This is where the problem begins.

The code running the player will probably not want to check for each type and decide what to do based on the different types encountered.

### 7.14.2 Making Use of Generic Functions

One benefit of a generic type is the fact that you can write your own types of data, vampires or zombies, to use as generic types. To begin with a simple example, we'll build a simple zombie class. After that we'll look at using a generic function to swap data between two variables. What should be a simple task will prove to be an interesting use of what we've learned so far. We'll start with the generic function and then observe how it can be used for more than one type of data.

```
public void swap<T>(ref T a, ref T b)
{
    T temp = b;
    b = a;
    a = temp;
}
```

Create a simple generic function in your code that looks like the above. We have a function called swap<T>, where T can be any sort of data. We use the ref T to indicate that we're making a reference to the data stored in the variable that's being used in the argument list directly, rather than making a copy of it. Then we make a T temp that holds onto the value of b. After that we tell b to take on the value stored at a. Then we tell a to take on the value that was stored locally in temp. Here's what the function looks like when in use.

```
//Use this for initialization
void Start ()
{
    int first = 1;
    int second = 2;
    Debug.Log(first);
    Debug.Log(second);
    swap(ref first, ref second);
    Debug.Log(first);
    Debug.Log(second);
}
```

This prints out 1 and 2 followed by 2 and then 1 after the swap has been applied. To explain what's going on here, first is assigned 1 and then second is assigned 2. From there we send their values to the Unity's Console panel to check their values; as expected we get a 1 followed by a 2. Then we apply swap(ref first, ref second); that swaps the values stored at first and second. When we log first and second to the Console again, the values return as 2 and 1. Without making any additional changes to the swap generic function, we're allowed to make some changes to the code in Start () and observe the same behavior with strings.

```
void Start ()
{
    string first = "one";
    string second = "two";
    Debug.Log(first);
    Debug.Log(second);
    swap(ref first, ref second);
    Debug.Log(first);
    Debug.Log(second);
}
```

This sends one and two followed by two and one to the Console, as you might expect. To make this more interesting, we'll create our own form of data.

```
public class zombie
{
    private string Name;//store the zombies name
    //constructor to assign a name on creation.
    public zombie(string name)
    {
        Name = name;
    }
    //override the ToString() command by
    //returning the zombies name instead of its type.
    public override string ToString()
    {
        return Name;
    }
}
```

Create a new zombie class that stores a Name variable. To do this, we'll want a constructor with a string argument to accept a zombie name. Then, to make the class return a more useful value when it's translated to a string, we'll override the ToString() function by returning the zombie's name instead of its type.

```
void Start ()
{
    zombie first = new zombie("stubbs");
    zombie second = new zombie("jackson");
    Debug.Log(first);
    Debug.Log(second);
    swap(ref first, ref second);
    Debug.Log(first);
    Debug.Log(second);
}
```

Now a simple modification to the Start () function, as in the above code, will print out stubbs and jackson, followed by jackson and stubbs in the Console panel. This brings up a few questions about how the <T> works. What happens when we mix data types?

```
void Start ()
{
    zombie first = new zombie("stubbs");
    string second = "jackson";
    Debug.Log(first);
    Debug.Log(second);
    swap(ref first, ref second);
    Debug.Log(first);
    Debug.Log(second);
}
```

For instance, if we try to use the above code with a string and a zombie, we'll get an error.

```
Assets/Generics.cs(41,17): error CS0411: The type arguments for method
'Generics.swap<T>(ref T, ref T)' cannot be inferred from the usage. Try
specifying the type arguments explicitly
```

When we try to mix different types, we won't be able to infer what we want to happen. When we tell a zombie that it's now a word, it's not likely to turn into anything comprehensible. This is very important for a C# to be able to parse your code. In the end there's no simple way to convert between different types that have very little in common. It's up to you to keep things organized in such a ways you won't have to worry about swapping types that don't match.

### 7.14.3 Generic Types

Speaking of types, a generic type can be created. That is to say, you can make a data type that has no specific type to start off with. In particular, these come in handy when we want to organize data in a particular fashion. For instance, if we wanted to create a short list of three zombies, we might want to create new data, that is, three zombies, but why restrict this data type to just zombies?

```
public class ThreeThings<T>
{
    private T first;
    private T second;
    private T third;
    //constructor for three things
    public ThreeThings(T a, T b, T c)
    {
        first = a;
        second = b;
        third = c;
    }
    //override ToString()
    public override string ToString()
    {
        return first + " " + second + " " + third;
    }
}
```

Start off with a new class with a constructor for holding onto three different things of the same type. The declaration of ThreeThings<T> infers that we're going to have an object that has objects of a single generic type. We'll be able to create a new class ThreeThings to hold three ints, floats, strings, or even zombies.

Next we'll want to create a new ThreeThings object in our Start () function and assign three different zombies to it using its constructor.

```
void Start ()
{
    zombie firstZombie = new zombie("stubbs");
    zombie secondZombie = new zombie("jackson");
    zombie thirdZombie = new zombie("bob");
    ThreeThings SomeThings = new ThreeThings(firstZombie, secondZombie,
thirdZombie);
    Debug.Log (SomeThings);
}
```

But wait; we're getting an error!

```
Assets/Generics.cs(57,17): error CS0305: Using the generic type 'Generics.
ThreeThings<T>' requires '1' type argument(s)
```

What does this mean? The `<Generics.zombie>` infers that the object being created is of type `Generic`. This means that when we deal with generic types, we need to inform `ThreeThings` what it's going to be. Therefore, to fix this, we need to tell `<T>` what it is.

```
    void Start ()
    {
        zombie firstZombie = new zombie("stubbs");
        zombie secondZombie = new zombie("jackson");
        zombie thirdZombie = new zombie("bob");
        ThreeThings<zombie> SomeThings =
        new ThreeThings<zombie>(firstZombie, secondZombie, thirdZombie);
        Debug.Log(SomeThings);
    }
```

We need to tell `ThreeThings` that it's going to be dealing with `<zombie>` as the generic type. However, there's a more clever trick to dealing with generic types.

### 7.14.4  Var

Normally, when we use types, we'd create a type by assigning it explicitly. For instance, `zombie firstZombie = new zombie("stubbs")` is an explicit type. It's a `zombie` and we knew that when it was created because it's a `zombie` class object. This is the same `int a = 10;`, which means that `a` is an `int` and it's assigned `10` as a value. This changes when the type can be anything and we don't necessarily know what it's going to be ahead of time.

To the computer, it's saying "The thing that SomeThings might turn into is going to be a generic of what ThreeThings is about to be assigned." We have to remind ourselves that computers aren't clever enough to figure this out. However, we can work with generics in a more straightforward way with the `var` keyword.

```
    void Start ()
    {
        zombie firstZombie = new zombie("stubbs");
        zombie secondZombie = new zombie("jackson");
        zombie thirdZombie = new zombie("bob");
        var SomeThings =
        new ThreeThings<zombie>(firstZombie, secondZombie, thirdZombie);
        Debug.Log(SomeThings);
    }
```

Here we use `var SomeThings` to tell the computer to expect any data type to store into `SomeThings`. That's right, *any* data type. There are some limitations, as one might expect with anything to do with computers, but `var` is a very open keyword. The `var` keyword means to implicitly get a type once it's been assigned. Only after the actual object is created and assigned to the identifier that was created with `var` will the identifier turn into a type. For instance, we can test this with a simple integer.

```
var whatAmI = 1;
Debug.Log(whatAmI.GetType());
```

Every object has a `GetType()` function that returns the data type of the variable in question. Therefore, when we create `var whatAmI` and assign it `1`, which is an integer, we get the following output to the Unity's Console panel.

```
System.Int32
UnityEngine.Debug:Log(Object)
Generics:Start () (at Assets/Generics.cs:61)
```

As it turns out, `System.Int32` is the integer that we've been using all this time. What happens when we do the same with `SomeThings`?

```
Generics+ThreeThings`1[Generics+zombie]
UnityEngine.Debug:Log(Object)
Generics:Start () (at Assets/Generics.cs:61)
```

Well, it's a bit less clear, but we do know that it involves a `Generics` class and `ThreeThings` and a `1`, which indicates how many different types are involved along with a `Zombie`. Quite informative, actually. Therefore, if `var` allows us to deal with any different type, why don't we use it more often? To be honest, the best reason is not because of code efficiency. The main reason why we don't want to use `var` so often is because of clarity. For instance, we can use the following code and give horrible nightmares to any programmer trying to follow our code.

```
public int tellMeLies(float f)
{
    return (int)f;
}
void Start ()
{
    var ImAFloat = tellMeLies(11.8f);
    Debug.Log(ImAFloat);
}
```

This sends `11` to the Console panel; `11.8f` is certainly not `11`, and as such the `var ImAFloat` is indeed telling lies. Were we to tell the truth from the beginning and use `int ImAFloat`, we might have a clue right away that something is amiss with the naming of the integer `ImAFloat`. This should prompt a meeting with the programmer concerned about naming variables clearly.

This can get a bit murky with generic classes, which don't have a specific constructor, but luckily the compiler will catch things for us.

```
public class Stuff<T>
{
    T thing;
    public void assignThing(T something)
    {
        thing = something;
    }
}
```

Here we can start with a generic class called `Stuff<T>`, that holds onto `T thing`. Then we make an available function afterward to assign `T thing` after the class has been instanced.

```
var what = new Stuff<int>();
what.assignThing(1.0f);
```

If we try the following assignment to assign a float to the Stuff<int>, we get an appropriate error telling us that we can't assign a float to an int.

```
Assets/Generics.cs(73,22): error CS1502: The best overloaded method match for
'Generics.Stuff<int>.assignThing(int)' has some invalid arguments
Assets/Generics.cs(73,22): error CS1503: Argument '#1' cannot convert 'float'
expression to type 'int'
```

This is a good thing as we'd be losing any numbers when converting a float to an int value. Therefore, there are some limitations indeed when it comes to dealing with generic types. They start off being generic, but once assigned they change into the assigned type and must be used accordingly. When Stuff or any generic class is created, it's referred to as an open type. Once it's been assigned with <type>, it's then considered a closed type. Once a generic has been closed, it can't be reassigned.

## 7.14.5 Multiple Generic Values

This is all fine and dandy, but what if we have more than one type that might be assigned later on?

```
public class TwoThings<T, U>
{
    T firstThing;
    U secondThing;
    public void AssignThings(T first, U second)
    {
        firstThing = first;
        secondThing = second;
    }
}
```

You need to have the forethought to anticipate having to deal with more than one thing as a good programmer, should you write a generic class that deals with more than one type. The above code uses <T, U> to assign the first and second types. You might consider a zombie followed by its rank in the zombie army or a glass of water and its percentage of fullness. These tasks can be completed in any way you feel needed.

```
var twoNumbers = new TwoThings <int, double>();
twoNumbers.AssignThings(4, 50.0);
var mixedThings = new TwoThings <zombie, float>();
mixedThings.AssignThings(firstZombie, 1.0f);
```

Once one instance of TwoThings has been assigned; you're able to assign the next instance of TwoThings to two different types. Each one stands on its own, but after they have been assigned, they can't necessarily interact with one another in any expected way. This feature, should not detract from the overall usefulness of a generic type or function.

This works in a similar way for a generic function.

```
public void LogTwoThings<T, U> (T firstThing, U secondThing) {
    Debug.Log(firstThing.GetType());
    Debug.Log(secondThing.GetType());
}
```

The first argument takes on the type of T and the second is assigned to the type of U. We can combine the examples in this chapter to fully demonstrate how generics can avoid type confusion.

```
public class TwoThings<T, U> {
    T firstThing;
    U secondThing;
    public void AssignThings(T first, U second) {
        firstThing = first;
        secondThing = second;
    }
    public T GetFirstThing() {
        return firstThing;
    }
    public U GetSecondThing() {
        return secondThing;
    }
}
```

Here we use T and U as return values for the TwoThings<T, U> class. The public T GetFirst Thing() returns T firstThing; and public U GetSecondThing() returns the value stored in secondThing. We can use LogTwoThings<T, U> to log the types of the objects that were used in the TwoThings class.

```
var mixedThings = new TwoThings<zombie, float>();
mixedThings.AssignThings(firstZombie, 1.0f);
LogTwoThings(mixedThings.GetFirstThing(),
mixedThings.GetSecondThing());
```

This code snippet produces the following log output in the Console:

```
Generics+zombie
UnityEngine.Debug:Log(Object)
Generics:LogTwoThings(zombie, Single) (at Assets/Generics.cs:78)
Generics:Start () (at Assets/Generics.cs:103)
System.Single
UnityEngine.Debug:Log(Object)
Generics:LogTwoThings(zombie, Single) (at Assets/Generics.cs:79)
Generics:Start () (at Assets/Generics.cs:103)
```

We have to get used to where the T appears throughout the function or class in which it makes its appearance. Once the type for T is assigned in the declaration of the class or function, T becomes whatever type it was assigned.

### 7.14.6 What We've Learned

This chapter has covered a great deal about generics. In short, "Generic" is the term given to a type that can be assigned once the function or the class it appears in is used.

```
public void LogTwoThings<T, U> (U firstThing, T secondThing) {
```

We can change the order in the signature from the declaration of the generic identifiers. Of course, this leads to confusion, so it's best to use them in order, although technically there are no adverse behaviors. The var keyword is handy, but mainly when dealing with generic types. It's important to try to use explicitly typed variables where possible. Generics should only be used when there are no other alternatives. With this in mind, it's good to know that you have options available to you when you find yourself cornered by your own data types.

Making collections of data by writing classes for each type is inefficient and excludes the ability to reuse code. When you need to make different functions for different situations that seem to behave in practically the same way, it's a good opportunity to look at a generic method to take care of the task at hand.

The main drawback of the generic methods is that once you start using them, it's difficult to break the habit. If your code begins with too many generic types, you'll end up writing code that depends on `var` and `<T>` in a myriad of different places.

This leads to type conflicts that are hard to track down. Debugging code with many generic classes and methods is difficult and can lead to a great deal of wasted time. In short, use them only when you have to.

In relation to Unity 3D there's a very useful function called `GetComponent<T>();`, which is used quite often.

```
var t = GetComponent<Transform>();
if (t is Transform)
{
    t.localPosition = new Vector3(1, 0, 0);
}
```

We might use the `GetComponent` function in a script to get a component in the game object our script is attached to. After we get the `Transform` component, it can be set. The alternative use is `GetComponent(typeof(Transform));`, which is a bit more verbose, but does the same thing.

## 7.15  Events

For many simple tasks, Unity 3D has provided some useful functions that update objects and execute when the object is first created in a world. There are event handlers in place ready for any mouse clicks which take place in the UI.

When an object receives a condition to act upon, any actions are usually limited to that object. With the tools we already know, we can probably find some way to spread out a message pretty easily, but they'd be awkward and use various static functions. This leads to spaghetti code: interdependent function calls leading to difficult debugging and long nights wondering why everything is broken.

Having a single large set of code that acts as the central switching board for the entire game becomes very cumbersome very quickly.

Delegates allow for many different cool tricks. Delegates with generic types allow for even more cool things, mosty notably, the event. An event acts as a container or a handy place to put any number of functions. When the event is called, all of the functions assigned to it are then called. It's a great system to notify another function that something has occurred that you were waiting for.

We identify a function using a declaration such as `public void functionName(){//code statements}`, something we've been doing already. Delegates are declared using `delegate void delegateName();` depending on what you're trying to accomplish. First we'll start with the minimal parts to explain what's required, and then we'll go into an example of why it's useful.

### 7.15.1  A Basic Example

Starting the Events Unity 3D project, we'll attach a new C# class to the Main Camera and name it `EventDispatcher`. We'll want to see the whole code sample to observe where a delegate like this needs to be declared.

First you need a delegate to assign any functions to. This can happen anywhere outside of the class declaration. Normally, we put them after the directives. The `EventHandler` should be named based on what sort of event it will be handling. We'll decide on better names after we know how they're used.

```
using UnityEngine;
using System.Collections;
public delegate void EventHandler();
public class EventDispatcher : MonoBehaviour
{
    public event EventHandler OnEvent;
    //Use this for initialization
    void Start ()
```

```
    {
    }
    //Update is called once per frame
    void Update ()
    {
    }
}
```

After declaring `public delegate void EventHandler();`, we'll want to make a variable to use the handler inside of the class. With the new keyword `event`, we declare a new event with the `public event EventHandler MyEvent;` statement, and now we have an event to assign functions to.

So far we've assumed that we can only assign data to a variable. An `event` means that we can assign a function to a variable. When an event is used, all of the functions assigned to it will be called. This comes with a few conditions, which we'll see in action after a bit more setup. Let's create another new class called `EventListener`, which should look like the following:

```
using UnityEngine;
using System.Collections;
public class EventListener : MonoBehaviour
{
    //Use this for initialization
    void Start ()
    {
        EventDispatcher dispatcher = GameObject.Find
        ("Main Camera").GetComponent<EventDispatcher>();
    }
    void CallMeMaybe()
    {
        Debug.Log("here's my number");
    }
    //Update is called once per frame
    void Update ()
    {
    }
}
```

In the `Start ()` function of the `EventListener`, we'll want to find the `EventDispatcher` component of the `Main Camera` where we have assigned the `EventDispatcher`. We can do this a number of ways which Unity 3D affords us, but using the `GameObject.Find()` function is the most simple for this example.

Once we've found `dispatcher` in the Main Camera by using `GetComponent<EventDispatcher>()`, we can then assign the event a new function. In this case, we have a short function called `void CallMeMaybe();` which prints "here's my number" to the Console in Unity 3D.

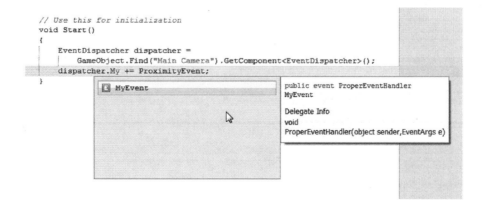

The `MyEvent` from `EventDispatcher` should show up in the Autocomplete pop-up.

```
//Use this for initialization
void Start ()
{
    EventDispatcher dispatcher = GameObject.Find ("Main
Camera").GetComponent<EventDispatcher>();
    dispatcher.MyEvent + = CallMeMaybe;
}
```

Here's where things get interesting. To add a function to `Class.Event`, you use + = and the function name, in this case, `dispatcher.MyEvent + = CallMeMaybe;`. Also notice that there's no () after the function name is assigned.

I've added a Point light to the scene and assigned the `EventListener` class to it.

Now back in the `EventDispatcher` class, we will want some way to activate the event.

```
using UnityEngine;
using System.Collections;
public delegate void EventHandler();
public class EventDispatcher : MonoBehaviour
{
    public event EventHandler MyEvent;
    public bool SendEvent;
    //Use this for initialization
    void Start ()
    {
    }
    //Update is called once per frame
    void Update ()
    {
        if(SendEvent)
        {
            MyEvent();
            SendEvent = false;
        }
    }
}
```

Here we've added a `public bool` called `SendEvent`. In the `Update ()`, add in a simple `if` statement to call the event and turn `SendEvent` back to `false`. This way we can have a sort of button that executes the event when we turn the `bool` to `true`.

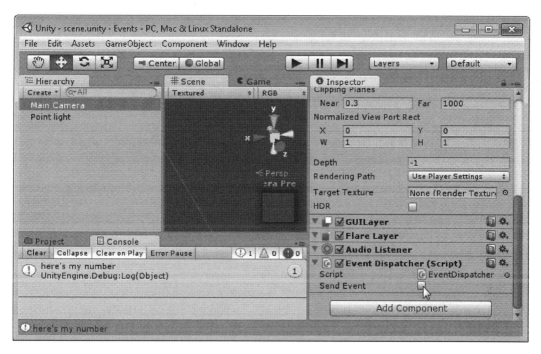

Now when we click on SendEvent bool in the Inspector panel, we get the CallMeMaybe() function on the Point light called from the EventDispatcher. This is about as simple as we can make an event. We have one EventListener in the scene; it's worth noting that any number of EventListeners can be added. Also, any number of functions can be added to the event MyEvent; in the EventDispatcher class.

## 7.15.2 A Proper Event

The .NET Framework has many conformant procedures, to which your code needs to comply. Microsoft has described many different best practices that cover everything from variable names to events. Therefore, it's somewhat necessitated by Microsoft that we take a look at how we should be writing our events should we want to comply with proper code procedures.

```
public delegate void ProperEventHandler(object sender, EventArgs e);
```

Let's add the above delegate to our EventDispatcher Class just after the old EventHandler. This has the addition of object sender and EventArgs e. We'll get into what these are for in a moment.

After the delegate has been declared outside of the class scope, add in a handler for the delegate in the scope of the class.

```
public event ProperEventHandler ProperEvent;
```

The above code should follow our `MyEvent`; just for sake of consistency. Next we'll want to make our event more useful by adding `EventArgs`, or rather Event Arguments, so our new event can have some additional functionality. `EventArgs` are used to pass parameters to anyone listening to the event. Before we can create a custom `EventArg`, we need to add in a new directive.

### 7.15.3 EventArgs

The `system` directive gives us access to a new class called an `EventArg`.

```
using UnityEngine;
using System.Collections;
using System;
```

The `EventArg` type is located in `System`, so to make a class based in it, we need to add the `using System`; at the global scope of the class. Once this is done, we'll want to create a new class at the global scope of the `EventDispatcher`.

```
class MyEventArgs : EventArgs
{
    public string MyNumber;
    public MyEventArgs()
    {
        MyNumber = "I just met you";
    }
}
```

This is a pretty simple class. Once the new `MyEventArgs` class is created or instanced, we should write that the `string MyNumber` is assigned `"I just met you."` This isn't super useful at the moment, but we'll add some more important details in a moment. What is important is that customized event arguments allow for specific event information to be passed to anyone who is listening for the event.

Now back inside of the `EventListener` class, we'll add in a new function within the class scope. We'll also need the `EventArgs` class to be included in the `EventListener` class; therefore the `using System`; statement needs to appear in the `EventListener` class as well.

```
void CallMePlease(object sender, EventArgs e)
{
    Debug.Log(sender);
    MyEventArgs args = (MyEventArgs) e;
    Debug.Log(args.MyNumber);
}
```

This should follow the `CallMeMaybe` function. Rather than have a void argument list in the function we're making use of `object sender` and `EventArgs e`. This is significant since we're going to want event-specific information passed to us later on. To have the function called, we'll want to add it to the new `ProperEvent` found in the `EventDispatcher`; this is done the same way as the previous assignment. To check the incoming parameters, we need `Debug.Logs` to print out what's being passed into the function.

```
void Start ()
{
    EventDispatcher dispatcher =
    GameObject.Find("Main Camera").GetComponent<EventDispatcher>();
```

```
        dispatcher.MyEvent + = CallMeMaybe;
        dispatcher.ProperEvent + = CallMePlease;
}
```

Now dispatcher has MyEvent calling the EventListeners CallMeMaybe function and ProperEvent calls the CallMePlease function. Finally, in the EventDispatcher, we need to add the ProperEvent to the if statement that makes calls.

```
void Update ()
{
    if(SendEvent)
    {
        MyEvent();
        ProperEvent(this, new MyEventArgs());
        SendEvent = false;
    }
}
```

MyEventArgs() is a class, so it needs to be instanced with new before it's used. In the ProperEvent argument list, we use this as the sender and new MyEventArgs() as the EventArg. These two values are passed to the listener. When the SendEvent bool is turned on in the game, we'll get the following output:

```
here's my number
UnityEngine.Debug:Log(Object)
EventListener:CallMeMaybe() (at Assets/EventListener.cs:14)
EventDispatcher:Update () (at Assets/EventDispatcher.cs:35)
Main Camera (EventDispatcher)
UnityEngine.Debug:Log(Object)
EventListener:CallMePlease(Object, EventArgs) (at Assets/EventListener.cs:18)
EventDispatcher:Update () (at Assets/EventDispatcher.cs:36)
I just met you
UnityEngine.Debug:Log(Object)
EventListener:CallMePlease(Object, EventArgs) (at Assets/EventListener.cs:20)
EventDispatcher:Update () (at Assets/EventDispatcher.cs:36)
```

Here's an important bit of information from the Listener. The sender is Main Camera, which makes sense, but depending on who sent the event, the sender might be someone different. Next we get I just met you from the EventArgs passed into the CallMePlease function. We can populate the EventArgs with more important data relevant to the event that occurred.

We've got some interesting parts here that we can put to use. The best situation is to have a clean event-driven game. Rather than wait for conditions to be met and perform some sort of task, it's better to do nothing until an event happens. This approach ensures we avoid having too many scripts updating all at once. On a PC this might not be an issue; however, you'll have a much lower ceiling once you want to put your game on a mobile device.

### 7.15.4 Update () to Event

We could have light react to the player. Thankfully, we started this project by adding the EventListener to the Point light in the scene. Therefore, when the player is away, we could have the light turned off. Once the player reaches a certain distance from the light, we can have the light pop on. This code is simple enough to add directly to the light object.

```
//Update is called once per frame
void Update () {
    GameObject player =
    GameObject.Find("Main Camera");
```

```
    Vector3 TargetVector =
    player.transform.position - transform.position;
    float DistanceToPlayer =
    TargetVector.magnitude;
    if(DistanceToPlayer < 10.0f)
    {
        gameObject.GetComponent<Light>().intensity = 2.0f;
    }
    else
    {
        gameObject.GetComponent<Light>().intensity = 0.1f;
    }
}
```

This code ensures that the light turns on only if the player is closer than 10 units from the light; otherwise it'll be fairly dim. This sets up some logic that's run every time the Update () function is called. However, the transition from one state to the other is very clear.

In this case, however, we will want to give the responsibility to the EventDispatcher or the Main Camera rather than the Point light. Therefore, first we'll want to move the code from the Update () into separate function calls so that they can be called by an event.

If we examine the above code, we can see we're checking for the Main Camera and calculating a distance. If the distance is within 10 units, then we set the intensity of the light to 2; otherwise the light is set to 0.1. Making the distance calculation and light intensity setting every frame is wasteful and is better served by a simple event when the player approaches or leaves the light.

We had an interesting look at generics in Section 7.14. It's time we put that to some use with an EventArg. It's easy to imagine that different events may require different arguments. Rather than having to figure out every situation ahead of time, it's easier to make a more generic event type.

### 7.15.5 Generic EventArg

After the MyEventArg, add the following generic event:

```
public class EventArgs<T> : EventArgs
{
public EventArgs(T v)
{
    Value = v;
}
public T Value;
}
```

This uses the standard <T> following an identifier. We're basing this on EventArgs like before, and in the constructor we're using (T v) to set the Value of the EventArg<T>. This does two things: First it means we can put any type of data into the EventArg. Then we get to pass the generic data to the listener. Now we can use it in our ProperEvent as follows:

```
ProperEvent(this, new EventArgs<float>(3.14f));
```

We'll want to replace the 3.14f with a distance, but we'll get to that in a moment. It's important to know that we're getting an expected value through to the EventListener first. However, if nothing is assigned to the ProperEvent, we'll get an error if we try to run it.

```
NullReferenceException: Object reference not set to an instance of an object
EventDispatcher.Update () (at Assets/EventDispatcher.cs:41)
```

If an event is called and there is nobody to receive the call, then we get a `NullReferenceException`. To fix this we simply put in a check to make sure that the event isn't null, which should always be done.

```
if(ProperEvent != null)
{
    ProperEvent(this, new EventArgs<float>(3.14f));
}
```

Next we'll want to have the light prepare a function to receive the call. In the `EventListener` class, we'll add in the following function to take the event as it comes in.

```
public void ProximityEvent(object sender, EventArgs e)
{
    EventArgs<float> eVal = (EventArgs<float>)e;
    Debug.Log(eVal.Value);
}
```

This will take the `EventArg` e and cast it to the proper generic version of the function we're looking for. `EventArgs<float>` eVal is the proper form for setting up a variable for a generic type. To cast e to `EventArgs<float>`, use `(EventArgs<float>)` e to do the cast to the expected type.

It's important to note the use of casting in this situation. The `(type)variable` structure is an explicit cast. Don't let the `EventArgs<T>` confuse you with the extra `<T>` in the parentheses. Once cast to `EventArgs<float>`, the `public T Value` inside of that class is now accessible.

`EventListener` should add itself to `EventDispatcher`'s `ProperEvent`. When `ProperEvent()` in `EventDispatcher` is called, `ProximityEvent()` in `EventListener` is also called.

```
void Start ()
{
    EventDispatcher dispatcher =
    GameObject.Find ("Main Camera").GetComponent<EventDispatcher>();
    dispatcher.ProperEvent + = ProximityEvent;
}
```

Therefore, we should be having 3.14 being sent out from `EventListener`. We can still use the same `bool` as we did earlier to check on the effectiveness of the event. Now it's a good idea to set up some a real system to raise these events. The `EventDispatcher` should be the only one with any code in the `Update ()` function.

```
private bool isClose;
void Update ()
{
    GameObject target =
    GameObject.Find("Point light");
    Vector3 targetVector =
    target.transform.position - transform.position ;
    float distanceToTarget = targetVector.magnitude;
    if(distanceToTarget < = 10 && !isClose)
    {
        ProperEvent(this, new EventArgs<float>(distanceToTarget));
        isClose = true;
    }
    if(distanceToTarget > 10 && isClose)
    {
        ProperEvent(this, new EventArgs<float>(distanceToTarget));
        isClose = false;
    }
}
```

Here we check to see if we're near the light target. We do the same sort of function to check for our distance away from the target. If we're close to the target, we change `isClose` to `true`, and if we're not, we turn `isClose` to `false`. This way we can keep the event from firing every time `Update ()` is evaluated.

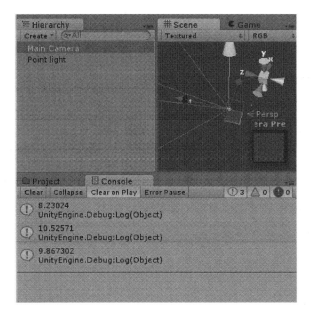

Now if we run the game and move the Main Camera around the light in the scene, we get some numbers popping up in the Console panel. Now all we need to do is make some decisions on what to do with the incoming `EventArg` within the `ProximityEvent` function.

Back in the `EventListener`, we change the `ProximityEvent` function to the following:

```
public void ProximityEvent(object sender, EventArgs e)
{
    EventArgs<float> eVal = (EventArgs<float>)e;
    if(eVal.Value > 10)
    {
        gameObject.GetComponent<Light>().intensity = 0.1f;
    }
    else
    {
        gameObject.GetComponent<Light>().intensity = 2.0f;
    }
    Debug.Log(eVal.Value);
}
```

With this we'll get the behavior we found in EventListener's Update () function earlier.

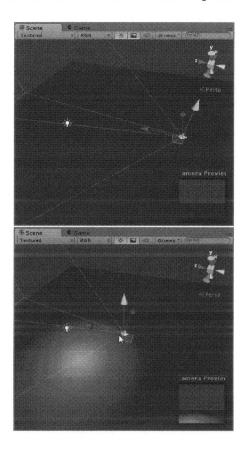

The key difference here is the fact that this evaluation is not happening in the Update () loop of the light. However, we have a dreadful problem. If we duplicate this light, the Main Camera's EventDispatcher will send the same EventArg to all of the EventListeners.

To solve this problem, we have to come up with a few different solutions. First is the fact that there will be multiple lights in the scene. This means that GameObject.Find will not be able to return everything in the scene. Next is our bool that prevents the event from firing multiple times.

The isClose is now a property relative to the light, not the Main Camera, so we'll move that to the EventListener class living on the light itself. Next we'll want to iterate through an array of lights, so that means a different system to finding each light in the scene.

FindByTag is a much better system, so we'll want to select all of the lights in the scene and assign them a new tag.

Select Point light on the Inspector panel, select the pop-up next to Tag, and pick Add Tag … at the bottom of the list.

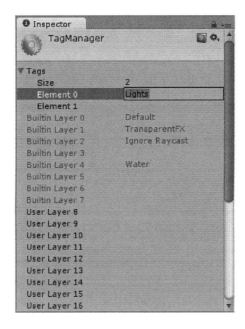

Enter Lights on the first Element and select all of the lights in the scene.

Then set Tag to lights. Therefore, our cleaned up and complete `EventDispatcher` code looks like the following:

```
using UnityEngine;
using System.Collections;
using System;
public delegate void ProperEventHandler(object sender, EventArgs e);
public class EventArgs<T> : EventArgs
{
public EventArgs(T v)
{
    Value = v;
}
public T Value;
}
public class EventDispatcher : MonoBehaviour {
    public event ProperEventHandler ProperEvent;
    //Use this for initialization
    void Start ()
    {
    }
    //Update is called once per frame
    void Update ()
    {
        GameObject[] Lights =
        GameObject.FindGameObjectsWithTag("Lights") as GameObject[];
        foreach(GameObject l in Lights)
        {
            Vector3 targetVector =
            l.transform.position - transform.position ;
            float distanceToTarget =
            targetVector.magnitude;
            EventListener el =
            l.GetComponent<EventListener>();
            if(distanceToTarget < = 10 && !el.isClose)
            {
                ProperEvent(gameObject.transform, new
                EventArgs<float>(distanceToTarget));
                el.isClose = true;
            }
            if(distanceToTarget > 10 && el.isClose)
            {
                ProperEvent(gameObject.transform, new
                EventArgs<float>(distanceToTarget));
                el.isClose = false;
            }
        }
    }
}
```

Therefore, we need to make a reference to `EventListener` in the script to determine whether or not we're close to the particular object or not. Then we send `gameObject.transform` as the sender.

And now the cleaned up `EventListener` code looks like this:

```
using UnityEngine;
using System.Collections;
using System;
public class EventListener : MonoBehaviour
```

```
{
    public bool isClose;
    //Use this for initialization
    void Start ()
    {
        EventDispatcher dispatcher =
        GameObject.Find ("Main Camera").GetComponent<EventDispatcher>();
        dispatcher.ProperEvent + = ProximityEvent;
    }
    public void ProximityEvent(object sender, EventArgs e)
    {
        Transform t = sender as Transform;
        Vector3 targetVector = t.position - transform.position ;
        float distanceToTarget = targetVector.magnitude;
        if(distanceToTarget > 10)
        {
            gameObject.GetComponent<Light>().intensity = 0.1f;
        }
        else
        {
            gameObject.GetComponent<Light>().intensity = 2.0f;
        }
        Debug.Log(distanceToTarget);
    }
}
```

We're not making use of the EventArgs<T> in this situation. We could send any value to the EventArgs parameter, for instance, the number of hit points, ammo, or number of brains we've eaten. Any particular information that isn't already present on the gameObject can be added to the EventArgs.

### 7.15.6 What We've Learned

It's important to use events in an intuitive manner. In any situation in which a frame-by-frame update isn't required, an event should be implemented instead. Thanks to inheritance, we can make the following script and attach it to any one of the lights.

```
using UnityEngine;
using System.Collections;
using System;
public class ColorChanger : EventListener {
    public Color CloseColor;
    public Color FarColor;
    public override void ProximityEvent(object sender, EventArgs e)
    {
        Transform t = sender as Transform;
        Vector3 targetVector = t.position - transform.position ;
        float distanceToTarget = targetVector.magnitude;
        if(distanceToTarget > 10)
        {
            gameObject.GetComponent<Light>().color = CloseColor;
        }
        else
        {
            gameObject.GetComponent<Light>().color = FarColor;
        }
        Debug.Log(distanceToTarget);
    }
}
```

To make this work, you'll want to change the `ProximityEvent` declaration to `public virtual void ProximityEvent(object sender, EventArgs e)`. A virtual function can be overridden to change the light's color rather than intensity.

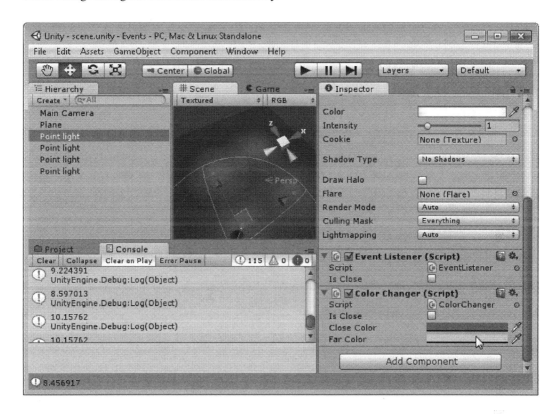

Adding a second script makes this light change both in intensity and color. We don't want to include a `Start ()` or `Update ()` function in the `ColorChanger` class either. We'll allow the base class to take care of the functionality that adds the `ProximityEvent` to the `EventDispatcher`.

When setting up weapons, events are a simple easy way to manage what happens when the trigger is pulled. When the weapon is equipped, you add any weapon's class functions that need to execute to an event handler that activates when the weapon is used.

Collision events and hit events are also great places to call functions. One last thing is the following code.

```
void OnDestroy()
{
    EventDispatcher dispatcher =
    GameObject.Find ("Main Camera").GetComponent<EventDispatcher>();
    dispatcher.ProperEvent - = ProximityEvent;
}
```

To clean up after an object is destroyed, you'll want to take the function out of the `EventHandler`. You use `- = ProximityEvent` to pull the function back out of the `EventDispatcher`'s event handler. This is very important; otherwise when the event is called, there will be a `NullReferenceException` error where the function's object used to be in the event handler.

If you write a similar proximity function in a `Zombie` class, you could use the same event handler that is operating calling the lights. However, reusing the same event handler for every situation isn't the best practice. Organizationally, it's better to create a different handler for each situation. Because you can use different event handlers, you can also name each handler based on what it's used for.

A ZombieProximityEvent should handle distances to zombies, a LightProximityEvent should handle only lights, and so forth. The brevity of the code allows for more complex behaviors to take up fewer lines of code. In this sense, it's more important to keep the lines of code as readable as possible.

## 7.16 Unity-Friendly Classes

When writing new classes, a classic programmer's mentality would be to write a single monolithic class that handles many different tasks in a single complex algorithm. As a programmer, you might approach many different problems with a single complex solution. The better, more Unity-friendly approach is quite the opposite.

When we think about building a solution for a complex problem, it's sometimes easier to start with a generalized solution. For instance, should we want to build a complex behavior for managing a group of zombies and humans chasing and eating one another, the first thought might be to write a crowd manager class that keeps track of each zombie and human, and then moves each one around based on a set of parameters.

This approach leads to what might be a single solution since we know everything about everyone in a scene. Writing this might be a difficult task, but getting it right would be quite an accomplishment; unfortunately, there are a few drawbacks. First off, now you have a single complex algorithm to debug, should small problems arise.

Next you run into an inflexibility problem. Rewriting anything to gain different behaviors turns into adding additional layers of complexity. Additional layers in an already complex class easily introduces more bugs and makes fixing those bugs more and more difficult.

The worst part of the monolithic approach comes when someone else needs to open your class and interpret what's going on. The more complex your code is, the more difficult it is to explain. What makes things worse, the longer your algorithm, the more the explanation that is required. Usually nobody likes to read every little comment, even if you wrote detailed comments throughout your code.

### 7.16.1 Extensions

When we're working with the built-in Unity 3D types such as GameObject, we're unable to extend those classes. If we try to use the following code, we'll get an interesting error:

```
public class MyGameObject : GameObject
{
}
```

This produces the following output:

```
Assets/Example.cs(29,14): error CS0509: 'MyGameObject': cannot derive from
sealed type 'UnityEngine.GameObject'
```

A sealed class means that it's final, and no one else is allowed to extend or make further modifications to the GameObject class. However, it doesn't mean that we can't give the GameObject new functions. For instance, if we wanted gameObject.NewTrick();, we're able to do this through Extensions methods.

### 7.16.2 A Basic Example

Let's start with the Extensions project in which we have a simple Example.cs class with a namespace added at the bottom.

```
using UnityEngine;
using System.Collections;
using Tricks;
public class Extensions : MonoBehaviour {
    //Use this for initialization
    void Start () {
```

```
        }
        //Update is called once per frame
        void Update () {
        }
}
namespace Tricks
{
using UnityEngine;
using System.Collections;
}
```

At the top we add `using Tricks;` to allow the `Extensions` class to use the contents of the namespace tacked on to the bottom of this class. In a more regular case, you should put the namespace into another file, but for clarity we're just going to merge these two objects together in this file.

In the namespace, we need to add a new class where we're going to be making use of our `GameObject` class.

```
namespace Tricks
{
using UnityEngine;
using System.Collections;
    public static class GameObjectExtensions {
    }
}
```

Here we use `GameObjectExtensions`, but this could be anything. So long as the name is descriptive as to what it's going to be doing, `GameObjectExtensions` is a good place to start. Inside of this class, we'll be adding our various functions that extend the `GameObject` class.

```
        public static class GameObjectExtensions {
            public static void NewTrick(this GameObject go)
            {
                Debug.Log(go.name);
            }
        }
```

The `public static void NewTrick()` is our extension function. To extend the `GameObject`, we use the argument `this GameObject go` where the `this` keyword informs C# that we're writing an extension method. In the argument list, we use the identifier `go` that appears in the function as `go.name`. This `NewTrick()` simply prints the name of the `gameObject` to the Console.

```
public class Extensions : MonoBehaviour {
    // Use this for initialization
    void Start () {
        gameObject.New|
        // gameO  ┌────────────────────────┐         public static void
        SimpleOk  │ Ⓜ NewTrick             │         NewTrick (
        UpdateEv  │                      ⬉ │            Vector3 pos
    }             │                        │         )
    public dele  │                        │
    public event │                        │         Extension Method from
    // Update i   │                        │         Tricks.GameObjectExtensions
    void Update   │                        │
        if( Upd   │                        │
        {         │                        │
            UpdateEvent();
        }
    }
}
```

Back in the `Start ()` function, if we write in `gameObject.N`, we get the above pop-up where we are shown `(Extension) void NewTrick()` in the list of functions available to the `gameObject` type. Perhaps our `NewTrick()` is not the most exciting trick for `gameObject` to have, but it is a good beginning. Selecting the `NewTrick();` and running the game prints `Main Camera` to the console.

Any additional arguments must come after the argument where the keyword `this` is used. Depending on the type that follows this in the first argument, you can change the function to extend a different sealed class.

```
public static void NewTrick(this GameObject go, Vector3 pos)
{
    go.transform.position = pos;
    Debug.Log(go.name);
}
```

Making the above addition of `Vector3 pos` and then using `go.transofm.position = pos;` will tell the `gameObject` to update its position. Therefore, in the `Start ()` function, we can use the following code to move the camera to `Vector3(1, 1, 1);` when the `NewTrick(Vector3.one);` is used:

```
void Start () {
    gameObject.NewTrick(Vector3.one);
}
```

The Extension functions can be applied to any sealed class. When working with third-party libraries, it's often useful to add your own functions to classes which you don't have source code for.

The `static` keyword is necessary to make the function appear in any context. The same goes for the class in which the Extension function appears. The `static` class in which the function is written in is a side effect of a function not being able live on its own. A function is always a member of a class, even though it might not be related to the class in which it's written in.

An extension function can technically be written into any `static` class, though it would be confusing if they appeared in an unrelated class. Clear naming practices are just as important as ever, in particular when naming functions unrelated to the class they exist in.

As a consequence of extensions, it's easy to keep adding to a `sealed` class. Often if you're able to do, it's far better to add the functions to the class itself. This sidesteps the necessity of writing any number of extension functions. This doesn't just have to work on a `gameObject`.

```
public static class GameObjectExtensions
{
    public static void NewTrick (this GameObject go, Vector3 pos)
    {
        go.transform.position = pos;
        Debug.Log(go.name);
    }
    public static void Zero (this Transform t)
    {
        t.position = Vector3.zero;
    }
}
```

In the above example, we can use `gameObject.transform.Zero();` to move the camera or any other object in the scene that has a transform to the center of the scene. However, this does highlight the fact that `Zero()` should probably appear in a different class called `TransformExtensions`, or should it?

Functions can be overloaded, so we can have more than one `Zero()` extension function in the class.

```
public static class GameObjectExtensions
{
```

```
            public static void NewTrick (this GameObject go, Vector3 pos)
            {
                go.transform.position = pos;
                Debug.Log(go.name);
            }
            public static void Zero (this Transform t)
            {
                t.position = Vector3.zero;
            }
            public static void Zero (this GameObject go)
            {
                go.transform.position = Vector3.zero;
            }
        }
```

Here we have a `Zero()` function that works on both the `GameObject` and the `Transform` types. Perhaps we should rename `GameObjectExtension` to something more like `GameExtensions`. Naming classes and functions is such a big part of writing code. Going back into your code only to rename a class or function is called refactoring.

It's good to know from the beginning some practices to avoid, as a project starts to grow. Unity 3D in particular works best when smaller components come together on each object in the scene. This feature is often referred to as the actor model.

`MonoBehaviour` has many benefits of the `Start ()` and `Update ()` loops. However, these come with a slight cost. Once several hundred objects have populated a scene, your scene now has to start the `Start ()` function and update it's `Update ()` function individually. This can cause slowdowns and loss of frame rate. Something like this might not be so apparent on a high-end PC, but it can have brutal effects on a tiny underpowered mobile device.

### 7.16.3 Inheriting from Object

The last resort, or possibly the first step in a lightweight fast Unity 3D game project, is to forget all about `MonoBehaviour`. The `Update ()` function tends to eat up a great deal of your game's frame rate. If there's one very busy `Update ()` function, you're better off than having a few hundred different simple `Update ()` function calls.

On a PC you'll never notice any slowdowns. It's only when you're on a mobile device you see a noticeable loss in frame rate. Phones have very tight processor and memory restrictions when compared to a desktop computer. It's important to limit how many resources and calculations your code uses to ensure optimal performance when running on a more limited system.

In the interest of keeping functions simple and easy to deal with, it's important that the single `Update ()` is kept short and organized. At the same time, it's important that the classes based on object and not `MonoBehaviour` are still allowed to update when needed.

### 7.16.4 OnUpdate

To continue with the previous exercise, we'll add a system to update the `SimpleObject` class with an event. This provides the lightweight class with an `Update ()` once we add the `OnUpdate ()` function to the `Update ()` in the `MonoBehaviour`-based class.

```
using UnityEngine;
using System.Collections;
using Tricks;
public class SimpleObject : Object
{
    GameObject gameObject;
```

```
        public SimpleObject(GameObject go)
        {
            this.gameObject = go;
            Debug.Log("im here: " + go.name);
        }
        public void OnUpdate ()
        {
            gameObject.Zero();
        }
}
```

First we'll want to have an `OnUpdate` () function in the `SimpleObject`. This makes use of a `gameObject` in much the same way that `MonoBehaviours` have a `gameObject`. We're using the newly added `.zero()` extension function.

Back in the `Extensions` class, we add in the following code for the simple object:

```
public class Extensions : MonoBehaviour
{
    //Use this for initialization
    void Start ()
    {
        SimpleObject so = new SimpleObject(this.gameObject);
        UpdateEvent+ = so.OnUpdate;
    }
    public delegate void UpdateHandler();
    public event UpdateHandler UpdateEvent;
    //Update is called once per frame
    void Update ()
    {
        if(UpdateEvent != null)
        {
            UpdateEvent();
        }
    }
}
```

We create an `UpdateHandler()` and an `UpdateEvent` to which we assign the `so.OnUpdate`. Once assigned, it's called on each frame by the `Update` () function. As soon as the game is run, the camera snaps to the center of the world at `Vector3(0,0,0);` and sticks there.

## 7.16.5 What We've Learned

After your scripts begin to deal with a great number of different variables, garbage collection (GC) begins to be an issue that also bogs down the game's performance. Intermittent hitches in frame rate can sometimes be the result of a large number of objects in memory being cleaned up.

Other interesting tricks that often come up in a small C# class in Unity 3D is limiting how much of a library is used. When you add directives such as `using System;`, you're including a heavy amount of memory that needs to be accessed. This memory isn't necessarily used when you're running the game; however, this is used when your code is compiled.

For ease of use, it's a simple matter to have a simple case like the following:

```
using Vect3 = UnityEngine.Vector3;
```

This shortens `Vector3` into `Vect3`. Doing so helps to reduce namespace conflicts as well as speeds up picking names in the Autocomplete feature in MonoDevelop. The normal behavior always has `Vector2` above `Vector3` in the pop-up list. After a while, this behavior can easily be replaced if you get used to using `Vect3` instead.

The usual practice is to use the regular name, in case the rest of the library is needed. However, it's good to know that tricks like this are possible, in case you come across something strange. Working in Unity 3D places specific constraints around what code will and will not work when it comes to the full feature set that the .NET foundation has to offer.

The developers at Unity 3D are hard set on supporting many different platforms, and the lowest common denominator sets the height of the bar. Getting to know a language with a focus is great; this is why Unity 3D is a great stage for learning C#. Once you've gotten into how the language works, it's a good idea to explore other development environments where you can make games with the full .NET Framework. Never limit yourself.

## 7.17 Destructors

While you're busy creating objects, Unity 3D is busy cleaning them up. If you clean them up quickly, you limit how often and how long it takes Unity 3D to do this for you.

We've looked at the constructor in Chapters 5 and 6. Destructors are the opposite construct from the constructor. C# is a garbage-collected language, so in most instances, you're not in need of a specific cleanup of your own data when your object is no longer referenced. However, when you begin to use unsafe code, some cleanup might be more necessary.

Unity 3D provides the `OnDestroy()` event after any object based on `MonoBehaviour` has been destroyed. If you want to destroy an object that isn't based on `MonoBehaviour`, you don't have an `OnDestroy()` event. Therefore, what else is there to do?

### 7.17.1 A Basic Example

In the Destructors project, open the `Example.cs` component attached to the Main Camera and also open the `DestroyMe.cs` file. The `DestroyMe` has both a constructor and a destructor.

```
using UnityEngine;
using System.Collections;
public class DestroyMe
{
    public string name;
    //constructor
    public DestroyMe(string name)
    {
        this.name = name;
        Debug.Log(name + " says hello.");
    }
    ~DestroyMe()
    {
        Debug.Log(name + " says goodbye.");
    }
}
```

The destructor can be identified by the ~, or tilde, preceding the class identifier. Somewhat like a very simple-looking constructor, the destructor is called any time the object is garbage collected. C# is a garbage-collected environment. Specific destructors aren't specifically written into the language. Even so, there are several ways we can force the object to be cleaned out of memory.

```
using UnityEngine;
using System.Collections;
public class Example : MonoBehaviour
{
```

```
        DestroyMe dm;
        //Use this for initialization
        void Start ()
        {
            dm = new DestroyMe("rob");
        }
        //Update is called once per frame
        void Update ()
        {
        }
}
```

In the Example.cs attached to the camera, we have a variable that is going to hold onto the DestroyMe class called dm. When we create a new DestroyMe and store it into dm, we give it a name so we can know what is being cleaned out and when. If we run the game scene, we see rob printed to the Console when the game starts.

Only when the game is stopped will we see "rob says goodbye." As long as the dm is holding onto the instance of DestroyMe, dm will occupy memory and will not be cleaned out. However, we can force the issue with a simple assignment.

```
        void Start ()
        {
            dm = new DestroyMe("rob");
            dm = null;
        }
```

When we create a new DestroyMe object, we see "rob says hello." As soon as dm = null; is called, we see "rob says goodbye." in the Console. Setting the variable dm to null releases the reference in this class to the DestroyMe object with the name rob. Once C# sees that there is nothing referencing the DestroyMe object named rob, it's cleaned out of memory and its destructor is called.

In general, GC in C# works automatically. For objects such as a struct, GC should be done very quickly. Only when you need to work with a large number of class objects do you need to pay close attention to the number of objects that are being created.

The automatic GC is done in random intervals. Usually there is little consequence of the GC on a PC. The memory and CPU are running so fast that it's imperceptible when the GC takes place.

On a mobile device, the GC can lead to a sudden loss in frame rate once every few seconds. The interval between GC cycles can be longer or shorter depending on how often objects are created. Because of this, it's important to build some sort of scheme to track and destroy objects on your own.

## 7.17.2 Clearing Out Objects

After an object has a reference to an event, it becomes a bit harder to get rid of. In the DestroyMe class, we'll add in a new OnUpdate () function:

```
using UnityEngine;
using System.Collections;
public class DestroyMe
{
    public string name;
    //constructor
    public DestroyMe(string name)
    {
        this.name = name;
        Debug.Log(name + " says hello.");
    }
    public void OnUpdate ()
```

```
    {
        Debug.Log(name + " is updating.");
    }
    ~DestroyMe()
    {
        Debug.Log(name + " says goodbye.");
    }
}
```

Then to make use of the function, we'll create a `delegate` and an `event` to update in the Example's `Update ()` function.

```
using UnityEngine;
using System.Collections;
public class Example : MonoBehaviour
{
    DestroyMe dm;
    int counter = 10;
    delegate void updateHandler();
    event updateHandler updateEvent;
    //Use this for initialization
    void Start ()
    {
        dm = new DestroyMe("rob");
        updateEvent + = dm.OnUpdate;
    }
    //Update is called once per frame
    void Update ()
    {
        if (updateEvent != null)
        {
            updateEvent();
            counter-- ;
            if (counter < = 0)
            {
                dm = null;
            }
        }
    }
}
```

In this version of the class, we want to update the `DestroyMe` object 10 times with an event and then get rid of it. If we look at what happens when our counter runs down to 0, we set `dm` to `null` like before. However, we don't get a message that the destructor has been called, and the `OnUpdate ()` function gets called every frame even after `dm` has been set to `null`.

```
    void Update ()
    {
        if (updateEvent != null)
        {
            updateEvent();
            counter-- ;
            if (counter < = 0)
            {
                dm = null;
                updateEvent = null;
            }
        }
    }
```

If we set the updateEvent to null, the OnUpdate () function stops getting called after 10 counts. However, we still don't see the DestroyMe's destructor being called. To force the GC we need to add in the using System; directive. This will give us access to the GC functions.

```
void Update ()
{
    if (updateEvent != null)
    {
        updateEvent();
        counter-- ;
        if (counter < = 0)
        {
            dm = null;
            updateEvent = null;
            GC.Collect();
        }
    }
}
```

By forcing GC to collect unreferenced classes, we can finally make sure that the object dm is cleaned out. Now after setting dm to null and updateEvent to null, and forcing GC, we get the expected hello, update, and goodbye from DestroyMe.

Therefore, if an updateEvent needs to get set to null, every other delegate that might be assigned to that event is also cleared out. If there were several objects relying on this event, we lose some of the ability to pick and choose which objects are added and removed from the event.

```
using UnityEngine;
using System.Collections;
using System;
public class Example : MonoBehaviour
{
    DestroyMe dm;
    private int counter = 10;
    delegate void updateHandler();
    event updateHandler updateEvent;
    ArrayList DestroyList = new ArrayList();
    //Use this for initialization
    void Start ()
    {
        dm = new DestroyMe("rob");
        updateEvent + = dm.OnUpdate;
        //dm = null;
        DestroyList.Add(new DestroyMe("white"));
        DestroyList.Add(new DestroyMe("stubbs"));
        DestroyList.Add(new DestroyMe("berney"));
    }
    //Update is called once per frame
    void Update ()
    {
        if (updateEvent != null)
        {
            updateEvent();
            counter-- ;
            if (counter < = 0)
            {
                //updateEvent - = dm.OnUpdate;
                dm = null;
                updateEvent = null;
```

```
                GC.Collect ();
            }
        }
        for (int i = 0; i < DestroyList.Count; i++)
        {
            DestroyMe d = DestroyList [i] as DestroyMe;
            if (counter < = 0)
            {
                if (d.name == "berney")
                {
                    DestroyList.Remove(DestroyList [i]);
                }
            }
            d.OnUpdate ();
        }
    }
}
```

To be more picky about which object is removed and updated, we can use an `ArrayList`. If we add three objects to the list, we can use their names to remove them from the list using a `for` loop. In the `for` loop, we can also call the object's `OnUpdate ()` function.

Once the `counter` drops to 0 or less, we check if one of the object names is `berney` and remove him from the list. By running the code, we'll notice that `berney` updates 10 times, but his destructor isn't immediately called. We have to wait a few seconds to see his `goodbye` message.

```
for(int i = 0; i < DestroyList.Count; i++)
{
    DestroyMe d = DestroyList[i] as DestroyMe;
    if(counter < = 0)
    {
        if(d.name == "berney")
        {
            DestroyList.Remove(DestroyList[i]);
            GC.Collect();
        }
    }
    d.OnUpdate ();
}
```

Even if we modify the `if` statement and add in a `GC.Collect();`, `berney` sits around for a few seconds before getting cleaned up. This becomes a problem if there are many different objects waiting to be cleaned up.

Here lies the problem with managed memory. When it comes to setting up and clearing out memory, C# has the bulk of the duties taken out of the programmer's hands. To have this sort of memory control, you'll need to use a programming language that allows for it. C# was engineered in such a way that prevents the software programmer from touching memory on this level.

This was done for a multitude of reasons. Prevention of access to objects that no longer exist or deletion of objects that are still in use are common problems in non-garbage-collected programming languages such as C or C++. C# was created to alleviate the work involved with allocation and deallocation of memory for every object.

The idea was that memory management was such a common problem that it would be better to have a more automatic system to take care of handling this job for you. The GC in C# is easy to work with, but it also prevents you from managing the memory more directly.

In most cases, this shouldn't ever be a major problem. GC is reliable; perhaps it just takes some faith to believe that it's doing as much as it can as quickly as it can. There are systems in place which allow for more direct control over the memory. Unfortunately, Unity 3D cannot make use of them without a Pro license. This limitation takes the lessons involved with that out of the scope of this book.

### 7.17.3 What We've Learned

Destructors are used when manual clean up of a class is needed. When using classes based on any of the Unity 3D class objects, it's recommended you use the OnDetroy() function to clear any extra data created by the class. It's recommended that any class not based on a Unity 3D class use a destructor, though it's not a common practice to create classes not based on Unity 3D.

When classes add a delegate to an event, the destructor can be used to remove the delegate. Unfortunately, we can't use `updateEvent - = dm.OnUpdate ();` to remove the reference to object `dm`. This still leaves behind some traces to the `dm` class in the memory and prevents GC from cleaning out the object.

Garbage collection happens in regular intervals, usually about a second between each pass through the heap. The heap is a pile of memory that can become disorganized. When an object is removed, it leaves behind a gap. After many hundreds of objects are created and destroyed, the heap can become a cube of Swiss cheese of usable and unusable spaces. Garbage collection tries to mitigate and clean the heap as often as it can. If the heap were processed any more, then performance in maintaining clean memory would take over your CPU cycles.

The balance between performance and memory management isn't always to your benefit. As improvements are made, there may be speed gains, but it's up to you to keep your use of memory as slim as possible to allow for quick GC passes.

This is one of the reasons why a struct is preferable over a class. Structs are allocated to a different section of memory for your game and thus don't need to be garbage collected at all. This isn't true if a struct is stored as a part of a class.

In the end, C# allows for so many different ways to use the language; the benefit far outreaches the limitation of memory management. Your task of creating a game shouldn't be hindered by the nitty-gritty of poking holes in memory and trying to fill them in manually. This sort of stuff isn't fun and should be left to the folks writing C# to figure out later on.

## 7.18 Concurrency or Coroutines

So far, everything that has been talked about has been for writing code that is executed in order. As the code is executed, each statement must wait until the preceding statement has completed its task. For the most part, this is done exceedingly fast.

### 7.18.1 Yield

We've gone over the use of `IEnumerator` earlier; it's a handy interface for more than one reason. The `IEnumerator` is notable for iterating over an array; in addition, it also allows the use of `yield`. The primary reason for the `yield` keyword was to allow a computer to continue with a function and allow something like our `Update ()` loop to come back to the function using the `yield` statement.

For instance, if we had a task that might take more than a single update frame to complete, we could use a function with a `yield`; this works only with a function that is an `IEnumerator`. This means that the function starts when it's called, but then allows us to come back to it again and check on how it's doing.

For instance, a really slow function, which fills the scene with 40,000 randomly placed cubes, might take a while to complete.

```
void Start ()
{
    FillUpObjects();
}
void FillUpObjects() {
    lotsOfObjects = new GameObject[40000];
    for(int i = 0; i < 40000; i++) {
        GameObject g = GameObject.CreatePrimitive(PrimitiveType.Cube);
        g.name = i.ToString() + "_cube";
```

```
        float rx = Random.Range(-1000,1000);
        float ry = Random.Range(-1000,1000);
        float rz = Random.Range(-1000,1000);
        g.transform.position = new Vector3(rx, ry, rz);
        g.transform.localScale = new Vector3(10,10,10);
        lotsOfObjects[i] = g;
    }
}
```

Unity 3D will lock up for several seconds waiting for this function to finish before the game is allowed to begin. One way to get around this is to use a coroutine.

```
IEnumerator FillUpObjects()
{
    lotsOfObjects = new GameObject[40000];
    for(int i = 0; i < 40000; i++)
    {
        GameObject g = GameObject.CreatePrimitive(PrimitiveType.Cube);
        g.name = i.ToString() + "_cube";
        float rx = Random.Range(-1000,1000);
        float ry = Random.Range(-1000,1000);
        float rz = Random.Range(-1000,1000);
        g.transform.position = new Vector3(rx, ry, rz);
        g.transform.localScale = new Vector3(10,10,10);
        lotsOfObjects[i] = g;
        yield return null;
    }
}
```

Change the return type of the function from `void` to `IEnumerator`, then at the end of the `for` loop, and add `yield return null;` so that the `IEnumerator` interface has something to return. The new sort function is called differently from a regular function as we see in the following code:

```
    void Start ()
    {
        StartCoroutine("FillUpObjects");
    }
```

`StartCoroutine()` calls the `IEnumerator` as a coroutine. When the game is started, we don't experience a lock, but we do get to watch cubes fill in the world. This is a simple example on how a coroutine is usually used. It's a great method to start an unusually long function and not have to wait for its completion before the rest of some code is executed.

### 7.18.1.1 A Basic Example

However, in terms of a game, there are more interesting uses for the coroutine. To see how this works, we'll start a Unity 3D Scene with a new script called `Concurrent` attached to the Main Camera.

```
using UnityEngine;
using System.Collections;
public class Concurrent : MonoBehaviour
{
    void Start ()
    {
        StartCoroutine (DelayStatement());
    }
    IEnumerator DelayStatement()
```

```
    {
        Debug.Log("Started at: " + Time.fixedTime);
        yield return new WaitForSeconds(3.0f);
        Debug.Log("Ended at: " + Time.fixedTime);
    }
}
```

With the above code, we can see that we're using the statement `StartCoroutine_ Auto()` to call on a function. The function is defined with the `IEnumerator` interface and is identified as `DelayStatement`. In the `DelayStatement` code block, we see that it starts with `Debug. Log("Started at: " + Time.fixedTime);` followed by a `yield` statement.

The `yield` statement `return new WaitForSeconds();` creates a concurrent task that then pauses the `DelayStatement` code block at the `yield`. Once the `yield` is done, it releases the function's operation and allows it to move to the next statement. It's also worth looking at starting multiple Concurrent coroutines.

```
using UnityEngine;
using System.Collections;
public class Concurrent : MonoBehaviour {
    public bool StartCoroutines;
    void Update ()
    {
        if(StartCoroutines)
        {
            for(int i = 0; i < 3; i++)
            {
                StartCoroutine_Auto(DelayStatement(i));
            }
            StartCoroutines = false;
        }
    }
    IEnumerator DelayStatement(int i)
    {
        Debug.Log(i + ") Started at: " + Time.fixedTime);
        yield return new WaitForSeconds(3.0f);
        Debug.Log(i + ") Ended at: " + Time.fixedTime);
    }
}
```

With the above code, we have the following output. Note that we're changing the `Debug.Log()` to include an index to identify each of the `DelayStatement()` functions as they are executed.

```
0) Started at: 0.9
UnityEngine.Debug:Log(Object)
<DelayStatement>c__Iterator0:MoveNext() (at Assets/Concurrent.cs:23)
UnityEngine.MonoBehaviour:StartCoroutine_Auto(IEnumerator)
Concurrent:Update () (at Assets/Concurrent.cs:14)
1) Started at: 0.9
UnityEngine.Debug:Log(Object)
<DelayStatement>c__Iterator0:MoveNext() (at Assets/Concurrent.cs:23)
UnityEngine.MonoBehaviour:StartCoroutine_Auto(IEnumerator)
Concurrent:Update () (at Assets/Concurrent.cs:14)
2) Started at: 0.9
UnityEngine.Debug:Log(Object)
<DelayStatement>c__Iterator0:MoveNext() (at Assets/Concurrent.cs:23)
UnityEngine.MonoBehaviour:StartCoroutine_Auto(IEnumerator)
Concurrent:Update () (at Assets/Concurrent.cs:14)
0) Ended at: 3.92
```

```
UnityEngine.Debug:Log(Object)
<DelayStatement>c__Iterator0:MoveNext() (at Assets/Concurrent.cs:27)
1) Ended at: 3.92
UnityEngine.Debug:Log(Object)
<DelayStatement>c__Iterator0:MoveNext() (at Assets/Concurrent.cs:27)
2) Ended at: 3.92
UnityEngine.Debug:Log(Object)
<DelayStatement>c__Iterator0:MoveNext() (at Assets/Concurrent.cs:27)
```

The three concurrent tasks 0, 1, and 2 started in order. After their `WaitForSeconds()`, they finish in the same order. `Concurrent` coroutines are useful for a good number of tasks. In combination with events, a concurrent task can add a great amount of behavioral variety to a group of characters.

## 7.18.2 Setting Up Timers

Setting up a timer is a pretty common task in programming. For instance, we could use the following code to perform a specific task every 3 seconds.

```
public float NextTime;
public float WaitTime = 3;
void Update ()
{
    if(Time.fixedTime > NextTime )
    {
        Debug.Log("Do some timed task");
        NextTime = Time.fixedTime + WaitTime;
    }
}
```

`Time.fixedTime` is the number of seconds since the game started. Once the time is greater than our `NextTime`, we execute a function, or in this case a `Debug.Log()`, and then we set `NextTime` to the `Time.fixedTime + WaitTime`. In this case, we get "`Do some timed task`" printed to the Console every 3 seconds.

Timers like these by themselves are not great CPU hogs, but they do build up quickly if there are many thousand instances running a comparison between `Time.fixedTime` and `NextTime`. This really only becomes noticeable when you're on a mobile device. With a coroutine, we get the same behavior but without needing to check a timer on every frame.

With the following code, you can have a repeating timer that uses a coroutine instead:

```
public bool KeepRepeating = true;
public float RepeatTime = 2.0f;
void Start ()
{
    StartCoroutine(RepeatTimer(RepeatTime));
}
IEnumerator RepeatTimer(float t)
{
    while (KeepRepeating)
    {
        Debug.Log("Starting timer");
        yield return new WaitForSeconds(t);
        Debug.Log("Restarting Timer");
    }
}
```

This uses a `while` loop in `IEnumerator RepeatTimer()`. The `WaitForSeconds()` uses an incoming parameter `RepeatTime` to give us some flexibility to decide how long to wait till the `RepeatTimer()` restarts. When this while loop is restarted, the first statement `Debug.Log("Starting timer");` is executed immediately.

Any code found before the `yield return new WaitForSeconds();` statement will be executed normally. This means that you can set up new `GameObjects`, add components, and build any number of systems before the `yield`. Once the `WaitForSeconds()` statement is finished, all the following lines are then executed normally. Therefore, anything that needs to happen before the timer is reset should happen here.

To stop the `RepeatTimer()`, just set the `KeepRepeating` bool to `false`, and the function will not be restarted. To restart the coroutine, we would need to have a `StartCoroutine` located in the `Update ()` loop. This will expand our code to something like the following:

```
public bool KeepRepeating = true;
public bool RestartCoroutine = false;
public float RepeatTime = 2.0f;
void Start ()
{
    StartCoroutine(RepeatTimer(RepeatTime));
}
IEnumerator RepeatTimer(float t)
{
    while (KeepRepeating)
    {
        Debug.Log("Starting timer");
        yield return new WaitForSeconds(t);
        Debug.Log("Restarting Timer");
    }
}
void Update ()
{
    if(RestartCoroutine)
    {
        KeepRepeating = true;
        StartCoroutine(RepeatTimer(RepeatTime));
        RestartCoroutine = false;
    }
}
```

This in essence is still taking up time in the `Update ()` function, so it would be better to use an event to tell the coroutine to begin. Each frame we need to check if `RestartCoroutine` is true. Again, if many hundreds of objects are doing this check, we're wasting valuable CPU time essentially not doing something.

There are still more things we can do with the `yield` keyword. In essence, adding additional `yield` statements means that we can have the loop start, do one thing, wait for a moment, do a second thing, and wait again.

```
IEnumerator RepeatTimer(float t)
{
    while (KeepRepeating)
    {
        Debug.Log("do first thing");
        yield return new WaitForSeconds(t);
        Debug.Log("do second thing");
        yield return new WaitForSeconds(t);
        Debug.Log("do third thing");
        yield return new WaitForSeconds(t);
        Debug.Log("start over...");
    }
}
```

With this in mind, we're able to take on a number of actions within the RepeatTimer() spaced out by time. With the above code, we can "do first thing," wait for some seconds, and then "do second thing." This is followed by a third thing, another pause, and then we start over and immediately "do first thing" again. This helps a great deal when building interesting behaviors in a game.

A character can stop, look around, actually build a list of objects, and then perform an action, wait, check results, and continue on to look around again. We can add more interesting possibilities if we add in some logic.

```
IEnumerator RepeatTimer(float t)
{
    while (KeepRepeating)
    {
        int random = Random.Range(0, 3);
        Debug.Log("pick a an option: " + random );
        yield return new WaitForSeconds(t);
        switch(random)
        {
            case 0:
                Debug.Log("doing first option");
                yield return new WaitForSeconds(t);
            break;
            case 1:
                Debug.Log("doing second option");
                yield return new WaitForSeconds(t);
            break;
            case 2:
                Debug.Log("doing third option");
                yield return new WaitForSeconds(t);
            break;
            default:
                Debug.Log("doing some other option");
                yield return new WaitForSeconds(t);
            break;
        }
    }
}
```

Switch statements lend themselves well to the particular task of picking from a list of things to do. In the first couple of lines, we pick a random number: 0, 1, or 2. Based on this random number, we skip to one of three different positions in the switch statement. At case 0, we have our first option followed by a yield and wait. The respective cases follow the same pattern.

This can be more interesting should we add in something to do other than just simple options.

### 7.18.3 Random Decisions with Logic

Here's a fun example of a system to keep several tasks in order, but also allow for random decisions. We start with a switch statement, where we decide what to do after waking up.

```
IEnumerator DayInTheLife(float t)
{
    while (KeepRepeating)
    {
        int rand = Random.Range(0, 3);
        Debug.Log("I woke up, then...");
        yield return new WaitForSeconds(t);
        switch(rand)
```

```
        {
    case 0:
        Debug.Log("drank some coffee with...");
        yield return new WaitForSeconds(t);
        goto hadCoffee;
        break;
    case 1:
        Debug.Log("ate toast with...");
        yield return new WaitForSeconds(t);
        goto hadToast;
        break;
    case 2:
        Debug.Log("ate brains with...");
        yield return new WaitForSeconds(t);
        goto hadBrains;
        break;
        }
hadCoffee:
    rand = Random.Range(0, 3);
    switch(rand)
    {
    case 0:
        Debug.Log("cream...");
        yield return new WaitForSeconds(t);
        break;
    case 1:
        Debug.Log("cream and sugar...");
        yield return new WaitForSeconds(t);
        break;
    case 2:
        Debug.Log("nothing in it...");
        yield return new WaitForSeconds(t);
        break;
    }
    Debug.Log("then i went to...");
    yield return new WaitForSeconds(t);
    goto goWork;
hadToast:
    rand = Random.Range(0, 3);
    switch(rand)
    {
    case 0:
        Debug.Log("butter and jam...");
        yield return new WaitForSeconds(t);
        break;
    case 1:
        Debug.Log("butter...");
        yield return new WaitForSeconds(t);
        break;
    case 2:
        Debug.Log("nothing on it...");
        yield return new WaitForSeconds(t);
        break;
    }
    Debug.Log("then i went to...");
    yield return new WaitForSeconds(t);
    goto goWork;
hadBrains:
    rand = Random.Range(0, 3);
```

```
        switch(rand)
        {
        case 0:
            Debug.Log("with ear and nose...");
            yield return new WaitForSeconds(t);
            break;
        case 1:
            Debug.Log("just an ear...");
            yield return new WaitForSeconds(t);
            break;
        case 2:
            Debug.Log("strawberries and bananas...");
            yield return new WaitForSeconds(t);
            break;
        }
        Debug.Log("then i went to...");
        yield return new WaitForSeconds(t);
        goto goWork;
    goWork:
        rand = Random.Range(0, 3);
        switch(rand)
        {
        case 0:
            Debug.Log("the office...");
            yield return new WaitForSeconds(t);
            break;
        case 1:
            Debug.Log("the gym...");
            yield return new WaitForSeconds(t);
            break;
        case 2:
            Debug.Log("the graveyard...");
            yield return new WaitForSeconds(t);
            break;
        }
        Debug.Log ("and after went home to sleep...");
        yield return new WaitForSeconds(t);
    }
}
```

After the initial decision, we are sent to one of three labels with goto. After the branch, all three results return to the same conclusion. The above system allows for many different behaviors in a solitary function. The first statement decides what we do when we wake up.

Do we drink coffee, eat toast, or eat brains? One of these things means that we're talking to a zombie. After coffee, we go to the coffee list of items, where we can pick one of three sets of things to put into the coffee; there's also an option for toast and brains. After consuming breakfast, we then go to the office, gym, or graveyard. At the end of the day, the subject goes home to sleep and repeats the cycle.

Using yield, we're able to make the decisions readable in the Console panel, and we get a fun little story out of it. I'll let you try this code out on your own. Of course, the random values can be set outside of the function allowing the game logic to handle the decision making rather than leaving the choice to a random number. As an example, you can set up the decisions to be more rash or drastic based on the condition of the character, each choice escalating as the character gets more desperate.

### 7.18.4 Stopping a Coroutine

To terminate any coroutines that endlessly loop, it's necessary to use the StopAllCoroutines(); function.

```
public bool StopTheRoutine;
void Update ()
{
     if(StopTheRoutine)
     {
          StopAllCoroutines();
          StopTheRoutine = false;
     }
}
```

A simple toggle will work to kill the `DayInTheLife()` coroutine in midday. To start and stop a specific coroutine, we need to use the following syntax:

```
void Start ()
{
     StartCoroutine("DayInTheLife", 2);
}
```

This will start a coroutine by a string to identify the function. The second parameter is the value given to the coroutine if it accepts any arguments.

```
public bool StopTheRoutine;
void Update ()
{
     if(StopTheRoutine)
     {
          StopCoroutine("DayInTheLife");
          StopTheRoutine = false;
     }
}
```

We can use `bool StopTheRoutine` to turn the coroutine off with `StopCoroutine` (`"DayInTheLife"`); using a string to identify the same function. The only way to specify which coroutine we are stopping is to start it by string.

### 7.18.5 What We've Learned

Coroutines are useful in games to manage various aspects of timing. Complex behaviors often involve movement, logic, and awareness. Creatures in general do not continuously move without pause. It's possible to use regular `Update ()` - style timers, but this gets cumbersome.

With coroutines, we're more free to make interesting combinations of behaviors with interesting decisions. The `DayInTheLife` coroutine we looked at earlier could easily execute various flanking and strategic behaviors. A coroutine can also call other functions, so it doesn't have to contain all of the logic in one block.

It's also possible for an `IEnumerator` to start its own coroutine. This can create overlapping behaviors, each one with its own timing. Combined with event handlers, you could trigger functions when a coroutine is started and when it is complete. If the event is raised before or after the `yield`, you can trigger an event when the coroutine begins or ends.

## 7.19 Dictionary, Stacks, and Queues

A dictionary type is an interesting version of an array. One basic use is setting up a list of items, say, zombies, vampires, and werewolves. Then we can give each one a value: 10 zombies, 13 vampires, and 7 werewolves. If we want to know the number of zombies, we can ask the dictionary what `"Zombies?"` and we'll get the value stored at `"Zombies"` as `10`.

The system works in a fairly similar way to an `ArrayList`, only we'll want to assign some specific types. The `Dictionary` data type is found under `System.Collections.Generic;`. We'll start a new Dictionary project. We'll assign a simple `Dictionaries.cs` component to the Main Camera in the scene.

### 7.19.1 A Basic Example

This example starts with the Dictionaries project. Open the scene and we'll have a Main Camera with a `Dictionaries` component attached.

```
using UnityEngine;
using System.Collections;
//new directive for dictionaries
using System.Collections.Generic;
public class Dictionaries : MonoBehaviour
{
    //declare a new dictionary called MyDictionary
    Dictionary<string,int> MyDictionary;
//Use this for initialization
    void Start ()
    {
        MyDictionary = new Dictionary<string,int>();
        MyDictionary.Add("Zombies",10);
        //prints 10;
        Debug.Log (MyDictionary["Zombies"]);
    }
}
```

We need to add a new directive named `Systems.Collections.Generic` that has the `Dictionary` data type in it. We can use it any number of ways, but one of the most common is the `Dictionary<string,int>` combination. This allows us to use a string to find a value in the dictionary.

The structure of the declaration of a `Dictionary` is < first type, second type >, where the first type you use is called a `key` and the second type is the `value` that is associated with that key. The `key`, or the first value, must all be unique throughout the dictionary.

```
        MyDictionary = new Dictionary<string,int>();
        MyDictionary.Add("Zombies",10);
        MyDictionary.Add("Zombies", 7);
```

If we try to use the above code, we'll get the following error:

```
ArgumentException: An element with the same key already exists in the
dictionary.
```

When a dictionary is used, the `key` is the value that is used to find the association to the second type. Therefore, in the above code, if you asked for "`Zombies`" the dictionary would not be able to tell you `10` or `7`.

To add dictionary entries to the dictionary, we use the `MyDictionary.Add("Zombies",10);` to push strings with associated values into the variable. To retrieve them, we use what looks like addressing an array.

```
        MyDictionary = new Dictionary<string,int>();
        MyDictionary.Add("Zombies",10);
        Debug.Log (MyDictionary ["Zombies"]);
```

`MyDictionary ["Zombies"]` acts as though it were the value assigned when using the `.Add()` statement. We can use different types in the dictionary as well.

```
Dictionary<int, Object> obs = new Dictionary<int, Object>();
Object[] allObjects = GameObject.FindObjectsOfType(typeof(Object)) as
Object[];
for(int i = 0; i < allObjects.Length; i++) {
```

```
        obs.Add(i, allObjects[i]);
        Debug.Log(obs[i]);
}
```

The above code will print out every `Object` found in the scene. The specific line `obs[i]` is all it takes to extract an object found in the scene by using an `int`. To make this a bit more clear, we can use the following three statements:

```
Debug.Log(obs[1]);
Debug.Log(obs[2]);
Debug.Log(obs[3]);
```

This code produces the following three messages in the Console panel:

```
Main Camera (UnityEngine.AudioListener)
UnityEngine.Debug:Log(Object)
MyDictionary:Start () (at Assets/MyDictionary.cs:19)
Main Camera (UnityEngine.FlareLayer)
UnityEngine.Debug:Log(Object)
MyDictionary:Start () (at Assets/MyDictionary.cs:20)
Main Camera (UnityEngine.GUILayer)
UnityEngine.Debug:Log(Object)
MyDictionary:Start () (at Assets/MyDictionary.cs:21)
```

Therefore, `obs[1]` is the Main Camera's `AudioListener,` which itself isn't so important as how we are currently referencing it. The dictionary `obs` is now an array, to which we use an `int`. At each entry in the dictionary, we have an associated object.

Dictionaries use generics to help make any combination of types to map from one type to another, not just referencing objects by a number. These can be used for any number of data systems. Usually, when addressing a large number of similar associations, we can use dictionaries to a great degree.

Scoreboards can be kept in a simple dictionary. `Dictionary<string,int>` can be used to associate player name with score. However, the advantage here is the number of built-in fail-safes that the `Dictionary` class comes with.

With this sort of data structure, we're allowed to ask how many zombies there are in the scene, with `int numZombies = MyDictionary["zombies"];`. Using a dictionary in this way adds a simple interface for storing an arbitrary number of values and things in the scene.

## 7.19.2 ContainsKey

To put this `Dictionary` to some use, we'll add in some code to give us the names of the objects in a scene.

```
//lists GameObject names in the scene
Dictionary<string, int> SceneDictionary = new Dictionary<string, int>();
//get all of the objects in the scene
GameObject[] gos = GameObject.FindObjectsOfType(typeof(GameObject)) as
GameObject[];
//iterate through them and add them to the dictionary
foreach(GameObject go in gos)
{
    //check if we've already found an object with the GameObject's name
    bool containsKey = SceneDictionary.ContainsKey(go.name);
    if(containsKey)
    {
        SceneDictionary[go.name] + = 1;
    }
    else
    {
```

```
                    SceneDictionary.Add(go.name, 1);
        }
}
```

This code added to the `Start ()` function will do two things. We create a new dictionary called `SceneDictionary` using a `string` to associate with an `int`. Then we get an array of all of the `GameObjects` in the scene called `gos`.

A `foreach` loop is used to iterate through each object in the `gos` `GameObject` array. To check if we've come across an object with the same name, we use a `bool` called `containsKey` and use the function `ContainsKey();` to check the dictionary. If the `ContainsKey()` returns `true`, then the dictionary already has a key with the value passed to the `ContainsKey()` function.

The argument passed to `ContainsKey()` must match the type used to initialize the dictionary. We used a string for the dictionary key, so we can use `go.name` as the string. The logic following this means that if the dictionary already has a key, then we need to increment the value in the dictionary of that key `+ = 1`. If the value is new and `ContainsKey()` returns false, then we add a new entry to the dictionary.

In the code below the `if-else` statement which uses `ContainsKey` uses the `SceneDictionary`. `Add(go.name, 1);` to both add a new key to the dictionary and increment the value for that key to 1. As we iterate through all of the objects, we populate the dictionary with both the names of all of the objects in the scene and the number of objects.

To expose these values to the editor, we'll add in a couple of regular arrays.

```
using UnityEngine;
using System.Collections;
using System.Collections.Generic;
public class Dictionaries : MonoBehaviour
{
    public Dictionary<string,int> MyDictionary;
    public string[] objectNames;
    public int[] objectCounts;
    //Use this for initialization
    void Start ()
    {
        //lists GameObject names in the scene
        Dictionary<string, int> SceneDictionary = new Dictionary<string,
int>();
        GameObject[] gos =
GameObject.FindObjectsOfType(typeof(GameObject)) as GameObject[];
        foreach(GameObject go in gos)
        {
            bool containsKey = SceneDictionary.ContainsKey(go.name);
            if(containsKey)
            {
                SceneDictionary[go.name] + = 1;
            }
            else
            {
                SceneDictionary.Add(go.name, 1);
            }
        }
        objectNames = new string[SceneDictionary.Keys.Count];
        objectCounts = new int[SceneDictionary.Values.Count];
        SceneDictionary.Keys.CopyTo(objectNames, 0);
        SceneDictionary.Values.CopyTo(objectCounts, 0);
    }
}
```

At the end of the `Start ()` function, we initialize the `string[]` array and the `int[]` array to the size of the dictionary. Then we use the function `SceneDictionary.Keys.CopyTo()` and assign all of the values of the keys to the `objectNames[]` array and the same for the `objectCounts`.

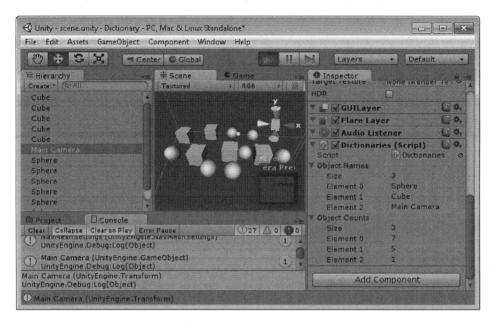

The scene reveals to the dictionary that we have three entries for names and numbers. The count for both the names and the numbers is 3. The first element is the `Sphere` that has a corresponding count of 7. There are five Cube objects and one Main Camera. Thanks to the Dictionary, we don't need to have two different arrays. This, of course, can be seen in the Inspector panel, but by no means is this easier to work with in terms of data and readability.

```
bool containsKey = SceneDictionary.ContainsKey(go.name);
if(containsKey)
{
        SceneDictionary[go.name] + = 1;
}
else
{
        SceneDictionary.Add(go.name, 1);
}
```

The clarity that this `if-else` statement offers allows you to very easily check and use a dictionary against what's already in the dictionary. The simplicity of using this dictionary is quite easy to remember.

Taking out a key and a value is just as easy. If we don't want the Main Camera in the list, we can just use the following statement:

```
SceneDictionary.Remove("Main Camera");
```

Do this just before copying the Dictionary to the `string` and `int` array, and the arrays will not have a Main Camera in them.

### 7.19.3 Stacks

A `stack` is basically an array with some added features. You get a `Push()`, a `Pop()`, and a `Peek()` function when you use a `stack`. The names of the functions might not mean a lot, but they can act as a clue as to what they do.

A stack is basically an array which you can mentally imagine as an actual stack of books. The top of the stack is where all of the functions perform their operations. Pushing an object onto the stack loads another book on the top of the stack. Peeking at it means to look at the contents of the book on the top of the stack. Popping the stack means to take the top item on the stack off, not that popping a book makes all that much sense.

### 7.19.3.1 A Basic Example

We will continue to use the project in Section 7.19.2, which had a few features we'll want to continue to use in the scene. This class was attached to the Main Camera.

```
public GameObject[] ObjectStack;
//Use this for initialization
void Start ()
{
        GameObject[] gos = GameObject.FindObjectsOfType(
        typeof(GameObject)) as GameObject[];
        //create a new stack
        Stack objectStack = new Stack();
        //assign objects to the stack using push
        foreach(GameObject go in gos)
        {
                objectStack.Push(go);
        }
        //initialize the class scope ObjectStack
        //to view in the inspector panel
        ObjectStack = new GameObject[objectStack.Count];
        //copy the stack to the array in Unity
        objectStack.CopyTo(ObjectStack, 0);
}
```

A stack used here makes a little less sense; however, the Push() function does make it very simple to read. The main benefit behind using a Stack is clarity and ease of use. This stack makes it clear what is happening and where the data is going.

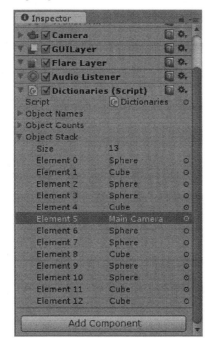

The result of the `stack` might not make much sense. The order in which the `FindObjectsOfType()` function don't necessarily guarantee any particular order. However, it's interesting to know that the item at the bottom of the `stack` was the first object found and the item at the top was the last object found.

To make better utilization of the `stack`, we can use a Trigger. To test this out we'll add to the scene a Capsule Collider and attach a Rigidbody component.

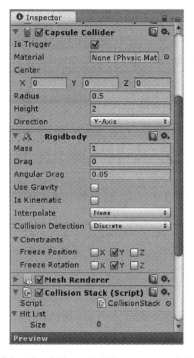

The settings on the Capsule Collider should have Is Trigger on, and then we need to have a Rigidbody where we've turned off Use Gravity and turned on a constraint on they position and rotation. This will keep our object easier to handle in the scene.

In a `Start ()` function, we'll initialize a new `stack` for use when the capsule touches another object in the scene. We will use the array for display in the Inspector panel in the editor. This will make the operation of the `stack` easier to see.

```
using UnityEngine;
using System.Collections;
public class CollisionStack : MonoBehaviour {
    //store the stack and array
    public GameObject[] HitList;
    public Stack HitStack;
    void Start ()
    {
        HitStack = new Stack();
    }
    void OnTriggerEnter(Collider other)
    {
        if(!HitStack.Contains(other.gameObject))
        {
            HitStack.Push(other.gameObject);
            HitList = new GameObject[HitStack.Count];
            HitStack.CopyTo(HitList, 0);
        }
    }
}
```

The code we'll want to look at is contained in the OnTriggerEnter() function. The if statement accomplishes two things. We can use the incoming parameter other and use the gameObject that collider is attached to. The Stack has a member function called Contains() where we can use other.gameObject to check through the entire stack if the object has already been added. If not, then we'll use Push() to add the gameObject component of other to the stack.

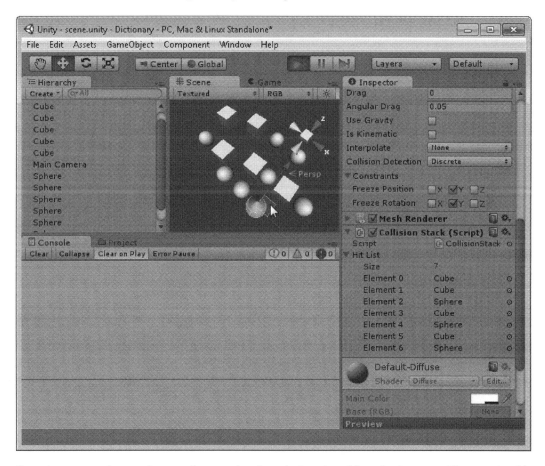

Start the game and move the capsule around and touch the other objects in the scene. The stack adds the touched object to the top of the HitList. Each time OnTriggerEnter is called, the HitList is reinitialized to match the size of the stack. Then the stack copies its contents to the HitList for viewing in the Inspector panel.

Of course, this isn't the only use. In something like a tower defense game, you can prioritize objects by their order in a stack. As new objects arrive and are added to a stack, you can have an artificial intelligence focus on the object at the top of the stack.

```
void Update () {
    if(HitStack.Count > 0)
    {
        GameObject lastObject = HitStack.Peek() as GameObject;
        Debug.DrawLine(transform.position,
        lastObject.transform.position);
    }
}
```

If we add a simple check in the Update () function, we can use it to draw a line from the capsule to the object that was added last to the stack. To get the object out of the stack, we need to use a cast.

The stack is a generic container. Everything in it is stored as object. This doesn't mean that any data is lost; it's just generically stored.

The Peek() function is used on the stack to observe the last object added to the stack. The statement GameObject lastObject = HitStack.Peek() as GameObject; assigns the data to the lastObject from the result of HitStack.Peek();. After this assignment, we can use the lastObject.transform.position as the other end of a line between the transform.position and the object that the code is attached to.

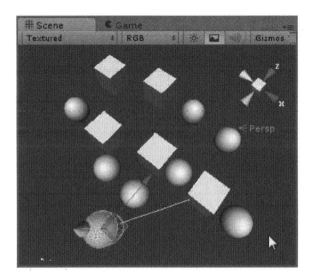

To remove an object from the stack, we use the Pop() function. Therefore, when a condition is met, for instance a timer ends, we can reduce the stack by one object. In the CollisionStack class we've been working in, we'll add a new IEnumerator popTheStack() function.

```
void Update () {
    if(HitStack.Count > 0)
        {
            GameObject lastObject = HitStack.Peek() as GameObject;
            Debug.DrawLine(transform.position,
            lastObject.transform.position);
            if(HitList[0] == lastObject)
            {
                StartCoroutine("popTheStack");
            }
        }
}
IEnumerator popTheStack()
{
    yield return new WaitForSeconds(2);
    if(HitStack.Count > 0)
    {
        HitStack.Pop();
        HitList = new GameObject[HitStack.Count];
        HitStack.CopyTo(HitList, 0);
        StopCoroutine("popTheStack");
    }
}
```

The popTheStack() will be started as a coroutine. Every 2 seconds, we'll pop the stack and draw a line to the next object at the top of the stack. To start the coroutine, we'll check if the top of the

`HitList` is the same as that of the `HitStack`. Once the `stack` has been popped, we'll rebuild the `HitList` array with the new version of the `HitStack`. After moving the capsule around in the scene, we'll collect some targets to draw a line to. Every 2 seconds, we'll move down the list and reduce the number of items in the `stack`.

### 7.19.4 Queues

The queue works in a similar fashion to the `stack`, but with a few handy modifications. The difference between a queue and a `stack` is the order in which new objects are added. When we add a new object to a `stack`, we add it to the top of the list. With a queue we're making a waiting list where the first object added to the queue will also be the first removed out of the list.

After a class scope variable is created with `Queue HitQueue;`, we add the statement `HitQueue = new Queue();` in the `Start ()` function of the class. This provides us with a class-wide `HitQueue` to work with. Then we can add the following code to the `OnTriggerEnter()` function:

```
if(!HitQueue.Contains(other.gameObject))
{
    HitQueue.Enqueue(other.gameObject);
    QueueList = new GameObject[HitQueue.Count];
    HitQueue.CopyTo(QueueList, 0);
}
```

This does the same thing as the `HitStack`. When the capsule touches another object, it's added to the queue, and then copied to a list so we can see the objects in the queue in the Inspector panel. In our `Update ()` function, we'll add more code, which looks like the following code used for the `stack`.

```
if(HitQueue.Count > 0)
{
    GameObject firstObject = HitQueue.Peek() as GameObject;
    Debug.DrawLine(transform.position,
    firstObject.transform.position, Color.red);
    if(QueueList[0] == firstObject)
    {
        StartCoroutine("dequeueTheQueue");
    }
}
```

This code does the same task as the `stack`. We'll draw a debug line to the first object in the queue and then start a coroutine to dequeue the `HitQueue`. Then, of course, we need to add code in for a dequeue-ing function.

```
IEnumerator dequeueTheQueue()
{
    yield return new WaitForSeconds(2);
    if(HitQueue.Count > 0)
    {
        HitQueue.Dequeue();
        QueueList = new GameObject[HitQueue.Count];
        HitQueue.CopyTo(QueueList, 0);
        StopCoroutine("dequeueTheQueue");
    }
}
```

This looks the same as the `stack pop()` function, only we're using `Dequeue()` to cut our queue back down every 2 seconds. Now when we move the capsule through the scene, we'll see a line being drawn to the first and the last object touched by the capsule.

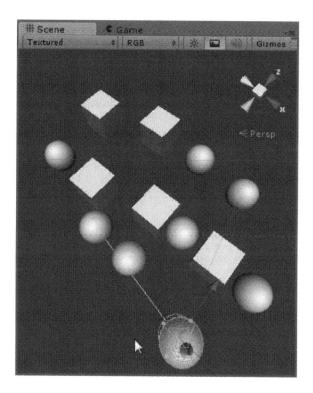

If this were something like a weapon turret, we could be aiming missiles or machine guns at some slow-moving zombies. The system that adds to the queue or `stack` can be anything, so too are the `pop()` and `Dequeue()` functions. They can be called as necessary like an event where the object at the top of the `stack` or the bottom of the queue has been destroyed.

### 7.19.5 What We've Learned

Organizing and referencing data is an important part of programming. Therefore, much of programming is collecting, organizing, and reorganizing data; there are already many mechanisms in place for use in your own code.

Learning every system in C# isn't our goal. What is important is remembering that there is a system that might be useful for many different situations. As you begin to remember them, you can look them up later to see how they're used.

The most important part of learning any language is the fact that there are words such as queue, `stack`, and dictionary, which all manage data differently. When you come across something that looks like a list of things that need to be handled, then you should look up what system might best suit your needs at the time.

It's impossible to learn everything at once. It's difficult to remember even half of the features that any programming language has. What's not difficult is looking things up on the Internet and remembering how they're used by reading some examples.

The best thing to do is observing how these constructs have been used here. When you're working on your own and come across something that seems familiar, it's a good idea to go looking around and try to remember what you learned here as a refresher. Then apply the discovery to your current task.

## 7.20 Callbacks

To overly simplify, a callback is a function that is executed when some other function is done with its work. A callback is often used when we need to begin work and want to know when it's done. This can be used when we start spawning monsters in a level and want to know when all of the monsters have finished populating a level. Likewise, in a complex game, we might spend some time opening several scenes and want to know when it's safe to allow the player to jump into the level and begin a game.

When one task begins, it's sometimes difficult to know when the task has finished. In a single function, it's easy to assume that you know a statement has completed when the following statement begins. When a statement triggers, an entire separate series of independent functions is executed; the following statement can execute before the independent functions finish. This happens most often with concurrent tasks.

A reference between objects can't be made unless both are present in a scene at the same time. This becomes a problem when we have objects in one scene that rely on objects in another scene that is yet to be loaded. To get around this order of loading, it would be useful to have an event, like events we just used, to fire off when a scene has finished loading.

Managing when and how a function is called is a simple matter of setting up a delegate to call when a task is done. Once the task is complete, the delegate is called and any assigned functions are then executed. The concept is to launch a task-specific function and make that function aware that there's some other function that has to be called when the task is done.

### 7.20.1 A Basic Example

In the Callbacks project, we have a `SimpleCallback.cs` attached to a Sphere. The following code has just a few functions to get us started with.

```
using UnityEngine;
using System.Collections;
public class SimpleCallback : MonoBehaviour {
    delegate void delegateCaller();
    delegateCaller caller = FunctionToCall;
    static void FunctionToCall()
    {
        Debug.Log("You called?");
    }
    void Start () {
        StartCoroutine(StartsATask());
    }
    IEnumerator StartsATask()
    {
        Debug.Log("starting");
        yield return new WaitForSeconds(1);
        Debug.Log("finishing");
        caller();
    }
}
```

This begins with a `delegate void delegateCaller();` that allows us to create a place to assign functions. The assignment here happens on the following line where we use the identifier of the new delegate `delegateCaller` and create a variable `caller`. The `caller` variable is then assigned `FunctionTocall;`, which simply sends "You called?" to the Console panel.

To test this out, we use a function `StartsATask()` that begins with "starting." The first `Debug.Log()` function is followed by a `yield return new WaitForSeconds(1);`, which tells Unity to hold off on executing the next line for a second. This is followed by "finishing" and then calling the assigned `delegateCaller caller()`.

The `StartsATask()` called `FunctionToCall()` when it was done. The callback in this case is `FunctionToCall()`, that waited a second for the `yield` to execute. As far as simple examples go, this is nicely self-contained. There are a couple of caveats here: `FunctionToCall()` is `static`. That is to say that the callback for this class is a static function and will be shared across all instances of the class.

The reason for this is the connection between the argument passed to `StartsATask()` and where the delegate function came from. The `StartsATask()` function can't see what the function belongs to, only that `delegateCaller` has an assignment. Just because there's something assigned to that argument doesn't mean that the instance that did the assignment is known.

To modify this behavior, we'd need to make the task with a callback less specific, but this has some more awkward drawbacks. We're in the `SimpleCallback` class. We can add a function called `PersonalCall()` to this class and be specific when calling it after a task.

```
void Start ()
{
    StartCoroutine(StartsPerClassTask(this));
}
public void PersonalCall()
{
    Debug.Log ("this is function");
}
IEnumerator StartsPerClassTask(SimpleCallback callThis)
{
    Debug.Log("starting");
    yield return new WaitForSeconds(1);
    Debug.Log("finishing");
    //this is quite specific
    callThis.PersonalCall();
}
```

In the above code, a class can be assigned to the function, by using the `this` keyword. Unfortunately, we need to call a specific function in the class when the task is done. This does accomplish calling a function after a task is complete, but it's inelegant and not reusable. What makes a callback useful is our being able to assign different functions to get the callback from the function. A more generic approach is required to make this more flexible.

## 7.20.2 Dynamic Callback Assignment

To gain some flexibility, we're going to want to be able to switch what function is called back. This means that different coroutines can be launched with different calls being made when they complete, which also means some differences in how the task-related function is created.

```
public class SimpleCallback : MonoBehaviour
{
    delegate void delegateCaller();
    public void PersonalCall()
    {
        Debug.Log ("wasssap?");
    }
    public void BusinessCall()
    {
        Debug.Log ("Thank you for calling.");
    }
    void Start ()
    {
        StartCoroutine(StartsATask(PersonalCall));
        StartCoroutine(StartsATask(BusinessCall));
    }
    IEnumerator StartsATask(delegateCaller callThis)
    {
        Debug.Log("starting");
```

```
        yield return new WaitForSeconds(1);
        Debug.Log("finishing");
        callThis();
    }
}
```

To revisit the `StartsATask()` function, we remove the assignment of the `delegateCaller()` and leave that up to the `StartsATask()` function for assignment. The main change here makes this far more flexible. By giving the `StartsATask()` function another function as an argument, we gain flexibility and reusability. To think about this a bit more, we can pass along variables to the coroutine to have an effect on the functions we pass to it as callbacks.

```
    void Start ()
    {
        StartCoroutine(StartEndTask(StartingMessage,3,EndingMessage));
    }
    void StartingMessage()
    {
        Debug.Log("im starting");
    }
    void EndingMessage()
    {
        Debug.Log("im done");
    }
    IEnumerator StartEndTask(delegateCaller startFunc,
    float delay,
    delegateCaller endFunc)
    {
        startFunc();
        yield return new WaitForSeconds(delay);
        endFunc();
    }
```

In the above code, we pass along two different functions and a `float`. This `float` value delays the execution of the start and end functions assigned to the coroutine. Of course, this can be expanded to provide any number of callbacks, but this can become somewhat cumbersome.

### 7.20.3 WWW

Now that we've got the basics of how a callback is structured, we might want to put this to some use. Callbacks, as we have seen, are functions passed along to other functions. A function which uses a function as a callback receives a value from that function once the callback is complete.

The `WWW` class in Unity 3D provides a multitude of functions that allow us to obtain various assets from the Web. We'll want to set up a new `WWW` delegate. The signature for this will be `(WWW www)`, where the uppercase and lowercase Ws are used throughout Unity's examples, so we may also follow along.

```
public delegate void delegateWWW(WWW www);
void Start ()
{
    StartCoroutine(getWWW("http://unity3d.com/robots.txt", readText));
}
public void readText(WWW www)
{
    Debug.Log(www.text);
}
IEnumerator getWWW(string url, delegateWWW funcWWW)
```

```
{
     WWW www = new WWW(url);
     yield return www;
     funcWWW(www);
}
```

Assign the `string` as `url` to the `getWWW` `IEnumerator` function as a callback. With this combo, we can use our `readText()` function to read the text being given to the callback. The `http://unity3d.com/robots.txt` points to a text file found on most websites. This tells search engines what it's allowed to look at when browsing on a website.

Another more useful function would be something that gets that www to find a texture and assign it to the model it's on.

```
public void readTexture(WWW www)
{
     Texture2D texture = www.texture;
     gameObject.renderer.material.SetTexture("_MainTex", texture);
}
```

Here's a simple function that does just that. The `Start ()` function gets a bit more awkward if we use that URL to download an image onto a sphere.

```
void Start ()
{
     StartCoroutine(
     getWWW("http://unity3d.com/robots.txt", readText));
     StartCoroutine(
getWWW("http://upload.wikimedia.org/wikipedia/commons/thumb/e/ea/
Clementine_albedo_simp750.jpg/800px-Clementine_albedo_simp750.jpg",
readTexture));
}
```

The URL is a bit long, but I've pointed it to a Wikipedia image. I'd suggest that you look for an image on the Internet on your own to assign to the `getWWW()` function. Using the same `getWWW`, we provide a different string as a `url` and a different function as a callback.

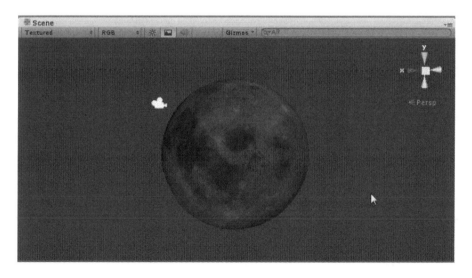

The above screenshot is the result of reading an image from the Internet and having it assigned to the `_MainTex` of the default shader that is added to a default sphere, which can be added to any scene.

Depending on how large the image is, you might have to wait longer till the image is done downloading before it'll show up on your object.

### 7.20.4 What We've Learned

Callbacks in C# allow for a wide range of flexibility. The main limitation is the signature of the delegate used to store the callback. A delegate with the signature of (WWW www) can only handle the WWW type going into its argument list. However, this is the strong typing that C# requires and will be enforced throughout the language.

Without this strong typing, what happens inside of a function might not match up with the callback that was assigned. Unexpected behaviors are harder to track down with very diverse types such as WWW.

The WWW type can return many different things such as sound and text or models for Unity 3D. If an unexpected type comes in, the cases for handling errors become all the more difficult to deal with, so be thankful for type enforcement.

Callbacks are often combined with concurrent tasks called from StartCoroutine(). This offers a simple system in which you're able to manage what do to when a coroutine is finished. The alternative is something running in an Update () loop waiting for a bool to flip.

```
void Update ()
{
        if(isDone)
        {
                //do something
                isDone = false;
        }
}
```

Here the isDone would be set to false when a coroutine is started. At the end of the coroutine, we could set isDone to true to execute the code in this block, and then set isDone to false to prevent the code from running again.

The mentioned pattern is common, and there's nothing wrong with it. The main problem with a coroutine in Unity 3D is the fact that it will never finish if the gameObject it's attached to is set inactive.

### 7.21 Lambda Expressions

Now that we're iterating through arrays, it's time to put those arrays to some work for you. Lambda expressions are relatively new to C#. The concept finds its origin in lambda calculus, an invention of the 1930s. The calculus form uses arrows with notation that looks a bit like the following:

```
(x) → x * x
```

Unity 3D took a while to upgrade from C# 2.0 to 3.5, and with that change came things such as lambda expressions. Lambda expressions were an upgrade from what is called an anonymous function. Anonymous functions were basically clips of code that could be stored as a variable. This sounds a bit like a delegate, and in some ways it is.

To clarify, we've made some uses of delegates with some basic uses in previous chapters. When we create a delegate, we need to do a bit of setup ahead of time to use them. We can use a delegate only if it's been created and a variable defined to hold onto the delegated tasks. Lambda expressions allow for creating and using a delegate in a single line.

The major difference is that an anonymous function can appear in the middle of your Start () or Update () function. Then be set to a variable, before being used. After the anonymous function is declared, its arguments are assigned in the same statement where it's used. Because anonymous expressions still work in C#, it's good to know how they work and why lambdas replaced them.

### 7.21.1 Anonymous Expressions

Anonymous expressions are basically short functions that can appear in the middle of a function. This seems a bit weird, but this will make more sense once we see what the code looks like.

#### *7.21.1.1 A Basic Example*

There are a few things to look for when we're creating an anonymous expression. The first is that it starts off like a regular delegate, where we create a delegate declaration with a signature. Where things get interesting is the fact that inside of the Start () function, we're adding the code to that delegate without having to write a separate function somewhere else.

```
using UnityEngine;
using System.Collections;
public class Lambdas : MonoBehaviour
{
        //declare a delegate like before
        delegate void AnonExpression(string s);
        //Use this for initialization
        void Start ()
        {
                //create and assign the delegate here
                AnonExpression delAnonExpression = delegate(string s)
                {
                        Debug.Log(s);
                };      //observe the ; after the}
                //delegates content has been assigned
                //after it's been assigned, we can use it.
                delAnonExpression("weird");
        }
}
```

In the above example, we're starting with the following line of code to declare the new anonymous expression. We've seen the delegate keyword before with the coroutine, so this is just another way to use the same keyword.

```
delegate void AnonExpression(string s);
```

This has a few important things which we have to remember. The delegate keyword is used followed by void AnonExpression(string s);. The void keyword means that this delegate returns a void when it's done, or rather, it really doesn't return anything.

The signature of AnonExpression is a single string parameter. Though this could have easily been nothing and the AnonExpression would have looked like void AnonExpression();, to make our example more interesting, we're adding in a string to observe the Anon in use.

Then things get interesting once we create an instance of this function.

```
AnonExpression delAnonExpression = delegate(string s){
    Debug.Log (s);
};
```

Once the Start () function is called, a new instance of a function of type AnonExpression is declared called delAnonExpression. Then the code for that delegated function is assigned using = delegate(string s) {};. This is a fairly clever feature of C#. This can be reduced a bit for clarity when we move on to lambda assignment as follows:

```
AnonExpression delAnonExpression = delegate(string s){Debug.Log(s);};
```

Of course, we're not limited to a short `Debug.Log` statement within the curly braces that fill in the `delAnon`expression. We can add much more complex code there in a bit. One important feature we must not forget is the final semicolon that finishes off the `delegate(){};` declaration. To further simplify without any parameters, we could use the following code:

```
using UnityEngine;
using System.Collections;
public class LambdaExpressions : MonoBehaviour
{
        delegate void MyDelegate();
        //Use this for initialization
        void Start ()
        {
                MyDelegate myDelegatedTask = delegate()
                {
                        Debug.Log("Hello from anon.");
                };
                myDelegatedTask();
        }
}
```

Before we get too far into using these anonymous functions, there's a reason for why these were replaced by a more modern version of the same system. Lambda expressions reduce the complexity further by allowing you to create an anonymous expression with even less setup.

Just for clarity, the above statement can be rewritten such that the `delegate()` looks like any other function.

```
using UnityEngine;
using System.Collections;
public class LambdaExpressions : MonoBehaviour
{
        delegate void MyDelegate();
        //Use this for initialization
        void Start ()
        {
                MyDelegate myDelegatedTask =
                        delegate()
                {
                        Debug.Log("Hello from anon.");
                };
                myDelegatedTask();
        }
}
```

### 7.21.2 Lambda Expressions

Lambda expressions are best recognized by the = > operator. This is sometimes called either the *becomes* or the *points to* operator. This wording is used because the left side becomes the expression to the right side of the = > operator. This works the same as the assignment operator =, only we're assigning a variable the result of an expression. The following code sample simply takes out some of the extra syntax used by the anonymous expression.

### 7.21.2.1 A Basic Example

To follow along with this section, take a look at the Lambdas project found in the downloaded Unity projects form GitHub. This code is found in the `LambdaExpressions.cs` file, which has been attached to the Main Camera in the scene.

```csharp
using UnityEngine;
using System.Collections;
public class LambdaExpressions : MonoBehaviour
{
        //create a delegate signature like before
        delegate void MyDelegate();
        //Use this for initialization
        void Start ()
        {
                //assign a new delegate and assign the expression at the same
time
                MyDelegate myDelegatedTask = () = > Debug.Log("Hello from
lambda.");
                //call the new delegated task
                myDelegatedTask();
        }
}
```

For some, this code might seem to oversimplify a task. The notation lacks some clarity because there's so little to it, but we'll break down the elements to understand what's going on a bit better. Once we get the hang of lambdas, we'll want to use them in place of anonymous expressions when possible.

The `delegate` is defined as before with `delegate void MyDelegate();`. Of course, this returns nothing and takes no parameters, as indicated by `void` and nothing within the parentheses for the delegate's argument list.

When we create an instance of `MyDelegate`, we call it `myDelegatedTask` and use `=` to assign it to `() = > Debug.Log("Hello from lambda.");`. The first two operators are important to see what's going on here. First the `()` should match the signature of the delegate we're instantiating. `MyDelegate()` had no arguments, so the `()` following the `=` assignment operator take no arguments.

Then we use the `= >` lambda operator to tell `myDelegatedTask` what it's to do when it's called. In this case, we're assigning it to `Debug.Log("Hello from lambda.");`.

Finally, to get the result of the expression, we call on `myDelegatedTask();` to get the hello message printed out to the Unity's Console panel.

To add in an argument in the lambda expression, we can use the following code:

```csharp
public class LambdaExpressions : MonoBehaviour
{
    delegate void MyDelegate(int i);
    //Use this for initialization
    void Start ()
    {
        MyDelegate myDelegatedTask = (x) = > Debug.Log(x * x);
        myDelegatedTask(5);
    }
}
```

Now we should see a reflection of what was being used in the 1930s. Mathematicians used $(x) \to x * x$, and today we can use $(x) = > x * x;$ in our code. Of course, this isn't the best way to use a lambda to get a value. More commonly, we'd see something where the lambda returns a value.

```csharp
    //Use this for initialization
    delegate int MyDelegate(int i);
    void Start () {
        MyDelegate myDelegatedTask = (x) = > x * x;
        int y = myDelegatedTask(5);
        Debug.Log(y);
    }
```

Change the delegate from void MyDelegate(int i); to int Mydelegate(int i);, and we'll be able to use myDelegatedTask() as a value. Later on, we'll see how much more useful this is rather than simply printing out Debug.Log(). Running this small code sample will print 25 to the Console panel.

### 7.21.3 When Lambdas Are Useful

Being succinct, or at the very least, brief is the main goal of the lambda. A lambda is basically a function written inside of a function. One strategy to maintain a clean-looking and smoothly running function is to break out the repeated tasks into another function.

When we write a bunch of different functions, we should think to keep tasks separate. A function should do a specific thing and only that one thing. When the task involves something more detailed which might require one or two other functions to get involved, it's sometimes easier to write a lambda instead.

### 7.21.4 Lambda Statements

The lambda statement follows the same basic setup with delegate() = > (input) = >expression, but we can extend this to include a full statement. Using delegate() = > (input) = > {statement;}, we can get a lot more use out of a lambda and its delegate.

This is similar to the delegate() which we looked at earlier; however, the lambda has some slight variations on the statements that can be done with the delegate function.

```
public class LambdaExpressions : MonoBehaviour
{
    //create a delegate signature like before
    delegate int MyDelegate(int i);
    //Use this for initialization
    //delegate int MyDelegate(int i);
    void Start ()
    {
        MyDelegate myLambda = (x) = > x * x;
        int y = myLambda(5);
        Debug.Log(y);
        MyDelegate myDelegate = delegate(int i)
        {
            return i * i;
        };
        int z = myDelegate(5);
        Debug.Log(z);
    }
}
```

These two function declaration statements for myDelegate and myLambda do the exact same thing. The formatting for the lambda is decidedly shorter, but not necessarily easier to read. Certainly, it's shorter and less verbose, but there is a problem so far as readability is concerned, unless you know what a lambda is and how it's used.

### 7.21.5 What We've Learned

Lambda expressions are more useful than simply printing to the Console; they're often used to sort through arrays of data. The same goes for anonymous expressions, but it's more important that we use a lambda expression to do this.

## 7.22 Leveling Up

We've reached the end of a very difficult chapter. One of the most important topics that have been covered more than once is inheritance. We looked at several different systems about controlling the inheritance of a class. Special classes such as the `abstract` class and the `interface` control how inheritance is managed.

We've been working to become a functional programmer, or at least being able to talk to one. At this point, it should be plausible that you would be able to build some interesting behaviors and write something compelling.

When talking about special programming tricks and learning new idioms and patterns, a great deal of work can be done by reading code. Finding interesting projects on GitHub or any other open-source code sharing site is a good place to start.

Studying code is more than trying to just understand what each statement is trying to do. The hard part is to interpret what an entire function is doing, determine how it works, and check if it's doing something you haven't seen before.

If the code contains a new trick, learn how it works. If the structure looks interesting, try to understand why it was built in that way. If there is new syntax, look it up and figure out how it works. The more code you read, the more you'll learn.

In Chapter 8, we'll take a look at some more interesting tricks and some common patterns, and syntax that is often used by more skilled programmers. Of course, not everything will be covered in as much depth as it deserves, but it's a starting point.

# 8

## *Extended*

### 8.1 What We'll Be Covering in This Chapter

If we've got this far together, we're in a good position to learn some of the more interesting aspects of the C# language. Not all of the things in this chapter will come up all too often in everyday programming tasks of a C# engineer, but they're all good to know, or at least know about.

We'll cover a few new tricks that include some style, some interesting syntax with LINQ, and more obscure number of tricks. A few design patterns and structure ideas will also be introduced. It's easy to get carried away with the tricks, so it's important to remember when and where some of these tricks should be used. Remember that everything is in moderation.

- Readability
- Source control, revisited
- Debugging techniques
- Recursion
- Reflection
- LINQ
- Bitwise operations
- Attributes
- Architectures
- Design patterns

This chapter is relatively short in comparison to the Chapters 2 through 7. At this point, it should only act as a launch pad to start you on your own into further study. Many of the basic concepts that will be covered have a wider scope into themselves than can be covered in this book.

Concepts like architecture and their related systems often cover entire volumes of text that dive deep into topics about optimizations and use cases. In this chapter, we'll cover the topics only in a very superficial way.

There are some important tricks here: bitwise operations are useful for enums and dealing with what are called flags. We'll also be covering some of the more tricky topics of attributes and reflection. We'll also cover the last looping system called recursion in which a function calls itself.

### 8.2 Review

Previously we looked over the topics of events and some interfaces. There are hundreds of other common interfaces, but thanks to implementing a few of them and making our own interfaces, we should be able to understand how to implement just about any other interface out there.

Delegate functions and anonymous functions are quite common in production. When you need to deal with Internet connections, the delegate and concurrent functions often work together to send and receive data from sources that aren't local to your own computer.

Accessors, also known as properties, are also very common in production. When working with a team of engineers, it's preferable to use `MyClass.property = data;` rather than `MyClass.SetProperty(data);` for setting variables. Because properties can be so flexible, it's good to know a bit about how to best think about them.

```csharp
using UnityEngine;
using System.Collections;
public class Example : MonoBehaviour
{
    //Use this for initialization
    void Start ()
    {
        HasProperties hp = new HasProperties();
        hp.MyFloat = 5f;
        Debug.Log(hp.MyFloat);//5
        Debug.Log(hp.HalfFloat);//2.5
        hp.HalfFloat = 9f;
        Debug.Log(hp.MyFloat);//4.5
    }
    class HasProperties
    {
        protected float myFloat;
        public float MyFloat
        {
            get
            {
                return myFloat;
            }
            set
            {
                myFloat = value;
            }
        }
        public float HalfFloat
        {
            get
            {
                return this.myFloat/2;
            }
            set
            {
                this.myFloat = value/2;
            }
        }
    }
}
```

In the above code, we have a `MyFloat` and a `HalfFloat` exposed to the class. We can get and set either one and get predictable values set by using either one. The `Debug.Log` files return half and can set them at half. Whether or not these values make sense is determined by how you intend them to be used. Should setting `HalfFloat` mean that you are giving a half value or giving it a value to be halved?

Like so many things, how the accessors are implemented is up to you; they're flexible in that you're allowed to write any form of logic into them. This power also opens up the opportunity for problems. Expecting one thing and getting another means only a miscommunication or a bug in the code.

Like so many things, writing code that makes sense means communication not only by your code to the reader but also between engineers. When you are working on your projects alone at home, you might be moving between different side projects. The systems you write should be portable and usable between your projects.

If you write a useful character controller, it's a shame to have to write another one for a different project that has a similar behavior. Any time you can reuse good code, you're saving time and effort and making advancements in your game's progress. Make enough parts for a game; eventually you'll be able to assemble an entire game by copying and pasting code from your other projects!

## 8.3 Readability Optimizations and Idioms

Reducing complexity and keeping the notation short is a simple way to make your code easier to read. Some of these notations follow specific patterns. For example, the `foreach()` loop is a more simple version of the `for(;;)` loop without an internally scoped `int`. There are other optimizations that you can use to make your code more brief, but in some cases the code becomes a bit less clear.

Some of these optimizations have become common enough to be called idioms, or commonly used programming patterns. C# idioms have been inherited from other programming languages like C and C++, which have had a longer history and more time to develop common patterns.

### 8.3.1 ?: Notation

A simple system to change a value based on a single comparison is the `?:` notation.

```
var result = condition ? true : false;
```

The above notation is a truncation of the following code:

```
var result;
if(condition)
{
    result = true;
} else {
    result = false;
}
```

The first notation might be confusing the first time you see it; however, its compactness is its advantage. There are many cases where keeping a simple "if true do this, else do that" to a single line makes sense.

```
int GreaterThan(int a, int b)
{
    return (a > b) ? a : b;
}
```

The above code simply returns the value of which `int` is greater than the other; it's simple and has only one line of code. If a is greater than b, return a; otherwise return b. The code is very simple and elegant and, more important, very hard to break. The above notation becomes less clear if you nest conditions.

```
int GreaterThan(int a, int b, int c)
{
    return (a > b) ? ((a > c) ? a : c) : ((b > c) ? b : c) ;
}
```

The above code compares all three values and returns the greatest, though from looking at the code it's not clear that this will actually work. The parentheses help, but they're not necessary. The above code could look like the following:

```
int GreaterThan(int a, int b, int c)
{
     return a>b?a>c?a:c:b>c?b:c;
}
```

Even though the above code is perfectly valid, it's fairly unreadable.

## 8.3.2 If

Another common strategy to keep code clean is to ignore curly braces {} when an `if` statement controls only one line of code.

```
if(condition)
     //do this;
else
     //do that;
```

The above code uses only tabs to determine the execution of each line. You're allowed to omit curly braces {} if each statement is only one line long. This works for a single `if` statement as well.

```
//doing things here;
if(condition)
     //do this;
//more code here;
```

The above code will only "do this" if the `if` statement is true. The line before and after the `if` statement will execute as normal. In general, most programmers tend to add in curly braces regardless of their necessity. If another line is required, curly braces will have to be added anyway, creating more work later on.

## 8.3.3 Smell

Programming style is sometimes referred to as either flavor or smell. As such there are good smells and bad smells. A bad smell doesn't necessarily mean that the code is broken and buggy. However, bad smelling code usually leads to problems later on.

This programming style is categorized into several groups.

### 8.3.3.1 Comments

Comments are descriptive but useless. They make up a part of your code as much as functions and variables. They're used to inform fellow programmers as to what a function or code block is used for. Poorly commented code smells bad, and such bad smells cause many headaches.

The real problems begin once any major overhaul of the code is required. Poorly formatted or organized code can become more problematic when finding and replacing field names or function names. Code that conforms to an expected formatting can more quickly and easily be updated, whereas bad smelling code will often result in botched renaming and replacing in a process called refactoring that will be covered in Section 8.12.5.

### 8.3.3.2 One Responsibility Rule

Long extremely complex functions often exude a certain bad smell. When a function gets too long, it's often a source for many different problems. Here, bad smell means that finding a problem in the function can take a long time to fix. Short functions are easier to debug as there are only fewer lines of code to fix.

The problem usually comes about when a single function tries to do too many different tasks. In other words, a function should have enough statements to complete a specific task and nothing more. Once a function completes more than necessary, it's time to split the function into two or more different functions.

A function should ever take care of only a single task. If there's a repeated task that needs to happen, then another new function should be written to take on that responsibility. This means that a number of different functions can also make use of a function that has that one task.

### 8.3.3.3 Duplicated Code

Long functions often have many repeated sections of code, leading to more problems. If one block of code needs a fix, the same fix will need to be applied to every other block that looks and acts in a similar fashion. Repeated code means repeated effort in fixing bugs.

Long functions often use too many parameters; more than two or three arguments in a function's list can also lead to bad smelling code. Often these long parameter lists can feed into longer logical chains.

A long ladder of `if-else` statements can become very difficult to decode and interpret. Too many conditions in a single `if` statement also lead to bad smelling code. In some cases, they're difficult to avoid, but they will leave a bad smell even if the code works.

There are always more simple and clever ways to solve problems like too many arguments and conditions. Clever solutions come once you've accumulated experience. To gain this experience, you need to expose yourself to a lot of clever code and read and understand how it all works.

We're not seeing many clever examples in this book, only pragmatic examples to explain basic concepts. There are programmers who are quite clever and willing to share their wisdom on the Internet. Forums are a great way to seek clever solutions to complex problems.

### 8.3.3.4 Long Names

Both variables and functions should follow a simple naming convention. When a name becomes too long and cumbersome, it's difficult to read statements that use long identifiers. Programming shouldn't feel like a restrictive set of rules that confine what you're allowed to do. However, there are some general concepts that help keep code readable and easy to understand.

For true false data types like bools, it's often useful to prefix the variable with "is" such as `bool isActive;` or `bool isEnabled`. If the prefixing is consistent throughout your own code, you'll be able to identify a variable as a `bool` simply by its name.

Classes and structs should be named as nouns. A `Zombie` class is a perfect example. A `classZombie` is a horrible name for a `Zombie` class. If it's a noun, you already know it's a class object, and having a type in the name of the variable is redundant.

Classes that inherit from certain interfaces should start with an uppercase `I`, so, for example, a `Graveyard` which inherits from `IEnumerable` should be an `IGraveyard`. In most cases, a naming standard should be followed. Usually, when you join a company or group of programmers, you'll want to come to agree on a shared set of coding standards.

### 8.3.4 What We've Learned

Coding standards are commonly thought about and shared, so there are many references on the Internet. General concepts can easily be followed to avoid bad smelling code and inconsistent identifier names. It's important to discover on your own why these rules have been written. This comes about only through practice and reading code on your own.

## 8.4 Source Control Revisited

Hopefully, you've been keeping up with using some sort of source control. Once you start working with a team of programmers, you'll need to know how to deal with managing multiple changes to a single file. When code overlaps, you'll need some additional software help to assist in merging multiple text files together.

### 8.4.1 Diff and Merge

As you write new code or make revisions, you'll want to push or check in your changes to the host. However, while you were making your revisions, another programmer might have also checked in some changes to the same file you have been working on. If we start with the code using the idea that we're fighting over what to name a variable, we could start with `OriginalNumber`.

To start your merge, you need to get or pull the latest revision from the trunk. Usually, the merge can be done automatically. It integrates the code from the trunk into your code. The merge gives you a chance to check whether your work still functions properly after you've integrated the latest revision.

If changes overlap, the automatic merge may fail. These conflicts require manual merging. Merging can sometimes cause headaches, especially if someone else changes a statement you were working on as well. To check for the differences between your code and his or her code, Git has a tool called diff, short for differences. To understand what's going on when checking for changed code, let's examine the following example.

```
using UnityEngine;
using System.Collections;
public class NewBehaviourScript : MonoBehaviour
{
    public int OriginalNumber;
}
```

On April's machine, she adds the following code to a `NewBehaviourScript.cs` and then pushes the change. Now `OriginalNumber` is replaced with `AprilsNumber`.

```
using UnityEngine;
using System.Collections;
public class NewBehaviourScript : MonoBehaviour
{
    public int AprilsNumber;
}
```

At the same time, you wanted to use your own number with this code, but you haven't had the chance to check it in yet.

```
using UnityEngine;
using System.Collections;
public class NewBehaviourScript : MonoBehaviour
{
    public int AlexsNumber;
}
```

This means that there are multiple versions of the same file: the file with the work you have done, the file with the work someone else has done, and the file on the server that both of you started with. Each file containing differences from the file on the server can be considered a branch. This is why the server is considered to have the trunk. Each deviation from the trunk can be considered a branch until it's merged back in.

Add in a comment that we want to change the name to Alex and press the Commit button. Once we press Sync to push the commit to the server, we get a problem.

Merging code back into the trunk needs to be done by adding your code and your fellow programmers' code together. In some cases, more than one merge may need to be done before your addition can be checked in.

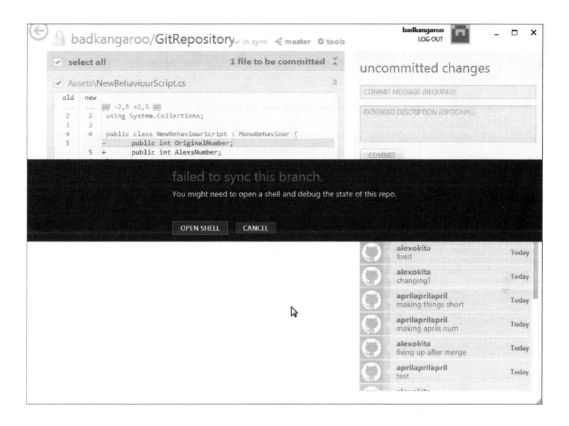

When you try to sync to the latest revision, you'll get a conflict. And it's unfortunate that we're told that we need to open a shell, but alas! GitHub is still new at the graphical user interface (GUI), so we'll have to deal with using a keyboard for a moment.

Enter the following command:

```
git mergetool -t kdiff3
```

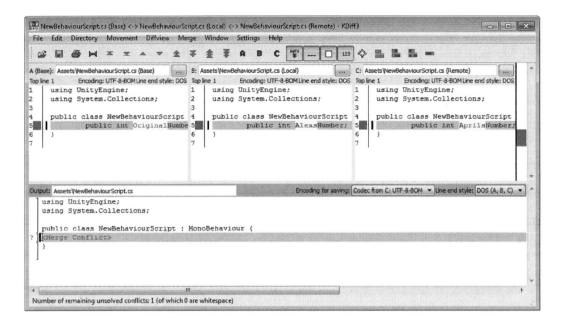

On the left is the original; you might be able to tell this because it's using `public int OriginalNumber`. In the middle is the local file on Alex's machine where the change is to make `OriginalNumber` to `AlexsNumber`. On the right is the remote change where April has changed the value to `AprilsNumber`. The bottom panel reflects which version we will want to use.

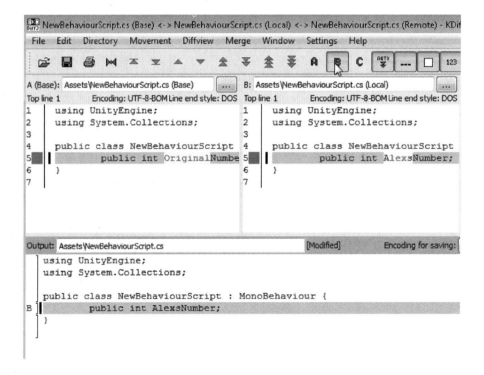

Pressing B resolves the conflict with our local change. Likewise C uses the remote file. Or we can use both B and C to add both `int`s to the file.

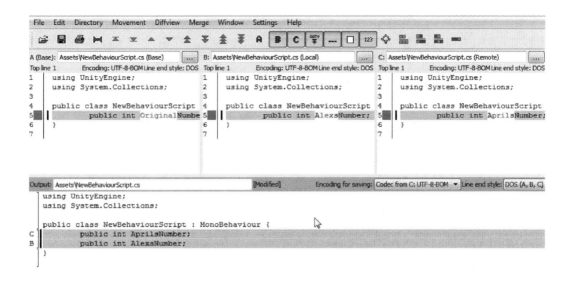

When we're done picking which versions to use, press Save and then close KDiff3.

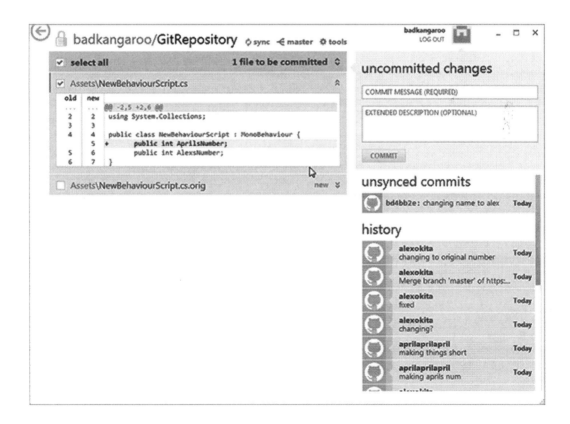

GitHub will pick up the change and note that you've resolved the conflict. There will be some leftover
.orig files which KDiff3 left behind, but we can uncheck those from the Commit.

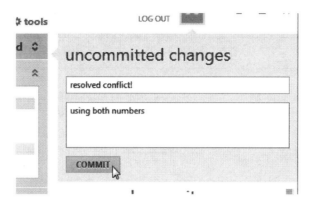

Code merging becomes a daily chore for a good programmer, and learning how to merge files takes some practice. To speed things along, yet another piece of software needs to be installed along with the GitHub. The GitHub software comes with its own diff tool called GitDiff. Because Git originates from the command line, the diff tool has no GUI. This is unfortunate as most beginning programmers find command-line interfaces difficult, and there are plenty of alternatives with a GUI.

### 8.4.2 KDiff3

A commonly used open source merging software called KDiff is available at http://kdiff3.sourceforge. net/, and the software is available on OS X, Windows, and Linux. WinMerge is another popular diff and merge tool but only works on Windows. There are other alternatives that look nicer, but you'll need to pay between $50 and $200 to get them, so we'll skip that investment for this chapter. Thankfully, they all do the same thing: compare two different files and allow you to pick which changes you want to keep.

Unfortunately, KDiff3 isn't the default merge tool used by GitHub; rather than use the built-in tools that operate in a shell, we're going to want something that actually looks like modern software. To do this, we'll have to edit a .gitconfig file.

On Windows, a .gitconfig file is located in your user directory; this file appears after GitHub is installed. For me this directory was C:\Users\alexokita; in this directory there's a .gitconfig file with a couple of settings already entered: [user] name = username and an e-mail address. To this file we're going to add in some new parameters to inform GitHub that we're using an external tool for diff and merge.

Merging involves the version you've been working on, which is the *local* file. The *remote* file is the incoming file from GitHub. Then there's the *base* file which both remote and local share as a common original.

KDiff3 is a simple merge tool. When you compare two different files, you're presented with your version on the left and the file from the server on the right. Color coding highlights the lines that have changed and can be automatically merged and which lines are in need of attention because an automatic merge isn't possible.

For each conflict, you need to pick which version to choose, A or B. Often if you have worked on a specific file for an extended amount of time, you may have touched many lines of code. This often increases the number of merge conflicts you'll have to merge with.

### 8.4.3 Avoiding Conflicts

Avoiding conflicts is easily done by using comments. Commenting out a broken section of code allows the automatic merge to more easily track differences and automatically merge files. Follow the commented section with a new section of code to keep everything working as intended.

### 8.4.4 What We've Learned

Once all of the merges have been made and you've tested your code to make sure that everything still works as intended, it's time to push your changes back up to the server. At this point, it's a good idea to remind your fellow programmers to get latest before they make too many more changes.

Communication remains the best form of code conflict resolution. Making sure that your code integrates well involves talking to everyone to make sure your changes don't stomp on something others have been working on. Everyone has his or her own coding style. C# is flexible enough to allow different philosophies to work together.

The tolerance of style is both good and bad. When programmers need to read each other's code, the philosophies can turn into arguments over how objects should interact or how code should be written. Coming to a peaceful resolution can happen only with proper communication.

## 8.5 Debugging

The call stack isn't something that is always referred to in a programming language book. The call stack, however, is an integral part of debugging code. Once in practice a call stack is an important part of any programming environment. The default setup for MonoDevelop allows you to write code. When you connect MonoDevelop to Unity 3D through its debugger, several new windows pop open. We'll go through the different windows and how they're used.

Accessors make debugging much easier. Let's take a look at the following scenario where we have a GUI object listing the GameObjects in a scene. In a setting without an accessor for a variable, we have the following class that accomplishes the required steps for this example.

In the Debugging project, we have a simple scene with a script Game.cs attached to the Main Camera, and in the scene we have a box with the attached Problem.cs class that at the moment does nothing. We'll look at how the Main Camera works right now.

### 8.5.1 Debugging Accessors

A side effect, as it is called, is the change that affects variables outside the scope of the function that is called. These side effects can be difficult to track down without a property accessor, as we will see.

```csharp
using UnityEngine;
using System.Collections;
public class Game : MonoBehaviour
{
    public GameObject[] GameObjects;
    public static string MyText = "";
    //Use this for initialization
    void Start ()
    {
        GameObjects =
        GameObject.FindObjectsOfType(typeof(GameObject)) as GameObject[];
        for (int i = 0; i < GameObjects.Length; i++)
        {
            MyText + = GameObjects [i].name + "\n";
        }
    }
    void OnGUI()
    {
        GUI.BeginGroup(new Rect(0, 0, 300, 100));
        GUI.Box(new Rect(0, 0, 300, 100), MyText);
        GUI.EndGroup();
    }
}
```

When this code is run, we get the following result. We have a simple dialog with Cube and Main Camera listed, quite simple.

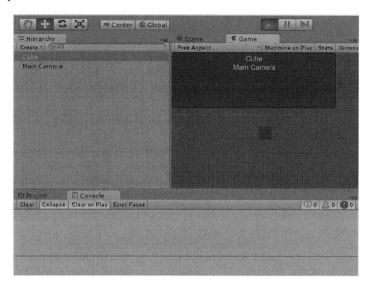

Where this becomes more interesting is when we add some code to the Cube, which affects the list of items. Attached to the cube is a class called `Problem.cs` that stomps on the list of items. The `Problem.cs` class uses the `Start ()` function to assign the variable `MyText` string found in `Game.cs`. This function is affecting a variable unrelated to the `Problem.cs` class; this is a side effect.

```
using UnityEngine;
using System.Collections;
public class Problem : MonoBehaviour
{
    //Use this for initialization
    void Start ()
    {
        Game.MyText = "nope.";
    }
}
```

With the above code, our nice dialog is denied:

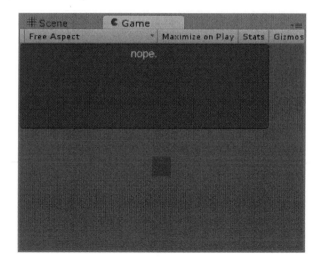

So why is this a problem? The `MyText` string is `static`; this makes it accessible from any other class so long as it can reach the `Game.cs` class. The `MyText` string is also `public`, so anyone can make changes.

This might be good if the Cube were able to update the `MyText` string with something useful, but right now it's just saying "nope" that might be a bug. If this scene had more than the two objects assigned, we'd have a more difficult time tracking down where this "nope" came from.

Once a scene has a few hundred properties, most of them might have any number of attached components, all of which can affect the text used in the box. Tracking down the one or many culprits in the scene, or elsewhere, might prove near impossible. It is not the best scenario for fixing a bug at 2 a.m. in the morning or the night before a deadline.

So we try to debug the error with the current code. Setting a breakpoint on the `MyText` variable makes sense, so let's put a breakpoint on that line where the variable appears. After attaching the debugger to Unity 3D, run the game with the breakpoint assigned to the variable.

```
◄  ►      Problem.cs                    ◉    Game.cs                         ✕

 ⓒ Game  ►  No selection

  1 ⊟  using UnityEngine;
  2 └  using System.Collections;
  3
  4 ⊟  public class Game : MonoBehaviour
  5    {
  6         public GameObject[] GameObjects;
  7         public static string MyText = "";
  8         // Use this for initialization
  9 ⊟      void Start()
 10         {
 11             GameObjects = GameObject.FindObjectsOfType(
 12             for (int i = 0; i < GameObjects.Length; i++
 13             {
 14                 MyText += GameObjects [i].name + "\n";
 15             }
 16 ┴      }
```

We get `nope` and the breakpoint was never reached. Why is this? A variable is not actually ever acted on in a way that will trigger a breakpoint. No action is actually happening on the line. The variable is indeed being accessed but not in a way that the breakpoint can stop.

How do we change this variable to allow a debugging process to find out when the variable is accessed? We use an accessor—that's how. An accessor has two parts: a `get` and a `set`. We can apply a breakpoint to either of these two actions and find out who was getting or setting the variable.

```
protected static string mText;
public static string MyText{
    get{return mText;}
    set{mText = value;}
}
```

We change the `MyText` to an accessor and add in a protected `mText` such that it can't be directly affected by an external class. This changes a few things. First of all, we have added a clean way to set the variable and give ourselves some room for double-checking that any values are valid. We've also given ourselves a place to set a breakpoint.

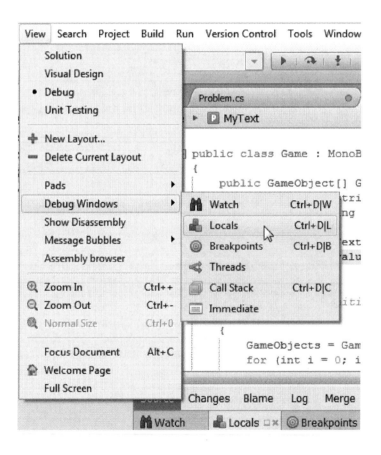

```
 8      public static string MyText
 9      {
10          get{ return mText;}
11          set{ mText = value;}
12      }
13
```

With the breakpoint on the line where the set occurs, we can then run the code again. Almost immediately, the debugger catches the first assignment. Now we can track who is setting `MyText` and what it's being set to.

## 8.5.2 Locals

When we first run into the breakpoint, we should look at the panel called Locals. If your Locals panel isn't showing, you can access it through the View → Debug Windows → Locals menu.

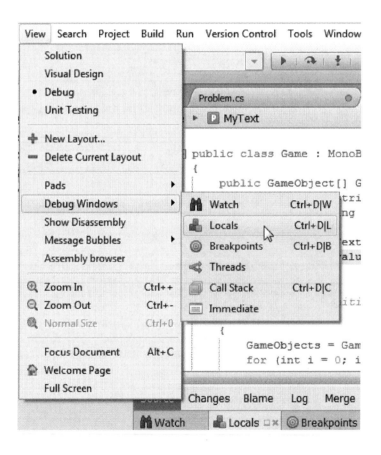

The first thing that happens to be in this Locals panel is value "`Main Camera\n`," which is the incoming data going into the `set{}` instruction of the accessor for `MyText`. By pressing F5, we allow the game to run normally until the breakpoint is hit again. This happens pretty much immediately as we're setting `MyText` inside of a simple `for(;;)` loop.

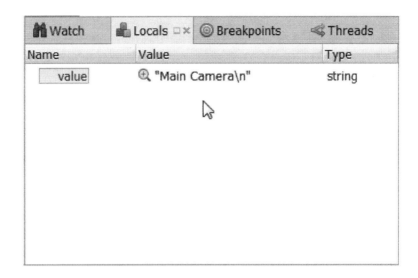

The second time we get another value that looks like the following:

Continue the execution.

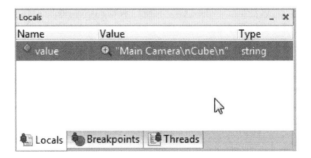

So far this is quite promising; these are the game objects in the scene. Hitting F5 again, we get the problem.

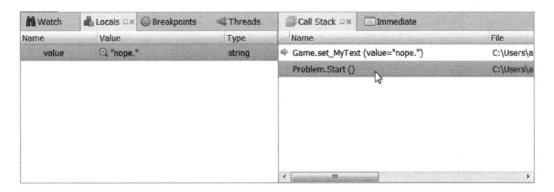

The string is set to "nope." If this were being set by some rogue class, somewhere we'd want to track it down and find out why it's being set to "nope" and ruining our lovely object list. There's another panel called a Call Stack.

### 8.5.3 Call Stack

A call stack is a list of functions or instructions that were active when the breakpoint was caught. With this list we can look at what was being done to produce the breakpoint.

  With the default MonoDevelop layout, you have the Call Stack set to the bottom right of the panel. This set shows you what's going on while the breakpoint is holding up the game. The start of the breakpoint is at the bottom of the list. As new calls are made, the new functions and operations are stacked on top of the first function, thus the name *call stack*.

  Here we can see that Problem.Start () is being called. Inside Problem.Start (), we are accessing Game.set _ MyText(value – "nope."), which lines up with what we're observing. From here is an easy step to double click on Problem.Start (), which takes us to that file and the line where the variable is being set.

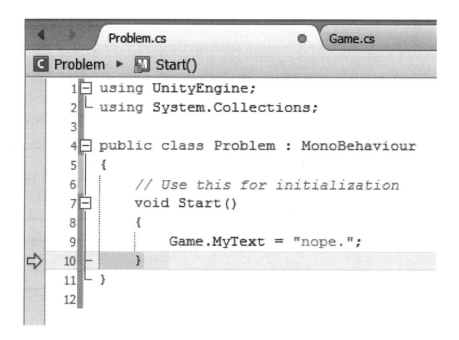

If an accessor was not set for MyText, we wouldn't be able to do this. Before your code gets unwieldy, it's important to make sure that certain measures are set in place. Setting up accessors for your variables should be a regular habit. This step might seem tedious at first, but once things get too far it gets harder and harder to debug your code without it.

### 8.5.4 Watch List

Another common feature that helps debugging is the Watch list. This list allows you to observe variables and classes as they are set.

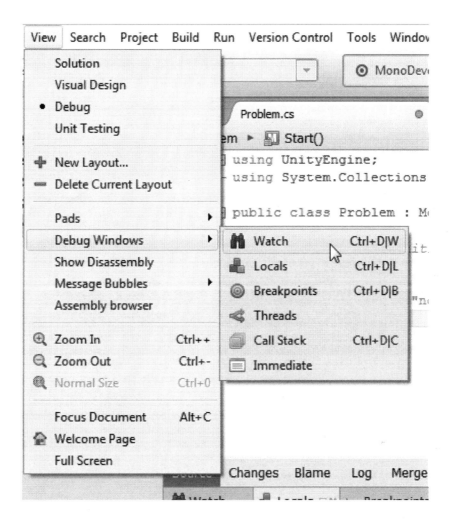

The Watch panel allows us to observe a variable in detail.

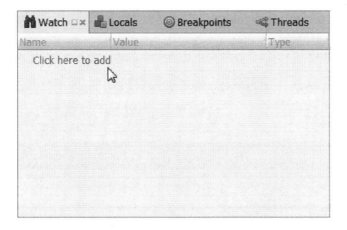

When the panel is open and you've trapped a breakpoint, the Watch panel gets activated. Click on the Click here to add line, and you'll be prompted to fill in a variable name.

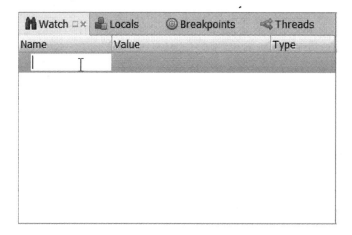

In this case, we can use mText to observe what's going on with that particular variable.

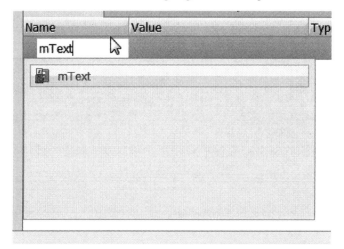

With mText entered into the field, we can see the current value as well as the type of that variable. There's more to this panel than just watching its current value. We can obtain any other value associated with the string class as it's used with mText.

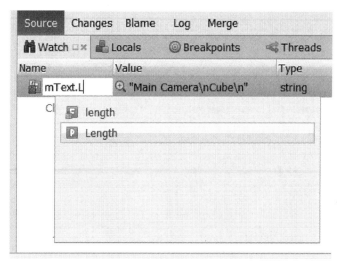

We can observe its Length value and see how many characters are being stored in that variable.

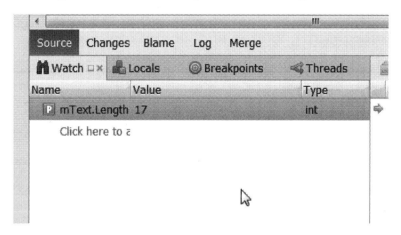

Even though we're not directly using the Length value anywhere, it's still an accessible part of the mText variable. What all of this really means is that the debugger, or more specifically MonoDevelop, is useful for many different reasons.

As a debugging tool, you can see who and where calls to functions are made. These systems are common among many different integrated development environments (IDEs) including Visual Studio. Once you're ready to move to different programming environments, you'll want to figure out their debugging tools.

### 8.5.5  What We've Learned

We've looked at a few contrived examples on how the debugger can be used. Most of the time a bug might creep in through unexpected paths. It's difficult to come up with a more specific unexpected example. Unfortunately, these cases are something you'll come across on your own more often than not.

Without a pro version of Unity 3D to use, we're really not able to take advantage of the Threads panel that you may see in some of the screenshots. Threads are basically operations running in parallel to one another. They work a bit differently than coroutines, but the general idea is the same.

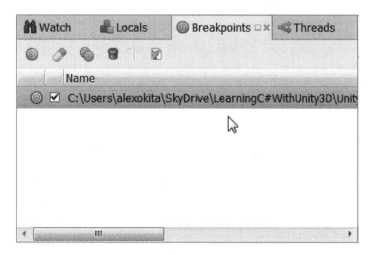

MonoDevelop remembers your breakpoints like bookmarks. The Breakpoints panel will show you where you have left them. If you're working with multiple classes, you may have forgotten where you have left them all.

The Breakpoints panel will show you what files and what line the breakpoints can be found on. This panel will also let you select some, delete them, or temporarily disable them. This doesn't have any effect on the code, but just on the selected breakpoint. So don't worry about breaking anything by removing or disabling a breakpoint.

As an integrated tool to programming, the debugger is indispensible. One of the big reasons why an IDE is useful is because of its debugging tools. Unity 3D by itself, along with a text editor, is functional only to a point. Once you've got used to working with a debugger, you'll find that you will absolutely rely on a good debugging tool.

## 8.6 Recursion

"To understand recursion, you must first understand recursion."—James Teal

We've studied most of the basic iteration loops. The `for`, `while`, `do while`, `foreach`, and even `goto` can be used to iterate through a task. Of all these options, we're left to adding them to the body of a function.

```
void Start ()
{
    //for loop
    for (int i = 0; i < 10; i++)
    {
        Debug.Log("for " + i.ToString());
    }
    //while loop
    int j = 0;
    while (j < 10)
    {
        Debug.Log("while " + j.ToString());
        j++;
    }
    //do while
    int k = 0;
    do
    {
        Debug.Log("do " + k.ToString());
        k++;
    } while(k < 10);
    //for each
    int[] ints = {0,1,2,3,4,5,6,7,8,9,10};
    foreach (int l in ints)
    {
        Debug.Log("foreach " + l.ToString());
    }
    //while alternate
    IEnumerator m = ints.GetEnumerator();
    while (m.MoveNext())
    {
        Debug.Log("IEnumerator " + m.Current.ToString());
    }
    //goto loop
    int n = 0;
    Start:
    Debug.Log("goto " + n.ToString());
    n++;
```

```
        if (n < 10)
        {
            goto Start;
        }
    }
```

Each one of these loops will count from 0 to 10, and all of them operate within the Start () function. However, if we wanted to create a self-contained function, we might want to consider a recursive function. A recursive function or method is any method that calls upon itself.

Recursion is often used to deal with complex sets of data. If we're not sure how many layers of data are buried within a set of parameters, we need to have a flexible system to deal with what we're given.

### 8.6.1 A Basic Example

Start with the Recursion project and open the Example class in MonoDevelop. A recursive function is a function that calls itself from within itself.

```
    void Recurse(int i)
    {
        if (i > 10)
        {
            return;
        }
        Debug.Log("Recurse " + i.ToString());
        i++;
        Recurse(i);
    }
```

This example fits in with the previous exercise of counting from 0 to 10. To add this to our list of loops, we use the following statements:

```
    void Start ()
    {
        Recurse(0);
    }
```

The above function and statement together create the same effect as the previous loop statements. We can add this to the growing list of interactive statements and systems, which we can use to deal with complex sets of data.

### 8.6.2 Understanding Recursion

Using a recursive function can be a bit mind-bending at first. It's all too easy to set yourself up for a loop that never breaks. It's important that we understand how recursion works in order to use it more effectively. The first rule for a recursive function is to have a clear condition where the function returns without calling on itself. This is how the function breaks out of itself. If we look at the above example, we use the statement:

```
if (i > 10)
{
    return;
}
```

This statement does not call on the `Recurse()` function again, so the recursion stops here. The reason recursion repeats itself is that the function calls on itself at some point. Once the function stops calling itself, the recursion terminates. To make this more clear, we can write a simple recursion function like the following:

```
void CountDownRecursion (int i)
{
    Debug.Log(i);
    If (i > 0)
    {
        i- ;
        CountDownRecursion(i);
    }
}
```

Here we can see that int i is decremented just before recurring. Once i is no longer greater than 0, the function doesn't call on itself. Once the function stops calling on itself, the function ends and we've reached the end of the recursive loop.

### 8.6.3 In Practice

When dealing with a set of data with many child components, we might have to use for loops within for loops to get through all of the data. If there's another tier of data underneath that, then we might pass over it without even knowing. To get started, building a simple blob of game objects will be our first goal. This way we'll have something to sort through.

```
//Use this for initialization
void Start ()
{
    int id = 0;
    GameObject g = new GameObject("A_" + id);
    for (int i = 0; i < 3; i ++)
    {
        id++;
        GameObject b = new GameObject("B_" + id.ToString());
        b.transform.parent = g.transform;
        for (int j = 0; j < 5; j++)
        {
            id++;
            GameObject c = new GameObject("C_" + id.ToString());
            c.transform.parent = b.transform;
            for (int k = 0; k < 2; k++)
            {
              id++;
              GameObject d = new GameObject("D_" + id.ToString());
              d.transform.parent = c.transform;
            }
        }
    }
}
```

The above code will produce a pretty interesting hierarchy of game objects in the scene. Some of the game objects were left collapsed. The above code is just a few different nested for loops creating and naming each game object as it's added to the scene. Once in the scene they're parented in such a way that they create the nested game object you see in the following hierarchy:

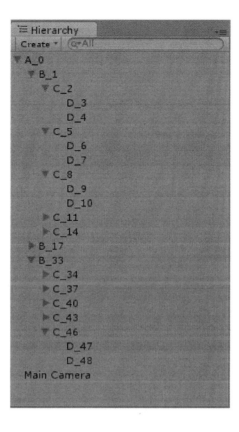

Now we'll want to make our recursive function that calls on itself to iterate through the whole lot of the game objects with a single call. After the recursive function is added, we just need to call it after the hierarchy of objects has been created.

```
void ListHierarchy(GameObject go)
{
    Debug.Log(g.name);
    for (int i = 0 ; i < go.transform.GetChildCount() ; i++)
    {
            GameObject g = go.transform.GetChild(i).gameObject;
            ListHierarchy(g);
    }
}
```

At the end of the nested `for` loops, we add in the `ListHierarchy()` function and give it the first GameObject `g` that was created for the hierarchy. Notice the line GameObject `g` = new GameObject("A _" + id);—here we create a variable g where we hold on to a gameObject in the scene. With this we can add every new game object under g.

```
//Use this for initialization
void Start ()
{
    int id = 0;
    //g is our gameObject to recurse through.
    GameObject g = new GameObject("A_" + id);
    for (int i = 0; i < 3 ; i ++)
    {
        id++;
```

```
        GameObject b = new GameObject("B_" + id.ToString());
        b.transform.parent = g.transform;
        for(int j = 0; j < 5 ; j++)
        {
            id++;
            GameObject c = new GameObject("C_" + id.ToString());
            c.transform.parent = b.transform;
            for(int k = 0; k < 2 ; k++)
            {
                id++;
                GameObject d = new GameObject("D_" + id.ToString());
                d.transform.parent = c.transform;
            }
        }
    }
    ListHierarchy(g);
}
```

With a complex hierarchy in the scene, we want to see each one of the game object's names printed to the Console panel with the recursive function ListHierarchy() by passing it a game object. It looks pretty simple, but there's a very interesting behavior that's going on with this simple function ListHierarchy(); in the Console panel.

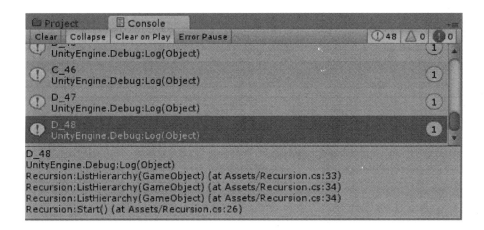

If you look at the log, you'll notice Recursion:ListHierarchy(GameObject) listed more than once! The first part of this log Recursion: indicates the class where the call is originating. It tells us what file is sending the Console output command. After that we get ListHierarchy(GameObject), which indicates what function has created the Debug:Log, highlighted in the Console panel. Then we get a line number, but ListHierarchy is listed three times for the D_48 Debug:Log sent to the Console panel.

The function has called itself two other times! This is, in particular, proof that the recursion is calling itself correctly. Also, it's quite interesting to see this behavior in action in the Console panel. Rather than just printing out the names of each game object in the hierarchy, we'd make something more useful with the information we're iterating through.

To build something more interesting to look at, we'll add in some GameObject primitives spawned rather than just emptying GameObject with a simple name in the hierarchy. We'll add in some simple transforms and rotations to some primitives. To set a goal, we're going to build a set of objects parented to one another; like in the hierarchy, we're going to have them orbit around one another.

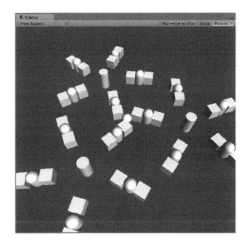

The above example will clearly show us a rotational relationship connected through the hierarchy.

We'll start off with the following `GameObject`:

```
//Class scope GameObject
GameObject a;
void Start ()
{
    a = GameObject.CreatePrimitive(PrimitiveType.Sphere);
    //create the a as a sphere
    int id = 0;
    a.name = "A_"+ id;//name the new sphere as we did before.
```

We'll add in `GameObject a;` at the class scope to begin. From here we'll try to stick to the same operation as we did before. However, after this we'll want to set some local offsets and rotations.

```
a = GameObject.CreatePrimitive(PrimitiveType.Sphere);
int id = 0;
a.name = "A_"+ id;
for (int i = 0; i < 3 ; i ++)
{
    id++;
    GameObject b = GameObject.CreatePrimitive(PrimitiveType.Cylinder);
    b.name = "B_"+id;
    //rotate the parent first!!!
    a.transform.localEulerAngles = new Vector3(0, (360/3) * i, 0);
    b.transform.localPosition = new Vector3(6.0f, 0, 0);
    b.transform.parent = a.transform;
    for(int j = 0; j < 5 ; j++)
    {
        id++;
        GameObject c = GameObject.CreatePrimitive(PrimitiveType.Capsule);
        c.name = "C_"+id;
        //rotate the parent first!!!
        b.transform.localEulerAngles = new Vector3(0, (360/5) * j, 0);
        c.transform.localPosition = new Vector3(2.0f, 0, 0);
        c.transform.parent = b.transform;
        for(int k = 0; k < 2 ; k++)
        {
            id++;
            GameObject d =
            GameObject.CreatePrimitive(PrimitiveType.Cube);
```

```
            d.name = "D_"+id;
            //rotate the parent first!!!
            c.transform.localEulerAngles = new Vector3(0,(360/2)*k,0);
            d.transform.localPosition = new Vector3(1.0f, 0, 0);
            d.transform.parent = c.transform;
        }
    }
}
```

The above code takes over the construction of the hierarchy that we created before. Notice here that the parent object from the previous for loop has its localEulerAngles set before the child is parented. This makes it critical to get the rotation to affect the child. Without this function the child object rotates in place rather than having an orbit set.

In addition, I've also created each different set of objects to different PrimitiveTypes; this gives some variety to the final solution to make different levels of hierarchy more clear. Then we'll add in a simple recursive function that rotates objects in the hierarchy.

```
void RotateHierarchy(GameObject go)
{
    go.transform.Rotate(new Vector3(0, 0.5f, 0));
    for (int i = 0 ; i < go.transform.GetChildCount() ; i++) {
        GameObject g = go.transform.GetChild(i).gameObject;
        RotateHierarchy(g);
    }
}
```

Rather than Debug.Log(), we'll use transform.Rotate and slowly rotate each object's *y*-axis. Using the first command go.transform.Rotate(new Vector3(0, 0.5f, 0));, we'll simply grab the object and add some rotation to it. Now it's only a matter of adding the RotateHierarchy() function to the Update () function.

```
void Update ()
{
    RotateHierarchy(a);
}
```

This is why we wanted to use GameObject a; at the class scope, otherwise we'd lose the handle to a as soon as the Start () function was finished. Now we have a rather strange set of objects rotating around one another.

With both the ListHierarchy() and RotateHierarchy() functions, the execution of the recursion was stopped because of the for loop's conditional statement. The second parameter in the for loop states i < go.transform.GetChildCount(); if this is not true, then the for loop isn't executed. This breaks the recursion stopping the recursive call.

### 8.6.4 Recursion Types

As programmers have a knack for giving clever names for systems, we've experienced what is commonly called linear recursion or sometimes single recursion. This is a recursive function that calls itself only once as a condition is met.

Linear recursion is the most simple type of recursive function. Basically, if we need to recurse then we do; otherwise we end the recursion. Because the linear recursion we wrote has the call to itself at the end of the function, it's in a subcategory of linear recursion functions called tail recursion.

Another common type of recursion is called indirect recursion. This occurs when two or more functions call on one another before ending. Indirect recursion is often useful for one function to be called that returns a completed set of data from the recursive function.

```
ArrayList GetList(GameObject go)
{
    ArrayList list = new ArrayList();
    BuildList(go, list);
    return list;
}
void BuildList(GameObject go, ArrayList l)
{
    l.Add(go);
    for (int i = 0; i < go.transform.GetChildCount(); i++)
    {
        GameObject g = go.transform.GetChild(i).gameObject;
        BuildList(g, l);
    }
}
```

The first function called `GetList()` calls the recursive function and gives it a list to fill in. This function is commonly referred to as a wrapper function. The task in the recursive function adds the incoming game object to the list given by the wrapper function. Then if there are children, it repeats the process for every child. Once it's done, the recursion ends and the function which called it gets the completed list. For instance, in the `Start ()` function, we can use these two functions with the following additions:

```
ArrayList myList = GetList(a);
foreach(GameObject g in myList)
{
        Debug.Log(g.name);
}
```

The above code fragment creates a list, then iterates through the list, and logs the names of each object in the `ArrayList myList` that was returned from the `GetList()` function. There are similarities between simple iterative loops like the one that created the original hierarchy of primitives and the recursive systems that look through them.

However, there are more differences at play than the superficial appearance of the code. In many cases, recursion functions often operate faster in the computer's memory than iterative functions. With increased complexity, the iterative function will slowdown more. Without going too far into how a computer's memory is managed, it's good to know that by using a recursive function you might be speeding things up, even if just by a tiny bit.

### 8.6.5 What We've Learned

As you might have guessed, there's a lot of information on recursion out on the vast sea of the Internet. It's one of those topics that people tend to write about to prove their competence. Aside from the somewhat confusing nature of a function calling on itself, the more important part of the recursion function is when the function *doesn't* call on itself.

The programmers writing Unity must know that recursion is a tricky topic. Many functions provided like `GetComponentsInChildren()` do some recursion to iterate through all of the components in the `gameObject`'s hierarchy. These functions supplant the necessity of writing your own function to do the same thing. That being said, at least now you know how the inner workings of the `GetComponent` functions work.

## 8.7 Reflection

A type like `int` or `string` is a clearly defined sort of data that we've been using quite a lot so far. When you create your own class, you're also creating a new type. While you're busy writing new classes, it's often the case that you'll want one class to read what another class can do or at least what sort of data it has. It's convenient to think that you'll be able to sort out which characters have a maximum run speed or a maximum flight height, but once you start adding in subclasses and multiple components, anything might change.

If you were able to read code, you'd be able to make more logical decisions based on the contents of a written class. One simple trick is to look at a class and find out what sort of variables it's hiding. When you look at a class, you can normally get its name; from its name, you might be able to guess what it's used for. Something like `MyZombieMonster()` might be fairly clear, but what does the zombie monster do?

### 8.7.1 A Basic Example

Reflection is a pretty interesting topic. Start with the Reflection project and we'll look at the `ReflectionA.cs` file that starts off with the following:

```
using UnityEngine;
using System.Collections;
using System.Reflection;
public class ReflectionA : MonoBehaviour
{
    class subClassA
    {
        public static int firstInt;
        public string secondInt;
        public int thirdInt;
        public subClassA(int first, int second, int third)
        {
            firstInt = first;
            this.secondInt = second.ToString();
            this.thirdInt = third;
        }
    }
    //Use this for initialization
    void Start ()
    {
        FieldInfo[] fields = typeof(subClassA).GetFields();
        foreach (FieldInfo field in fields)
        {
            Debug.Log(field.Name);
        }
    }
}
```

The above code shows the use of `typeof(subClassA).GetFields();`. This returns a new array of type `FieldInfo[]` which we're naming `fields`. By using a `foreach`, we can inspect each of the fields contained in the subClassA type. If we Debug.Log() the field.Name, we simply get firstInt, secondInt, and thirdInt printed to the Console.

By itself we now know that there are three fields, and we know their names. We can expand the Debug.Log() to the following and get more information:

```
Debug.Log(field.Attributes + " " + field.FieldType + " " + field.Name);
```

The above code gives us a pretty good view of the different fields in the subClassA's variables.

```
Public, Static System.Int32 firstInt
Public System.String secondInt
Public System.Int32 thirdInt
```

The above code is a slightly edited version of the output from the Console showing us that the firstInt is public and static; it's an Int32. From this we're able to do a few tasks, like making decisions based on the attribute and type. This sort of information can be used for many different tasks.

From the information extracted from FieldInfo[] fields, we're able to understand what we can do to each variable inside of subClassA. Even with deceptively named variables like string secondInt;, we can tell that it's not actually storing an int value.

### 8.7.2 Reflection MethodInfo

Aside from the fields found in a class, it's also possible to find functions. Because each class may or may not have a function of the same name, it's possible to sort through a number of classes and find functions in each one.

By starting with a few different subclasses, we can observe a very short list of different classes.

```
class subClassA
{
    public static int firstInt;
    public string secondInt;
    public int thirdInt;
    public subClassA(int first, int second, int third)
    {
        firstInt = first;
        this.secondInt = second.ToString();
        this.thirdInt = third;
    }
    public void OnUpdate ()
    {
        Debug.Log("subClassA Updating A");
    }
}
class subClassB
{
    public void OnUpdate ()
    {
        Debug.Log("subClassB Updating B");
    }
}
class subClassC
{
    public void NotUpdate ()
    {
    }
}
```

In the above code, we have three subclasses: subClassA, subClassB, and subClassC. These have no relation to one another. However, subClassA and subClassB happen to have a function in between called OnUpdate (), which has its own instructions. The subClassC has a NotUpdate () function, not an OnUpdate () function. Without knowing anything in all three classes, we can check for a function called OnUpdate () and call it with the following few statements in the Update () function.

Before we get into that, we'll want to make an instance of each class.

```csharp
subClassA ca;
subClassB cb;
subClassC cc;
//Use this for initialization
void Start ()
{
    ca = new subClassA(1,2,3);
    cb = new subClassB();
    cc = new subClassC();
}
```

In the Start () function, we create the three classes and hold them around in ca, cb, and cc. These can be anywhere; for example, in the above code, we're keeping them close, so we can see everything at once. In actual use, we might sort through the entire scene and find all of the different classes attached to every gameObject we can find. Once these are in an array, we can examine all of the different objects returned to an ArrayList. Instead of our example, we'll just use the following code in the Update () loop.

```csharp
void Update ()
{
    ArrayList subClasses = new ArrayList();
    subClasses.Add(ca);
    subClasses.Add(cb);
    subClasses.Add(cc);
    foreach(object o in subClasses)
    {
        MethodInfo method =
        (MethodInfo)o.GetType().GetMethod("OnUpdate");
        if(method != null)
        {
            method.Invoke(o, null);
        }
    }
}
```

Once the three classes have been added to an ArrayList, we can use a foreach to look at each object in the ArrayList. MethodInfo method is assigned to something rather tricky. The object o is a boxed look at each item in the ArrayList. In this list, we have subClassA, subClassB, and subClassC. However, we might not know whether they have an OnUpdate () function or not. Therefore, we use (MethodInfo) cast to turn the value into a MethodInfo data type.

To do this, we start with o.GetType() that returns the object's type. This is how we convert the object found in o to its type; otherwise we'd have to use the typeof(type) to get the type's method. Since the type in question can be anything, we can't do this.

If we knew what types to expect, then we'd be able to use an unboxing cast such as the following:

```csharp
if (o is subClassA)
{
    subClassA sc = (subClassA) o;
    sc.OnUpdate ();
}
```

```
if (o is subClassB)
{
    subClassB sc = (subClassB) o;
    sc.OnUpdate ();
}
```

However, we'd need to do this for every class that has the OnUpdate () function. Once a project grows past a few dozen C# files, this isn't a practical solution as there would need to be a check for each and every class you've written. Furthermore, if you forgot a class, then you'd need to add it to this ladder of if statements.

After we get the type from the object o, we use the .GetMethod("OnUpdate"); to check the class for a method called OnUpdate. If the function exists, then method is not null, so we can call it. To call OnUpdate () function, we use method.Invoke(o, null); to invoke the OnUpdate () function now stored in MethodInfo method. The first argument o tells the method.Invoke() function what we're calling the function in, and the null argument tells the method.Invoke() what parameters we're passing to the function. Since the function takes no arguments, we need to pass the function null.

Because subClassC has no function called OnUpdate (), we don't try to invoke it. If we were to simply try o.OnUpdate ();, we'd get an error, simply because on subClassC there is no OnUpdate () function, just a NotUpdate () function.

To a limited effect, the above method is a more simple way to update classes that are not derived from the MonoBehaviour class. When trying to prune down the amount of central processing unit (CPU) time your C# is taking up on a low-end device, this is an important step toward speed improvements. Now we can find fields and methods in each class we write without having to memorize our entire project. This is great if we're working with an already established code base.

We could have used gameObject.BroadcastMessage("OnUpdate");, but this code assumes two things: First, this makes the assumption that the class we're calling is a component of the gameObject, and second the class is inheriting from MonoBehaviour. If the class is not inheriting from MonoBehaviour, then BroadcastMessage won't find the OnUpdate () function.

The only way to know if a class has an OnUpdate () function is to either have read the contents of the class in person, in MonoDevelop with your own eyes, or use type reflection. However, there's so much more we can do. Scrolling through the various options in the pop up that appears after adding the dot before the method, we can see a whole number of function attributes and parameters.

It looks something as simple as the following:

```
MemberInfo[] memberInfos = typeof(subClassA).GetMembers();
foreach(MemberInfo m in memberInfos)
{
    Debug.Log(m.ToString());
}
```

The above fragment reveals all of the functions, fields, and attributes associated with the function and field. It would be quite rewarding to investigate all of the different options on your own. As there are so many things that reflection has to offer, it's impossible to go through too many examples in a single book.

### 8.7.3 What We've Learned

If we modify the foreach loop in the Start () function, we can set the value of any strings we find in a class.

```
void Start ()
{
    ca = new subClassA(1,2,3);
    cb = new subClassB();
    cc = new subClassC();
    FieldInfo[] fields = typeof(subClassA).GetFields();
    foreach(FieldInfo field in fields)
```

```
        {
            Debug.Log(field.Attributes + " " + field.FieldType + " " +
            field.Name);
            if(field.FieldType == typeof(string))
            {
                field.SetValue(ca, "I found a string!");
            }
        }
    }
```

The above code includes the added `ca = new subClassA();` declaration. If we know that we have an object, we can apply some type reflection to what we can see as an example of setting a field in an object. In our check through `typeof(subClassA).GetFields()`, we find three variables: `firstInt`, `secondInt`, and `thirdInt`. Even though `secondInt` isn't actually an `int` but a string, the `field`. `FieldType` knows what it actually is. By checking if `field.FieldType` is a `typeof (string)`, we can use `field.SetValue()` to change the `secondInt` in `ca` to "`I found a string!`"

The power that we have with type reflection is broad and quite encompassing. You should feel a bit like this is a super power, x-ray vision for code. Like any super power, it's to be used wisely and only when necessary. A good use case would be when there are too many different classes where the function is a known name, but there's no common parent function to call.

Likewise if classes share a common field like a life or an armor setting that needs to be modified, using reflection will allow you to find it and make those changes. There are still many new tricks left to discover with reflection.

## 8.8 LINQ

LINQ helps sort through objects and data.

Let's think for a moment about a large-scale game in Unity 3D. If we're doing a large role-playing game, we will want to store a mass of data in either an Excel spreadsheet or an XML. Either of these things will generate a long list of items with respective stats. How then will we need to find and organize the items? One simple method is using LINQ, pronounced "link." LINQ stands for *language-integrated query*, something Microsoft introduced to C# and the .NET Framework several years ago.

### 8.8.1 Lambdas and Arrays

As we had seen earlier in Chapter 7 on `IEnumerator`, we can use the interface with the array. With the upgrade to C# 3.5, we also gained the `System.Linq` library. This is a very powerful library when it comes to finding specific bits of data in an array.

Instead of what might have been a rather tedious manual task of sifting through a scene with a bunch of monsters looking for the ones with the most hit points, you can now use the LINQ library to sift through that data for you.

#### 8.8.1.1 A Basic Example

We'll start with a simple way to find every third number in an array of `ints`. I've assigned a new C# file to the Main Camera in the scene and added the following code to the `Start ()` function. We can follow along in the `Linq` example from the project files.

```
//Use this for initialization
void Start ()
{
    int[] numbers = {0,1,2,3,4,5,6,7,8,9,10};//declare an array
```

```
        //some crazy new Linq stuff...
        var divisibleByThree =
        from n in numbers where (n% 3) == 0 select n;
        //do something with everyThird
        foreach (int i in everyThird)
        {
            Debug.Log(i);
        }
    }
}
```

The above code will produce the following log output when the game is started.

```
        var divisibleByThree =
System.Collections.Generic.List<int> divisibleByThree % 3) == 0 select n).ToList();
```

Whoa, what's going on there?

## 8.8.2 Var

The System.Linq library introduces some new keywords we're going to get to know. Let's take a look at the crazy new Linq stuff. The first word var is not necessarily specific to Linq, but it's quite useful for dealing with the type of data that Linq will return.

If we look at the variable we created called divisibleByThree, we'll see that it's an ArrayList of int values. Though the var can be different everywhere, it's used in your code as the type is assigned dynamically depending on how it's used. For instance, if we create a few different things assigned to var, we can see how MonoDevelop sees the types being assigned to var.

```
        var aThingHere = 9;
        var anotherThingThere = (object)9;
        var aDifferentThing = (float)9;
```

```
    int[] numbers = {0,1,2,3,4,5,6,7,8,9,10};
    var aThingHere = 9;
    var  int aThingHere  gThere = (object)9;
    var              hing = (float)9;
```

```
    int[] numbers = {0,1,2,3,4,5,6,7,8,9,10};
    var aThingHere = 9;
    var anotherThingThere = (object)9;
    var  object anotherThingThere  (float)9;
```

```
    int[] numbers = {0,1,2,3,4,5,6,7,8,9,10};
    var aThingHere = 9;
    var anotherThingThere = (object)9;
    var aDifferentThing = (float)9;
        float aDifferentThing
    var  divisibleByThree  =
```

The first is seen as int, the second as an object, and the third as a float. The var type is fine with any type of assignment, even arrays. So the var's type is assigned based on the value it is assigned. In the statement var divisibleByThree = from n in numbers where (n% 3) == 0; var becomes an array of int values.

## 8.8.3 LINQ From

We can break this down into the following statement: from n in numbers where we've seen a similar use with a foreach statement. The foreach statement uses foreach(int i in numbers), so we've seen the in keyword before. After the word from, LINQ expects to see an identifier; in this case, we used n to identify a variable. This becomes the variable that holds an individual object in the numbers array declared at the beginning of the Start () function.

Then we get into where (n% 3) == 0, which is a conditional operation on the n variable. The result of where should be either true or false. When it returns true, the last part of the statement select n; assigns the n to the divisibleByThree var declared at the beginning of the statement. Because we're selecting multiple things, var has its type automatically set to an array.

To be more informative, we'll add more detail to the operation of the LINQ expression.

First in our new Linq class, we'll add in a nested class called Zombie.

```
public class Zombie
{
    //a place to hold hitPoints
    public int hitPoints;
    //the class constructor
    public Zombie()
    {
        //assign a random number between 1 and 100
        this.hitPoints = Random.Range(1, 100);
    }
}
```

We'll even give the zombie some hit points that will be randomly assigned between 1 and 100 when a new Zombie is instanced. Then in our Start () function, we'll create an array of them and then instance new zombies into the array with the following block of code:

```
Zombie[] zombies = new Zombie[100];
for (int i = 0; i < 100; i++)
{
    zombies[i] = new Zombie();
}
```

After the array is populated with some Zombie objects, we'll make an array of them, the hit points of which are less than 50, with the following LINQ expression.

```
var weakZombies = from z in zombies where z.hitPoints < 50 select z;
```

Then to prove that we've got a list of zombies with less than 50 hit points, we'll print out the hitPoints of each zombie in the new weakZombies var.

```
foreach(Zombie z in weakZombies)
{
    Debug.Log(z.hitPoints);
}
```

From this little exercise, we'll get the following output to the Console panel.

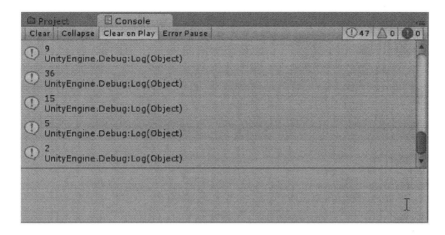

The multitude of tricks you can deploy using LINQ can fill a book on its own. When dealing with a large number of different objects to sort through, LINQ is often the most flexible option. Another bonus is that it's quite fast. Implementing various tricks to sort and find data was done by a large team of experienced developers.

### 8.8.4 Strange Behaviors in LINQ

When a LINQ query is created, it's not immediately executed. We can take a look at the numbers array that we started with and observe some interesting behaviors by adding to the list after the linq statement is used.

```
//Use this for initialization
void Start () {
    int[] numbers = {0,1,2,3,4,5,6,7,8,9,10};//declare an array
    //some crazy new linq stuff...
    var divisibleByThree = from n in numbers where (n% 3) == 0 select n;
    numbers[0] = 1;
    numbers[3] = 1;
    numbers[6] = 1;
    numbers[9] = 1;
    //do something with divisibleByThree
    foreach(int i in divisibleByThree)
    {
        Debug.Log(i);
    }
}
```

After the divisibleByThree Linq query is created, we can change the numbers in the array to something which isn't divisible by 3. This is done after the array is created and after the statement divisibleByThree is written. It's only when the foreach statement uses the var from the linq statement the actual query is made.

The above code prints out nothing since in the array there are no numbers left to divide by 3. It's important to keep this in mind when using LINQ; this can lead to strange bugs if you're not aware of what's going on here.

### 8.8.5 Greedy Operator

The LINQ statements offer additional functionality through the dot operator. Some of the functions force the data type returned by a LINQ statement into a specific type. These are called Greedy Operators.

```
var divisibleByThree = (from n in numbers where (n% 3) == 0 select n).ToList();
```

We can avoid the strange behaviors by converting the query into a list by using what is called a greedy operator. If we encapsulate the `Linq` statement in () and add.`ToList` () afterward, we can force the `Linq` statement to fulfill the `var` into a list.

This tells us that the `divisibleByThree` query is set before the `numbers` array is modified. This becomes a very important change to the operation of this query. The `var` type is important to the query, but not to how it's used. Because `var` is flexible, we don't have to figure out what we're getting back from the query.

### 8.8.6 What We've Learned

The LINQ library is a power tool made available through `System.Linq`. For sorting through and finding bits of information, we are able to use LINQ to find and use data quickly and easily. Rather than using `for` loops and complex `foreach` loops for inspecting each object in an array, we're better able to use LINQ to find what we're looking for.

Practically any data type can be sorted out with a LINQ expression, even if it's a list of zombies, weapons or colors. A LINQ expression can use an external function to provide additional logic. In the following fragment, the LINQ statement uses a function `moduloThree()` to fulfill the LINQ condition.

```
public int moduloThree(int n)
{
      return n% 3;
}
var divisibleByThree = (from n in numbers where (moduloThree(n)) == 0 select
n).ToList();
```

We're even able to put functions into the LINQ expression that gives us even a better control over the logic used to find the data we're looking for. Once you see how the LINQ expression is used, it's important to remember the notation. When you see it again, you'll be able to use these expressions to understand what's going on and how it's being used.

## 8.9 Bitwise Operators

In school when you are taught to count, you're learning the decimal system. The decimal system is a base-10 numeral system, but there are many other systems as well. Your computer uses binary or a base-2 numeral system. The transistors in your computer have only two states; they are either on or off. To be more technically correct, they are in either a charged state or a ground state.

Manipulating individual bits seems a bit low level for the common game-building tasks, but it seems that once you get the hang of flipping individual bits, they can be used for many different tricks. Going back to the basics, we'll review a bit about how numbers are stored in the computer's memory.

A byte is a collection of eight 1s and 0s. Therefore, the binary 0000 0000 represents the decimal 0. The binary representation is what is stored in the computer's memory. A decimal 1 is stored as binary 0000 0001, and a computer represents decimal 2 as 0000 0010. The second place is actually a decimal 2. More interestingly, decimal 128 is binary 1000 0000.

### 8.9.1 Big Endian and Little Endian

The arrangement of the digits we're looking at is called little endian. The name comes from the position in the line of 1s and 0s where the biggest value is stored. Since the lowest value is stored at the end, the far right, it's called little endian. If we were to represent 128 as 0000 0001, then we're looking at a big endian number.

Each digit is a value of a power of 2. The first number is either 0 or 1; that is to say, the first value is either 0 or 2 to the power of 0. The second digit is either 0 or 2 to the power of 1, which is 2. The third digit is 0 or 2 to the power of 2, which is 4. The pattern repeats for each digit in the binary number.

To explain we can take a look at how binary actually works and consider what the 1s and 0s actually represent. Because binary is made up of 1s and 0s, each one represents a power of 2. So, 1, 2, 4, 8, and then 16, 32, 64, 128 are what each digit in a byte actually means. With these we're able to represent each number between 0 and 255.

As a simplified example, we'll look at a 2-bit number. To count to 3, we'd start with 00, 10, 01, and then 11. The first digit is 0 or 1 followed by 0 or 2. To count 0, we use 00. The combination 10 counts 1. To count to 2, we use 01. Last, the number 3 is indicated with a 10 and a 01, added together as 11. If you add 1 and 2, you get 3. This is how your computer counts.

### 8.9.2 Signed or Unsigned

The same system as above works for a byte that is eight 1s and 0s. An int stores 32 1s and 0s, but there's a catch. The words signed and unsigned indicate if a number is allowed to have negative values. If the number is signed, then you lose a bit to indicate a plus + or minus − sign; though you don't usually see a plus + symbol in front of a positive number, it is inferred.

To go back to our 2-bit number, we'd only be able to count to three values again. To begin we can start with 10 that would translate into −1. When the first bit represents a value, the second bit indicates a sign.

We can use 00 to indicate a 0 and 11 to indicate a +1. We still have three usable values: −1, 0, and +1. Whether or not a bit is used to indicate a plus + or minus − sign is called signed or unsigned. When we have only positive values, we consider that an unsigned number; if we can show both positive and negative numbers, programmers call this signed.

A signed byte or an sbyte is a number from −128 to +127. An int is a number between −2,147,483,648 and 2,147,483,647. Notice that the number reaches one more negative than positive; we will see why in a moment. A uint or an unsigned int is a number from 0 to 4,294,967,295. To get these numbers, the last digit is the only one that is considered negative.

In terms of the byte, consider the following: 1000 0000 is simply −128 where the rest of the digits are 0. To count back up as start filling in 1s like normal till we reach 1111 1111, which is −128 + 64 + 32 + 16 + 8 + 4 + 2 + 1, which sums to −1. Adding one more resets the byte to 0000 0000, which is 0. This is why we can always count one more negative than positive.

So the regular math operators work as we'd expect, but we get an interesting behavior when we reach the limit of these numbers.

```
void Start ()
{
    int a = 2147483647;
    int b = 1;
    int c = a + b;
    Debug.Log(c);
}
```

Normally, you might expect c to print out 2147483648; however, we get the following output:

```
-2147483648
UnityEngine.Debug:Log(Object)
BitwiseOperators:Start () (at Assets/BitwiseOperators.cs:18)
```

The result −2147483648 is a negative number, but why is this? To clarify, we might use a uint to make more clear what's happening.

```
uint a = 4294967295;
uint b = 1;
uint c = a + b;
Debug.Log(c);
```

This results with 0. When a is assigned, you can imagine 32 1s filling up the 32-bit number. When we add 1, they're rolled over and the result turns into 32 0s instead. Therefore, the numbers in the computer, because they are binary, act weird. This is a simple awkward fact of computing. In a small example, rather than looking at 32 numbers, we'll look at just a few digits.

A 4-bit number, 0000, sometimes called a nibble, starts off as a collection of four digits. If we add 1, we get the following result 0001, which is then pushed to the left; when we add another 1, we get 0010 to get 2. Remember that the second digit is $2^1$.

Adding another 1, we get 0011 to get $1 + 2$ or $2^0 + 2^1$, so we have 3. By adding another 1, we get 0100; the first two numbers are reset and the 1 is pushed to the left again, so we have 4. Adding another 1, we get 0101 to get $1 + 4$. To continue we add another 1 and we get 0110; then we add another 1 and we get 0111 or $1 + 2 + 4$ to get 7.

Finally, by adding another 1, we get 1000, which is the last digit for 8. The process continues until we have 1111, and following the pattern of adding another 1 will push the 1 to the right, but there's no space left, so we get 0000. The 4-bit number has rolled over. With a 4-bit number, we get a range from 0 to 15. If we have a signed 4-bit number, we get a range from −8 to 7.

This whole business of counting with $2^0 + 2^1 + 2^2 + \ldots$ was invented in 1679. A mathematician named Gottfried Wilhelm von Leibniz concocted the system. He also happened to invent calculus, so if you're having trouble in math class, you can blame Gottfried.

Though without him we wouldn't have computers. After he created the system, he said, "When numbers are reduced to 0 and 1, a beautiful order prevails everywhere." Indeed, computers have led to many beautiful things.

The system works for larger numbers. In the case of a 32-bit number, we'd be counting till we hit the 4294967296 number before we roll the number. When we use a signed number, we lose either the first or last digit to store the sign, either + or −. Technically, it's a 31-bit number with a sign whose range is either $+2^{31}(-1$ for holding a 0) or $-2^{31}$, which means 2147483647 to −2147483648. Even though computers are limited by the bits per number, we can work with this, so long as we keep these limitations in mind.

### 8.9.3 Bitwise Or |

The bitwise operators |, &, ^, and ~ are used to manipulate numbers on the bit level rather than on the math level where we assume $1 + 2 = 3$. We can also use $1 | 2 = 3$, though this is not working in the way you might think it is. The or operator | is used to merge bits together. Looking at the previous 4-bit number, we can use the following notation:

```
1001//9
|1010//10
= 1011//11
```

Or in C# we can use the following notation:

```
uint a = 5;//1 + 4
uint b = 6;//2 + 4
uint c = a | b;
Debug.Log(c);//1+2+4
```

The above example looks at the 1s, and if either bit is 1, then the resulting bit is set to 1. If both numbers are 1s, then the final result is only another 1. Therefore, in the above example, we get the result 7, not 11 as you might imagine.

At first glance, we might not immediately see the advantage of using numbers by the bits that they are made of. However, programmers like to think in strange ways, and to learn how to write code is to learn how to think like a programmer, which is never an easy task.

### 8.9.4 Enums and Numbers

Should we use an enum, we can set each value to a number.

```
enum characterClass
{
    farmer = 0,
    fighter = 1,
    thief = 2,
    wizard = 4,
    archer = 8
}
```

If we use the above enum, you can see some assignments to number values. You should also notice that they are being assigned the same values that are used when counting in binary. Therefore, if 0000 is a farmer, then 0001 is a fighter. This means 0010 is a thief, 0100 is a wizard, and 1000 is the archer. What should happen if we want to have a multiclass character who is a fighter wizard?

```
public enum characterClass
{
    farmer = 0,
    fighter = 1,
    thief = 2,
    wizard = 4,
    archer = 8
}
//Use this for initialization
void Start ()
{
    characterClass classA = characterClass.fighter;
    characterClass classB = characterClass.wizard;
    characterClass multiclass = classA | classB;
}
```

Therefore, we can use the code multiclass = classA | classB; to merge both values into the enum. Hidden on the inside of the multiclass value is a 0101 from using 0001 | 0100 to combine the bits. This might seem strange, since the result is actually 5, and there is nothing actually assigned to the number 5. However, that's assuming we're using the enums as numbers, not bits, or in this case, we're using them as flags.

### 8.9.5 Bitwise And &

To find out which bits are in use, we use the and bitwise operator &. Therefore, to see if the bits match up, we can use the & operator to compare two sets of bits.

```
 1001
&0101
= 0001
```

The above notation returns a 1 only when bits in both values match 1. There is only one condition where the & operator will return a 1; this works like a key filtering out everything but the bits that match. To use this to check what classes our character is, we can use the following fragment:

```
characterClass classA = characterClass.fighter;
characterClass classB = characterClass.wizard;
characterClass multiclass = classA | classB;
//check if multiclass has fighter
characterClass f = multiclass & characterClass.fighter;
//check if multiclass has wizard
characterClass w = multiclass & characterClass.wizard;
bool isFighter = f == characterClass.fighter;
bool isWizard = w == characterClass.wizard;
Debug.Log("chass is fighter? " + isFighter + " class is wizard? " +
isWizard);
```

In the above code, the use of `characterClass f` returns a value based on whether or not multi-class `& characterClass.fighter` has any overlapping 1s. Therefore, if `multiclass` is 1010 and `fighter` is 1000, then we get 1000, so `characterClass f` is assigned 1000 or 1. When we compare `f == characterClass.fighter`, `isFighter` is assigned true. The same goes for the wizard comparison where we compare `multiclass` 1010 `& 0010 characterClass.wizard`, where the result 0010 is assigned to w.

By using | to assign bits and & to check for bits, we can use an enum to store more than one value, but again this works only if we specifically assign power of 2 values to the enum.

### 8.9.6 Bitwise Exclusive Or ^ (xor)

We can also see which bits are mismatching.

```
int a = 5;//1001 1 + 4
int b = 6;//^0101 2 + 4
    //= 1100 1 + 2
int c = a ^ b;
Debug.Log(c);
```

The ^ operator in the above code fragment shows us where two sets of bits misalign. The 0s are ignored, but if there are 1s, then we take action. In this case, we get the first and second bits mismatching. The following bits are the same, so they are left at 0.

To go back to the enum we were just using, we have a multiclass fighter and wizard, but how do we take the fighter out from the enum? This is what the xor operator is for. Multiclass is a combination of the bits from the fighter and the bits from the wizard. The fighter was 0001 and the wizard was 0100, so multiclass is 0101. To remove the wizard, we want to end up with 0001 again.

```
int fi = 1; //0001
int wi = 4; //0100
int fiwi = fi | wi;//0101
Debug.Log(fiwi ^ wi);//0001
```

Therefore, `int fi = 1;` is the same as the `int` assigned to the fighter, and wi is 4, the `int` for the wizard enum. Using `fi | wi`, we get 0101 or 5 and assign that to `fiwi` or a fighter wizard. To remove the bits in use for wi from `fiwi`, we use `fiwi ^ wi`; the final result is 1, and so far as our enum is concerned, the fighter.

From the previous example, our code will look like the following:

```
characterClass classC = multiclass ^ characterClass.fighter;
Debug.Log(classC);
```

To add bits we use the or operator |, to check for bits we use the and operator &, and to remove bits we use the exclusive or operator ^. In the above case, we'll be looking at classC and we get fighter sent to the Console. This works with any number of classes.

```
characterClass classA = characterClass.fighter;
characterClass classB = characterClass.wizard;
characterClass classC = characterClass.thief;
characterClass multiclass = classA | classB | classC;
```

The | operator is able to compound as many values as there are bits to work with. With the above code, the multiclass is now a fighter, a wizard, or a thief. To check which of these classes multiclass is, we use the same statement as we did earlier. To check if multiclass contains the bits required to be a thief, we use the same statement:

```
characterClass t = multiclass & characterClass.thief;
```

and t is indeed a thief.

```
bool isThief = t == characterClass.thief;
```

Therefore, isThief in this case is true. However, now we're starting to repeat ourselves, and as any programmer should do, we should make our lives easier by writing a function to do all of this stuff for us. So where do we start? Logically, we'll want to begin with the same processes. We started with adding bits to a value, so we should start there.

### 8.9.7 Setting Bitwise Flags

After assigning a characterClass, it's time to add one. The enum isn't something we can extend, so we'll want to use something like addClass(my current class, class im adding) that would look like the following:

```
public characterClass addClass(characterClass a, characterClass b)
{
    return a | b;
}
```

So we have something like the following:

```
characterClass newbie = characterClass.farmer;
newbie = addClass(newbie, characterClass.wizard);
```

Now newbie is a wizard. To extend to a second class, we'd use the following.

```
newbie = addClass(newbie, characterClass.archer);
```

By using newbie in the addClass() function, we're adding a second value to the newbie enum. To remove a class, we'll want to do something similar.

```
public characterClass removeClass(characterClass a, characterClass b)
{
    return a ^ b;
}
```

This means that if we use removeClass(newbie, characterClass.archer);, we'll take the archer flags back out.

Of course, we could use a bool to check if a class contains a value with the following function:

```
public bool containsClass(characterClass a, characterClass b)
{
    return (a & b) == b;
}
```

This simply checks if the flag is present, and if it is then our return is true; otherwise it's false. This can be used to check if a character, given its characterClass, can be allowed to fire a bow or pick a lock. This changes the nature of the enum that is usually intended to be fixed at a single value. Of course, it would be easy to store these as boolean values, but where's the fun in that?

### 8.9.8 Bitwise Shortcuts | = and ^ =

When assigning these enums, we can shorten some of the assignments by using the same operators. If we want to assign a = a | b;, we can use a | = b;. You can imagine that this is similar to a = a + b; and a += b; from Section 5.6. The same goes for a = a ^ b;, which can be replaced with a ^= b;.

### 8.9.9 Bits in Numbers

Remember that we're still dealing with numbers, not just bits. Being numbers we can use this to check for odd or even numbers with a simple & operator. Odd numbers always have a 1 in them, but even numbers do not. What does that mean? We can use bool even = (number & 1) == 0 ? true : false; to check if a value is odd or even.

```
int number = 758;
bool even = (number & 1) == 0 ? true : false;
Debug.Log(even);
```

This returns true, quick and easy. In addition, performing checks like this happens very quickly on most CPUs. We'll want to keep this in mind for some later math tricks in C#.

### 8.9.10 Bit Shifting >> and <<

Our enum was written in the form farmer = 0, fighter = 1, through archer = 8, and so on. However, if you had many different classes, we might easily miscalculate one of the numbers. Off the cuff, it's not too easy to remember what 37^2 is; your higher numbers turn into rather difficult to remember the power of two values. Therefore, again bitwise operators can help here as well. We can add the >> and the << between numbers to indicate a movement of bits.

```
public enum characterClass{
    farmer = 0,
    fighter = 1<<0,//1
    thief = 1<<1,//2
    wizard = 1<<2,//4
    archer = 1<<3 //8
}
```

The above code is simply numbered 0–3, and if we need a fifth class, we simply add monk = 1<<4 at the end. What does the << do? It's taking the value of 1 and moving it over to the right the number of digits indicated by the number following the operator. Therefore, in the bits we start off as 1000, which is 1. Then if we look at fighter, we shift the bits 0 places, and we still get 1.

```
public enum characterClass{
    farmer = 0,//correct
    fighter = 1<<0,//1
    thief = 1<<1,//2
    wizard = 1<<2,//4
    archer = 1<<3,//8
    monk = 1<<4,//16
}
```

The opposite works in a similar way: 0011 or 3 turns into something else altogether when shifted one space. Looking at 3 or 0011 << 1 = 0110, which is 6. Then, 6 << 1 = 12 or 1100, so there is a pattern! This is the same as multiplying by 2—altogether another useful math operation that can be done by shifting bits!

Of course, we're just looking at the little end of the value range of a 32-bit `int`; it's just more simple than writing out 0000 0000 0000 0000 0000 0000 0000 1100 to show 12. Shifting the numbers << can happen many times before we run out of digits.

### 8.9.11 What We've Learned

Computers do math in a unique way, different from what we are accustomed to. Thinking in 1s and 0s requires a fundamental restart in learning how to do math. Multiplication, addition, subtraction, and even counting require a whole unique system.

Some of these systems have effects outside of math. Using the binary system as a collection of flags or using them as enums allows for a greater ability to control a breadth of information in a single value. A 64-bit integer allows for 64 unique boolean values to be stored.

## 8.10 Bitwise Math

The strange thing about bits is that they are numbers that operate with a system aside from what we've been taught in your usual math class. If you wanted to make 10 into –10, you might normally think to simply multiply 10 by –1. However, the usual tricks don't work in the context of the computer's binary world.

Remember what happens when we add 1 to a number at the limit of the binary range. For a nibble, that would be 1111 or 15. However, the nibble we're looking at is unsigned, or rather the four digits are all used for counting. Should we use a signed nibble, or perhaps a snibble, our limit would be either –8 or 7, which is either 1000 or 0111.

The interesting fact going on with the nibble is that it's a range from 0 to 15, which is 16 values, or $2^4$. This is called a hexadecimal. You come across this term fairly often when making colors for a web page.

When we're taught to count, we use 10 different characters, 0 through 9. To count to 10, we add another digit to fill in the 10s' place. When we count past 99, we add another digit for hundreds, and so on. When computers count, they use 16, or a nibble; to represent this, we use a few letters to fill in the extra six characters.

To count like a computer, we use the sequence 0, 1, 2, 3, 4, 5, 6, 7, 8, 9, a, b, c, d, e, f, before getting to another digit. For the computer to count from 0 to 255, it uses eight binary digits, but if we use two nibbles we can represent that with two digits. This is actually two nibbles, not one nibble, or a nibble. A nibble is a specific number of bits in a computer's memory. This can tell the computer that 1 in decimal is 01 in hexadecimal, and ff is 255 in hexadecimal.

```
byte b = 0xff;
Debug.Log(b);
```

The above code prints 255 to the Console panel in Unity. Here the prefix 0x informs C# that we are representing a byte followed by two digits in hexadecimal. This can be considered easier to read than byte b = 11111111;. If we want to use a signed byte or an sbyte, we can represent negative numbers with the following:

```
sbyte b = -0x80;
Debug.Log(b);
```

This prints out -128 in the Unity's Console panel. If we try to assign a value outside of the range of the sbyte, we get an error reminding us that we can't assign 255 to an sbyte. However, after a valid assignment, anything can happen.

```
sbyte b = -0x80;
b-;
Debug.Log(b);
```

If we subtract 1 from -0x80, we get a 127 printed to the Unity's Console panel, not -129. Again, we roll numbers even though we're using a different notation. The difference in notation hasn't changed the nature of how the data is stored or calculated.

### 8.10.1  Two's Complement

To change an `int` from 10 to -10 using binary operations, we use a method known as two's complement. If we wanted to use multiplication, we could go that route; however, by using a bitwise operation, we can speed up the process. Starting with a value, say an `int` -1 that would look like binary 1111 1111 or

```
int n = -0x01;
```

We can use the complement bitwise operator ~ to flip the bits. Therefore, if we look at the important bits, we'll have 0000 0000;, which turns into decimal 0.

```
int n = -0x10;
int p = ~n;
Debug.Log("before: " + n + " after: " + p);
```

The code fragment produces the following output:

```
before: -1 after: 0
```

Therefore, to get the correct value, add 1 to ~n and assign that to p.

```
int n = -0x10;
int p = ~n+1;
Debug.Log("before: " + n + " after: " + p);
```

This prints out the following:

```
before: -1 after: 1
```

And we get the same as if we had used `int p = -n;` on the value. So why do things this way? In short, bitwise operations are faster. When performance becomes an issue, bitwise operations are the closest thing we can use in C# to talk to the computer's hardware. In a way, we're using the native instructions that the CPU already uses. Because of this near one-to-one translation from your code to computer instructions, bitwise operations can be faster in some situations.

### 8.10.2  Unary Operator ~

The unary operator ~ works on `int` values, and if you use `byte b = 0x01;`, then ~b; C# will automatically upcast the `byte` to an `int` before performing the operation. In general, the `int` is the more universal of the different integer numbers used in C#.

Aside from the casting implications of using the ~ operator, this operator does an interesting trick. If we have 0001, the ~ operator applied to this nibble gives us 1110. This two's complement is used for many different things, including addition.

### 8.10.3  Bitwise Addition and Subtraction

The computer's CPU actually has no + and – circuits built into it. It's actually a collection of these bitwise operators. Because of this reason, it's an interesting exercise to understand what it's actually doing when you do something simple like 7 + 3.

Looking at the nibble again, we have the decimal 7 represented as `0111` and 3 being `0011`; adding these together makes the bits look like `1010` or `10`. There isn't a direct process by which `0111` and `0011` can be added together in one operation. To add we need to move bits from one number into the other.

```
int a = 7;
int b = 3;
int c = a & b;
int r = a ^ b;
while(c != 0)
{
    int s = c << 1;
    c = r & s;
    r = r ^ s;
}
Debug.Log(r);
```

`while (c != 0)`, we are done taking all of the bits from the carry `c` and adding them to the result `r`. A breakdown of the code, one line at a time, shows what's happening to the bits and their decimal values. There are only three significant lines we need to observe. The first line is just a temporary storage of `a` for clarity.

The loop begins by finding all of the digits that match. This loop will tell us which digits need to be carried over. The carried-over digits are the ones where 1s appear in both numbers. So `a & b` shows us where 1s appear in both numbers, and we get `0111 & 0011 = 0011`. After this we need to find where the digits are mismatched with `0111 ^ 0011 = 0100`.

In the first line where we begin adding the numbers, we start with a shifted digit.

```
int s = c << 1;
// 0011
// <<1
//s = 0110
```

We move the digits over by one space and find the next digit to carry over.

```
c = r & s;
// 0100
//&0110
//c = 0100
```

After shifting the digit and finding the one that needs to be carried over, we need to reassign `r` to the next digit to carry.

```
r = r ^ s;
// 0100
//^0110
//r = 0010
```

We've reduced the number of carry digits by 1. However, we still have one digit to merge in, so we go back to the beginning of the loop.

```
int s = c << 1;
// 0100
// <<1
//s = 1000
```

We have a digit carried over from the previous loop that needs to be merged back into the result. But we need to check whether there are any digits overlapping to check if we need to do the loop again.

```
c = r & s;
// 0010
//&1000
//c = 0000
```

Here we see that `0010 & 1000` has no overlapping digits. Therefore, we can merge to our final result.

```
r = r ^ s;
// 0010
//^1000
//r = 1010
```

Now our result is a correct merging of `0010` and `1000`, which is `10`. Inside the computer's CPU, there is a section of circuits called an adder that does the same thing. When you have a computer running several billion operations per second, this operation happens incredibly fast. However, if you need to do this operation a hundred million times, then you'll see a performance difference between this operation and perhaps a more complex operation.

To turn the above code into a function, we'll use the following:

```
int BitwiseAdd(int a, int b)
{
    int c = a & b;
    int r = a ^ b;
    while(c != 0)
    {
        int s = c << 1;        //shift digits to add
        c = r & s;             //find overlapping digits
        r = r ^ s;             //merge digits that don't overlap
    }
    return r;
}
```

Subtraction is actually an addition with a negative number. To get the negative number, we use the previous two's complement. So in the case of

```
int a = 7;
int b = 3;
int c = BitwiseSubtract(a, b);
```

Subtraction involves flipping the b into a negative number using two's complement and then adding them together. To use this feature, we can simply reuse the `BitwiseAdd()` function a couple of times; the first one is basically two's complement without using a `+ 1` to get the negative version of b, and then we use `BitwiseAdd()` again to get a result.

```
int BitwiseSub(int a, int b)
{
    b = BitwiseAdd(~b, 1);
    return BitwiseAdd(a, b);
}
```

## 8.10.4 Bitwise Multiplication

The bitshift operators can be used to multiply by 2: `4 << 1 = 8` or `0100 << 1 = 1000`; this is rather handy when finding a specific half or double of a value. However, when multiplying, we need to do something similar to that of addition. We need to find out how many times we can multiply by 2, and then to an odd number we add the last number. So in the case of 7 * 3, we use (7*2) + 7; the code that can do this operation is shown below.

```
int BitwiseMultiplication(int a, int b)
{
    int r = 0;
    while (b != 0)
    {
        if ((b & 1) != 0)
        {
            r = BitwiseAdd(r, a);
        }
        a = a << 1;
        if (b == 0)
        {
            r = a;
            break;
        }
        b = b >> 1;
    }
    return r;
}
```

The above code shifts a << 1 for each multiple of 2 we find in b. Each time b is shifted >> 1, it's moved toward 0. When we check if b is odd using (b & 1) != 0, we add to int r whatever is at int a before it's shifted again. When we're done shifting and thus done multiplying by 2, our while loop exits and we're done.

Division can be simplified to the number of times b can be subtracted from a.

```
int BitwiseDiv(int a, int b)
{
    int divideStart = a;
    int timesDivided = 1;
    while(true)
    {
        divideStart = BitwiseSub(divideStart, b);
        if(divideStart <= 0)
            break;
        timesDivided = BitwiseAdd(timesDivided, 1);
    }
    return timesDivided;
}
```

The above code is a very simple version of an integer division solution using our BitwiseAdd() and BitwiseSub() functions. Multiplication can also be a simple addition of a to a by b times. Though not as efficient as the system used in the multiplication function, the division system is a very rudimentary example of how the most basic bitwise operators can be used to do mundane math functions. The problem with an integer is that you're not allowed any fractions, so division will end up with an incorrect value unless a is evenly divided by b.

### 8.10.5 Bitwise Tricks

One simple task now is that we know how bits work on a more fundamental level; we can use them to our advantage to perform quick operations. Rather than checking if an int is odd or even by using n%2 == 0, we can use the faster n & 1 == 1 to check for an odd number. We can tell if a number is negative using a bit; if (someNumber & (1<<31)) != 0, then we have a positive number. This checks for the last digit, which is at 1<<31 and looks to see if it's a 1 or a 0. If it's 1, then it's negative; otherwise it's positive.

Not all of these tricks are necessarily faster than using more regular math functions. We can check the 1<<31th bit. But perhaps it's just easier to check if someNumber > 0 to see if it's positive or not. However, knowing how bits work is pretty interesting.

If you need to know whether two values are both negative, both positive, or different, then you can check with the following:

```
int a = 20;
int b = 1;
bool same = ((a ^ b) > 0);
Debug.Log(same);
```

If a and b are positive, the same is true; otherwise if a and b are different signs, then the same is false. This condition works only when the bit at 1 holds a sign for positive or negative. Simple tricks like this can be used in various situations.

The following function will help with the above examples by printing out each digit.

```
string bitsToString(int number, int digits)
{
    char[] binary = new char[digits];
    int digit = digits-1;
    int place = 0;
    while (place < digits)
    {
        int d = number & (1 << place);
        if (d != 0)
        {
            binary[digit] = '1';
        }
        else
        {
            binary[digit] = '0';
        }
        digit- ;
        place++;
    }
    return new string(binary);
}
```

The above code uses int d, which is a check for a 1 or a 0 at the place in the given number. Each iteration of the while loop increments the place and decrements which digit we're looking at. If d is 0, then we add a 0 to the char[] array; otherwise we add a 1. With the above code, we can check out the first 4 bits or all 32 bits of an int.

## 8.10.6 What We've Learned

These tutorials got into quite low-level concepts. Finding practical game play applications for these concepts may not be readily evident. However, the concepts do provide an important foundation for your understanding of C#.

The ability to create complex algorithms means being able to create more complex and more interesting game play scenarios. Adding in various logical parameters and making use of them in creative ways means providing more interesting puzzles.

Outside of games, many of these concepts are also useful for processing data. A modern game requires many different tasks, from collecting and analyzing data from users to sorting through databases to building leader boards.

## 8.11 Attributes

When working with the editor, we are able to add new menu items, windows, and other useful tools for helping with the level design. Many of the new menu items are done through Unity 3D-specific attributes. Attributes is another layer added to the C# language that augment how the code is read by the computer.

Attributes in some ways look out of place; like preprocessor directives, they have their own set of rules and uses. They use the square brackets [] to indicate their use and function. Attributes allow your code to read additional information about your code. Reflection occurs when your code is able to look up additional information on a function or type. This includes any field in a class as well as any function or the class itself.

Often in Unity 3D we use [Serializable] to indicate a field or value which you want to have saved by the game. For instance, you've created custom data structures and other public settings that show up in the editor; normally any form of plain old data (POD) will be automatically serialized. However, in times where you've written your own data, you need to tell Unity 3D that your new data types must also be serialized to be saved.

In many cases, you might be getting used to using a struct or class to store a complex assortment of different types of data. This is fine; however, it's better to consider using a class to hold data rather than a struct.

This serves two purposes: first, you're better able to handle data coming in and going out of each variable, and second, you're able to use the class in Unity 3D as a clever container for your variables which you can edit in the Inspector panel.

### 8.11.1 A Basic Example

We'll need to add the using System; directive to start. This will give us the [Serializable] attribute for use in the editor. Our code will start off like the following:

```
using System;
using UnityEngine;
using System.Collections;
public class Attributes : MonoBehaviour
{
    public class nestedClass
    {
        public int myInt;
    }
    public nestedClass MyNestedClass;
}
```

This gives us a simple public class nestedClass{} to which we'll add a solitary field. The public int myInt will serve as our basic example of serialization. After this we'll add in a public nestedClass MyNestedClass where we can hold some data we just set up in nestedClass. If you look into the editor's Inspector panel, you'll notice that there is nothing in the panel where we're able to set any values.

To get the `MyNestedClass` to show up, we simply add a single attribute to the class.

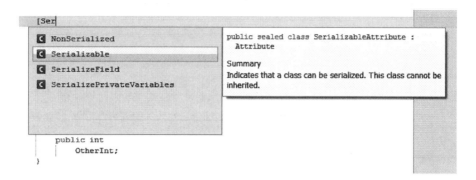

As we begin to type in the word `Serializable`, MonoDevelop prompts us with `SerializableAttribute`; this leaves us with the following:

```
[Serializable]
public class nestedClass
{
    public int myInt;
}
```

After the `Serializable` attribute was added to the `nestedClass`, the member `myInt` variable becomes visible under the `MyNestedClass` object in the Unity 3D Inspector panel. The result in the editor is our new `NestedClass`, which is now available in the editor:

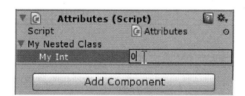

Adding the `Serializable` attribute makes the data stored inside of the class savable. That is to say, once we make changes to the values in the serialized class, the editor can save them with the scene. The attribute tells Unity 3D to look at the class as a chunk of information which it needs to both expose to the Inspector panel and save with the scene.

The other attributes that `System` gives us are also useful for different reasons.

Should we add an `int` to the class outside of the nested class, we'd get what you'd normally expect to see in the Inspector panel.

```
public int PlainOldInt;
```

This shows up as an `int` value in the editor as we have seen earlier.

However, we can add an attribute to keep this out of the editor but also maintain the variable's public accessor setting.

```
[NonSerialized]
public int PlainOldInt;
```

Adding the attribute magically hides the value from the Inspector panel. This has two effects: first, any values assigned to the Plain Old Int variable will not be saved with the scene, and second, the value cannot be set from the editor. The variable still acts as any normal public int, only that we're not able to manipulate it from within the editor.

### 8.11.2  Custom Attributes

Beginning with a simple scenario, we can imagine that you have a main game class that handles the bulk of the behaviors and record keeping in your game. As new objects are added to a scene, it's often useful to know whether a class has a specific function or not. When we get away from using MonoBehaviour to decrease our dependency on Update (), we need a new system to keep our classes updated.

C# allows us to add a label to a function to apply additional information to each function. Once a function is labeled, another class is able to inspect a different class and find labeled functions. Once found, a function's attributes can be inspected and proper adjustments can be made to use it.

An attribute is a tag which classes can add to functions. We've used an attribute before called [Serializable], which tells Unity 3D that the variable function or class has information that needs to be saved. Then Unity 3D inspects different members of a class to keep track of what needs to be saved.

```
[serializable]
int number = 0;
```

The concept of a class being able to collect information on another object is called reflection. When using the System.Reflection class, an object is allowed to inspect another class or struct in depth. When you write code, you're able to actually look at and see another object before using it.

By reading a function like int AddInts(int a, int b);, you're able to understand that it's a function with two arguments and an int return type. Reflection gives us the ability to read the function's arguments, return type, and its name. However, this might not be enough information to work with.

Reflection allows your code to make decisions based on attributes assigned to functions. Once your code can read these attributes, you're able to apply logic and make decisions on which function to use. If we were able to assign additional information to a function or field, we would be able to better scheme up new ways to make our code smarter.

Attributes need to be prepared before they are used. A custom attribute is a class that inherits from the System.Attributes class. The class itself is also labeled as a special class that is used to define custom attributes.

### 8.11.3  Finding Custom Attributes

The prepared Attributes project contains a class named MyAttribute.cs.

```
using System;
using UnityEngine;
using System.Collections;
[AttributeUsage(AttributeTargets.All)]
public class MyAttribute : Attribute
{
    public string name;
    public string Name{
        get{return this.name;}
    }
    public int number;
    public int Number
```

```
    {
        get{return this.number;}
        set{this.number = value;}
    }
    public MyAttribute(string name)
    {
        this.name = name;
    }
}
```

We have a field for a name and a number as well as a constructor that sets the name. Most important is the [AttributeUsage(AttributeTargets.All)] attribute applied to the class that is inheriting from Attribute. This might seem a bit redundant, but it's all necessary.

First, we're inheriting from the Attribute base class. This class contains many different functions, which we'll be using in a moment. In the MyAttribute class, we get to add any information which we might want to use later on. In this case, we're going to look for a name and number.

The last is an attribute applied to the MyAttribute class. Inside the square brackets [], we have the AttributeUsage() function with AttributeTags.All enum in the argument list. This indicates that the attribute can be applied to any type of data. We'll see how this can be modified later on.

## 8.11.4 Attribute Constructor

The MyAttribute class has a public MyAttribute() constructor. This constructor accepts a string name that is then assigned to this.name. The attribute's constructor is important when using an attribute as it's fulfilling the various attribute properties that can be seen when using reflection.

For the MyAttribute to be assigned to a class member and have some information, it needs a constructor, which adds any data inside the attribute that will be needed later on. Assigning multiple arguments to the constructor allows for more than one property of the attribute to be assigned.

Once we've got a useable constructor, we're ready to use the attribute. To see the attribute in Unity 3D, open the SpecialAttributes.cs file in the project, and we'll be seeing the following code:

```csharp
using System;
using UnityEngine;
using System.Collections;
using System.Reflection;
public class SpecialAttributes : MonoBehaviour
{
    [Serializable]
    public class nestedClass
    {
        public int myInt;
        [MyAttribute("So Special.")]
        public int SpecialInt;
    }
    public nestedClass MyNestedClass;
    [NonSerialized]
    public int PlainOldInt;
    void Start ()
    {
        MemberInfo[] memberInfos = typeof(nestedClass).GetMembers();
        foreach (MemberInfo info in memberInfos)
        {
            Debug.Log(info);
            object[] myAttrib = info.GetCustomAttributes(true);
            foreach(MyAttribute ma in myAttrib)
```

```
                    {
                        Debug.Log(ma.Name);
                    }
            }
        }
}
```

In the SpecialAttributes class, we create a new nestedClass{} where we have a regular public int myInt;, followed by a more special public int SpecialInt; that has the [MyAttribute("So Special.")] assigned to it.

Here, we have extended our Start () function with some reflection tests to get each member from the nestedClass. To do this, we used the typeof(nestedClass).GetMembers() that returns an array of MemberInfo[] objects. On each information in the memberInfos array, we need to scan for each custom attribute using the info.GetCustomAttributes();. The bool true in the Get-CustomAttributes() argument list tells the function to check any inherited classes for attributes as well.

It's also important to see how we're using MyAttribute ma in the foreach statement. The object[] myAttrib is an array of type object and not MyAttribute. When the MyAttribute ma is used against an array of a different type, it's automatically cast to the MyAttribute type. Only if the cast succeeds, then the contents of the foreach loop are executed.

### 8.11.5 Multiple Attributes

Each custom attribute should be fairly specific. The special instructions or hint which you mark a field or function with should be for a specific use. If you need to add multiple attributes to a class member, then you can stack them.

```
[AttributeUsage(AttributeTargets.All, AllowMultiple = true, Inherited =
true)]
```

The addition of AllowMultiple = true tells the attribute that you can stack different attributes over a class member. In addition, we can add the Inherited = true option to this attribute as well. This code tells anything inspecting this attribute that any child class inheriting the member will also have the accompanying attribute.

```
[SpecialAttribute]
[SuperficialAttribute]
public int myInt;
```

or

```
[SpecialAttribute, SuperficialAttribute]
public int myInt;
```

The myInt in the above example will have an array of attributes associated with it. So in the case with the code we just used, object[] myAttrib will have two different attributes associated with it.

```
        foreach (MemberInfo info in memberInfos)
        {
            object[] myAttribs = info.GetCustomAttributes(true);
            foreach(Attribute attrib in myAttribs)
            {
                if(attrib is MyAttribute)
                {
                    MyAttribute ma = attrib as MyAttribute;
                    Debug.Log("found "
                        + info.ToString()
```

```
                    + " attrib is a "
                    + ma.Name);
        }
        if(attrib is MyOtherAttribute)
        {
            MyOtherAttribute ma = attrib as
            MyOtherAttribute;
            Debug.Log("found "
                    + info.ToString()
                    + " attrib is a "
                    + ma.OtherName);
        }
    }
}
```

To make things a bit more simple, we can check the types of attributes and cast them as they are found. Once they have been cast, we can extract the expected information and make use of it. In this example, we're just looking at simple casts to find the attributes. Once the attribute is found, we have both the information from the attribute and the member of the class that the attribute is associated with.

## 8.11.6 Putting Attributes to Work

To make an attribute useful, we can make associations with some classes that aren't necessarily based on `MonoBehaviour` having an active `Update ()` function. The MonoBehavior base class makes them considerably more controllable. Starting with a simple class that isn't based on `MonoBehaviour`, we have something like the following:

```
using UnityEngine;
using System.Collections;
public class BaseClass
{
    public string name;
    public BaseClass(string n)
    {
        this.name = n;
    }
    public void OnUpdate ()
    {
        Debug.Log(name + " is updating...");
    }
}
```

This gives us a fast, light class to start with. Then over the `OnUpdate ()` function, we'll add an attribute called "Update." In this case, we'll give the attribute the name `Update`, which we'll look for when using the reflection system we had earlier. Inside of the new base class, we add the following attribute above the `OnUpdate ()` function.

```
[MyAttribute("Update")]
public void OnUpdate ()
{
    Debug.Log(name + " is updating...");
}
```

The small fragment shows the `MyAttribute` added to the function. Now it's a matter of creating a few different instances of this in the scene. This provides a simple test that if there are many different objects in a scene, they can all share an attribute over different functions. We'll add that to our example in a moment.

```
    void Start ()
    {
        baseClasses = new BaseClass[10];
        for (int i = 0; i < 10 ; i ++)
        {
            BaseClass bc = new BaseClass(i.ToString());
            baseClasses[i] = bc;
        }
    }
```

This will create a number of `BaseClass` objects and add them to an array. These objects can also be done with an `ArrayList` and using `GameObject.FindObjectsOfType(typeof(object));` to get everything in the scene. After that, we would be able to sift through all of the objects, including all C# classes, and look for `MyAttribute`.

Next in the `SpecialAttributes.cs` class, we'll implement an `Update ()` function as well as an event to get updated in the `Update ()` loop.

```
    public delegate void UpdateHandler();
    public event UpdateHandler UpdateEvent;
    void Update ()
    {
        if(UpdateEvent != null)
        {
            UpdateEvent();
        }
    }
```

This will create a handler and an event which is called inside of the `Update ()` function called on each frame, thanks to `MonoBehaviour`. The `BaseClass` cannot do this on its own as it's not a child of `MonoBehaviour`. For this reason, we'll be using an `UpdateEvent` to call any function with the `MyAttribute("Update")` assigned.

Now the tricky part begins. We need to look at the class, find all the functions in the classes, get the attributes of those functions, and then add the function to the `UpdateEvent`. First we'll start with getting each object.

```
foreach(object o in baseClasses)
{
    Type t = o.GetType();
    MethodInfo[] methods = t.GetMethods();
}
```

The above code does two things: It looks into our array of found objects and then gets the type of the object with `Type t = o.GetType()`, so we can get the methods from t with the `GetMethods()` reflection function. This turns into a `MethodInfo[]` array. Once we have this array, we can sort through each one and look for attributes.

```
foreach(object o in baseClasses)
{
    Type t = o.GetType();
    MethodInfo[] methods = t.GetMethods();
    foreach(MethodInfo method in methods)
    {
        object[] attributes = method.GetCustomAttributes(true);
    }
}
```

To continue we'll look at the object's custom attributes assigned to the `object[]` attributes variable. So `foreach` method in method is how we'll look through the array `MethodInfo[]` obtained from `t.GetMethods()`. For each method, we need to look for its attributes. Therefore, we use `object[]` attributes and assign the `object[]` array with `method.GetCustomAttributes(true)`. As a reminder the `true` is used to tell the function that we want to include parent classes which `BaseClass` might be inheriting from.

Now that we have an array of attributes for each method, we need to look at each attribute.

```
foreach(object o in baseClasses)
{
    Type t = o.GetType();
    MethodInfo[] methods = t.GetMethods();
    foreach(MethodInfo method in methods)
    {
        object[] attributes = method.GetCustomAttributes(true);
        foreach(object attribute in attributes)
        {
            if (attribute is MyAttribute)
            {
            }
        }
    }
}
```

Once we have an attribute, we should check whether it is the `MyAttribute` attribute we expect. If so, then we can check what the attribute's name is.

```
foreach(object o in baseClasses)
{
    Type t = o.GetType();
    MethodInfo[] methods = t.GetMethods();
    foreach(MethodInfo method in methods)
    {
        object[] attributes = method.GetCustomAttributes(true);
        foreach(object attribute in attributes)
        {
            if (attribute is MyAttribute)
            {
                MyAttribute ma = attribute as MyAttribute;
                if(ma.Name == "Update")
                {
                }
            }
        }
    }
}
```

Therefore, we assign `MyAttribute ma` to `attribute as MyAttribute`. We know this works since `attribute is MyAttribute`. Then we can check whether its name is "`Update`," and if so, then we'll add the method we started looking at to the event. So here's the final algorithm:

```
foreach(object o in baseClasses)
{
    Type t = o.GetType();
    MethodInfo[] methods = t.GetMethods();
    foreach(MethodInfo method in methods)
    {
        object[] attributes = method.GetCustomAttributes(true);
        foreach(object attribute in attributes)
```

```
    {
        if (attribute is MyAttribute)
        {
            MyAttribute ma = attribute as MyAttribute;
            if(ma.Name == "Update")
            {
                EventInfo ei
                typeof(SpecialAttributes).GetEvent("UpdateEvent");
                Type et = ei.EventHandlerType;
                Delegate d = Delegate.CreateDelegate(et, o,method);
                ei.AddEventHandler(this, d);
            }
        }
    }
}
}
```

This takes a few steps. First we need to get the EventInfo of the event we're assigning it to. So in SpecialAttributes, we assign EventInfo ei to the return value from typeof(SpecialAttributes).GetEvent("UpdateEvent"). Then we need to get the type from it. This is done with Type et = ei.EventHandlerType, where the EventHandlerType is the UpdateHandler which the UpdateEvent is assigned to.

Each function found in the object of the correct type gets a new delegate assigned to it using Delegate d = Delegate.CreateDelegate(). The CreateDelegate() function of Delegate takes three arguments: The first one is the type that it's creating a delegate for, so in this case it's Type et; then it wants to know what owns the function we're assigning to that event, so in this case it's object o; and finally we need to know what function is being assigned to the event, which is the function we scanned for MethodInfo method attributes.

Then we assign Delegate d to EventInfo we got from the SpecialAttributes class ei by using AddEventHandler(). The first argument in the statement is the object the event is assigned to; we use the this keyword to assign the class itself as the object. The call back assigned to this object is Delegate d.

Now when the game is run, objects are created. After the objects are created, they are scanned for functions that have attributes. If the attribute's name is "Update," then the function is assigned to the UpdateEvent, which is called the MonoBehaviour's Update () function.

This sort of utility allows for a great number of simple ways to connect classes together. Better interobject communication allows for your code to work smarter and more intelligently. Of course, this is dependent on how well you understand what is possible with Reflection and how to use Attributes to enhance the abilities of Reflection.

The example shown here isn't the best way to operate a scene. This is a brute force way to make sure that objects in a scene have their OnUpdate () functions added to a singular Update () handled in MonoBehaviour. A more simple method, of course, would be to use eventHandler+ = object. OnUpdate ();, but this might not always be an option. In a situation where you simply can't create the scene manager before the objects, something like this might be more useful.

### 8.11.7 Attribute Flags

Attributes can be applied to classes, functions, and variables. We should also consider keeping track of what an attribute should be applied to, limiting where an attribute can be used to prevent an attribute being applied to an object which you don't want to have a specific attribute assigned.

When declaring the new attribute class, we've got several options we can apply.

```
[AttributeUsage(AttributeTargets.Method)]
public class MyOtherAttribute : Attribute
{
}
```

The above code makes the `MyOtherAttribute` applicable only to your class functions. We can also add additional `AttributeTargets` using the bitwise operator | to add multiple flags. Such flags were covered in Section 8.9.

```
[AttributeUsage(AttributeTargets.Method | AttributeTargets.Field)]
public class MyOtherAttribute : Attribute
{
}
```

This changes the option to include both functions and variables. As we've just seen the bitwise operator | in Section 8.9.3, we know that the `AttributeTargets` enum is set up for bitwise checks.

### 8.11.8 What We've Learned

The special attributes exercise at the end of this chapter prints out each class member to the Console panel. The function's output describes each member and its custom attribute. With a custom attribute, we can put it to work to help with many different tasks. An `Update` attribute with a time delay `[UpdateAttribute(3.0f)]` could indicate if a function should be added to an update event and how often it should be updated.

Each monster could have a different version of the `UpdateAttribute` with different time values. Smarter, faster monsters can update more often than slower, dumber monsters that have long delays between updates. If you revive a character, various stats may need to be reset to their default values. If each different character had a different set of stats, the bookkeeping might get more difficult. A `[RestoreAttribute(int restoredAmount)]` attribute would make the bookkeeping automatic. Just get all of the fields that need to be restored and restore them to the indicated restored amount.

Using the custom attributes provides an easy readable system to attach important information to a function or variable.

## 8.12 Architectures and Organization

So far in this book we've focused on writing individual classes or inheriting one class to another. This is fine to learn the mechanics of the language, but it doesn't help toward building a larger project. Take a moment and step back and think about how all your classes fit together to build an entire project. This takes another frame of mind altogether.

When you're building a structure for your game, it's important to keep C# files separated by task. Tasks can be added or merged as needed far more easy when separated into different files. The more separation you keep, the less often files will have to be merged when working in a team of engineers.

If each class is limited in scope to just a few related tasks, you also decrease the number of places you need to look to fix bugs. This also helps when using the debugger; if the file isn't long and the scope is limited, you only have to find a problem and fix it in a smaller file.

When you're working by yourself, it's easy to claim ownership over your code base. You know where everything is, and you have a better idea of what it's doing. However, when it comes to working in a team, each person needs to focus on smaller, more specialized part of the code base. When you're able to concentrate on a specific task, you're better able to limit your scope and build a more thoughtfully crafted class.

Once each task lives in its own file, it's unlikely that too many people will have to touch the file while you're working on it. This reduces the number of merging you'll need to do when using version control systems like Git or Subversion (SVN). If a single C# script file spans many different operations, then more and more people will need to make changes to the file. When you check in the file, having to merge your changes with many other changes can create problems if the merge isn't done correctly.

Approaching a project with the intent to build a complex game involves a great amount of thought; luckily, if you've written functions that have little or no side effects, then you're better able to rearrange and separate the classes and functions into different files much more easily.

This example is found in the Architecture directory in the Unity 3D Projects resources for this book. Although we're not necessarily going to be writing too much code for this chapter, it is a nice reference to look at; should you feel, you need to follow along with the actual files.

### 8.12.1 Planning Structure

Even the smallest project can be a huge undertaking. There's almost no such thing as overly organized when it comes to programming. When programming is well organized, it also becomes much easier to both read and write. Your specific tasks become precise and sometimes more simple.

The root or base of your game should be named something fairly generic, but something you can remember. Most often it's your team or company's name such as `AwesomeGameCo` or perhaps `AwesomeGameSystem`. This serves as a container for the most generic functions and classes for your project. We'll come back to what sort of classes should live in this namespace.

If you intend to make only one game ever, then a game-specific namespace may not be necessary, but I'm sure that you've got bigger vision than that. After a broad namespace, a slightly more specific namespace for your game should be considered. So we might be looking at `AwesomeGameCo.ZombieGame` that would contain classes which are in particular useful for a zombie game.

`ZombieGame` should be composed of more classes and functions that are specific to a zombie game, but not to implement an actual zombie. The `ZombieGame` namespace should implement things like starting the game, creating a scene, and observing and ending the game. Inside of the `ZombieGame` namespace, you can implement more specific namespaces for scene management, player management, input managers, and so on.

The different categories are intended to separate your classes into categories to prevent the overlapping of tasks. If something in the zombie animation is talking to the network to update a score, then you've got a chance for problems.

The purpose of a namespace is to create a structure of organization for the different tasks in your game, for example, a namespace for the player, the environment, effects, monsters, and weapons. Each major category should have its own namespace.

### 8.12.2 Fixing Namespaces

You may have noticed that `MonoBehaviour` uses a particular spelling which isn't common in American English. If this bothers you, it can easily be fixed, with a starting namespace for your own Game Company.

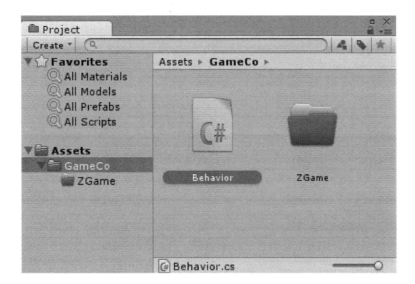

Here we can create a simple renaming of MonoBehaviour to Behavior.

```
using UnityEngine;
using System.Collections;
namespace AGameCo
{
        public class Behavior : MonoBehaviour
        {
        }
}
```

This means you can inherit from Behavior rather than MonoBehaviour for your own classes if the spelling has been bothering you.

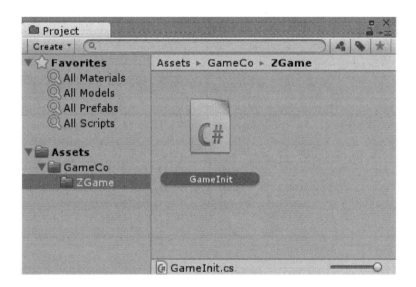

Inside of a ZGame directory under your GameCo directory, you can give the following GameInit class a base class of Behavior rather than MonoBehaviour so long as you add the using AGameCo; directive.

```
using UnityEngine;
using System.Collections;
using AGameCo;
public class GameInit : Behavior {
     //Use this for initialization
     void Start () {
     }
     //Update is called once per frame
     void Update () {
     }
}
```

This works in the same way as MonoBehaviour; however, it's shorter and not spelled with an extra u. Therefore, we can use a namespace to make a generalization of other classes for our benefit. The AGameCo namespace can also be used to store general information for your game. A GameInfo.cs class could contain the following:

```
using UnityEngine;
using System.Collections;
```

```
namespace AGameCo
{
    public class GameInfo
    {
        private static int timesPlayed;
        public static int TimesPlayed
        {
            get
            {
                return timesPlayed;
            }
            set
            {
                timesPlayed = value;
            }
        }
    }
}
```

Of course, this code can be expanded considerably to include much more information, but, as a general idea, this is an interesting concept to follow. If you're planning on collecting user data, then a `GameInfo` class at the root of `AGameCo`'s namespace is a good place to start.

So why `AGameCo` and not `AwesomeGameCompany`? Shorter names are far more easy to type. There's also the simple fact that more letters means more space is needed. Keeping all of your naming short helps prevent giant namespaces.

Of course, some naming conventions and coding standards dictate using full names. The decision to use long names is up to you for your own project. In some cases, long names can make more sense. In terms of clarity and description, long names can make sure that you know what object you are referencing. Shorter names can mask the true purpose of a class or namespace. In either situation, if it's your project, then feel free to do as you will. If you're working with code already in place, then go with the flow and try not to upset the *status quo*.

The `AGameCo` namespace is also a good place to store any number of structs. In a `GameStats.cs`, you can have a short struct that looks like the following:

```
using UnityEngine;
using System.Collections;
namespace AGameCo {
    public struct GameStats
    {
        public int timesPlayed;
        public int timesDied;
        public int zombiesKilled;
        public float hoursPlayed;
    }
}
```

And that's it, by limiting the scope of each class, you limit the number of places you need to look to find where the `GameStats` struct was created. It's in `GameStats.cs`; no need to look anywhere else. This means that the previous `GameInfo.cs` can use the `GameStats` struct.

```
using UnityEngine;
using System.Collections;
namespace AGameCo
{
    public class GameInfo
    {
        private int timesPlayed;
```

```
        public int TimesPlayed
        {
            get
            {
                return timesPlayed;
            }
            set
            {
                timesPlayed = value;
            }
        }
        public GameStats GetGameInfo()
        {
            GameStats gameStats = new GameStats();
            gameStats.timesPlayed = timesPlayed;
            return gameStats;
        }
    }
}
```

Now we can write a GetGameInfo() function in the GameInfo class. So a namespace can couple structs with classes in a neatly organized system. Naming classes and files is easier when you have to worry about only one object at a time in each file. Also notice if you're using the namespace AGameCo, you don't need to add the using AGameCo; directive. Adding in the namespace both uses that namespace and extends its contents.

This also makes errors easier to spot when you're only looking at a few dozen lines of code. If the struct GameStats lives in GameStats.cs and has only a few lines of code, how can this break? Debugging a file with just a few lines of code to inspect is much easier as well.

When you're working with a version control system, you can check who was the last to modify the GameStats.cs file and what he or she had changed. So if something breaks in that file, you know who to ask about the change and why it was made.

**NOTE:** Some version control systems have a built-in blame feature. If you're working with a large team, then this might be a preferred system to use to tell people that they have something to fix. If they take too long to get around to fixing their bug, then you can shoot a Nerf dart at them as motivation.

### 8.12.3 Namespace and Directory Structure

Directories for your classes add to the structure of the project. It's a good practice to keep the names of the directories matching the names of the classes and namespaces. For instance, if you started adding a few different classes to ZGame like an enum for picking a different effect when hit by a bullet, knife, or other weapon in a DamageType.cs:

```
using UnityEngine;
using System.Collections;
namespace AGameCo.ZGame
{
    public enum DamageType : byte
    {
        bullet,
        knife,
        axe,
        rocket,
        fire,
```

```
            ice
        }
}
```

Then a way to communicate to an affected target how it was damaged in a `DamageInfo.cs` is as follows:

```
using UnityEngine;
using System.Collections;
namespace AGameCo.ZGame
{
    public struct DamageInfo
    {
        public DamageType damageType;
        public int damageAmount;
    }
}
```

Then finally a way to set and apply that damage between objects in `Damage.cs` is as follows:

```
using UnityEngine;
using System.Collections;
namespace AGameCo.ZGame
{
    public class Damage {
    public DamageInfo GetDamage(DamageType dType, int amount)
        {
            DamageInfo damageInfo = new DamageInfo();
            damageInfo.damageType = dType;
            damageInfo.damageAmount = amount;
            return damageInfo;
        }
    }
}
```

These all coordinate together to make `Damage` apply to them and work on zombies. The general theme here should be grouped together in a namespace and directory called `Damage`. So a `Zombie.cs` should live in `namespace Zombie` and its own directory `Zombie`.

```
using UnityEngine;
using System.Collections;
using AGameCo.ZGame.Damage;
namespace AGameCo.ZGame.Zombie
{
    public class Zombie : Behavior
    {
        private int hitPoints = 10;
        public void OnTakeDamage(DamageInfo damage)
        {
            hitPoints - = damage.damageAmount;
        }
    }
}
```

Include the `Damage` namespace by adding a directive. Now `Zombie` can make use of all of the different types and systems found in that namespace. By building up directories and systems like this, we can limit the number of lines of code in each class. However, when systems get very complex, it's also handy to break down a class into multiple files using the `partial` keyword.

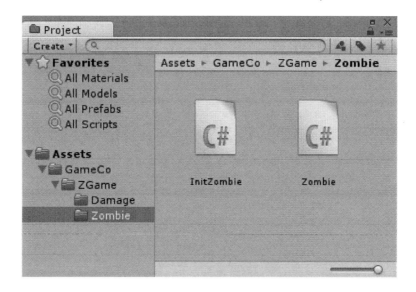

### 8.12.4 Using Partial

Modify Zombie.cs to public partial class Zombie : Behavior and then create a new C# script file called InitZombie.cs, which could contain one function. The partial keyword will allow us to break apart a single class across multiple different files. The reason for this is to allow you to spread your work across multiple files.

```
using UnityEngine;
using System.Collections;
namespace AGameCo.ZGame.Zombie
{
    public partial class Zombie : Behavior
    {
        void InitZombie()
        {
            //create a zombie here.
        }
    }
}
```

This allows you to have one location for the initialization of the Zombie class. In our scene, we can add a ZGame.cs based on Behavior to the Main Camera. Handy shortcuts like this allow for a huge amount of expandability. This allows for a single class to have many functions and options without needing to cram them all into a single file.

```
using UnityEngine;
using System.Collections;
using AGameCo;
using AGameCo.ZGame;
using AGameCo.ZGame.Zombie;
using AGameCo.ZGame.Damage;
public class ZGame : Behavior
{
    //Use this for initialization
    void Start ()
```

```
    {
        Zombie stubbs = new Zombie();
        stubbs.InitZombie();
    }
}
```

This uses all of the new namespaces, and when we create a new `Zombie()`, we have access to the `InitZombie();` function. Again, now we're free to inspect the code in that one function in a solitary class. This also means that we can avoid any side effects as that can sometimes lead to unexpected behaviors.

A large project can have many dozens of directories and hundreds of files. Each file can be trimmed down to just a few lines of code or a short collection of a few functions that are closely related. It's up to you to decide on how these are organized, but in the end a project that starts off simple will almost always grow into a beast if you start off with writing large monolithic files.

It's easy to make namespaces, and it's also easy to get carried away. Once you've gone more than four or five levels deep, you might be making too much work for yourself. Something like `AGameCo. ZGame.Damage.Magic.Spell.Scrolls` is certainly a bit too much. Keeping things simple should always be a primary focus. Making specialized code for very specific tasks should be handled in a more generalized way.

A simple layout can end up being many different folders, each one containing any number of related classes and partial classes designed to work together. It's also important to keep your C# script files separated from your game assets.

You should be managing these files in some form of source control. This allows your heavy assets like art and audio to run on a different version control system from your code. Combining binary files like an image with text makes for a messy version control system. Art files also tend to take up a lot more space than text files. Large files that make pulling an update from a server take a long time. In the interest of keeping code versioning quick, it's best to keep the two under different revision control servers.

By starting a project with isolated classes and functions, it's harder to create cross-dependent functions. If `funcA()` relies on `funcB()` setting a variable before it's able to update properly, you can run into various timing problems. Different devices operate slightly differently, and variables may or may not have an expected value before another function is called.

## 8.12.5 Refactoring

When you've decided that a class or type name needs to change, the work to change it has multiplied once the name has spread across many different files. Searching for every place that a particular name appears isn't always so easy.

A Find and Replace will find something like `Damage` in `DamageType` and `DamageInfo`. This means inspecting each instance and deciding whether or not it should be changed. So long as the name only appears in a few places, this might not be too bad. If the word were more common, then you might be looking at many dozen instances that can easily lead to creating bugs.

The Refactor tool in MonoDevelop as well as many other IDEs was created to help this process. A refactor is aware of the name's use and where it appears. Because of this, it's easy to find any instance of a name and allow you to make global changes.

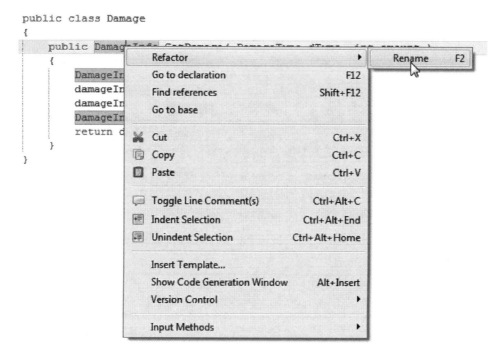

If we right click on a class name, we can pick Refactor → Rename. This is followed by a dialog asking what we would like to rename the class to.

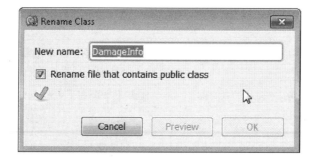

To see what files it's touching and what it's changing, we can use the Preview button that opens the following dialog box.

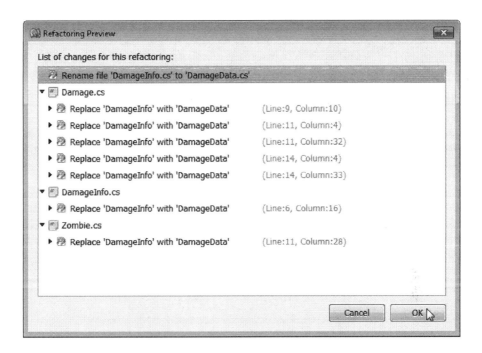

This shows us each place the DamageInfo class makes an appearance. In this project, we can see that it's appearing several times in Damage.cs as well as once in DamageInfo.cs and Zombie. cs. We can expand each entry to see what the line will look like before and after the refactoring is done.

This works the same for fields in a class. If we had a Weapon base class that just stored some information for Ammunition and Damage, we'd be able to see the refactor work across multiple classes.

```
using UnityEngine;
using System.Collections;
namespace AGameCo.ZGame.Weapon
{
    public class Weapon
    {
        public int Ammunition;
        public int Damage;
    }
}
```

An important test is to check if refactoring will broadly search for the appearance of the word Ammunition.

```
using UnityEngine;
using System.Collections;
namespace AGameCo.ZGame.Items
{
    public class Ammo : Pickups
    {
        public int Ammunition;
    }
}
```

Here we show two different classes: Weapon and Ammo. The Weapon class keeps track of the number of times the weapon can be used. The number for this record is Ammunition. The Ammo class stores a number of Ammunition which we can use to resupply the player with more firepower.

This situation shows a Shotgun inheriting from Weapon. Here we see that the Shotgun has a function making use of the Ammunition inherited from the Weapon parent class. Find and replace in files will also find Ammunition in the Ammo class. However, Refactor is smarter than that.

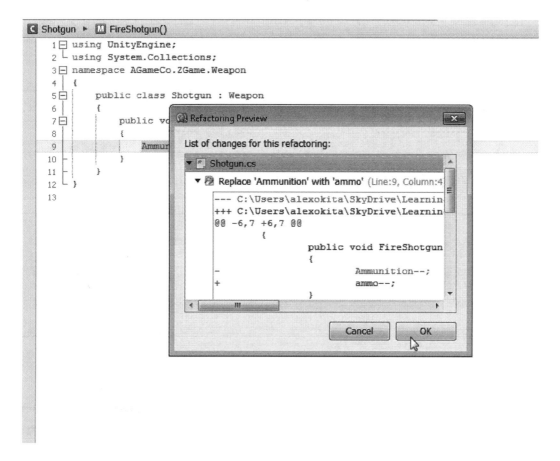

The Refactor sees only the places where the Ammunition is used and makes the proper changes to the objects related to the use of Ammunition in relation to the class it's actually being used in. The context is clearly related to the Weapon class and its children, not in unrelated classes like the Ammo pickup item.

### 8.12.6 What We've Learned

Creating and using a structure for your game takes a lot of experience and practice. Coming to a final decision on structure before you've started writing the code for your game is unlikely. By creating namespaces and writing small classes in each one, you're also giving yourself a much easier way to reorganize the files into new namespaces and new directories.

Even after things get established, it's not so difficult to make widespread changes. One of the best ways for making these changes is by keeping categories and types clearly separated. Ensuring that the crossover between classes is limited to only specific functions is difficult, but no less important.

The less each class needs to depend on another class to operate, the less chance you have of one object causing a cascade of errors. If each function can act on its own, then you have a better chance of preventing bugs. If a class can be fragmented into many different parts, then assigning work to different team members is easier.

By splitting off functions to different people, you've also made decisions that make the design more clear. If the design is still undecided to make clear tasks for a given project, then it might be a good idea to spend more time thinking about what you're building before writing any code.

## 8.13 Design Patterns

We can't get the feeling that we've learned how to speak the same language as a programmer unless we've studied something called a design pattern. Computer programmers have been solving the same problems time and again, so it should come as no surprise that some common solutions for similar problems have been discovered and shared.

The solutions to these reoccurring problems became to be known as design patterns. With the long history of programming, many complex problems are solved with known patterns. The more common the problem, the more likely there's already a known pattern. These solutions are described by how the problem has been solved.

Design patterns are reusable solutions. The patterns become established when they are reusable, and they are proven to work. They are also general enough to be modified to suit the situation you need it for.

Often the patterns have been tested enough and optimized to the smallest fastest code required for a solution to the problem. When properly understood and applied, the pattern will often prevent edge cases from escaping the solution. If a pattern stands the test of time, it becomes established and relied upon.

Learning patterns means you get to build up your vocabulary and overall ability as a programmer. There are a great number of established design patterns. The list of design patterns is extensive and the topic concerns many matters beyond the scope of this book. However, we can still talk to some of the main points behind why the design patterns matter.

There are three categories of design patterns in computing: creational, structural, and behavioral. When writing software for the first time, you're going to be coming across tasks thinking that they're all new. In fact, they're the same problems which everyone has had to solve many times before you.

### 8.13.1 Creational Design Patterns

Creational design patterns are named so because they relate to how an object is created and later used. These systems are often used in games to instance new creatures and items. When you start a game, it's a good idea that you're starting one game and referencing the one game that was started. Other patterns are useful for creating a variety of similar objects.

Creational design patterns represent the idea of creating and setting up any object from a class using a consistent system. To list a few common creational design patterns, we can start with the Factory, Prototype, Singleton, and Builder.

#### 8.13.1.1 Singleton Pattern

A singleton pattern is a creational pattern which limits the number of instanced objects to one instance. If a problem comes up like "I'd like to make ensure there's only one instance of an object," then you might look on the Internet to how someone has solved this particular problem. After a few searches, you'll come across a "Singleton pattern" which ensures that only once instance of an object is ever created.

The first time the object is asked for like `CommandCenter MyCommander = CommandCenter.Commander;`, you can use an accessor to create and return the commander. If the commander has already been created, then you can pass him along, and not create a new one.

The Singleton pattern is useful to ensure that a game only has a single game state controller. If you want to keep track of the player's navigation through your menus and into your game, it's better to have a single class instructing the rest of your game to start, stop, and post results through one class.

The reason why we don't simply use a lot of static fields and functions is more an effect to memory. If everything was static, then they're never cleared out of memory. If you're managing a lot of data, then the static field storing them will never be freed, and your game's memory will bloat and take up all the room left for the rest of your game.

Like the "singleton pattern," many different patterns have a specific role and description. The "factory pattern" uses a class whose only purpose is to instance and create objects. Much like a candy factory produces various sweets. The "builder pattern" is similar to the "factory pattern" but requires another class called a director to control its activity. The "prototype pattern" is another variation on the factory pattern, but copies from a preexisting copy of a class to create a new object.

### 8.13.2 Structural Design Patterns

Structural design patterns help consolidate how data and functions are organized and arranged in a class. In this category, we've got the Decorator, Facade, Flyweight, Adapter, and Proxy. Of these the Decorator pattern comes up often in games.

The Decorator pattern is used when instancing objects into a scene. We use this pattern extensively in Unity 3D. For each component you attach to a `gameObject`, you're decorating it with new behaviors. See that you've been using design patterns all this time and didn't even know it.

When you create a template for creating a zombie or a vampire, you're creating a system to decorate a `gameObject` with the appropriate components. By keeping movement, armor, attack patterns, and other behaviors separated into different components, you're allowing yourself more freedom to create new objects with different decorations.

Add a blood-sucking component to a Plymouth Fury and you've got a 1980's movie car. Add a talking component to a toaster and you've got a British situation comedy in space. Various components allows for unexpected and sometimes fun results.

### 8.13.3 Behavioral Design Patterns

Behavioral design patterns focus on communication between objects in a system. Some behavioral patterns include Iterator, Mediator, Observer, and Visitor. In this section, we'll take a close look at the Iterator and Observer patterns.

The Observer pattern is a common system of behavioral design. Combine this with the Singleton, and you've got a game state manager. Combine this with a character, and you've got a level boss. The Observer pattern means that a single class orchestrates the behavior of many child classes.

The children are actually the observers; they watch a central class for changes in the game. Based on the events in the game, a condition will change, and they'll all change their behavior, or rather they observe a state change and react accordingly.

When building your game, it's often a good idea to make sure that data isn't duplicated anywhere it's not necessary. If every child had a record of the player's health, then you're wasting space on redundant data. The player's health should only ever be located in the player object.

When new conditions are met, an event can be raised to tell the game state that the player's health is low. When this event is raised, anyone observing this change should be notified. Then the observing objects can rush in to finish off the player.

### 8.13.4 What We've Learned

It's unfortunate that we don't have another few hundred pages for this book to go into more depth on the different design patterns. Each one has not only benefits but also some interesting drawbacks. A Singleton pattern is great for centralizing all of your object management. The main problem here is the fact that the Singleton tends to get very big once it's managing a lot of different things.

There's no perfect answer for which pattern any situation should use. In the end, a blend of a few different patterns is usually how the final implementation ends up. Holding too close to any single pattern will only accomplish slowing down overall development time and limit what your game can do.

The final product should be something fun for your player. Even if the code is a little bit awkward in some places, your player isn't reading your code. So long as the code runs fast, reliable, and is easy to read, you're on the right track.

## 8.14 Continuing on Your Own

Where to go from here. You'll want to explore more of the different function calls that are found within .NET and the Unity 3D application programming interfaces. Google and Bing are both great to help search for answers. Also, now that you know a lot of different programmer jargons, you're less likely to be ignored when asking questions on forums.

One of the hardest lessons to learn is less about code and more about time management. The time management I speak of is not the amount of work any given task is going to take. The amount of time your work takes up of your life is more about what I'm speaking of.

After talking to many vets in the games and software industry is the amount of time left after work and dedicated to living *away* from your keyboard. When first getting into any new topic, it's natural to want to dedicate a large portion of your life to learning more and getting better. However, when this becomes the majority of your life to the degradation of your health, it's time to pull back.

Only after experience can one clearly see that overzealous dedication was a mistake. Of course, getting to that point leads to the experience necessary to see where things went wrong, a horrible Catch-22 if there ever was one. Because of this I'll just leave you with a final word of caution to not let your computer take over your life.

Personally I've realized that I don't draw as often as I used to. I appreciate my weekends more, and I'm learning a wider variety of things trying not to focus so heavily on a single topic any more. This comes after realizing that putting your life's work into a single project can all too easily lead to disaster. Though I haven't really had any giant plans crushed by being overfocused, I have seen friends having family problems and personal issues due to lack of a life outside of work.

Anything can happen, and a project can get canceled before it sees the light of day. The end result can be months or worse yet years invested into a lost cause. Nothing is worse than walking away from a gigantic project with nothing to show for your work.

The games industry is volatile; it's filled with politics and instability. The more you know, the easier it is to remain relevant. The more skills you have, the wider your opportunities. Eventually, once you've accumulated enough skill, it's time to work on personal projects that mean more to you.

# 9

## *Stuff We Couldn't Cover*

Right now, Unity 3D is limited to older versions of the C# library. Today, C# is in its fifth version and it's continuing to grow. Not all features added to C# are allowed in Unity 3D for reasons of security or platform compatibility.

When C# is compiled into other platforms, such as iOS or Android, many of the tricks we discussed don't exist. The desktop environment is still the more powerful, not just because of the central processing unit and the graphics processing unit: As of today, the operating system (OS) of a desktop still has plenty more ability than that of a mobile OS.

Some features in C# are limited to specific OS or hardware features. Some features are tied to specific dynamic link libraries (DLLs) provided by third-party developers. Whenever a new feature is introduced, there's always someone willing to describe how it's used. These tutorials assume that you're already familiar with C# and are interested in how the new feature is used in this context.

At this point, you should be able to approach these new features and understand their context. It's unfortunate that many online learning resources assume that you're already familiar with general programming features; at least now, you are.

## 9.1 The Extern and Unsafe Keywords

With Unity 3D, we're limited to the types of code we're able to use in C#. The free version of the engine disallows the use of external DLLs, and without them, some of the keywords become rather pointless.

The `extern` keyword is specifically used to point a function at the contents of a DLL. Another tricky element that wasn't covered here is `unsafe` code. Unfortunately, C# in Unity 3D only allows the use of the `unsafe` keyword, in Unity 3D Pro. This feature allows for more direct access to locations in memory and is disallowed in mobile and web builds of a Unity 3D game, as it can lead to security breaches in your computer's memory.

## 9.2 Dynamic

We've used `var`, but there's also a keyword `dynamic`. How is this different? The `dynamic` keyword is intended to allow for more compatibility with different systems. It works in many ways the same as `var`.

### 9.2.1 Dynamic versus Var

When we are unsure of the type we're going to get from unboxing an object, we need to use `var` to store the resulting type. In other words, if we use `var objects = GameObject.FindObjectsOfType();`, we may find a large variety of different objects. The following code shows what the above function returns.

```
void Start ()
{
    var objects = GameObject.FindObjectsOfType(typeof(Object));
    Debug.Log(objects.GetType());
}
```

This statement prints the following output to the Console panel:

```
UnityEngine.Object[]
```

This statement means that `objects` is a `UnityEngine.Object[]` or an array of Unity 3D objects. This then means that `objects` becomes a `UnityEngine.Object[]` type once it's assigned. If we change `Object` to `GameObject`, `var objects` is now of type `UnityEngine.GameObject[]` when it's checked.

Now `var objects` has a type that can't be changed any more. The following code will throw an error:

```
void Start () {
    var objects = GameObject.FindObjectsOfType(typeof(GameObject));
    Debug.Log(objects);
    objects = 1;//assign var objects an int
}
```

As soon as we make this change, Unity 3D shows us the following error:

```
Assets/MyDynamic.cs(10,17): error CS0029: Cannot implicitly convert type
'int' to 'UnityEngine.Object[]'
```

Therefore, `objects = 1;` throws an error, telling us that `int` isn't a `UnityEngine.Object[]`; and it's right. Once a `var` gets assigned, that variable becomes the type it's been assigned to. However, we can do something more with `dynamic`.

```
void Start ()
{
    var objects = GameObject.FindObjectsOfType(typeof(GameObject));
    Debug.Log(objects);
    dynamic d = objects;
    d = 1;
}
```

The first thing we do is assign `dynamic d` to `objects`, making `d` a `UnityEngine.Object[]`. Then, we make a new assignment with `d = 1`, which changes the type form `GameObject[]` to int. The `var` would immediately raise an error; however, `d` isn't going to raise an error. `dynamic` variables can be changed any time they need to, even after an initial assignment.

If we're doing a lot of boxing and unboxing of various different types, we usually use `var`. The `var` and `dynamic` keywords are different, based on when the variable is turned into the type that's being used.

This means that you can assign `d` to a class and do something like `d.DoSomething();` and call a function in the class assigned to the `dynamic` variable. Often, `dynamic` types aren't as useful, as they begin to break the strong type principles of C#. If every variable were `dynamic`, many problems could arise when the compiler tries to interpret your code. Not all operators work on all different data types. With dynamic data it becomes more difficult to catch data type mismatches before using them in an expression.

As yet, the `dynamic` type hasn't been fully integrated into Unity 3D and breaks in many cases. Assigning anything to `d` after this case throws an error.

```
Internal compiler error. See the console log for more information. output
was:error CS0518: The predefined type
'System.Runtime.CompilerServices.CallSite' is not defined or imported
error CS0518: The predefined type
'System.Runtime.CompilerServices.CallSite'1' is not defined or imported
```

Not all of the features in the latest version of .NET have been incorporated into the Unity 3D version of Mono.

There are several bitwise operators which we didn't cover: the coalesce operator ?? that is used for dealing with null variables; the operators bitwise left assignment, <<= and the bitwise right assignment, >>= that are used for shift assignments; and the bitwise or, |= and bitwise xor, ^=, which are similar to xor and are assigned at the same time.

We couldn't cover everything in much detail, and there's still a lot left to learn. At least now, we can browse a bookstore's shelf of programming books and pick out more reading material and continue to learn. Of course, we shouldn't just read books; the best way to learn is to do.

Learning by doing, testing, and playing is the best experience anyone can have. To start a project and find problems that might be easy or tough to solve is all a part of the experience. When things get too difficult, start over using a different approach. Never let a single problem keep you from learning. Start something else and see how far you get.

Start and complete enough projects; eventually you'll finish one.

# 10

## *Good Luck*

If you've gotten this far, then thank you. Even though you've read through miles of material, you've still got a long way to go to be a full-fledged programmer. However, don't let this dull your motivation.

The most important advice I can give you is that you remain focused on learning with your first few projects rather than finishing that massively multiplayer online role-playing, first-person World War II zombie shooter game. It's important that you understand what you're capable of, and to do this, you need to learn your own limitations.

Your strengths aren't just about what you're able to do, but how long it takes to do them. Eventually, you'll be able to write a fairly complex multiplayer game. It might take a few years, but it'll eventually get done. If you think you'll still be interested in working on one project for many thousands of hours, then I commend your focus and dedication.

For many people, a weekend or an evening project should remain fairly simple and small. A puzzle game, an endless runner, or a simple adventure game can still be done by one person. Once your game requires several hundred assets, sounds, effects, and the like, you're now looking at a product requiring a large-scale effort.

Such efforts require teams of people simply because of the hours involved to finish the product. Even a team of less than a dozen people means that there is several times more hours dedicated to a project than you can dedicate alone. Even if you dedicate 2000 hours a month to a project, it would not be enough, as many large-scale projects require tens of millions of hours to complete.

Finishing a project, even a small one, means you have something to show for your effort. You may well start down the path of a super cool game that no one has ever seen before; but is it something you can stay focused on for a few million hours? It's likely that even after a few hundred hours into the project, you'll realize that you need to start over anyway.

Learning how to write code is an ongoing process. Halfway through a large project, you'll learn that the beginning of your project had many mistakes because of bad programming habits. Usually, fixing all of the problems means throwing everything out and starting over. Don't let this discourage you. You've learned something, and you've become a better programmer!

# *Index*